AVANTI!

Mussolini
And the Wars of Italy
1919-1945

By
J. Lee Ready

Acknowledgments

A work of this magnitude draws upon years of assistance from many people, including veterans of the wars in question from the Italian, British, American and German armed forces. Librarians in many countries have been most helpful. Of especial notice should be the men and women of the Imperial War Museum, the University of London, and the London School of Economics and Political Science. On a more personal note the solid support of my family together with Rick Christensen and David Charnley was crucial. This book is theirs too.

Contents:

PART ONE
In Search of a Cause

Chapter One
The Creation of Mussolini

Benito Amilcare Andrea Mussolini was born July 29 1883 in the poor Italian village of Varnano dei Costa. His father, a revolutionary rabble-rouser, named the boy after famous revolutionaries. The boy inherited his father's rebellious character and when challenged he reacted violently without a hint of regret. He obviously had a charismatic personality, though, because despite his indifference to friendship he always had some sort of following in the playground. Violent as he was, he was not stupid, nor did he lack vocabulary: far from it. He inherited these good points from his schoolteacher mother.

At age nine he was sent to a boarding school at Faenza run by Salesian priests. It is possible that his mother sent him there as much to get the boy away from his father's influence as to gain a spiritual and academic education. However, within a few months his violent temper forced the priests to expel him. This angered him: all he had done was stab a fellow pupil with a knife.

His mother persevered and managed to place him at the Giosue Carducci School in Forlimpopoli. Here he was on his best behavior and was only suspended a few times. Passing his exams at age eighteen he qualified to take a job teaching small children. The terror of the schoolyard had become a teacher.

Yet he was still his father's son and he challenged school rules that he could not bend. After a year of frustration he turned his back on his job, his education and his country, and emigrated to Switzerland. His emigration surprised no one in an age when a high proportion of young Italian men were leaving for the United States, South America or Italy's African colonies. Nor did his destination surprise his father. In 1902 Switzerland was the place to go if one wanted to become a revolutionary. Settling at first in the Italian-speaking region of that nation he soon attracted a following of inspired intellectuals, pseudo-philosophers and misfits, who changed political ideologies quicker than they changed lodgings, and that was often.

Initially to eke out a living Mussolini worked freelance as a French/Italian translator, but he had carried with him the baggage of insubordination and violence, and soon fell afoul of the local police. The authorities particularly objected to his pamphlets and speeches that urged local agricultural laborers to strike. Sometimes he adopted the symbol of the fasces, i. e. a sheaf of wheat, which not only had farm connotations, but also was an ancient symbol of the Roman Empire. Hence his group was known as fascists.

Hounded by the local police in town after town, at times he had to work as a butcher's apprentice, errand boy, mason's mate and manual laborer, but he was always a freelance journalist and pamphlet writer. From April 1904 onwards he knew he could not go back to Italy without facing a jail sentence, because he had failed to acknowledge his conscription into the Italian Army. He had in fact already seen the inside of a cell. He was imprisoned in Berne, Switzerland for a time for political rabble-rousing.

Late in 1904 King Vittorio Emmanuele II of Italy declared an amnesty for draft-dodgers if they returned to do their duty. Mussolini, evidently concluding that Italian drill sergeants could not be any worse than Swiss policemen, chose to accept the offer. Mussolini the draft dodger became a soldier serving from January 1905 to September 1906 in the 10th Bersaglieri (light infantry) Regiment. He served in Italy. Surprisingly his supervisors judged him to be a good soldier.

Unfortunately, once out of uniform he fell under the spell of his father again, his mother having passed away, and together the two wooed women and audiences. Both served time in prison, but the younger Mussolini spent his two weeks confinement studying for a university exam. He passed and within months he was working as a substitute teacher.

Ironically in 1909 his political activity gained him a job as editor of a Socialist Party newspaper, a respectful position, at least among socialists. More noteworthy is that the offer had come from Trento, a city of Italians ruled by the Austrian Empire. As a boy, like countless other Italian boys of his age, he had dreamed of liberating those Italians who lived under Austrian oppression. Now he had been given a chance to preach revolution to them. Mussolini, who had once turned his back on Italy, now began to preach pan-Italian nationalism as well as socialism.

Despite part of 'Italy' being under Austrian occupation, the remainder of Italy itself was by no means homogeneous. Italy controlled Sardinia, where most spoke Sardinian or Catalan. Italy also controlled Sicily, where many still spoke their native tongue. In Southern Italy there were Greek-speaking enclaves and along the east coast several Albanian-speaking towns. On the northwest border many villagers spoke Provencal or French.

The Austrian police did not care for rebels any more than their Swiss counterparts had, and it is astonishing that they put up with his antics for eight months before deporting him. This made him a hero to the socialists and nationalists alike. With the death of his father in December 1910, Mussolini was at last his own man, and he had a sense of destiny. To Mussolini, who had been an expelled student, but also a teacher, a draft dodger, but also a soldier, an ex-patriot and yet also a nationalist, it did not seem odd that he could merge the seemingly opposite ideologies of socialism and nationalism into one force.

——————

Many Italian politicians had become increasingly angry that their fellow Europeans had left nothing for Italy in the colonial game, except Eritrea, Somaliland and Ethiopia. The Italians had eagerly snapped up these lands, but for Ethiopia, which had repelled the Italians at the humiliating battle of Adowa in 1896.

However, in 1898 the Americans had turned on their fellow white men, the Spaniards, and had stolen colonies. They got away with it. Then the Japanese imitated them and stole colonies from the Russians. As a result the Italians decided to get into the colony stealing business. They planned their move well, wooing Libyan Arabs away from their Turkish masters using methods of which Machiavelli would have approved. This included making investments in the coastal cities of Libya and loaning money generously. In 1906 the French wandered into the Tibesti mountains in southern Libya. The Italians suspected the French were at the same game.

Back home in Italy the government had a dilemma: how to encourage the unemployed to emigrate from Italy, while retaining them for military duty if needed. In this day and age it was believed that national security could only be retained by large armies of reservists. But those Italians who had left for other countries might end up in foreign armies, such as the US Army, if there was a major conflict. The government's solution to the problem was to provide opportunities for the unemployed in the colonies as farmers, miners, construction workers etc. Eritrea and Somaliland soon lured 100,000 Italians from Italy's bulging population, and Libya would, it was hoped, lure many more, if it could be wrested from the Turks.

On 29 September 1911 the Italians made their move. Their warships bombarded Turkish coastal defenses in Albania, but this was a feint. On 3 October the Italians landed on the Libyan coast at Tripoli, Homs, Tobruk and Benghazi. Ever innovative, the Italians were the first in history to drop bombs from aircraft. The war went well as the Turks were hopelessly outclassed.

Mussolini was furious. Using his new job as editor of a socialist newspaper in Italy as a platform, he publicly denounced the war, reminding the people that a million Italians were still living under Swiss, French and Austrian rule, but instead of liberating them, the gutless politicians of the day had challenged the ailing Turks for control of a few miserable mud huts. He led anti-war demonstrators, urging them to burn cavalry hay, derail military trains, sack recruitment offices and cause havoc. Understandably the government took a dim view of this and jailed him for one year.

The war went on. Italy took the Greek-populated Dodecanese

Islands and the coast of Libya from Turkish control, and in October 1912 the Turks sued for peace. Italy was satisfied with her modest gains.

––––––––––––

The king survived an assassination attempt and the three holders of the only parliamentary seats the socialists had managed to acquire congratulated the king. Mussolini, now out of prison denounced their hypocrisy. His internment had raised his prestige among socialists and nationalists and he was offered the position of editor of Avanti, the leading Socialist Party newspaper. Mussolini had arrived on the national scene.

In 1913 he was arrested for inciting riots, but he successfully defended himself in court. He was able to use Libya as a political crutch, because the nomadic Arabs and Berbers of the Libyan Desert, especially those of the Senussi religious sect, refused to accept Italian rule. In March 1913 Italian troops destroyed the Nefusah Berbers at the battle of Asabaa, and in July they occupied Mizda Oasis. By year's end Italian troops had penetrated 500 miles into the desert. Actually most of the troops were colonials: Arabs from Libya's coastal cities, Somalis, Eritreans, Italians born in those colonies, and mercenary Yemeni Arabs. Even they found the Libyan Desert to be an inhospitable place. Meanwhile, back in Italy the government convinced the people that the desert war had been won.

This was, therefore, the wrong time for Mussolini to continue to protest the war. Nor would the Socialist Party back him. Running for the constituency of Forli as an independent socialist in November 1913 he suffered a sobering defeat. He was forced to return to the Socialist Party with cap in hand.

They welcomed him because they were planning their biggest move yet, namely a major attempt to take over the country, and they desperately needed his oration and writing skills.

The upheaval began in June 1914 with mass strikes, riots and demonstrations, and workers everywhere were encouraged or coerced to down tools. Within a day the nation was at a standstill. The upper class, upper middle class and reactionary elements also took to the streets. The police took a blatantly anti-worker stance, and shot some of the strikers. Italy was on the brink of civil war. After a week the death toll was in the hundreds. Then suddenly the beaten workers limped back to their jobs.

Naturally Mussolini was disgusted at the failure of Red Week, as it came to be known. Worse news came from Libya. The troops had been unable to maintain their lines of communication owing to Senussi snipers, and had retreated back to the coast. However, Mussolini was not given time to brood, for an even more threatening crisis suddenly loomed.

The civilized world failed to live up to its own standards and in the summer of 1914 a terrorist incident sparked off a family quarrel that degenerated into the most horrific slaughter in human history to date. The manner in which war came has been likened to falling dominoes, each passing on an unstoppable energy. The first domino fell when a Serbian terrorist assassinated the heir to the Austrian throne. The second domino was Austria's reaction to this latest and worst insult by Serbia. They invaded Serbia. From then on each national domino followed in line: the Russian Tsar backed Serbia; his cousin the German Kaiser supported Austria; France allied with Serbia; the Kaiser rose to fend off France by sneaking around the Belgian flank; Britain, whose king was a cousin of both the Kaiser and the Tsar defended Belgium.

Italy was obligated by treaty to defend Austria, one of those obligations that weak governments sometimes acquire. The crisis came immediately after Red Week and the Italian government did not feel strong enough to hand out rifles to its army reservists, the very workers it had just crushed. Nor did it want to defend the Austrians, who were still in occupation of a large acreage of land that was historically and culturally Italian. As a result the government refused to make war. Their legal standing for this was that Austria was the invader not the invaded. The fact that Italy was able to extricate herself from the line of dominoes proves that the conflict soon known as the Great War was not inevitable. [Aka World War I]

The socialists were happy, as they believed that both sides in the war were warmongers who were willing to shed the blood of millions of workers for profit. The government's refusal to make war did have its opponents, though: the more naive nationalists who felt Italy's honor was at stake, and those who hoped that in gratitude for their presence on the battlefield alongside the Austrians, the Austrians would free that part of Italy they still held. Mussolini was of another mind. He believed Italy should go to war, but to fight Austria not defend it. This caused Mussolini's final break with the socialists. In November the Socialist Party expelled Mussolini, and in response he began his own newspaper 'The People of Italy'. It proved popular.

Mussolini's popularity went up in March 1915 when he fought a duel to defend his cause and was slightly wounded. By spring 1915 Austria and Germany were close to victory: they had devastated entire Russian armies, slaughtered the French and British by the hundred thousand, conquered Belgium and northern France, all but destroyed Serbia, and enticed Turkey into their alliance. This was not a good time to challenge them, but Mussolini was much more emotive than logical. On May 20 the Italian parliament voted whether to attack Austria. The vote was a victory for Mussolini and his cause: 407 yes,

———

General Luigi Cadorna's plan was to cross the Isonzo River into Austrian-controlled Italy with 875,000 regulars and reservists, his goal being Gorizia, then Trieste, then if necessary into Austria proper and on to Vienna. But after thirty-six days of butchery Cadorna called off the offensive. His peasant soldiers had been thrown against barbed wire, magazine-fed rifles, machine guns and massed artillery, a mincing machine for human flesh, and they had not even crossed the river.

On July 18 Cadorna asked his men to try again, and try bravely they did, but by August 3 they had yet to cross the river, so he called off the attack. By now Cadorna's casualty list had 60,000 names on it.

Mussolini was many things, but not a coward. He had fought a duel over his principles and had fully expected to serve his country in war against Austria, for he was a reservist and still only thirty-one years of age. However, he had not reckoned with the generals, who felt he was the last person they wanted in their army, this anti-war activist who had announced he would write a dispatch every day from the front line. They refused to call him up, and Mussolini begged them to in every issue of his newspaper. Eventually realizing they could control him better if he was in uniform under their gaze, the generals agreed, and on 31 August 1915 Benito Mussolini put on the gray-green uniform and helmet with black plume of the 11th Bersaglieri Regiment, assembled the accoutrements of a light infantryman, and grabbed his trusty 6.6mm Mannlicher-Carcano rifle, and entered the lines as a lance corporal.

Despite his notoriety among the generals he was still a celebrity and disregarding his rank many an officer invited him to dinner. He accepted, believing that as a war correspondent as well as a soldier he had a duty to report the war from all points of view. His fellow mud crawlers seem not to have minded, for he shared the danger and hardships, and he achieved genuine friendships among them. His commanders reported he was a good soldier.

By October 1915 Cadorna wanted to use the latest batch of reservists and youthful volunteers to make one more big push before snow blocked the mountain passes. Using six times the amount of artillery as he had during his first onslaught, he assaulted the Austrians for eighteen days of unbelievable horror. Not one Italian penetrated the enemy line and lived to talk about it.

With winter fast approaching Cadorna tried once more on 10 November, but by 2 December he had to accept defeat and called off all attacks. Six months of war had cost Italy 160,000 casualties.

Mussolini received leave, and shocked everyone by marrying. His bride, Rachele, was one of his many mistresses. Marriage was very common as soldiers came home from the front suffering a terrible loneliness and an eagerness to set things right with the world before they left it for good. They had lost their innocence and their belief they were immortal. For the first time Mussolini could see at first hand the reality of violent bloody death in snowy mud, and it obviously affected him deeply.

Ever the writer he spent much of his honeymoon sending off dispatches. Then within days he was back at the front, sleeping in a freezing trench in the mountains.

Cadorna's great spring offensive began 11 March 1916 just as the first melted snow began to trickle down from the mountain passes towards the warm sea. Corporal Mussolini was here. The battle came to a halt after nineteen days. There had been no gains worth mentioning.

On May 16 the Italians in the Trentino area were attacked by the Austrian Third and Eleventh Armies. General Brusati's First Army was overrun, but by 10 June the Italians had brought the Austrians to a bloody stop, and then they rose up and chased the Austrians all the way back to their original positions. On 17 June both sides fell exhausted. The Austrians claimed a victory for they had killed or maimed 107,000 Italians and captured 40,000. The Italians claimed a victory for they had killed or maimed 55,000 Austrians and captured 26,000.

On 6 August the Italians tried once more to smash their heads through the stubborn Austrian line, and this time they brushed aside the bullets and shrapnel slicing into their flesh and crossed the river, liberating the province of Gorizia. At last the Italians had a real victory to celebrate and it had only cost them 51,000 men.

Nonetheless, this was the only good news as the remainder of the year gained them nothing but the loss of another 75,000 sons of Italy.

In January 1917 good soldier Mussolini was promoted to sergeant. Mussolini had also proved a dutiful war correspondent, for he wrote the truth, but allowed government censorship to rule his version of the truth. The generals did not want Italian mothers to know that their sons were sleeping in rat-infested holes with a piece of a human corpse for a pillow.

On 23 February 1917 Mussolini was ordered to test a new type of mortar. He placed it according to instructions, but it proved defective: it blew up. Comrades rushed their dazed and bleeding hero to the nearest medical tent. His wounds were severe with shrapnel embedded in both legs. It was several days before he was well enough to write his dispatch and explain his condition. Weeks later he was released from hospital, but only to be sent home on crutches to convalesce. He knew his military service was over.

———

It was incomprehensible to the poor semi-literate masses who read Mussolini's articles that a country that had never been able to pay her workers a decent salary, heal her sick, house her homeless or support her destitute could now afford to continue the war for a third year spending money like it was water.

The soldiers went over the top once more, on 12 May 1917, just as their generals ordered, but their heart was not in it and the generals noticed that by 8 June the men were exhausted and nothing had been gained. They called off the affair: too late for the 157,000 whose blood was already flowing down from alpine meadows into the streams of the Trentino and Isonzo.

On 18 August General Luigi Capello's Second Army attacked the enemy lines in Northern Gorizia, while the Duke d'Aosta's Third Army advanced against the fortifications of Southern Gorizia. Capello's men broke through the shattered remnants of the Austrian armies, and liberated Bainsizza Plateau. The Austrians, now at the end of their tether, swallowed their pride and asked Germany for help. The Germans could afford to provide it because they had practically annihilated the Russians and had brought the French to the verge of mass mutiny.

On 24 October 1917 the Austrians and Germans launched their offensive against the Italian Second Army near Caporetto, first unsettling the Italians with poison gas, then advancing with small but heavily armed parties of infantry who infiltrated into the Italian trenches. These shock troops as the Germans called them were a new innovation. One of the junior German officers among them who found these tactics overwhelmingly successful was a certain Erwin Rommel. Behind them followed twenty-eight Austrian and seven German divisions. Two days later the Austrians used similar tactics to break into the Italian Third Army. Of the Italians, their Third Army was forced into retreat, their Carnic Force was surrounded and their Second Army was annihilated.

The Italian generals reacted with drastic measures, ordering the Carabinieri (military police) to shoot deserters on the spot. The generals within the warm comfortable walls of their villas drew a line on the map, naming it the Tagliamento Defense Line and expected it to stop the enemy. Lines on maps do no such thing. Drawing the Livenza Line was equally futile. Only by mid-November did the Italians manage to stop the onslaught of Teutonic invaders. The generals were too much in shock to breathe a sigh of relief: thousands of tons of precious supplies had been overrun, a good slice of Italy had been lost, 2,500 artillery pieces had been destroyed or lost and 315,000 men were missing. The scale of this defeat, named Caporetto, was one of the most humiliating in Italy's three thousand year history

Mussolini was caustic in his criticism of the Italian general staff, but forever loyal to the Italian soldier. He found it shameful that the

Italian government had asked for British, French and American reinforcements. Worse, the British were at the end of their tether too. Having ditched Prime Minister Asquith for Lloyd George, and having recently suffered a revolt by their Irish subjects, they were desperate for a morale builder. The British needed to keep their men in battle lest the Russians and French collapse altogether, and they had to hold on until their new partner the United States raised an army, so they began to chant that their boys could take it, unlike the Italians. This myth of Italian cowardice, one of the greatest myths of the twentieth century, was thus born out of political necessity. In truth before British reinforcements could arrive at the Italian front, the Italians had stabilized the line and were successfully counter-attacking in some areas.

Of course in Italy heads had to roll for such a debacle. Many blamed Major General Pietro Badoglio, who had commanded the artillery of the XXVII Corps, and who had failed to halt the avalanche of Austrians in a crucial sector. Fortunately for him he had friends in high places including Prime Minister Vittorio Orlando. Cadorna had no friends, so the blame fell on him and he was replaced by General Armando Diaz.

Seven months later, though, Diaz had yet to move. The defeat had been so severe he dare not risk a major fight. The Germans had left the scene to use their shock troop tactics on the British and French in France to excellent effect. Only the arrival of American divisions and a last minute revival of French courage prevented the Germans from winning the war there and then.

On 15 June 1918 two Austrian army groups attacked across the Trentino and the Piave, but unbelievably they gained only three miles, then the Italians counter-attacked with impressive bravura and won a major victory. Orlando's faith in Badoglio proved well founded for as a deputy army chief of staff he worked wonders.

So on 23 October 1918 a year after Caporetto Diaz chose to launch his own offensive around Vittorio Veneto. Attacking alongside a token presence of British, French and Americans the Italians turned the tables on the Austrians completely. On the ninth day of battle the Austrians collapsed like a house of cards. On 4 November, as the Italians counted their 300,000th prisoner, Austria surrendered. Five days later Germany also threw in the towel.

———

As much as any individual Mussolini had been responsible for sending Italy into war against Austria. It was now time to reap the spoils of war. Mussolini read with avid interest the results of the post war treaties. The Austrian Empire was dissolved and its ethnic parts given their freedom, more or less. The Italian-speaking districts of Trentino, Istria and Dalmatia went to Italy, these being Mussolini's own personal goals. But Italy gained more: the districts of Gorizia and Friuli [where a million people speak Friuli-Ladin], a slice of Croatia, a slice of Slovenia, some enclaves of Greek-speaking people on the coast of mainland Turkey, and the South Tyrol where the people are real Austrians. Furthermore the German colonies in Africa would be divided equally among the victors.

Italian mothers read the results too and wondered if it had been worth the price tag of 612,000 Italians dead and 954,000 maimed.

———

Chapter Two
The Street War

Everyone who survives a war wants to remake the world, and some
are more naturally inclined or luckier or better placed to do just that.
In Italy new political parties sprang up in a bloom of confusion and
anarchy. The Communist Party was the most militant and the best
organized as its leaders had been to Russia to study the works of
Marx, the speeches of Lenin and the firing squads of Trotsky.

Mussolini and his newspaper were at the forefront of these debates.
Most veterans had been sickened by the slaughter on the battlefield,
but a few had become immunized against squeamishness. Mussolini
was not one of these, but he did recognize their usefulness if they
could be harnessed as political followers.

On 23 March 1919 Mussolini gathered his trusted followers
together, still calling themselves Fascists from the old days in
Switzerland, and he created Action Squads of 'bully-boys' consisting
of veterans that had seen so much combat that they had become
institutionalized into it, and also of teenagers who had been too young
to see action and were out to 'prove' themselves. Initially referred to
as Squadristi, in time they adopted a black shirt as their uniform. The
first such unit to be so dressed was that of Gabriele d'Annunzio.
Eventually all of the Squadristi donned a black shirt. Political
uniforms were common in this age: for example a rival nationalist
party called its thugs the Blueshirts.

Mussolini needed his Blackshirts to protect Fascist Party rallies
from attacks by rival groups and for attacking other parties' meetings,
but he gave them no political direction as yet. They fought for
Mussolini not for an ideal.

Mussolini soon found an idea to fight against: Communism. In a
bloody civil war Russia was falling acre by acre to the Communists;
Hungary too went Communist; Germany was in the throes of civil
war against the Communists; France was in turmoil; the British were
at war in Ireland but were actually sending troops from Ireland to
England for fear of a Communist revolution. In Italy the Communist
Party's Red Guards were already using pistols to settle political
arguments.

With hindsight, this author believes, the creation of the Blackshirts
was one of Mussolini's greatest errors. They soon gained a reputation
for attracting loafers, thugs and petty crooks that would rather prance
up and down the street in uniform than get a job. They invariably
moved in gangs and beat up anyone who did not show the proper
respect. Mussolini's political protests were valid and he need not have
sunk to the savagery of the other extremist groups.

Yet Mussolini believed civil war was near and he wanted to be in a position to win it. He kept the Blackshirts under a very loose control, which pleased them, and he listened to their officers as if their opinions mattered.

Then the final signatures were placed on the Treaty of Versailles to formally end the war. The revised and final draft came as a shock to the Italian people. The French and British had gobbled up the German colonies without so much as a 'please' or 'thank you', leaving nothing for the Italians. Furthermore the Turkish Army announced it would fight any Italian attempt to gain the enclaves on the Turkish coast promised by the treaty. The British and French refused to help the Italians if it came to war with Turkey. Furthermore they ordered Italy to give the Italian-speaking city of Fiume to Serbia. They also reneged on their promise to give the Dalmatian coast to Italy, with the exception of Zara and the island of Lagosta, giving it instead to Serbia. Additionally the British and French ordered Italy to renounce all claims to Albania and all claims to the Italian-speaking villages on the French side of the Franco-Italian border.

The Italian perception was that the French and British were treating them more like a conquered foe than a brother in arms.

While Mussolini fumed, ranted and raved about the treaty in his editorials, a well-known poet and war hero Gabriele D'Annunzio took action. With 300 Blackshirts, he occupied several buildings in Fiume and declared the city to be an independent nation.

In November 1919 came elections, which everyone had been waiting for with dread. Mussolini was well and truly loved, but his Blackshirts were loathed. His Fascist Party earned so few votes that they became a laughing stock. In fact the elections settled nothing, for there were so many parties now that none gained a clear majority, so the street battles continued.

Mussolini shrugged off the election results with jokes, but he knew he had to distance himself from the monster he had created, the Blackshirts. He began to meet with industrialists and the nobility, reminding them that he would be a better catch than a Communist, who would steal the factories from their owners and throw the nobility out of their palaces.

In May 1920 in Rome the Royal Guards attacked a mob of Blackshirts and killed fifteen in a bloody incident. The wealthy and powerful saw this as a costly error: 'gun down the Communists, not the Fascists', they told the government. Within a month Prime Minister Nitti was forced to step down.

The new Prime Minister, Giovanni Giolitti, was more compliant, but he too had his embarrassment. At the port of Valona in Albania civilians began shooting at Italian warships berthed there. Giolitti ordered his ships to make a shameful retreat.

Naturally Mussolini denounced this cowardice, and this time his words bore fruit. Giolitti offered to buy him off with a post in the government. Mussolini refused, but at last he knew he was gaining sufficient credibility to be taken seriously.

In August 1920 the Socialists and Communists allied together to create another 'Red Week' with mass strikes and demonstrations in every town. Instead of policing the rebels Giolitti took a most unusual step. He gave them free rein. This new 'Red Week' lasted a month and true to the boasts the rebels brought the nation to a standstill, but then realized that they could not make anything work, for only managers and owners knew how to do that. The workers, feeling betrayed by the rabble-rousers, drifted back to work and waited for the managers to return. The Socialists and Communists blamed each and began fighting among themselves again. And there was a major split among the Socialists, with many of them joining the Fascist Party.

But at the moment of triumph Giolitti threw away his lead: he signed the Treaty of Rapallo, which gave the requested lands to Serbia. At Serbian insistence Italian Royal Guards attacked D'Annunzio's rebels in Fiume and rounded them up in a bloody five-day house-to-house battle.

Mussolini publicly denounced the treaty and the attack on D'Annunzio, but secretly he must have been happy that his rival for leadership of the Fascist Party had been defeated.

The street battles got worse. In Bologna Blackshirts led by Dino Grandi fought the Socialists, killing three and wounding twenty, for no serious injuries to themselves. In February 1921 two Blackshirts were gunned down by Socialists. In March there was an assassination attempt on Mussolini. On 23 March a Communist bomb went off at a Milan theater during a gala event, killing 18 and wounding 127. Many beautiful society heiresses were maimed. The Milan Blackshirts retaliated by going on a rampage, burning down the offices of the Communists and Socialists.

In late March the Blackshirts seized several towns in Sardinia, an island that had long been in Italy's possession, though the people are indigenous not Italian. The Blackshirts looked to Mussolini for justification, but found none. Once again their rashness had made him look bad. Then to make matters worse the commander of the Blackshirts, Italo Balbo, declared that he now had 20,000 men and to prove it he would demonstrate in every town in Italy.

Perhaps this show of strength did some good, for in the May 1921 elections the Fascist Party won 35 seats in parliament. Mussolini personally represented the dual-constituency of Milan and Bologna. Long kept out of the cold, Mussolini had finally become a politician.

He was soon ranting in parliament, for on 26 June Prime Minister Sforza surrendered the town of Porto Baros to Serbia. This shameful cowardice sparked riots throughout the nation.

On 21 July a Blackshirt parade in Sarzana was ambushed by

Socialists and police working together. For no loss the attackers killed twenty and wounded over a hundred. The Blackshirts were now in the mood to kill every Socialist on sight, but Mussolini took everyone by surprise by making a truce with the Socialists on 2 August. Many a Blackshirt swore at Mussolini for this and clamored for his head, so he gave it to them. He resigned from the Fascist Party!

Italy was stunned. The Fascists had not really wanted him to go: who else could hold them together and give them direction. The leading Fascists and Blackshirts went begging to Mussolini to reconsider, which is exactly what he had wanted. He agreed to rejoin, but only if they agreed to obey him without a whimper. They accepted. It was a brilliant move.

Of course the leading Fascists were not stupid and saw through the act, and they were simply giving Mussolini enough rope to hang himself. They planned their own operation to seize control of Italy. In the future the Fascists, Blackshirts and Mussolini would all use each other, presenting a unified front to opponents, but behind the scenes there would be backstabbing, intrigue, plots and counter-plots.

In January 1922 in separate incidents three Fascists were gunned down. The Blackshirts responded by burning down more offices.

The pope had died and the new successor to this powerful office was Achille Ratti, who would reign as Pope Pius XI, and in February 1922 he announced he would not allow the church to become involved in politics. This was magnificent news for Mussolini, for it left the strong Catholic Popular Party bereft of financial support. Then Moscow abandoned the Italian Communist Party. Only the Nationalists and Socialists were still a threat to the Fascists, and daily the Fascists were recruiting disaffected members of both parties.

In March 1922 an assassination attempt wounded Achille Starace, a member of Mussolini's inner circle. Now the Blackshirts launched their own operation, occupying government buildings in Ferrara, hoping to force Mussolini to accept their action. Mussolini bit his tongue and smiled on the affair. He needed the Blackshirts now more than ever. Mussolini even defended the act in a duel wounding his Socialist challenger.

In August the Blackshirts ignored Mussolini's pleas for restraint and occupied more government buildings in Cremona and other towns. He saw his grip on them slip away. The news from Parma sent a shockwave throughout Italy, because here Italo Balbo led a Blackshirt army to seize the city, but armed socialists, Catholics and Communists resisted in a ferocious gunfight for six days. After suffering thirty-nine killed and a hundred and fifty wounded the Blackshirts retreated.

As a last desperate measure Mussolini ordered the demobilization of the Blackshirts, sending them home. Few heeded his order. Instead, Italo Balbo, Cesare Maria de Vecchi, General Emilio de Bono and others called for a march on Rome by all Blackshirts to seize power. Mussolini warned them that they would have to face the Italian Army and police. They ignored him. The march was scheduled to begin 30 October, 1922.

That morning King Vittorio Emmanuele invited Mussolini to his palace in Rome and asked him to take the position of Prime Minister until new elections could be held. Before the marchers had reached the first village they were told by telephone that Mussolini had beaten them to it. The marchers continued nonetheless and in every town they passed through they destroyed the offices of rival political parties. As almost his first official act Mussolini ordered the police not to hinder the Blackshirts. He knew the Blackshirts were only venting their frustration with him. From now on if they wanted a piece of the cake they would have to let Mussolini choose the recipe.

Mussolini went back to the king with his suggestion for a new cabinet. To everyone's relief, he picked mostly non-Fascists. As a result parliament approved his assumption of power with 306 for and 116 against.

The schoolyard bully boy, the teacher, the anti-war activist, the warrior, the Socialist, the Fascist, the enigma that was Mussolini had achieved the highest position in the nation, and was still only thirty-nine years old.

———

Chapter Three
The Libyan War

On 12 January 1923 the Fascist Party absorbed the Nationalist Party. Prime Minister Benito Mussolini was proclaimed the leader of this new super party, and was saluted as Il Duce, a term extrapolated from the ancient Roman title of Dux meaning war leader. He achieved this by bribing the Nationalist bosses with gifts, titles and government jobs.

The term Dux did not refer to Mussolini's leadership in any external war, nor did it mean he was the commander in chief of the armed forces. The king held that position. Dux was in fact a simple recognition that the Fascists and Blackshirts had won the street war. It was purely an honorary title.

On 1 February he rewarded his Blackshirts with the title Voluntary Militia of National Security (MSVN), and legitimized their activities. Their administration was divided into sixteen geographic zones, which gave sixteen of the most power-hungry Blackshirts the title of Lieutenant General. It seemed at first that the Blackshirts had taken over, but all Mussolini had done is remove fifteen of the highest-ranking Blackshirts from Rome and divide them into squabbling provincials. They would remain harmless from now on in their new pretty black uniforms. They had a rank system and structure based on the ancient Roman Army with cohorts and legions, and saw themselves as the vanguard of a new Roman Empire. They even saluted in the ancient Roman style, the right arm extended forward.

Of course the Blackshirts wanted to participate in governing the country, so Mussolini fobbed them off with the creation of the Railway Militia, i.e. railroad police. It would be manned by Blackshirts, but Mussolini made sure it would be controlled by the Ministry of Communications.

There is no doubt that the Fascists were extreme right wing, but they were not anti-Semitic like some other similar parties in other countries. In fact many Jews were Fascists and some were Blackshirts.

The most important change for the ordinary Blackshirt Squadristi was that full-time units were created who were paid well and barracked in good conditions. Currently every Italian man reaching adulthood had to serve in the military, as Mussolini had been forced to do, but now any conscript could choose to serve in the Blackshirts rather than the army, navy or air force. The military agreed to this. After all, they did not want Fascists in their ranks anyway. The vast majority of Blackshirts were still reservists who held down civilian jobs. However, the generals and admirals did not like the idea of a new rival armed force, even if it was only armed with rifles. To appease the military Mussolini introduced new programs. The air force, hitherto part of the army and therefore beholding to ground generals for a budget, was given its independence by Mussolini as the Regia Aeronautica. At one fell swoop a whole gaggle of air force generals owed their positions to a man who only six years earlier had been a mere sergeant.

Mussolini needed to find a way to appease the army and navy, and an opportunity arose on 27 August 1923 when in Greece General Tellini and four members of the Italian Armistice Commission were murdered by unknown assailants. At once Mussolini demanded Greece apologize, pay a large amount in reparations and perform several other duties that no self-respecting government would ever agree to. He was confident the Greeks were too proud to agree and too crippled by their recent defeat at the hands of the Turks to fight him. When a journalist suggested that a show of strength might convince the Greeks that Mussolini was serious, he seized upon this proposal, not really to impress the Greeks but to impress the Italians. He ordered Admiral Solari to bombard the island of Corfu using the battleship Conte di Cavour, then to land marines and occupy the island. The operation took place on 31 August. Unfortunately there were civilian casualties.

The world saw this as an act of unwarranted aggression, but to the Italians it was a sign that at long last they had a prime minister that would not back down shamefully. Having achieved his goal, Mussolini brought the marines home.

———

Ironically Mussolini had actually inherited a real war, but because Italian arms were not succeeding in this war the press had not been giving the conflict the attention it deserved. For over a decade the nomadic Arabs and Berbers had denied Italians passage into the Libyan Desert. The colony of Libya that the Italians had created after conquering it from the Turks was a success, as Italians had settled on the coast in towns and were attempting some agricultural progress on the coastal plain, which was up to eighteen miles wide. But the desert remained off limits.

In 1915 a column of Italian and Eritrean cavalry, patrolling a supposed pacified coastal area near Sirte, was ambushed and destroyed by the followers of Ramadan Suwayhili of Misurata, who had once pledged peace to the Italians. This act of treachery gave new hope to those tribes still holding out against the Italians, and they were soon helped by a shipment of arms from Austria [then at war with Italy]; and this spurred them on to resist the Italians.

Some of these nomads were followers of the Senussi religious sect led by Sayyid Ahmed, and fortunately for the Italians the Senussi became cocky enough that they challenged the British in neighboring

Egypt. British forces repelled them.

So in 1917 the new Senussi leader Sayyid Idris signed a peace treaty with Italy and Britain. In return the Italians recognized provincial parliaments in two regions of Libya [Tripolitania and Cyrenaica], and in 1919 Italy gave citizenship to all Libyans. In October 1920 Italy recognized Sayyid Idris as Emir of Cyrenaica and in April 1922 recognized him as ruler of Tripolitania.

Meanwhile the colonization program had been continuing and soon the coastal cities of Tripoli, Benghazi, Homs, Tobruk and Bardia had sprouted thriving Italian neighborhoods.

However, throughout all this the desert still lay off limits to all but large well-armed parties, because many of the nomadic bands were fiercely independent. By this time almost all the 'Italian' soldiers in Libya were in fact coastal Arabs. The Italian name for an African soldier was ascari. They served in sand colored uniforms under white officers and at a few yards distance could be mistaken for Italians, though Italians wore pith helmets, whereas ascaris wore fez caps.

By summer 1922 it was the Italians' turn to feel cocky, and Giuseppe Volpi the Governor of Tripolitania took it upon himself to conquer the desert. Hearing of the invasion, Sayyid Idris called off all deals and declared a religious war against Italy. In October Mussolini became Prime Minister and inherited this war.

Volpi immediately cried out for reinforcements, but Mussolini was apprehensive. It was too early for him to start risking the sons of Italian mothers. Nonetheless he did send reinforcements, almost all of them ascaris from Eritrea and Somaliland. Let Black African mothers weep for their lost sons, he decided. He also sent some Yemeni Arabs. These were mercenaries that came from a British colony. Thus the only actual Italians involved in this new war would be officers, some rear-echelon personnel and airmen. However, the Blackshirts changed that, for they demanded a share in the glory, and they sent the Velino CCNN Legion from Avezzano, the Vespri CCNN Legion from Sicily and the San Efisio CCNN Legion from Sardinia. The initials CCNN stood for Blackshirt. A legion contained two cohorts [rifle battalions] and a company of machine guns and mortars. These Blackshirts in Libya wore an army uniform, but with a black shirt and MSVN insignia. This was to help them blend in a little better, but the army resented them. Not least of the reasons was that the Blackshirts were paid much better than army soldiers of equal rank, in fact more than a skilled machinist.

Together the fez capped ascaris and pith helmeted Blackshirts searched a mountainous wasteland larger than Italy while aircraft scanned the far horizons. They found no guerillas. However, on occasion the guerillas found them, ambushing small patrols.

Mussolini soon realized that he had to win this war, because his power base would only support him as long as he was strong: lose

Libya and he would lose Italy. Therefore, he ordered his troops to occupy oasis after oasis. The local civilians appeared peaceful enough, but this had always been the easy part. Maintaining the lines of supply was the hard part, because the guerillas were mounted on horses and camels and were highly mobile. In this cat and mouse game it was difficult to judge the battle performance of the Blackshirts.

In 1924 the colonists on the Libyan coast raised two Blackshirt legions for self-defense, the Oea CCNN and the Berenice CCNN. By now eighty per cent of the oases had been occupied, but only ten per cent of the land.

———

Meanwhile Mussolini was consolidating his grip on power at home, putting off that proposed election time and again. In June 1924 he made a treaty with Serbia, regaining the Italian-speaking city of Fiume, while allowing the Serbs to have the Serbo-Croat suburbs. This came as great news for the Nationalists, lifting the nation's self-esteem. On the home front he pleased the industrialists and investors by raising industrial production and rooting out Communist union bosses. This in turn brought in new investment from home and abroad. He pleased the land owners of all sizes by raising agricultural production, draining marshes and bringing in the newest equipment, and quashing peasant rabble-rousers. He pleased the workers and farm laborers by ensuring everyone got a fair shake, and he introduced a socialist agenda that would eventually be copied by every industrialized nation in the world. He encouraged the aviators of the Regia Aeronautica to engage in the newest sport, air racing, and this proved to be a great public morale builder, for the Italians soon led the world in this daring sport. Generally speaking he gave the nation a long overdue shot in the arm. Fascist Party membership remained low, but Mussolinism was on the rise.

Unable to stave off the election any longer, it was held in April 1924: the Fascists winning a fine victory, 356 seats. The Catholic Popular Party was suddenly not so popular, winning only 40 seats. The Socialists took 25 and the Communists 18. Smaller parties took the remainder. Regrettably the election run-up had been marred by street warfare again: eighteen Fascists had been killed and 147 wounded, mostly by Communists.

Giacomo Matteoti the Socialist leader challenged the election result as a fraud, and to be sure it was probably not as honest as it should have been, but the Fascists would probably still have won, because Mussolini was working wonders. Then suddenly one incident obstructed Mussolini's quest for respectability. Mussolini certainly must have wished out loud that Matteoti would disappear, but this author doubts that he actually ordered it. Probably, one of Il Duce's less pensive followers took it upon himself to murder Matteoti. The killing caused a sensation in the world press. Indeed the outcry was so strong that evidently Mussolini actually considered resigning. However, on 12 September a trade union leader murdered a Fascist member of parliament. This somehow seemed to silence the Matteoti affair: an eye for an eye, so to speak. By the year's end Mussolini felt strong enough to start curbing the press. He who had used the freedom of the press for so long now began to deny it to others. He, who had been a teacher, now ensured that only Fascists taught schoolchildren. Italy was slowly, without fuss, sliding into a totalitarian dictatorship.

———

In Libya the conflict that claimed the lives of a few ascaris each week was becoming an embarrassment. If Italian aviators could win air races, why could they not find guerillas in a treeless desert? Mussolini decided to kill two birds with one stone: he sent a military commander of renown to win the war, and simultaneously removed the most powerful Blackshirt commander in Rome to become the political commander in Libya. The political commander was white bearded Blackshirt General Emilio de Bono. The latter knew the real reason for his appointment as Governor of Tripolitania. It was an exile in disguise. In a similar move Mussolini had sent the powerful Cesare Maria de Vecchi to Somaliland.

The military commander was Major General Rodolfo Graziani. He was one of the world's greatest survivors. He had fought in Libya in 1911 and had been medically discharged following a severe illness. Having once trained as a priest, but not willing to return to the cloth and with no military future ahead of him he joined the police. However, when the trenches of 1915 created a shortage of army officers, he was reexamined and ordered to return to military duty. Before the war ended he was wounded by poison gas and invalided out of the army a second time. In 1921 he reapplied, passed the medical, and returned to duty. He did a tour in Libya. Now in 1925 Mussolini was sending him back to Libya with orders to do all that was necessary to win.

Graziani knew that his opponent was not a professional military man. In fact Omar Mukhtar was a sheik of the Minifa tribe, a religious teacher, by now 61 years old. Never possessing more than a thousand men he gave the Italians a run for their money. The Italians had aircraft, trucks, radios, artillery and machine guns, whereas Mukhtar had horses, camels, swords and rifles with little ammunition. Graziani had noticed on his first tour in Libya that only when the Italians fought like Senussi did they stand a chance, such as when they used the Somali Camel Force. This unit of ascaris was currently commanded by Major Amedeo, the young, handsome and tall son of

General the Duke D'Aosta. Amedeo was as popular with the magazines as a film star, and the darling of the social scene in the coastal cities.

Graziani was an innovator, and to help win his victory he brought tanks to the desert. The Italians had already been using Lancia armored cars in the desert, but it was hitherto thought that tanks were far too heavy and would sink into the sand. Graziani experimented, and found the L3 [CV29] at less than three tons and only four feet high was light enough and its tread wide enough that it did not sink. While the two-man crew was protected from rifle fire they could spray the guerillas with a 6.5mm machine gun. However, this 'tank' did not possess a turret. It was in fact a tankette, based upon a British design.

———

Now that Mussolini had the generals and admirals where he wanted them, he decided to go one better. Not being happy as an ex-sergeant, he promoted himself on 26 January 1926 to Minister of War, Minister of Air and Minister of the Navy -- jobs traditionally held by uniformed members of those services. He also made himself commander of the MSVN.

Mussolini had continued to buy off the Blackshirts. By now, in addition to the Blackshirt-manned Railroad Militia, Blackshirts were also manning the Forestry Militia, which was responsible for the protection and exploitation of nature and wildlife [under the control of the Ministry of Agriculture and Forests]. They also manned the Port Militia, which guarded the main ports in both Italy and its colonies, and was controlled by the Ministry of Communications. They also manned the Post and Telegraph Militia, a police force responsible for the prevention of fraud in postal, telephone and telegraph services. This too was controlled by the Ministry of Communications.

In 1927 the MSVN Anti-Aircraft Militia was formed, responsible for the anti-aircraft gun defense of Italy. (Not to be confused with the anti-aircraft units operated by the military). This militia manned guns, searchlights and observation posts, and its personnel were reservist Blackshirts. Also this year the full-time MSVN Frontier Militia was established, and these Blackshirts were responsible for guarding the frontiers against smuggling and illegal border crossings.

In 1928 the MSVN Highway Militia was created, and these Blackshirts became highway police. It was controlled by the Ministry of Public Works.

On the face of it the Blackshirts had expanded rapidly, but in truth each of their militias was under civilian control. This was Mussolini's method of divide and rule.

———

Graziani took Blackshirts with him into the desert. This was to appease the leadership of the Blackshirts, not because he thought highly of their capabilities. Over the next three years he extended Italian rule to all but a handful of oases in the extreme south of the colony. Graziani hoped to bring Mukhtar to a final battle in the Sirtica Desert, because long-range sniping and nightly raids by horsemen were fraying the nerves of Graziani's troops.

At this point Mussolini chose someone new to be the political commander of Libya and his choice was highly controversial, none other than General Badoglio, the scoundrel of Caporetto, whom Mussolini also admitted to the nobility as the Marquis of Sabotino.

Badoglio was smart enough not to risk his reputation in the desert so he allowed Graziani to continue as commander in the field, and ordered him to advance across the great Fezzan Desert to the French outposts in Chad. In a truly magnificent feat Graziani took his column of men, animals, tankettes and trucks across trackless wastes to occupy small village oases that no army had visited for over a thousand years. Periodically Caproni CA 73 bi-planes landed on the flat desert by the side of the column to bring in emergency equipment and messages. But it was March 1930 before Graziani reached the Chad border.

Throughout this time Badoglio had tried to negotiate with Mukhtar, but the old man was obdurate, so Badoglio ordered random searches of villages. If any sign of guerilla activity was found, he imprisoned all males in the village. Moreover, all nomad men, women and children were arrested and placed into concentration camps [an idea he got from the British]. His most impressive move was an incredible engineering project, the creation of a barbed-wire fence complete with watch towers and searchlights stretching southwards from the sea along the Egyptian-Libyan border for 180 miles. Its purpose was to force Mukhtar's gunrunners to go around the fence to the south thus considerably lengthening Mukhtar's resupply time.

Believing that all Moslem holy men were preaching treason, Badoglio had them all arrested and their mosques closed. This almost caused mutiny among his ascaris, most of whom were Moslem. When this did not bring an end to the war, Badoglio began to execute his prisoners. But then again his prisoners were already dying. Italian sanitary methods were never all that impressive even in Italy, so they certainly saw no need to upgrade them for prisoners who were dark-skinned, non-Christian and suspected of rebellion. Libyan estimates of deaths of men, women and children in these camps are highly fanciful, but certainly they numbered in the thousands.

In late 1930 Graziani's column finally reached Mukhtar's last waterhole, the community of Kufra. The inhabitants panicked as they saw the cloud of dust that heralded the approach of the Italians. Graziani expected this and called in aircraft, which appeared on cue and began strafing and bombing the mass of fleeing humanity. The survivors were rounded up by ascaris. Mukhtar was not among them.

In fact for many more months Mukhtar and a handful of guerillas hid in the mountains. Venturing down in small teams they ran into Italian patrols and were killed off one by one. In September 1931 Omar Mukhtar was finally captured and publicly hanged. By January 1932 believing that only a handful of ill-armed holdouts were left, Badoglio and Graziani declared the war was over.

Mussolini had won the Street War, and now the Libyan War. It had taken the Italians twenty years and three months to pacify Libya, but this is not a poor reflection on Italian military prowess. After all, it had taken the British twenty-five years to defeat the Mad Mullah in Somaliland/Sudan, the Americans forty years to pacify the Apache of Arizona, and the French never did pacify all of Algeria in 125 years.

Despite the length of the war it never merited more than a small column mid-way through an Italian newspaper, and actual white Italian casualties were few, most of the losses being ascaris, who were never mourned in Italy. Enemy casualties were frightful, and once released by the Italians many of the nomads fled to British Egypt or French Algeria.

In 1934 Mussolini used Libya again as a political exile by sending Italo Balbo there as governor to replace Badoglio. Balbo instituted an increased colonization drive and within five years 200,000 Italians were living in Libya.

———

Chapter Four
The Ethiopian War

    By the early 1930s Italy was a prosperous modern nation, whereas the rest of the world was suffering from the Great Depression. Mussolini had taken this half-medieval peasant society by the scruff of the neck, rubbed its nose in industrialism and technology and was dragging it along to catch up with Britain, France and the United States. His draconian economic measures had worked. Productivity was higher than in most nations, the transportation system was revolutionized, vast marshes and coastal swamps were drained to make room for agriculture, and Italy was making her mark everywhere. Mussolini made sure that everything that was positive was laid at the door of Fascism. Children were schooled by Fascists and attended weekly scout type Fascist Party functions: rifle training for boys and athletics for girls. The new ocean liner Rex was a triumph of Fascist Will. Sports heroes were Fascist sports heroes. Movie stars were Fascist movie stars. Everything that was negative was laid at the door of anti-Fascists.
    More than anyone, the man responsible for this transformation into a Fascist state was Achille Starace, an inner circle member, who in 1931 became Secretary of the Fascist Party. He went as far as ordering the Fascist salute to replace the handshake.
    People no longer looked to the Roman Catholic Church for advice and comfort, and the congregations became smaller each year. The church was becoming alarmed and Mussolini decided he had to bribe the Pope to keep him quiet, and he came up with a brilliant method. He offered complete sovereignty to the Pope's palace in Rome, the Vatican. It would be the smallest country on earth, but equal to the largest. The Pope would become a head of state. Popes had once been political leaders and had led soldiers in battle over land as recently as thirteen years before Mussolini's birth. But since that time the Vatican had been part of Italy. This restoration would give the Pope the right to place an ambassador in every capital city in the world and thus make his opinion heard in private among the world leaders. In other words it placed the Pope on the world stage even in non-Catholic and even non-Christian countries. The offer was too good to turn down. Pope Pius XI made the deal. Francesco Pacelli negotiated on behalf of the Pope. In return the Pope ignored the darker side of Fascism: the midnight arrests by the secret police [OVRA: Organization for the Vigilance and Repression of Anti-Fascism], beatings by mobs of Blackshirts, tortures by the police and imprisonment for anti-Fascist activity. Mussolini also had an unusual punishment for his enemies: tens of thousands of outspoken anti-Fascists were arrested, driven to the border and dumped, their citizenship revoked. Many settled in

France or the USA, where they usually had relatives to go to. To be sure the Italian people were no longer free.

However, the world saw only the acceptable face of Fascism. In Italy there were no concentration camps and no death squads. In the first eighteen years of Fascist rule Italy averaged only one execution per year for a political offense, not much different than the democracies of the day. Mussolini made treaties with Spain, Hungary, Greece, Austria, Serbia [now calling herself Yugoslavia] and Ethiopia. In the latter case Mussolini showed a very fair minded attitude when it came to race. Treaties between white nations and black African nations were almost unheard of. When Ras Tafari, the regent of the Ethiopian Empire, came to Rome on a state visit he was treated as a European. Mussolini showed how magnanimous he was by sponsoring Ethiopia's entrance into the League of Nations, the first black African nation to be so honored. In magazines and newspapers throughout Britain, USA, France and other countries Mussolini was 'Man of the Year'.

Mussolini had expanded and modernized Italy's armed forces, which was actually welcomed by Britain and France, who looked upon Italy as a member of the Old Boys Club from the Great War. In their arrogance they did not realize that the Italians had a deep mistrust of the British and French for their acts of betrayal at Versailles, and for Britain's wartime suggestion that all Italians were cowards. British tourists had been coming to Italy for two hundred years to see the ancient architecture. It was obvious to Italians that British tourists looked down their noses on Italians as a nation of waiters, organ grinders and ice cream salesmen.

Under Mussolini the Italian Army was reconstructed with five ordinary grades, three non-commissioned officer ranks and eleven commissioned officer ranks. The gray-green uniform remained, but a flat cap replaced the peaked hat, a new round helmet replaced the old boat-shaped helmet, and the high-buttoned collar was eliminated. For desert use the khaki uniform with pith helmet was retained. Ascaris still wore the fez. These changes were popular.

Ascari brigades still retained four battalions, but for white Italians the brigade system was abandoned in favor of a divisional system. Three infantry battalions made a regiment, and three infantry regiments made a division. Each division also had an artillery regiment and an engineer battalion. Most divisions were raised locally and bore the name of the region or largest town or a regionally known symbol, such as Lupi di Toscana – the Wolves of Tuscany. However, not all members of a regional unit were recruited in that region.

Mussolini kept the light bolt-action 6.5mm Mannlicher-Carcano rifle, though it was very unpopular. Each section of ten men possessed one Moschetto-Beretta automatic carbine, which fired a 9mm slug from a 25-round magazine. Independent machine gun companies were armed with 6.5mm bipod and tripod weapons and a few Breda 8mm tripod guns. The main complaint about the 6.5mm was that a Senussi on a charging Arabian steed waving a razor-sharp curved sword could not be stopped by just one bullet. In fact some complained the 6.5mm could not knock down a goat.

At least the infantry did have support from the new 45mm and 81mm mortars.

Mussolini bragged about his armored force, but in truth he was woefully behind in modern tank design. His most numerous tank was the new two-man three-ton L3 [CV29 and CV32] armed with two 6.5mm machine guns. Designated a tankette, it was really not a tank, but a self-propelled gun, as it had no turret. It was more noisy than effective. Of slightly better quality was the two man six-ton Fiat 3000. A real tank, it possessed a turret with two machine guns, and one derivation had a 37mm gun.

Mussolini was right to be proud of his artillerymen. Unfortunately their guns were old. They ranged from 65mm, to 70mm, 75mm, 100mm, 105mm and 150mm.

The Regia Aeronautica was the envy of the world, not just for its quantity of aircraft but its quality of planes and crews. Its fliers were considered heroes throughout the world.

The only cause for alarm as far as the British were concerned was the growth of the Italian Navy. By 1934 Italy had four battleships, twenty-four cruisers, ninety-four destroyers and fifty-nine submarines, plus a host of small craft including the MAS, which was an excellent motor torpedo boat. Under construction were another two battleships, six cruisers, eight destroyers and eight submarines. It was the fifth largest navy in the world, behind only Britain, USA, France and Japan.

———

In 1934 a very trivial incident at a place with a silly name suddenly gave Mussolini an opportunity to flex his military muscles. Wal Wal Oasis contained the only water for a day's walk either way deep in the Ogaden Desert. Two clans of Somalis used the oasis, one which owed a loose political allegiance to the Ethiopian Empire and the other which owed about the same degree of loyalty to Italy. All others who drew water did so only with the approval of one of these clans. In October a British boundary commission arrived to find the oasis occupied by both clans and an Italian army unit about a hundred strong. This unit was a 'bande'. The Italians had shown good foresight in realizing that some tribesmen would make good soldiers if they were allowed to make up their own rules. Thus the bande were born. Unlike ascaris, who were simply native Africans in the Italian Army, the bande wore what they wanted, behaved as they wanted and went home from time to time as the mood took them. Their Italian officers had to go through clan and tribal chieftains to pass on major orders. In fact the only reason anyone joined a bande was to gain access to Italian guns and ammunition.

The British arrived at Walwal to find trouble brewing, because the bande here was protecting a deserter from the Ethiopian Army. The pro-Ethiopian clan became angry, as this was Ethiopian territory they said. The pro-Italian clan knew it was part of Somaliland and thus Italian territory. The boundary commission had in fact come here to map the area and answer such questions. The tension grew for weeks, and became worse with the arrival of an Ethiopian army unit under General Gabremariam. [Ethiopian ranks were often hereditary.]

On 5 December someone fired a shot. Immediately the Ethiopians attacked. The one hundred members of the bande defended themselves very well, while their Italian officers radioed for support. Two Italian-manned L3 tankettes arrived, and this weighted the scales in favor of the bande, and when Italian warplanes strafed the Ethiopians, they fled in panic. Many had never seen an aircraft before. The Ethiopians left 107 dead on the battlefield.

Such incidents on African frontiers were not all that rare. A few weeks earlier a body of Ethiopians had attacked a French Army patrol. And this incident could have been swept under the rug. Both Mussolini and Ras Tafari could care less. But the incident at Walwal had been witnessed by outsiders, the British, who reported it. Then the world news media got a hold of it.

Tafari was a nobleman of the Amhara, the ruling ethnicity of the Ethiopian empire, and he was a hereditary Ras [a sort of Field Marshal]. Following a revolution in 1916 he had been made regent. In 1930 he declared himself to be emperor with no basis for doing so, except his popularity among the Amhara. This tribe is mostly Christian, and knowing this Tafari assumed the title 'Power of the Holy Trinity' [in the Amharic language 'Haile Selassie']. He even nurtured a few overzealous devotees who practically looked upon him as divine. They became known as Ras Tafari-ans.

Naturally Haile Selassie had many enemies, not least the rightful heir to the throne, and he knew he could not show weakness. He had to stand up to Mussolini now that the British had told the world about the fight at Walwal. He had already begun to suspect the Italians were laughing at him. The white man had never conquered Ethiopia, and Haile Selassie hoped to modernize his people so that this would never happen. Spurning Adowa, the empire's traditional capital, he had chosen Addis Ababa as his capital city, and had brought in European architects and engineers to transform it. He hired Belgian military advisors to create an Imperial Guard, and contracted for Swedish Army advisors to establish an officer's candidate school. His army had some trucks and one tankette – a present from Mussolini. However, this nation that stretched hundreds of miles across only possessed one road, dirt all the way.

On 9 December 1934 Haile Selassie lodged an official protest with the League of Nations. Mussolini was startled: this jumped-up little revolutionary would not even have the right to protest if Mussolini had not sponsored his membership of the league, and besides the Ethiopians had attacked first. Mussolini demanded that Gabremariam apologize, that his men salute the Italian flag and that he hand over the officer immediately responsible for the attack. Haile Selassie did not have the power to force Gabremariam to do this, even had he wanted to. Each Somali clan was a law unto themselves, paying only lip service to one faction or another.

Worse was to come. Italian reconnaissance aircraft reported Gabremariam was mobilizing an army at Gerlogubi Oasis twenty-five miles from Walwal. Assuming another attack was coming, Mussolini authorized a pre-emptive strike. He sent a bande supported by tankettes to Gerlogubi and timed an air strike with their arrival. They easily dispersed Gabremariam's warriors.

Mussolini hoped this was the end of the affair. He could not afford a major military exercise at the moment. His eyes were on Europe. The continent was still in the throes of the depression. Germany was now under a volatile dictator, the Austrian Adolf Hitler. Austria had recently been engulfed in civil war. As Italy still controlled the South Tyrol and its Austrian population, the last thing Mussolini needed was a German-Austrian strong man on his border.

But the British and French press would not let Walwal go. They declared that Mussolini had begun the affair in revenge for the Battle of Adowa, an 1896 defeat of an Italian army by Ethiopians. Behind the scenes Mussolini was in contact with Haile Selassie's enemies. He did not wish to topple the emperor, but just wanted to be prepared no matter who was thrown to the top of the heap in the next revolution. Furthermore the British and French press called Italy an aggressor nation. This was rich, thought the Italians, coming from the two largest empires the world has ever known. If war was to come, the Italian press replied, it would be caused by the jibes of the foreign press.

However, behind closed doors the British and French governments sang a different tune, secretly offering Mussolini a free hand to crush the Ethiopians if he signed a pact aimed at preventing Hitler from remilitarizing Germany. To clarify their position the British sent a new ambassador to Rome, Sir Eric Drummond, known to be pro-Fascist. The Belgian Army told its officers of Selassie's Imperial Guard not to become involved, reminding them that the heir to the Italian throne was married to the Belgian king's daughter.

On 12 February 1935 Mussolini ordered the Gavinana [Venezia] and Peloritana [Piemonte] Divisions to recall their reservists. He also recalled the class of 1911, namely those males who had been born in

1911. Currently all twenty-one year old Italian men were conscripted into the military for a year or so of training. Thus the 1911 class had only been out of uniform sixteen months.

The Fascists were clamoring for an invasion of Ethiopia. They did not believe Haile Selassie's claim that he had two million warriors. The Blackshirts bragged the usual boasts that they had become known for....one Blackshirt is worth a thousand Ethiopians, etc.

On 22 February General Rodolfo Graziani boarded ship at Naples with elements of the Peloritana Division destined for Somaliland. Days later the Gavinana Division of Major General Villa Santa followed. In March Mussolini recalled the class of 1912 and in May he mobilized the Gran Sasso [Pinerolo] and Sabauda Divisions. His activity seemed sluggish, and many thought he was giving Haile Selassie time to back down.

The British reacted by stopping arms shipments to Italy and Ethiopia. It was obvious whom this would hurt most.

There had been no combat since the pre-emptive raid on Gerlogubi, so when Graziani arrived in Italian Somaliland he found everyone at peace. Mussolini gave him command of the Peloritana Division, the new 6th Tevere Blackshirt Division and Colonel Luigi Frusci's brigade of four battalions of Yemeni and Somali ascaris. And he was ordered to build a new division from smaller units of Yemenis, Somalis and Eritreans, many of whom had served under him in Libya. He gave Major General Guglielmo Nasi that command. He also had supervision of thousands of Somali bande. But to his chagrin he was given a secondary role in the coming offensive.

The main part of the Ethiopian expeditionary force was commanded by Blackshirt General Emilio de Bono and was assembled in Eritrea. It consisted of three corps: Major General Pirzio Biroli's Eritrean Corps, Major General Santini's I Corps and Lieutenant General Maravigna's II Corps.

Biroli controlled Major General Salvatore di Pietro's 1st Colonial Division and Major General Achille Vaccarisi's 2nd Colonial Division. Both were made up of Eritrean ascaris. Also there were two battalions of Libyan ascaris.

Santini drew his combat troops from the following divisions: Major General Enrico Riccardi's Assietta, Major General Italo Gariboldi's Sabauda and Major General Luigi Cesi's Pusteria Alpini.

Maravigna commanded Major General Nino Villa Santa's Gavinana Division and Major General Adalberto Principe's Gran Sasso Division.

These divisions were named after locations in Italy. De Bono also had independent battalions of Alpini, a Blackshirt Frontier Guard formation and thousands of Eritrean bande.

The standard MSVN Blackshirt unit was the CCNN legion, but Mussolini had authorized the Blackshirts to create six new divisions.

Major General Enrico Boscardi's 6th 'Tevere' Division was sent to Italian Somaliland, but the others were sent to Eritrea: Major General Ettore Bastico's 1st '23 March', Major General Umberto Somma's 2nd '28 October', Major General Giacomo Appiotti's 3rd '21 April', Major General Alessandro Traditi's 4th '3 January' and Lieutenant General Attillio Teruzzi's 5th '1 February'. They were named after important dates in Fascist history. The artillery and rear-echelon of the Blackshirt divisions were mostly army soldiers not Blackshirts.

The colonial divisions contained about 12,000 men each, most of them veteran soldiers. The Blackshirt divisions were small with about 7,000 persons each, and contained many Great War veterans. The army divisions contained around 10,000 men, mostly conscripts and recalled reservists aged between twenty-one and twenty-four.

The ascaris were discerned by their fez caps. Actual Italians wore pith helmets. Ascaris preferred sandals to boots. Other than that the ascaris were pretty much dressed like Italians in their sand colored uniforms. Bande warriors dressed in their tribal clothing.

General Aimone Cat controlled the air component manned by volunteers. They were eager to try out the newest warplanes: Saiman 202 liaison aircraft; Breda BA65 monoplane reconnaissance plane; Caproni CA101 tri-motor monoplane bomber; CA111 monoplane fighter; CA133 tri-motor biplane bomber; Fiat CR30 open cockpit biplane fighter; Savoia Marchetti SM81 tri-motor monoplane bomber; and IMAM RO37 biplane fighter.

Many of the fliers were Fascists, for unlike Nazi Germany, where leading Nazis sent others to do the fighting for them, in Italy the bombastic inflammatory Fascist orators were willing to risk their own lives. Regular officers such as Lieutenant Morgantini and Major Criniti were surprised to hear of the arrival of leading Fascists. Serving in air units were Mussolini's sons Bruno and Vittorio and his son-in-law Count Galeazzo Ciano. Achille Starace, Secretary of the Fascist Party, came to command a motorized column. The commander of the MSVN [i.e. all Blackshirts] Attilio Teruzzi came to lead the 5th Blackshirt Division. Army officers commanded the other Blackshirt divisions, but their deputies were Blackshirts.

Armored vehicles were here too: L3 tankettes, Fiat 3000 tanks, and Fiat armored cars. The latter were a good size at seven tons, with a five man crew and carrying a 37mm gun in a turret.

The natives of Eritrea must have been convinced that every Italian in Italy had come here, to parade, strut, sing, salute and wait under the hot African sun. All they needed was a war.

———

On 13 September 1935 the British mobilized their Royal Navy. Mussolini ordered his navy to respond. Suddenly the stakes had been raised. The world held its breath.

On 1 October some Eritrean bande occupied Moussa Ali Mountain just inside Ethiopia. Haile Selassie ordered his generals to take his army to the border. Once on the move, there would be no stopping them.

Two days later a few Eritrean bande and ascari horse cavalry moved into Ethiopia. Behind them marched 100,000 men. Italy was on the march.

Within four days Mussolini fulfilled the boyhood ambition of many an Italian: his troops occupied Adowa, not quite forty years after that ignominious defeat. Mussolini bragged that the world was trembling to the sound of Italian boots marching to the drums of war. On 6 October Lieutenant Morgantini got all the glory he had ever wished for, when he became the first Italian killed in the new war.

On the 11th Marshal Haile Selassie Gugsa [the emperor's son-in-law] led his 1,200 Ethiopians towards the II Corps, but not to fight, but rather to join the Italians. This was a major coup for Mussolini. Clearly his secret agents had been doing their job well. Many Italians hoped that most Ethiopians would defect like this, at least the Christian ones. After all, the Pope had given his blessing to the war.

By the 15th the invaders had occupied the holy city of Axum. As yet the Italians had encountered no organized resistance, and after penetrating a hundred miles inside Ethiopia no one had seen a sign of Selassie's so-called two million strong army. However, the heat and dust were already overheating truck engines, and the L3 tankettes were breaking their tracks on the rough ground.

When General Badoglio arrived uninvited on an inspection tour he found de Bono's men building roads as they advanced, so naturally the advance was slow and predictable. He reported to Mussolini that everyone was waiting for sixty-nine year old de Bono to make up his mind.

Mussolini read the report, but his mind was on Britain. British elections were coming up and the opposition Labour Party had declared that if elected they would send the Royal Navy to blockade the British-controlled Suez Canal, which would cut off the Italian expeditionary force from home. Mussolini decided he needed a major victory before that election. On 3 November he urged de Bono to advance on Amba Alagi, but the arrogant Blackshirt general refused curtly.

———

The Eastern Lowlands Column under the leadership of Major General Oreste Mariotti was still advancing. He and thirty Italian officers controlled two Eritrean and one Libyan battalions of ascaris and three bande designated Massawa, Northern Dankalia and Southern Dankalia. His artillery consisted of 120mm guns and 77mm pack guns. By 11 November they had reached Au, to find 200 defectors awaiting them, far short of the entire Danakil Army that was supposed to be willing to surrender.

On 12 November Marriotti's column began stumbling through a rocky gorge along the Enda River. No fool, Marriotti recognized this as a good ambush site, so he ordered his guns unpacked and the troops dispersed, when suddenly everyone came under inaccurate rifle fire. The supply camels took many of the bullets, while the disciplined ascaris ran to either side of the gorge and began to reply. The bande reacted in a mixed manner: some fled, others hid, and still others fought. Aircraft called in by Marriotti failed to budge the enemy. General Kassa Sebhat had planned his ambush well, but his warriors were poorly trained and they retreated during the night.

On 14 November Stanley Baldwin's nationalist government won the British election, thwarting the Labour Party's ambition to challenge Mussolini. Baldwin was happy to go no further than impose trade sanctions on Italy. Mussolini could breathe easier. On 17 November Mussolini kicked de Bono upstairs. Badoglio was already on his way to replace him. Mussolini decided to use the team of Graziani-Badoglio to win in Ethiopia as they had won in Libya. Of course the Blackshirts felt insulted that a Blackshirt general had been relieved by an army general. [Though de Bono was also a retired army general.]

Meanwhile Graziani had been squirming in Somaliland, incensed at his second fiddle role. He sent a bande to occupy Gerlogubi. They took it for ten casualties. Then he advanced to Dolo Oasis, and thence to Tafere Ketemma, where he learned the Ethiopians were fighting among themselves. On this intelligence he launched a major strike. Hearing that Gorrabei was held by a battalion of Haile Selassie's famed Imperial Guard, supported by a horde of Ogaden desert warriors, Graziani brought up six battalions of Yemeni and Somali ascaris in trucks with nine tankettes and twenty armored cars to attack them, preceded by an air raid of twenty aircraft. Evidently the air raid killed the local commander, whereupon the Ethiopians fled. It was an easy victory.

But the Ethiopians rallied a few miles further on. Frusci was cautious, and he decided to study them rather than rush them. Over the next week 2,000 defectors joined him.

On 11 November Colonel Pietro Maletti's armored column was ambushed in a narrow rocky pass, and his tankettes could not elevate their machine guns sufficiently to shoot the ambushers. He was forced to abandon three tankettes. Haile Selassie himself flew to the area in one of his few aircraft to reward the tankette captors and berate his field commanders.

———

As Badoglio arrived at the port of Massawa in Eritrea on 26

November he learned the main invasion force had reached the Tembien Mountains, and Italian warplanes were bombing the enemy who had massed to the south at Dabat. He also heard that Haile Selassie was reported to be in Dessie, so he ordered an air strike, hoping to kill the little emperor. He failed, but among the buildings hit was the American Hospital. Though the hospital was currently being used for military as well as medical purposes, this was a public relations victory for Selassie.

Mussolini ordered Badoglio to advance. Surely the Ethiopians massing at Dabat were already worn out, because some of them had walked as much as six hundred miles over rough terrain to get here. From 4 December onwards Badoglio pounded them with air strikes. Thousands of warriors screamed and waved swords at the slow deliberate aircraft. Italian spies reported that General Gessesse had led his personal units out of the city in retreat.

At dawn 15 December in the mountains north east of Dabat an outpost of the Bande Altopiani was wiped out in a sudden rush of razor-sharp swords. As the dawn rays created weird shapes along the craggy canyon sides a patrol of horsed Eritrean bande was mobbed by scores of Ethiopians. The horsemen turned and rode for the nearest outpost to report to their commander, Major Criniti. He ordered the remainder of his bande into battle stations and he radioed for reinforcements. Luckily he had ten tankettes with him.

Within minutes this position was swamped by thousands of Ethiopians. One enemy warrior ran up to a tankette, flung open the hatch and in the twinkling of four terrified eyes he decapitated the two crewmen. Seeing this, the bande fled, and some threw up their hands in surrender. The Ethiopians did not kill their bande prisoners, but they did slice off their hands. Criniti, his officers and the remaining tankettes were able to back out and cover the escape of most of the bande.

In the nick of time reinforcements arrived: infantry of the 3rd Blackshirt Division riding in trucks. Aided by the tankettes, they counter-attacked and regained the lost ground.

They then drove into a canyon, but here they were ambushed, with the Ethiopians rolling large rocks down on them, which blocked the advance and retreat of the tankettes and trucks. Moreover the tankette machine guns could not traverse high enough to hit the enemy on the crest. The tankettes and trucks were abandoned, and the whole party retreated on foot.

The day had cost the Italians about two hundred dead and missing. Spies later informed them that they had been attacked by the entire Simien Army commanded by General Ayalew Birru and the Shoa Army of Marshal Ras Imru.

———

On Christmas Day Maravigna's II Corps advanced into Af Gaga Pass, where his Italian infantry soon came under fire from the Shoa Army. They continued to advance until noon, having taken two hundred casualties. The next morning aircraft reported that the enemy was in retreat.

Meanwhile the Eritrean Corps had also advanced, and Lieutenant General Biroli identified a strategic point, Abbi Addi, where a mule track sliced through the Tembien Mountains, so he sent Consul General Filippo Diamanti's 1st Blackshirt Gruppo towards it. Like most Blackshirt gruppos, it consisted of two legions, each of two cohorts of about 500 men each, and one machine gun company. On 18 December these Blackshirts drew a swarm of no less than ten thousand charging Ethiopians, most of them armed with spears and swords. The two thousand Italians scythed down the charging warriors with their rifles and machine guns, and they called in artillery support from 100mm and 77mm guns. The few Italians that fell were struck by inaccurate enemy rifle fire and by three Ethiopian machine guns perched high on hills. Biroli sent up his Eritrean 1st Colonial Brigade in support.

The following day the Ethiopians charged again, meeting the same bloody fate. After this the Eritrean ascaris advanced and captured the immediate mountain peaks.

Badoglio was irate. His columns were going nowhere fast, so he decided to take the time to readjust his lines. To protect Makalle he concentrated a large part of his artillery, and to protect his long lines of supply he formed IV Corps under Major General Ezio Babbini using Somma's 2nd Blackshirt, Teruzzi's 5th Blackshirt and Major General Pietro Pintor's Cosseria Divisions. To defend Adowa and Axum on his right [west] he ordered II Corps to dig in, and he told the Eritrean Corps to guard Abbi Addi. On his left [east] Santini's I Corps protected Amba Aradem. The air force continued to harass the enemy.

On 20 January 1936 the 1st Colonial Division advanced through Warieu Pass, but heavy rifle fire from the Wag Army forced them to stop by late afternoon. The following day these troops moved forward again, this time helped by the 2nd Blackshirt Division and 1st Blackshirt Gruppo. They inflicted heavy losses on the enemy, but were nonetheless forced to fall back slightly at day's end. The third day they advanced again, and now they did not halt at dusk, but continued to attack all night, in some cases with bayonet versus sword. Come dawn on the fourth day the opposing forces were too close to each other for Italian aircraft to bomb or artillery to bombard. Biroli brought up the 2nd Colonial Division to join the battle, and finally on the evening of the fifth day the Ethiopians fled.

Biroli praised his troops, thinking they had shattered the Wag Army. But prisoners soon confirmed he had also been up against the Beghemder Army of Marshal Kassa, the Tigre Army of Marshal

Seyoum, the Lasta Army and the Iejjiu Army --- a total of 100,000 warriors. The corpses of the enemy desecrated the landscape by the thousands.

———

Graziani was chafing at the bit, convinced he could advance further if allowed. Instead he impatiently awaited orders, while his bande sniped at the enemy. Finally, in January the enemy solved his problem. They advanced towards him en masse in full view of Italian reconnaissance pilots. Graziani prepared to meet them with Major General Giuseppe Pavone's Peloritana Division, Colonel Frusci's brigade of Yemeni and Somali ascaris, Major General Nasi's division of Libyan, Yemeni, Somali and Eritrean ascaris, Major General Annibale Bergonzolli's armored column, Major General Enrico Boscardi's 6th Blackshirt Division and thousands of bande.

Graziani's aircraft slaughtered the oncoming enemy, and then on 10 January Graziani seized the initiative and ordered Bergonzolli to charge the Sidamo Army of Marshal Desta Damteur. In the flat Ogaden Desert Bergonzolli's armored cars and tankettes shattered Damteur's ranks with machine gun fire. The enemy fled. Graziani now ordered an offensive. After advancing for nine days the Aosta Lancers riding in trucks captured Neghelli, and by the 23rd they had entered the Wadara Forest.

This was the sort of battle Mussolini had been waiting for, and he made sure the Italian press put the right slant on things. The news of the joint victories of Neghelli and Warieu Pass were eagerly grabbed by the journalists that until lately had been offered nothing but Fascist oratory.

Unfortunately, there were incidents that Mussolini wanted to keep out of the press. Nasi had organized his sixteen battalions of ascaris into four gruppos, but they were now in a mutinous mood. They were not eager to die to expand the Italian Empire, and one night several hundred of Colonel Maramarcio's 4th Colonial Gruppo deserted. At daybreak Italian planes looked for them, but about six hundred reached British Kenya and were given sanctuary. A few defected to the Ethiopians. Nasi reassigned the remnants of the 4th Gruppo to other units. No one realized it at the time, but this was an early sign of a war weariness that would eventually grip the entire Italian Army.

———

By February Badoglio had seven divisions in front of Makalle, while 170 of his warplanes picked off enemy warriors in small bunches in a mountainous road less zone of 15,000 square miles. Simultaneously his 280 guns pounded those Ethiopians that came within range. On 10 February Badoglio launched his next offensive, aiming for Amba Aradem an eighteen square mile plateau, leading with Santini's I Corps and the new III Corps of Lieutenant General Ettore Bastico. The latter had the Sila Division of Major General Francesco Bertini and the 1st Blackshirt Division of Major General Filiberto the Duke of Pistoia. Santini controlled Traditi's 4th Blackshirt and Gariboldi's Sabauda Divisions.

Only snipers were encountered for two days, but then a battalion of the 4th Blackshirt was pinned down on the slopes of Enda Gabor Mountain by heavy rifle and machine gun fire. At nightfall the impetuous Badoglio withdrew the entire Division, claiming the Blackshirts were not combat ready, and he replaced them with the army's Pusteria Division of Alpini, Italy's crack mountain troops. This insult to the Blackshirts did not go unnoticed in Rome.

At dawn 13 February advanced listening posts of the Sabauda were silently overrun by waving swords, but the enemy did not push his advantage, and come daylight the Sabauda and others advanced, hoping to trap a large force of Ethiopians.

On the 15th the enemy suddenly realized their predicament, and the Center Army of Marshal Muluqueta tried to break out of the closing trap. A party of Alpini managed to climb a peak from which they soon poured down machine gun fire on the mass of warriors. The Italians found that some Ethiopians had holed up in caves, and it took a fearsome effort to root them out.

The first to reach Amba Aradem Plateau was the 1st Blackshirt Division, but their rejoicing was half-hearted once they realized most of the enemy had escaped. Cleaning up the battlefield the Italians were astonished to find hundreds of machine guns, thousands of rifles, some of them hand-made and crude, and eight thousand Ethiopian dead.

Badoglio's spies informed him that the Moslems of Raya Galla were slaughtering the fleeing Ethiopians, most of whom were Christians. Within days the Wollega and Shoa Armies were both retiring. Badoglio would have been happier still had he known that the commander of the Wollega, Marshal Demissie, who was also Chief Counselor to the emperor, had been killed, as had Marshal Muluqueta the emperor's Minister of War.

On the 26th Badoglio sent III Corps from Amba Alagi into the Tembien Mountains to approach Abbi Addi from the rear, while the Eritrean Corps attacked frontally. As an ace up his sleeve Badoglio possessed Lieutenant Tito Polo's team of thirty-five Blackshirts of the 114th Legion and twenty-five Eritrean ascaris of the 12th Colonial Battalion. Using ropes they climbed a precipitous face during the night, crept past enemy sentries, and then captured a summit defensive position. Another team failed at a similar move.

Come dawn and the start of the Italian offensive Polo's team shot down into the enemy, and throughout the day they held against fourteen counter attacks. By dusk the Beghemder, Tigre, Lasta and

Iejjiu Armies were seriously hurt, mostly by air and artillery bombardment. But yet again the Italians moved too slowly to catch the retreating enemy.

On the evening of 29 February III Corps, which had swung behind the Ethiopian Wag Army, was struck by a horde of fleeing enemy warriors, who in their flight were astonished to find Italians here. Well into the night the Italians aided by air dropped flares butchered the fleeing warriors with their rifles, machine guns and artillery. Thousands of Ethiopians including two generals ran straight into this mincing machine.

Badoglio was on a roll now and he urged his commanders to keep up the pressure. To crush the Shoa Army, he ordered II Corps westwards from the Adowa-Axum area and IV Corps southwards from the Mareb River.

II Corps kicked off with the 3rd Blackshirt, Gavinana and Gran Sasso Divisions, an Eritrean ascari brigade and the Eritrean Camel Corps. Near Selaclaw two battalions of the Gavinana were counter-attacked by 6,000 warriors, and though outnumbered five to one they held their ground until the remainder of the division could become engaged. Their courage decided the issue and the enemy drew back.

On the afternoon of 2 March the whole II Corps front was charged by the Shoa Army and elements of the Simien Army. Italian artillery gunners had to lower their sights and fire point blank to keep from being overrun. Badoglio complained of the halt, but Maravigna explained that in places surviving warriors were coming close enough to stab his men with swords and spears. All that night and into the next morning the charge continued.

Finally the attack stopped. The Italians were in a daze, a stupor. Many of them were shaking uncontrollably, unable to speak coherently. The mass of blood and flesh piled high in front of them heaved and moaned as Ethiopian wounded tried to crawl from under the bodies of their friends.

Unbelievably, that afternoon the Ethiopians charged again, trying not to step on corpses, and once again the Italians scythed them down with bullets and shells. Then suddenly it was over.

Badoglio readied two columns to make for Gondar, the Eritrean 3rd Brigade to follow the fleeing stragglers and Starace's motorized detachment to cross the flatlands with 433 trucks in order to outflank the enemy on the west.

———

By mid-March 1936 the Italians had reached the Takazze River and there they rested. On the 21st Badoglio's radio interception unit heard Haile Selassie give orders for his reserves to make an attempt to drive back the invader. At once Badoglio alerted all commands. Selassie still had the remnants of the Kaffa, Wag, Wollo, Shoa,

Beghemder, Tigre and Lasta Armies. Each man had his trusty blade or spear, and in addition thousands had rifles. Furthermore they had 400 machine guns, twelve 75mm artillery guns, six mortars and a few anti-aircraft guns. By any standards it was still a formidable array.

Badoglio formed his line with from right to left the Pusteria, 1st Colonial and 2nd Colonial Divisions under Biroli's Eritrean Corps. Behind them, stood I Corps with the Sabauda, 1st Blackshirt and Assietta Divisions. All faced the Mai Ceu Plain towards Lake Ashangi, and they were all dug in behind barbed wire with rifles and machine guns. Artillery of 77mm, 120mm and 149mm caliber was close by, and air support was on call.

At 5:45 am 31 March before dawn the Italians came under fire from Ethiopian mortars and artillery: the shooting being alarmingly accurate. Minutes later through the darkness they heard a nerve tingling wail. Ethiopians by the thousand were singing and chanting and advancing. As soon as the first figures could be seen in the misty dawn the Italians opened fire with their magazine-fed rifles. Machine guns traversed the field dealing out death. Italian artillery opened fire.

The attack was quickly broken, but soon after dawn a second wave fell on the Italians. It too was broken, and in mid-morning it was followed by a third wave. This time in places the Ethiopians came close enough to match their swords and spears against the bayonets of the ascaris of the 2nd Division.

Behind this wave came the uniformed Ethiopian Imperial Guard, attacking with European-style fire and movement tactics. They broke through at the junction of the 1st and 2nd Colonial Divisions, but the ascaris counter-attacked and broke the back of the Imperial Guard. That afternoon the Ethiopians came on again, and soon the entire Italian front line was in fierce hand-to-hand combat. Towards day's end the surviving Ethiopians began falling back.

The Azebo Gallo tribe viewed this great slaughter from a mountaintop. Finally deciding to intervene, they chose the winning side, and horse-mounted they slammed into the retreating Ethiopians with spears and swords, wreaking untold carnage.

Meanwhile Badoglio's front line repaired their trenches, plucked dead bodies off the barbed wire and restrung it, and brought up food and water. Many soldiers were out of ammunition, despite having been resupplied. Some companies fired more bullets this day than they had originally been allotted for the entire war. The psychological effect of such bloodletting affected Biroli's men to the point that they were in no state to advance for the next week.

However, once they did start to advance on 9 April they were welcomed with cheers in town after town: some citizens hating Haile Selassie, others just glad their town was to be left unscarred, and others hoping that smiles would help them survive. Once the Italians reached Dessie, Badoglio brought up his mechanized forces, because

Dessie had a road, and it led straight to Addis Ababa, Haile Selassie' capital.

———

Graziani was forgiven by Badoglio for having jumped the gun, and he was now given permission to advance. Sending Major General Ranza's air units to blast the towns of the Ogaden Desert, Graziani advanced with from left to right [south to north] Nasi's division of Libyan, Yemeni, Somali and Eritrean ascaris from Webbe Shebelli, Frusci's brigade of Yemeni and Somali ascaris from Gorrahei and Major General Augusto Agostini's Blackshirt Forest Militia on the flank. Graziani held the 6th Blackshirt and Peloritana Divisions in reserve. The fact that the Blackshirts had a Forest Militia, let alone had sent it to a desert war, shows how political necessity rather than military necessity flavored all Blackshirt decisions.

On 14 April Nasi's men encountered the main enemy column made up of a mixture of Semitic and Negro tribal warriors under the grand titles of the Kulu, Gemugofa and Wollega Armies. For three days Nasi's ascaris battled this motley assembly. Aircraft dropped bombs into the mass of enemy humanity, creating craters that from the air appeared to be roses blooming instantly, blood red roses. On the 17th the surviving Ethiopians fled.

On the 24th Frusci's troops clashed with a rearguard of warriors and Imperial Guardsmen, overcame them, and over the next three days they advanced, overcoming similar rearguards. On 30 April Frusci's troops entered Daghabur, the capital of the Ogaden. They had taken untold thousands of prisoners.

———

On 28 April Starace led his column of Blackshirts, Bersaglieri and artillery to victory at Debra Tabor. Badoglio now readied his dash for Addis Ababa. As the trucks moved out along the road he warned his men to expect a rearguard at Ad Termaber Pass. On the 30th Brigadier General Sebastiano Gallina's Eritrean brigade was guided through the mountains by local villagers, and this enabled him to surprise the Ethiopian rearguard of a hundred Imperial Guardsmen and officer cadets. The ascaris killed half and drove off the rest.

A rail line led from Addis Ababa to French Djibouti, and Haile Selassie used this to leave the country along with many foreigners: businessmen, adventurers and missionaries. The emperor left Marshal Imru in charge as regent. Drunken stragglers began running amok through the city burning down foreign buildings. French Embassy troops were trying to quell the riot.

On the evening of 4 May Mussolini's son in law, Galeazzo Ciano, flew low over the great city watching inquisitively as the Eritrean 1st Brigade quietly slipped into the suburbs. The following morning

2,000 vehicles filled with Italians drove into the city. Fascist war correspondents dubbed this the 'Column of Iron Will'.

The news was received in Italy with rapture. Some cheered because Italy had been victorious. Most cheered because the conscripts would be coming home. Mussolini appeared on the balcony overlooking the Piazza Venezia in Rome and to ecstatic cheers he declared the war was over.

That night Badoglio slept at the Italian Embassy in Addis Ababa, while in the streets his men rounded up filthy exhausted stragglers by the thousands.

On 8 May Graziani entered Harar, just in time to see Ethiopian warriors running away. His bande attacked and killed 200 before their officers regained control.

Mussolini appointed Badoglio to be Viceroy of Italian East Africa, and he promoted Graziani to Marshal and made him the Marquis of Neghelli. Mussolini did not forget Italy's long silent king. He made him Emperor of Ethiopia.

The war had cost Mussolini 3,600 dead, of which 2,000 were actual Italians. His wounded numbered twice this. Haile Selassie claimed to have lost 275,000 dead, but this is ludicrous. A figure of 110,000 killed and wounded is probably as accurate as anyone can get.

The Italians had performed well. It is true the young army conscripts had fought more ferociously than the older Blackshirts, but in every army ferocity dissipates with age. The ascaris and bande had done far better than their Italian masters had a right to expect. One alarming piece of news reached Mussolini's ears: Italian military equipment was found to be shoddy and unreliable.

———

Chapter Five
The Ethiopian Guerilla War

Within two weeks of his victory Badoglio resigned. He had no intention of withering on the vine in Africa. Besides, Ethiopia no longer proved useful to him. In fact, it was a liability, because the war was not over, despite his announcement to the press. Sentries were still being stabbed and convoys ambushed.

His successor was an old hand at fighting guerillas. Marshal Graziani willingly inherited this headache with orders to pacify the nation, something that the ruling Amharas of Ethiopia had never been able to do. His mission was to find the guerillas and crush them, but the monsoon rains were beginning and that would make major movement impossible. Meanwhile he accepted the surrender of the beaten nobility of the nation, many of whom walked hundreds of miles for the opportunity of humiliating themselves in front of him in Addis Ababa. The surrenders involved speeches of loyalty followed by many Fascist salutes and a few Italian songs.

As all colonial masters are wont to do, Graziani began to recruit locals. He employed an entire bande of 1,000 Ethiopian warriors led by Marshal Hailu, a sixty-eight year old illegitimate son of a king. Graziani's only restriction on him was that he could not return to his homeland of Gojjam.

The Italians saw much room for improvement in their new colony. There was only one road and one rail line, and there were not any health facilities, modern schools or industries. The rains were unbearable to the Italians, and the fear of being stabbed in the back made life tense. Even the ascaris who remained as a garrison wondered if they were being punished.

On 27 June General Magliocco the colony's new air force chief flew with eleven staff officers to Wollega to coordinate air activity with local Moslems who were willing to hunt down Ethiopian Christian guerillas. Unfortunately the airstrip proved to be in the hands of Haile Selassie's officer cadets and their Swedish advisors. They killed all the Italians.

Graziani felt safe in Addis Ababa, as he was protected by 10,000 ascaris in several forts under General Italo Gariboldi. He also had an air unit based at the airport. Furthermore Consul General Diamanti's 1st Blackshirt Gruppo provided sentries, and there were also plenty of Italian rear-echelon personnel and Carabinieri [military police]. Moreover Italian civilian construction workers were arriving in their hundreds.

On the morning of 28 July 1936 in a light rain guerillas sneaked into the city, passing silently along winding alleys. Running into a party of Italian army engineers they massacred them in seconds. But, the guerillas were soon discovered, and the alarm was given. The guerillas continued to march towards St. George's Square, singing war chants.

Gariboldi quickly sent the 8th Colonial Battalion and 221st Blackshirt Legion to Graziani's headquarters, while he gave Major General Tessitore two battalions of ascaris, some Carabinieri, a few rear-echelon troops and some armored cars and ordered him to defend the square. They reached it just in time, and their firepower forced the guerillas to withdraw back into the alleys and side streets.

Next morning Gariboldi ordered an advance to cut the guerillas off from the countryside, but all units soon reported they were under full-scale assault, and therefore could not advance. However, Hailu's loyal bande was able to reach the square to join Tessitore. The guerillas here were led by Petros the Christian Bishop of Dessie. They suffered hideous losses charging against massed rifle and machine gun fire.

During the course of the day some Italians were able to advance, but at the Qebana River they were counter-attacked by guerillas led by General Fikremariam. The Italians drove them off.

On day three of the battle the Italians advanced again, while Hailu's bande eagerly searched every house for enemy stragglers, and slaughtered them.

Meanwhile, Marshal Abeebe Aregai's guerillas launched a major assault on the airport, and almost caught the Italians off guard, but air force ground crews and army rear echelon soldiers successfully defended themselves. They would have been overrun, had it not been for the fact that several guerilla units chickened out at the last moment.

On day four, the city was cleared of guerillas. Mussolini ordered Graziani to execute all captured guerillas. Graziani publicly executed all captured officers including the Bishop of Dessie, but he refused to execute the rank and file. He was the guerilla expert, he boasted, not Mussolini.

————

When the rains ended in October Graziani sent Hailu's bande to Ambo along with a column of ascaris, where they linked up with Moslems led by Abba Jobir of Jimma 150 miles southwest of Addis Ababa.

On 5 November Colonel Princivalle's ascaris were ambushed near Jimma, but his machine guns all but wiped out the enemy. At Gore, having travelled another fifty miles west, he publicly executed the local bishop. This was certainly an immoral act, but under international law it was legal, and the Ethiopians understood this kind of law.

On 14 November Major General Carlo Geloso directed a column of bande and ascaris into the Sidamo region midway between Jimma and Gore. He encountered guerillas at once. His troops wounded General Gabremariam, but were unable to pursue the scattering guerillas owing to the rough ground. A major problem was that the Italians advanced at the speed of their mules.

Under Geloso's orders Captain Tucci and his bande negotiated with 5,000 Galla tribesmen and convinced them to join the Italians.

Graziani's strategy was to use these many columns and air strikes to tighten a noose around the separate guerilla groups. On 13 December Princivalle and Abba Jobir caught Marshal Imru's main body along the Naso River and gained a resounding victory. Imru's guerillas fled to the Gogeb River, where they found Colonel Minniti's Italians awaiting them. Minniti negotiated with Imru, warning him that his planes would drop mustard gas unless Imru surrendered. Imru agreed. Minniti radioed Brigadier General Malti of the momentous news, and he passed it along the chain of command. Mussolini ordered Graziani to execute Imru. Graziani ignored Mussolini, and sent Imru to a prison on the island of Ponza off the coast of Italy, to share a cell with anti-Fascist Italians.

Graziani hoped that by sending five columns towards Fikke he could trap the many holdouts led by the three Kassa brothers, and his plan began bearing fruit almost at once. Captain Farello's bande of Wollos, part of Brigadier General Tracchia's command, clashed with guerillas in caves near the Takazze River headwaters. Within days both Tracchia and Hailu had considerable success talking the die-hards into giving up, and they captured and executed the rebel chief Wandossen Kassa.

On 21 December Colonel Belly accepted the capitulation of General Aberra Kassa and his brother Asfawossen Kassa. Tracchia had them brought to his field tent, where he ordered his Carabinieri to shoot them. He had now killed all three Kassa brothers and he displayed their heads in St. George's Square in Addis Ababa. Hailu seemed unmoved by this barbarity, though one of the brothers was his son-in-law.

Yet Graziani was frustrated. He knew that thousands of guerillas were still hanging on: the train from Addis Ababa to Djibouti was sniped at daily; sentries were still being murdered; sabotage was rife. Unable to command from an armchair any longer he flew one hundred and sixty miles south of Addis Ababa to Yirga Alem on 7 January 1937 to lead the hunt in person. He accused Major General Carlo Geloso of failure and gave his command to Nasi with orders to destroy the die-hards at all costs. Spies told him that Marshal Desta and Generals Gabremariam and Beiene Merid were still at large with 6,000 men. Nasi directed Brigadier General Kubbedu's ascaris to drive the guerillas northwards towards two other columns, emphasizing that no assault be made until the guerillas were in one mass.

On 17 February Captain Tucci's bande and his Moslem allies sighted a guerilla force being driven towards them by Kubbedu. Suspecting this was the enemy main body Tucci ordered an all-out attack. Much of the combat was medieval style with the Moslems fighting the guerillas with spears and swords. Here and there Tucci's bande were able to get a shot in. Gabremariam was cut down. Merid was captured and executed. Prisoners reported that Desta had crawled away wounded. Tucci radioed Nasi, who alerted Graziani, who sent word to Mussolini, who publicly declared the war was over --- for the second time. He had to admit that his previous announcement had been somewhat premature. The Italians had suffered 600 casualties since that first announcement.

———

Chapter Six
War in Spain

Mussolini was flattered that many far right political parties
imitated his Fascists and Blackshirts, such as the Romanian League of
Archangel Michael and its Iron Guard Greenshirts, the British Union
of Fascists and its Blackshirts, the Irish Army Comrades and its
Blueshirts, the Dutch National Socialist Movement and its
Blackshirts, the American Silver Legion and its Silvershirts, and the
German Nazi Party and its SA Brownshirts, to name but a few. In
Spain General Primo de Rivera ruled from 1923-1930 in a fascist
style. In 1928 General Salazar seized control of Portugal and
instituted a regime that owed much to Mussolini.

However, in 1931 the Socialists won the Spanish election, and
King Alfonso fled the country. Spain's major problems were
threefold: poverty; the Roman Catholic Church that tried to keep the
peasants and workers downtrodden; and the presence of three non-
Spanish ethnicities [Catalans, Basques and Gallegos] that lived under
cultural oppression.

Mussolini could care less about Spain as long as it did not affect
him, but as Spain descended into political chaos the chances of a
Communist victory there grew, and that scared him. The Spanish
Falangist Party of Antonio Primo de Rivera (son of the general) aped
Mussolini's Fascists, and they had their Blueshirts, and because of this
Mussolini gave Rivera considerable monetary support. In 1934 the
rival Carlists, a right wing Spanish monarchist faction, sent
representatives to Mussolini asking for aid. The arch-peacock was
flattered and could not refuse.

In October 1934 the Spanish boil burst. A new conservative
government was on the scene, but the Socialists, Anarchists and
Communists organized a strike by the coal miners, hoping to bring
down the government. Instead the government decided to take
military action. Not trusting Spanish Army conscripts, they called in
General Francisco Franco and his Moroccan ascaris. The result was a
massive battle, in which the troops arrested 30,000 strikers and shot
dead 1,800, many by firing squads. The public outcry was loud,
naturally. The result was another election in February 1936. The
Socialists won.

But by now the generals of the Spanish Army had tired of this
seesaw rule and they decided to finish it by ending democracy. On 18
July 1936 they ordered their troops to seize control of government
buildings throughout Spain. However, many of the young conscripts
doing their short obligatory service disobeyed their officers, and they
opened the arms rooms, handing out weapons to civilians: Socialists,
Communists, Anarchists, Catalan Nationalists, Basque Nationalists,

Gallego Nationalists, and indeed anyone who would fight the generals. Most male civilians in Spain had done some military service, so they knew how to handle a rifle. In response the generals also armed civilians: Spanish Nationalists, Conservatives, staunch Catholics, Falangists, Carlists and Bourbonists, indeed anyone within the right-wing spectrum. Within hours in every town a full-scale battle began, including the use of artillery and warplanes. The Spanish Civil War had begun.

For convenience sake the foreign press dubbed all Spanish left-wingers 'Republicans' and all right-wingers 'Nationalists'. For propaganda purposes the Nationalists claimed that all the Republicans were Communists of one hue or another. The Republicans in their propaganda declared that all the Nationalists were Fascists of one shade or another. Both claims were nonsense. The situation was far more complicated than that.

After a week of sheer butchery, a series of front lines developed with the Nationalists holding the southern tip of the country and the north central region. The Republicans held the remainder. However, there were many trapped garrisons throughout the nation. Using warships of the Spanish Navy manned by professional sailors, the Nationalists quickly captured the islands of Minorca, Majorca and Ibiza from their Catalan defenders.

The cocktail party intellectuals of the world had expected the philosophical struggle of right versus left would one day break out into war somewhere, and they quickly took sides. In several countries trade unions organized volunteers to fight for the Republican cause: entire battalions of Germans, Britons, Americans and Italians. Leading Italian anti-Fascists Luigi Longo, Walter Audisio and Mario Ricci joined the Garibaldi Battalion.

Because the foreign supporters of the Nationalists had no grass roots recruiting base, such as the trade unions, they arrived as individuals rather than in units. They were a motley crew of bored playboys, aristocrats, Christian fanatics and refugees from Russian Communism.

The strongest Nationalist military force was the ascari garrison of Spanish Morocco commanded by General Francisco Franco. But he had a problem. A narrow stretch of sea lay between Franco and Spain. A fleet of Spanish warships had been seized by left-wingers, following a few fistfights aboard ship, and they blocked Franco's passage to Spain.

Franco hit upon a brilliant solution. He would fly his army to Spain! No one had ever done this before. However, there was one slight hurdle to overcome. He did not have enough planes. Of necessity, he asked Hitler and Mussolini for aircraft.

Mussolini refused. After all, this was not his war, and he was still bogged down in Ethiopia, despite having told his people the war was over. But Hitler said 'yes', and loaned not just Luftwaffe planes but fliers and ground crews. Mussolini suddenly saw that Hitler might become the leading Fascist in the world… Hitler to the rescue, so to speak... and Mussolini's ego would not allow that. So, Mussolini changed his mind and agreed to send transport aircraft and crews to Franco. Within days the Regia Aeronautica was transferring tens of thousands of troops from Spanish Morocco to mainland Spain in their SM81 tri-motor monoplane aircraft. However, both Mussolini and Hitler shied away from sending combat personnel.

———

In October 1936 it was learned for sure that Soviet tank units and air squadrons were entering the line on the Republican side. Franco asked for aid from the three extreme right-wing governments in Europe: Salazar's Portugal, Hitler's Germany and Mussolini's Italy. Salazar responded with 20,000 Portuguese soldiers. Hitler sent tanks and air squadrons.

Mussolini had to support Franco, he felt, or lose his lead as the top Fascist in the world. So he asked for volunteers. This proved to be even more popular than the Ethiopian War. No fewer than 27,000 Blackshirts and tens of thousands of soldiers and civilians stepped forward. The Italian press and the Roman Catholic Church declared this war to be a crusade against the atheistic left, and the Pope blessed the fortunes of the new expedition. The civilians would have to be trained, of course, but those volunteers already in the army or in the reserves were placed into the Littorio Division [another word for Fascist], which would contain three infantry regiments [of three battalions each], an artillery regiment, an engineer battalion and support units, for a total of about 12,000 men. Supposedly they were all volunteers, but in truth some were ordered to 'volunteer'. The Blackshirts were placed into three new Blackshirt divisions: the 1st God Wills It, 2nd Black Feathers and 3rd Black Flames. Though these Blackshirt divisions were new, they did contain some veterans of the recent Ethiopian conflict. The Blackshirt divisions, at about 8,000 men each, had three infantry gruppos rather than regiments. Each gruppo consisted of two legions, and each legion consisted of two cohorts and a heavy weapons unit. Each Blackshirt division also had an artillery gruppo and an engineer cohort. There were also two independent Blackshirt gruppos, the 5th and 7th. Actually not all Italians in the Blackshirt units were Blackshirts. Many of the artillerymen, engineers, technicians and specialists were army troops. And several of the officers were on loan from the army. The weapons were much the same as used in Ethiopia. However, the army would now be able to try out its new 20mm and 75mm anti-aircraft guns.

Mussolini named this expeditionary force 'the Voluntary Troops Corps'. Most of it had to go by sea, so the Italian Navy escorted the troopships in case of attack by Republican ships. Furthermore Mussolini ordered his warships and submarines to intercept Republican warships or any merchant ship on its way to a Republican-held port.

Mussolini also sent an air component flying IMAM RO-37 biplane fighters, SM79 tri-motor monoplane bombers, SM81 tri-motor monoplane bombers, Fiat BR20 twin-engine monoplane bombers, Caproni CA111 monoplane fighters, Fiat CR32 open cockpit biplane fighters, Caproni CA101 tri-motor monoplane bombers and Caproni CA133 tri-motor biplane bombers.

The Spanish fliers of the Nationalist Air Force were impressed. They flew anything that would take off including millionaire's playthings.

On 10 December 1936 the first of the Italian ground troops arrived in Spain. The shore was warm and sunny, but the further inland the soldiers moved the colder it became. The Volunteer Troops Corps was commanded by General Mario Roatta. This forty-nine year old Italian officer was a descendant of Spanish Jews, and he had recently been Mussolini's liaison officer to Franco, so he knew what to expect. His field commanders were Italian generals: Edmondo Rossi, Amerigo Coppi, Luigi Nuvoloni and Annibale Bergonzolli. The latter was a hero of the Ethiopia War, and his men affectionately called him 'Electric Whiskers' owing to his wild beard.

Franco wanted to reinforce each Nationalist unit with a handful of Italians, but Roatta would have none of this. He knew Mussolini wanted glory and only a solid phalanx of Italians could earn that. However, the troops witnessed no glory as they marched into the cold mountains. Many were still wearing the tropical sand colored uniforms they had worn in Ethiopia. As they reached the front line and jumped into filthy trenches of frozen mud and snow, enemy artillery welcomed them. Those that had fought in the Great War believed they had gone back in time.

After two months in the Spanish trenches, the Italians launched their first offensive. On 3 February at Malaga the Italians went 'over the top', that is they climbed over the lip of their trenches and charged into 'no man's land' screaming for the enemy to do his worst. The Republicans panicked and either surrendered or ran like rabbits. For five days the Italians chased them on foot across muddy hillsides. Wherever possible, Italian tankettes and tanks churned the mud alongside the infantry. Here and there the Italians encountered small rearguards and the odd artillery salvo.

Taking advantage of the Italian advance, the Nationalists attacked on 6 February, trying to break out of the Jarama Valley. In one instance Irish Blueshirts (Nationalist side) fought Irish Republican Army (Republican side). By the end of the first day 20,000 Nationalists and Republicans lay bleeding.

It certainly seemed to everyone that Franco had made a wise choice in asking for Italian aid. The Italians had suffered 74 killed and 221 wounded in their five day offensive, but had taken 4,000 prisoners and had inflicted hundreds of casualties, and had covered much ground. As part of their agreement with Franco the Italians handed their prisoners over to the Nationalists, who, to the astonishment of the Italians, murdered most of them. Roatta voiced his complaint, but Franco ignored him. The Italians started to wonder what kind of war they had got themselves into.

Franco's next choice of battlefield was the Guadalajara sector, and he wanted to use the Italians again. So, on 24 February Roatta transferred his corps to this sector, putting the Black Feathers and Black Flames Divisions into the line, while the other units were allowed to remain inside warm buildings in the rear.

By 7 March it was still cold when Roatta's officers briefed their men. The following dawn the Italians opened fire with 160 guns, while aircraft bombed and strafed. Then Coppi's Black Feathers Division went over the top. This time the Republicans stayed and fought back with rifles, mortars, machine guns and artillery. Indeed the action was rough for several hours. But before dusk the Republicans broke. Next day the Black Feathers were joined by Nuvoloni's Black Flames Division and also by Colonel Enrico Francisci's 5th Blackshirt Gruppo as they all chased after the enemy. The advance was swift. In two days the Italians advanced thirteen miles!

On 10 March Nuvoloni held his Black Flames back, because he had outrun his supplies, but Coppi's and Francisci's units captured the town of Brihuega. Late in the day Nuvoloni unleashed his Black Flames again, but they soon ran into Soviet T-26 tanks. These were formidable nine ton machines armed with a 45mm gun in a turret. Furthermore the tanks were supported by Republican infantry, including the Garibaldi Battalion of anti-Fascist Italians. On the next day the Blackshirts attacked the Soviet tank force again, but made little headway.

On the 12th the Republicans counter attacked with air, tanks and infantry. The Blackshirts held. Sensing his troops were tiring, Roatta relieved them with Rossi's God Wills It Division, Bergonzolli's Littorio Division and Consul General Mario Pittau's 7th Blackshirt Gruppo. The Republicans, equally exhausted, did not interfere.

There is no doubt, looking at it objectively, that this was another Italian victory. Certainly Franco was pleased.

But on 18 March the Second Battle of Guadalajara began when the Italians were hit by a massive Republican onslaught. Almost at once Pittau's 7th Blackshirt Gruppo came under pressure from the Garibaldi Battalion, and Pittau ordered a withdrawal across the Tajuna River. Within Rossi's God Wills It Division Colonel Frezza tried to rally his

1st Gruppo after they were struck by Soviet tanks, but he was killed. Colonel Salvi brought up his 2nd Gruppo to hold a stopgap line west of Brihuega, and by late afternoon he was collecting remnants of the 1st Gruppo. The 6th Gruppo also fell back to this line, as did Colonel Mazza and his 3rd Blackshirt Gruppo.

The Littorio had also been hard hit, but Bergonzolli ordered an immediate counter-thrust, though he knew his own armored vehicles were no match for the T-26.

That night Pittau and Mazza reported to Rossi that they could not prevent their Blackshirts from drifting to the rear, and this forced Rossi to order a divisional retreat. Bergonzolli was determined to hold, but when Rossi's retreat uncovered his flank, he had no choice but to fall back as well. Even then he left a large rearguard along a rail line. Among the Blackshirts only Salvi's 2nd Gruppo had remained cohesive.

Next morning the God Wills It Division walked in retreat through the lines of the Black Feathers Division. The enemy did not challenge them. Over the next few days the Italians were relieved by Nationalists so that they could regroup.

Taken together, in the two battles of Guadalajara the Italians had lost twenty-five field guns, ten mortars, eighty-five machine guns, sixty-seven trucks, 415 killed, 1,832 wounded and 496 taken prisoner.

This was not good, but all in all they had still gained ground from the enemy and had inflicted heavy losses. However, the Italians were soon astonished by the ferocity of the editorials in the world's left-wing press. The British press, always eager to insult Italians, claimed that once again Italians had been exposed as cowards. They failed to mention that the Italians had been victorious in their two previous battles, and that some of the heroic Republicans were themselves Italians of the Garibaldi Battalion. The Republican cause was dying on its feet and the left-wingers throughout the world needed a victory, so they manufactured one. The truth was that Roatta's corps, for a total of 2,743 casualties and the loss of a regrettable but nonetheless affordable amount of equipment, had inflicted well over 6,000 casualties and had destroyed or captured equipment that was worth its weight in gold to the Republicans, and even after their short retreat they were still twelve miles inside the Republican lines! This is all the more remarkable when it is remembered that the Soviet T-26 outclassed every Italian vehicle. Three quarters of a century later, left-wingers would still be laughing at the great Italian defeat. Truth is the first casualty in war, and myths live longer than truths.

———

The British and French were constantly complaining of Italian piracy at sea: no less than forty Soviet merchant vessels were sunk by Nationalist and Italian warships and submarines in just a few months.

The Italians were always stopping neutral ships and searching them. Any found to be carrying goods destined for the Republican cause were either confiscated or sunk after the crew was taken off. One Italian submarine entered Barcelona harbor and sank a ship that had just brought in foreign volunteers.

In June 1937 the Italian cruiser Barletta was damaged by Republican aircraft while lying in Palma harbor, Majorca.

———

Mussolini recognized the truth about Guadalajara and he brought Roatta home to be lavished with honors, but Mussolini did not judge his generals on military prowess alone. He also judged them for political liability. He felt Roatta had never really gained control of the battlefield, nor did he like Roatta's complaints about Nationalist massacres, so he replaced him with General Ettore Bastico.

Franco knew that the British stories of Italian cowardice were nonsense, and he hoped that Italian courage and ability could stiffen the backbones of his Spanish troops. Therefore, he suggested to Bastico when he arrived that the Nationalist units should be corseted with Italian troops. Roatta had refused to consider this suggestion, but Bastico was willing to compromise. He agreed to form three new Italian divisions: the Black Arrows, Green Arrows and Blue Flames, which would contain Italian soldiers of the Blackshirts and army, but over time the enlisted men in the infantry components would be replaced by Spaniards. The Blue Flames would retain one all-Italian infantry gruppo. Furthermore, each infantry gruppo in these divisions would be corseted by four Blackshirt companies that would retain their Italian personnel. Thus Bastico controlled seven divisions.

Franco was already looking to Northern Spain for his next victory, where he intended to cut off the Basques from the Republican main body. The Basques were fighting for independence from the Spaniards. Franco's offensive began with a German air raid on an undefended Basque town, Durango. On the front line the Nationalist troops attacked, and at once ran into fanatic opposition from the Basques. Franco asked for Italian reinforcements, and Bastico sent him the Black Arrows Division, though it was still being created and was only at one third strength. It had few Spaniards on board. These Italians found the going tough, exhausting and dangerous.

In sheer frustration Nationalist General Mola sent German planes against another undefended town, Guernica. It was 26 April 1937, market day. The civilians were slaughtered. Alarmed by the bad press, Mola claimed the town had been hit accidentally. Later the Nationalists changed their story again, claiming the Republicans had committed the crime.

For several days in May the Black Arrows were held up by a rearguard at Bermeo, so Bastico sent the God Wills It Division to reinforce them. At last on 12 June the Italians and Nationalists broke through the Basque line. On the 19th the Black Arrows took Bilbao. Franco now called a halt to resupply. Italian losses in the two month campaign were 105 killed and 427 wounded.

On 13 August Franco launched the second phase of his Basque offensive. He placed Bastico's corps just west of Burgos. Here the Italians attacked along the north coast with the God Wills It, Black Flames and Littorio Divisions. In immediate reserve was the Black Arrows Division, which was now led by General Roatta. The latter had pleaded with Mussolini to be allowed to return to Spain, even at a lesser command, in order to redeem himself in Mussolini's eyes. Il Duce agreed, and demoted Roatta to divisional commander. The Italians were held up in the Magdalena Mountains for two days, but on the 15th they broke out towards Reinosa, and quickly took Santander and Santona. The Blue Flames Division was still only at one-third strength, almost all Italian, but it was brought into the battle, and performed well near Belchite.

Bastico accepted the surrender of Santona and gave generous terms to the Basques, but Franco refused to honor the agreement, and once he got his clutches on the prisoners he murdered thousands of them.

In fact the alliance was at breaking point. Owing to the brutality of the Nationalists, most Italian officers were barely on speaking terms with their Nationalist counterparts. The Italians did not mix with the Germans either, considering them arrogant. Likewise, the Germans looked down upon the Italians, Portuguese and Spaniards as immoral, filthy and ignorant. The Nazis among the Germans even considered their allies to be subhuman. Any references to Italians, Spaniards, Portuguese and Germans fighting shoulder to shoulder against the common enemy came solely from the imaginations of propaganda writers not from reality.

In September the second phase of the Basque offensive ground to a halt. Bastico's Italians had suffered 486 killed and 1,546 wounded.

———

Chapter Seven
The Ethiopian Terrorist War

The Italian people were confused. The Ethiopian War would not go away. It had ended in May 1936 had it not? Here it was 18 February 1937 and according to Graziani it had only just ended now. The following day Graziani held a party at his headquarters in Addis Ababa, which was ostensibly in honor of the recent birth of an Italian prince, but was opportune following the announcement of the end of hostilities. At the height of the festivities the room was devastated by an explosion: everyone was knocked down by the concussion amid shattering glass, and then a second explosion sent shockwaves throughout the room.

One guest was killed, and among the thirty wounded were Archbishop Cyrillos, Armando Petretti the Vice-Governor General, General Liotta and Graziani himself. Within seconds Carabinieri were running wildly around the building shooting at any Ethiopian who looked suspicious. Within an hour Guido Cortese, the chief Fascist Party functionary in East Africa, was haranguing anyone who would listen, and he gave license to commit any crime against the native population. Most Italians took this as permission to get drunk, but some took the opportunity to vent their frustrations upon the helpless populace. These rampaging soldiers and civilians looted buildings, set fires, raped and shot dead anyone who protested. They went berserk. Some ascaris joined them. Most soldiers and policemen tried to stop the riot, but short of shooting their fellow Italians there was little they could do until the alcohol wore off. The natives hid behind closed doors in terror.

After three days of lying in pain, Graziani issued an order from his hospital bed that the rioting must cease at once. Cortese, shamed by this, issued similar orders.

There will never be an accurate count of the cost to the citizens of Addis Ababa. Perhaps as many as 2,000 men were murdered and thousands of women were raped.

There were also legal executions. Within hours of the explosion sixty-two Ethiopian prisoners of war were dragged from their cells by Carabinieri and shot. Four days later a patrol captured Marshal Desta and executed him in front of his own people.

On 1 March Graziani still abed ordered General Nasi to shoot all noblemen in Harar Province. Nasi was dumbfounded. He was a soldier, he replied, not a hired assassin, and he refused. Graziani reaffirmed his order and this time included all of Nasi's prisoners of war, who should have already been killed according to Mussolini's directive.

By the 21 March Graziani could report to Mussolini that 324

prisoners had been executed, but he did not mention that Nasi had disobeyed orders. Nasi found himself in the dilemma in which all citizens of a dictatorship find themselves. If he refused the order, someone else would do it and he would have sacrificed his career for nothing. Eventually Nasi compromised with his conscience. He executed 600 prisoners, and asked if he could spare his remaining 4,000. Graziani knew Nasi was too good a general to lose, so he agreed.

The Carabinieri investigated the explosion and found that the two terrorists had connections to the German Embassy! Yet Mussolini saw this as proof that the British were behind it! The terrorists also had links to the monastery of Debra Libanos. Graziani commanded Brigadier General Maletti to massacre the monks at the monastery. Maletti was astonished. He was a tank commander not a murderer, he replied, and certainly not a murderer of Christian monks. However, he agreed to pass the order to Colonel Garelli, and this officer had no morals: he ordered his troops to shoot the 320 monks. However, the order said nothing about students at the monastery so Garelli spared them. Graziani found out and demanded the job be finished. Garelli returned and killed the 129 students.

Graziani issued an even more horrific order. Italians were to shoot any suspicious looking vagabond, in this a nation where everyone looked like a vagabond. It was obvious that Graziani had lost control of his colony, his men and himself. On 8 May he was allowed to leave hospital. Once again the great survivor had beaten the odds. He moved to the better climate of Asmara in Eritrea, and from there he convinced Mussolini that Ethiopia had been pacified. Mussolini swallowed this hogwash, so once again the Italian people were told the Ethiopian War was over.

Indeed Mussolini decided to allow Ethiopians into his army. The Italians had used Ethiopians as allies since the beginning of the campaign, but Mussolini was ordering the recruitment of them as ascaris and bande. He also encouraged Italians to seek their fortune in the colony.

In August 1937 an outpost at Debra Tabor was attacked, a patrol near Bahr Dar was ambushed, and sniping and sabotage began everywhere. In Gojjam a convoy was assaulted. A relief expedition of five battalions was sent, and was ambushed. The 6th Colonial [Somali/Yemeni] Battalion suffered especially high losses. It was obvious that the guerillas had not read the Italian newspapers telling them the war was over. The news of this new outbreak of violence reached Mussolini's ears, and it made him look like a fool, for he had told the new colonists the region was safe. Naturally they demanded protection.

The Italian diplomatic corps wanted someone in Addis Ababa who was neither a general nor a Blackshirt nor a Fascist nor a mass murderer, but who could restore confidence with the Italian people, with the colonists and with foreign ambassadors. Mussolini listened and made a shrewd choice. He retired Graziani for health reasons, and replaced him with Amedeo the new Duke D'Aosta. He was young [thirty-nine], handsome, popular with women, the darling of the social set, a member of the air force, a veteran of Libya, good with Africans, the son of a Great War hero, a nobleman, fluent in English and French, and married to a French aristocrat. He was perfect. Only the king complained, but Mussolini could care less what that old fool thought.

Mussolini named Attilio Teruzzi, ex-commander of the MSVN, to represent the duke in Rome, and this pleased the Blackshirts. Mussolini gave the duke General Ugo Cavallero as his commander in the field, which pleased the army. The business world was also pleased for Cavallero was a senior executive with connections to Pirelli Rubber and Ansaldo Shipbuilders. Mussolini also dismissed all of Graziani's senior commanders, except for Nasi. The latter had risked his career by defying Graziani, but it had paid off.

In December 1937 the duke arrived in Addis Ababa like a whirlwind. He stopped the executions, released most political prisoners, allowed freedom of travel, abolished Ethiopian serfdom and outlawed slavery. His orders created a cheap labor supply for Italian contractors, and he advertised in Italy for Italian engineers, technicians, teachers and doctors. He began a major construction program: schools, hospitals, irrigation systems, modern housing, sanitation facilities, trash collection, post offices, aqueducts, telegraph lines, railroads, telephone exchanges, bridges and industrial estates. He wanted a colony fit for Italian colonists and for Ethiopians too. He not only introduced Ethiopia to the twentieth century, but married them in a shotgun wedding.

There is no doubt that Duke D'Aosta impressed the Ethiopian people, but it did not seem to faze the die-hard guerillas. So, in late January 1938 the duke sent a punitive expedition into the mountains looking for guerillas. On 15 March the barracks at Debra Markos was attacked. So, more troops were sent into the mountains. By month's end Cavallero had 60,000 troops in the field in Gojjam Province alone. Everywhere army engineers built forts. In June the duke launched an expedition against 'Prince', a rebel who had declared himself emperor. The duke thought the colony had too many rulers already. Prince's 500 followers were soon dispersed.

By summer 1938 the colony resembled the American Wild West with its miners, new towns, entrepreneurs, confidence tricksters, gamblers, prostitutes, gangs of thieves, missionaries and 'somewhere in those hills' bands of marauding tribesmen.

———

Chapter Eight
Victory in Spain

Franco chose as his goal for 1938 the destruction of Catalonia. Spain had long ruled the Catalans and he needed to reaffirm his Greater Spain ideology. He began by cutting off the Catalans from the French border over which they drew supplies.

In order to give his troops something to fight for on a personal level, and to appease Hitler and Mussolini who wanted a document to take to their people, Franco wrote the Labor Charter. Many of its tenets were borrowed from Fascism: compensation for the sick and unemployed, pensions for the disabled and elderly, a minimum wage, paid holidays, allowances for people with children, and similar such radical ideas that the business world had fought against for generations. But as in Italy and Germany, the businessmen and industrialists in Spain could not oppose these Fascist goals, for the alternative was Communism. The Fascist nations led the world in caring for the common man, and their wealthy classes cried all the way to the bank. Whereas, in the democracies the wealthy classes fought the workers tooth and nail.

Franco also gave the Roman Catholic Church protection. This was a bribe so that the pope would look the other way while Franco butchered helpless prisoners. In any case, the pope and the bishops knew that their choice was limited, either support Franco or risk a Communist takeover.

To help repay Hitler for his support Franco diverted much of the iron ore from the mines of Spanish Morocco to Hitler's industrial machine.

In the world's right-wing press the Portuguese, Spanish Nationalists, Germans and Italians were brothers-in-arms, but in reality there was constant friction among them. Franco continually had to intervene to prevent the Germans and Italians from simply going home. Bastico complained so much about Nationalists killing prisoners that Mussolini had to take action - he fired Bastico, and replaced him with General Mario Berti. But when Berti saw the cruelty of the Spanish Nationalists he suggested that Italy pull out of the war completely. Mussolini kept Berti, but gave field command to Major General Frusci.

Exacerbating the situation was the dogma of the Falangists in Spain, the Fascists in Italy and the Nazis in Germany. These groups were never the majority, but they were the most vocal. Nazis in Spain had a habit of laughing at the 'primitive and dirty' Spaniards and Italians. Italian Fascists in Spain behaved with unbearable arrogance towards Spanish men and with unbridled lust towards Spanish women.

However, when the Italians came into contact with German equipment they were shamed into silence, because of the glaring inequality. German equipment was solid and innovative. Italian equipment was shoddy and unreliable. At least there had been one change for the good. After years of complaints the Italian soldiers began to receive new weapons: a 7.35mm bolt-action rifle, a 7.35mm tripod machine gun, a new L3 tankette armed with two 8mm machine guns, and a greater issue of the 9mm parabellum sub-machine gun with magazines that could hold forty rounds. The only Italian aircraft of quality was the SM79. The Germans had the excellent JU52 bomber/transport, and in 1938 they introduced the startling JU87 Stuka dive-bomber.

A serious rift had also occurred between the Italian Army and the Blackshirts. Never pals, their differences were major. Most Blackshirts came from Southern Italy, Sicily and Sardinia. Many had joined because of the high pay. The army drew from everywhere and pay was low. More than half the Blackshirts were over age thirty. The army still largely consisted of conscripts in their early twenties. In the eyes of the army generals the Blackshirts had performed poorly, and the generals had sent 3,700 individual Blackshirts home from Spain in disgrace by the end of 1937.

Furthermore the training of Spaniards by the Italians had not gone according to plan. When the God Wills It and Black Flames Divisions were rotated home, their soldiers were kept in Spain and transferred to the Black Feathers, Black Arrows and Blue Flames Divisions. In other words the rotation was on paper only, a trick to fool the Italian public. Franco had never provided sufficient soldiers to fill out the Black Arrows and Blue Flames Divisions, so Berti redesignated them as all-Italian gruppos and placed them both inside the new Arrows Division. However, they would not fight as a division. The Blue Flames Gruppo was sent to Estremadura, and the Black Arrows Gruppo was sent to Northern Spain. Franco had never sent enough Spaniards to replace the Italians of the Green Arrows Division, so Berti disbanded the division and sent its personnel to other units. The army's Littorio Division was still the mainstay of the Italian Volunteer Troops Corps, about forty per cent of its personnel being regular army, the rest being conscripts and volunteers. Thus the corps was reduced from seven divisions to three, and some smaller units.

The variable weather conditions of Spain, the dislocation of war, and the fact that the nation had never possessed good sanitary facilities caused a high sick list among the Italians. Many had to be sent back to Italy to recuperate. Actual casualties were not prohibitive: a total of 5,750 killed and wounded in one year.

Losses among Spaniards on the other hand were atrociously high. A relatively insignificant action at Teruel cost Franco 50,000 men.

To begin his Catalan offensive Franco chose to attack west of

Tortosa. Four Nationalist divisions would assault Belchite, while Frusci would attack on their right (southern) flank around Segura with four divisions [three Italian and one Nationalist]. On Frusci's right would be another five Nationalist divisions and 150 German tanks. The massive offensive would be supported by 600 guns and a thousand Nationalist, German and Italian aircraft.

Preliminary assaults began 7 March 1938 and two days later everyone went 'over the top'. Belchite fell at once, but the Italians were stopped at Rudilla until the Black Arrows Gruppo broke through. By the 13th the Italians had captured the important crossroads of Alcaniz on the Guadalupe River. So far the attackers had done well against some of the best troops the Republicans had. Alongside the Republican Catalans were some anti-Fascist German troops. Between 16 and 18 March Italian bombers struck Barcelona, devastating the Catalan capital and killing perhaps 3,000 civilians.

The second phase began 30 March with the Italians now less than fifty miles from the coast. An armored column of the Littorio encountered an infantry defense line. After sunset, unable to see where they were going in the dark on rough ground the tank and tankette drivers should have stopped, but instead they crept forward slowly. Despite the snail's pace these vehicles together with Italian infantry battled the enemy all night. Their enemy here proved to be a battalion of about 650 Britons. By noon the next day the Italians had inflicted 290 casualties on the British, and had pushed back the remainder. [Needless to say the British press did not publicize this.]

The advance continued and on 15 April the Italians reached the coast. Exultant, the Italian soldiers washed in the surf, repaired, slept and thanked Jesus and Mary that they had survived. The two-phase offensive had cost them 641 killed and 2,398 wounded.

The Pope saw the way the wind was blowing and he recognized Franco's government as the legitimate government of Spain and he praised the efforts of Hitler and Mussolini. He also declared that all nuns and priests murdered by the Republicans would have martyr status.

Now Mussolini began to rotate his troops from Spain. In Italy the arrival of troopships was met with a rapturous welcome. Outgoing troopships sailed without fanfare. This gave the Italian public the impression that Mussolini was winding down his presence in Spain.

On 13 July 1938 the Italian corps launched yet another offensive using the Littorio and Arrows Divisions and the Nationalist 5th Navarrese Division. The result was another victory as the Italians captured Albantosa and Sarion, though it did not come without cost on the ground. However in the air Italian squadrons flew 3,126 sorties for a loss of only eleven planes.

Then the Republicans launched a counter thrust, sending 80,000 men over the Ebro River. Facing such an onslaught, the Nationalists turned and retreated for twenty-five miles over the next seven days. Following this, Nationalists, Germans and Italians counter-attacked. Spearheaded by L3 tankettes and Fiat 3000 tanks and covered by aircraft the Littorio swept the enemy from the field. The Italians took thousands of prisoners and advanced sixty miles in five days!

————

In September 1938 Mussolini was distracted by a major confrontation in Europe. Hitler demanded that Czecho-Slovakia hand over the Sudetenland, a German-speaking remnant of the old Austrian Empire. The British and French were obligated by treaty to defend the Czech state. Mussolini became involved because he did not want to see a war that would compromise him. He would have to support Hitler, he knew, but he too ruled over a German-speaking remnant of the Austrian Empire, the South Tirol. Would Hitler want this region as well? So Mussolini chose to intervene as a referee instead, and his mediation paid off when the British and French abandoned the Czechs. German troops occupied the Sudetenland without firing a shot. Mussolini suddenly looked to the world like a restraining voice, a moderate among the extreme right wing.

Within days Mussolini announced that he was bringing the Blackshirts home from Spain, leaving only the Littorio Division of Major General Gervasio Bitossi. The equipment of the Arrows and Black Feathers Divisions was handed over to Franco. Mussolini also declared a new commander for the remaining Italians in Spain: Lieutenant General Gastone Gambara.

The French government, now in full appeasement mode, agreed to Franco's demands to close their border with Republican territory.

In November Franco called a halt to his latest assault. It had cost him 37,000 casualties. However, he knew he could not let up for long. The Republicans were in dire straits. Of the 60,000 foreign volunteers who had come to fight for them only 12,500 remained: the others had become casualties or had become disillusioned and had deserted. The Soviets too began pulling out their forces.

On 23 December 1938 Franco launched an offensive against Barcelona despite snow, frozen mud and terrible blizzard conditions. The Littorio was here, as were 675 Italian officers and sergeants serving in Nationalist units as cadre. There were also 100 tanks and tankettes with Italian crews and maintenance personnel. Supporting the offensive were 2,000 Italian engineers, 8,000 Italian rear-echelon troops and 7,000 Italian gunners manning 600 field pieces. Above them flew Italian planes with Italian crews, maintained by Italian ground crews. In all 33,000 Italians were involved in the battle.

The whistles blew and the infantry charged forward into the teeth of rifle and machine gun fire. The combat was tough and the advance slow, but an advance it was, and after thirty-four days of fierce battle

Gambara's Italians and General Yague's Nationalists captured Barcelona. Like a starving rat chewing its own leg, the Republicans turned on themselves fighting a suicidal civil war within a civil war. Then on 1 April 1939 the Republicans laid down their arms. It was over.

————

In the last offensive the Italians suffered 527 killed and 2,141 wounded. Thus the war had cost Italy in dead 1,824 army soldiers; 1,777 Blackshirts; 180 airmen; and 38 sailors. Together with a total of 10,600 wounded this meant that Mussolini's crusade in Spain had cost 14,400 casualties out of a total of 150,000 men sent there. The Portuguese had lost 8,000 casualties and German losses were a few hundred.

The Spanish loss was monumental: 300,000 wounded Nationalists and 196,000 dead of whom 86,000 had been murdered after surrendering. The Republicans claimed 175,000 killed or died of disease plus 40,000 murdered in Nationalist prisons. Republican foreigners suffered 9,934 killed and 7,686 wounded. In addition, of the two million Republicans taken prisoner at the final surrender about 150,000 were murdered by order of Franco. Add to this the total of about 600,000 dead civilians, and it is readily understood that the war had devastated Spain.

When Pope Pius XI died, a new pope had to be chosen, and the cardinals picked a man who could capitalize on the rise of extremism in politics. Eugenio Pacelli accepted the See of Rome as Pope Pius XII. An Italian favorable to Fascism, he remembered that the Vatican only existed as a sovereign state because Mussolini allowed it. His brother, Francesco, had negotiated that treaty. As a cardinal, Pacelli had authored the special relationship between the church and Hitler, whereby the church ignored Hitler's excesses in return for a protected presence in Germany. He publicly announced that the world owed a debt of gratitude to Franco, Hitler and Mussolini.

With the Christian world looking to Mussolini as a savior, the British and French calling him a peacemaker, and Hitler begging him for an alliance, Mussolini the victor of three wars in seven years was at the pinnacle of his success.

————

Chapter Nine
Mussolini the Peacemaker

In March 1939 Hitler's armies marched into the Czech half of
Czecho-Slovakia, while Polish troops occupied the Polish-speaking
part of that nation, and Hungarian forces conquered the ethnically
Hungarian region. Slovakia and Ruthenia declared independence from
the Czechs, and Hungary invaded and crushed the Ruthenians. All of
this happened within a twenty-four period!

The world was stunned. The British felt betrayed, not so much by
Hitler as by their Prime Minister Neville Chamberlain. In a knee-jerk
reaction the British parliament guaranteed Polish and Romanian soil
from invasion by Germany. The French made similar noises.

Hitler also sent troops to annex Memelland from Lithuania.

Mussolini was extremely jealous of Hitler. He had only just begun
to bask in the glory of his victory in Spain, even if he had to share it
with Hitler, and now the Fuehrer had gone and spoiled it all with his
seizure of the Czechs and the Memellanders. Everybody in the world
was talking about Hitler. Obviously Mussolini had to do something
quickly, and it had to be spectacular.

By the end of the Great War in 1918 the Albanians believed they
had deserved independence, but their neighbors had rapacious
appetites. Greece sliced off a chunk of Southern Albania, and Serbia
demanded and received Kosovo. This left a remnant of the nation to
be granted independence. There were also a few villages of
Macedonians and Greeks on the Albanian side of the badly drawn
border. And there was a smattering of Gypsies and Jews, whom
nobody wanted. The actual Albanians were 68% Moslem, 21%
Orthodox Christian and 11% Roman Catholic.

In an attempt to stabilize this remnant nation Ahmed Zog seized
power in 1924, and he asked Mussolini for financial aid. Mussolini
accepted the position of Sugar Daddy to the poor Albanians. In 1928
Zog promoted himself to king. Nobody minded. The Albanians were
much more concerned about corruption in government agencies,
especially from 1932 onwards when the Great World Depression
reached the sluggish economy of Albania. Both Mussolini and the
Albanian people began to lose faith in the self-made king when he
outlawed religious schools. Furthermore by March 1939 Mussolini
could see no return on his investment.

Mussolini had influenced several wars. During the 1911 Italo-
Turkish War he was an anti-war demonstrator. Come the Great War,
he was an instigator and warrior. In the Street War he was an
opportunist. In Libya he was the inheritor. In Ethiopia he was a
warmonger. In the argument between Germany and the Anglo-French
over Czecho-Slovakia, he had been a peace broker. And in Spain he

had become a savior.

But now he needed another victory. He needed to become a conqueror. So, on 7 April 1939 on Good Friday, the Roman Catholic Feast Day that recalls Jesus dying for man's sins, Mussolini committed the sin of international aggression. He sent his navy to bombard the Albanian coast and to land an expedition under General Alfredo Guzzoni of the Parma, Arezzo, Puglie and Firenze [Florence] Divisions. [All named after locations in Italy] The Albanians had no navy, and their tiny army had Italian advisers, who advised the Albanians not to resist. The invaders took Durres the first day. On Saturday the Italians repelled a counter attack and captured the capital Tirana. On Easter Sunday they seized Shkoder and Gjirokaster. King Zog fled.

To be sure not all Albanians were aghast at the invasion. Mussolini's henchmen were quickly able to create a miniature Italy with local Fascists aiding them. The Albanian police remained armed and together with Italian Carabinieri they hunted down those die-hards who wanted to wage a guerilla war against the invader. Soon two large guerilla bands were formed: the Nationalists of Abas Kopi, and the Communists of Milan Popovic and Dustan Mugosa. The Italians created a new Albanian Army of six battalions, and the MSVN created four Albanian legions. Even King Vittorio Emmanuele got into the act by recruiting an Albanian detachment for his Royal Guard, made up of young men who could see no further than a pretty uniform.

To be fair the country was in much better hands now, for despite being part of the European mainland the nation was as primitive as Ethiopia. The Italians began a modernizing campaign.

But Mussolini had not gained his real goal, namely displacing Hitler from the front pages of the world press. It seemed that no one cared about Albania. Hitler was in the big tent now, and Mussolini had been relegated to a mere side show.

Oddly enough Hitler was not worried about Britain and France, because this great gambler had two aces up his sleeve. First he intended to make a deal with Stalin's Soviet Union. Surely the British and French would not attack him if he had Stalin on his side. Hitler's second ace was Mussolini. Specifically, if the British and French did pluck up enough courage to attack Hitler, his friend Mussolini would use the Italian Navy to destroy the British colonial lifeline of Gibraltar-Malta-Suez, and send the Italian Army to invade France.

However, there was a flaw in Hitler's calculations. Mussolini had allied with Hitler in the so-called Rome-Berlin Axis for defensive purposes only. True, Mussolini's army was large, but it consisted of poorly trained reservists, and their equipment was inadequate. It would be another year before the next generation of weapons could reach the troops. Mussolini's navy was powerful, but he could not fight both the French Navy and the British Royal Navy. Moreover, Mussolini started to suspect that the Italians were sick of war by now. Libya, Ethiopia and Spain had provided all the young hotheads with an outlet for seventeen out of the last twenty years. The war gods had been sated. Italians now looked forward to a period of prosperous peace.

On 23 August 1939 Hitler drew his first ace. His foreign minister went to Moscow to sign a non-aggression pact between Nazi Germany and the Communist Soviet Union. Throughout the world left leaning intellectuals, philosophers, professors, trade unionists, workers and Republican veterans of the Spanish Civil War all threw up their hands asking: 'How could Stalin make a pact with Hitler the arch-reactionary?' Conservatives, Fascists and devout Christians cried out: 'How could Hitler make a pact with Stalin the arch-atheist, the anti-Christ?'

Mussolini was equally surprised, for Hitler had not briefed him on the coming pact. Il Duce now realized that Hitler obviously wanted to gobble up Poland, which lay between Germany and the Soviet Union, and he expected Mussolini to keep Britain and France off his back while he did it. Alarmed, on 25 August Mussolini wrote Hitler: he required military equipment and supplies if he was to protect Germany. The shopping list was colossal. Only eighty-six Italian planes had been shot down in Spain, but twice that number had been worn out. Additionally he had given Franco 763 warplanes. He needed German replacements for all these. Hundreds of tanks had been worn out in Spain and Ethiopia. He needed German replacements for these. Mussolini had also given Franco 1,930 artillery guns, 10,000 machine guns and tens of thousands of small arms. He needed German replacements for these. It was true that Mussolini had the manpower for sixty divisions, but he had little equipment for them!

When Hitler read the letter his face went white. Mussolini was not his ace in the hole, after all. He was the joker in the deck! Hitler frantically telephoned his generals to call off the invasion of Poland scheduled for the very next day!

This gave Hitler a breathing space, and over the next few days his advisers assured him the British and French would never fight for Poland, so Italy would not be needed. Becalmed, Hitler took their advice and ordered the invasion to begin 1 September 1939.

For two days following the invasion it looked like his advisers might be right, because the British and French bickered and prevaricated. But on the morning of 3 September the British declared war on Germany. The French followed suit. As the two largest empires in the world were now at war with Germany, the press dubbed this the beginning of the Second World War.

Just as Italy had refrained from jumping into the First World War in 1914, so Mussolini kept Italy out of this war. To the Italian people he became much more of a hero for keeping out of the conflict than he could ever have become for entering it.

———

Chapter Ten
Mussolini the War Maker

While Europe crept into war, the Italians in Ethiopia were trying to creep into peace. In October 1938 the Duke D'Aosta ordered one last expedition to finish off the guerillas once and for all. But by month's end intelligence was reporting that major groups were still in existence on the Menz Plateau under Marshal Abeebe Aregai and General Auraris and around Wolisso sixty miles southwest of Addis Ababa under Olona Dinkel and Gurassu-Duke.

General Cavallero directed Captain Rolle's Eritrean bande towards Wolisso, and sent Major Criniti's Bande Altopiani and Major Farello's bande of Wollo Gallas towards the Menz Plateau. Harassed by snipers in daylight and infiltrators at night the Italians advanced slowly. A column of Eritrean ascaris was sent to Mount Faguta, where they quickly became involved in major combat. Yet by December the guerillas had faded away as if into a mist.

Mussolini sent Blackshirt General Attilio Teruzzi to Ethiopia to find out why sixty-five battalions were still tied down in a conflict that he had declared at an end three times. Teruzzi got one story from the Duke d'Aosta, but another from Cavallero. As a result on 10 March 1939 Mussolini ordered the duke to Rome. Cavallero could not help but smile, for he had been left in charge without recrimination.

Once the duke and the dictator were alone Mussolini chastised the duke for hours in a torrent of Fascist rhetoric. Italian East Africa was surrounded by British and French territory and if war came the colony would be isolated. It was imperative the guerilla conflict be wound up immediately. The duke was surprised. He realized he was not being relieved, but was being ordered to prepare to wage war on his own against France and Britain.

On his journey back to Ethiopia the duke was courteous to his potential enemies, stopping off for British dinner parties in Cairo and Khartoum, and once back in Addis Ababa he was polite to the British and French diplomats.

But he was not polite to Cavallero. He sent him back to Italy, and took over actual military command himself. Obviously Cavallero stopped smiling. The duke would use Lieutenant General Luigi de Biase as senior military adviser and Major General Edoardo Majnardi as deputy adviser, and he promoted General Nasi to Vice-Governor General of Italian East Africa. Cavallero was not in the doldrums for long, however, for he learned Mussolini wanted him to command the entire Italian Army.

In May 1939 Mussolini ordered the duke to mobilize as per instructions. The duke ordered all bande to come back from their unofficial vacations, and commanded all ascari reservists to report for duty. He also drafted every white Italian male in Ethiopia, Eritrea and Somaliland aged twenty-one to fifty-five.

When the German invasion of Poland came and went, and Italy remained at peace, the duke breathed a sigh of relief as much as anyone. He released his reservists, and allowed the drafted white men to go back to their jobs, though he told them not to leave the colony.

On 27 September 1939 the duke chaired a most unusual ceremony. He honored three Ethiopian field marshals for their loyalty to Italy: Hailu, Haile Selassie Gugsa and Seyoum; and he promoted Ayalew Birru to marshal (Ras). By now the guerillas in the mountains were spending most of their time just trying to survive. They no longer had the support of the villagers or the priests, and thousands had taken advantage of the duke's amnesty and had gone home. Olona Dinkel was murdered for the price on his head.

———

But in spring 1940 Mussolini ordered another mobilization. Again the duke implemented the plan. While the duke was short of manpower, hence his call up of all white males aged twenty-one to fifty-five, in Italy Mussolini had no shortage of manpower. But he was short of weapons. As a result the call up in Italy was selective, often taking men because of their trade rather than their age. Moreover, Mussolini could not take men away from the factories; otherwise he would never make enough equipment for his manpower. Among those reservists that he did call up, there was a shortage of trained officers and sergeants. It was understandable that the recall of a white reservist who had not served in ten years and then only in peacetime was not an adequate replacement for a skilled professional soldier whether white or ascari. And unfortunately too many skilled soldiers lay buried in Libya, Ethiopia and Spain. And too many had been rendered unfit by wounds and sickness.

Some of those being recalled had seen war at first hand in the Great War, Libya, Ethiopia or Spain, but these non-professional veterans were not as valuable as it might seem, because they knew they had cheated death once. To enter into another war was just plain 'asking for it', surely. In fact Italians of all ages reported for duty most reluctantly.

Every community in the world produces young men eager for war. Every war produces weary men eager for peace. Italy's war spirit was Fascism, but that ideology had proven inadequate against bullets. No German infantry had fought in Spain, and Hitler's current combat troops aged nineteen to thirty-five were too young to have fought in the Great War. It would take a couple of years for the Germans to become disillusioned with war. The Italians were already disillusioned.

Mussolini mobilized the reservists of the MSVN Anti-Aircraft

Militia and MSVN Coastal Defense Militia. The former manned anti-aircraft guns, searchlights and observation posts, and the latter manned coastal artillery. Most of them were issued the old boat shaped helmet, as there were not enough of the new round helmets to go around.

On 18 March Mussolini and Hitler met face to face in the Brenner Pass, and Il Duce begged the Fuehrer not to attack the French, who, despite their declaration of war, still lay dormant. But Hitler explained he could not continue to allow a French dagger to be held at his throat. He had to remove it, and he invited Mussolini to join him. Il Duce declined.

Regardless of his victories and his war service Mussolini was in fact highly ignorant of military affairs. He knew nothing of strategy or logistics. Indeed he was in the process of making a very bad mistake by reorganizing most of his divisions into binary formations, i. e. forming the infantry component into two regiments or brigades instead of three as in a ternary division. By disbanding one third of each division's infantry, he hoped to solve his equipment shortage problem. The Americans had only just chosen to reorganize their divisions into ternary divisions to match the rest of the world. A ternary division could put a regiment on its left and one on its right with one in reserve. But a binary division had no reserve! Yet Mussolini expected his binary divisions to complete the same mission as a ternary formation, though they only had two-thirds the required infantry strength.

Once mobilization was completed in spring 1940 Mussolini's ground forces possessed the following: five divisions in Albania [one Alpini, one armored and three infantry]; one infantry division in the Dodecanese Islands; fourteen divisions in Libya [two Libyan ascari, three Blackshirt and nine infantry] plus two armored gruppos; seven divisions in East Africa [a grenadier, a Blackshirt, three Eritrean ascari and two Yemeni/Somali ascari], plus several Ethiopian ascari brigades and hordes of Ethiopian, Eritrean and Somali bande; and fifty-one divisions in Italy [two armored, four Alpini, two cavalry and forty-three infantry] plus several smaller formations.

Mussolini's most loyal soldiers were the Blackshirts, but the army generals were constantly complaining that the Blackshirts were sullen and unresponsive. An army officer could ask a Blackshirt to do something, but he could not order him, and there lay the root of the problem. Mussolini listened to his generals, and he now declared that all MSVN combat formations would henceforth come under army orders. This included the anti-aircraft and coastal artillery militias. The Blackshirts were not amused.

Marshal Francesco Pricolo was aware that morale was poor in his Regia Aeronautica. His fliers had been shamed in Spain when they compared their Italian machines with the German Stuka dive bomber and the new Bf-109 fighter. The Italian Fiat CR42 fighter plane was just one year old, but this open cockpit bi-plane radial engine aircraft that flew a maximum of 267 mph resembled a museum piece. The Fiat G50 radial engine fighter was better, but still only had a top speed of 293 mph. The radial engine Macchi MC200 fighter flew at 312 mph, but it was arriving in a trickle. The Reggiane Re2000 radial engine fighter flew at 323 mph and had two heavy machine guns, but again delivery was slow. Some fighter squadrons were still using the old CR32 inline engine biplane fighter [maximum speed 248 mph].

Pricolo's bomber force had the Savoia Marchetti SM79 trimotor heavy bomber and SM81 trimotor medium bomber, Cant Z1007 trimotor heavy bomber, Caproni Ca309, Ca310, Ca311 and Ca313 twin engine light bombers, Breda Ba65 single engine and Ba88 twin engine ground attack planes, and the Fiat BR20 twin engine heavy bomber. The Ca313 could carry a torpedo. Defensive armament was poor on all these planes, though some BR20s were equipped with a powered top turret. The heaviest bomber was the SM82, but only a dozen were currently available. The Italians did have a four-engine bomber, the Piaggio P108, but it had yet to reach the squadrons. Only the SM79 continued to shine. It could carry 3,300 lb. of bombs or two torpedoes or be adapted with cannon in the nose for ground attack, and some models reached 295 mph.

The Regia Marina [Italian navy] had the Cant Z501 single-engine reconnaissance flying boat, Fiat RS14 twin engine torpedo bomber float plane and the Z506 trimotor torpedo bomber float plane. Large Italian warships carried the IMAM RO43 single engine catapult launched reconnaissance float plane.

Mussolini bragged to the newspapers that he had 3,300 planes, but failed to mention most were worn out deathtraps. There was a new dive-bomber, and Giuseppe Cenni, a famous hero from the Spanish war, was ordered to test it. He reported it to be obsolete and suggested the Italians buy German Stukas. When an Italian aviator asked for a non-Italian product something was amiss. It is ironic that Italian aircraft designers reached the peak of their capabilities in the early 1930s while the British, Americans and Germans were only just reaching their best by the late 1930s. When aviation was a sport the Italians ruled, but now that it was a matter of national survival they lagged behind.

If Mussolini's army lacked decent equipment, and if the Blackshirts were sulking because their dreams of becoming an independent army were dashed, and if his airmen were unable to fly without apprehension, there was at least the navy. Naval morale was high: in fact far too high. Of the four larger navies in the world, the Americans and the Japanese were busy watching each other. This left only the French and British to challenge the Italians in European waters. The Mediterranean Sea was the playground of the French fleet and the highway of the British fleet, which guarded this route to their Asian empire by the use of naval bases at Gibraltar, Malta and Alexandria.

The Italian Navy [Regia Marina] had gained considerable experience in the Spanish Civil War, but unfortunately it was the wrong kind of experience, for their opposition had been negligible. The submarine force was especially way over confidant.

Admiral Domenico Cavagnari possessed the fifth largest navy in the world: seven battleships, seven heavy cruisers, twelve light cruisers, 124 destroyers, 115 submarines and scores of frigates, minesweepers and small craft. The battleships varied from the 1910 vintage with ten 12.6inch guns to the new vessels with nine 15inch guns. The destroyer force was extremely diverse. The largest were of the Navigatore class of 1,870 tons mounting six 4.7inch guns in three turrets and four 21inch torpedo tubes, plus depth charge launchers and manned by 230 men each. The smallest were of the Pilo class of 615 tons mounting five 4inch guns in five turrets and four 17.7inch torpedo tubes, plus depth charge throwers and manned by a crew of 95. The most numerous of the small craft were the MAS boats ranging from 75 feet and 20 tons to 50 feet and 11.8 tons. They were armed with two heavy machine guns, two 17.7inch torpedo tubes [no reloads] and depth charges that could be rolled off the side. Crew size ranged from 15 to 30. There were also a few 120 feet MAS boats that carried two 20mm cannon in addition to the above armament.

———————

By 10 June 1940 the Germans had conquered Poland, Norway, Denmark, Luxemburg, the Netherlands and Belgium, had driven the British Army into the sea and had overrun Northern France. Even the Germans were astonished at the speed of their victories. At 4:30 pm this day Count Galeazzo Ciano [Mussolini's son-in-law] in his capacity as Italy's Foreign Minister received the French ambassador at the Palazzo Chigi in Rome and informed him that as of midnight Italy would be at war with Britain and France.

The French were indignant. France was drowning in a sea of blood, and Mussolini was jumping in just in time to pick her pockets before she went under for the last time. Surely this was Mussolini's most shameful moment.

When Mussolini spoke from a balcony to the thousands who had gathered to hear him, he gave them the reasons for his decision. They cheered. However, these were the party faithful. The rest of Italy did not cheer. For all their dislike of the French and British, the people thought it unbelievable that they were now at war with their Great War partners, and allied to their Great War enemy.

The following morning General Tedeschino Lulli ordered the aircraft on his Sicilian airfields to strike British bases on Malta: thirty

SM79s escorted by twenty-six CR32s, seventeen CR42s and twenty-six MC200s under the command of Colonel Umberto Mazzini. The second wave was made up of one hundred and thirty-seven SM79s and forty-nine reconnaissance planes of various types. This same morning twenty fast SM81 trimotor heavy bombers took off from the Dodecanese Islands to bomb British bases in Egypt. Simultaneously, a few SM81s left Eritrea to bomb British facilities in Sudan. Over every target the British flak opposition [anti-aircraft guns] was negligible, and fighter opposition was almost non-existent.

After dark the British Royal Air Force replied with counter strikes of their own, two of which made the most impact: two Whitley bombers struck the city of Genoa, and nine Whitleys hit Turin. These cities in Italy were well lit and only when the bombers were overhead did the civil defense shut off the lights. The British crews reported heavy but inaccurate flak. At Turin seventeen civilians were killed. The reality of war had come to Italy.

Also this evening the British cruisers Gloucester and Liverpool and four destroyers engaged the Italian cruiser San Giorgio and four smaller vessels off Tobruk. The Italian gunboat Berta was sunk.

In Italian cities the anti-aircraft guns were manned by the Blackshirts of the MSVN Anti-Aircraft Militia. Military bases and airfields had army gunners, and naval bases had naval gunners. By now the MSVN Coastal Defense Militia also had its own Blackshirt anti-aircraft gunners in addition to anti-shipping guns.

In theory the Italian high command owed their allegiance to the king. But in truth this would be Mussolini's war. He was Prime Minister and Chief of Comando Supremo [armed forces high command] and Minister of War [army] and Minister of Air [air force] and Minister of the Navy. Of course he could not perform all these jobs adequately, and he relied heavily on the chief of staff of Comando Supremo, Marshal Pietro Badoglio the conqueror of Ethiopia. The real military commanders were General Cavallero [army], Marshal Pricolo [air force] and Admiral Cavagnari [navy].

The air force continued to bomb the British and French every day, and the navy began a series of coastal raids. In the first week of war the submarine Alpino Bagnolini sank the British cruiser Calypso. The destroyers Baleno and Strale sank the British submarine Odin. The destroyers Circe, Calliope, Polluce and Clio sank the British submarine Grampus and damaged others. And the destroyer Turbine sank the British submarine Orpheus. Italian naval spirits soared. The much-lauded British Royal Navy had been met and vanquished. The British, fed on a diet of Italian cowardice myths, were shocked by the courage of Italian sailors. Even the loss of the Italian submarine Provana to the French sloop La Curieuse did not dampen Italian morale.

On 18 June the Duke D'Aosta sent an expedition against French

Djibouti. He was content to make a show only, for the previous day the new French Prime Minister Henri Petain had announced he was going to surrender. Mussolini met Hitler this day in Munich, and he expected to be given a slice of the French pie, but Hitler told him he was going to be lenient on the French. Mussolini would not even get crumbs.

Angered by this rebuff, Mussolini ordered his generals to attack France and gain a victory before the French spoiled everything by giving up.

Umberto di Savoia the Prince of Piemonte commanded Italian troops on the Franco-Italian border. He was a generation younger than his generals, and owed his position solely to the fact that his father was the king. The border consisted of 200 miles of rugged mountains, with only a few passes and one coastal road. In the foothills overlooking the blue Mediterranean was General Pietro Pintor's First Army of three corps: Lieutenant General Francesco Bettini's II Corps, Lieutenant General Mario Arisio's III Corps and Lieutenant General Gastone Gambara's XV Corps. Bettini had three and a half divisions: Acqui Mountain, Forli Mountain, Cuneense Alpini [of Cuneo] and Pusteria Alpini (half). Arisio controlled four divisions: Ravenna Mountain, Livorno Mountain, Pistoia and Friuli. Gambara commanded five divisions: Cosseria, Modena Mountain, Cuneo, Cremona and Cacciatore delle Alpi of Major General Dante Lorenzelli [the Hunters of the Alps]. Under Pintor's personal command were the 4th Bersaglieri Regiment, Nizza Mechanized Cavalry Regiment and 2nd Alpini Gruppo. The 36th CCNN [Blackshirt] Legion was attached to the Modena.

General Alfredo Guzzoni's Fourth Army was inland in the Alps, divided into three corps: Lieutenant General Luigi Negri's Alpini, Lieutenant General Carlo Vecchiarelli's I and Lieutenant General Camillo Mercalli's IV. Negri led five and a half divisions: Taurinense Alpini [of Turin], Tridentina Alpini [of Trento], Pusteria Alpini (half), Trieste Motorized and Littorio Armored. He also had the Levanna Alpini Gruppo. Vecchiarelli commanded the 3rd Alpino Gruppo and four divisions: Superga Mountain, Pinerolo, Cagliari Mountain and Legnano. Mercalli controlled three divisions: Pasubio, Piave and Brennero [Brenner]. Under Guzzoni's personal command were the 1st Bersaglieri Regiment, Monferrato Mechanized Cavalry Regiment and 1st Alpini Gruppo. In reserve were the Lupi di Toscana [Wolves of Tuscany] Division, Julia Alpini Division, seven CCNN battalions and several alpini battalions.

The Pinerolo of Major General Giuseppe de Stefanis had fought in Ethiopia under the name Gran Sasso. Most of these divisions were named after localities in Italy, but Cacciatore delle Alpi was a historic name. Julia is a mountain range. Superga is a mountain. Pasubio and Piave were World War One Battlefields.

Major General Bitossi's Littorio Division had fought in Spain and had been reconstituted as an armored formation. Some of his tanks were the L6 with a 20mm gun in a turret, and the Fiat 3000 with a 37mm turreted gun, but most were the useless tankettes. The Littorio and Trieste Divisions possessed enough trucks to allow the infantry to ride to battle. The Bersaglieri either rode in trucks or on motorcycles with sidecars. All other Italian infantry walked. Those divisions labeled 'mountain' had pack artillery and special climbing equipment, but only the alpini units contained actual mountaineers.

At the last moment the Julia Alpini Division was ordered to leave behind those soldiers who came from the Slovenian and Croatian districts of Northeast Italy. Obviously Mussolini did not trust these ethnic minorities. The order was never carried out by the outraged officers, but the damage to morale was done.

The troops in their green uniforms and round metal helmets began their march up uphill in warm June sunshine, sweating to carry their loads. They walked alongside trucks that crawled up the winding roads in low gear at a snail's pace. Mule columns moved to the roadside when necessary. After a day's march ever upwards the troops entered a cooler climate of pine forests. The next day they reached the tree line and now walked upwards among rocky scenery, and they felt the cold wind now and were short of breath from the altitude. By the third day they were walking up precipitous slopes in a freezing rain, and by evening the narrow winding roads had iced over.

Mussolini urged the prince to hurry up. Once again he was behaving like a politician not a soldier. Italian artillery began trading shots with French artillery, and on the 20th the fight began in earnest.

At an altitude of 6,500 feet Negri attacked through the Little St. Bernard Pass and the Seigne Pass with the Levanna Alpini Gruppo and three divisions: Major General Paolo Micheletti's Taurinense Alpini, Major General Ugo Santovito's Tridentina Alpini, and half of Major General Amedeo de Cia's Pusteria Alpini. French artillery fire was exceedingly accurate, for they had had years to sight in these guns. In addition French alpine troops fired down from lofty heights. But the Italian infantry continued to walk forward.

Within hours Negri called up the Trieste Motorized Division, and under the cover of a dense fog and the noise of the shellfire its Bersaglieri motorcycle battalion charged right past the French guns for over a mile and crossed the Isere River, despite the bridge having been destroyed.

Next morning the Trieste brought up tankettes and trucked infantry and advanced towards Seez. The Littorio's tanks and tankettes followed.

Meanwhile Vecchiarelli's I Corps was also advancing with the 3rd Alpini Gruppo and three divisions: Major General Count Curio Barbasetti di Prun's Superga Mountain, Major General Antonio

Scuero's Cagliari Mountain and Major General Edoardo Scala's Legnano.

By the third day of fighting the Cagliari Mountain Division had broken through Belcombe Pass, Glazette Pass and Little Monte Cenis Pass. And the Levanna Alpini Gruppo had broken through Chapeau Pass and Etache Pass, and had linked up with the Cagliari.

On the fourth day of fighting the Cagliari and Levanna advanced towards Modane. Meanwhile Major General Arnaldo Forgiero's Brennero Division broke through Monte Cenis Pass.

While General Guzzoni was attacking in the freezing mountains, General Pintor was pushing forward along the coastal mountains. Bettini sent forward his three and a half divisions: Major General Francesco Sartoris'Acqui Mountain, Major General Giulio Perugi's Forli Mountain, Major General Alberto Ferrero's Cuneense Alpini and half of Major General de Cia's Pusteria Alpini. Arisio advanced with three divisions: Major General Edoardo Nebbia's Ravenna Mountain, Major General Benvenuto Gioda's Livorno Mountain and Major General Mario Priore's Pistoia. Gambara attacked with Major General Alberto Vassari's Cosseria Division and Major General Alessandro Gloria's Modena Mountain Division.

Mussolini's military ignorance was made worse by his generals' sycophantic groveling. The French could not believe their luck. The Italian infantry, engineers, muleteers, medics, couriers and radio operators were queuing behind each other, each waiting their turn to charge forward into the French dicing machine. The shrieks of mules, their bellies slit open by shrapnel, were indistinguishable from the cries of humans. Only after four days did the insane slaughter stop.

————

Meanwhile at sea the war leveled out. Near Aden the submarine Galileo Galilei was crippled and captured by the British corvette Moonstone. The submarine Galvani was sunk by the British gunboat Falmouth. The submarine Toricelli fought well in a surface action against several warships, damaging the British sloop Shoreham and crippling the British destroyer Khartoum. But the Toricelli was crippled, and her crew scuttled her. The Khartoum was afire, and her captain beached her to prevent her from sinking, but she blew up. The British were so loathe to admit the 'cowardly' Italians were responsible, they listed the ship as an accidental loss - and do so to this day!

The submarine Diamante was sunk off Libya by the British submarine Parthian. French warships bombarded Genoa on the Italian coast and Bardia on the Libyan coast. French planes raided Trapani and Livorno in Italy.

On 24 June in the Villa Olgiata in Rome Marshal Badoglio stiffly handed the French General Huntziger the surrender documents. The

Frenchman signed them. The two-week war with France was over.

Italy gained a few villages on the French side of the border, some of them ethnically Italian. In private Mussolini's generals knew Italy could not afford many more such victories, because their assault on the French border had cost them dearly: 1,247 killed in action, 2,632 wounded, 3,878 captured [many of them wounded] and 2,151 maimed by frostbite that often necessitated amputations. The French lost thirty-seven killed!

———

PART TWO
Making the World Tremble
Chapter Eleven
War against England

The Duke D'Aosta had been looking forward to the war with dread, because he genuinely liked the French and the British. His only hope was that as the French were folding up and the British Army had been kicked out of mainland Europe, the British government would see how futile it was to continue the war. The duke knew that if the British felt obliged to continue they would invade Italian East Africa. Just as British possession of the Suez Canal cut off Italian East Africa (Eritrea, Somaliland, Ethiopia] from Italy, so Italian East Africa cut off the Suez Canal from Britain's Asian and East African colonies. As long as he held onto East Africa, the British would be forced to send their ships the long way around western Africa. This did not just mean more fuel used and longer voyage time, but it put their ships at risk of German and Italian submarine attack for a longer period.

Besides, he did not need to be a great strategian to figure out British intentions. Their officers were so open about their plan to invade East Africa that they invited Italian officers to cross the border into Sudan to view their preparations! Surely this was owing to their arrogance towards the Italians. The duke's strategy was to knock the British off balance, so that it would take them months to recover, by which time their parliament would probably have decided on peace. The duke's current chief of staff, General Claudio Trezzani, was in full agreement with the duke's strategy, as was Comando Supremo.

Upon his mobilization the duke found he had 250,000 African and 92,371 Italian uniformed personnel, sixty-three tanks and tankettes, 136 armored cars, 323 aircraft and a small naval flotilla of a few submarines and destroyers. This was the largest army on the African continent. This was the good news. However, behind the scenes he was concerned about the loyalty of his Ethiopian ascaris and bande. Furthermore his L3 tankettes were useless, his armored cars were worn out, his aircraft were almost grounded for lack of spare parts, his navy was very low on fuel, and his border consisted of two thousand five hundred miles of inhospitable scrub, desert, mountains and jungle with few tracks. He was surrounded by British Somaliland on the northeast, British Sudan on the west and British Kenya on the south, plus the French colony of Djibouti in the north.

On the first day of Italy's participation in World War II, 11 June 1940, the duke sent planes to bomb the British, who countered by bombing Gondar and Assab. On the evening of the 14th a British soldier in Gallabat fired his rifle across the border in the direction of Fort Metemma. The Italian garrison of Colonel Castagnola thought this quite unsporting, so they fired back in indignation. The Anglo-Italian ground war had begun three hundred miles northwest of Addis Ababa.

The French surrendered on 24 June, but the Italians did not march into Djibouti. Hitler warned them not to, and Mussolini acquiesced!

Now the flaw in Mussolini's plan was evident. The British refused to surrender, which took both Hitler and Mussolini by surprise. Even when German bombs fell on peaceful English coastal towns they refused to consider surrender. Even when offered a 'let bygones be bygones' treaty, they refused.

On 28 June a party of Ethiopian guerillas with British advisers and thirty Sudanese ascaris of the British Army set up an ambush near Fort Metemma, and a bande of the Beni Amer under Colonel Castagnola's command walked right into the sights of the ambushers during the night. The fight was on, but the bande fought well and at dawn they drove the 'British' back across the border. Haile Selassie had come to Khartoum in the Sudan to await the British liberation of his country. Obviously he was premature. However, Sudanese troops did capture a small outpost on the Gilo River from some of Major Praga's 3rd Gruppo.

The British assumed the duke would remain on the defensive, but he had other plans. He ordered an attack for 4 July. Colonel Castagnola in Fort Metemma crossed the border and assaulted Gallabat in the Sudan with his 27th Colonial Battalion. The British withdrew at once, though Sudanese camel-mounted troops did harass the Italians. This same day Major General Frusci launched an attack against Kassala in the Sudan, five hundred miles northwest of Addis Ababa, which cost him 157 casualties, and the next day he threw in aircraft, artillery, armored cars and infantry under Major General Tessitore, while Eritrean horse cavalry outflanked the town. It was a text book operation and a pity the British were not there to see it: they had fled during the night. Italian bande captured the Sudanese police outposts at Kurmuk, three hundred and twenty miles northwest of Addis Ababa, and Karora six hundred miles north of Addis Ababa.

Only now did the chief of British Middle East Command in Cairo, General Sir Archibald Wavell, realize that the duke was aggressive after all, and he was obviously going for Khartoum in the Sudan, a city that controlled the Nile River and rail and air traffic in the region. More importantly, if the Italians took Sudan they might then strike west and link up with the Italians in Libya. Winston Churchill, British prime minister since 10 May, took special notice of this, for he had campaigned in the Sudan as a young officer. He knew its importance to the British Empire. So he increased British air strength there and sent an extra battalion to reinforce Khartoum.

On 1 July Lieutenant General Pietro Gazzera of the 24th Colonial Division probed the border of Ethiopia and Kenya four hundred miles south of Addis Ababa with his 9th Colonial Brigade, but his ascaris were immediately thrown back by the King's African Rifles [KAR] [British Army ascaris mostly from Kenya and Uganda].

On the 14th Gazzera launched his real invasion. He sent a very large bande to swarm all over three battalions of KAR, and captured Fort Moyale. Two hundred miles south east of here on the Somali and Kenya border a bande of Somalis was assaulted by a battalion of the British Army's 23rd Nigerian Brigade, but the Somalis regrouped, counter attacked on camels and defeated the Nigerian ascaris and a KAR battalion. Satisfied, Gazzera now stood still. Wavell and Churchill decided that the Kenya move was a feint and that the duke was still aiming for the Sudan and would invade as soon as the rainy season ended in October.

————

Haile Selassie urged the British to provide weapons for his guerillas, but the British were loath to do this so they compromised, forming the 1st Ethiopian Battalion from guerillas. This unit was trained in the Sudan by Sudanese sergeants and British officers, following which it invaded Ethiopia, wandered around for two weeks, skirmished with a bande, and then moved on into Kenya.

While the British were thus involved in playing at war, the duke had seized the initiative and his troops were doing well against the British. His next move would show he was for real. General Nasi gathered 20,000 troops at Harar three hundred and sixty miles east of Addis Ababa, and on 3 August he led them northwards across the border into British Somaliland in four columns commanded by Consul General Giovanni Passerone, Brigadier General Sisto Bertoldi and Major General Carlo de Simone. Passerone was a Blackshirt, and Bertoldi had once been Inspector General of the Italian Army. Both had fought in the invasion of Ethiopia.

Passerone had a Blackshirt battalion, a Yemeni-Somali battalion and an Ethiopian bande, and he was aiming for Dobo Pass. Bertoldi with two battalions of Yemenis and Somalis and two battalions of the Savoia Grenadiers Division targeted Jireh Pass. De Simone with the Harar Colonial Division and 2nd (Eritrean) Colonial Brigade was shooting for Tug Argan Pass. The fourth column was a Somali bande heading for Sheikh Pass. Their opposition, the British Somaliland Camel Corps, fell back when challenged by horse-mounted ascari scouts, and within three days Bertoldi's men were bathing in the blue Gulf of Aden. Passerone's men reached the beach soon afterwards. Naturally the duke expected these men to strike Sheikh and Tug Argan Passes from the rear, but Bertoldi and Passerone were Fascists who disliked anti-Fascists such as the duke, Nasi and de Simone. On 6 August de Simone's men captured an outpost defended by British Army Rhodesian ascaris, but then he stopped for two days under a heavy rain. [Rhodesia is now Zambia and Zimbabwe] On the 11th he finally reached Tug Argan Pass and soon found his work cut out for him. His Eritrean ascaris charged into narrow gorges held by four battalions of Rhodesians, KAR and Punjabis [the latter of the Indian Army]. Meanwhile at Sheikh Pass the bande was stopped by other Punjabis. The Indian Army drew its recruits from India [today's India, Pakistan and Bangla Desh], but most of its officers were ethnic British. The Indian Army was a sort of reserve team for the British government.

Owing to heavy losses de Simone withdrew the Harar Division's 14th Colonial Brigade and threw in Colonel Lorenzini's well-trained 2nd Colonial Brigade. Despite his professorial appearance with his glasses and beard, Lorenzini was a warrior. His force too made little progress, until they managed to ambush an all-Scottish battalion, causing the Scots to run away. To see White British troops run from Black Africans helped Eritrean morale considerably.

Trezzani visited Nasi and demanded to know what was going on. It seemed Bertoldi had not only failed to help, but had recalled one of his units that had almost cut off the British escape route. On the 15th de Simone sent tankettes into Tug Argan Pass, and they too failed to break through, and that afternoon Lorenzini's men were stopped by a bayonet charge of Scots, who had regained their composure. However, on the 17th the Italians found the enemy gone.

It was now the turn of the Regia Aeronautica to prevent the British Royal Navy from evacuating the Allied troops in British Somaliland from the port of Berbera. But the bombers flew too high to be accurate. It took de Simone's men three days to reach the port, dodging enemy naval shells over the last few miles. They arrived just in time to wave goodbye to the British from the pier.

The duke had triumphed. His feint against Kenya and the Sudan, while secretly aiming to conquer British Somaliland, was a masterstroke. The British had been taken off guard so much, that they had only been able to reinforce British Somaliland with a battalion of Scots and one Englishman, Major General A. R. Godwin-Austen, both of dubious value.

The Italian invaders had braved enemy fire from the British and Indian Armies, New Zealand and British warships, and air strikes by British and South African warplanes, and had emerged victorious. This made great headlines back in Italy, but behind the scenes the duke was furious. In a just world Bertoldi and Passerone would have been shot. Instead the duke had to restrain himself, because the two had friends in Rome. Their betrayal had caused de Simone to make frontal assaults. His losses were 465 killed and 1,530 wounded. Total Allied casualties were 250.

———

General Wavell had seven strategic problems. First, the Italians in East Africa blocked the southern approaches to the Suez Canal and had the potential to neutralize the British naval base at Aden and to conquer the Sudan and Kenya. Secondly, the French in Syria-Lebanon were now under a pro-Fascist government and might invade the British territories of Jordan and Palestine at the behest of Hitler. Thirdly, within Palestine Jewish terrorists were revolting against British rule. Fourthly, the Egyptian people were openly hostile to the British. From the moment that Italian aircraft began bombing British installations in Egypt, the Egyptian troops on the Libyan-Egyptian border had fled back to the Nile. They passed British troops moving up to the border. Churchill and Wavell agreed that the way to protect the Suez Canal in Egypt was to protect all of Egypt, even if the Egyptians did not want protecting. Mussolini knew that the Egyptians would see the Italians as liberators from British oppression. He had agents there trying to stir up a revolt. Wavell's fifth problem was that Italian aircraft based in the Dodecanese Islands were interfering with British shipping in the Eastern Mediterranean and were close enough to bomb British bases in Egypt and Palestine. His sixth problem was the Italian Army in Libya, poised to invade Egypt and capture the Suez Canal. And his seventh problem was that any British ship that tried to reach him from Britain had to run a gauntlet of Italian planes and warships for the entire length of the Mediterranean.

In fact only three locations stood in the way of Italian domination of the Mediterranean, which Mussolini referred to as 'our sea': namely Malta, an island group in the Central Mediterranean; Gibraltar, a British-controlled peninsula on the coast of Spain; and Alexandria, a British naval base in Egypt. There were also British bases at Cyprus and Palestine, but they were too far off the supply route to have effect. As a result Italian planes bombed Malta daily, and Mussolini pleaded with Franco to invade Gibraltar.

————

Currently the Royal Navy had three battleships, five light cruisers and twenty destroyers in the Mediterranean Sea, and other vessels were on call. The Italian admirals knew the secret of British sea power was not more or better ships, but better commanders. They hoped this tradition was no longer true. Admiral Cavagnari ordered Vice Admiral Edoardo Somigli not to confront the British with his main battle fleet until he was absolutely sure of victory.

Italian submarines were not doing well. In late June the Bezzi scuttled after being damaged by several British destroyers. Likewise, the Uebi Scebeli was scuttled following damage inflicted by several destroyers. The Argonauta engaged several destroyers and was sunk by depth charges. The submarine Rubino was bombed and sunk by a British Sunderland flying boat. It was 3 July before another Italian victory at sea: the Marconi torpedoed and damaged the British destroyer Vortigern. A few days later the Marconi torpedoed and crippled the British destroyer Escort.

Italian destroyers were holding their own. The Espero, Ostro and Zeffiro (Turbine class 1,070 tons) ran into a squadron of the Australian light cruiser Sidney and British light cruisers Orion, Gloucester and Liverpool and destroyer Neptune. Hopelessly outgunned, the Espero nonetheless tried to hold off the enemy while the Ostro and Zeffiro escaped. Espero's 179 crewmen opened fire with their 4inch guns while the enemy replied with 6inch guns. The Espero was hit repeatedly. Soon rendered dead in the water, she began to sink with her guns still blazing. The British picked up 47 survivors.

Thus in the first three weeks of the war with England, the Italians had sunk a cruiser and four destroyers and had lost a destroyer and nine submarines. Then the Italians were suddenly blessed with an incredible piece of good fortune. Churchill, who was responsible for some of the greatest blunders in warfare, turned on his former ally France by attacking them at sea and on the coast of French Algeria, sinking two warships and damaging four, thus throwing the French into the arms of the Germans and Italians. The surrender of France had taken the French fleet off the list of Italy's enemies, but this British attack placed the French fleet on the list of Italy's friends! Mussolini himself could not have planned it better. The Italians were now confident that they could win the naval war against Britain.

On 5 July British Swordfish bi-plane torpedo bombers from the carrier Eagle raided Tobruk and sank the destroyer Zeffiro and a merchant ship, and damaged the destroyer Euro. Simultaneously Swordfish flying from Malta raided Catania in Sicily. Next day Swordfish from the carrier Ark Royal damaged the French cruiser Dunquerque. On the 8th Swordfish and motorboats attacked the French battleship Richelieu at Dakar. This day Italian SM79s braved anti-aircraft fire and damaged the British light cruiser Gloucester and destroyer Escort.

On 9 July Vice Admiral Inigo Campione took a battle squadron to sea to attack a British convoy. He had the battleships Giulio Cesare (flag) and Conte di Cavour, heavy cruisers Trento, Fiume, Zara and Pola, eight light cruisers and sixteen destroyers. The two 29,000 ton battleships had been launched in 1910 and each carried ten 12.6inch guns in four turrets which had a range of 17.5 miles, and also twelve 4.7inch guns in six turrets with a range of 12 miles. The heavy cruisers had 8inch guns with a range of 16 miles. Off Calabria they sighted the convoy, which was protected by the light cruisers Orion, Gloucester, Liverpool and Sidney. Just as the Italians opened fire, however, from over the horizon came a British squadron under Vice Admiral Sir Andrew Cunningham: battleships Warspite (35,000 tons), Malaya (33,000 tons) and Royal Sovereign (28,000 tons) each with

15inch guns with a range of 26.5 miles. They were escorted by seventeen destroyers and the carrier Eagle. The Italians were now heavily outgunned and outranged.

It was difficult for the Italian gunners to take aim while their ships were swerving from side to side to avoid torpedoes dropped by Swordfish launched from the carrier. Furthermore the ships' anti-aircraft defenses created quite a racket, firing 3.9inch and 37mm anti-aircraft guns. Both sides closed on each other, and Campione ordered Rear Admiral Riccardo Paladini to take the cruisers in closer yet for better accuracy, but then a 15inch shell fired from the Warspite thirteen miles away struck the Giulio Cesare in the boiler. As his flagship was crippled, Campione decided to call it a day. Paladini's heavy cruisers fought a rearguard action, to let the battleships withdraw, and then while he withdrew, the light cruisers manned the rearguard. Finally they withdrew, leaving the destroyers to fire torpedoes to ensure the British did not follow.

Although only two vessels had been damaged in the fight, the Giulio Cesare and the Liverpool, the Italian Navy had met the famed Royal Navy and they had survived. The Italians felt like the spectator going one round with the champ at a boxing carnival. They learned two lessons: their flak defenses were inadequate, and the Regia Aeronautica was slow. Campione had called for air support, but the Italian planes arrived too late to make a difference, though they did succeed in damaging the Gloucester.

In mid-July Italian bombers damaged the cruiser Liverpool; the destroyer Pancaldo (1,870 tons) was damaged by Swordfish; and the Italian oil tanker Dora was torpedoed by the British submarine Phoenix, but the Italian destroyer Albatros depth charged the Phoenix and sank her.

Then on the 19th two light cruisers, Bartolomeo Colleone and Giovanni delle Bande Nere [flag] under Rear Admiral Ferdinando Casardi sighted four British destroyers off Cape Spada, which immediately ran from him. Casardi chased them, and at only 5,000 tons each his two ships could make 37 knots. However, the British had been running for the protection of the Sidney, at 9,000 tons a much larger vessel, and once the Allied force was united they turned to fight. For an hour the two sides traded shells. While Casardi conferred with the Nere's Captain Franco Maugeri, the Colleone's Captain Umberto Navara radioed that his ship had been badly damaged in the engine room. Suddenly shells slammed into the Nere. Casardi ordered a retreat. Then the bow of the Colleone was blown off, and her crew abandoned her. She was finished off by British destroyers. Italian planes arrived, but their bombs fell harmlessly into the sea. The British picked up some survivors including the mortally wounded Navara.

On 20 July the destroyers Ostro and Nembo were sunk off Tobruk by Swordfish, but elsewhere the destroyer Achille Papa (890 tons) damaged a British submarine with depth charges. Two days later the destroyer Ugolino Vivaldi (1,870 tons) rammed and sank the submarine Oswald. The Italians rescued the British crew. This day Italian bombers damaged the cruiser Liverpool again.

When Mussolini declared war on Britain the British police arrested Italian civilians currently in Britain, including an inordinately high number of ice cream vendors! Most were anti-Fascist and wanted to serve the British against Mussolini. But the British would not listen. Of these internees, 717 were placed on a passenger ship Arandora Star alongside hundreds of German internees. Their destination was an internment camp in Newfoundland, but they never made it. A German U-boat [submarine] torpedoed the vessel. Of the 743 who went down with her, 453 were Italians.

On 25 August an air raid by just three Swordfish sank a depot ship, a destroyer and the submarine Iride. Unknown to these courageous fliers they almost caused Italy a major setback. The idea of human torpedoes was not new. The Americans had used them in the 18th century. The Italians had revived this idea, and had created a special warfare unit called the 10th MAS Flotilla. [The name was meant to confuse the British]. And on this particular day the submarine Iride of Lieutenant Francesco Brunetti was carrying four experimental human torpedoes, nicknamed Maiale (pigs) by the Italians. Moreover, aboard were the two men behind the whole project, Lieutenants Teseo Tesei and Elios Toschi. The pigs were lost along with the Iride, but fortunately Brunetti, Tesei and Toschi survived.

In addition to air raids Italian ports had to be on the lookout for British warships that might sail in close during the night. The Royal Navy was becoming quite impudent, shelling Bomba, Pegadia, Scarpanto and Bardia, the latter four times between June and September.

———

Italo Balbo the Governor of Libya was well aware that his troops on the Libyan coast had become unnerved by the sight of Swordfish coming in low over the water, and they were on edge at night in expectation of a naval bombardment. Furthermore he knew his Libyan ascaris in the desert were terrified of British armored cars. Being a man of action he felt he had to become involved in this war to restore morale, so he flew in an SM79 over British camps to see for himself what preparations his enemy was making, dodging flak and British fighters to do so. On one occasion he directed a unit by radio to capture a British armored car he had spotted from the air. He then landed nearby and conversed with the captured Britons.

On 28 June his plane was returning to Tobruk when nine British bombers struck the city. Every flak gunner of the navy, army and

Blackshirts opened fire and cheered when one of the bombers crashed in flames. Then it was discovered it was an SM79. Italo Balbo, the handsome 44-year-old darling of the magazines, was dead. A nephew and a brother-in-law died with him.

———

Mainland Italy was also under nightly air raids. By October 1940 San Giovanni and Genoa had each been bombed once, Milan had been struck three times and Turin had been raided ten times. Italian night fighters and flak gunners had not shot down one British bomber. Mussolini lost face because of this, so he sent Cant Z1007s, BR20s and CR42s to Belgium, from which they could bomb England in retaliation.

The Dodecanese Islands also received some attention: twenty Swordfish from the carriers Eagle and Illustrious bombed Rhodes on 4 September. Stampalia was shelled by the Orion and Sidney on 2 October, and Leros was hit by fifteen Swordfish from the Illustrious on 2 October and eight from the Eagle on 27 October.

The naval war continued like a race that was neck and neck, neither side gaining a clear advantage. An Italian sea mine ruined the British destroyer Hostile, and two Italian SM79s torpedoed and crippled the heavy cruiser Kent on 17 September. In October the submarine Enrico Toti sank the British submarine Triad in a surface fight. Sea mines sank the British submarine Rainbow, and Italian SM79s devastated the cruiser Liverpool, setting her afire and blowing up a gun turret. However, the Italians took losses too. The destroyer Palestro (862 tons) was sunk off Albania by a British submarine. The destroyer Borea (1,070 tons) was sunk off Tobruk by Swordfish. The Borea's sister ship the Aquitore was hurt when she struck a mine. The destroyer Cozenz (650 tons) was crippled in an air raid on Benghazi. The submarine Lafole challenged two British warships, Hotspur and Griffin, and paid the price. The destroyer Nullo (1,058 tons) was hit in a destroyer action and forced to beach. Come next day, Allied planes bombed the Nullo. The submarine Durbo was bombed by two London flying boats and attacked by warships. Damaged, she scuttled. On 12 October the destroyers Airone, Ariel, Artigliere, Camico Nere, Aviere and Geniere fought the light cruisers Ajax and York. Though outgunned, the Italians managed to damage the Ajax, but the Airone and Ariel were sent below the waves and the Artigliere was turned into a blazing hulk. The submarine Berillo had to scuttle following her encounter with the British destroyers Havock and Hasty. The Italian submarine Foca was lost, probably to a mine. In a tragic accident the Tricheco sank the Gemma. Both were Italian submarines.

The 10th MAS Flotilla launched another raid. Off Alexandria Lieutenant Brunetti, survivor of the Iride, was now in command of the submarine Gondar and four pigs, but his mission was nipped in the bud when the boat was spotted by a British Sunderland flying boat and damaged with depth charges. Later the Gondar was depth charged by the Australian destroyer Stuart. Owing to damage the Gondar had to surface, but rather than risk the capture of the secret pigs Brunetti scuttled his submarine and surrendered the crew.

———

Mussolini needed someone to replace Balbo, so he brought Graziani out of retirement. The famed desert warrior studied the situation and realized that though the French in Tunisia to the west of Libya were no longer a threat, and therefore the Italian troops on that border were now available, there were still not enough troops in Libya to conquer Egypt. He chose a strategy similar to that of the Duke D'Aosta: put the British off balance, and then stop. Attending a strategy meeting with Mussolini and General Ubaldo Soddu [Cavallero's deputy] at the Palazzo Venezia in Rome, he unveiled his plan. He would send General Berti's Tenth Army into Egypt for a few miles where they would build several camps, but he would do nothing else until Mussolini provided him with enough tanks to fight the new British 7th Armored Division. It is ironic that Graziani who had built the border fence to keep Senussi gunrunners out of Libya was now asking that it be torn down so he could invade Egypt, and also ironic that he who had first used tanks in the desert was now afraid to move because of British tanks.

Most Italian troops arriving in Libya came with the normal green uniform and round metal helmets. Few were issued pith helmets and sand colored uniforms.

So far on the Egyptian border Libyan ascaris had been facing the British with nothing but their uniform to stop a bullet, whereas the British had armored cars. These Libyans certainly did not want to lay down their lives for that dictator in Rome. Understandably therefore in the first ninety days of conflict an average of thirty-three ascaris surrendered each day, whereas British losses were but 150 and most of them to Italian air raids. This all changed on 13 September when Graziani sent the mighty Tenth Army into Egypt. The column consisted of motorcyclists of the Bersaglieri, Italian infantry, Blackshirts, ascaris, artillerymen, engineers, armored cars, supply trucks, tanks and tankettes and support troops, and a host of Fascist war correspondents. The British backed away.

———

Chapter Twelve
War against Greece

It has been suggested by some historians that Mussolini had long had his eye on Greece, but a search by this author finds no such evidence. True he had attacked Corfu at the beginning of his rule, but that had been for domestic consumption. The fact that the island was Greek was irrelevant. The Greek-speaking Dodecanese Islands had been conquered by the democratic Italians in 1911 not by the Fascists. Mussolini had ordered the occupation of some uninhabited rocky islets claimed by Greece and from June 1940 onwards his planes did shoot at Greek merchant vessels, but the pilots claimed they had mistaken them for British, a very plausible explanation given the rudimentary identification methods of the day. Greater evidence for this theory is the amount of anti-Greek propaganda in Italy. But Fascist propaganda insulted most countries, not just Greece. The greatest evidence of this theory is the Helle incident. The Helle was a Greek warship that on 15 August 1940 was carrying a Greek Orthodox religious icon as part of a religious holiday. But the Italian submarine Delfino torpedoed her. It was a shameful act, and Mussolini at once denied it. The fact that he denied it is evidence, to this author, that he knew nothing about it. It is doubtful that he would have issued such an order and then denied it, for this would have damaged his reputation among the Fascists as a man of action. After all, this is the man who once fought a duel in order to support someone else's action. Mussolini bragged and boasted. He never denied unless his denial was based on truth. The truth probably lies elsewhere. It is possible the submarine commander had initially thought the vessel was British. Or perhaps he had been overly influenced by anti-Greek propaganda and had fired without orders. It is even possible he had secret orders from someone other than Mussolini, such as the Aegean Sea theater commander, General Count Cesare de Vecchi. The latter had been a thorn in Mussolini's side for years.

Of course the Greeks assumed the attack had been ordered by Mussolini. They too were ruled by a dictator, who relied on a militant faction for support. Mussolini was aware that General Joannes Metaxas might react to the attack by invading Albania. And here is more evidence that Mussolini was innocent of this particular incident. He had taken no extra precautions to defend Albania from Greek attack.

On 4 October Mussolini met Hitler in the Brenner Pass and had to sit for hours listening to the Fuehrer pontificate how he planned to restructure the post war world. This galled Il Duce, who believed that only he had a right to such dreams. Mussolini was still angry with the

Fuehrer for having restricted Italian gains when the French surrendered.

Eight days later Mussolini learned that Hitler had made a deal to buy oil from Romania. Il Duce went into a tirade. This oil was currently flowing into Italian storage tanks. Hitler had not even notified him of this pending deal, let alone asked his permission. This was too much. Mussolini searched his brain for a way to outmaneuver Hitler in the fame game. Then it came to him. He would conquer Greece. He knew Hitler had a tremendous respect for ancient Greek classical culture.

Comando Supremo already had a plan for the invasion of Greece, because it is the job of military planners of all nations to have such plans. On 20 October Mussolini ordered his staff officers to dust it off and bring it to him. It called for an expedition of at least twenty divisions entering from Albania and an amphibious invasion of the west coast. Mussolini liked the plan and ordered the invasion for ten days hence!

When each senior Italian officer was informed, it took several minutes for the message to sink in to their brains. Ten days? No one could mount such an invasion in so short a time. And, by the way, there was the little matter of the ongoing war with Britain, the largest empire in the world, or had Il Duce forgotten about that? Mussolini was insistent. He also remembered that the Bulgars hated the Greeks, so he invited them to the party. On the 22nd they expressed their regrets that they would be unable to attend.

The following days saw one of the greatest feats of military logistics ever undertaken. Truck convoys raced to the ports. Ships massed at the dockside. The six airfields in Albania received every kind of plane conceivable, parking them nose to tail. Reservists were called up and hastily equipped. Maps were issued and tactical plans drawn up. There was one advantage. The Greeks never thought an invasion could be mounted so quickly.

On 28 October 1940 one hundred and seven Italian bombers, fifty-five fighters and twenty-five reconnaissance planes took off from Albania; eighty-two aircraft took off from the Dodecanese Islands; and fifty-four fighters and one hundred and forty bombers took off from Italy. Their targets were the airfields of the Greek Air Force, which consisted of thirty-eight fighters and eighty-five bombers. Many were destroyed on the ground, and in desperation the Greeks had to use training aircraft in combat. Furthermore, the Greeks used machines made in five different countries, and spare parts were hard to find. In addition there were only two all-weather airfields in all of Greece, one of them being Athens airport.

The Greek Army had not mobilized, and only their 8th and 9th Divisions lay on the Albanian border.

This morning Hitler was on board his personal train on his way to

Florence to see Mussolini when he heard by radio of the invasion. He was enraged! A smug Mussolini met him on the platform with the words: "Fuehrer, we are on the march." Once again young Italians would die in a war in order to inflate Mussolini's ego.

Mussolini gave command of the offensive to General Sebastiano Visconti-Prasca. He was a political general, who had recently been Mussolini's attaché to Berlin. Visconti-Prasca placed Lieutenant General Angelo Rossi's Tsamouria Corps in the Epirus Mountains and on the coast road and he sent Lieutenant General Gabriele Nasci's XXVI Corps into the Macedonian Mountains. To link the two corps he put the Julia Alpini Division into the Pindus Mountains. The San Marco Marines stood by in ships ready to invade the coast. In reserve were the Arezzo and Venezia [Venice] Divisions.

However, Marshal Badoglio, as ranking officer at Comando Supremo, named General Roatta as the field commander. Badoglio did this as an affront to Mussolini and Visconti-Prasca.

Rossi's corps consisted of the Ferrara, Siena and Centauro [Centaur] Divisions, a grenadier regiment, three horse cavalry regiments and eighteen batteries of artillery. He found the going to be awkward as the terrain of the Epirus Mountains was primitive indeed, and the coastal plain offered little width. The land shot upwards to 5,500 feet in just a few miles. Therefore he was not able to lead with the Centauro, an armored formation, as he had hoped.

Nasci's corps in the Macedonian Mountains consisted of the Piemonte Division [and attached 166th CCNN Legion] and the Parma Division [and attached 109th CCNN Legion], plus a battalion of the Albanian Army, a machine gun battalion, a tank regiment and fourteen batteries of artillery. The Parma was bigger than most Italian divisions.

The Venezia and Piemonte Divisions had fought in Ethiopia as the Gavinana and Peloritana. The Parma and Arezzo had invaded Albania in 1939. The Julia, being an Alpini division, was much better equipped to handle the weather and the rocky craggy ground, and its 10,800 men were supported by mountain artillery and a machine gun battalion.

Politically speaking the invasion was unbelievably stupid for it gave Britain a European mainland ally at a time when she had none. Propaganda wise, it was an error, because it showed the world that Britain really was fighting the world's war as her propaganda claimed. Economically speaking the invasion was a blunder for Italy could not afford to wage another campaign: e.g. each division only had twenty-four trucks. Furthermore, Greece was now likely to invite British long-range bombers to use Greek airfields, which would put them within range of Romania's oilfields, which were supplying Mussolini and Hitler. In terms of command the campaign was idiocy, because no one really knew who was in command. Militarily the invasion was a colossal error for it was launched at the wrong time [the rainy approach of winter], in the wrong manner [charging through mountain passes without regards to who was sitting on the bypassed peaks], and in the wrong place [a primitive mountainous region with an inadequate base and a tenuous supply line stretching along Albanian goat tracks and thence across the sea to Italy]. Mussolini should have remained a sergeant.

Of course this army was made up of human beings: men such as Lieutenant Franco Sampietro, Lieutenant Colonel Udalgiso Ferucci, Colonel Felice Trizio, Colonel Luigi Zacco and Colonel Giannini; who wondered how they would behave under fire. Would they have the courage to fight, and moreover the courage to lead, when the going got tough? Back home the members of this army might have been Fascists or anti-Fascists, good men or bullies, career soldiers or reservists, family men or playboys, but now they were just scared little boys being asked to do a man's job.

As early as the third day Nasci asked for reinforcements. The 10,000 men and fifty guns of Major General Silvio Bonini's Venezia Division [and attached 72nd CCNN Legion] were sent into the Macedonian Mountains to join him.

The next day Major General Licurgo Zannini's Ferrara Division, reinforced to 12,785 men by the addition of the 82nd CCNN legion and some horse cavalry, was caught in a well-prepared artillery ambush in the Epirus Mountains. Some officers were stricken with indecision, but others like Lieutenant Colonel Ferucci and Colonel Trizio rallied their men.

On 1 November in the Macedonian Mountains the Venezia's 83rd Regiment was counter attacked by part of the Greek 9th Division, but the division's 84th Regiment came to the rescue.

On 2 and 3 of November Major General Mario Girotti's Julia Division assaulted a rearguard of elite Evzones, horse cavalry and mountain guns. These alpini did well, but on the 4th the Julia was struck in flank as Greeks poured down from the bypassed mountain peaks. Within minutes the divisional mule convoy was sliced into pockets. Visconti-Prasca ordered the Centauro to help, and this division did so, but refused to send in tanks, a wise move, and instead sent its 5th Bersaglieri Regiment.

This same day Major General Gualtiero Gabutti's Siena Division [and attached 141st CCNN Legion] was counter attacked in the coastal plain by elements of the Greek 8th Division. Heedless of this, Colonel Giannini led his 32nd Regiment across the rain-swollen Kalamos River, though at a cost of 98 men, including himself.

On 6 November, while the 5th Bersaglieri Regiment rushed forward in a bitterly cold rain to try to rescue the Julia, Girotti the commander of the Julia ordered his men to turn about and attack to the rear, the only method by which he could save his supplies and link up with the Bersaglieri. He succeeded, but countless small pockets of troops were cut off in narrow defiles.

The Ferrara Division [and attached 82nd CCNN Legion] in the Epirus Mountains was also counter attacked, and they too fought bravely, and suffered high losses including Lieutenant Colonel Ferucci.

In the Macedonian Mountains the Albanian battalion was counter assaulted, and at once half its personnel ran away and the other half surrendered. Some Albanians panicked so much they shot at the Italians. As Nasci had already committed his reserves, the Venezia Division, he had no infantry to plug the gap, and in desperation he called upon his Carabinieri [military police] to stop the Greeks!

On 6 November General Soddu [Cavallero's deputy] ordered the Italian command in Greece to be split into two, with Visconti-Prasca taking control over everyone west of the Macedonian Mountains under the title Eleventh Army, and General Mario Vercellino taking command in the Macedonian Mountains under the title Ninth Army. To please Badoglio, Soddu left Roatta as field commander. Badoglio was irate, nonetheless, because Soddu had gone behind his back, but he could not complain publicly for he knew Soddu would not sneeze without getting Mussolini's permission.

———

Chapter Thirteen
Naval Debacle

By 10 November Mussolini's Italy was at the peak of her military expansion. Having defeated the Senussi in Libya, conquered Ethiopia, found victory in Spain, crushed Albania, taken land from France, and overrun British Somaliland, she was holding her own against the British Royal Navy, was bombing British bases from Aden to England, had invaded Kenya, Sudan and Egypt, and was now entering Greece.

11 November 1940 was one of those salient days that appear in every nation's life now and then. Many Italians reflected on the irony that this was the 22nd anniversary of their defeat of Germany in World War One. Then their emotions turned to grief as the bad news began coming in. This day off the coast of England thirteen of their planes were shot down within minutes, a very high loss for the small force engaged. After sunset, four merchant vessels were on their way to Albania with an escort of the destroyer Fabrizi and the armed banana boat Ramb III, when they were pounced upon by a British flotilla including the light cruiser Sidney. The Ramb III was driven off, but the Fabrizi fought until she was crippled by shellfire. The Sidney then sank all four merchant vessels. This made eleven merchant losses in four nights. This same night southeastern Italy, hitherto immune from war, was bombed by British planes flying from Greece. However, the worst news came from Taranto naval base. At 8:40pm lookouts peering into the darkness sighted a handful of the flimsy Swordfish bi-planes skimming over the waves. By the time the sirens shrieked and the gun crews ran to their battle stations the planes were already among the ships dropping flares to light up the eerie scene. Then the planes banked sharply in a circle and came in again so low on top of the waves that the ocean spray was striking the pilots' goggles in their open cockpits. The Italian gunners opened fire, but the pilots ignored this, and let loose their torpedoes. These death dealers ran true and struck the ships, causing explosions that sent shrouds of white water high into the air. Other Swordfish dropped bombs. The flak gunners sent two Swordfish plummeting into the sea, but the remainder escaped. Then the damage reports started to reach the admirals: destroyer Libeccio (1,417 tons) severely damaged by bombs; heavy cruiser Trento (10,500 tons) hit by bombs; battleship Caio Duilio (29,400 tons) torpedoed and crippled; and battleships Conte di Cavour (29,000 tons) and Littorio (46,000 tons) torpedoed and sinking.

Mussolini went into a rage. Twelve obsolete Swordfish from the carriers Illustrious and Eagle had crippled his navy. The only response from his admirals was to apologize and ask to move the fleet to Naples further out of range of British planes. The Italian admirals could not really be blamed for they had supposed Taranto harbor too shallow for aerial torpedoes and had expected nothing worse than a daylight high-level bombing raid. The results were beyond the wildest dreams of the British officers who planned the affair. [The Italian admirals learned from the raid. And so did the Japanese. The American admirals did not, and suffered an identical defeat at the hands of the Japanese at Pearl Harbor a year later. The Italians had an excuse. The Americans had none.]

Days later Italian warships approached a British convoy out of Gibraltar, which turned tail as soon as it was learned the Italians were near.

On 23 November Comando Supremo learned that a British battle fleet code name Force H had left Gibraltar heading east, and Admiral Cavagnari ordered Vice Admiral Campione to intercept it with two battleships and seven destroyers. The Vittorio Veneto (45,700 tons) was armed with nine 15inch guns in three turrets with a range of 26.5 miles and twelve 6inch guns with a range of 15 miles. The Giulio Cesare (29,000 tons) was armed with ten 12.6inch guns in four turrets with a range of 17.5 miles and twelve 4.7inch guns with a range of 12 miles. Joining him would be Rear Admiral Angelo Iachino with the heavy cruisers Pola, Fiume and Gorizia (11,500 tons each) armed with 8inch guns, plus four destroyers. They would rendezvous with Rear Admiral Luigi Sansonetti with his heavy cruisers Bolzano (11,000 tons) and Trieste and Trento (both 10,500 tons) armed with 8inch guns, plus three destroyers.

Before dawn on the morning of 27 November the destroyer Sirio sighted British cruisers and sent a couple of torpedoes towards them without result. Come daylight off the toe of Italy at Cape Spartivento [Teulada] a reconnaissance plane from the Bolzano sighted British cruisers Berwick, Manchester, Newcastle, Sheffield and Southampton, and at once Campione ordered a retreat, hoping to entice the British into an ambush. But Rear Admiral Pellegrino Matteuci misunderstood the order, and his Fiume opened fire. Therefore Campione countermanded the order and his cruisers began to slug it out with the British. Within minutes planes from the British carrier Ark Royal began to make life quite uncomfortable for the Italians. As their ships' 37mm flak guns fired shells by the hundreds at the diving planes, the warships swayed this way and that, trying to dodge bombs and torpedoes and not to collide, and meanwhile the Italian gunners tried to aim at the enemy vessels. Despite such conditions, Italian shells struck the cruiser Berwick and set her afire.

However, the destroyer Lanciere (1,620 tons) was crippled by falling shells fired by HMS Manchester. Then very heavy shells began landing near the Italian cruisers, obviously coming from British capital ships over the horizon. They proved to be the battle cruiser Renown [30,000 tons] and the battleship Ramillies [28,000 tons].

Both had 15inch guns.

Eventually the Vittorio Veneto approached the scene and opened fire at 25 miles. The Giulio Cesare charged on hoping to close the distance, and finally at 15 miles she too opened fire. Several Italian ships received near misses that sent shrapnel slicing through bulkheads. At last the Regia Aeronautica joined the free for all, but their bombs missed. Other Italian aircraft were driven off by British carrier-borne fighters…obsolete Skuas and new Fulmars.

Miraculously no further damage was done to either side, and all ships returned to port when they ran low on fuel. Though inconclusive, the battle helped Italian naval morale considerably. However, the sailors had a few choice epithets for the Regia Aeronautica.

Also in November in the Atlantic the Italian submarine Argo torpedoed and damaged the Canadian destroyer Saguenay, while the Italian submarine Faa di Bruno was sunk by the British destroyer Havelock.

———

Chapter Fourteen
Greek Debacle

General Alexandros Papagos the Greek commander saw a weakness in the Italian strategy following his counter assault on the Julia Division. He decided to repeat the movement on a large scale, now that he had been reinforced to seven divisions. On 14 November his Greeks swooped down from the mountain crests to strike the long thin supply lines of the divisions of the new Ninth Army: the Parma [and attached 109th CCNN Legion], Venezia [and attached 72nd CCNN Legion], Bari and Piemonte [and attached 166th CCNN Legion]. This caused total and utter confusion among the Italian commanders from corps on down as they were directed to 'attack towards the rear'. In one place Lieutenant Franco Sampietro ran around collecting panicky and dazed stragglers from combat units and rear echelon outfits and he formed them into an ad hoc unit and counter-attacked. His award of Italy's highest honor, the Gold Medal, was well deserved.

Seeing success within his grasp Papagos ordered similar attacks on all Italian formations. On the 18th Comando Supremo reluctantly acknowledged the need for a complete withdrawal from Greece in order to regroup. On the battlefield the Venezia and Julia Divisions fared best because they launched short sharp counter-attacks to front and rear. Colonel Zacco was killed leading his 84th Regiment in a bayonet charge. Only by the use of sacrificial rearguards did all the divisions withdraw safely. In one incident Customs Police were thrown in as a rearguard to save Major General Achille d'Havet's Bari Division. When Lieutenant General Bancale was given command of the new VII Corps, his first order was to retreat. The Julia fought extremely well and actually had to be ordered to retreat time and again, for they believed staying put was the best strategy. By 21 November the XXVI Corps had withdrawn all the way to Korce fifteen miles inside Albania.

Obviously the fact that Mussolini had only given his generals ten days to prepare for this new war was now having its effect. For infantry to have to call upon Carabinieri and Customs Police to man the line is evidence of a lack of strategic foresight.

———

By the end of November 1940 Italy's warriors at sea and in the air were fighting a stalemate campaign, and in Greece they were fighting the weather, the terrain and the Greeks, whereas in East Africa they were sheltering from the rain, and in Egypt they swatted flies, while the generals and admirals in Rome bickered among themselves. Badoglio was at loggerheads with Mussolini, and on 11 November he fired Il Duce's man Visconti-Prasca, and replaced him as head of Eleventh Army with General Carlo Geloso.

Mussolini was livid, but he also knew that he needed these generals. It took him a while to sort the wheat from the chaff, but on 6 December he named Visconti-Prasca as field commander in Greece, replacing Roatta, and he dismissed Badoglio from active duty, replacing him as deputy commander of Comando Supremo with General Cavallero. He picked Roatta to run the army, in Cavallero's place, and he made Soddu the deputy of Roatta with particular responsibility for the Greek campaign. Thus the Greek campaign had four different command structures in thirty-nine days. There is little wonder that it was a fiasco.

―――――

Chapter Fifteen
Egyptian Debacle

In Egypt the Tenth Army waited while Graziani pleaded for more tank brigades. He had only been given two. He even threatened to resign if he did not get them. Meanwhile in Cairo the British commander of the Middle East and North Africa Field Marshal Wavell was bombarded by officers each of whom claimed to have a war-winning strategy in his pocket. Some wanted to retreat to the Suez Canal, others to attack Graziani, others to harass the Italians and some like Churchill wanted to ignore Graziani and concentrate on saving the Sudan. As if he did not have enough headaches Wavell was given command of British operations in Greece as well. The Greek experience with the British in World War I had left a bad taste in their mouths, so Metaxas wanted no British troops, but he did accept air support, and British planes were now based in Greece. These planes and their fliers were a godsend to the Greeks. The bombers such as the Blenheims were little more than a nuisance to the Italians, but the Hurricanes and Tomahawks [Warhawks] were fine fighters.

The British press made things decidedly worse by still claiming that Italians were faint-hearted. Wavell knew this was claptrap. The Italians had so far shown courage especially in East Africa. They were bombing British forces in Crete, Malta, Egypt, Sudan, Kenya, Aden and Bahrain. At sea they showed no reluctance to give battle. They had driven the British out of Somaliland in a miniature 'Dunkirk', and had invaded Egypt.

Lieutenant General Richard O'Connor wanted to use his scant forces of the Western Desert Force to raid the Tenth Army camps in Egypt, and Wavell gave him permission, figuring a raid would do no harm to his cause and might lead to something substantial. O'Connor would have Major General Michael Creagh's British 7th Armored Division and Major General Noel Beresford-Pierce's Indian Army 4th Division. Like most Indian Army divisions its infantry consisted of three British Army and six Indian Army battalions, and the artillery was British-manned. The support troops were a mixture of Britons and Indians. Wavell held out hope for the Indian troops. He was an Indian Army officer not a British Army officer. Furthermore O'Connor planned to use blitzkrieg tactics on the Italians, which had proven so successful when the Germans used them on the British the previous spring.

Graziani had no illusions, but he did believe his defense in depth was the best strategy, hence his construction of camps. With water scarce he had to keep these camps apart and relatively small. Furthermore, he knew an attacking force could not ignore these camps, for the attackers also needed water. His intelligence network was very good, informing him that something besides tea was brewing in the English camp.

At 5:40am 9 December 1940 Brigadier General Pietro Maletti was sleeping in his drafty cold tent at Nibeiwa camp. This veteran of the Ethiopian War was not a friend of Graziani, for he had once refused to obey Graziani's order to execute prisoners. His so-called brigade of armor consisted of two Italian-manned and one Libyan-manned tank battalions. His L6s were armed with a turreted 20mm gun and machine gun. His M11s were armed with a hull-mounted 37mm gun and a turreted machine gun. They were parked in the center of the cold flat windy desert camp. His men had been alerted in case of an attack. Suddenly artillery bursts awoke him from his dreams. Some of his men were pierced by shrapnel before they left their tents. Others were cut down as they ran for their tanks, and as each L6 only carried a crew of two it could not function with a man short. The gunners of the brigade's artillery detachment manned their pieces, but as yet were offered no targets. The British guns had a greater range. For a solid hour the Italians stood up under fire.

At last the Italians could see enemy infantry to the east, the direction of the British lines, and now their artillery opened fire on the British, while Maletti ordered his tanks to charge. For an hour the British eluded him, until his lookouts back in the camp sighted another force attacking from the west, i. e. from the rear. Obviously the initial British advance had been a feint. This new British threat consisted of tanks and 2,000 British and Indian infantry. Maletti recalled his tanks, but the British force was the first to reach the wide-open camp. Hundreds of unarmed Italian and Libyan rear-echelon personnel threw up their hands. Those that tried to run for it were machine-gunned or mashed under tank treads. However, the Italian artillerymen swung their guns around and fired over open sights at point blank range. When these gunners were charged by British and Indian infantry, they remained at their guns and were soon locked in deadly hand to hand combat using shovels, crowbars and ramrods against British bullets and bayonets. At last the Italian tanks returned and entered the furious fight, but their 37mm shells could not penetrate the 80mm armor of the British Matildas, whereas the British 2-pounder (40mm) tank guns sent solid shot piercing right through the Italian 29mm armor like a hot poker through butter. Some Italian tanks blew up in spectacular explosions as the red-hot shot hit their fuel or ammunition. But more often the shot simply hit a track, breaking it in twain and spilling it onto the desert floor, rendering the vehicle motionless, and as an M11's main gun was in the hull this rendered the tank defenseless too. Other M11s were hit in the engine, which simply stopped running. In others the armor piercing shell entered the vehicle and spun around inside at incredible speed mashing heads, lopping off arms and legs and smashing equipment before it eventually lodged somewhere. At 11:30am after six hours of bloody struggle the Italians and Libyans began giving up. The British and Indians were astonished at their victory, and they were also surprised at the bravery of Italian artillerymen. They took over 2,000 prisoners, many of them wounded, and they counted about a hundred dead Italians and Libyans. Maletti had fought to the death. Allied losses were just 56 killed and wounded. Maletti, who had refused to kill prisoners, had become a victim of Mussolini's lust for glory.

When the early morning reports reached O'Connor he realized he was onto a good thing. He ordered an assault against Tumar West at once. This camp was defended by one third of Major General Armando Pescatori's 2nd Libyan Division. Pescatori and his staff knew something was up, and suspected the previous night's air raid had been intended to drown the sound of British tanks on the move. Of course they hoped the tanks would attack someone else for they had no real anti-tank defenses themselves. Moreover these 2,000 Libyans had no wish to die for Mussolini. In fact recent air raids and a naval barrage had already caused considerable panic among them. Then Pescatori was informed that Nibeiwa Camp was under attack.

Beginning at 11:25am the Libyans at Tumar West were subjected to artillery fire. Here too the Libyan artillery gunners had to sit and take it, for they did not have the range to reply. Then the camp was assaulted by forty British tanks and 2,000 infantry. Now the gunners had a target within range. As the shells fell and the bullets buzzed past, the Italian officers and sergeants began yelling orders, commanding, pleading and begging the Libyans to stand and fight. It is amazing that they managed to convince the Libyans to stand up to tank fire, artillery salvoes, machine gun bullet and massed rifle fire for two and a half hours. In fact the Libyans only surrendered when they ran out of ammunition.

The remainder of the 2nd Libyan Division was stationed at Tumar East and they did not need radio messages to know what was happening, because the sound of battle to their west [their rear] told them they were cut off. In the afternoon shells began landing among them, and shortly afterwards they were assaulted by one British and two Indian infantry battalions. The Libyans fought until nightfall, and then when no longer in sight of their officers they began giving up. The Italians in the division...officers, sergeants and technicians... chose to fight on, and once it was fully dark they charged the enemy, broke through and continued running into the cold black desert night. They knew that if they ran westwards for two days they would reach the security of the city of Sidi Barani. The Indians and Britons were too exhausted to chase after them.

Lieutenant General Gallina passed the news to Tenth Army headquarters, that after one day of combat, 8,000 men were missing. This Ethiopian War veteran would have been even more numbed with shock had he learned his troops had only inflicted 125 casualties on the enemy. He still had the 1st Libyan Division and the 4th 3 January Blackshirt Division, but the Libyans at Meiktila were being bombed from the air and shelled by warships out to sea, and they had already begun to show signs of panic. The Blackshirts of Consul General Fabio Merzari at Sidi Barani had also been suffering from air raids, and they had been shelled by warships no less than seven times in the last few weeks.

Wavell now gave his approval to continue. On the morning of 10 December the garrison of Sidi Barani came under British artillery fire. The Libyan civilian population and the Italian colonists living here went crazy, but the defenders held their positions and waited. The garrison was made up of the 4th Blackshirt Division and rear-echelon personnel of the Italian army and Regia Aeronautica. Here too the Italian artillerymen suffered in frustration, because their guns did not have the range to reply. Finally after two hours of shelling the 204th Artillery Regiment saw a target: one Indian and three British infantry battalions were approaching. The gunners now began to throw shells into the attackers, but bravely they kept coming. When the enemy came close enough, the Blackshirts opened up with mortars, machine guns and rifles. They stopped the assault.

But then another flank was charged by a hundred British tanks. Impervious to bullets, these vehicles straddled Italian trenches and machine-gunned the defenders. Once again it was proved that a rifle was no match for a tank even if held by a Fascist fanatic. The bloodletting lasted all day and continued all night long.

The noisy darkness was periodically lit by muzzle flashes. It appeared to some defenders that they would be overrun by the tanks come dawn, so they decided to charge head on against the British lines. This made the fight very intense, as no one was quite sure who was shooting whom, but before the first rays of the sun shone on this battlefield some of the Italians had broken through the British lines and were running westwards across the flat cold desert.

Just after dawn the British tanks advanced into the city, and the garrison surrendered. The twenty-four hour battle had cost the Italians and Libyans several hundred killed and wounded, and the British and Indians had suffered five hundred killed and wounded, but this morning fifteen thousand Italians and Libyans capitulated.

While the Blackshirts were fighting for Sidi Barani, Major General Luigi Sibille's 1st Libyan Division of 150 Italians and 5,000 Libyans was retreating from Meiktila in full view of every Allied plane in the region. Each time an aircraft swooped low to bomb and strafe, more Libyans fled the column, running off wildly into the desert. Come dawn on 11 December the tail end stragglers could see a cloud of dust behind them: British tanks. As the British approached the column, many Libyans scattered in all directions. A few Libyans were picked off by British machine guns, but the British knew that those who were not caught would soon die of thirst. Surprisingly Sibille managed to retain enough troops to give battle, and their sting was sharp enough that the British thought better of it and pulled back. For the next twenty-four hours the British plastered the defenders with artillery, while three British destroyers sailed close to shore and shelled them, and all the while British aircraft bombed and strafed. The following day, the Italian staff surrendered the division, rather than see everyone slaughtered. Over the next week Libyan stragglers would come to the coast road to surrender to British truck drivers and beg for water.

Even now a few Italians of the 1st and 2nd Libyan Divisions tried to carry on the fight by running towards Sidi Barani, not realizing this town had already fallen.

When General Berti, the Spanish War veteran, returned to the headquarters of the Tenth Army from sick leave he was informed by his embarrassed staff officers that Gallina's corps of 30,000 men had disappeared. Berti was obviously stunned by the report. The British use of tanks had been unbelievably successful. Berti only had one armored force left, Valentino Babini's brigade, but his tanks were little better than Maletti's. Berti ordered all available personnel to concentrate on defending the city of Bardia in Libya, which had a thirty-year old Italian residential community.

Meanwhile a rearguard of a thousand troops of the 1st Blackshirt 23 March Division was ordered to hold Sidi Omar. On 16 December British tanks rolled right over them. Within hours 900 bewildered Italians were marching off to a makeshift barbed wire cage, leaving behind a hundred Italians lying still on the cold lonely desert floor.

———

The year had failed to bring glory to Italy. The inhabitants of Catania, Cagliari, Elmas, Taranto, Bari, Turin, Milan, San Giovanni, Genoa, Benghazi, Tobruk and Bardia had been bombed, and some had been bombarded by heavy naval shells. Despite the bravery of Italian fliers their machines had proven unreliable. Spectacular actions like the 28 August long-range bombing of Gibraltar were seen for what they were: publicity stunts. The colonists of Bardia, some of them born and bred there, were under siege by year's end. Italian merchant ships no sooner set sail than they were sunk. The invasions of France, Sudan, Kenya, British Somaliland, Greece and Egypt had brought nothing but casualties. Italian artillery gunners had once again enhanced their reputation for courage, and the engineers and tank crews were building their reputation, but the infantry had performed in a very mixed fashion, some running in blind panic, others exhibiting suicidal bravery. Italian generalship was also mixed. Badoglio's dismissal was a popular move among the soldiers, but they thought other heads should roll too. Fascist slogans now rang hollow.

For the first time in twenty years Blackshirts were spat upon and insulted by angry crowds.

On 14 December heads did roll. Mussolini replaced Admiral Cavagnari with Admiral Arturo Ricciardi, and fired Vice Admiral Edoardo Somigli, putting Vice Admiral Inigo Campione in his place, and dismissed Vice Admiral Guido Bacci di Capaci. Vice Admiral Angelo Iachino took his job. Mussolini also dismissed General de Vecchi from his Dodecanese command. The surviving generals and admirals decided that no offensive should be made into Greece for at least a couple of months, that Graziani should hold what he could, that the air force and navy had to create a better liaison system and that the navy should continue to try to lure the Royal Navy to its doom. They also agreed that the Duke D'Aosta was doing splendidly.

———

Chapter Sixteen
East African Stalemate

In East Africa the duke's most pressing problem was that he was cut off from Italy, bar a few aircraft bringing in essentials. Furthermore he knew he had merely put the British off balance. He had not defeated them. In September 1940 his forces had skirmished with Ethiopian guerillas at Mount Zibist and had found evidence of British advisers. Indeed Churchill loved the idea of tiny bands of hero officers straight out of boy's magazines leading native guerillas. Italian aircraft scoured the mountains seeking signs of guerillas. A spy reported that a British adviser was in Dangila District, so Brigadier General Torelli sent the 22nd Colonial Brigade to hunt him down. They found guerillas but no Englishman.

The duke had confidence in Frusci at Kassala five hundred miles north of Addis Ababa, Castagnola and his ascaris at Gallabat three hundred and fifty miles northwest, and in Gazzera at Gore two hundred and fifty miles west, but these officers were too busy with the British to hunt guerillas. So the duke ordered Brigadier General Prina to take the 11th Colonial Brigade and the Rolle Bande to Kurmuk three hundred miles northwest of Addis Ababa to hunt guerillas along the Sudan border. But Prina only provided the bande with four days rations, and instead of finding guerillas they ran into Sudanese troops of the British Army, and after they lost fifty casualties they returned to base.

By now the British had come to the conclusion that penny packet raids and feints was all the duke was going to do, and that he had become defensive. Moreover Churchill continuously demanded action. After all, since April the British had been in retreat from the Arctic to the Equator, and English towns were under German air raids. He needed good news.

Castagnola's scouts told him the British were planning an attack now that the rainy season was over. This was true. Brigadier William Slim had been given two Indian battalions, a squadron of tanks, artillery and planes with which to retake Gallabat. However, at the last minute he was given a British battalion to 'stiffen the backs of his Indians'. Though Slim was British he was an Indian Army officer not a British Army officer and he resented this racist inference that Indians needed 'stiffening'.

Starting 1 November Gallabat's outer perimeter defended by the 27th Colonial Battalion came under daily sniper fire, and on the 6th the ascaris were shelled and then bombed from the air. An hour later Indian troops charged out of a field of eight-foot tall elephant grass, and the ascaris quickly fell back. Meanwhile Castagnola watched from Fort Metemma with pride because everything was going according to plan. When the Indians were halfway between Gallabat and the fort he opened fire with machine guns manned by a company of the Savoia Grenadiers Division, plus artillery and mortars. Then he counter attacked with the 25th and 77th Colonial Battalions. The fighting was quite fierce, and fortunately for the Italians there was no sign of British tanks. Then on schedule thirty of General Pietro Pinna's bombers arrived and pummeled the Indians. They were challenged by seven Gladiator bi-plane fighters of the South African Air Force, but Italian fighters arrived to shoot down all seven in full view of the ground troops. The British 'stiffening' battalion did nothing until a nearby ammunition truck was hit and blew up, whereupon the Britons ran away. Slim tried to stop them, but some in a truck almost ran him over. The Italians actually thought this was some sort of trick. That night Italian aircraft returned, but the Indians would still not budge. The panicky Britons regrouped, but when the Italians threw some smoke-emitting shells at them they panicked and ran away again. As for the twelve British tanks, nine had thrown treads on rough ground. The following day in anger and embarrassment Slim withdrew his forces.

Castagnola had lost the village of Gallabat and 428 casualties, but he had brought the duke a much-needed victory. Two days later he and his exhausted troops were relieved by Brigadier General Polverini's 4th Colonial Brigade. The Fascist press made much of the victory. The Ethiopian ascaris were proud of their accomplishments. The British press all but ignored the defeat. British policy was to hide the news of Italian victories and overemphasize Italian defeats.

Unknown to the Italians their greatest threat arrived in the Sudan at this time: Major Orde Wingate. This officer was as masochistic, controversial and brilliant as his cousin Lawrence of Arabia. He soon made friends with Haile Selassie, then gained permission to use Sudanese troops to escort the camel convoys that were resupplying the guerillas, and then he suggested the British establish an Ethiopian Liberation Army administered in companies of 200 guerillas, each cadred by five British or Sudanese sergeants and a British officer. His superiors agreed but only if he used the existing British-trained Ethiopians. They wanted this 'army' to be small and disciplined, not large and unruly.

Meanwhile the unruly guerillas had become a serious problem for the duke, especially in Gojjam one hundred and forty miles northwest of Addis Ababa. In November an entire truck convoy was wiped out by them, and another suffered high loss.

General Nasi believed the guerillas should be crushed as soon as possible before they coordinated their efforts with the British. He had recruited additional bande and had bribed chieftains to remain loyal, and his spies fomented trouble between guerilla bands. In order to pacify the Gojjam-Debra Markos area Nasi stuck his neck out by allowing Marshal Hailu to return there against Mussolini's orders. This king's welcome to his homeland was tumultuous and within days several guerilla bands had defected to him. Hailu was the carrot. Nasi's troops would provide the stick. By coincidence British air raids ceased at this time and many Ethiopians came to the conclusion that Italy was winning the war.

———

Chapter Seventeen
Libyan Debacle

In Libya Berti organized the best defenses for Bardia that he could. In the last two weeks of 1940 the perimeter was tested by a few British armored cars and infantry, while the main city was bombed regularly, and on one night the Italians were shelled by warships. Berti's air defenses were not successful, his CR42 fighters barely matching the enemy Gladiators, and when the British introduced the sleek new Hurricane monoplane fighter, the Italian machines were hopelessly outclassed.

In direct command of the defenses was Lieutenant General Bergonzolli, old electric whiskers, and his fighting troops consisted of Lieutenant General Lorenzo Dalmazzo's XXI Corps of Major General Ruggero Tracchia's Marmarica Division and Major General Alessandro de Guidi's Cirene Division both recruited in part from Italian colonists in Libya, so that some of these men were defending their hometown. Also present was the XXIII Corps of Major General Francesco Antonelli's 1st Blackshirt 23 March Division and Major General Francesco Argentina's 2nd Blackshirt 28 October Division. In reserve was a battle group of Major General Giuseppe Amico's Catanzaro Division, plus some extra tank companies, armored car companies, artillery battalions and anti-tank teams. Antonelli's division had already lost a thousand men in a sacrificial rearguard, and in the city were the survivors of the 1st Libyan, 2nd Libyan and 4th Blackshirt Divisions. In the city the flak gunners were in constant action, but there were also thousands of noncombatant personnel of the army, police, Carabinieri, navy and air force. The Catanzaro had been created by siphoning off the army personnel attached to the 3rd Blackshirt 21 April Division, and then adding new recruits.

The British decided to test the defenses with tanks, spraying the front line with machine gun fire as they did so. The Italian anti-tank gunners with their 47mm guns had to sit and take this until the British tanks were within 250 yards before their shots could penetrate, but when they opened fire they did so with a vengeance. The Italians cheered when they saw their anti-tank gunners drive off the enemy.

On 2 January 1941 the British XIII Corps launched a full-scale assault. First the Italians were shelled by long-range artillery and three British destroyers, and then they were bombed and strafed by aircraft. The following morning the outer perimeter was assaulted by Major General Ivan McKay's Australian 6th Division and thirty tanks of the British 7th Armored Division. Instantly the Italian infantry pinned down the attackers, but eventually British and Australian artillery blasted a gap in the front line. Italian anti-tank gunners were given one opportunity to strike the tank coming towards them in the confusion of battle amid smoke and blowing sand. If they missed they had the option of running, surrendering or dying. Meanwhile Italian infantry launched violent bayonet charges to try to close the gap, while elsewhere they clung to their trenches like grim death, oblivious to the pounding of Blenheim bombers, Hurricane fighters, artillery shells and a bombardment from the sea by seven destroyers, a monitor and the battleships Barham, Valiant and Warspite. One salvo from a battleship could wipe out a hundred yards of trenches. Casualties were fearful. Some men quite literally disappeared in a puff of smoke.

An Italian platoon of about thirty men would be overrun, twenty of them limping to the rear, half a dozen fighting to the death, half a dozen surrendering or taken while incapacitated by wounds. The twenty survivors would then counter attack, losing five or six to machine guns and rifle fire, but recapturing their position. Within minutes the incident would be repeated and matched by other platoons along the line.

Only after twenty-four hours of this seesaw action did one section of the line collapse enabling the Australians to pour through. Once again Italian leadership proved inadequate.

Bergonzolli recognized the signs of defeat at once, and bypassing the chain of command he made a super-human effort to personally direct a counter-thrust. But by dusk on the 4th there was nothing left to stop British tanks from driving into the Italian rear. Therefore he called for volunteers to break out to fight another day. That night he, Giuseppe Amico and a mixed bag of personnel, most of them from the 2nd Blackshirt Division, charged on foot into the Australian lines, and sliced their way through and ran onwards into the darkness towards the west.

Back in Bardia the battle still raged all night and into the dawn. But on the afternoon of 5 January the remaining staff officers surrendered the garrison. The cost to the Australians was 456 killed and wounded. British casualties were very light. Italian casualties were well over a thousand. The British press played down the aspect of death on both sides and seized upon the fact that two Allied divisions had taken the surrender of four and a half Italian divisions, capturing a port city, a hundred armored vehicles, 462 guns, a thousand trucks, tons of supplies, aircraft, merchant ships and naval vessels and 35,949 personnel.

Bergonzolli's mob was still running along the coast road, diving into the sand periodically to avoid the bullets and bombs of Allied fighters and bombers, and miraculously most of them reached Tobruk seventy miles away. Without resting Bergonzolli inspected the city's defenses of Lieutenant General Enrico Pitassi Manella's XXII Corps and found the only significant force was Major General Vincenzo della Mura's Sirte Division of colonists. Most of the troops in the city were rear echelon. At least there was some artillery and the old cruiser

San Giorgio in the harbor.

Bergonzolli did not expect the British to give him time to prepare, and indeed their infantry and armored cars were already testing the perimeter when he arrived. However, the British refrained from pressing the defenses too hard, preferring to punish Tobruk with artillery fire, shelling by three destroyers and continuous air raids for two weeks. The Sirte men were quite aware that six Italian garrisons had already fallen, and their morale was bad even before they were subjected to this hellacious bombardment. Moreover they were worried about the Italian women and children in the city.

On 21 January the ground attack began. The Sirte was assaulted by the Australian 6th Division and three British battalions, odds of two to one. The Italians did well and late in the day they launched a fearless counter attack that repulsed the Australians and worried the Allied commanders. However, Manella was captured during the day, and Bergonzolli once again witnessed evidence of an imminent collapse. He chose to lead another marathon across the desert, and in the dark he and his die-hards ran right through the exhausted Australians. Unfortunately British tanks were waiting for them, and many among this mob were gunned down.

The next morning della Mura surrendered Tobruk. The twenty-four hour fight had cost the Allies 355 killed and wounded. They had captured a port city, tons of supplies, scores of guns, hundreds of vehicles, merchant ships and naval vessels, aircraft and 25,000 personnel of all branches.

Before noon this day 22 January, the perimeter of Derna, a hundred and fifty miles west of Tobruk, was approached by British tanks. Here Lieutenant General Fernandino Conaco's XX Corps held the town with elements of the Sabratha and Catanzaro Divisions, plus gunners with 65mm and 105mm guns, anti-tank teams with 47mm guns and thousands of support troops. The Sabratha was also drawn from Italian colonists. This afternoon the defenders were attacked by the British tanks, and they repelled them.

On the 24th the garrison of Mechili forty odd miles south of Derna was made up of a regiment of the Sabratha and a few guns, and this day it was assaulted by British tanks, and here too the ferocious defense came as a shock to the British. The Italians also produced a surprise. Conaco had withheld Babini's tank brigade, and now he unleashed it. Babini's thirteen-ton M13s with 40mm armor were highly vulnerable to the British tanks, but with a turret-mounted 47mm gun the M13 could repay in kind. When Babini charged forward he forced the British 26 ton Matilda tanks to retreat, at a cost of just two M13s. Later the British attacked again, this time with 12 ton Cruiser tanks, which only had 30mm armor, but were speedy and maneuverable. After another seven of his tanks were knocked out, Babini ordered his support troops to withdraw while his tanks fought a rearguard action. As few of his tanks had radios he could not have ordered a retreat had he wanted to. Both sides were relieved that darkness brought a halt to the tank battle.

Next day the garrison of Mechili repulsed another tank onslaught, but that night the entire garrison retreated westwards.

Babini had orders to move north to reinforce Derna, which was now under heavy tank/infantry assault, and he did so soon becoming embroiled in the whirlwind of battle. For four days the Italians and Allies battled and by the 29th Conaco concluded his men were near breaking point. So he ordered a retreat.

Come dawn the Italians were strung out along the coast road for miles and were subject to anything the Allied air forces wanted to throw at them. The Italians were hungry, thirsty, exhausted, cold, dazed, demoralized, filthy and sick and felt like ducks in a shooting gallery. Oddly enough they were not being followed, because the British in their tanks and trucks were racing past them across the flat desert hoping to circumvent Benghazi. In that town the Arab populace was already rebellious, and nomads had drifted in hoping to loot the homes of Italian colonists. The latter were terrified and demanded protection, and as a result the police and Carabinieri had their hands full hunting for Libyan deserters, dispersing looters, directing traffic and patrolling Italian neighborhoods, and all under air raids. Then suddenly the British were at the gates.

Graziani relieved Berti of command and brought in Lieutenant General Giuseppe Tellera, whose first order to Tenth Army was to reassemble west of Beda Fomm. All towns to the east were to be abandoned, as were the sick and wounded. Indeed the plight of the sick and wounded was terrible, for they had to calmly await the arrival of the Allies, not knowing if they would be killed or taken prisoner, and not caring either way, such was their state of demoralization.

The main body of retreating Italians was still ready to fight if only they could at first sleep, eat, rearm and reequip. Once they passed through the bottleneck of Beda Fomm they would be able to do this, but on 5 February they received depressing news: the British had looped around them and had cut them off. So in order to reach safety they would now have to charge through a British blocking position consisting of an infantry brigade, four tank battalions, an armored car battalion, a battery of anti-tank guns and two batteries of 25pounder field guns. The Italian officers began prodding their sergeants, and they began to round up remnants of their platoons, and the men began to psyche themselves up to attack. Some had walked 500 miles under air attack to get here.

Boldly crying 'Avanti' in their dry mouths they charged forward, throwing wave after wave against the British, and as had been the case since the invention of gunpowder mere flesh was not strong enough to repel hot piercing bullets. Next day the infantry and combat engineers charged forward again, while Babini attacked with 110 tanks. By day's end hundreds of Italians lay bleeding and eighty Italian tanks had been knocked out. A British 25pounder shell could turn an M13 into a pile of scrap. The Italians continued to attack throughout the night. General Tellera fell mortally wounded.

By dawn on the 7th it was over. Everybody knew it, but Babini, never one to be called a quitter, attacked one more time. The remnant of his brigade was destroyed. Now the Italians gave up. British newsreel cameras filmed the event and gave the impression of a happy crowd at a sports event. But the Italians were smiling because they did not want to antagonize a trigger-happy British soldier at this stage. The cameras did not film the corpses that littered the desert. The British counted 25,000 live Italians. One of them was Bergonzolli.

By mid-February the Allies had registered their losses as 1,900 killed and wounded since 9 December in Egypt and Libya. Graziani could only assume they were telling the truth. He was surer of his own losses for only 7,000 men of Tenth Army had reached him, meaning that 100,000 Italians and 30,000 Libyans were missing. About 10,000 of these had been killed, the remainder including sick and wounded had been taken prisoner. Graziani asked to be relieved, and Mussolini acquiesced and sent General Italo Gariboldi to Libya in his stead.

———

Chapter Eighteen
Bloody East Africa

When the British in East Africa commanded by Lieutenant General Alan Cunningham heard of their peers' spectacular successes in Egypt they became more determined than ever to do something about their own predicament. They reminded Churchill how large the area of Somaliland, Ethiopia and Eritrea was and that any invasion would need a large number of vehicles just to carry drinking water.

The duke and his generals knew their days were numbered, for the British would hardly think of surrendering now that they were advancing in Egypt. On the Kenya-Somaliland border British Major General Godwin-Austen was massing four brigades of East African ascaris, two brigades of West African ascaris, two divisions of the South African Army [almost all white troops], white colonist East African horse cavalry, British tanks, armored cars and artillery and several groups of tribal warriors, the British equivalent of bande. To defend this thousand mile border Lieutenant General Gustavo Pesenti had only Major General Alfredo Baccari's 101st and Major General Amedeo Liberati's 102nd Colonial Divisions, and Colonel Garino's 191st Colonial Battalion, all consisting of Somali ascaris, plus a few Somali and Ethiopian bande.

On 16 December 1940 the garrison of one thousand bande at El Waq was assaulted by planes, artillery, two companies of KAR, two companies of armored cars, a company of tanks, a South African brigade and the 24th Gold Coast Brigade [Ghana]. These bande were not expected to hold against modern European troops, let alone a force five times their number, and it is to their credit that they stood up to the attackers for three days before retreating. They left behind eight Italian and 200 native dead and 44 wounded.

The duke flew to Mogadishu in Somaliland to ask Pesenti why the position had been lost. Pesenti was obviously shaken, for he asked the duke to seek surrender terms. He was lucky. The duke simply fired him. Graziani would have had him shot for defeatism.

The duke replaced him with de Simone, who was not a defeatist, but then again neither was he much of a general. The duke knew that Pesenti had only been echoing the thoughts of millions of his countrymen, for the Italian people had been dragged from war to war and the current conflict was unpopular. The stories of the defeats in Greece and Egypt went the rounds in East Africa in many languages and became embellished with the telling. Certainly no one could disguise the fact that the great Badoglio had been dismissed and the great Graziani had been defeated.

One cannot overemphasize the rough conditions in East Africa. Even peacetime tourists found the land almost impossible to traverse, and the climate ranged from wet, cold and miserable to hot, dry and miserable. Another cause for concern, that the duke noticed, was that those Italian troops who had come here as colonists with their wives and children, were now worried about their families. After all only a handful of police and Carabinieri stood between their loved ones and murder or rape by marauding bands of Ethiopian deserters and guerillas. Their families were also under air attack. The thought of leaving a wife, daughter, mother or sister at the mercy of 'black savages' was too much for some, and they deserted to protect their womenfolk.

In the security of his Addis Ababa headquarters the duke studied his maps. He knew the assaults on Gallabat and El Waq had been probes. He wondered where the British would launch their real invasion. His intelligence staff said they were strong enough to attack everywhere. The duke suspected this was alarmism and the British would only attempt an attack from Khartoum in the northwest or Port Sudan in the north or both. Victory here would give the British the Eritrean ports of Massawa and Assab and would link them with the Gojjam guerillas, which would give British merchant ships unrestricted passage south from the Suez Canal. Once done they could let the duke and his men wither on the vine. Just in case he was wrong the duke kept his best reserves, the Savoia Grenadiers and Cacciatore d'Africa Divisions, centrally located at Addis Ababa.

Then spies reported that Beresford-Pierce's's 4th Indian and Lewis Heath's 5th Indian Divisions and an Australian division plus tanks were disembarking at Port Sudan seven hundred miles north of Addis Ababa. And at the junction of the Eritrean-Ethiopian-Sudanese border four hundred miles northwest of Addis Ababa a patrol of the 1st Colonial Brigade was attacked by a unit of anti-Fascist French. It looked like the duke had been right after all. The duke readjusted his forces at once. He told Major Quigini's bande to withdraw from Gubba three hundred miles northwest of Addis Ababa, and ordered Frusci to abandon Kassala in Sudan five hundred miles to the northwest.

Unknown to the duke the British knew of these moves, because they had broken the duke's signaling code and could read almost every order he gave!

Haile Selassie got in on the act. He entered a border hamlet and declared the beginning of the liberation of his country.

The duke gave Frusci the job of protecting Eritrea and for this he was allowed eleven brigades. Frusci placed five on the Sudanese border, five near Asmara in case of an amphibious landing and one at Keren between them. His plan was to allow the enemy to enter and hold them at the Agordat-Barentu Line. As per instructions the last troops pulled out of Kassala on the 17 January, half withdrawing to Agordat, half to Barentu, and three days later Kassala was assaulted by the British. It appeared to Frusci that the evacuation had gone unnoticed by the British. It had, to every Briton except General Cunningham. Only he knew the truth. He could use the information gained by the British code-breakers, but could not tell anyone how he got his information.

On 21 January 1941 Brigadier General Ugo Fongoli's 41st Colonial Brigade reached Keru Gorge on the Agordat road after a tiring march of four days. Here he turned and launched a riposte against the Indian battalion that had been following him, sending them packing with 150 casualties. Then British artillery arrived, so Fongoli ordered a cavalry charge. Lieutenant Guillet, the commander of the Gruppo Bande a Cavallo Amhara sent Lieutenant Togni and sixty of his native horsemen to charge the guns on their flank. At the gallop, firing carbines as they rode, the horsemen almost reached the guns, but then the gunners swung their pieces around and opened fire pointblank. The last horse fell just twenty-five yards from the guns. Togni had nearly succeeded, but he lost all his horses and twenty-three men killed and sixteen wounded. An hour later Lieutenant Guillet launched another charge with his remaining 440 horsemen, but by now the guns were protected by Sudanese infantry in two lines. Naturally the horsemen were slaughtered by artillery shells, machine guns and rifle fire, yet incredibly some managed to jump over the first infantry line, but were massacred before they could gain the second line. Guillet lost eighty-nine horses killed and sixty-eight wounded, and one hundred and seventy-nine men killed and two hundred and sixty wounded. Guillet's command had been wiped out.

Fongoli's command was now subjected to three days of air raids and artillery barrages and infantry probes, after which Fongoli learned he had been cut off, because a brigade of the Indian 5th Division had found a route around the gorge. Fongoli's men were attacked in the rear by a Scottish battalion at Biscia, and they repelled the assault, but Fongoli knew it was hopeless. He had barely seven hundred men left. He surrendered.

The other column that was retreating from Kassala on the Barentu road left a rearguard at El Gogno, which was challenged on 25 January by a brigade of the Indian 5th Division. This day Frusci was visited by Generals Prinna and Trezzani and together they inspected the defenses of Agordat. It was agreed to bring up Colonel Lorenzini's 2nd Colonial Brigade. The duke had already reinforced Frusci with the 11th Regiment of the Savoia Grenadiers Division. The duke knew Lorenzini had performed well at Tug Argan Pass, and to the astonishment of many the duke now promoted him two ranks to major general and gave him responsibility for Agordat. He would have his own Eritrean brigade, another Eritrean brigade, a Blackshirt battalion, artillery, some tanks and armored cars and support troops for a total of 12,000 men, and he named this formation the 4th

Colonial Division. Frusci ordered Major General Bergonzi to defend Barentu with his 6000-man 2nd Colonial Division.

When Lorenzini was informed the Allies were near he sent tanks to greet them, but when two were knocked out by anti-tank guns the others withdrew, as did the enemy. But this was just the opening of the curtain. The real battle began an hour later, when the Indian 4th Division launched an assault. Unknown to these Italians, this division had fought the Italians in Egypt. Its British and Indian soldiers were aware that Italians could fight well, regardless of what British propaganda told them, and they were soon reminded of this when they were beaten back from the Italian barbed wire trenches by rifle and machine gun fire and barrages from mortars and artillery.

On the evening of the 29th the Indians tried to infiltrate the mountains around the town of Agordat, and they ran into ascari outposts that fought them in hand to hand combat. The action lasted all night into the dawn and all day, and Lorenzini's troops were victorious. The following day the Indians attacked again, but the Eritrean ascaris repulsed them and then counter attacked with the bayonet. Some ascari platoons were all but wiped out. When British tanks tried to advance, the Italians replied with tanks of their own supported by Blackshirt infantry. Eleven Italian tanks were blown up, and the Blackshirts were mowed down by machine guns.

Lorenzini decided it was time to leave Agordat, but unfortunately this meant he would have to abandon a thousand sick and wounded. A small force of Eritrean cavalry held the rearguard.

Meantime at Barentu forty miles to the south Bergonzi's 2nd Colonial Division was holding out against attacks by the Indian 5th Division, and on 1 February he counter attacked and pushed the enemy back. However, news of the evacuation of Agordat meant that his right flank was turned, so this night he ordered a retreat, and he too had to abandon his sick and wounded.

A few miles further to the south Colonel Postiglione's 1st Colonial Brigade was retreating along the Um Hagar-Asmara road, trying to stay one jump ahead of Sudanese and French troops. And one hundred and eighty miles south of Barentu Polverini's 4th Colonial Brigade was in retreat from Metemma towards Gondar. To the south of Polverini's unit, the Gruppi Bande Frontiere made up of Ethiopian Gojjam warriors was covering his flank.

On 23 January three hundred and fifty miles west of Addis Ababa on the Baro River Major Praga's 3rd Bande Gruppo lost Jokau to an attack by Nuer tribesmen led by a British officer. Two days later Praga's scouts on the Gilo River forty miles south sighted a mass of Anuak tribesmen led by a British officer. Praga attacked and sent the Anuaks packing.

On the 25th Major Gobatto's 2nd Bande Gruppo at Eribo was attacked by Sudanese troops of the British Army, and he held.

So far the only Allied forces that had advanced into Eritrea had come from Khartoum, but now they came on from Port Sudan too, as the duke had expected. On 28 January Italian customs police, whose real job was to arrest smugglers, found themselves fighting as infantry at Karora on Eritrea's northern border against a swarm of Beja tribesmen led by a British officer. The following day near Karora Italian planes sighted a British truck column stuck in soft sand, so they strafed them. Frusci responded by sending his 5th and 44th Colonial Brigades to Karora. The duke reinforced Frusci further, sending the 6th and 11th Colonial Brigades from Shoa.

Meanwhile Lorenzini and Bergonzi had fallen back to Keren and had joined forces, and their engineers had blocked the road with demolitions. The pass here is one of the most inaccessible in East Africa and so rugged that by 1941 none of the eleven major peaks in the area had been explored by white men. To bypass Keren the Allies would have to make a 150 mile detour. However, if they broke through at Karora they could come up behind Lorenzini and Bergonzi.

On 3 February Bergonzi's ascaris watched as British infantry of the 11th Indian Brigade approached, clambering up the steep slopes of Mount Sanchil. The ascaris opened fire, but were soon driven off a small peak, whereupon they counter attacked, failed, counter attacked again, failed and counter attacked yet again, and failed to recapture the small peak. But the British fire was highly inaccurate and by day's end Bergonzi had lost only eighteen ascaris.

Next day a hasty repositioning of ascaris kept another small peak from falling to the British. But after dusk the Forcuta peaks were lost to an Indian night attack.

On the 5th Frusci reinforced Bergonzi with two battalions of Savoia Grenadiers, and these Italians counter attacked with the bayonet immediately, scrambling over sharp rocks and uneven slopes, and they shoved an Indian battalion back to its jump off line. Encountering a second battalion there the Italians prudently fell back.

Lorenzini had put two battalions on Acqua Col, a wise move, for on 7 February an Indian company was seen approaching it. The ascaris allowed the Indians within their perimeter, but would not let them out again, despite the Indians having artillery support on call. Only nine Indians escaped the trap.

This day the duke himself inspected the Keren defenses. The chain of command was straightened out: Frusci would be in charge of Eritrea, and under him Lieutenant General Nicolangelo Carnimeo would command at Keren, with Lorenzini holding the northern half of the line and Bergonzi the southern. The duke strolled with Carnimeo's staff, but without Carnimeo, who rarely left his bunker, and he gave advice where necessary. Lorenzini was told to place his 2nd and 11th Colonial Brigades up front to block the Indian 5th Brigade from breaking through at Acqua Col. The 6th Colonial Brigade was ordered to hold the main road and rail line at Dongalaas Gorge. The duke contradicted Frusci's orders and sent Bergonzi's 5th Colonial Brigade to the far northern flank. The duke, assuming his actual Italians were his best soldiers, put four battalions of Savoia Grenadiers and two battalions of Blackshirts on Mount Sanchil under Bergonzi. This gave Carnimeo twelve battalions of Eritrean and Ethiopian ascaris and six battalions of Italians, plus Italian combat engineers. His artillery was commanded by Colonel Lamborghini and manned by both ascaris and Italians…one hundred and forty-four guns of 65mm and 105mm. It was believed that the enemy facing him consisted of twelve Indian and six British infantry battalions, plus Indian and British engineers, and one hundred and forty-four guns. Thus the two sides were more or less equal, though the Allies had air superiority and their guns had a greater range.

At midday on 10 February the defenders of Keren were struck by a heavy artillery barrage that continued for hours. At dusk the 97th Colonial Battalion was attacked by Indians, and they reported that they could not hold for long under this pounding, but at the last minute a Bersaglieri company reinforced them and they held. Deeper into the night three minor peaks were lost to the Indians, but the Bersaglieri counter attacked across ground that sloped perilously steep and recaptured one peak. Then the Indians counter attacked and the Bersaglieri fell back.

At dawn Lamborghini gave what gun support he could while the Bersaglieri joined by a battalion of Alpini charged over open terrain and retook the lost peaks. Not only did this knock the Indian 11th Brigade back where it had started a week earlier, but the brigade was so badly crippled it had to be relieved.

Meanwhile this day the 2nd and 11th Colonial Brigades defended Acqua Col from an assault by the Indian 5th Brigade supported by Sudanese machine gunners. The fighting degenerated into hand-to-hand combat. The ascaris fought magnificently and held their ground. One Indian company was whittled down to eighteen men at day's end. The Italians and ascaris breathed a sigh of relief come nightfall. They had just defeated the finest troops in the British Empire.

By now the Italians and their ascaris were living in atrocious conditions. Everything from socks to artillery shells had to be hand carried up craggy precipitous slopes. And all wounded and sick had to be hand carried down these slopes. Many men were injured in falls. The nature of the ground meant that often parties of two or three men had to fight on alone, becoming convinced their compatriots had deserted them. The nights were nerve-wracking, because Indians that had been recruited from the warlike tribes along the Indian/Afghanistan border would infiltrate the Italian positions with long knives. Artillery explosions, aerial bombs and sniper's bullets added to the discomfort. Under such conditions the Italian supply system broke down. Even the tedious Italian tinned sausages failed to show up. Drinking water became scarce and medical materials were in short supply. The road and rail line between Keren and Asmara was under constant surveillance by Allied aircraft. Most of the Italian planes were grounded for lack of trivial spare parts. By this date the duke could put up no more than fifty aircraft per day in all of East Africa. It is understandable why many ascaris fell out of love with Mussolini at this time. Over a period of a few weeks the 11th Colonial Brigade suffered 40% desertions. Other ascari units had rates almost as high.

———

The war was still mobile throughout the rest of East Africa. On 17 January an Ethiopian bande on the Kenya border four hundred miles south of Addis Ababa repulsed a South African attack. At first the duke asked for confirmation, not believing that these bande could defeat a modern white military formation. South African combat troops were white [English-speaking and Afrikaans-speaking], though some of their support personnel were native Africans. Then on 31 January the 54th Colonial Battalion at Moyale on this border was assaulted by Major General Isaac de Villiers South African 2nd Division, and despite odds of six to one against the ascaris repelled the South Africans! The ascaris were elated. Not only had they defeated the enemy, but they (black men) had defeated an army of white men. The British generals were shocked and demanded that de Villiers' division be retrained! To be fair to de Villiers he was not a professional soldier, but was a civilian policeman, and he should never have been placed in this position. He was eventually sent home.

With no worries over Keren, and news of these two victories on the Kenya border, the duke was feeling better, and his propaganda office convinced the colonists of East Africa that there was no cause to be concerned. To show his faith in Ethiopian loyalty the duke acknowledged Marshal Seyoum as King of Tigre and allowed him to be crowned at Adowa. He was even given a personal bodyguard under Colonel Delitala. The duke also allowed Marshal Ayalew Birru to return to his homeland, Gondar, with a bodyguard under Brigadier General Martini.

———

However, just as this sense of relief was spreading across the land the British launched four new invasions of Italian East Africa.

Having secured a Northern Eritrean fishing village the British brought in a brigade of Frenchmen and French ascaris, and together with British troops they assaulted Cub Cub. The four hundred Eritrean ascaris here gave up after a short futile fight. Frusci was not concerned though, despite the fact that Cub Cub was seventy miles to the rear of Keren, because between Keren and Cub Cub lay Mescelit

Pass guarded by L3 tankettes. However, two days later British open-topped Bren gun carriers [similar to the tankettes] chased away the Italian tankettes, and by 26 February the invaders were just seven miles north of Keren at Mount Engiahat. Fortunately the 5th Colonial Brigade held that mountain, courtesy of the duke's foresight, and they stopped the British and French.

––––––––––

The second Allied offensive came out of Kenya on 14 February, spearheaded by Major General George Brink's South African 1st Division. The only formation in its path was an Ethiopian bande at Mega four hundred miles south of Addis Ababa supported by some 122mm guns. The bande folded quickly. About a hundred miles west of Mega Major Gobatto's bande retreated in the face of an advance by the 25th East African Brigade of Major General Harry Wetherall's 11th African Division. The British were aided by Turkhana tribesmen. Fortunately for Gobatto he was able to draw support from Merille and Donjiro tribesmen, not because they loved Italians, but because they hated Turkhanas. British air power decided the issue.

The third invasion also came from Kenya. De Simone was worried about the British build up in Kenya opposite the Somaliland border, and once he had inspected the defenses of Baccari's 101st and Liberati's 102nd Colonial Divisions he became even more concerned, and he urgently requested a reinforcement by actual Italian troops. The duke turned him down and told him to do the best he could to hold the Juba River eight hundred miles southeast of Addis Ababa.

On 4 February the British crossed into Somaliland. A Somali bande tried to hold Beles Gugnani, a desert oasis in front of [i. e. south of] the Juba River, when they were attacked by Brigadier Charles Fowkes' British 22nd East African Brigade of the 11th African Division reinforced by South African armored cars, but within hours the bande warriors fled or surrendered. The invaders pressed on northwards towards the river, and six days later they approached Afmadu. Here fifteen Allied aircraft bombed and strafed the 94th Colonial Battalion. This caused panic among these ascaris, who had never faced planes before, and that night they abandoned the town and retreated northwards towards the river.

De Simone tried to stop the advance on 13 February at Bulo Erillo, where he had reinforced his Somali ascaris with armored cars and a battery of 65mm guns, and they did indeed fight well against the oncoming 24th Gold Coast Brigade of Godwin-Austen's 12th African Division, at least for a few hours, but then the Somalis collapsed and withdrew, leaving one hundred and forty wounded to be captured.

Next de Simone intended to stop the enemy at Jelib on the Juba River, and here he placed the remainder of Liberati's 102nd Colonial Division. They did bring the Gold Coasters to a halt.

De Simone had a decision to make: should he fight for the port of

Kismayu, which lie south of the river or cut his losses and hold the river only? Already de Simone in his headquarters at the port of Mogadishu was under British naval bombardment, which might be the herald of an amphibious invasion. So he ordered Kismayu to be abandoned. Strategically this was the right decision, but unfortunately the Italian and ascari uniformed personnel there obeyed this order so quickly that they did not destroy the port. Thus the British inherited an intact port in working order, a Somali city with its half-century old Italian quarter, a mountain of supplies, 330,000 gallons of fuel and twenty-five merchant ships. When the British arrived the Italian colonists cheered them! These women and children had been terrified of being raped and murdered by the local Somalis. With the British in control they knew they would be safe.

On 16 February at Gobwen on the Juba River de Simone's ascaris fought well enough to prevent Brigadier Dan Pienaar's South African 1st Brigade of the 12th African Division from crossing. De Simone suspected the enemy would try a flanking movement, and his scouts identified other South Africans crossing in boats fifteen miles upstream, so he sent ascari battalions rushing to the threatened sector and for two days they stopped the invaders. However, on the 19th South African engineers finished a pontoon bridge that enabled their armored cars to cross. Outflanked by these machines, the ascaris retreated.

Meanwhile the ascaris at Jelib were still holding, and on 20 February some Gold Coasters crossed the Juba River at an undefended ford and swung round to strike Jelib in flank. When de Simone was informed of both crossings and that desertion had increased dramatically, he ordered a complete retreat from the river. In fact he now intended to abandon all of Somaliland.

On the 22nd the Italian garrison of the port of Brava, ninety miles north of the river, began to destroy as much as possible before retreating, but when a British cruiser began shelling them they left hurriedly. In Mogadishu one hundred and twenty miles north of Brava de Simone and his rear echelon Italians were already destroying that port, and on the 24th de Simone and his troops abandoned the city when he heard that Allied motorized infantry were near. That night the British 23rd Nigerian Brigade drove into the city amid the cheers of the Italian civilians. However, at the dockside some Italian sailors decided to resist. They had been appalled at the panic at army headquarters. Of course they were outclassed by the Nigerian infantry, and by morning the Nigerians had taken the port. Here the Nigerians captured 430,000 gallons of fuel and a great amount of supplies.

The fourth Allied invasion in February did not begin so noisily as the others. Without fighting or fanfare Major Orde Wingate and his

Gideon Force entered Ethiopia from Sudan at a point three hundred and fifty miles northwest of Addis Ababa. This British officer commanded Ethiopian guerillas through a cadre of Sudanese and British sergeants and British officers, supported by Sudanese infantry of the British Army, and by 19 February he had reached Makatal Pass. From here Wingate sent a hundred men to raid Bahrdar at the southern tip of Lake Tana, while his main force moved on to Engiabara.

General Nasi at his headquarters in Gondar north of Lake Tana was in control of this entire region, and he had little faith in the few Ethiopian bande at Engiabara, so he ordered them to retreat. However, he expected Brigadier General Torelli to hold Bahrdar, because he had a garrison of a few hundred ascaris and 10,000 bande. Furthermore just seventy miles south of Bahrdar was Burie, where Colonel Natale possessed the 3rd Colonial Brigade and a mob of bande too numerous and volatile to count. In addition fifty miles southeast of Burie was Debra Markos, where Colonel Saverio Maraventano had a garrison of ascaris and bande. Thus on the map it appeared that Nasi had a good defense line: Gondar, Lake Tana, Bahrdar, Burie and Debra Markos. But in truth there were gaps in the line big enough for an entire army to squeeze through, especially if Italian planes could be kept at bay.

Nasi's military intelligence believed Wingate was aiming for Burie, so he informed Natale, who sent up spotter aircraft. They sighted Gideon Force and shadowed it until the 25th when it suddenly disappeared. Natale waited tensely. At dawn on the 27th one of his outposts near Burie was attacked by Sudanese infantry, but Natale wisely saw this as a feint and he did not take the bait. Finally Wingate's main attack came at Burie itself, and Natale met the guerillas with artillery fire, which broke them, and then Natale charged them with cavalry. The tactic worked well, and a second charge threw the guerillas into a panic. Wingate himself narrowly escaped capture. As a finishing tough Natale's planes strafed the fleeing remnant of Gideon Force. He radioed Nasi that he had won the first round, but was concerned for the safety of the Italian women and children in Burie.

———

At Keren no one was going anywhere. The battle was one of attrition, each side hoping the other would wear down first. On 23 February Colonel Persichelli led his 4th Colonial Battalion of Eritreans and some armored cars into the attack and took a segment of the enemy line. Following this good news the duke sent more reinforcements to Carnimeo: three more battalions of the Savoia Grenadiers and some ascaris.

At the beginning of March Carnimeo reorganized his Keren

defenses. The 2nd Colonial Brigade was finally pulled out for a rest. He gave the Zelale sector to Colonel Ossoli's 11th Colonial Brigade with a battery each of 75mm and horse-drawn 65mm guns. He gave the Dologorodok sector to Colonels Prina and Corsi with the Savoia Grenadiers' 11th Regiment, a battalion of ascaris and a battery each of 65mm guns, 47mm anti-tank guns and 20mm flak guns. Mount Amba would be held by the 5th Colonial Brigade, and a battery each of 65mm guns, 75mm flak guns and 105mm guns. The Samana area was given to Colonel Bonelli, who would have the 12th Colonial Brigade, an extra ascari battalion and a battery each of 65mm and 75mm guns. The northern flank would be defended by the 2nd and 6th Colonial Brigades, 44th CCNN Battalion, and three batteries of 65mm and one battery of 75mm guns. In reserve he held back the 44th Colonial Brigade, 11th CCNN Legion, three Blackshirt companies and some horse cavalry and tanks.

At 7am 15 March these impressive defenses were assaulted by the Indian 4th and 5th Divisions, starting with a heavy rolling artillery barrage. Suspecting the enemy was creeping behind the moving barrage the Italian artillery opened fire, and good job too, for the British and Indians were caught in the open. The six mortars assigned to each Italian infantry battalion also joined in the bloodletting. Nonetheless one position of the 5th Colonial Brigade was overrun by an Indian battalion. A counter attack failed to retake it. Unknown to the Italians they had inflicted 50% losses on the Indian battalion.

In the Samana sector Bonelli's 12th Colonial Brigade lost their first line of defense, but refused to give up their secondary line. At Dologorodok the Savoia Grenadiers were struck very hard indeed by two Indian and two British battalions, but they pinned down the attackers. Their anti-tank guns stopped a charging wave of Bren gun carriers. Dusk brought no cessation to the struggle as the grenadiers continued to shoot at the enemy. Three times the Italians repulsed the British and Indians, but on the fourth attempt they had to withdraw. Not for long though, because they counter attacked with two companies of Italians and two of ascaris. This failed, and both sides settled down, though the British artillery continued to pound the Italians, who must have thought the British possessed all the artillery shells in the world. Come dawn the defenders of Fort Dologorodok could see the British massing 300 feet below and they opened fire. British shells fell in the fort, while the British infantry scrambled up the incline and climbed over the walls. The British found two medics and forty wounded in the fort. Later in the morning two Italian battalions tried to retake the fort but failed.

That night the 5th Colonial Brigade was struck by the Indian 10th Brigade, but they drove off the Indians and British by dawn inflicting 316 casualties. In the darkness two Italian companies ran into a British battalion and had to pull back, losing forty men.

On the 17th the Savoia Grenadiers repelled another attack. In addition to a host of ailments and wounds the Italians were now suffering from heat stroke owing to a change in the weather.

Carnimeo became obsessed with retaking Fort Dologorodok and he gave Lorenzini control of this dubious venture. Leading three battalions of grenadiers and one of ascaris Lorenzini climbed the slope under fire. The three L3 tankettes with him proved useless. His attack failed, but the worst news from this endeavor was that Lorenzini had breathed his last.

———

Fort Mankusa was six miles from Burie, and Natale had garrisoned it with two companies of ascaris. These men were assaulted by a large element of Gideon Force, while British officers using loudspeakers called upon the ascaris to surrender, but encouraged by their Italian officers the ascaris fought back bravely. The Ethiopian guerillas retreated when they were accidentally mortared by a Sudanese unit. The fort commandant radioed Natale to assure him he would hold.

Meanwhile Burie was under Allied air attack, which panicked both the Italian and Ethiopian civilians. The Ethiopian Prince Mammo decided to make the best of a bad situation and he marched one thousand five hundred bande out of the town and declared neutrality. Naturally Natale was disgusted by this treachery, and he radioed Nasi for permission to retreat as he was even more concerned now for the Italian civilians. Nasi agreed.

So on 4 March the garrison of Burie withdrew and was soon stretched out in a miles long column aiming for Debra Markos, flanked by horse cavalry and armored cars. Natale had three thousand five hundred ascaris, four thousand bande and five hundred actual Italians serving as officers, clerks, technicians, medical orderlies, artillerymen, armored car crews and truck drivers, and interweaving in the column were hundreds of Italian women and children and some Ethiopian civilians. Italian planes flew overhead to reconnoiter the way to Debra Markos. The first two nights were tense, as guerilla snipers kept up a continuous fire. But incredibly on 6 March this noisy, sluggish, clumsy column actually surprised an Ethiopian unit led by a British officer. At once Natale sent forward four armored cars and some horse cavalry. Two of the cars were destroyed, but the others caught the enemy in the open and began to machine gun them. Then the ascari horsemen reached the scene and they attacked. One Italian plane came down to watch the slaughter and was shot down for its trouble. Ascari infantry joined the fight, which was fierce, and eventually the Ethiopians withdrew. Natale was stunned by the news that he had lost no fewer than two hundred and fifty ascaris killed and as many wounded. Worst of all the main column had been held up, and Gideon Force was now only an hour behind.

Therefore Natale left 500 ascaris at nearby Fort Dembecha with orders to delay Wingate. They held for forty-eight hours.

Nasi came to the conclusion that Natale had not handled the affair very well, for not only had he abandoned many supplies and placed his troops and civilians at risk in the open, but also he had abandoned four forts. When Natale's column finally reached Debra Markos, Nasi ordered Colonel Maraventano to take charge of Natale's men in addition to his own. Natale was ordered to fly to Massawa to await orders.

At Debra Markos Maraventano had control of the 3rd Colonial Brigade and the bande that had retreated from Burie, plus his own 19th Colonial Brigade, some independent ascari battalions, 10th CCNN legion, some bande, artillery, air units and support troops: a total of two thousand Italians, three thousand bande and ten thousand ascaris. With this strong force, and with Torelli's ascaris and bande at Bahrdar a hundred miles to the north and with Marshal Hailu's bande in the Chokey Mountains between, Maraventano felt safe. In fact Nasi was ready to go on the offensive, and he advanced some troops who quickly captured Fort Emmanuel. Nasi asked Marshal Hailu and the people of Gojjam to join with him to repel the invaders. Marshal Hailu immediately opened negotiations with Wingate. This was not what Nasi had in mind!

———

On 16 March the British launched their first successful amphibious invasion of the war by bombarding Berbera the capital of British Somaliland, which had been under Italian occupation since the previous August. They followed the bombardment by a troop landing. The garrison of Somali ascaris fled, leaving sixty men to surrender. This maneuver three hundred and fifty miles east of Addis Ababa and seven hundred miles north of Mogadishu outflanked de Simone in Somaliland, but he was already whipped in any case. Following his abysmal performance in February, the duke had agreed that de Simone's forces should join the main body of defenders in Ethiopia. Baccari's 101st Colonial Division was on its way to Neghelli, and Liberati's 102nd Colonial Division was marching to Jijiga. Following Baccari was the British 12th African Division, and hard on their heels of Liberati was the British 11th African Division.

Meanwhile de Simone went to Harar to converse with the duke. The latter insisted that the Jijiga Line, two hundred and fifty miles east of Addis Ababa, had to be held at all costs. De Simone pleaded for reinforcements, and the duke let him have the 70th Colonial Brigade, a Blackshirt battalion, some Carabinieri and police and customs police and a mob of bande, in all 5,000 Italians and 26,000 native Africans.

The pep talk did no good at all. Brigadier General Bertello waited until he could see British Army Nigerian troops arriving at the Jijiga Line and then he jumped onto a mule and rode away - he had no choice for his 70th Colonial Brigade had already deserted.

The men Liberati had brought with him to Jijiga were exhausted and sick, for they had marched 800 miles in six weeks. However, the Allies following in trucks had outrun their supplies and they halted for three days. De Simone and Liberati used this time to establish a rearguard at Marda Pass, though that night the bande and ascaris began to desert, as did those Italians who had families in Harar.

Throughout the morning of 21 March Allied planes bombed the pass, causing more ascaris to flee. At noon South African artillery shelled the pass. The Italian guns replied. Half an hour later the 23rd Nigerian Brigade attacked, and the ascaris began backing up, but their officers demanded a counter attack, and this took place, and so they were able to hold the Nigerians until dark. However, that night the ascaris fled in droves and the Italians had no recourse but to retreat after them.

De Simone now built a rearguard at Babile Pass using artillery alone. They held off the Nigerians for a day.

The last defense line before the city of Harar was the Bisidimo River and de Simone organized another rearguard here, which fought well on the 25th. Meanwhile he notified the British he was declaring Harar an open city, so that the Italian civilians there would not be in danger. At 7am on the 26th the Bisidimo defenders withdrew and allowed the British to occupy Harar.

The colonist soldiers' fear for their families was very real, because as soon as the troops pulled out of Harar the native population attacked the Italian quarter defended by a few Carabinieri. As soon as Nigerian troops arrived their British officers ordered their men to disperse the rioters. The Italian police chief of Diredawa, thirty miles northwest of Hara, telephoned the Nigerians and asked them to occupy his town too as ascaris and bande had gone on a rampage looting, raping and murdering. South African troops rushed in and shot any rioters who did not surrender.

De Simone's survivors were now retreating westwards towards Addis Ababa, where 18,000 Italian civilians were living next to 250,000 oppressed Ethiopians.

———————

At Keren disease had ravaged the Italians. Thousands lay on cots or grass piles with scant medical attention. At 4:30am on 25 March the defenders of Dongalaas Gorge came under assault from Britons, Indians and Palestinian commandos [Jews and Arabs]. Most of the Ethiopian ascaris had already deserted by now, and only a few die-hards remained along with the trustworthy Eritreans and the actual Italians. At 7am a company of Bersaglieri counter attacked, but these

Italians were either gunned down or surrounded in small pockets. By now the British had brought up engineers to the road and they began clearing obstacles.

Carnimeo ordered a counter attack to retake the peaks overlooking the engineers, but this was broken up by British artillery. He ordered another. It failed, as did a third.

On the 27th Carnimeo accepted the reality of the situation and ordered a withdrawal, just as sixty-one British tanks and Bren gun carriers began driving through the cleared obstacles. By 10 am the British were in the streets of Keren town. They took no fewer than three thousand prisoners: sick, wounded and small pockets that had not received the withdrawal order in time.

The duke took a hard look at his future: the road to the 'Italian' cities of Asmara and Massawa was wide open; Somaliland had been lost as had the Ogaden, British Somaliland and the Great Lakes region; the forts in Western Ethiopia were under siege; Addis Ababa was defenseless; there was no hope of relief from Italy; indeed it seemed Mussolini had written them off. De Simone reported that of all the troops under his command to date eleven thousand Italians and forty-two thousand Africans were missing. The British recorded ten thousand three hundred and fifty Italians and eleven thousand seven hundred and thirty-two Africans as prisoners of war, a high number of them taken in their hospital beds, meaning that about thirty thousand Africans and a few hundred Italians had deserted.

Therefore the duke decided to take the field himself and carry on the fight. His first act was to rid himself of the responsibility for the Italian civilians in Addis Ababa, so he declared his capital an open city. Upon conferring with Trezzani and his staff the duke chose to head northwards hoping to pick up retreating columns along the way as well as garrisons on route and unite with Frusci in the mountains in order to hold out until the rainy season arrived which would put a stop to all Allied movement. It was a slim chance, he accepted, but then again he had known he did not stand a cat's chance in hell even before the war began.

On the Awash River east of Addis Ababa two battalions of Blackshirts, the Rolle Bande, a company of Savoia Grenadiers machine gunners and six tanks manned a rearguard to hold up the British until negotiations could take place. On 3 April they fought off an attack, but the following day they were outflanked by armored cars. At once the Blackshirts ran for Addis Ababa and the bande scattered. The grenadiers withdrew in good order. A few fought to the death. That night the last members of the capital's garrison withdrew. On 5 April Major General Mambrini met the advancing British and informed them the city was wide open. In order to protect civilians the duke had left 10,000 police and Carabinieri behind. The British entered the city and allowed these uniformed Italians to remain armed and continue their duty!

British Lieutenant General Cunningham was well satisfied. His invasion from Kenya into Somaliland had conquered an area twice the size of England, had inflicted 55,000 casualties, had put the enemy's commander and main force on the run and had handed Haile Selassie his capital city - and all for the loss of just 445 killed and wounded!

————

In Eritrea Frusci decided he could not afford any more stands like Keren. Between the Sudanese border and that mountain position his men had been bombed continually for ten weeks, had been struck by 11,000 artillery shells, and had fought two reinforced divisions, and had only retreated when tanks broke through on the road. His survivors were worn out with combat fatigue, malnutrition, dysentery, skin sepsis and mental depression. Carnimeo ordered Colonel Borghese to leave some Savoia Grenadiers and four battalions of ascaris behind as a rearguard, while the remainder made for Asmara fifty miles to the southeast.

Frusci ordered Colonel Delitala at Adowa, eighty miles south of Asmara, to ensure Marshal Seyoum's loyalty, but his reply was that Seyoum could not be trusted. Therefore, Frusci decided he would take the remainder of the troops in Eritrea southwards towards the duke at Addis Ababa. Frusci ordered Delitala to join him at Adigrat forty miles east of Adowa.

On 30 March Borghese watched as the Allies tried to outflank his rearguard near Keren, and he fought skillfully, making good use of 65mm guns. But after two days of battle his Savoia Grenadiers were cut off by a surprise move and they began to surrender. The ascaris retreated, but Borghese fought to the death.

This evening Frusci declared Asmara an open city to protect its fifty thousand Italian civilians. There was already shooting in the city between police and ascari deserters.

————

Colonel Maraventano had been reorganizing his troops at Debra Markos with the object of undoing the calamity Natale had brought on the town. Maraventano knew only one method to fight Wingate's Gideon Force and that was by attacking. He had no idea how strong Wingate was, but he did know that daily Wingate was being joined by guerillas and deserters from the bande and ascaris, the latter bringing their Italian weapons and Italian training with them.

Maraventano began his move by advancing two battalions to Gulit Ridge to tempt Wingate. But Wingate did not fall for the trap, preferring to just shell the ridge with mortars. In light of this Maraventano sent two battalions to recapture Fort Emmanuele fifteen miles to the northwest and another battalion to take Mota eight miles to the southwest.

On 24 March Maraventano launched his major offensive. His Sudanese opponents did not put up too much of a fight until after dusk when they counter attacked. The ascaris held.

On the 27th as part of Maraventano's plan Brigadier General Torelli advanced southwards from Bahrdar with five ascari battalions, a thousand bande and artillery, but he ran into stiff resistance at once from guerillas. By the 29th Torelli had suffered a hundred and seventy-five casualties, and asked permission to fall back. Nasi allowed this.

Maraventano's troops were now subjected to a major counter thrust by Wingate, and on the 31st he ordered Fort Emmanuele to be abandoned, but as the troops pulled out in trucks two of their vehicles struck landmines inflicting twenty-three casualties. By the end of 2 April most of the outer forts had been lost, yet Maraventano's men were able to retreat right past a guerilla force, too nervous to stop them.

Back in Debra Markos, while under an enemy mortar barrage, Maraventano came to the conclusion that he had to withdraw from the town and link with Nasi's personal command at Gondar two hundred miles to the north. Marshal Hailu declared to him that he and his 6,000 bande would remain in Debra Markos. Therefore, Maraventano gave the orders to the 3rd and 19th Colonial Brigades, 10th CCNN Legion, and a host of support troops including air force ground crews, a total of one thousand one hundred Italians, seven thousand ascaris and two thousand Italian civilians. Next morning the column left the town in trucks, cars, horse-drawn wagons, on camels and on foot.

Hailu immediately declared his independence from Mussolini, but neither did he open the gates to the British. He negotiated with Wingate until he was sure Maraventano's column was safely across the Blue Nile River. Furthermore Hailu had bribed a guerilla group in Maraventano's path not to hinder the Italians.

When Maraventano learned that the duke was retreating northwards from Addis Ababa on a parallel line a hundred and sixty miles east of Maraventano's route, he decided to aim for Debra Tabor and hoped to rendezvous there with the duke.

———

General Gazzera at Gore wanted to join with the duke too, but Nasi ordered him to stay put. Gore was two hundred miles southwest of Debra Markos, and there was no way Gazzera could reach the duke who was already marching to the northeast of Debra Markos.

Having abandoned Asmara Carnimeo's veterans of Keren had fallen back to Massawa on the coast of Eritrea, and they were soon settling into Forts Umberto and Montcullo. This port had been raided by British carrier planes once already, and on 1 April the port was hit by Swordfish and Gladiators from the carrier Eagle. The destroyer Leone (1,700 tons) dodged the aerial torpedoes, but in so doing struck a rock. Rendered unseaworthy she was scuttled. This left eight warships at the port. Though they had nowhere to go, the crews took the vessels to sea anyway, and 3 April they were caught by the Eagle's Swordfish. The Suaro was sunk and the Marin and Batista were crippled and forced to scuttle. Later the Pantera and Tigre were damaged by Wellesley bombers and scuttled. The Acerbi was also crippled. However the gunboat Eritrea and armed banana boat Ramb II managed to elude the enemy and set sail for Japan.

On 6 April at Massawa the defenders of Forts Umberto and Montcullo were subjected to air attack by British and South African planes, and a ground assault by British tanks, British artillery, Charles Monclar's French Brigade, the Indian 7th Brigade and Indian 10th Brigade. The forts were bravely defended by the Blackshirts, ascaris and Savoia Grenadiers that had fought at Keren, and by two battalions of the San Marco Marines and some customs police. On the second day of battle some sectors were overrun, and more on the third day. Now Admiral Bonetti ordered all ships to scuttle and that afternoon he surrendered all forces at Massawa. The small port of Assab had yet to fall, but the British could afford to isolate it.

The loss of Eritrea was the greatest defeat so far for Italy, because the air and naval bases here were the only prize in East Africa worth fighting for in terms of war winning strategy, and their loss freed the southern approaches to the Suez Canal for the Allies. Defending the colony had cost the lives of three thousand Italians and two thousand ascaris and bande, and four thousand five hundred Italians and three thousand five hundred Africans had been wounded. Of the ten thousand taken prisoner on the last day a high proportion were bedridden. Allied losses were four thousand killed and wounded.

————

By 17 April the duke and his personal forces had retreated a hundred and fifty miles north of Addis Ababa to Kombolcha, and there he conferred with Frusci, whose personal forces were coming southwards from Eritrea. It was decided that a rearguard should be left at Kombolcha, while the bulk of their joint forces should unite at Amba Alagi Ridge, one of the most inhospitable and highest mountains in the territory. It was one hundred and thirty miles north of Kombolcha. Frusci agreed to remain behind to command the rearguard. The duke had been followed by South Africans, who had not needed guides: they simply followed the trail of discarded coats, packs, helmets, tins, broken vehicles, dead horses, dead camels, dead mules and dead people. They found many a live Italian lying in the dirt too weak and sick to speak.

Ironically the rainy season was beginning, and a battalion of South

Africans was isolated by a flash flood near Kombolcha. Frusci might have thought that divine intervention was on his side when he saw this. His rearguard here took advantage of this and shelled the enemy in the rain. His rearguard consisted of two ascari and four Blackshirt battalions, gunners, engineers and some sailors, a total of 4,500 personnel. For the next five days this rearguard was attacked in pouring rain by a South African brigade and thousands of Ethiopian guerillas. Of course the latter were not exactly guerillas any more, but more of a mob. By 22 April Frusci was in danger of being outflanked, so he ordered a withdrawal, and it was performed in an orderly fashion, and the last defenders did not slip away until the 25th. Here his 4,500 men had suffered 400 killed and 1,200 wounded or sick. The bedridden had to be abandoned.

Frusci left a small rearguard at Dessie just five miles from Kombolcha, but it did not fight well, especially when South African engineers blew a bridge to their rear. The rearguard commander offered to surrender if the South African brigade commander, Dan Pienaar, agreed to protect his Italian women and children and look after his sick and wounded. Pienaar gave his word and informed his few score medical personnel to come up front. When they entered the town they found the buildings crammed with one thousand five hundred Italian women and children and a shockingly high number of bedridden wounded and sick soldiers: two thousand seven hundred and sixty-six ascaris and five thousand two hundred and fifty-eight Italians!

On 27 April the Italian forward artillery observers at Amba Alagi sighted enemy troops coming down from Eritrea and they called for a barrage. Amba Alagi Ridge stretched for ten miles and was divided by the main road with the Pyramid on the extreme west and Wireless Hill on the extreme east. The duke put General Valetti-Borgnini in command, who placed most of his faith in the one thousand two hundred Ethiopian ascaris of the 43rd Colonial Brigade and ten mountain guns. Spread out along the ridge were two Blackshirt battalions, a Savoia Grenadiers machine gun battalion, four artillery batteries, two flak batteries and provisional companies of sailors, airmen, support troops, customs police, Carabinieri and police. All of these formations faced the north.

On 30 April the eastern flank was attacked by Palestinian commandos, who gained a foothold. By now the entire ridge was under artillery fire, air raids and sniping, not to mention sporadic heavy rains. On 3 May the eastern defenders held when assaulted by the commandos and armored cars. In the center the defenders drove off an Indian attack. However, two companies of customs police were driven back by Indian infantry from two peaks near the Pyramid. Middle Hill protected by Savoia Grenadiers came under a ferocious assault by Indians, which lasted all night. Only when the last grenadiers were killed off at dawn could the Indians claim victory.

For two days the Allies rested, but on the 6th the ascaris and grenadiers defending a position near Middle Hill sighted Indians crawling towards them. They opened fire, but could not stop the enemy from squeezing through the barbed wire entanglements, and thus the fight turned into a hand to hand melee with bayonets and rifle butts in the trenches. However, the Italians and ascaris were victorious, and they drove the Indians down the slope.

On the night of the 7th the Italian and ascari defenders of Castle Ridge in the east repelled an Indian attack, but those on the nearby Tongue were overrun. Again both sides stopped to draw breath.

On the 11th the Italians and ascaris came under attack from the south, that is their rear, by South Africans and thousands of guerillas under Marshal Seyoum. To add to everyone's discomfort the sporadic rains turned into a steady heavy downpour. The duke could have surrendered with honor at this moment: fighting under cold heavy rain that flooded his trenches, bereft of supplies, pounded by artillery fire, surrounded and outnumbered perhaps ten to one. Instead he told his officers to fight on.

That afternoon in a heavy rain the defenders of the Twin Pyramids were overrun by a swarm of guerillas, many of them deserters from the ascaris and bande. They captured several wounded Italians. However, when the guerillas continued on to the Triangle, the defending Italians slaughtered them by the hundreds with machine guns and rifle fire. Many of the guerillas in their loose clothing became entangled in the barbed wire and were thus easy prey for the Italians. The remaining guerillas fell back amid explosions of Italian artillery shells. The guerillas were frustrated, and they took out their anger on the wounded they had captured, torturing them within earshot of the Italians and then throwing them off cliffs.

The following night the defenders of the Triangle were overrun by a sensible assault launched by South African and Indian troops using bangalore torpedoes to blow gaps in the barbed wire.

The duke now took stock of the situation in East Africa. Most of the bande had deserted, as had most of the Ethiopian, Yemeni and Somali ascaris, some of the Eritrean ascaris and some of the Italians. Maraventano had been unable to intercept with the duke's forces, and was at Addis Dera two hundred miles southwest of the duke surrounded by thousands of guerillas. Colonel Ignazio Angelini and five thousand men at Debra Tabor one hundred and fifty miles southwest of the duke were besieged by Gideon Force and a large group of guerillas. Torelli at Bahrdar one hundred and eighty miles to the southwest was surrounded by thousands of guerillas. Nasi had twenty-five thousand men, but he was surrounded at Gondar one hundred and fifty miles to the west. Also in this area five thousand men were surrounded at Wolchefit Pass, two thousand five hundred at

Chilga and two thousand five hundred at Kulkaber. General Gazzera was at Jimma five hundred miles to the south of the duke. He had twenty-five thousand men, but outside the walls was the British 12th African Division. At Soddu six hundred miles to the south the 21st and 25th Colonial Divisions with remnants of the 101st Colonial Division were surrounded by guerillas and British East African troops. Six hundred and fifty miles to the south two Eritrean brigades held out at Wadera watched by a Gold Coast brigade. Several smaller garrisons were also surrounded. The duke himself was hanging on to three square miles of Amba Alagi Ridge surrounded by guerillas, South Africans, Indians, Britons, Sudanese and Palestinians supported by artillery, armored cars and aircraft. For almost a year the duke had been cut off from Italy. At Amba Alagi alone he had lost a thousand killed in two weeks. Therefore he asked the British for terms.

At 11:15am on 19 May 1941 the duke and his die-hard defenders began to crawl out of rocky crevices and caves to surrender. Despite being filthy and wet and suffering from wounds and disease, they tried to walk with dignity. The Britons and others had been so impressed with the Italian defense that they created avenues of soldiers on parade and with bagpipes playing they saluted the duke and his men! The duke surrendered one hundred and eighty-five officers, including generals Valetti-Borgnini, Frusci and Pinna, four hundred and twelve ascaris and four thousand one hundred and eighty Italians. All of them were at death's door from their ordeal. The duke, only forty-three years old, did not recover and soon died.

———

Chapter Nineteen
War at Sea

The ground war was certainly going against Italy, but the war at sea was harder to judge by the end of 1940, despite the spectacular raid on Taranto and the inability of Italian submarines to remain undetected. Italian aircraft sank the British submarine Regulus in November. In December the Italian submarine Naiade was scuttled following damage inflicted by the British destroyers Hyperion and Hereward. The submarine Tarantini was sunk by the British submarine Thunderbolt. The destroyer Clio redressed the balance somewhat by sinking the British submarine Triton. This was Clio's second victory. Italian SM79 bombers damaged the cruiser Glasgow in Suda Bay, Crete, despite heavy flak from warships and shore guns.

Sea mines were also a frightful weapon. In December the Italian destroyers Calipso (640 tons) and Cairoli (615 tons) were blown up by British mines.

By the beginning of 1941 German submarine losses in the Atlantic were heavy. The Italian submarines Nani, Argo and Marcello successfully ran the gauntlet of the British naval base at Gibraltar in order to reach the Atlantic - no mean feat - but the Marcello was sunk when attacked by several British destroyers in January. The Nani did not survive the rough Atlantic storms. However, the submarine Argo survived the Atlantic and torpedoed the Canadian destroyer Sagueney.

The Axis powers knew that the British were struggling to keep their convoys afloat, and as a result the British were slowly dragging the US Navy into the Atlantic conflict day-by-day, incident-by-incident. The reality was that by late 1940 Germany and the USA were in a naval war.

In early 1941 Italian intelligence learned that the British were planning a great convoy to take urgently needed supplies from Gibraltar to Malta, and the Italians planned to sink it. They got first blood on 10 January, when one of their mines crippled one of the convoy's escorts. That night the destroyers Circe and Vega (both 640 tons) courageously tackled the escort of two light cruisers, a carrier and several destroyers. The Circe was demolished and the Vega blown out of the water. British recruits aboard ship were astonished, because British propaganda had told them that Italians were cowards. At dawn on the 11th German aircraft flying from new bases in Sicily made a superb raid on the convoy, damaging several merchant ships and the carrier Illustrious and crippling the light cruiser Southampton [that had to be scuttled]. This was followed by a raid of Italian SM79s. The convoy reached Malta, but the British realized soberly that even the presence of a large escort would not deter the Italians · and Germans from attacking.

On 31 January SM79s made up for earlier failures by sinking the British minesweeper Huntley off Sidi Barani.

The main Italian battle fleet had withdrawn to Naples following the Taranto disaster, and the warships were fitted with 20mm flak guns in addition to their normal anti-aircraft armament. The admirals felt safer here as the docks had its own naval flak defenses and the city had its Blackshirt flak defenses. However, their complacency proved ill judged, because on 8 January the port was raided by British aircraft and the battleship Giulio Cesare was damaged.

On the night of 9 February British planes from the carrier Ark Royal bombed the docks at La Spezia and Livorno and the rail yards at Pisa, while the battleships Renown and Malaya bombarded the port of Genoa, sinking four vessels and damaging eighteen. Also this month the Italian light cruiser Armando Diaz was torpedoed and sunk by the British submarine Upright off Kerkenah Bank. This same month an Italian mine sank the British armed trawler Ouse, and German planes sank the British destroyer Dainty and crippled the Terror.

Castelorizzo was a small island off the south coast of Turkey and its garrison of forty-eight Italians must have thought they were in for an easy war. But on 25 February the island was invaded by British marines and commandos. The Italians fought back and only after thirteen had been killed and others wounded did they give up. Italian planes arrived and damaged a British gunboat. The Italians in the Dodecanese Islands took this as a challenge and the following day they retaliated, sending a hundred marines and sixty-five army special troops in the destroyers Crispi, Liva and Libra. First the destroyers shelled the shore: then the marines and soldiers landed under fire. Almost at once they realized they were outnumbered, but they battled on, taking many British prisoners, and the following day the British evacuated. Naturally Italian propaganda made this a bigger victory than it was, and equally British propaganda made it a smaller defeat than it was.

In March the sea God continued to show no favoritism: the destroyer Clio gained her third victory, sinking the anti-Fascist French submarine Narval; the submarines Dagabur and Ambra launched torpedoes at the British light cruiser Bonaventure and sank her; the Italian destroyer Andromeda (640 tons) was sunk in an air raid; the submarine Capponi was sunk by the British submarine Rorqual; and the destroyer Chinolto (890 tons) was lost to a mine. The Italian submarine Anfitrite was scuttled after being damaged by the British destroyer Grayhound.

Admiral Arturo Ricciardi was eager to use his still potent battle fleet to swing the balance in Italy's favor; the mission Mussolini had given him three months earlier. If Italian capital ships went to sea at all they did so as convoy escorts, and both Mussolini and Ricciardi believed this was a waste of their best sea-going weapons. On 16 March German planes reported they had sunk two British battleships. Ricciardi knew the report might not be true, because fliers of all nationalities were notoriously full of exaggeration when it came to ship identification and damage reports, but surely if ever there was a time to strike it was now. So, Ricciardi ordered Vice Admiral Iachino to sea at once.

On 25 March an Italian reconnaissance plane sighted two British cruisers in Suda Bay, Crete. Ricciardi decided this would be a good moment to use a new secret weapon created by the 10th MAS Flotilla: one-man motorboats crewed by suicide warriors. In darkness the destroyers Crispi and Sella sailed within ten miles of Suda Bay and disembarked six of the boats. Lieutenant Vascello Luigi Faggione led the tiny flotilla so as to arrive just before dawn. The six men knew they were on a one-way mission. They got close enough to identify four cruisers in the bay, but then they were spotted, and British warships and shore guns opened up at once. Faggione signaled the others to run the gauntlet of fire and attack. The men aimed their explosives-laden boats to ram and at the last possible second jumped overboard. Three of the boats were damaged and veered off out of control, but one struck a Norwegian oil tanker and two slammed into the cruiser York. The six Italians swam to shore, where they tried not to get caught. There was always a chance the British might shoot them in anger. But they were caught, and they were not shot. It was an incredible escapade. The oil tanker sank and the York was a write off. No wonder the six men were awarded the Gold Medal.

On the morning of the 27th a British flying boat circled the Italian battle fleet. Iachino did not mind being discovered. He wanted a fight. He had thrown down the gauntlet. The British Admiral Cunningham picked it up.

The forward echelon of Iachino's fleet was Rear Admiral Sansonetti's cruiser squadron of the Trieste (flag), Trento and Bolzano. Behind him was Vice Admiral Carlo Cattaneo's cruiser squadron of the Zara (flag), Pola and Fiume. Behind him was Vice Admiral Antonio Legnani's light cruiser squadron of the Giuseppe Garibaldi and Duca degli Abruzzi, both of 9,400 tons and armed with ten 6inch guns. Behind him was Iachino in the battleship Vittorio Veneto. Eleven destroyers protected the flanks and rear. Spies alerted Ricciardi that Cunningham was putting to sea from Alexandria, Egypt that evening. The wily Brit had the carrier Formidable, battleships Valiant, Warspite and Barham, cruisers Ajax, Gloucester, Orion and Perth, and sixteen destroyers.

At 8:12 next morning Sansonetti's squadron sighted the British cruisers and opened fire. The Gloucester replied, whereupon Sansonetti retreated: standard Italian tactics hoping to suck in the British. The Gloucester and her pals fell for it, perhaps having believed some of that wretched anti-Italian propaganda that colored British conceptions. At 11am the British cruisers came within range of the Vittorio Veneto, twenty-six and one third miles. Captain Sparzani gave the word and her three massive gun turrets each shot three 15inch shells into the air. Each shell weighed as much as a small car. It took forever before the Italian spotters using strong binoculars could see spouts of water burst near the British ships. Time after time the battleship reloaded and fired a barrage, many of her shells throwing geysers of water over the Orion and sending shrapnel into her. Moreover, Sansonetti had turned around to give battle. The guns of the British cruisers could not reach the Vittorio Veneto, but they did engage Sansonetti's cruisers: Trieste, Trento and Bolzano.

The British had one advantage in this unequal struggle. They had a carrier, and within minutes Swordfish, Walrus, Fulmar and Albacore aircraft swooped down from the sky to challenge the Italian ships' flak gunners. From captain to helmsman and engine room the orders were fast and furious as the ships tried to dodge aerial torpedoes and bombs. Under such conditions it was impossible for the gun aimers to draw a bead on the British ships. A torpedo just barely missed the Bolzano. Then more British planes arrived, having flown from Crete. Iachino and Sparzani held their breath as torpedoes spiraled towards the Vittorio Veneto, passing with but a few feet to spare. The Italian ships sent a handful of catapult seaplanes aloft to assault the British ships and direct gunfire. Finally Axis air reinforcements arrived, German JU-88s, which attacked the British cruisers. The struggle was a brawl: water shooting up hundreds of feet when hit by bombs and 15inch, 8inch, 6inch and 4.7inch shells, torpedoes plowing furrows through the waves, 3.9inch anti-aircraft shells bursting in air, and 37mm and 20mm shells and heavy machine gun bullets whizzing their way upwards at incredible speed.

At 12:54pm two SM79s arrived and took on the carrier Formidable. Her flak guns and patrolling fighters were enough to put the Italian crews off their aim and their torpedoes missed. At 2:20pm the Vittorio Veneto's flak gunners tossed up such a wall of metal in front of three attacking Blenheims that their bombs missed. At 2:50pm six more Blenheims arrived and dropped their bombs from a high altitude, while at the same moment seven of Formidable's torpedo bombers came skipping over the waves. Every one of the one thousand eight hundred and thirty men aboard the Vittorio Veneto prayed to his personal god: but a bomb exploded deep into the aft deck, and a torpedo screwed right into the stern, as a British bomber tumbled into the sea. The mighty battleship was stopped dead in the water. Then eleven Blenheims tackled the Pola, Zara, Fiume and Giuseppe Garibaldi, while nine Blenheims assaulted the Trento, Trieste and Bolzano.

After two hours Sparzani's damage control parties got the

battleship moving on two engines, and he and Iachino agreed they had to make for Taranto at once. The fleet withdrew. At dusk British planes searched in vain for the Italians, but when they finally saw a ship, the Pola, they were too low on fuel to attack. Yet, one lone plane left the flock and ignored the flak to put a torpedo straight into her. After this last event mother nature pulled a dark shroud over the entire scene, putting an end to human insanity.

Iachino's orders were cruel, but correct: the Pola was to be left to her own devices. He wanted all other ships in port before dawn. He was also leery of the British battleships: where were they, he wondered?

Cattaneo felt terrible, for the Pola was in his squadron. Eventually his sense of honor won out over his common sense. He ordered his squadron of the Zara and Fiume and five Oriani class (1,600 tons) destroyers to turn back and help the Pola. He also allowed most of his men to sleep as they were exhausted, but he did at least urge his lookouts to peer into the darkness. He did not realize that the British possession of radar, a new invention, was a major advantage. Cattaneo had in fact sailed right towards the battleships Barham, Warspite and Valiant. Using radar the British identified the Italians before Cattaneo's lookouts saw anything. In fact when the British battleships came within shooting range they turned on searchlights that lit up their targets and blinded the Italian lookouts. Before the Italian crews could reach battle stations, deadly 15inch shells began straddling the Italian cruisers, sending slivers of white hot metal through bulkheads. Cattaneo and Captain Louis Corsi aboard the Zara yelled orders as did Captain Giorgis on the Fiume, but in minutes the British had the range and their shells began ramming into the deck and superstructure of the destroyer Vittorio Alfieri, mashing metal like it was paper and flinging bits of human flesh into the air.

The remaining four Italian destroyers charged towards the British battleships hoping to come close enough to use their small guns and torpedoes. When the Giosue Carducci was hit by a 15inch shell she practically disappeared. The others were struck too and turned to limp away, the Oriani with just one engine. However, as the British closed on the Vittorio Alfieri like wolves, the plucky Italian vessel suddenly burst into life, launching three torpedoes and firing four salvoes from her 4.7inch guns, despite a shower of shells cascading down upon her until she sank.

The Fiume and Zara had also started to take serious punishment, but kept firing for as long as possible. Thirty minutes after the shooting began the Fiume slid beneath the waves. By now the Zara was in terrible shape, and Corsi gave the order to scuttle. Commander Dominic Bastianini and Lieutenant Umberto Grosso went below to set off explosive charges, while the crew abandoned ship. Within minutes the Zara blew up. Now the British turned their attention to the immobile Pola, and offered to accept the crew before sinking her. This was done. By dawn the British had fished nine hundred Italians out of the water, but then withdrew when they sighted Axis planes. The Allied Greek destroyer Ydra picked up one hundred and twelve Italians, and later that day the Italian hospital ship Gradisca located one hundred and sixty burned, wounded and oil-soaked survivors. Fully two thousand four hundred Italians had died. Cattaneo, Corsi, Bastianini and Grosso were awarded the Gold Medal posthumously.

The British returned to port for a hero's welcome. The battle of Cape Matapan had repercussions far greater than the Italian losses, for bad as they were Italy could afford them. The ultimate result, not realized immediately, was that the Italian admirals became convinced they could not risk capital ships in daylight until the Regia Aeronautica and their German partners gained air supremacy, nor could they risk them in darkness until they possessed radar.

———

Chapter Twenty
Greek Stalemate

During the early days of Mussolini's Greek invasion he had used
every method of propaganda he could muster. One statement was that
he was liberating the land of the Chams. Cham land was Albanian
territory that had been forcibly annexed by Greece twenty years
earlier. It became embarrassing when his troops not only failed to
'liberate' these people, but actually retreated several miles into
Albania proper and thus placed even more Albanians/Chams under
Greek rule. Indeed several members of the Italian-sponsored Albanian
Army had defected to the Greeks and had formed their own Greek-
sponsored military unit, which aimed at liberating all of Albania from
Italian rule.

During the winter of 1940-41 in Albania those Italian troops
unlucky enough to be stationed in the high mountain passes suffered
frostbite in snow-covered foxholes at temperatures lower than minus
20 Fahrenheit [-27C], while those unlucky enough to be stationed in
the valleys developed hypothermia and pneumonia under a constant
cold rain and biting wind. Mussolini had agreed to a massive
reinforcement, and in late November 1940 several divisions arrived:
Acqui Mountain [with attached 27th CCNN Legion], Brennero [with
attached 35th CCNN Legion], Cuneense Alpini, Cuneo [and attached
24th CCNN Legion], Lupi di Toscana, Modena Mountain [and
attached 36th CCNN Legion], Pinerolo [with attached 136th CCNN
Legion], Pusteria Alpini, Taro [and attached 164th CCNN Legion] and
Tridentina Alpini. The Pusteria and Cuneense had fought in Ethiopia
and in France, and the Acqui, Tridentina, Modena and Brennero had
fought in France.

Another formation arriving was Lieutenant General Enzo
Galbiati's CCNN Raggruppamento [of the 8th, 12th, 16th and 29th
CCNN Battalions], which was to provide support to the Acqui and
Cuneo Divisions.

Additionally, the Littorio Gruppo was formed with three
regiments: 3rd Grenadiers, Aosta (Horse) Cavalry and Milan Lancers
(armored cars). This brought Italian forces in Albania up to nineteen
divisions, the number that the original plan had called for.

Personnel replacements were also arriving to take the places of
those killed, missing, wounded, sick and crippled by frostbite. There
was an especial shortage of officers. Men like Colonels Adolfo
Rivoir, Gaetano Tavoni, Vincenzo Carla and Rodolfo Psaro were
ready to do their duty, but fear gripped everyone tightening the knots
in their stomachs.

Unlike the leading German Nazis, who only appeared at the front
lines for propaganda photographs and sent others to battle on their

behalf, the leading Italian Fascists were at least willing to risk their own lives. Several had served in Ethiopia and some had fought in Spain, despite holding a high position. Many an Italian unit in Albania was surprised to see leading political figures arrive to take up war-time jobs: Renato Ricci a Fascist and Blackshirt from the early days and now a government cabinet minister arrived to fight as a Bersaglieri battalion commander. Achille Starace the Secretary of the Fascist Party had led Blackshirts into battle in Ethiopia. He now arrived as a Bersaglieri lieutenant colonel. Giuseppe Bottai the Minister of Education and Dino Grandi the Minister of Justice came to serve as Alpini officers. Carlo Alberto Biggini a cabinet minister showed up as an infantry captain. Alessandro Pavolini a leading Fascist official donned the uniform of an air force major. Mussolini's own sons Bruno and Vittorio and his son-in-law Galeazzo Ciano had flown bombing missions in Ethiopia and now came to Albania to do the same. And Mussolini's daughter, Edda Ciano, made it a family act by serving as a nurse aboard a hospital ship off the coast of Albania. Unknown to the public some of these Fascists were ordered to serve by Mussolini, who wanted them out of his hair.

On 1 December 1940 the Ferrara Division lost Colonel Trizio, who was killed in action. On 8 December the Pusteria Alpini Division launched an attack using its 7th Alpini Regiment, but failed with the loss of the regimental commander Colonel Rodolfo Psaro. To date in the campaign the 8th Alpini Regiment of the Julia Alpini Division had suffered 80% casualties. The remainder of the Julia's infantry was down by 30%. On 10 December on the coastal plain the Siena Division [with attached 141st CCNN Legion] began making a fighting withdrawal in the face of a major Greek onslaught, and was only able to halt after ten days. On 14 December Lieutenant Colonel Adolfo Rivoir of the Tridentina Alpini Division was severely wounded. The loss of so many senior officers was a serious blow to the Italians, for these were fighting men. They were not fops who feared going near the front and therefore never got shot. All too often though, they were replaced by officers who were politically correct but inadequate in all else. By now the Siena suffered from poor morale. An accidental bombing by Italian planes did not help matters.

At Christmas the Pusteria Alpini Division was hurt by a Greek attack, but the Julia came to the rescue. In this two-day battle these mountain troops gained nothing but casualties including the death of Colonel Tavoni, leader of the 9th Alpini Regiment.

Mussolini became exasperated with General Soddu's running of the Greek campaign and dismissed him. Cavallero, the chief of staff at Comando Supremo, chose to command the next offensive himself, but some of Soddu's mistakes could not be rectified. For example Soddu had ordered Major General Carlo Melotti to attack with his Cuneo Division [and 24th CCNN Legion], and yet had then proceeded to strip the division of its combat elements to reinforce other units!

Cavallero's own offensive opened on 3 January 1941, but the Greeks counter attacked almost immediately. The fresh eager faces of the Italian replacements - young conscripts, teen-age volunteers and middle-aged reservists - suddenly lost their eagerness for glory as the reality of hot slicing shrapnel took its toll. Many of the new guys abandoned the line. The veterans shook their heads in dismay. The Julia was quickly reinforced by Major General Ottavio Bollea's Lupi di Toscana Division [and attached 15th CCNN Legion] and together they held their ground.

On 9 January the Italians tried attacking in a different sector, but again the Greeks proved to be outstanding mountain warriors. The next day the Lupi di Toscana withdrew slightly and a regiment of the Bari Division retreated four miles. Not everyone retreated. Lieutenant Ugo Passalacqua of the Centauro was awarded the Gold Medal for his sacrificial courage.

As a result of the failed offensives, some divisions were withdrawn for a rest: Centauro Armored, Ferrara [and attached 82nd CCNN Legion], Modena Mountain [and attached 36th CCNN Legion], Parma [and attached 109th CCNN Legion], Siena [and attached 141st CCNN Legion] and Venezia [and attached 72nd CCNN Legion]. The Littorio Gruppo was dissolved. Fresh divisions were brought up: Cagliari Mountain [with attached 28th CCNN Legion], Feltre, Forli Mountain, Legnano and Sforzesca Mountain [and attached 30th CCNN Legion].The latter division was named after the Sforza family. The Cagliari, Forli and Legnano had fought in France. The Julia Alpini and Piemonte [and attached 166th CCNN Legion] should have been rested, but were deemed to be too valuable to be withdrawn.

Mussolini visited Hitler at the latter's personal playground, Berchtesgaden, and for the first time Il Duce met Hitler's mistress, Eva Braun. Her sister, Ilse, had fallen in love with Bruno Mussolini, Il Duce's son, and Eva was very much infatuated with Italians too, especially Ciano, Mussolini's son in law. Surely Hitler noticed this and there is a possibility that good old-fashioned jealousy was Hitler's motive when he told Mussolini that his spies had learned that his son-in-law, Ciano, was 'playing the field', sexually that is. Of course Mussolini was insulted, for first of all it suggested that his own secret police, the OVRA, was inept, and secondly the report implied that his daughter Edda was possibly implicated in the 'goings on'. Il Duce felt bad enough having to tell Hitler how poorly his army was doing in Greece and Libya. Now he was indignant. He had toyed with dismissing Ciano from his foreign minister job - after all, he was currently off flying bombers - but now he resolved to keep him just to anger Hitler.

Someone had to be blamed for Mussolini's military inadequacy, so more heads rolled. Colonel Vincenzo Carla of the Bari Division was court martialed for retreating. Lieutenant General Bancale, commander of VII Corps, was replaced by Lieutenant General Gastone Gambara, an officer who had shown Fascist spirit in Spain. General Vercellino was ordered to hand his Ninth Army to General Alessandro Pirzio-Biroli, who had performed well in Ethiopia.

On 18 February the Italians launched another offensive against the Greeks and for an entire week they threw men against bullets. Casualties were horrific and no gains were made.

Now the Arezzo, Cuneense Alpini, Cuneo [and attached 24th CCNN Legion] and Piemonte [and attached 166th CCNN Legion] Divisions were withdrawn for a rest, while the Ferrara [and attached 82nd CCNN Legion] went back in to participate in the daily terror of trench warfare. The hard-pressed Julia was still not withdrawn.

In early March the Julia Alpini Division and Sforzesca Mountain Division [and attached 30th CCNN Legion] performed very well, repelling a major Greek offensive.

It was at this time that Mussolini visited Albania to harangue his generals in person. He had provided massive reinforcement, had he not? He had given them five hundred and fifty-nine warplanes, had he not? Even God was on their side: the Greek dictator Metaxas had died on 29 January had he not? The new Greek leader Alexandros Koryzis was a poor substitute for the wily old general. Koryzis had agreed to accept British ground troops, but he had sent them to the quiet Bulgarian border, not to the front line! Therefore why were the Italians not winning, Mussolini inquired?

On 10 March the Italians launched yet another major offensive. The combat was bitter and deadly, and it accomplished nothing, apart from ridding Italy of a sizeable portion of her young manhood. Lieutenant Carlo Borsani of the 7th Regiment led his men into the attack, but was severely wounded. Ignoring this he continued the fight, until mortar shrapnel ripped away a piece of his skull. Unbelievably, he survived. [He was awarded the Gold Medal]

During this engagement British aircraft bombed and sank the well-marked hospital ship Po. Among the dead were three female nurses. Naturally the Italian press made much of this despicable act, especially as Edda Ciano was aboard: she survived.

The Bari Division [and attached 152nd CCNN Legion] and Feltre Division were withdrawn for a rest and the Siena [and attached 141st CCNN Legion] went back into action. The Puglie Division had only just arrived, yet needed resting too!

———

Chapter Twenty-One
Hitler to the Rescue

Hitler had offered to help Mussolini on the battlefield, but the arrogant and proud Italian had refused. Later Il Duce accepted some air units to help control the Mediterranean, but by early 1941 he had to swallow his pride and allow German forces to aid the Italians in Libya. Fascist propaganda put the best spin on this that they could, reminding the Italian people that Italian air units were aiding the Germans in the bombing of Britain, and Italian submarines were helping German U-boats in the Battle of the Atlantic.

Hitler sent ten thousand Germans to Libya and quickly formed them into the new 5th Light Division under the leadership of Lieutenant General Erwin Rommel. Many German generals were jealous of Rommel. Unlike most of them he was not an aristocrat: his name was not 'von' Rommel. Furthermore unlike most of them he had never been a member of the Prussian Army. He disliked stiff necked Prussians. An infantry expert, who had written a book on the subject, he had come to Hitler's attention while commanding his personal bodyguard in Poland in 1939. Thus, as far as the German generals were concerned, Rommel was a 'political' officer. Rommel had hoped his relationship with Hitler would lead to the command of an infantry division for the May 1940 Western Offensive. Instead Hitler had given him a panzer division [armored]. Rommel was at first puzzled, for he was not an armor expert, but Hitler's decision proved to be an inspired move, because Rommel turned out to be a natural tank leader. Yet ironically Hitler did not send him to Libya because of his tank expertise, but rather because of his lack of it. Hitler needed all the real tank experts for his coming invasion of the Soviet Union. In other words Rommel was sent to Africa because he wasn't needed in Russia.

Rommel was aware of this, and he did not like it one bit, though he put on a brave face. He saw Libya as a sideshow and the British Army as no more than a nuisance. Moreover he hated the idea of being under Italian command. He had fought the Italians in World War I, and had more than once witnessed hundreds of Italians surrendering to a handful of Germans. The Italian defeats in the winter of 1940-41 had come as no surprise to him. It is unfortunate that Rommel had only fought the Italians at Caporetto in 1917, not one of their shining moments. Had he witnessed their victory at Vittorio Veneto in 1918, he might have arrived in Libya with a little less arrogance.

By 1941 a new nomenclature was being used to designate armored vehicles, which generally speaking was to remain in force for the rest of the century. Under the new designations a tank was an armored vehicle mounting either its primary or secondary armament in a turret, and manned by members of the armored branch. A vehicle of this description without a turret was now called an assault gun: i.e. in order to aim the gun the driver had to aim the vehicle. Thus the Italian L3 tankettte was really an assault gun. Assault guns might be manned by members of the armored branch or the artillery. The self-propelled gun was still another weapon, simply any artillery piece mounted on top of a vehicle and often only partially armored, and operated by artillerymen. The tank destroyer was still another weapon: an assault gun specifically designed to knock out a tank, and operated by artillerymen. There were also many armored transport vehicles, such as the British Bren Gun Carrier, the prime mission of which was to carry people or materiel or a Bren gun [machine gun]. All the above vehicles were tracked. The armored car was an armored vehicle with or without a turret, but with wheels and tires, not tracks. It might be manned by members of the armored, reconnaissance or mechanized cavalry branches. Armored vehicles were usually accompanied by soft skinned vehicles, i.e. not armored: either trucks [all wheeled] or half-tracks [tracked in the rear, but with front wheels for steering].

As Rommel watched his various vehicles being unloaded at the dockside he was already planning his first move. His tanks impressed the Italians. The Mark I was only 5 feet 7 inches high, so it could hide in the flat desert, and weighing in at just 5.9 tons it could speed along the desert at 25 mph carrying two machine guns in its turret. It was ideal for rounding up enemy infantry. The Mark II was still small enough to hide, at 6 feet 9 inches high, but slower as it weighed 9.34 tons. It carried a 20mm cannon in a turret and could wreak havoc among soft-skinned vehicles. Furthermore it had a range of one hundred and twenty-four miles before refueling, which would be an advantage in the lonely desert. Both Marks I and II were two-man vehicles. The Mark III was a heavy tank at 19.2 tons, 7 feet 9 inches high, mounting a 37mm gun and a machine gun in its turret and two machine guns in its hull, manned by a crew of five.

Rommel also brought a tank destroyer, the Panzerjaeger I, which was a Mark I hull mounting a fixed 47mm anti-tank gun. Its greatest advantage was its low silhouette.

His armored cars were the Sd231, at 7.7 tons and 7 feet 10 inches high, armed with a 20mm cannon and a machine gun in a turret. Manned by four men, it had a high speed of 50 mph and an incredible range of five hundred and sixty miles.

For armored transportation he would have the Sd11, a 3-ton open-topped half-track armed with two machine guns, with a speed of 33 mph and a crew of two. It was able to carry supplies or ten infantrymen or an artillery gun crew while towing the gun behind. Some mounted a 20mm anti-aircraft gun.

All of these vehicles were far better than their Italian counterparts, but their crews knew their work would be cut out for them, because the British were now receiving new tanks too: the Matilda II, a 26.5 ton monster armed with a 2-pounder turreted gun; and the Cruiser A9 a 12-ton fast tank with the same armament. Either tank could knock out any of the German armor, except the Mark III. The Mark III and Panzerjaeger I could knock out a Cruiser, but not a Matilda.

The Italians took one look at the German vehicles and breathed a sigh of relief. At last they finally stood a chance against British armor. General Italo Gariboldi who had fought Ethiopian guerillas, and who was now in command in Libya, ordered Rommel to head for the front at once, but Rommel soon found out that the front and the battlefield were two different things. The most advanced British units were miles from the Italian defenses. Gariboldi had created a line of trenches using the X Corps [Brescia and Pavia Divisions]. Gariboldi admitted he was amazed that the British had not continued their advance, and Rommel too expressed surprise that the British had let the initiative pass to the Italians.

However, Rommel did not like Gariboldi's next order, which was to remain inert. To the Germans Libya appeared to be a relatively flat rocky desert, splattered with a few fly-infested hovels, a row of coastal cities, a pleasing climate and a population of Arabs and Italians who moved in slow motion. Luftwaffe squadrons also arrived (not under Rommel's command), and they too were told to remain quiet. But the Germans were eager to advance. They were not here for a vacation. Rommel could not help but remember he had smashed through British forces in Belgium just nine months earlier. He knew it was not the quality of the armor so much as how one used it.

In late March the caged-in Rommel rebelled and ordered his armored cars and half-tracks to reconnoiter the British positions. As the Germans in their new sand-colored uniforms and pith helmets drove across the desert they became bolder and bolder. Gariboldi warned Rommel that the British had replaced the worn out veterans of the Libya fighting, the British 7th Armored and Australian 6th Divisions, and had brought up fresh divisions: Major General M. Gambier-Parry's British 2nd Armored, Major General Bernard Freyberg's New Zealand 2nd and Major General Leslie Morshead's Australian 9th. In addition the British had four brigades: one Indian, one Australian, one Polish and one French. They also had some independent battalions, including Libyan defectors from the Italian Army. Gariboldi preached that until the Luftwaffe and Regia Aeronautica gained control of the skies, and the Italian Navy gained control of the coastal waters, any ground offensive was out of the question.

On 31 March Rommel's reconnaissance unit ignored this advice and entered Agheila, taking the British garrison totally by surprise. It was an easy capture. True, Gariboldi was conservative, but he was not timid, and he was pleasantly surprised at this news and he agreed to ask Cavallero in Rome for permission to attack in a month's time.

Rommel was far too impatient to wait a month, and forty-eight hours later he attacked on his own – his one division against the equivalent of five divisions. Rommel also convinced the Luftwaffe to attack. The Germans had brought with them their Bf109 single-seat monoplane fighter, which matched anything the British had in North Africa including their Hurricane, Tomahawk and Martlet [Wildcat] fighters. Seeing the German planes take off, the Regia Aeronautica also disobeyed orders and they too took to the air. Fortunately, they had just received a shipment of the new Macchi MC200, a fighter that was almost equal to the Hurricane in speed - though some pilots missed the maneuverability of their old CR42s.

As the Germans advanced along the coastal plain, British General Ronald Neame, military governor of Cyrenaica, ordered his armor to withdraw, and he told his support troops in Benghazi to destroy that port and evacuate.

On 5 April the Germans met serious resistance for the first time, encountering the Indian 3rd Brigade at Mechili, and it took two days to destroy it.

Churchill demanded to know what was happening. He insisted that Beresford-Pierce hold the Libyan ports at all costs, if not Benghazi then certainly Tobruk. On 8 April the Germans entered Salum Pass just in time to see French troops leaving. By 10 April Rommel had reached Tobruk and was surveying the old Italian perimeter of trenches and barbed wire, which was now manned by the Australian 9th Division plus an additional Australian brigade, some British tank battalions, Indian armored cars, and a host of rear-echelon personnel including Libyans and Mauritians, all under the command of Australian Major General Morshead. Next day German and Italian planes struck the port, inflicting severe damage on a troopship and the docks. Following this raid, Rommel's 5th Light Division attacked the city's defensive perimeter. For three days over the Easter weekend the Germans battled the defenders, and on Monday thirty-eight German tanks broke through, only to be ambushed by Australian artillery, losing sixteen tanks. Rommel was smart enough to know when to quit. He called off the attack.

The Italians were jubilant by his advance. They were not ashamed that Germans had won where they had lost. On the contrary, the German victory proved that the British had beaten the Italians because of their superior strategy and tactics, not because they were braver than Italians. The Germans, who in 1939 had been the first to use blitzkrieg tactics, and had since perfected them, had now used them on the British for a second time. In nine days the Germans had liberated five hundred and fifty miles of coastline, had captured the ports of Benghazi, Bardia and Derna, and had destroyed the Indian 3rd Brigade and British 2nd Armored Division, and had captured

Generals Gambier-Parry, Neame and O'Connor, and had surrounded Tobruk. In fact so many British tanks had been captured undamaged that the Italians were able to issue entire tank companies with Matildas and Cruisers to replace their useless L3s, L6s and almost useless M11s.

Gariboldi released his Italians and they walked and drove across the desert, hoping to catch up with Rommel, but they reached Tobruk just when the battle had ended. Rommel informed the Italian generals that if a German armored division could not crack open the port, an Italian one certainly could not, and he expected the Italians to be relieved they would not have to fight. Instead he watched in astonishment as they prepared to assault the defenses. It was a matter of pride, they explained. Tobruk was 'their' city - it had an Italian colonist quarter - and moreover they had been humiliatingly defeated here just eighty-two days earlier. This was the beginning of Rommel's education into the idiosyncrasies of the Italian mind. For the assault they brought up Major General Ettore Baldassare's Ariete Armored Division [Aries, a God], which consisted of the 8th Bersaglieri Regiment [two battalions of light infantry, one of which rode in trucks and one on motor cycles], an armored regiment [one battalion equipped with L3s, one battalion with M13s, several companies of M11s, and a few ad hoc companies of captured Matildas and Cruisers], a battalion of combat engineers, some 20mm flak guns, and two batteries of 75mm towed guns. As the Bersaglieri dismounted and crept towards the lines, the black plumes in their helmets blowing in the desert wind, they were hit by a powerful artillery barrage. Though some of these Bersaglieri had fought in Albania in 1939, it was the first fight for most of them, and they retreated, and it took the remainder of the day to regroup them. The next day Major General Giuseppe de Stefanis' Trento Motorized Division arrived. The Trento possessed the 7th Bersaglieri Regiment in addition to its two infantry regiments. De Stefanis, who had commanded the Pinerolo Division in the French Alps, ignored the failure of the Germans and Bersaglieri and decided to attack at once, aided by eighteen M13s of Ariete. The attack failed with high loss, whereupon Australian infantry counter attacked and took many prisoners included most of the Italian wounded. Having wasted a thousand men, the Italian generals decided that their honor had been satisfied. The attacks were called off and the battlefield became quiet.

As Rommel had no troops to spare to guard his prisoners, he handed them over to the Italians. Naturally the Italians berated these unfortunates about the anti-Italian propaganda of the British government.

———

Chapter Twenty-two
Decision in the Balkans

Italy was Nazi Germany's first partner. Together they had created
the Rome-Berlin Axis. Hitler and Mussolini were warmongers, but
they acquired partners through diplomacy. Slovakia was persuaded to
join them in 1939. France joined the Axis alliance (in effect) when the
British turned on them in July 1940. Romania joined that same month.
Japan joined in September 1940, Hungary in November and Bulgaria
on 1 March 1941. Finland was amenable to joining by this date.

On 25 March the government of Yugoslavia (the name of the Serb
Empire) joined the Axis alliance, but the ink was barely dry on the
signed document when the Serbian people, the controlling ethnicity in
the nation, rose in revolt in the capital city Belgrade. The government
was forced to resign and an air force general, Dusan Simonovitch,
took control and repudiated the treaty. The Serbs were naive if they
thought Hitler would take this rebuff lying down. He needed
Yugoslavia's raw materials, but more than this he could not afford to
let a bunch of 'peasants' stand in his way. Upon hearing the news, he
went into a violent rage and the very word 'Yugoslavia' became
anathema to him. He ordered his army to crush the Serbs at once. His
advisers leaned over to remind him that these 'peasants' had an army
of three hundred and forty-four thousand, an air force of five hundred
planes and a terrain built by God for defensive warfare.

There was one way out of this mess. The only nations that liked the
Serbs were the Russians, French and British, and the latter two had
created the Serbian Empire because they needed a friend in southeast
Europe. The French were now part of the Axis, though. The Russians
pretended to be Serbia's big brother when it suited them. At the
moment it did not suit them. Thus Serbia's only friend was Britain,
which was in no position to help. Inside Yugoslavia were many ethnic
groups that longed for independence from Serb rule: pockets of
German-speakers, whom the Nazis called Volksdeutsch, left over
from the days of 1918 when Austria ruled the region; ethnic Italians
along the Dalmatian coast; ethnic Albanians in Kosovo; Slovenians;
Croats; Moslems in Bosnia and Herzegovina; Montenegrins;
Macedonians; Magyars who wanted reunification with Hungary;
ethnic Romanians who wanted reunification with Romania; and
ethnic Bulgars who wanted reunification with Bulgaria. It was no
wonder that Yugoslavia's neighbors mistrusted the Serbs. Many held
the Serbs responsible for starting World War I, and since 1918 the
Serbs had been insufferable. Hitler therefore did not have to look far
to find partners who would help him crush the Serbs.

Hitler asked Romania, Hungary and Bulgaria to allow his troops to
use their soil. They agreed. Hitler also approached Mussolini, for that

dictator had claimed to be the protector of all ethnic Albanians and this included those in Kosovo. He had also been playing host to Ante Pavelic a Croat Fascist rabble-rouser. One topic they had discussed was the piece of Croatia that Italy had occupied since 1919.

Mussolini agreed to help Hitler. This would be the eighth time he ordered his troops into a war. Quickly the Italian and German generals came up with a plan.

On the spring morning of 6 April 1941 German aircraft flew into Yugoslavian airspace and dropped bombs on the residential neighborhoods of Belgrade. This was Hitler's answer to the Serb people who had defied him. Simultaneously the German Second Army supported by five hundred and seventy-six aircraft invaded Yugoslavia from Austria, and the German Twelfth Army invaded from Bulgaria. In reply Yugoslavian planes struck the German supply lines in Hungary, Bulgaria and Romania, giving those nations an excuse to attack, as if they needed one.

The Italian Second Army of General Vittorio Ambrosio supported by one hundred and ninety-two planes crossed the border from northeast Italy into northwest Yugoslavia. His army was divided into the following: Lieutenant General Balocco's V Corps, Lieutenant General Lorenzo Dalmazzo's VI Corps, Lieutenant General Robotti's XI Corps, Lieutenant General F. Zingales' Motorized Corps, and Lieutenant General Federico Ferrari-Orsi's Celere Corps.

Balocco had the Lombardia Division [with attached 137th CCNN Legion] and the Bergamo Division [with attached 89th CCNN Legion], plus three regiments of Frontier Guards. Dalmazzo controlled the Assietta Mountain Division [and attached 17th CCNN Legion], the Sassari Division [and attached 73rd CCNN Legion] and the Friuli Division [and attached 88th CCNN Legion]. Robotti possessed the Ravenna Mountain Division [with attached 5th CCNN Legion], Re [King's] Division [with attached 75th CCNN Legion] and Isonzo Division [with attached 98th CCNN Legion], plus the 3rd Alpini Gruppo and four regiments of border guards. Zingales led the Littorio Armored Division, Pasubio Motorized Division and Torino (Turin) Motorized Division. And Ferrari-Orsi commanded the Eugenio di Savoia Celere Division, Emanuele Filiberto Celere Division and Amedeo Duca d'Aosta Celere Division. All three were named after great military leaders.

Each celere division consisted of a Bersaglieri regiment, two regiments of horse cavalry, some armored cars, some L3 tankettes and L6 tanks and towed artillery.

Of the above divisions all were green, but for the Assietta that had fought in Ethiopia, the Ravenna and Friuli that had seen limited action in France and the Littorio that had fought in Spain and France. Some of the Bersaglieri of the Emanuele Filiberto and the Amedeo Duca d'Aosta had invaded Albania in 1939.

The Italian soldiers found this to be a confusing war. Yugoslavian Army units manned by Croats welcomed them as liberators, while others manned by Slovenians either resisted or ran away, but all Serb-manned units fought them tooth and nail. Two days into the invasion the Serbs surprised the Italians by attacking into Albania with their Yugoslavian Sixth Army against a force of Italians that was guarding the Yugoslavian-Albanian border under the personal command of General Ugo Cavallero. Here he had placed Lieutenant General Vecchi's XIV Corps, Lieutenant General Pafundi's XVII Armored Corps and Lieutenant General Nasci's Librazid Command.

Vecchi led the Cuneense Alpini Division and half the Puglie Mountain Division, plus the 6th Aosta Cavalry Regiment (horsed). Pafundi commanded the Centauro Armored Division, Marche Division [and attached 49th CCNN Legion], Messina Division and half the Puglie Mountain Division, plus the 19th Cavalleggeri Guide Cavalry Regiment (horsed) and the Diamanti CCNN Raggruppamento [made up of the 23rd, 28th, 108th, 115th, 136th and 152nd CCNN Legions and the Skanderbeg CCNN Legion of Albanian Blackshirts]. Nasci was in charge of the Arezzo Division, Pinerolo Division and Firenze Division [with attached 92nd CCNN Legion] plus the 7th Milan Lancers Regiment [armored cars], the Biscaccianti CCNN Brigade [80th and 109th CCNN Legions], the Brisotto Infantry Regiment, the Agostini CCNN Forest Militia Regiment and the 4th Bicycle Regiment.

The Arezzo and Firenze had invaded Albania in 1939. The Puglie, Arezzo, Pinerolo, Cuneense and Centauro Divisions and 28th, 109th, 136th and 152nd CCNN Legions had fought on the Greek front, and the Cuneense and 28th had also fought the French. Cavallero could have held his ground, but this would have disrupted the invasion timetable. Instead he ordered his men to back up and allow the enemy in for up to thirty miles around Scutari. He was content to bomb the invading Serbs with two hundred and forty-six Italian and one hundred and sixty-eight German planes.

By dusk on 8 April the Luftwaffe and Regia Aeronautica had taken just three days to destroy three quarters of the Yugoslavian Air Force, and by this date Ambrosio's troops in the northwest of the country had the Yugoslavian Fourth Army if not on the run, certainly on the walk. The Yugoslavian First, Third and Fifth Armies were definitely on the run from the Germans. Their Sixth Army had been sucked into Albania. Only their Second Army in reserve was still in good shape.

This day a German armored force charged out of Yugoslavia into Greece. The Greeks had troops in Albania and on their Bulgarian border, but none in between along the Yugoslavian border. Thus the Germans were able to swing around the Greek defenders of the Bulgarian border, cut them off and capture the port of Salonika, where thousands of Allied troops were simply rounded up: Greeks, Britons,

Poles, Cypriots, Canadians, Palestinian Arabs and Palestinian Jews.

The British did have a fighting force in Greece, consisting of the recently arrived Australian 6th and New Zealand 2nd Divisions and the British 1st Armored Brigade, but their commander General Henry Maitland Wilson ordered a retreat at once. They had practically yet to fire a shot! This retreat uncovered the flank of the main Greek army that was facing the Italians in Albania.

On 9 April in Northern Albania Cavallero now counter attacked the Yugoslavian Sixth Army with his Cuneense Alpini, Marche, Arezzo and Firenze Divisions, and they soon cut off those Yugoslavs inside Albania. At the same time the Italian garrison of Zara [which was pre-war Italian territory] on the coast attacked inland into Yugoslavia, and the Bafile and Grado Battalions of the San Marco Marines made an amphibious invasion on the coast.

On 10 April Mussolini recognized Croatia as an independent state with Pavelic as ruler. Most of those Croats that had not yet surrendered did so now. On 11 April Hungarian and Bulgarian troops invaded Yugoslavia.

The Italian forces in southern Albania facing the Greeks moved up to launch a major assault. Here the Italian Eleventh Army of General Geloso controlled the VIII and XXV Corps. The VIII commanded the Pusteria Alpini Division, Cagliari Mountain Division, Cacciatori delle Alpi Division [with attached 105th CCNN Legion], Siena Division [with attached 141st CCNN Legion] and Bari Division. The XXV Corps controlled the Julia Alpini Division, Sforzesca Mountain Division [and attached 30th CCNN Legion], Modena Mountain Division [and attached 36th CCNN Legion], Ferrara Division [with attached 82nd CCNN Legion], Brennero Division [with attached 35th CCNN Legion], Lupi di Toscana Division and Legnano Division.

Pirzio-Biroli's Italian Ninth Army also faced the Greeks. He commanded the III and XXVI Corps. The III had the Venezia Division [and attached 72nd CCNN Legion], Forli Division and Taro Division [with attached 164th CCNN Legion]. The XXVI had the Tridentina Alpini Division, Piemonte Division and Parma Division.

In reserve were the Casale Division, Cuneo Division and Acqui Division [with attached 27th CCNN Legion].

On the 12th Geloso's and Pirzio-Biroli's armies launched a major offensive against the Greek Epirus Army in Albania. For three days the combat was as bitter as any that had been witnessed on this front.

On the 14th the Regia Aeronautica caught the remnants of the Greek Air Force at Paramythia airfield and destroyed them. This day the British retreated past Mount Olympus thus allowing the Germans to advance a hundred and sixty miles behind the Greeks Army, and Maitland Wilson ordered the retreat to continue towards Thermopylae Pass.

On the 15th Italian soldiers captured Split in Yugoslavia, while in

Albania the Italians began to advance against the collapsing Greeks.

On the 17th the Yugoslavian government capitulated. Those Yugoslavs trapped by the Italians inside northern Albania fought on for another forty-eight hours before accepting reality.

On the 18th Greek General Zolakoglou asked for terms, the Greek Prime Minister Koryzis shot himself, and the Greek King Giorgios, who had been a mere figurehead until now, appointed Emmanuel Zouderos to lead the nation and keep fighting, but it was already too late. The Italians were now advancing rapidly into Greece taking thousands of prisoners. To add one last insult against the Italians several Greek divisions deliberately sought to surrender to German troops.

The British chose to evacuate by sea to the Greek island of Crete, and soon the Greek king and government followed suit. Fifty-seven Italian aircraft flying from the Dodecanese Islands and scores of German planes flying from captured Greek airfields bombed the British embarkation area and sank several merchant ships.

There is no escaping the fact that the Yugoslavian campaign was a magnificent military offensive. It was solely a German-Italian victory. The Bulgarians and Hungarians just came in to grab territory that had already been conquered. The Nazis, being Nazis, claimed the victory was theirs and theirs alone. The German accomplishment was superb, to be fair. Following only ten days planning they had killed or captured a third of a million Yugoslavian troops in eleven days at a cost to themselves of just one hundred and fifty-one killed!

But the Italian contribution was impressive too. They had even less time to prepare than the Germans, yet Ambrosio's Second Army had advanced an average of twenty-three miles per day, all the more noteworthy when it is remembered that they were under fire all the way and that this area is rugged mountainous terrain. The total Italian tally of Yugoslavian prisoners was thirty thousand, and this did not count those Croats who defected. Mussolini annexed Dalmatia, Kosovo, Montenegro, much of Bosnia and Herzegovina, a slice of Macedonia and a chunk of Slovenia. He acknowledged Croatia as an independent state ruled by Pavelic, but not only did he refrain from handing over to Pavelic the slice of Croatia occupied by the Italians since 1919, but he took another slice of Croatia, just to remind Pavelic who was boss.

Mussolini had won his Greek war too, but he could not hide the fact that it had taken German intervention to uncover the Greek flank. The Greek conflict had exhibited four things to the discerning eye: the arrogance of Mussolini; the incompetence of Italian generalship; the shoddy quality of Italian military equipment; and the outstanding courage of the ordinary Italian soldier.

The Italians now occupied all of Greece, but for the ethnic Bulgar and Macedonian areas, which they gave to Bulgaria, and they permitted the Germans to have some influence in Western Thrace, Athens, Salonika and on some islands. Of all Greek territory, only the island of Crete still held out for the Allies.

The Italian people found that Mussolini's purchase of Greek real estate had come at a high price in terms of Italian blood: thirteen thousand seven hundred and fifty-five killed, twelve thousand three hundred and sixty-eight permanently maimed by frostbite, fifty thousand wounded and twenty thousand taken prisoner, many of them after becoming crippled by wounds or frostbite. Moreover, the Greeks had sent these prisoners overseas to British camps, so they were not liberated.

———

Chapter Twenty-three
The Battle for Our Sea

The Italian Navy benefited greatly from Italian land victories in spring 1941. No longer was the supply line from Italy to the Dodecanese fraught with danger, for now the Italians had naval and air bases all along the Greek coast and in the Aegean Islands. Additionally the navy regained the lost ports in Libya, except Tobruk which remained stubbornly defiant.

In April 1941 in the Mediterranean the Italian motor torpedo boat MAS213 ignored the tremendous long range firepower of the British cruiser Capetown and torpedoed her, knocking her out of commission for over a year: Italian aircraft damaged the cruiser York, which was still at Suda Bay; German planes sank three British destroyers; and Italian mines sank three Allied warships.

Notwithstanding these losses the Royal Navy ruled the Mediterranean in April, for not only were they able to safely embark most of the Australian, New Zealand and British troops from mainland Greece to Crete, and take reinforcements into besieged Tobruk, but they bombarded Italian coastal positions in Libya at Bomba, Sollum, Gazala, Tripoli and Bardia.

On 16 April a British flotilla intercepted an Italian convoy of four merchant vessels escorted by three destroyers: Baleno, Lampo and Luca Tarigo. At once Commander Pietro di Cristoforo in command of the large destroyer Luca Tarigo (1,870 tons) charged towards the British. Incoming shells shattered the bridge badly wounding Cristoforo, but he demanded the attack continue. Once within range, the destroyer launched torpedoes, then curved around and fled to escape further damage, but more shells struck home. Casualties were terrible, and the last living officer Lieutenant Ettore Bisagno ordered the tubes to be reloaded and told the helmsman to aim for the enemy. By now the Luca Tarigo was an unrecognizable pile of scrap, her wiring afire, smoke billowing throughout her and the passageways blocked with dead sailors, yet the surviving crewmen managed to launch more torpedoes, one of which slammed into the British destroyer Mohawk, wrecking her. But already the Luca Tarigo was disappearing beneath the waves.

The Baleno was hit by so many British shells she foundered and went down like a rock, and the Lampo was set afire and her captain was forced to beach her. The British then leisurely sank the four merchant ships. The Mohawk had to be scuttled.

———

In Libya on the night of 16 April 1941 Italian infantry had only just caught up with German reconnaissance troops at the port of

Bardia, exhausted from their long march across the desert, when they were shelled by British warships. The British returned for another bombardment on the night of the 18th. However, the next night they not only bombarded the port, but unloaded commandos into launches. Italian artillery on the shore engaged the warships and shelled the arriving launches. When the commandos reached the shore they encountered a mob of Italian airmen, sailors, army rear-echelon troops, Blackshirts, marines and Carabinieri armed with rifles and machine guns, which offered resistance. In fact the British commandos were so taken aback by the fierce defense that they re-embarked. This was the second time that the Italians had defeated the elite British commandos. The ferocity of the Italian response forced the British to rethink their entire commando strategy.

————

In May 1941 in the central Mediterranean German planes sank three British destroyers; Italian mines claimed one British destroyer and a submarine; and the Italian destroyers Zeno and Pigafetta sank the British submarine Usk. However, to balance the scale, the Italian destroyers Schiaffino, La Farina and Carlo Mirabello were sunk by mines; the armed banana boat Ramb III was torpedoed and sunk in Benghazi harbor by the British submarine Triumph; the Curtatone was crippled by a mine; the Canopo was lost in an air raid; and the ocean liner Conte Rosso, now used as a troopship, was sunk by the British submarine Upholder. Of her two thousand seven hundred and twenty-nine crew and passengers, one thousand two hundred and nine drowned.

Lieutenant Count Junio Valerio Borghese attempted a pig raid, but when one accidentally sank he aborted the mission. The whole pig project seemed to be jinxed.

In the Atlantic the Italian submarine Marconi sank the British naval tanker Cairndale.

This month the major air-sea action was around Crete. This remnant of Greece was held by an Allied garrison: the local Greek troops known as the Crete Division, the Australian 6th Division, New Zealand 2nd Division, two British Army brigades and one British Royal Marine brigade. Mussolini wanted Crete for political reasons, and his admirals wanted it for naval strategic reasons, but they did not want to launch a major amphibious invasion while the Royal Navy still held the upper hand. Hitler wanted Crete too, because British bombers based there could reach his precious Romanian oilfields. Moreover Turkey had watched recent events carefully. Hitler hoped to impress the Turks enough to bring them into the Axis. He thought his capture of Crete might do the trick. But the German generals reminded Hitler that they would have to ask the Italian navy to carry them to Crete. Hitler overruled his generals, and Mussolini overruled his admirals.

The aim of the first phase of the plan was to gain complete air supremacy over the one hundred and sixty mile long island. To this end Italian and German planes began bombing. On 18 May German aircraft were especially accurate, damaging three British destroyers and sinking several merchant vessels. The following day the Allies withdrew all their planes from Crete's airfields, sending them to Egypt. Phase one had been won.

Now came phase two. On 20 May a division of German paratroopers dropped onto Crete's airfields. The combat was tough in places, but the Germans were astonished to find that the Allies were not defending the airfields, because they had believed the wild statements by Nazi propaganda that had boasted that the German JU-52 transport aircraft could land anywhere and did not need an airfield!

Now came phase three. On the night of 21 May a hodge-podge invasion fleet set sail. It consisted of trawlers, barges, caiques, yachts, coasters, fishing smacks and anything that was seaworthy. The vessels were provided by the Italians and the Romanians, and many were stolen from Greeks. Most of the crewmembers were Italian, and every vessel was crammed with German soldiers. However, unknown to Axis intelligence the British knew about the amphibious invasion and this night they met the armada with three British light cruisers and four destroyers. All of a sudden muzzle flashes lit the black horizon: two caiques burst into flames and a Romanian coaster blew up in a multi-colored display. The armada turned back, while its escorting Italian destroyers charged the British. The destroyer Lupo was hit no fewer than eighteen times by 6inch shells until she was riddled with holes, yet she managed to damage the British cruiser Orion. Meanwhile the destroyer Lira braved shellfire to rescue soldiers and sailors floundering in the water. Italian seaplanes also set down on the water to rescue survivors. Through these magnificent efforts one thousand six hundred and fifty men were plucked from the sea, so that only three hundred actually died in the disaster.

Hitler was shocked and refused to countenance another amphibious invasion, but his paratroopers now possessed the airfields, so phase four could begin: the German 5th Mountain Division was brought in aboard passenger aircraft.

Phase five was to be an amphibious invasion by Italian troops. Though the German attempt had been massacred, the Italians insisted on trying it. In fact it went smoothly as the British Royal Navy did not interfere. They were too busy evacuating as many of the Allied troops on the island as possible. Owing to limited space the British abandoned most of the Greek soldiers.

The lessons of Crete were odd indeed. The capture of the island solely by airborne troops was the final evidence to the Allies that it was imperative they begin creating airborne divisions of their own.

Yet the high casualties suffered by the Germans convinced Hitler that airborne operations were impractical and he never again launched a drop of this size. The successful British evacuations from mainland Greece and now from Crete convinced the Italians that the Royal Navy would always be there to rescue a trapped Allied force. However, the Royal Navy had suffered such terrible losses to air attack during the Crete evacuation that the British admirals vowed never to perform such an evacuation again. In other words while the British admirals and generals accepted they had been defeated, Hitler and the Italian admirals acted as if their victory had been a defeat. It is understandable why the British admirals made this decision. Italian and German planes had inflicted serious damage on the carrier Formidable, battleships Barham, Valiant and Warspite, light cruisers Ajax, Carlisle, Naiad, Orion and Perth (Australian), and on two Australian and seven British destroyers. More importantly Italian and German planes had sent to the bottom the light cruisers Calcutta, Fiji, Gloucester and York, plus seven destroyers, four submarines, two launches and five motor torpedo boats. And this only counts the naval vessels. Many cargo ships, troopships and civilian boats were also sunk or damaged.

The Italian performance in the Crete campaign was heroic. Not only did Italian airmen help gain air supremacy, and Italian sailors risk their lives to save German soldiers, but the Italian willingness to make their own amphibious invasion despite having seen what happened to the Germans was inspiring. Yet, the entire world ignored the Italian contribution to the victory. The British press consoled themselves by claiming that the Italian pilots never hit anything owing to their cowardice and that the Italian soldiers deliberately arrived late because they were cowards. By this date the ordinary Brits in the street were so bitterly prejudiced against Italians that they were ready to believe any old tripe. The German Nazis naturally claimed they had won the battle all by themselves.

———

Chapter Twenty-four
The Long Death

As the strictly censured Italian newspapers, magazines, cinema newsreels and radio broadcasts proclaimed Mussolini's great victories, it is understandable that even the anti-Fascist majority became convinced they were going to win the war against Britain. Of course, this was no recompense for the mothers and widows and orphans that Mussolini's glory hunting had left in bereavement.

Rommel paid scant attention to press reports coming out of Rome or Berlin. He was all too aware that the Royal Navy still moved with impunity and therefore the besieged troops in Tobruk would be continually resupplied by sea.

However, he too had been resupplied, and he had been reinforced by the German 15th Panzer Division. So, on 30 April 1941, he once again sent his armor against Tobruk's defenses, supported by German and Italian planes and German and Italian artillery. His tanks advanced in the face of Allied artillery fire, while his panzergrenadiers (infantry armed with extra automatic weapons) walked behind them for safety. After a mile they were pinned down by heavy fire from tanks, anti-tank guns and artillery, and at dusk they withdrew. The Germans were angry and, not wishing to blame themselves for their failure, they blamed their defeat on the Italian armor, which had not supported them. The Italians explained that they had not attacked because the Germans had insisted they didn't need help. The two Axis partners argued constantly. Gariboldi gave few orders to Rommel, knowing he would do as he wished anyway. The truth was that the Germans had been defeated by landmines, Australian artillery and British tanks.

On the night of 3 May the Australians counter attacked. They were met by some panzergrenadiers and the Italian Trento and Pavia Divisions, the latter performing well in this their first real action. The Australians were driven back.

From now on the siege of Tobruk took on a scene of nightly patrols, long range sniping, occasional artillery salvoes, regular air raids, choking sandstorms, blistering heat, fly-infested food, foxholes shared with sand fleas, brackish drinking water, sickness and maddening frustrating boredom. Soon the Germans were walking as slowly as the Arabs and Italians, having learned their lesson to conserve energy in such a climate.

The battle for Tobruk was also fought at sea. Allied and Italian supply vessels both dodged planes, mines, warships and submarines. On 4 May two Italian merchant ships and an oil tanker were sunk by planes. On 8 May four Italian ships reached Benghazi only to be sunk in an air raid. Days later an onshore Italian fuel depot was blown up in an air attack.

———

In May 1941 the Italian people received the news of the Duke D'Aosta's surrender at Addis Ababa with solemnity, but there was too much good news elsewhere for there to be national mourning, especially as the wily duke had surrendered only his own direct field command at Amba Alagi, not the many garrisons still holding out in Ethiopia! It would take much time for the British to conquer these, and even longer if they waited for them to surrender.

To be sure some British voices argued that these garrisons should be left to wither on the vine, but there were three reasons why the British could not afford do this. First, the British government considered Haile Selassie's regime to be an ally, and his Ethiopian guerillas could not crush the Italians by themselves. Secondly, the Italian garrisons might unite somewhat and strike at one or more of the airfields or ports in Eritrea, thus blocking the entrance to the Suez Canal yet again. Thirdly, the idea of an Italian advance from southern Libya to rescue these garrisons was still not beyond the realms of possibility, especially as the Italians were already back on the Egyptian border. Surely there was another reason. British propaganda was consistently underselling Italian ability, and the British generals could not bear the thought of backing off from the kill. They believed the Italian garrisons would fall like ripe apples.

As a result the British continued to put pressure on the Italians in Ethiopia. In late May they forced the garrison of Colito to surrender, putting another four hundred and eighty-nine Italians and three hundred ascaris behind British wire. Days later they captured Siolo. The garrison of Abalti was offered a choice: capitulate to the 23rd Nigerian Brigade of the British Army, who pledged to care for them, or wait to be overrun by thousands of Ethiopian guerillas who pledged to torture them to death. The Italians chose to surrender to the Nigerians.

But Soddu there was still heavy fighting, where the 21st, 25th and 101st Colonial Divisions held out against attacking Ethiopian guerillas and the British 12th African Division. But even here the garrison ran out of food and ammunition, and being given an opportunity to surrender to the civilized British, rather than to the vengeful Ethiopians, the garrison gave up.

The two thousand five hundred strong garrison of Chilga repulsed an assault by Ethiopians and Sudanese on 17 May. The five thousand defenders of Wolchefit Pass not only drove off a major Ethiopian attack, but captured Ayalew Birru, a senior guerilla commander.

By now Colonel Maraventano was at the end of his rope. His column numbered eight thousand uniformed personnel of all descriptions and two thousand civilians. He had halted at Addis Dera, his rendezvous with the duke having failed, and his people were exhausted and sick. In the hills surrounding him were an unknown number of bloodthirsty guerillas. The arrival of the seasonal rains brought to life a host of bronchial ailments, and everyone's immunity system was already dangerously low. Nonetheless when Sudanese troops and Ethiopian guerillas approached his defenses, he ordered a counter attack and for three days his soldiers did his bidding with incredible fortitude, eventually driving off the enemy. Then the colonel ordered his column to march another forty miles to Fort Agibar. The ordeal was accomplished, but only at the cost of tremendous suffering for civilians and soldiers alike. As soon as they arrived, they were attacked by guerillas. Only the fittest men were able to fight, but they repulsed the enemy.

On 19 May an emissary from Wingate arrived at the fort to inform Maraventano that the duke had surrendered, and that Marshal Kassa was waiting in the hills ready to unleash his tens of thousands of guerillas upon the hapless force, and that Wingate urged a capitulation to him at once to avoid a massacre. On 23 May Maraventano agreed.

Meanwhile Brigadier General Torelli, who had been seriously wounded, decided to abandon Bahrdar and march to Gondar to join Nasi. Against the odds he accomplished this hundred mile journey.

General Pietro Gazzera was also on the move with four thousand five hundred Italians and two thousand ascaris. He had abandoned his sick and wounded at Jimmu: twelve thousand Italians and three thousand ascaris, with orders to surrender to the British 22nd East African Brigade, which they did on 21 June. Gazzera brushed aside two brigades of British African troops at Demli and Gimbi, but after marching a hundred and fifty miles he found his path blocked by a column of Belgians. Trapped, he gave up on 6 July.

Colonel Angelini and his five thousand man garrison at Debra Tabor had repulsed several attacks by Ethiopian guerillas, but his men were now under daily air raids by South African planes, and as he watched the guerilla army grow in size and saw the arrival of Indian infantry, British artillery and Indian armored cars, he came to the conclusion that his men would be wiped out. On 6 July he surrendered. His 79th Colonial Battalion of Ethiopians defected to the guerillas at once.

In late July the defenders of Wolchefit Pass refused a call to surrender, and when the onslaught came, launched by Indian infantry, British artillery, South African aircraft and the ever-present mass of Ethiopian guerillas, the Italians repelled them all.

General Guglielmo Nasi, by now the highest-ranking Italian officer in all of East Africa, knew that the longer he held out, the longer he tied down the British. He instilled in his men at Gondar, Chilga and Kulkaber the thought that they might be fighting in Ethiopia, but it was the same war as that being waged in Libya or at sea or in the skies over Italy. By August 1941 his men were still tying down the equivalent of two British divisions, several South African air squadrons and a mountain of supplies, and this did not count the guerillas.

On 27 September the garrison of Wolchefit Pass surrendered to the 25th East African Brigade, but only because they had been on starvation rations for months and had finally run out of food.

Throughout October Nasi's Italian die-hards repulsed continuous attacks by the 25th and 26th East African Brigades, the Sudan Defense Force, South African armored cars and artillery, British artillery and three squadrons of South African planes, plus thousands of Ethiopian guerillas. In this fighting the last Italian plane in East Africa was shot down. Nasi could have surrendered at any time with honor, but he knew the British were really becoming impatient at the length of this campaign, hence their vigorous attacks. On 11 November the Chilga garrison inflicted serious losses on the Sudanese.

The British changed their plan, deciding to concentrate on Kulkaber defended by Colonel Ugolini and some Blackshirts, ascaris and a battalion of Carabinieri. They struck him with South African armored cars, British East African infantry and Ethiopian guerillas, but the Italians drove them all back. Two weeks later the British came on again, attacking with Sudanese troops, and Ugolini sent in his last reserves to repel them. However, unknown to him these attackers were not Sudanese infantry, but were Sudanese pioneers. In other words in desperation the British had handed rifles to these labor troops and had thrown them against the Italian line in a feint. The real attack struck two miles away with the 25th and 26th East African Brigades, armored cars and a swarm of Ethiopians. The British tactic worked. Ugolini was outflanked and forced to surrender his survivors: one thousand six hundred and forty-eight Italians and seven hundred and seventy-five ascaris.

On 27 November with his supply dumps all but empty, Nasi finally accepted British terms and surrendered all remaining Italian forces in East Africa. When his men walked out with their hands up, the British stood at attention and paid respect to the stamina of their Italian enemy.

―――――

This was the end of Italy's East African empire. Mussolini's sojourn here did not have a happy ending. His yearn for glory had cost Italy ten thousand five hundred killed and wounded to conquer Ethiopia in 1935-36. He had then spent another three thousand killed and five thousand wounded trying to govern it over the next four years. Trying to defend East Africa between June 1940 and November 1941 cost him twenty thousand dead (of which five thousand were actual Italians) and two hundred and seventy thousand missing [captured or deserted]. Furthermore, three hundred thousand Italian colonists now came under British rule.

The Duke D'Aosta had foreseen this disastrous outcome even before he had begun the campaign. He was not a Fascist, but he believed in his country and he fought to the best of his ability. To be sure his resistance and that of his successors caused the Allies tremendous problems. First of all the Allies could not use the southern exit from the Suez Canal/Red Sea for almost a year. And many neutral nations such as the United States would not allow their merchant ships to sail these waters. Secondly the campaign sucked in an inordinate amount of Allied provisions and supplies owing to the longevity of the campaign and the primitive state of the terrain and the sheer size of the battlefield. Thirdly it took the equivalent of seven divisions of Allied troops [not counting the guerillas] and several air squadrons to bring the campaign to a close. No one will ever know what would have happened in Greece or Libya if the British had been able to call upon these units. Throughout the seventeen-month campaign Generals Wavell and Cunningham were under constant pressure by Churchill to withdraw units from East Africa, because they were desperately needed elsewhere. The British Army was large, but between July 1940 and November 1941, matching exactly the time frame of the East African campaign, Churchill's fear of a German invasion of Britain was so great that he kept the vast majority of his troops home in Britain, and relied almost exclusively on non-British soldiers to do his fighting for him, beefed up when necessary by small numbers of Britons. During this entire period not one infantry division recruited in Britain saw action!

As a result of Churchill's reluctance to commit Britons to battle Wavell simply did not have the manpower for all the missions Churchill thrust upon him, and consistently he had to 'rob Peter to pay Paul'. For example, the Indian 4th Division fought in Egypt in December 1940, and then Wavell rushed them to Eritrea in January 1941, and immediately following their victory at Keren he rushed them to back Egypt with no rest between combats. The Indian 5th Division served in Eritrea and Ethiopia until May 1941, and then Wavell whisked them away to fight the French in Syria. The Australian 6th Division fought in Libya, Greece and Crete and all within one hundred and fifty days. In December 1940 two British-controlled divisions were fighting in Egypt, and two and a third such divisions were battling in East Africa, but by January 1941 the figures were two divisions in Libya and seven and a third in East Africa, and in April-May three and two thirds British-controlled divisions fought in Libya, while three fought in Greece and Crete, and six and a third were still fighting in East Africa.

The Italian stand in East Africa should have gone down in history as a great epic. Instead it has been forgotten. There are several reasons for this. For one, the Germans were not there, and of all the Axis partners only the Germans and Japanese retained any post-war mystique and interest among the world's general public. Moreover, English-speaking people have a tendency to want to read only of the exploits of other English-speaking people, and the battles fought by Nigerians and Kenyans do not have much appeal to them. Naturally the Italian press has never put too much emphasis on a campaign they lost. The fact that British code breakers could read the duke's orders to an Italian unit practically as quickly as the intended recipient was naturally not revealed by the British during the war. The duke therefore could never really surprise the British, whereas they often surprised him. However, the British generals had to explain their victories to the world's press. They could mention that they had better equipment and a superior strategy, but they could not mention their ability to read Italian signals. Therefore they fell back on that old nonsense about Italians being cowards. The British rarely reported that many of their 'Italian' prisoners were in fact Ethiopian defectors demanding permission to join the guerillas. They simply gave out the statistics and allowed the British public to 'assume' these prisoners were all ethnic Italians. Moreover on days when the Italians won, the British generals shunned the war correspondents, but on days when the Italians lost the British generals demanded headlines. British propaganda had two purposes: keeping up the morale of the British people, who were suffering the greatest onslaught of aerial bombing in history, and trying to convince the Americans to escalate their military activity to help Britain.

The downside to this was that Allied troops who fought the Italians received less praise from their friends and neighbors back home than those who fought the Germans or Japanese! Nor was this injustice ever remedied in the post-war years. Some wives for the rest of their lives told people that their husband had 'only' fought Italians, and was not deserving of the respect given to those that fought Germans or Japanese.

In truth the Italian defense of North Africa in the winter 1940-41 was pitiful. Yet, this Italian reaction on the receiving end of blitzkrieg tactics was little different than that of the British when they were on the receiving end of such tactics. In December 1940 seven Italian brigades were destroyed in four days by seven British-controlled brigades. In April 1941 three British-controlled brigades were destroyed and four others were made to retreat by just two German 'brigades' in nine days. In the former the Italians faced odds of one to one. In the latter the British faced odds of seven to two in their favor.

The loss of a third of a million Italian-controlled troops in seventeen months in East Africa was a disgrace, to be sure. But compare it with the loss of a third of a million Yugoslavs in twelve days! And the Yugoslavs were defending their homes, not some far off primitive colony! In May 1940 an all-British army of a half million was kicked into the sea in seventeen days. It was the strategy that counted not the nationality of the belligerents!

Having said that, the participation of non-white troops was a major factor. The British use of Africans and Indians was justified, for these men whose families had been under British rule for generations fought in a disciplined and aggressive manner. Likewise the Italian reliance on Eritreans, under Italian rule for two generations, was also justified, some Eritreans being outstanding soldiers. But the Italian reliance on Yemeni mercenaries and Somalis was not justified, and the use of newly conquered Libyans and Ethiopians was courting disaster. Many fled at the first shot, and others defected to the enemy. The British accepted the Libyan defectors into their army, but quickly found them to be worthy of sentry duty at best. The British did not even attempt to recruit Ethiopians, including Wingate's personnel, nor did they ever consider using the Ethiopian guerillas outside of Ethiopia.

Some Italians panicked under fire. Fact. Some Britons panicked. Also fact. Witness the abysmal performances of Britons at Tug Argan Pass and Gallabat. In the early days white South Africans were known to run away at the mere suggestion that Italians were nearby.

The Duke D'Aosta was arguably the best Italian military leader of the war, and if given free rein by Mussolini and a better aerial supply system he could have held out months longer and indeed might have seriously affected the progress of the war. He was fortunate to have some good subordinates: sensible fighting men like Gazzera, Nasi, Frusci, Carnimeo, Maraventano, Lorenzini and Ugolini, who were true warriors and priceless. Some of the combat in East Africa was as tough as World War I trench warfare. Men who witnessed both claimed this. The British awarded several Victoria Crosses for the campaign, their highest medal for valor. On the very last day of fighting in the campaign British-controlled forces suffered three hundred casualties and the Ethiopians lost even more. The Indian Army lost four thousand seven hundred and eighty-five killed and wounded in East Africa, one combat soldier in four! The British and Indians who fought the Italians at Keren eventually left East Africa and went on to battle French, Germans and Japanese, but at the end of World War II they declared that Keren had been their toughest fight!

———

Chapter Twenty-five
Crusade in Russia

By May 1941 Britain was near the end, or so it seemed to many: her island waters infested with German submarines, her cities devastated by German bombers, her armies driven from Greece and Crete and Libya. A gambling man would not have bet on Britain to win the war. As a result Hitler believed he was now free to pursue bigger fish. On May 31 he called Mussolini to an urgent meeting at the Brenner Pass in two days' time. Il Duce had suspected that Hitler would announce his invasion of the Soviet Union, as a rumor to that effect had been around for a while. However, Hitler spent the meeting discussing past events. There seemed to Il Duce to be nothing new and certainly no reason for urgency. Mussolini returned to Rome none the wiser.

On the night of June 21 a courier brought Il Duce an urgent letter from Hitler. In clouded terms it told Mussolini that the Germans were indeed invading the Soviet Union. The attack would begin within hours.

Unfortunately Mussolini had backed himself into a corner. While preaching for years that his arch-enemy was Communism, only in Spain had he in fact waged war against Communism, and even there the Communists made up only a small portion of his enemies - the Republican forces.

Stalin had ruled the Communist Soviet Union since emerging as the victor in the Russian Civil War in 1921, and he had exported Communism as a revolutionary ideology. He was also the most prolific brutal murderer in the history of the world, massacring his fellow beings by the million. Communists were not immune from his insanity: indeed he decimated the Communist Party throughout the world. In September 1939 he had invaded Poland, as part of a deal made with Hitler - surely one devil in league with another devil - and then he had followed this with the invasion of Finland. In 1940 he took over Latvia, Lithuania, Estonia and a piece of Romania. In each land he had sent in his NKVD security forces to massacre the intelligentsia, namely anyone who might have organizational skills such as doctors, lawyers, managers, teachers, scientists, clergy etc. As many as one person in every hundred was murdered or imprisoned.

There was no doubt in the mind of most Italians that Stalin was the anti-Christ, the devil incarnate, who preached atheism and subservence to the state. Yet the Italian Fascists had toned down their anti-Communist propaganda as of late because Stalin and Hitler had made an 'accommodation', and Mussolini did not want to embarrass Hitler. But with Hitler's attack on Stalin, all restraints were gone and Mussolini had to join in now, in other words put his 'money' where his mouth was.

Italy's armed forces were in no state to take on another major enemy, but Mussolini could hardly refuse Hitler. How could he tell his people that it was noble for Italians to attack harmless Ethiopians, bomb the British and invade the French, Yugoslavs and Greeks, but they should now stay out of the crusade to kill the devil in his den? He had managed to convince the pope to bless the flags of Italian regiments when they marched off to kill Christian Englishmen and Frenchmen. How could he now say to the pope he was refusing to make war on the world's greatest atheist? This was not feasible, so he ordered Comando Supremo to prepare to make war on the Soviets. There was the possibility, some thought, that Britain might forget their past differences and join the Italians in this crusade. After all, the British had raised an army to fight Stalin as recently as fourteen months earlier.

On 22 June 1941 German artillery and planes bombarded the entire western border of the Soviet Union from the Baltic to the Black Sea. They then launched three massive invasions out of Poland: Army Group North charging into Lithuania, Army Group Center attacking into Byelorussia, and Army Group South advancing into Ukrainia.

Within days the reports were excellent: the Germans had caught the Soviets unawares. Soon the German armies were joined by troops from Hitler's crusading partners: Finland, Hungary, Romania, Slovakia, Spain and Croatia. Those nations under Hitler's thumb also sent contingents of soldiers: Belgians, Danes, Dutch, French and Norwegians. There were also volunteers from Sweden and Switzerland. The Germans even raised units of Soviet citizens, who wished to cleanse their country of Communism.

Mussolini honored his pledge and sent elements of all three branches of the armed forces to aid the Germans. His navy would be represented by a flotilla of MAS boats and six midget submarines, which would operate from the Romanian coast. The Regia Aeronautica sent a gruppo of bombers, fighters and reconnaissance planes. The Italian Army organized a corps of 55,000 men commanded by Lieutenant General Zingales, divided into three divisions – Brigadier General Mario Maranzzani's Amedeo Duca d'Aosta Celere, Major General Vittorio Giovannelli's Pasubio Motorized and Major General Luigi Manzi's Torino. All three had fought in Yugoslavia two months earlier. The Pasubio, which had also fought in France, gained the 1st CCNN Legion.

The expedition was given a traditional Fascist send off with parades, salutes, songs, speeches, pomp and fanfare. Italians at the cinema saw a newsreel of Il Duce in Verona taking the salute of marching troops. They were keen to get to grips with Stalin's soldiers before the Germans killed them all. It is easy to be a warrior when pretty girls in clinging summer dresses are cheering and throwing flowers.

The excitement was too much for Zingales. He had a heart attack. Quickly a new commander was found, Lieutenant General Giovanni Messe, who had fought in Ethiopia, the invasion of Albania and the Greek campaign.

Within a few days these Italians became greatly overawed by the size of the Soviet Union as they marched mile after mile along hot dusty dirt roads never wholly coming to grips with the illusive Soviets. Soviet civilians welcomed them by the roadside with water and food, obviously glad to see the backs of Stalin's NKVD. The most numerous losses among the Italians were caused by sore feet. After an entire month the soldiers started to wonder if their generals were leading them in circles: surely no country was this large? At the end of August the troops were grateful when they were ordered to halt and man the Dniepr River line. They had marched 500 miles! Mussolini joined Hitler in an aircraft and together they flew over the vast territory that the Italians had 'conquered'. Mussolini enjoyed seeing the conquered lands, but there was a pang of regret in all of this too, for on August 7 his son Bruno had been killed test flying the new P108 bomber.

Mussolini saw at first hand the deplorable state of Russian/Ukrainian roads. Owing to a heavy rain Messe had to come to a meeting in a horse-drawn cart, as all the motor vehicles were stuck in mud.

In August Messe's corps in Russia gained the 63rd CCNN Legion, of which one coorte [battalion] came from the 1st CCNN Legion. All his Blackshirts now came under the 63rd CCNN Battalion Gruppo.

After resting a few weeks, the Italian artillery bombarded the far bank of the Dniepr, and then the 3rd Bersaglieri Regiment of the Amedeo Duca d'Aosta Celere Division crossed in small boats under fire. The Soviet defenders folded up at once. Then the remainder of Messe's corps crossed and began advancing.

Overcoming rearguards, the Italians aimed towards Stalino, spearheading an entire German army group! The Soviet opposition was poor, but the Italians were astonished when they encountered the Soviet T-34 tank. It was bigger and faster than anything they had ever seen and it carried a 76.2mm gun.

Come October the rains began to fall and now the dirt roads turned into rivers of mud. Soon every artillery piece had to be hand-carried, and trucks sank up to their door handles in mud. Those Italians that had studied history were reminded of Napoleon's invasion of Russia in 1812, in which many Italians had participated. They were now moving at the same speed as their 19th century predecessors.

On 17 October the horse cavalry of the Amedeo Duca d'Aosta Celere Division approached the Sukyie Yalli River - the Savoia Dragoons dismounted and crossed in small boats to take the far bank from a rearguard. Next day the Novara Lancers crossed on a makeshift bridge and walked their horses through mud into Uspenovka, which turned out to be a dirty ugly market town identical to all the others. Once they had cleared the buildings of Russian stragglers and a few die-hards, they resumed their slipping, sliding, slithery mud march towards Stalino.

Then the frost came. This froze the ground, which was good, but it also froze the muddy ruts into rock-hard channels that vehicles had to follow. The steering wheel was useless. On 29 October the Italians finally reached Stalino, and in two days of hard fighting they captured the city.

The Russians had never been subjected to that silly British propaganda that 'all Italians are cowards', so they could only judge the Italians by what they saw with their own eyes. They found the Italian soldier to be disciplined, dedicated and aggressive. The Russians saw no difference between them and the Germans.

The news that the Italians had met Stalin's Red Army and had been victorious was elixir for the people back home in Italy. There was one flaw. At Stalino it was turning colder and colder with each passing day, and like the Germans the Italians had not brought any winter clothing with them.

————————

Chapter Twenty-six
Beware of Balkan Entanglements

In April 1941 Mussolini made Albania a gift of the Chams, i.e. their long lost brethren in those parts of Albania that had been occupied by the Greeks and Serbs since 1919. Unfortunately this was a hollow gift, because Mussolini kept a chokehold on all Albanians as Albania was a mere puppet state. In Kosovo the newly 'liberated' ethnic Albanians turned on the Serbs, who had been their masters these last twenty-two years, and not just on those Serbs who had come from Serbia in 1919 to take the best jobs, but also those Serbs who had lived among them for centuries. Years of frustration spilled over into violence and some Serbs were murdered. Many fled to Serbia.

The Italians turned a blind eye to this, as they did not want to antagonize these Albanians and turn them into anti-Fascist guerillas. In Albania proper small bands of guerillas had been waging war against the Italians since the 1939 invasion, but their efforts were mostly paltry and the Albanian police and Italian Carabinieri were able to handle them without calling upon the Italian Army.

In fact in all those parts of Greece and Yugoslavia that now came under Italian occupation the locals found the Italians to be easy going taskmasters, certainly in comparison to Germans, Hungarians and Bulgarians. The Bulgarian Fifth Army, which occupied most of Macedonia, behaved with intolerable arrogance, and the Bulgarian police were brutal in their treatment of anyone who spoke ill of their ruler Tsar Boris. The Hungarian Army behaved well, for after all the majority of the people they occupied were of the same ethnicity, but close behind the Hungarian soldiers came members of the Arrow Cross. These Hungarian imitators of Mussolini's Blackshirts began to hunt down the minority of Serbs and Jews in the zone occupied by Hungary, and on their very first day of operations they murdered two hundred and fifty of them in Subotica. In their first week they murdered five hundred in Novi Sad.

Though Hitler had made the Serbs the specific target of his war, he ironically did not place Serbia itself under German military government. His advisers, who were more humane and realistic than he, had convinced him to make Serbia an autonomous state under the protection of Germany, and they found a puppet who would rule Serbia for them: Milan Acimovich. To give his rule some teeth without bogging down actual Germans, he was allowed to recruit a seventeen thousand man armed police force and a five thousand six hundred strong Frontier Guard, both of which would have German advisers. A Factory Guard was also created to prevent sabotage by anti-Fascist elements. Pre-war Yugoslavia had been a refuge for anti-Communist Russians and many of these fellows joined the Factory

Guard.

Banat was an area of Serbia where the population spoke German, as they were descended from Austrians. In other words they had been the top dog in this region until 1919. Hitler now gave these Volksdeutsch as he called them a special status and allowed them to establish their own defensive militia. The SS soon arrived here with slogans and pretty uniforms to recruit naive youngsters. The Volksdeutsch were jubilant at their liberation. After all, Hitler himself was an Austrian. The only thing that marred this joyous period was that local gangs of thugs dragged three thousand Jews and hundreds of Serbs out of their homes and beat and robbed them. Fortunately, SS troops stepped in and restored order! In fact the SS solved the problem by deporting the Jews and Serbs to Serbia. The Serbs welcomed their ethnic brothers, but did not welcome more Jews, so Acimovich's police arrested them and placed them in a hastily built concentration camp.

In 1919 Austria had lost almost all her non-Austrian territories owing to her defeat in World War I at the hands of the Italians, but the new Austrian Republic had retained Carinthia, a Slovenian-speaking district, which became part of Germany in 1938 when Hitler annexed Austria. Because of Hitler's twisted sense of logic, he thought that as he already 'owned' these Slovenians, he had a right to annex the remainder of Slovenia from Yugoslavia. Mussolini had the same weird attitude. He believed that as Italy had grabbed a piece of extreme Western Slovenia in 1919, he should be entitled to annex the remainder of Slovenia in 1941. He and Hitler compromised and they each took half of Slovenia.

Italy had also occupied a slice of Croatia in 1919, but now Mussolini and Hitler agreed that Croatia should become independent, though Mussolini held on to his bit. Ante Pavelic had learned much from Mussolini while living in Italy and he now set up his own Blackshirt imitation, the Ustaci. Upon their inauguration they needed money for uniforms, weapons and equipment, so they taxed every Jew in the new state and then conscripted all male Jews for slave labor. On 26 June 1941 they tired of this partial anti-Semitism and just went ahead and arrested all Jews regardless of age or gender and incarcerated them in newly erected concentration camps at Danica and Jasenovac. Within weeks they had executed six thousand Jews. Most Croats were devoutly Roman Catholic, and they hated the Ustaci, but this force had the support of Pavelic, Hitler, Mussolini and the Catholic bishops in the country.

Mussolini and Hitler agreed to award most of Bosnia and Herzegovina to Croatia, despite the fact that only a quarter of the population in these locales was Croat. The remainder consisted of Serbs, Gypsies, Jews and Moslems. The latter were in fact only different in their religion, not ethnicity. When Croat troops occupied these provinces the Ustaci followed them, raping, burning, looting and murdering with the express purpose of ethnic cleansing - kicking out everyone who was not a Croat. The helpless people ran, carrying a pitiful few of their belongings in suitcases, horse-drawn carts and in wheelbarrows and they crossed the mountains: the Serbs towards Serbia, and the others towards the Italian-occupied zones of Yugoslavia.

However, where Serbs were able to arm themselves they resisted this oppression, and took the opportunity to kick out their Croat, Moslem, Jewish and Gypsy neighbors.

Thus the Italians found themselves in the unusual position of providing sanctuary, shelter, food and medical aid to the Moslem, Jewish and Gypsy victims of Mussolini's partners. Every day they heard atrocity stories. In Foca the Ustaci murdered four hundred Serbs, while nearby armed Serbs massacred three thousand Moslems.

The Italians were appalled by this attitude, and to be sure Pavelic had not learned anti-Semitism in Italy. The Italian Fascists were not anti-Semitic, and a third of Italian Jews belonged to the party. But in Yugoslavia outside the big cities the Jews spoke their own languages, either Yiddish or Ladino, and they dressed and acted differently. They were easy to spot and could not very well melt into a crowd. But there had been Jews in Italy since before the days of Jesus, and by the twentieth century about forty-five thousand Italian were Jewish. Italy had inadvertently gained other Jews during her conquests: twenty-four thousand in Libya, forty thousand in Ethiopia, four thousand four hundred in the Dodecanese. The oppression of Jews under the Germans, Hungarians, Romanians, Serbs, Croats and others became intolerable in Europe, but Mussolini was not anti-Semitic and by summer 1940 he was already housing ten thousand refugee Jews. Any anti-Jewish laws he passed were to placate Hitler only, and they were usually not enforced. Mussolini did much to keep Hitler happy: e.g. allowing ethnic Germans [Volksdeutsch] of Italian citizenship that lived in the South Tyrol to volunteer for service in the German armed forces rather than the Italian.

Hitler declared that anyone, regardless of religion, who had more than two grandparents who had practiced Judaism was to be treated as a Jew. Thus even Protestant pastors and Catholic nuns and priests could be arrested as a Jew.

In Italy the pope had insisted that Mussolini exclude Jews who practiced Catholicism from his anti-Jewish legislation. However, Protestant Jews were fair game. The pope cared about Catholics, but evidently not about anyone else. Nonetheless Mussolini's new anti-Jewish laws damaged his cause as they became ever more strict. Countless Jews were dismissed from their positions, including Aldo Finzi a leading member of the Fascist Party, Dante Almansi the deputy chief of police, Guido Jung an ex-Minister of Finance,

Maurizio Rava a Blackshirt general, and Margherita Sarfatti one of Mussolini's mistresses. Moreover Jews were dismissed from Mussolini's armed forces, including no fewer than five admirals and twenty-four generals. However, Mussolini listened to the pope and did not bother Catholic Jews. Nor did he physically harm any Jews, and he continued to take in Jewish refugees. About six thousand Jews were formally baptised into the Catholic Church in order to keep their jobs. Another six thousand asked to emigrate to the USA, and as the Americans were still neutral in this war, Mussolini agreed.

As can be seen, compared to the other Fascist ruling bodies in Yugoslavia the Italians were mild. But the Montenegrins did not see it that way. To them any occupier was seen as an enemy. Montenegrins worshipped God in the Serbian Orthodox manner, spoke Serbo-Croat, and culturally borrowed much from Serbs and Croats, but their independence was fierce nonetheless. One point in Mussolini's favor was that Italy's queen was a Montenegrin. Recognizing this fiery spirit among them, Mussolini allowed the Montenegrins to control their own police, set up village militias and establish a four-battalion auxiliary police force to hunt down Yugoslav soldiers who had yet to surrender.

But the kid glove treatment did not work. On 13 July 1941 Montenegrin peasants rose in revolt, shooting at an Italian Ninth Army truck convoy near Kolasin in the Tara Valley, besieging the Italian garrison at Bioce and surrounding the Italian outpost at Danilovgrad. It was obvious to Italian military intelligence that these were concerted moves by a well-organized guerilla force: the incidents were just too far apart to be otherwise. Mussolini ordered General Pirzio-Biroli the commander of the Ninth Army to send his XIV Corps to crush these guerillas at once. The Italians wondered if British agents were at the bottom of this.

Over the next few days a Carabinieri post at Baranc was overrun, the Carabinieri post at Mojkovac was destroyed, the Bioce garrison broke out and the Danilovgrad troops marched out under a truce. The worst incident was the ambush of an infantry battalion at Podgorica, in which two hundred Italians were killed and wounded. Mussolini now realized he had another war on his hands.

Pirzio-Biroli's strategy was to occupy the mouths of the Zeta and Maraca Rivers with infantry and the Grado Battalion of the San Marco Marines, and then to march the divisions of his XIV Corps into the Veljobrdo Mountains and Trijebac Mountains. The following divisions began winding their way up narrow mountain tracks: Venezia [with attached 72nd CCNN Legion], Taro [with attached 164th CCNN Legion], Pusteria Alpini, Messina [with attached 108th CCNN Legion], Ferrara [with attached 82nd CCNN Legion] and the newly created Alpi Graie Alpini of Major General Girotti. These troops encountered small clusters of badly organized guerillas, and they dispersed them with artillery fire and air raids. An unexpected ally here was the local Moslem minority, who decided it must be open season on Montenegrins, so they murdered them whenever possible.

The Montenegrin rebellion was in fact very poorly organized, and despite being on the run the guerillas launched several attacks in divergent directions. Indeed only when Milovan Djilas, a Communist rabble-rouser, began going from group to group preaching unity, did their activities start to make sense. In the first week in August Major General Bonini's Venezia Division attacked the towns of Lipov, Kolasin and Krnovo, driving out hundreds of guerillas. Following this, Pirzio-Biroli declared Montenegro secure. Mussolini now demanded that the Italians rule the occupied areas with an iron hand.

Of all the instigators of Yugoslavian rebellion against the invaders, two men stood out: Josip Broz and Draza Milhailovich. The latter, a Serb and a Yugoslavian Army colonel, had refused to surrender in April 1941, and had gathered together a band of Serb soldiers, mostly officers, to hide in the mountains of southwest Serbia. In July he felt his 'Officer's Movement' was strong enough to launch attacks, but the target of his aggression was not one of the invader armies, but rather the puppet state of Acimovich. His guerillas began by urging Acimovich's Serb police, frontier guards and factory guards to defect and bring their weapons with them. However, many of Milhailovich's guerillas thought this was a waste of time, especially as thousands of ethnic Serbs in Bosnia-Herzegovina were in dire need of protection from roaming bands of Moslem guerillas and Croat Ustaci.

Broz on the other hand was a Communist, half Serb and half Croat, who after twenty years of speeches had managed to convince about a thousand people to follow him. In the confused situation in spring 1941 Broz seized his chance, creating a guerilla movement by using his Communist cell infrastructure. Knowing that Communism was anathema to the people, most of whom were devout something or other, he denied his connections to Moscow and even downplayed his own Communism, and furthermore he used a nom de guerre instead of his own name. He chose 'Tito', a play on the words "you, do it", in the Serbo-Croat language. At first Stalin in Moscow did not want Tito to act, for in April 1941 Stalin was still at peace with Hitler, but once Hitler invaded the Soviet Union, Stalin changed his mind and urged Tito to rebel against the Fascist occupiers in order to pin down as many Fascist troops in Yugoslavia as possible, and thus keep them away from the Soviet Union. Therefore, while preaching to his guerillas that he wanted to rid his country of the enemy, Tito was in fact under orders from Stalin to do the opposite. When Tito heard of the Montenegrin revolt he sent one of his deputies, Milovan Djilas, to seize control of the various factions there. Meanwhile Tito launched an offensive of his own, and like Milhailovich he chose to begin by trying to convince members of the Serb puppet state to defect.

Another guerilla leader was Kosta Pecanec. A staunch monarchist, he was a politician among the Serb minority in Bosnia-Herzegovina, and his main aim was to protect his Serb neighbors from attacks by Croats and Moslems. His followers took the name Cetniks, an old word often used by Serbs in past history. However, he did the exact opposite of Tito and Milhailovich - he urged his followers to cooperate with Acimovich's state and use that territory as a safe haven.

There was much soul searching among Serbs. Should they follow Tito, Pecanec, Milhailovich or Acimovich? One of Milhailovich's sons joined Tito. Acimovich was supported by the leading classes: lawyers, business owners, academics and priests, but the remainder of the Serb population was divided.

The Germans decided to stay out of this 'Serb Civil War', maintaining only enough troops in the region to show the flag. However, on 29 August 1941 they reminded the Serbs who was really in charge by dismissing Acimovich and replacing him with Milan Nedic, a former Yugoslavian Minister of War. He ordered an immediate offensive against all guerillas. The Germans gave him permission to recruit an army.

This interference by the Germans backfired, for it divided Pecanec's Cetniks into three: those who wanted to continue to support the puppet state and who therefore enlisted into Nedic's new army named 'the Volunteer Corps'; those who realized that Tito had been speaking the truth and therefore joined his ranks; and those who thought Milhailovich had a hold on the truth. Indeed so many of the Cetniks joined Milhailovich's Officers Movement, that their name 'Cetniks' began to be applied to all of Milhailovich's followers.

On 21 September Tito's guerillas (Titoist partisans) took over the town of Uzice close to Milhailovich's stronghold at Ravna Gora. Three days later some Titoists bullied a bunch of Milhailovich's supporters (henceforth known as Cetniks) into leaving the town of Boza. Nedic's propaganda was trying to pry Tito, Pecanec and Milhailovich apart with the use of truths, half-truths and lies, and it was working.

On 11 October the Macedonians decided they could take the oppression by the Bulgarian invaders no longer and they revolted. Tito sent representatives to seize control of the Macedonian rebels.

Near Kraljevo Cetniks killed thirty German soldiers. This sparked an act of cruel retribution. The Germans in Kraljevo executed every adult male in the town whom they suspected of harboring anti-German sentiment, all one thousand seven hundred. Thirty miles away in Kragujevac a band of Cetniks killed ten Germans. The Germans replied by massacring two thousand three hundred Serbian men, women and children. By the end of October in the city of Belgrade, Nedic's capital, his Serbian police together with German police and German SS security police had executed four thousand seven hundred and fifty men and women for treason.

Milhailovich was horrified at the German response, and he called off all attacks, though some hotheads disobeyed him. The Titoists believed they should continue to attack the Germans, regardless of such atrocities, and on 28 October a band of Titoists tried to argue this attitude with a band of Cetniks, but gunplay broke out. The Cetnik-Titoist War had begun.

In response on 1 November Milhailovich ordered an all-out offensive against the Titoist headquarters at Uzice. His point was that if he could not rid Yugoslavia of Fascists he would at least rid his country of Communists. However, the Titoists fought well and quickly reversed the situation by besieging the Cetniks in their own camp at Ravna Gora. During the action the Cetniks captured thirty female Titoists and executed them.

On 11 November Milhailovich contacted Pecanec by radio and asked him to pass on to Nedic that as long as Tito's Communists were a threat he would refrain from attacking Nedic's Serbs or the Germans. Nedic seized this opportunity to join the Cetniks in their fight against the Titoists and he asked the Germans to do the same. They agreed.

As a result in late November Nedic's Volunteer Corps together with two and a third German divisions attacked the Titoists. Tito immediately called off his siege of Ravna Gora and frantically ordered a full-scale retreat across the border into Italian-controlled Montenegro.

Inside the supposedly pacified Montenegro, the local police, auxiliary police and village militias continually failed to report signs of guerilla activity to their Italian masters and certainly took no action. Indeed the Italians suspected that many were in cahoots with the guerillas. Near Kuci an Italian infantry battalion was ambushed and it took two days to fight their way out. On 18 October an Italian truck convoy was stopped by guerillas and the seventy drivers were taken prisoner. The militia in the nearby village of Jelin Dub had obviously not been vigilant. In response Italian troops marched into the village, called the militiamen to formation, picked out ten at random and executed them! This punishment of the militia, an ancient Roman method called decimation, was publicized and it seemed to do the trick. Throughout Montenegro the militia became more vigilant.

However, in late November 1941 the Montenegrin campaign

changed completely as the Titoist partisan army backed into northeast Montenegro, fleeing the Nedic offensive. Tito and Djilas met and the two groups of Serb Titoist partisans and Montenegrin guerillas fused together. Despite his Communism, Tito accepted all races and religions. He even had Italian-speaking Dalmatians and German-speaking Volksdeutsch in his army. Many of his guerillas were women.

This 'invasion' caught the Italian Ninth Army's XIV Corps totally by surprise, for neither Nedic nor the Germans had bothered to inform them that thousands of Titoist partisans were headed their way. An Italian patrol was surprised and captured by Titoists near Nova Varos on the Lim River. A nearby Italian garrison retreated when they witnessed hordes of partisans pour out of the hills. But an Italian infantry battalion at Pljevlja fought back fiercely when the partisans attacked them, and they drove off the Titoists who left three hundred dead on the battlefield.

On 12 December the Italians counter attacked at Drenovo with two divisions - Venezia [and 72nd CCNN Legion] and Ferrara [and 82nd CCNN Legion], and they quickly put Tito's partisans to rout. They missed taking Tito himself by minutes. Indeed the Italian riposte had been so fierce, that Tito decided to return to Serbia, for he'd rather face the Serbs and the Germans.

———————————

In Central Slovenia the Italians had organized a local force, the Anti-Communist Volunteer Militia, to protect the people from Tito's followers. Most of these militiamen served part-time, but there was one full-time unit - the Legion of Death. The day-to-day name for Italian-sponsored Slovenians was 'whites'. The Titoists were referred to as 'reds'. However, Slovenian guerilla bands had also arisen that were anti-Italian as well as anti-Communist, such as the Slovenian Legion of Roman Catholics, the Falcon Legion of Liberals and Socialists, the National League of extreme-right Slovenians, and some smaller bands. The collective name for these was 'blues'.

General Ambrosio and his Italian Second Army took the following course: allow the blues to fight the reds, and let the whites tackle both. The plan worked and actual Italians only suffered if they got in the way.

———————————

Chapter Twenty-seven
The Air-Sea War June-December 1941

Throughout the second half of 1941 Mussolini was directing seven campaigns: in East Africa, where Nasi's die-hards were holding out; in North Africa where Tobruk remained obdurate; in the Soviet Union where his troops were defeating the Red Army; in Albania where his Carabinieri were containing the guerillas; in Yugoslavia where the Montenegrin guerillas had joined with the Titoist partisans; and in the Mediterranean Sea where his naval and air forces battled to retain 'Our Sea'.

Italian coastal depots were often under British air attack and their only real defense was a few flak guns. Italian fighter pilots tried their best, but even the new MC200 fighter plane was barely a match for the British Tomahawk, was proving to be inadequate against the British Hurricane and was totally outclassed by the British Spitfire. The Italians had also produced the Reggiane Re2000 inline engine monoplane fighter, but it showed itself to be even worse than the Mc200, and was soon relegated to provide air support for ships as a catapult-launched aircraft.

Much had been written in the world's press about the great German fighter aces of the Condor Legion that had flown in Spain. Their highest scorer was Werner Moelders with fourteen kills. There had been little publicity about the Italian flyers, but the Italian Colonel Mario Bonzano had gained fifteen kills in Spain. Mussolini knew that his fighter pilots were equal to the world's best, but they needed better machines. Finally, in late 1941 the new 371 mph MC202 and 336 mph Re2001 inline engine monoplane fighters began reaching his squadrons. Now the Italian fighter pilots could compete with their British counterparts.

Northern Italy had easily recovered from the British air raids of the previous year, but their tranquil nights were shattered on 10 September 1941 when seventy-six British bombers arrived over Turin, the largest British raid on Italy to date. Searchlights crisscrossed the sky and flak gunners threw up shrapnel, but the bombers were able to strike the Fiat steel works. Sixteen nights later British bombers struck Genoa and again two nights after that.

Meanwhile the Regia Aeronautica was still bombing Malta, an aerial campaign that had begun on the first day of Italy's entry into the war. Daily flights of SM79s, SM81s, SM84s, CA133s and CA111s flew the short span of ocean between Sicily and the islands of Malta and Gozo. One of their opponents was the British fighter pilot Sandy Robagliatti, an ethnic Italian. Another was John L. Lynch, an American who had tired of waiting for Roosevelt to make up his mind, and had joined the British Royal Air Force as a fighter pilot.

Savoia Marchetti had a new dive-bomber, but it failed miserably. Mussolini swallowed his pride and took Major Cenni's advice and bought the German JU-87 Stuka dive-bomber. One reason he was willing to bend his nationalism in this instance was that the Stuka could hit ships, and Mussolini knew that the sea campaign was the most crucial. If he lost control of the sea, he would lose Italy.

Yet Mussolini's naval forces were offered an opportunity that they failed to seize. Come June 1941 the ships of the British Royal Navy in the Mediterranean were either licking their wounds from the Crete evacuation or were tied up fighting the French off the coast of Syria. In April and May British warships had shelled the Libyan coast twelve times, but in June the British were noticeable by their absence from that shore.

Yet the main Italian battle fleet did not sail during this time, preferring to leave the naval war to smaller forces. The Italian admirals were steeling themselves for another major encounter, but the city of Trieste shipyards had not finished repairing the battleships Littorio and Conte di Cavour, and the new La Roma was not yet completed. This still left the battleships Giulio Cesare, Caio Duilio, Vittorio Veneto and Andrea Doria ready for action. Yet the admirals would not budge. They missed a major opportunity.

On 24 June German planes sank the New Zealand light cruiser Auckland off Tobruk. On 29 June Major Cenni in one of the recently delivered Stukas sank the Australian destroyer Waterhen. On 11 July other Italian Stukas annihilated the British destroyer Defender. On 20 July the famous Italian destroyer Circe sank the British submarine Union.

Italian submarines continued to try valiantly, but their poor training and shoddy equipment placed them in serious jeopardy. In June the submarine Salpa was sunk by the British submarine Triumph, and while attacking a convoy the Glauco was sunk by the British warship Wishart. In July the Jantina was sunk by the British submarine Torbay.

On the evening of 21 July Italian spies reported a British convoy of six merchant vessels leaving Gibraltar for Malta. In the Atlantic, where the British only had to worry about the German Navy and the Luftwaffe and a handful of Italian submarines, a convoy of six ships would have had an escort of two small warships at most. However, in the Mediterranean this convoy would have to run the gauntlet of the Regia Marina and Regia Aeronautica and a few Luftwaffe planes. It was evident that the British admirals had a new found respect for the Italians, for they chose to escort these half dozen ships with none other than the battleship Nelson, cruisers Edinburgh, Manchester and Arethusa and several destroyers. On the morning of 23 July Italian planes struck the convoy, Stukas bombing the destroyer Fearless into a ruin, and SM79s torpedoing the Manchester. That evening Italian planes returned to cripple another destroyer, Firedrake. After nightfall Italian MAS boats charged the convoy - MAS532 and MAS533 managed to dodge heavy shells to torpedo a merchant ship. Yet the British accomplished their goal, namely resupplying Malta.

On 27 July Doglio in his MC202 was shot down over Malta in a dogfight. A famous aviator from before the war, he had shot down seven fighters in this conflict.

––––––––––

Teseo Tesei had yet to inflict damage on the enemy with his pigs, which the Italian admirals had started to believe were expensive accident-prone toys, but they gave him and the 10th MAS Flotilla one last chance. A tiny flotilla of sixteen craft appeared in the darkness just off Malta: specifically the submarine Diana, ten motor launches, an electric boat, MAS451 and MAS452 and two of the precious pigs. The swell was so rough that it swamped a launch and the electric boat so quickly that the crew of the Diana thought these men had drowned, but surprisingly during the night they were picked up by a British warship. When interrogated they refused to talk, but their very presence alerted the British that something was up and the harbors of Malta were alerted.

Hours later during this dark night British warships ran into the remaining nine launches and shot them to pieces. The pig jinx seemed to be at work again. However, the two pigs had survived with two men riding on each, and as they approached the harbor of Valetta in Malta they submerged, but only to find a metal net blocking their path. Tesei himself was on one pig, and he chose to use his pig to blow a hole in the net to allow the other through, though he was quite aware there might not be enough time for he and his partner Petty Officer Alcide Pedretti to swim to safety. They settled their pig into position, set the timer and swam away as swiftly as possible. The explosion did indeed rip the net apart, but it also flung Tesei and Pedretti around like sea horses, collapsing their lungs and crushing their brains. Their sacrifice proved to be for naught, because the second pig failed to get through the small hole in the net.

Come dawn the two MAS boats were strafed by no fewer than thirty Hurricanes. Twelve of the twenty-six sailors were killed, but the boats remained afloat. Ten Italian fighters arrived in the nick of time. They traded three MC200s for one Hurricane. The MAS boats escaped.

The raid had cost the lives of forty-one seamen and had gained nothing.

––––––––––

On 30 July Italian Stukas crippled the submarine Cachalot. Later that day the destroyer Achille Papa raked the Cachalot with gunfire and then rammed her until she sank. The British crew was rescued. Also in July the Italian submarine Bianchi was sunk by the British submarine Tigris.

In August Italian mines claimed the British submarine P32. Also in August the Italian submarine Tembien was rammed and sunk by the British destroyer Hermione. The Italian destroyer Partenope sank the British submarine P33.

In September Italian naval losses continued to be serious: the light cruiser Bolzano was bombed at Messina harbor losing twelve killed and thirty-four wounded; a convoy was devastated by a British air attack; the destroyer Albatros was sunk by a British submarine; the submarine Maggiore Baracca attacked a convoy, but was mortally damaged by the British destroyer Croome; the submarine Fisalia assaulted some merchant ships, but was sunk by the British corvette Hyacinth; the submarine Adua did not survive her engagement with the British warships Legion and Gurkha; and the submarine Smeraldo was lost probably to a mine. The ocean liners Oceania and Neptunia, which were carrying six thousand five hundred Italian soldiers, were both torpedoed and sunk by the British submarine Upholder. Fortunately only three hundred and eighty-four men died. The troopship Andrea Gritti was sunk by British planes and went down with three hundred and forty-seven men.

Commander Junio Valerio Borghese and his submarine Scire had already failed in two attempts on Gibraltar harbor, and despite the pig jinx the Italian admirals approved one more raid, and on the night of 10 September 1941 Borghese took the Scire to within 7,000 yards of Gibraltar and launched three pigs on a one-way mission. The pigs silently slid beneath the waves and made their way under the port's defenses. Then the six crew members silently placed the three pigs under two oil tankers and a merchant ship, and then the six men swam away. The explosions sank both tankers and crippled the merchantman. The British were taken completely by surprise, and thinking a submarine had done the damage they depth charged the waters. Two pig crewmen were killed by the concussion. However, the four survivors swam to the coast of Spain. Franco's Spanish police interned the four briefly, then allowed them to return to Italy. Tesei's faith in the pig had finally been vindicated.

The sea war was having political consequences that Mussolini did not like. It was dragging the USA into the war. So far there had been three types of Americans who had become involved in the war: the unlucky, the volunteers, and those in the armed forces.

The unlucky had begun to suffer on 3 September 1939 when a British passenger liner, the Athenia, was sunk by a German submarine and twenty-eight innocent American passengers had been killed. A year later a US merchant ship was sunk by the Germans. By October 1941 three more had been sunk. These were the unlucky.

The volunteers were those Americans who on an individual basis had joined the British and Canadian armed forces to wage war against Fascism. By 1940 over seven thousand had done so. Indeed by 1941 the British had enough American fighter pilots to form three all-American squadrons. Others like Lance Wade and John L. Lynch flew in British squadrons. Joe McCarthy from Brooklyn was such a good bomber pilot, the British put him in their all-star squadron. Henry Ferris signed up as a medical orderly with the RAF, but the British assigned him to a commando unit.

These Americans served with not only the knowledge of the US government, but with its assistance! In fact most of the American pilots were trained by British and American instructors in the USA at Tulsa, Dallas, Glendale and Bakersfield.

Then there were those in the American armed forces. In 1939 US Navy warships began escorting convoys bound for Britain, at first just a few miles into the Atlantic, but by 1941 they were coming half way across, to rendezvous with a British escort. US warships and aircraft were also ever on the lookout for German and Italian submarines, and when they found them they radioed the British to 'come and get 'em'! American pilots and other technical personnel were also loaned to the British, legally speaking as 'observers'. One of the 'British' pilots who found the German battleship Bismarck at sea was in fact an American 'observer'.

Beginning 30 March 1941 the US Navy began to arrest German and Italian merchant ships! During this period the USA committed several acts of war against Germany and Italy, but wisely Hitler and Mussolini turned a blind eye, for the American public was still blissfully ignorant of their true involvement in this war.

But it was only a matter of time. On 4 September 1941 a German U-boat commander became tired of watching the destroyer USS Greer reconnoiter for British bombers, so he fired a brace of torpedoes at her. He missed. In response the Greer dropped depth charges and missed. A day later a U-boat sank a US merchant vessel. On 11 September President Roosevelt ordered US forces to shoot on sight at any unidentified submarine in the Atlantic: a de facto declaration of war on Germany and Italy. Just four days later the destroyer USS Kearsarge, while protecting a convoy, sensed that a German U-boat was trying to attack, and she went to battle stations - but a German torpedo plowed right into her. The explosion damaged the warship, killed 11 American sailors and wounded others.

On 30 October 1941 a U-boat torpedoed the destroyer USS Reuben James. She quickly slid beneath the freezing waves, and of her 160-man crew, only 45 were rescued.

In October the Italian submarine Marconi disappeared. She had seven confirmed kills in her brief operational life.

———————

Italian planes continued to bomb Malta. It was frustrating work for these flyers, who thought surely the island would sink under the weight of their bombs. Lieutenant Colonel Carlo Romagnoli, an Italian fighter ace in the Spanish Civil War, was now leading fighters to escort the bombers to and from Malta. They braved the flak thrown up by British and Maltese gunners and fought off British fighters. On 4 September 1941 his group of MC200s had just completed another mission and had almost reached Sicily with nearly empty fuel tanks, when they were jumped by eighteen Hurricanes. Romagnoli's aircraft was blasted by machine gun bullets and went straight down into the sea. He probably never knew what had hit him.

On 24 September another British convoy left Gibraltar for Malta. The last such convoy had suffered, and the British admirals did not want to take chances with this one. They assigned an escort, the size of which was unprecedented. No British convoy passing through a purely German gauntlet had ever been so well protected. The amount of respect the British now had for the Regia Marina and Regia Aeronautica was obvious, for they assigned the battleships Nelson and Rodney, battle cruiser Prince of Wales, carrier Ark Royal, five cruisers and eight destroyers as escort to just nine merchant ships.

On the 27th this convoy's battle began as Italian and German pilots swooped in, ignoring the British carrier-borne Fulmar fighters, the wall of flak, air turbulence, the buffeting by aerial explosions and the risk of collision in order to concentrate their minds on the swerving vessels. The Italian pilot of a new SM84 trimotor bomber dropped his torpedo perfectly on target towards the Nelson, and then he began a slow climb under pummeling fire from flak guns, while his rear gunner called out that the torpedo had spiraled straight into the bowels of the mighty warship. The Nelson remained afloat, but her escorting duties were over for a while. Nightfall brought no respite as Italian and German planes continued to bomb the ships in darkness, using the white wakes as target indicators. One merchant ship was sunk. Next day the convoy reached Malta.

———————

By October 1941 it was still impossible to foretell whether the Mediterranean would remain Mare Nostrum or become Mare Britannica. This month the Italians lost the destroyer Pleiade (640 tons) to an air strike off Tripoli, the Altair and Aldebaran (both 640 tons) to mines off Athens, and the submarine Ferraris after her surface battle with the British destroyer Lamerton. The Italian submarine Malaspina was sunk by an Australian Sunderland flying boat.

British warships only resumed bombardment of the Libyan coast on 19 October, but they no longer did this with impunity. German U-boats had recently entered the Mediterranean and they torpedoed two British destroyers. German planes sank a British destroyer.

October was a good month for Sergeant Teresio Martinolli and his new MC202: on the 4th he shot down a Hurricane; on the 19th he severely damaged two more; on the 22nd he shot down another; and on 1 November he shot down a Blenheim and crippled another.

If the British were forced to use battleships to protect a handful of merchant vessels, the Italians had an opposite problem: too few admirals who were willing to risk their battleships. This is one reason why by the end of October 1941 of the last two hundred Italian merchant ships to sail, forty had been sunk. But there was another reason. The British had broken the Italian naval code and were able to intercept a convoy at will.

On the evening of 8 November in the Mediterranean one German and four Italian merchant ships and two Italian oil tankers were trying to sneak past the British and reach Libya. They were escorted by the light cruisers Trieste and Trento and some destroyers. However, they were intercepted by the British light cruisers Aurora and Penelope and destroyers Lively and Lance. The Italian destroyers charged at once, despite 6inch shells falling among them immediately. The Grecale (1,417 tons) was hit and badly damaged, and the Fulmine (1,220 tons) was blown apart by shellfire. The Libeccio stopped to pick up survivors, but was struck by a torpedo. The crew had not known the British submarine Upholder was in the vicinity. Now the British cruisers kept the Italian cruisers busy, while the British destroyers ran amuck among the convoy, sinking every ship. The crew of the Trieste and Trento were no doubt glad to survive the fight, but they were surely ashamed that they had lost all their charges, which they were supposed to protect.

On 21 November the light cruisers Trieste and Duca degli Abruzzi were attacked by aircraft. Flak gunners strained their eyes to see the tiny targets, and the captains ordered their ships to swerve to avoid falling bombs. No one saw the British submarine Utmost, which slipped in to torpedo both of them. Damaged severely both vessels returned to port.

By the end of 1941 after eighteen months of war Mussolini had lost two hundred and fifty merchant ships either captured or sunk.

The British could not read German naval signals and this is one reason why the U-boats in the Mediterranean had better success than their Italian counterparts. On 12 November a U-boat sank the British carrier Ark Royal. On the 25th a U-boat torpedoed the battleship Barham, which rolled over and sank with the loss of eight hundred and sixty-two crewmen. Two nights later a U-boat sank an Australian sloop and an Indian sloop.

Mussolini kept his eye on the American situation. On 13

November the US congress authorized the US Navy to place guns and gunners on all American merchant vessels, and furthermore the congress removed all war zone restrictions. Thus armed American merchantmen could now sail anywhere to aid the British. At the beginning of December U-boats sank two American merchant ships.

———————

Chapter Twenty-eight
Tobruk

In April 1941 the British managed to outrun Rommel's offensive in Libya, but left behind a garrison at the port of Tobruk. Rommel's Germans and then the Italians failed to take Tobruk, and they settled down into a siege.

The Italian command was divided into rear-echelon support troops, flak units, coastal artillery and the front line echelon. The latter consisted of Lieutenant General Enea Navarini's XXI Corps, Lieutenant General Gastone Gambara's XX Corps and Rommel's Afrika Korps. Gambara was a fascist who had proven his spirit in Ethiopia, Spain, the French Alps and Greece.

XXI Corps contained Major General Bortolo Zambon's Brescia Division, Major General Antonio Franceschini's Pavia Division and Major General Stampione's Trento Motorized Division, all currently besieging Tobruk. The corps also contained Major General Fidele de Giorgis' Savona Division (reinforced), manning the frontier defenses near Halfaya Pass, and Major General Alessandro Gloria's Bologna Division in reserve. Gloria had led the Modena Division in the assault against the French and the Greeks. Some members of the Brescia and Savona had served with the Sila Division in Ethiopia.

Gambara's XX Corps included Major General Mario Balotta's Ariete Armored Division and Major General Alessandro Piazzoni's Trieste Motorized Division. The latter was beefed up with the 9th Bersaglieri Regiment. This corps was in reserve, but Gambara had loaned out a few troops here and there to the frontier and to Tobruk.

Rommel's Afrika Korps controlled the 5th Light Division, which he had brought with him from Germany, which would soon be redesignated the 21st Panzer Division. He also had the 15th Panzer Division, which had been in Libya since April, and he was currently receiving the Afrika Light Division. Hitler hit upon the idea of combing his armed forces for men who had desert experience, including some who had served in the French Foreign Legion, and they were sent to Rommel. All Rommel's men were in reserve, except a few that he had loaned out to the Italians.

The British approached the new front line on the Libyan-Egyptian border in May 1941, ostensibly to rescue Tobruk, but the Savona Division easily repelled them. It was obvious this was only a probe, but Mussolini's propaganda machine made it into a great victory. British propaganda all but ignored their defeat. The real British offensive came in June when the Indian 11th Brigade [of the Indian 4th Division] and the British Guards Brigade and 4th Brigade attacked through Halfaya Pass. The Savona's artillery inflicted losses on the advancing Britons and Indians, and then the Germans counter-attacked with a few tanks: the Mark III upgraded with a short 50mm gun; and the 8 feet 7 inch tall 20-ton Mark IV armed with a short-barrel 75mm gun. The Italian 1st Artillery Regiment also counter-attacked! As a rule artillery does not attack unsupported, but this unit was equipped with Semoventi 47s and some new Semoventi 75s. These were self-propelled assault guns fully encased in armor. The 47mm was a passable gun, but the 75mm was outstanding. At 13 tons, with a speed of 20mph and a height of just 6 feet the Semoventi 75 could show up in the most unlikely places. This Italian weapon proved to be a winner at once, and even the Germans were impressed. Its weakness was that it could not absorb punishment, because its frontal armor was only 30mm and in other places as thin as 10mm. E. g. in this assault a British artillery shell landed on top of one of them, blowing it apart and killing two of the three crewmen. The wounded survivor Major Leopoldo Pardi, should have crawled out and sought medical attention, but he found the gun to be in working order and he continued to man the gun alone. After four days of battle the British withdrew. Again the British press played down the affair, whereas the German and Italian propaganda machines touted their victory.

Meanwhile at Tobruk the Australians had tried to break out, but they were quickly shut down by the Italian Trento, Brescia and Pavia Divisions. The British press made excuses about this defeat.

There was another affair in Libya at this time. Jalo Oasis was in the south hundreds of miles from nowhere and its small Italian garrison most likely thought the war had passed them by. Suddenly, they were surrounded by two British, one Indian and one Sudanese battalions with South African armored cars. The Italians surrendered. To resist would have been pure suicide.

At Tobruk the British brought in reinforcements by sea, including commandos to patrol the perimeter at night. Despite the commandos' elite status, the ordinary Italian infantrymen who encountered them saw nothing 'elite' about them. Night and day, the summer's oppressive heat controlled everything at Tobruk, and flies, sandstorms and disease were major concerns for both sides.

General Ettore Bastico was now the supreme commander of Axis forces in North Africa. Navarini doubled as commander of XXI Corps and as Bastico's chief of staff. Italian spies reported to Bastico that the Tobruk garrison had begun to rotate its Australians back to Egypt by sea, and was replacing them with fresh units. In fact the British brought in General Ronald Scobie's British 70th Division, a Polish brigade and a Czech battalion, and retained a couple of Australian battalions. This was the first British infantry division to see action anywhere in well over a year.

The hot summer gave way to a moderate autumn, and then by November the desert wind was cold. 16 November brought a cold rain that ruined the sandy roads and turned airfields into muddy pools.

The Italians of the Ariete were damp and cold in their tents or they tried to sleep inside cramped armored vehicles. The division had been restructured and now consisted of four regiments: a tank regiment of ninety-nine M13s; a reconnaissance regiment (made up of thirty-three L6 tanks, an armored car company and a Bersaglieri motorized battalion); the 8th Bersaglieri Regiment of two motorized battalions; and an artillery regiment of thirty-two towed 75mm guns and sixteen Semoventi 75s.

The 15th and 21st Panzer Divisions each contained eighteen Mark IVs, seventy Mark IIIs, thirty-five Mark IIs, some Panzerjaeger I tank destroyers, a regiment of panzergrenadiers and a regiment of self-propelled guns (most of them makeshift hybrids of a Mark I or II chassis with an artillery piece atop). The Afrika Light Division was strictly a panzergrenadier formation.

The British had renamed their Western Desert Force. Now known as the Eighth Army, it was in the hands of General Cunningham, the victor in East Africa. He had with him several Ethiopia veterans including Major General Godwin-Austen to whom he gave XIII Corps and Major General Frank Messervy, who had led an Indian brigade at Keren, to whom he gave the Indian 4th Division. He also received Lieutenant General Charles Norrie, a tank expert from Britain, to command XXX Corps. Cunningham planned to use the experience he had gained fighting the Duke d'Aosta, but unfortunately for him this would be an armored clash, nothing like the Ethiopian campaign. However, Churchill wanted a victorious British general to lead the offensive, and Cunningham was the only one in existence. Neame and O'Connor were in Italian prison camps, and Wavell had been dismissed and sent to command forces in India, where there was no war. This was a dirty shame, for Wavell was paying for others' mistakes. Wavell's chair of Middle East Commander had been taken by another Indian Army general, Claude Auchinleck. The 'Auk" had fought in World War I and against the Fakir of Ipi on the Indian Northwest Frontier, and had then seen action in Norway in 1940.

In the early rainy hours of 17 November 1941 the Savona's forward listening posts at Halfaya Pass, Sollum, Sidi Omar and Bardia were completely annihilated by Indian and British infantry of Major General Frank Messervy's Indian 4th Division. As the first combat reports came in to de Giorgis, he passed them on to Navarini, who sent them to Bastico, so that his senior staff officers could gather to discuss their meaning. By mid-morning de Giorgis was reporting that his Savona infantry, combat engineers and artillery were fighting for their very lives. As the day progressed it became apparent that the British were launching a major offensive. The British called it Operation Crusader.

Towards late afternoon German reconnaissance vehicles probing the open desert south of the Savona sighted an entire British armored division of two brigades advancing westwards.

Rommel was currently visiting Greece, but he flew back at once, and after being briefed on the day's events he ordered his Afrika Korps to counter attack the British armor on the morrow. Bastico agreed and loaned him the Ariete Armored Division.

To keep up with rapidly advancing armor technology the British had replaced their Matildas and first generation Cruisers with the Crusader Cruiser, which at 19-tons with 40mm armor, only 7 feet 4 inches high and a speed of 27mph was a major improvement. Yet it was armed with the same old 2pounder gun that had proven inadequate. Worse, the tanks had only been issued with armor piercing solid shot for anti-tank work, whereas Italian and German tanks carried high-explosive shells too for anti-personnel work.

The US Army generals knew they would soon be involved in armored warfare. They already had their own tanks which were invincible, or at least that is what US propaganda said, but after American officers had observed the British in action, the Americans looked at their own tanks and concluded they were crap. The result was a new American tank, the Stuart. It was armed with an excellent 37mm gun in a turret and no fewer than five machine guns, but it was small at 12.3 tons with a short range, and yet was 8 feet 3 inches high. Still, any tank in the desert was a treasure, and because the British could not build Crusaders fast enough, they had bought the Stuart. The British troops in the desert took one look at it and ripped out three of the five machine guns to save room and weight, and they added extra fuel tanks to give it range. It's only advantage over the Crusader was that its main gun could fire high explosive shells. They nicknamed this new version the 'Honey' [American slang for sweetheart].

The British hit upon another idea, dividing their tanks into 'tank brigades' and 'armored brigades'. The former were ordered to protect the infantry and were equipped with Matildas, Valentines, old Cruisers and captured Italian M11s and M13s. Valentines were 7 feet 5 inches high, weighed 17 tons and were not as well armored as Matildas. The new 32nd Tank Brigade was sent by sea to Tobruk.

The 'armored brigades' would operate independently and needed to be fast so they were equipped with Honeys and Crusaders.

Rommel's armored counter-attack began on the morning of the 18th, and early on some Italian M13s of the Ariete encountered one hundred and twenty Crusaders of the British 22nd Armored Brigade of Major General W. H. E. Gott's 7th Armored Division. At once the

Italians turned and ran, and the British chased after them, joking among themselves that the stories they had heard of Italian cowardice must be true. Suddenly the M13s stopped, turned and opened fire, and simultaneously Italian 47mm anti-tank guns that were hidden in sparse clumps of vegetation opened fire on the British from the flanks, and then Semoventi 75s came out of depressions in the sand and fired their 75mm guns point-blank into the British. The Ariete Armored Division had suckered the British into an ambush. The British brigade managed to back out and retreat, but they left a quarter of their new tanks on the field broken, busted and burning.

The Ariete knew that if they could stop the British 22nd Armored Brigade, and they had, then obviously the Germans with their two panzer divisions could stop the other brigade of the 7th Armored Division, namely the British 7th Armored Brigade, and that would be the end of Cunningham's offensive. Therefore it came as a shock when they heard that the Germans had turned and run for real! Further bad news reached them: the brigade the Germans had run from was the hitherto unseen 4th Armored Brigade. Because no one had challenged the British 7th Armored Brigade, it had driven onto Sidi Rezegh airfield along with some South African armored cars and was shooting up the place. Only three German planes escaped by taking off in a spray of mud.

Navarini had to think quickly to stave off disaster. He saw on the map that a thirty-foot high ridge overlooked the airfield, and he ordered it to be occupied at once by a scratch force from his XXI Corps. These Italian infantry and German panzergrenadiers reached it ahead of the British with just minutes to spare. When British and White Rhodesian infantry (of the 7th Armored Division) supported by Bren gun carriers started coming up the slope, Navarini's ad hoc force opened fire and repulsed them. Rommel decided his 15th and 21st Panzer Divisions could be best used to liberate the airfield, but it would take time to reach it.

On the 19th, Day Three of the battle, the Italian/German force on the ridge repelled another British assault, while the remainder of XXI Corps stopped a British attempt to break out of Tobruk. Meantime the Savona at the frontier continued to hold back the Indian 4th Division.

On Day Four Rommel's tanks engaged the British on the eastern approaches to the airfield, but the fight was inconclusive.

On Day Five the Italian/German defenders of the ridge were assaulted by British infantry and thirty tanks of the British 7th Armored Division. Unable to stop the tanks, the defenders simply allowed them through, then closed ranks behind them, and opened fire on the following infantry! The British tanks could have turned around and assaulted the defenders from the rear, but instead they drove on towards Tobruk, hoping to strike the XXI Corps in the rear, but Navarini had been alerted and he had prepared an ambush by using

Italian artillery and anti-tank guns and some German 88mm flak guns manned by members of the Luftwaffe. The plan worked. Not one British tank survived the Italian ambush! Meanwhile Rommel's tanks attacked the airfield from the east again, resulting in a major tank battle. Also this day British and Australian troops at Tobruk made a sortie at the junction of the Italian Bologna Division and the German Afrika Light Division [now renamed 90th Light]. In the wild melee the Italians and Germans fell back, abandoning their wounded and several isolated pockets – upwards of a thousand men. Then they regained their breath and counter-attacked, restoring their position, liberating some of their men and taking several hundred Allied prisoners.

On Day Six Rommel's tanks failed to prevent the British from reinforcing the airfield with their 4th Armored and 22nd Armored Brigades. The tank battle was ferocious - tanks blew up and men screamed with burns and shrapnel wounds. In both Allied and Axis hospital tents the wounded lay, Germans, Italians and Britons together.

Five miles south of the airfield an entire German panzergrenadier battalion with attached armored cars was taken prisoner by South African infantry. In the open desert Major General Bernard Freyberg's New Zealand 2nd Division overran the field headquarters of the Afrika Korps. Rommel was not at home, as he had just been promoted. The Italians complained because the Germans had not yet retaken the airfield. The Germans complained they were running low on fuel.

Lieutenant General Ludwig Cruewell, new commander of the Afrika Korps, conferred by radio with Rommel, who in turn radioed Bastico, and together they decided that Cruewell should not only continue to try to recapture the airfield but should crush the impudent South African infantry to the south. However, the assault on the airfield was rendered unnecessary when that night the British abandoned the airfield and joined the South Africans on a plateau.

As the dawn rays created long sinister shadows across the airfield on Day Seven the Italians on the ridge wiped the grit from their exhausted eyes and stared at the black burned-out vehicles, pieces of shattered equipment, charred bodies and unrecognizable piles of scrap metal, some of which still burned with an ugly black oily smoke. They looked at each other in shock, scared, shaking, almost hysterical, but the enemy had gone and they were eternally grateful to God who had permitted them to see one more sunrise.

Cruewell ordered the Afrika Korps and Ariete to drive the enemy off the plateau, but the Ariete called to say they would be late. Tired of waiting, the Germans attacked in the afternoon. The Ariete had driven as fast as possible, but by the time they reached the plateau it was already a scene of burning vehicles and exploding swirling tornadoes of sand. One Italian column ran into anti-tank guns and twelve M13s were knocked out one right after the other. The Germans lost seventy Mark IIIs to anti-tank guns and artillery. But just as the sun was setting the British jumped into their vehicles and fled eastwards towards Egypt, abandoning the South African 5th Brigade, which was afoot. Ariete's 8th Bersaglieri Regiment then advanced against the South Africans and spent the night rounding up three thousand prisoners.

This evening Rommel urged an all-out advance to chase after the British, but the Italian generals wondered if that might not push the men too much. After all, they had been fighting and laboring for a week at breakneck speed in extremely hazardous conditions. They had kept the noose around Tobruk, repelled an offensive at Bardia and Halfaya Pass, repulsed several attacks on Sidi Rezegh Ridge, recaptured Sidi Rezegh airfield, destroyed an enemy brigade and crippled three British armored brigades. Surely this was enough? Nonetheless Bastico let Rommel sway him. He agreed to let Rommel advance and gave him the Afrika Korps and XX Corps. The latter had just been reinforced by the Giovanni Fascisti Gruppo [Young Fascists Group] of two infantry battalions beefed up with considerable heavy weapons, some L3 tankettes and elements of the 8th and 9th Bersaglieri Regiments].

The defenders of Sidi Rezegh Ridge were still thanking their lucky stars, when this evening they were suddenly attacked by enemy forces from the east. This move by the enemy was totally unexpected. One battalion of the 9th Bersaglieri Regiment and three battalions of panzergrenadiers fought back frantically in the dark. Radio interception and prisoner interrogation convinced them they were under assault by the British 1st Tank Brigade and New Zealand 2nd Division.

Rommel rode in a vehicle to the battle site to see for himself how serious this attack was. He was particularly worried about the Italians, even now still not convinced of their fortitude. He was an incredibly hard man to please. However, once he reached the ridge he saw that the Germans and Italians were holding, though they had no tanks of their own, so he left them to it and went back to planning his armored counter stroke.

On the morning of the ninth day of battle the Afrika Korps launched the counter-offensive and was immediately pinned down by artillery and infantry of Brigadier Harold Briggs' Indian 7th Brigade [of the Indian 4th Division] aided by South African anti-tank guns and air strikes. The Italian XX Corps, leading with Ariete, advanced on the flank, until they encountered a box (fortified camp) defended by Brigadier Dan Pienaar's 1st South African Brigade and British 4th Armored Brigade, which had just received new tanks. The Italians charged the box repeatedly, but could not break through.

While Rommel was directing this part of the battle he was

informed that the German panzergrenadiers on Sidi Rezegh Ridge had fallen back, allowing the New Zealanders to reach Tobruk. The siege had been broken. However, the heroic Bersaglieri still held their part of the ridge. At once he sent a German panzer regiment to their aid, and a few hours later these tanks ran into the New Zealander's rear headquarters and captured it. Fortunately for the 'Kiwis', their commander, Freyberg, was not caught.

And now Bastico lost his nerve and ordered a complete retreat. Rommel was stunned. He stated privately that the brave Italian soldiers deserved better generalship. In response he ordered the Afrika Korps and XX Corps to call off their fight, turn around and attack to their rear towards the New Zealand 2nd Division and the British 1st Tank Brigade.

There was constant bickering in the Allied camp too. Auchinleck came forward to watch Eighth Army in action and to ask why no breakthrough had been made. Unable to hear a satisfactory reply, he relieved Cunningham on the spot and gave the army to Lieutenant General Neil Ritchie. This may have been a harsh judgment on Auchinleck's part, but he was under constant pressure from Churchill to achieve a victory. It was also a controversial decision, for Ritchie was a staff officer and his last command had been that of a battalion in World War I.

By Day Twelve, despite receiving orders to retreat three days earlier, the Brescia, Pavia, Trento and 90th Light Divisions were still standing their ground, preventing the British from breaking out of Tobruk. This evening the Afrika Korps reached the rear of the British 1st Tank Brigade, but the Germans were so exhausted that a brief maneuver by the slow Matildas was enough to stop them.

On the morning of Day Thirteen, after a few hours rest, the Afrika Korps attacked again, by now joined by the equally exhausted Ariete. Only the 21st Panzer Division managed to advance, capturing Ed Duda Ridge, but then fell back and its divisional commander was captured.

Rommel ordered a change in tactics. He directed his tanks to concentrate on the New Zealand infantry and not on the British Matildas. Rommel was always of the belief that tanks should never attack tanks even slower ones. On the morning of Day Fourteen his tankers did as ordered. But unbelievably, while the German recovery units, engineers and support troops were watching their tanks and panzergrenadiers move out, they themselves were struck in the rear, that is from the east, by the South African 1st Brigade, British 1st Tank Brigade and 4th and 22nd Armored Brigades. Some of the German tanks were recalled to meet this new emergency and they reached their base camp just in time to drive off the attackers. It was a close run thing. However, Rommel's plan was working - his tanks took six hundred New Zealand prisoners this day.

On Day Fifteen, 1 December 1941, Rommel demanded that his German and Italian mobile forces make one last superhuman effort. However, the New Zealand commander, Freyberg, had requested permission from Ritchie to withdraw from Tobruk. Ritchie was aware that if Freyberg thought this necessary then it really was, for this New Zealander was one of the greatest fighting men of the war. He granted him permission, and the New Zealanders and Matildas withdrew, leaving Tobruk surrounded again.

Ritchie had failed. Therefore, Auchinleck fired him too, and this time he took over command personally. He ordered the South African 2nd Division to crush the stubborn defenders of Bardia and Halfaya Pass once and for all.

Bastico, who had evidently forgotten about his order to retreat, agreed with Rommel that this was the time to take Tobruk. So on Day Sixteen this great struggle began again, as the infantry of the Bologna, Brescia, Trento, Pavia, Trieste, Ariete and 90th Light Divisions rose up out of the perimeter trenches and charged forward into withering enemy fire, while their artillery pounded the city. Quickly the Italian officers were pinned down by machine gun fire, so they grabbed their radio operators and begged for reinforcements and more support - mortar, artillery and air concentrations on identified strong points. More Italians crawled forward: combat engineers dragging explosives and carrying wire cutters; stretcher bearers to carry away the bleeding; medics to bandage the screaming; priests to comfort the dying; couriers with messages; artillery observers to call in support.

The bitter combat lasted all day, then all night, then all day again and through another night. By Day Eighteen Bastico was forced to conclude there would be no victory at Tobruk. Aerial reconnaissance reported that the British armor was advancing from the frontier again having received a fresh shipment of tanks. Bastico suggested to Rommel that they all should retreat, regroup, resupply and rest, and try again some other time. Rommel, downhearted, agreed.

So now the mad scramble began. Almost all the Germans had access to vehicles and they jumped into them and accelerated towards the west. Those Italians with vehicles did the same, but by far the majority of Italians had walked here and would have to walk back. Advancing British armor nearly caught them in the open desert, but a rearguard, peeled off from the Ariete, stopped the British.

The retreat was an incredible act of endurance, because the long columns were under the ever-watchful eye of Allied planes. Many a German and Italian soldier that had fought courageously was now killed by a bomb while hugging the sand. One of them was the commander of the 90th Light Division. Quite a few Italians were trapped at Bir el Gubi by the Indian 7th Brigade [of the Indian 4th Division]. When Rommel heard that these Italians were staunchly fighting back, refusing to give up, he diverted some German tanks to their rescue. Between them the Germans and Italians destroyed the Indian brigade.

On Day Twenty-one of the campaign the Pavia Division drew the short straw of rearguard duty. They brought the British armor to a halt until nightfall, and then ran like hell. It was easy to navigate in the dark. They just followed the trail of vehicles burned out by Allied air raids. In some the corpses had been fused into the vehicles.

On Day Twenty-six, 12 December, the Italian infantry finally reached the fortress that was the Gazala Line, their goal of sanctuary that they had heard so much about from Fascist propaganda. They found the armored and motorized troops already resting here.

But the men stared in disbelief. The 'Line' was merely a few holes in the sand and a roll or two of barbed wire. In other words it was a propaganda fortress not a real one. The line existed only in the minds of Hitler and Mussolini. They would have shed tears, but were too exhausted with mental strain, so they just fell in a stupor and slept.

These men should have been given weeks if not months to recover. Instead they were given just forty-eight hours, for on Day Twenty-eight they were assaulted by the Allies. On the coastal end of the line the Brescia Division was struck by the New Zealanders. Further inland the Trento Motorized and Pavia Divisions were attacked by a Polish-Czech brigade. Brigadier General Giuseppe Borsarelli di Rifredo of the Trento was killed in an airstrike. On the open desert flank the XX Corps of Major General Francesco la Ferla's Trieste Division and Major General Piazzone's Ariete Armored Division was hit by the British 70th and Indian 4th Divisions. The only Germans up front were a few small battle groups.

That the Italians held here is remarkable, because their units were mere shadows of their former selves: the Ariete was at 10% strength! Yet, they held, though outnumbered nine to one in places. Only on the following day did the enemy break through - Poles pushing back the Ariete's 8th Bersaglieri Regiment - but elements of Ariete and Trieste counter attacked and restored the line.

At the end of Day Thirty Rommel agreed to another retreat, hoping the Allies would outrun their supply lines. Unfortunately panic started to grip the men now. Nazis, who found their transport destroyed or missing, stole vehicles from Italians at gunpoint! Nazis abandoned their fellow Germans too, whom they blamed for the calamity. Fascists behaved equally appalling towards their fellow Italians. Furthermore most German officers did not bother to inform their Italian neighbors they were pulling out. Indeed only come dawn did most of the Italians realize what was going on. Radios were not as plentiful among them as in German units.

The Italians had already abandoned much equipment. Now they had to abandon even more, including engineering and maintenance equipment, tents, artillery pieces, tons of precious supplies, and trucks and tanks that were simply in need of minor repairs or had empty fuel tanks, and saddest of all they had to leave their bedridden wounded and sick. Wearing overcoats they struck out across the cold windy flat desert marching to the west, totally naked to the prying eyes of Allied pilots.

On 19 December Rommel's conscience got the better of him and he ordered his German armor to stop for twenty-four hours to allow the Italians to catch up somewhat, while a rearguard composed of elements of the Ariete Armored and Trieste Motorized Divisions held back the enemy. Then for three days a battalion of Carabinieri paratroopers held back the British at a cost of three hundred Italian casualties.

On December 21 Bastico's bedraggled army reached Beda Fomm. The Axis partners were right back where they had started from nine months earlier.

For mile upon mile as the Allies advanced they picked up Italian stragglers. These Italians sat in the sand, their bellies empty and bloated, their glazed eyes fixed in space, their bodies racked with disease, throats parched, tongues swollen with thirst, minds confused, sense of time and place lost, hopes ridiculed and dreams forgotten, as they waited for death. They had been forced to fight for worthless land with broken down equipment and obsolete weapons, embarrassed when they compared them to German or Allied equivalents. Some Italian officers had shown value, but many only left their tents to relieve themselves from their latest vino binge. On the move Italian officers almost always rode in vehicles and few shared the privations of their men. Some Italian generals had even brought their mistresses with them to the desert! When limited supplies arrived they were first doled out to the Italian mobile formations, then to the remainder on a prestige basis. Italian infantrymen were often forced to beg from passing Germans for the most rudimentary items, including food and water. The real Germans, the decent Germans, shared their last piece of black bread and last drop of water, but the Nazis would laugh at the Italians. As a result discipline among the Italians was poor. The Allies always claimed that a captured German dugout was far cleaner than an Italian one.

Therefore, all things considered it was a miracle that the Italians fought at all, let alone as well as they did. Rommel was famous in the German Army for his strict expectations. He did not exactly throw valor medals to his men like confetti. He believed that courage was the duty of every soldier, but even he could be impressed on occasion. The Germans knew that if Rommel decorated a man, then that man really must have earned it. Rommel awarded bravery medals to several Italians. Nor was Rommel known for lavish praise, but this top German Army infantry expert declared that the Bersaglieri were as good as any German infantry. Rommel's anti-Italian bias had mellowed considerably.

For some the battle was not in fact over, because the Italian and German defenders at the Egyptian-Libyan frontier had never retreated! Under relentless attacks by Indian, British and South African infantry, South African armored cars and British tanks, and under constant artillery salvoes and air strikes, these Italians and Germans held on by the skin of their teeth. De Giorgis held a staff conference that resulted in a decision to hold until the last round or last bite of food. German Major General Schmidt controlled one part of the line with four thousand five hundred combat troops, mostly Italians of the Savona Division, and in mid-December these fellows had been assaulted by three tank battalions, five artillery battalions and six infantry battalions. With but one man for every thirty feet of line his defense was exceptionally weak, but the Italians fought with steadfast courage. Schmidt replaced his infantry losses by throwing in Italian engineers and support troops, and when they were lost he tossed in his one thousand five hundred German rear-echelon personnel. When things became crucial, he gave rifles to Italian and German airmen and sailors and threw them into the line. On 30 December British warships shelled the coastal end of his line. They put up a magnificent effort, but it was not enough and just after New Year 1942, after forty-seven days of hell, Schmidt surrendered.

But De Giorgis with the remainder of the Savona Division and a few Germans were alive and kicking at Lower Sollum and Halfaya Pass in the middle of a waterless mountainous desert. They too had been pommelled by tanks and infantry, and only on 11 January after fifty-six days of battle did Lower Sollum capitulate. Next day de Giorgis surrendered. The last defenders, mostly Germans, threw in the towel on the 17th, Day Sixty-two of Operation Crusader.

The feat of the Savona Division (reinforced) has almost been lost to history. It may not have been Italy's Alamo or Thermopylae, or even Italy's Vicksburg or Mafeking, but it was an incredible feat of endurance under the circumstances. Yet, most so-called scholarly histories of this campaign do not even mention the division by name let alone recount the deed. Rommel had nothing but praise for de Giorgis and his thirteen thousand eight hundred Italians and four thousand Germans, calling the general's performance 'superb'.

But why did they hold? What was the value of their accomplishment? The answer is that they denied the Allies the use of the valuable port of Bardia for eight weeks; and denied the Allies the use of Halfaya Pass for nine weeks; and forced the Allied main thrust to circumvent their positions thus putting the Allies at greater risk of Axis air strikes; and they soaked up a large amount of Allied provisions, supplies and munitions; and they inflicted casualties on the Allies; and they kept considerable Allied forces occupied for two months.

As for the Tobruk siege, it is true that the Axis powers had failed, and the British claimed a great victory here, and rightly so. But herein lies the rub. The British and their allied partners lauded their stand at Tobruk as a tremendous accomplishment and would commemorate it for years, and still do, but by so doing they inadvertently caused praise to fall upon the Italians, for the siege had in reality been an Italian affair. Few Germans had been assigned to the Tobruk perimeter. The besiegers were the Trento, Pavia and Brescia Divisions.

The entire struggle in Libya from 16 November 1941 to 17 January 1942 cost the Axis forty thousand casualties. Allied losses were seventeen thousand seven hundred. The breakdown for the Allies is two thousand nine hundred killed, seven thousand three hundred wounded and seven thousand five hundred missing (Australians, Britons, Cypriots, Czechs, French, Indians, Libyans, Mauritians, New Zealanders, Palestinians (both Arabs and Jews), Poles, Rhodesians (white), Rodriguez Islanders and South Africans (mostly white).

Among the Axis troops the dead numbered one thousand one hundred Germans and two thousand three hundred Italians, the wounded were counted at three thousand four hundred Germans and two thousand seven hundred Italians, and the missing were six thousand one hundred Germans and six thousand Italians. Additionally four thousand Germans and thirteen thousand eight hundred Italians were killed or captured on the frontier.

Statistics can be misleading. On the face of it for every shot German one in four died, but for every Italian hit almost half died. This discrepancy can be explained by the nature of the unit. All the Germans had access to motorized transportation and could be taken to medical facilities much quicker than many of the Italians, who had few or no vehicles. Likewise Germans in retreat could usually take their wounded with them in vehicles. Italians in retreat had to hand carry most of their wounded and many were left behind, and thus fell into the 'missing' category. Furthermore the Italians were not as physically healthy as the Germans owing to poor provisions, and this aggravated their wounds. Additionally Italian medical services were bad in comparison with German. Considering the fact that a German in a truck can escape faster than an Italian on foot, there is evidence that an Italian was not any more likely to surrender than a German. Of all German casualties 57.6% were captured. Of all Italian casualties 54.5% were captured.

———————

Chapter Twenty-nine
War Against the USA

Of all Mussolini's wars the one with the greatest social aspects and ultimately the most damaging results for Italy began on 7 December 1941, for that evening Mussolini and the Italian people heard with astonishment that the Japanese had attacked the USA and Britain. Though an Axis partner Japan had so far not taken part in Italy's wars. But suddenly Japan was at war with Britain, Italy's enemy. Did that mean that Italy as Japan's partner was now at war with the USA too? Mussolini clarified the situation four days later by making a public statement in his typical bombastic style from the balcony of the Palazzo Venezia in Rome. He declared war on the United States. Most Italians heard him over the radio, but for those seeing him in person it was noticeable that the usual frenetic adulation from the crowd was missing this time. The reason was that even the Fascists in the audience reacted to the words with horror. Mussolini saw the response and shortened his speech to five minutes, his shortest ever.

The reaction of the people was logical, because every Italian had a relative or neighbor that had emigrated to the USA. This was especially true of Sicilians and Southern Italians. Some of these emigrants had returned home to serve in the current war and they spoke highly of America. Anyone who did return was always addressed from then on as 'Il Americano'. Many young Italian soldiers had American cousins of military age.

For Italians 'Hollywood' was the window by which they viewed America, no matter that it was all make believe. Every Italian village had its 'Ronald Coleman' and 'Jean Harlow' imitators and the cinema was often the focal point of small town life. As a result every Italian knew that in America the good guys wore white hats and they always won and got the girl. In America everyone was rich with an automobile and a telephone. But now Mussolini was expecting the Italians to kill them.

Returned emigrants began to worry that they might be arrested by Mussolini's political police, the OVRA. Families with a relative in America worried that the FBI would arrest that relative as a spy and throw him into prison like George Raft and James Cagney. A worse concern was that cousin would fight cousin. Pity the Italian grandmother who had an Italian grandson and an American grandson, both of military age. It would be like a disguised civil war.

Of course unknown to the Italian people this 'civil war' was already in its early stages. In Spain Mussolini's Italians had fought anti-Fascist Italians. In Yugoslavia Tito had recruited ethnic Italians from Dalmatia. In 1939 anti-Fascist Italians living in France, Canada, Australia and Britain had joined those armed forces. The first British paratrooper hero was in fact an Italian immigrant. Moreover, of all the Italians taken prisoner by the British so far, no fewer than one in ten, 13,000, had joined the British and were serving as labor troops, i.e. pioneers of the British Army or artisans of the Royal Navy.

The Italian people tried to understand Mussolini's side of the situation. Many had seen the Ethiopian War as a civilizing mission. And many had accepted the war in Spain because the enemy had included Communists. They could certainly see the logic of attacking the Soviet Union, the heart of atheistic Communism. As for the Albanians, well they were surely better off than under King Zog. War against the Greeks was harder to justify. But the Serbs had been in occupation of Italian soil for twenty-two years, had they not, so they deserved what they got. Perhaps war with the British and French was necessary, who with their massive empires and hypocrisy to match had wanted to keep the Italians 'in their place'. And now had come war with America. Even Fascists began to question the wisdom of this move.

There was method in Mussolini's madness, though. The Americans had been sneaking into this war for two years, and the US had made overt acts of aggression against Italy time and again, but for political reasons Hitler, Mussolini and Roosevelt had not publicized this state of camouflaged war. The Japanese onslaught on the Americans had caught Mussolini and Hitler totally by surprise. However, the Japanese had also attacked British Asian bases and both dictators loved this, for it would siphon off British supplies, deny the British much-needed raw materials, and draw away a portion of the British armed forces. This could prove too much for the British to bear and might bring them to their knees. Moreover the Australians and New Zealanders would have to recall their forces in case the Japanese expanded to the southeast, and the South Africans would have to do the same if the Japanese expanded to the southwest. Naturally the Indian Army would have to rush home to defend their soil. Furthermore the British had been dipping into Roosevelt's arsenal of democracy as he called it, and the British were using American weapons against the Italians. Now Roosevelt would have to close his doors to his British client surely, for the Americans could not fight two major wars on opposite sides of the planet at the same time, could they? And if by some miracle they could, they would not be able to continue to supply the British as well. Thus most of Italy's enemies might simply melt away. Mussolini had to encourage the Japanese to continue their offensive, hence his declaration of war. Indeed the gunboat Eritrea and armed banana boat Ramb II that had been in Japanese ports since March were now given orders to support Italian submarines in the Indian Ocean and western Pacific against British and American shipping.

This very moment the Germans were so close to Moscow they

could see the city's factory chimneys. The Soviet Union was obviously about to collapse. Therefore Mussolini laughed at the apprehension visible on his generals' faces. It would never actually come to Italians shooting Americans on the battlefield, of that he was quite sure.

————

Chapter Thirty
The Balkan Cauldron 1942

By late 1941 Yugoslavia was a maelstrom of warfare. It was not just a war of artillery, planes, infantry and horse cavalry, but also a war of throat slitting, massacre, rape, pillage, smuggling, black market extortion, robbery, betrayal, frostbite, pneumonia, disease and starvation. The entire nation was dying.

On orders from Moscow the Titoists killed anti-Communist Russian immigrants wherever they found them. As a result these Russians founded their own defensive force of horse cavalry equipped with items they begged, borrowed and stole from the various armies in the country.

In Croatia part-time Ustaci members were very brave hunting down and arresting 'enemies of the state', such as Jews, but they stayed out of the way of Cetnik and Titoist partisans, because partisans shot back. Bullies do not risk their own lives. They did form two rail security battalions to prevent sabotage. There were also two full-time Ustaci units, the Poglavnik Battalion and the Black Legion, which in theory were raised to hunt partisans, but instead they spent their time 'ethnically cleansing' Croatia, Bosnia and Herzegovina. However, the Croatian government did desire the eradication of the partisans and for this they relied on their fifty five thousand man army, commanded by Field Marshal Slavkovitez Kwaternik, which was divided into five divisions, a horse cavalry regiment and an armored car unit. In addition one regiment and a battalion were serving on the Russian front. Four field regiments of police assisted the army. Acting defensively were the normal police and a police militia of seven thousand five hundred part-timers. Pavelic also had a small air component.

The Italians and Germans got along very well with ordinary Croatians, but not with the Ustaci, and they complained that the Ustaci was undisciplined, cowardly and bloodthirsty. Eventually the Germans demanded that Pavelic dismiss the Black Legion commander Jure Francetic for his unbridled cruelty towards innocent people. Pavelic responded by promoting Francetic!

There was in fact much 'unbridled cruelty' towards innocents in all areas of Yugoslavia. In December 1941 the Serb police rounded up all Jews in Belgrade and marched them to the rail station. Any that protested were shot on the spot. In freezing cold weather these men, women and children were crammed like sardines into freight cars with no heat, no food, no water nor a place to relieve themselves. Those who fainted could not fall, such was the press of standing bodies. Then guards of the German Concentration Camp Service boarded a passenger car and the locomotive began to pull the train of tragedy. Their destination was Zemun, a concentration camp where the Germans put the Jews to work under horrific conditions. Within six months fifteen thousand inmates would be dead.

In those regions 'liberated' by Hungarian forces the majority population of ethnic Hungarians were happy enough, but the minorities were miserable. This produced an uprising by Serbs and Jews, who in the first eight months of occupation killed seventeen Hungarian soldiers. In January 1942 the Hungarian General Ferenc Feketehalmi-Czeydner used these killings as an excuse to retaliate against minorities and anti-Fascist Hungarians. Near Ujvidek his Arrow Cross militia forced five hundred and ninety-two Jews and two hundred and ninety-two Serbs onto a frozen river. Their weight cracked open the thin ice and they fell in and drowned. Those few who climbed onto ice flows were shot. The laughing executioners then walked off in search of more victims. Over the next week they murdered another two thousand four hundred and twenty-five unarmed civilians. Jewish historians claim this was strictly an anti-Semitic exercise, but in truth Serbs, Gypsies and outspoken Hungarian anti-Fascists were also murdered.

At this time Hitler asked Tsar Boris to loan him some Bulgarian troops to hunt partisans in Serbia. The young tsar could hardly refuse. He had already hurt Hitler's feelings by refusing to take part in the war against the Soviet Union. He sent Hitler three divisions.

Hitler's request is evidence that he was already stretching his armed forces too thin. He needed help in Serbia because in January 1942 the Titoist main force, having been rebuffed by the Italian Ninth Army, reinvaded Serbia from Montenegro. The Serb Volunteer Corps and Serb Frontier Guard were caught off balance and they retreated.

The Italians had suspected Tito would do this, once they defeated him, but they did not bother to inform the Serbs, perhaps in anger at not being warned by the Serbs the previous November. Generals can be petty.

The Germans came to the aid of the Serbs as best they could by sending an infantry division and a security division. The latter was smaller than an infantry division and was manned by army soldiers aged thirty-six to forty-five equipped with second-rate material. In a German infantry division the combat-echelon rank and file was aged eighteen to thirty-five, and only rear-echelon troops and officers were older. The Germans also asked for Italian air support. Tito found all this attention to be too much, so he turned around and re-invaded Montenegro again, deciding he would take his chances with the Italians. As his long narrow columns shuffled through snow-covered mountains, Cetnik horse cavalry harassed them.

But the Italians had been keeping an eye on the situation, and they weren't caught napping this time. Their XIV Corps was waiting and as soon as they saw the Titoists crossing the Lim River the Italians attacked near Prijepolje with the following divisions: Venezia [with attached 72nd CCNN Legion], Taro [with attached 164th CCNN Legion], Pusteria Alpini, Messina [with attached 108th CCNN Legion], Alpi Graie Alpini and Ferrara [with attached 82nd CCNN Legion] and after a fierce battle the Italians gained the field. It was soon evident though that the Italians had only been fighting a flanking unit. The climate was so bad that visibility was poor, and Tito's main force had broken through. It was so cold that many Italians were maimed by frostbite.

However, Tito knew it was only a matter of time before the Italians discovered his main force, so in February he chose to reinvade Serbia. He got seventy miles north to Valjevo on the Kolubara River before the Serbs and Germans counter attacked and inflicted a serious defeat on his partisans. Simultaneously the Cetniks destroyed several Titoist camps in the Sinjajevina Mountains.

Once again Mussolini's generals had reported the total destruction of the enemy and once again he accepted their word and announced this to his people and once again his generals were shown to be premature in their judgment, to say the least.

On a warm spring day in early April 1942 near Kolasin in Montenegro a Cetnik unit was attacked by a strong Titoist force using artillery. Pirzio Biroli and his staff of Italian Ninth Army realized that the Titoists were still a powerful force and he chose this moment to launch a major offensive against them. However, now he was willing to coordinate activities with the other Axis partners - the Serbs, Croats, Germans, Bulgarians, Hungarians and even the Cetniks. Naturally this took time to plan and there was much mistrust on all sides, especially by the Cetniks who wondered why they were suddenly being treated like an equal. In order to acquire German participation Mussolini had allowed them to pick the field commander for the international force. Of course they chose a German: Lieutenant General Paul Bader.

On 16 April 1942 the offensive began. The Titoists must have thought the whole world had ganged up on them when they were attacked by planes bearing German, Croatian and Italian markings, and were then assaulted by the following: a large mob of Cetniks, a German security division, ten battalions of Croatian Army and Ustaci, and the Italian XIV Corps - Taurinense Alpini Division, Pusteria Alpini Division, Cacciatore delle Alpi Division [with attached 105th CCNN Legion], San Marco Tank Gruppo and the 1st Alpini Gruppo. The Taurinense was fresh and at full strength having not fought since June 1940.

The plan went well, but the Italians moved slower than anticipated owing to administrative foul-ups and this gave the Titoists a chance to regroup on 3 May and entrench themselves. Bader was hereafter content to use aircraft against them.

On 16 May the Italian garrison at Kolasin reported they were under attack from Titoists, so Italian reinforcements rushed to that sector, outfought the Titoists and drove them off in disarray. In their usual manner the Italians now spent several days congratulating themselves.

———————

Chapter Thirty-one
Italian Victory in Africa

It is quite understandable that at the end of 1941 Bastico's Italians were heartbroken that they had been forced to relinquish everything they had won in Libya and once again hand over the Italian colonist towns of Bardia, Tobruk, Derna and Benghazi to the British. The Germans were also in bad shape for they had come to save the Italians, had they not, and they had failed. It was embarrassing for everyone.

However, Rommel was one of those leaders that were always planning the next battle. Just before abandoning the port of Benghazi he had unloaded thirty new Mark III tanks with long barrel 50mm guns, and on 30 December 1941 he had used them as a rearguard to stop the entire British 22nd Armored Brigade. This gave him food for thought, suspecting the Allies were stretched dangerously thin like a rubber band, and his engineer officers assured him the Allies would not have the docks at Benghazi and Derna in full working order for several weeks.

On 18 January just one day after learning that the garrisons around Bardia had surrendered, Rommel sent a force of tanks and panzergrenadiers against the closest Allied unit, the British 201st Guards Brigade. The Brits jumped into their trucks and fled. This told Rommel that the enemy was indeed spread too thin and had no strength up front. Immediately he ordered the Afrika Korps to launch an offensive. The Italians were astonished, for the Germans were down to their last one hundred tanks.

The Afrika Korps ran straight into a battalion of fifty Crusaders, part of Major General Herbert Lumsden's fresh British 1st Armored Division, and in a fearsome tank battle lasting several hours the Germans devastated the British force. Here Rommel experimented by advancing with field artillery in the lead, including towed 88mm flak guns with Luftwaffe crews. Though these flak gunners were completely unprotected, their 88mm gun was superb and could fire rounds that pierced tanks and blew up infantry. As they fired along a direct trajectory, the enemy did not hear the shells coming in. It was like sniping with a cannon. Within twenty-four hours the entire British 1st Armored Division was on the run. To add to British confusion, Lumsden was wounded in an air attack. The Germans might have advanced as far as Mechili, but on the 25th they ran out of fuel!

Bastico was so convinced that Rommel would extend himself too much that he refused permission for his Italians to follow the Germans. Not until 4 February did he change his mind. His men probably needed the extra time to rest and regroup, anyway. But finally recognizing a winner when he saw one, Bastico increased Rommel's powers, putting him in charge of the new Armored Group Africa (in Italian: Armata Gruppo Africa; in German: Panzergruppe Afrika). Once Rommel had received more fuel, he swiftly advanced to Msus, Mechili and Benghazi, and knocked out or captured ninety-six British tanks, thirty-eight guns and 190 trucks and took a thousand prisoners. Then he halted. Like any professional he knew to quit while he was ahead.

The British used the next three months wisely to rebuild their Eighth Army, which was once again under the command of Lieutenant General Ritchie, but with Auchinleck looking over his shoulder. Equipment arrived from Britain and the USA by ship. Italian possession of the Mediterranean forced these ships to sail across the South Atlantic to South Africa, thence along the East Africa coast across the Red Sea, through the Suez Canal and then along the Egyptian and Libyan coasts to Alexandria, Bardia, Tobruk, Mersah Matruh or Derna, where they were unloaded. The British tank brigades retained their obsolete Matildas and Cruisers, and the armored brigades retained their Honeys and Crusaders.

American observers serving with the British had informed Washington that the Stuart [Honey] was inadequate, so yet another American tank design was approved, the Lee, which was rushed to the British, who could not produce enough tanks on their own. When the Brits saw the Lee at the dockside they were dismayed, for the Lee was huge. Far too heavy for the desert at 27 tons (heavier than the Matilda), it would stick out in the flat desert like a sore thumb because it was 10 foot 3 inches high. It appeared to be a composite of several vehicles in one, a tank built by a committee: a 75mm gun in the hull; a 37mm gun in a turret; and machine guns in a cupola on top of that. It required a crew of six. In order to reduce the height by eight inches, the British dismantled the machine gun cupola. Following other modifications the British named their version the Grant. [Because in 1865 Grant had bested Lee] The men assigned to the tank did like the 51mm frontal armor plate and the fact that unlike British-built tanks they could fire anti-personnel high explosive shells as well as solid shot. But they felt naked because of the vehicle's height.

British troops had complained consistently about the lightweight 2-pounder gun on British tanks and that they had no self-propelled anti-tank guns, so in desperation British troops in the field had created a self-propelled anti-tank gun by placing a 25-pounder field gun on top of a Valentine hull. These "Bishops" were clumsy and tall, but they worked well nonetheless. A hit by a 25-pound shell would blow a German or Italian tank to smithereens. By spring 1942 British factories began to send the Eighth Army 6-pounder guns for their

Crusader tanks and 6-pounder anti-tank guns. Both were vast improvements.

By May 1942 the Eighth Army was holding the Gazala Line with from north to south [i.e. from the coast inland] Major General Pienaar's South African 1st Division, then Major General John Nicholls' British 50th Division, both under orders from Lieutenant General Gott's X Corps. Then further south were Major General Lumsden's British 1st Armored Division and Major General Frank Messervy's British 7th Armored Division, plus the Indian 3rd Brigade and French (anti-Fascist) 1st Brigade all controlled by XXX Corps. British 1st and 32nd Tank Brigades were in reserve. The Eighth Army's support troops came from a host of nations and its air support consisted of British, South African, Australian, Greek, Polish and French squadrons. Without publicity a small unit of Americans arrived to test the Lee tank in battle and gain some experience. At last Italians and Americans would be shooting at each other, something Mussolini promised would never happen.

Facing the Allies was Rommel, whose command had once again been upgraded and was now called Armored Army Africa (in Italian: Armata Corazzini Africa; in German: Panzerarmee Afrika). His main punch was Major General Walther Nehring's Afrika Korps of the 15th and 21st Panzer Divisions, with the 90th Light Division temporarily attached. Nehring had served in Poland, France and Russia. If the Afrika Korps was Rommel's right fist, then surely Lieutenant General Ettore Baldassare's Italian XX Corps was his left fist, containing the Trieste Motorized Division of Major General Arnaldo Azzi, the Ariete Armored Division now led by Major General Giuseppe de Stefanis, and the new Gruppe Cruewell, which was a German all-arms force led by Major General Ludwig Cruewell. Rommel's infantry was divided into two corps. Lieutenant General Benvenuto Gioda's X Corps had the Brescia Division of Major General Giacomo Lombardi and Pavia Division of Major General Franceschini and the 9th Bersaglieri Regiment. Gioda had fought in Ethiopia and on the French border. Lieutenant General Enea Navarini's XXI Corps had the Trento Motorized Division of Major General Carlo Gotti, Sabratha Division of Major General Mario Soldarelli, the new German 15th Guards Brigade of Colonel Menny and the 7th Bersaglieri Regiment. It says a lot for Rommel's current attitude towards the Italians that he allowed Italian generals to command German formations, something he would not have even considered a year earlier.

For reconnaissance Rommel could call upon a German unit, Sonderverband 288, and several Italian armored car companies of the Auto-Sahara Company. There were also some smaller units and a large rear-echelon, mostly manned by Italians.

Bastico retained the Italian Littorio Armored and Bologna

Divisions in reserve. All of the Italian divisions had fought in this desert before, but for the Littorio, which had seen action in Spain, France and Yugoslavia.

Italian armored formations had now received some new M14s, which were little better than the more numerous M13s. The Ariete's artillery was beefed up with twenty Semoventi 75s and eight 88mm flak guns. The Trieste had loaned out an infantry regiment and the 9th Bersaglieri Regiment, but had gained a Bersaglieri battalion and a tank battalion. The Trento had loaned out its 7th Bersaglieri Regiment. The Italians had two hundred and twenty-eight armored fighting vehicles: M11s, M13s, M14s, captured machines, the useless L6s, Autoblinda armored cars and the excellent Semoventi 75s.

The Germans had a mixture of armor. The Mark I had gone, but they still used the Mark II and Sd 231 for reconnaissance. Their tank battalions were armed with Mark IIIs with medium barrel 50mm guns, some better Mark IIIs with long barrel 50mm guns and some very good Mark IVs with short 75mm guns. Their artillery used towed guns, but for anti-tank purposes they had the Panzerjaeger Mark I self-propelled anti-tank gun and a few of the brand-new Lorraine Schlepper, a 75mm self-propelled anti-tank gun. Counting all of these, the Germans possessed about four hundred armored fighting vehicles.

The Axis was ahead of the Allies in towed anti-tank gun design, using the Italian 47mm and German 50mm, and of necessity the 88mm. Only the latter though could knock out a tank at a distance. The British had yet to realize the latter was merely a flak gun manned by Luftwaffe personnel.

––––––––––––

On 26 May 1942 Rommel's Italian and German artillery opened fire on the unsuspecting Allies, and Italian and German planes began to bomb and strafe. Then at the command 'Avanti' the two infantry regiments of the Sabratha Division began a slow run across a half-mile of flat scrub desert until they were pinned down by South African machine guns. The Italian radio operators yelled into their microphones ordering artillery and air support to hit specific enemy locations. Forward artillery observers used radios to fine tune the gunfire. Also crawling along under fire were telephone linesmen, messengers chosen for their agility, stretcher bearers and medics, the latter always working their healing magic as if they were immune to the bullets buzzing past them. The precious combat assault engineers, whom the Italians called 'destroyers', were here as well to blow up obstacles with satchel charges, cut barbed wire and lift mines all in full view of those chattering South African machine guns.

A few miles to the south of the Sabratha's battlefield an identical struggle was taking place as the Trento Motorized Division sent forward its two infantry regiments to assault the South African southern flank. Still further southwards the Brescia's two regiments charged against two brigades of the British 50th Division, and yet further southwards the Pavia's two regiments advanced upon the remaining brigade of the 50th Division.

Meanwhile Rommel's two-fisted armored attack was taking place a full fifteen miles south of the Pavia, as the Afrika Korps and XX Corps drove past the southern flank of the Gazala Line.

But things began to go wrong quickly. First the two-fisted punch was caught by Allied planes, then the Trieste got lost, quite easy to do in a landscape with no landmarks, and then the Trieste unexpectedly ran into Allied troops. During the confusing combat the Trieste officers figured out that instead of bypassing the southern flank of the Gazala Line as planned, they had run into it, where it was manned by the British 150th Brigade [of the 50th Division], which was already under assault from the Pavia Division. The Trieste remained stuck here.

All along the Gazala Line the Italians were pinned down and they soon found to their horror that the Allied infantry was being reinforced by tanks. Italian intelligence had failed to notice the presence of the two British tank brigades. Italian radio operators excitedly called for anti-tank guns. The struggle retained its intensity into the night, the men's scared faces periodically lit by lightning-like gun flashes.

Come dawn the British armor on the open desert flank began to withdraw, thus abandoning two lonely boxes, one manned by an Indian brigade, the other manned by a French brigade. De Stefanis trimmed a battle group of all arms from his Ariete and sent it southwards into the open desert to attack the French box, which was at Bir Hakeim (Chief's Well). As the Italians approached the Frenchmen, they were met by a truly fierce response from machine guns, mortars, anti-tank guns, flak guns and artillery. They also found the ground strewn with landmines. Several M13s and M14s were knocked out, though they did overrun a trench manned by the French Foreign Legion. In late morning the Italians pressed on and this time the Italian assault leader had his M14 blown up beneath him. Though in shock he climbed out, but rather than run to the rear, as one would expect, he remained in the path of bullets and shrapnel until he could hail a passing tank and hitch a ride. But within minutes this tank too blew up beneath him. Still alive, he acquired yet a third tank and this too was blown up beneath him. Severely wounded by now and under fire he had no option but to surrender.

Meanwhile this morning the Afrika Korps clashed with the British 7th Armored Division, and by afternoon the German tanks had defeated the British, had broken into their rear and had captured Major General Messervy, but they were then stopped by a counter attack by Lumsden's British 1st Armored Division from the east and south and by the 1st Tank Brigade from the west. Messervy took advantage of the confusion among the Germans and he escaped. The forward elements of the 21st Panzer Division were royally chewed up and Nehring had to order a withdrawal to the southeast to seek the safety of open terrain.

Rommel's officers tried to put the two days into perspective: they had destroyed hundreds of British armored fighting vehicles, had taken a thousand prisoners, had pushed back the famed Desert Rats of the 7th Armored Division, and had come within thirty miles of the Allied land supply route. At the moment Rommel was using 88mm guns to hold off the British armor.

Rommel decided to continue the attack against the British armor, while the Ariete crushed the French and Indian boxes. As directed, de Stefanis sent against these Indians his 132nd Armored Regiment and the Semoventi 75s of the 132nd Artillery Regiment with his 8th Bersaglieri Regiment following behind the armored vehicles. The defending Indian 3rd Brigade [two thirds Indians and one third British] fought for a few hours then dispersed into the desert. The Italians took six hundred British and Indian prisoners, but as they had no provisions for them, Rommel approved that they could be set free! To the prisoners' astonishment, this was done.

By Day Four of Rommel's offensive the fighting on the Gazala Line had reduced in intensity somewhat, but the Sabratha was losing heavily and the Trieste was still engaged at the southern tip of the line. A violent sandstorm put an end to the shooting for a while as both sides lay flat, their faces covered. Perhaps this was God reminding them he was still in charge?

To the southeast of the Gazala Line the armor of both sides fought a sort of mechanical gladiator contest. When some Ariete tank crews joined this fight they could only see out of narrow slits and their vision was further curtailed by sand swirling from turning vehicles, explosions of sand and shrapnel, smoke from burning tanks and dark engine exhaust fumes. In fact most tanks on both sides drove around blindly wasting precious fuel.

Rommel was aware his vehicles were low on fuel and water, and unfortunately his supply trucks could not drive the forty miles straight to his forward dumps, but had to detour a hundred miles in order to remain clear of the French artillery at Bir Hakeim and avoid the belt of mines between Bir Hakeim and the Gazala Line. Not only did this reduce his supply turnaround time, but it placed the trucks in full view of Allied planes for a longer period. Bir Hakeim had really become a serious nuisance.

Rommel demanded that Baldassare take his entire XX Corps and destroy the French once and for all. The Italian general went to see for himself, accompanied by his chief of artillery Major General Guido

Piacenza and his chief of engineers Colonel Vittorio Raffaelli. These officers were some of the few that had earned respect from the ordinary Italian soldiers. The first order from this trio was for the engineers of the Trieste to lift the landmines between Bir Hakeim and the Gazala Line. The engineers obeyed the order, knowing that mine lifting in good visibility with plenty of time and no ground vibrations was still a deadly business, but in the middle of a battlefield and carrying on into the night without lights it would practically be suicide.

Unbelievably by the dawn of Day Five Trieste's engineers had opened a path wide enough for two trucks at a time, and at once Axis supply vehicles began using this much shorter route, though the bottleneck made them vulnerable to Allied aircraft.

As for the French, Baldassare wanted to know why they had not been crushed yet. The Ariete staff officers replied that by the end of Day Four the Ariete had lost thirty-two tanks and six Autoblinda armored cars at Bir Hakeim. Each night the 8th Bersaglieri had put out patrols searching for gaps in the perimeter minefield. Each day Italian and German planes plastered the French camp.

On Day Five the French counter attacked in Bren gun carriers and battled with the 8th Bersaglieri. After a few hours both sides retreated. Late on Day Five under Baldassare's direction Ariete's tanks charged again and were met by Bren gun carriers, but soon the French thought better of it and withdrew into their camp.

On Day Six as the Trieste's engineers cleared more paths for the supply trucks, the remainder of the Trieste disengaged from the British 150th Brigade. This was not what Rommel wanted, and in bitter frustration he arrived at the Trieste to personally lead an assault on the 150th Brigade using the Trieste Motorized and 90th Light Divisions, plus most of Ariete and also the panzergrenadiers of the 21st Panzer Division. The combat was frenzied, but by the end of Day Seven Rommel had destroyed the British brigade.

However, Baldassare was having no luck cracking the defenses of Bir Hakeim. On Day Eight the French counter attacked again with a truck column of legionnaires and Pacific Islanders. An Italian truck and tank column met them and both sides machine-gunned each other.

Baldassare sent emissaries to ask the French to surrender, but Bir Hakeim's commander, Brigadier General Pierre Koenig, refused. Baldassare then called for an air strike. On Day Nine the Ariete approached the French perimeter, and were met by two thousand five hundred artillery shells! This same day the Italians watched as Allied fighters shot down seven German planes over Bir Hakeim.

Meanwhile Rommel had sent the Afrika Korps ahead to occupied Aslagh Ridge far to the Allied rear and just twenty-five miles from Tobruk. Rommel now called for the Ariete to leave Bir Hakeim and advance to Aslagh Ridge. He was straining at the leash, but he had insufficient fuel to continue the advance, and the Gazala Line and Bir Hakeim were still in his rear threatening his supply lines. He obviously had faith in the Italian soldier, otherwise he would not have put them on the crucial Aslagh Ridge, but he did have little faith in Italian generalship, so he sent the 90th Light Division to do what the Ariete had failed to do: take Bir Hakeim.

These Germans bashed their heads against the stubborn French defenses for two days, and then reported they had failed. It is possible that some Italians smiled secretly at this news, with a sort of 'I told you so'.

On Day Eleven (5 June 1942) the 8th Bersaglieri of the Ariete had only just settled into the defenses of Aslagh Ridge, when they were assaulted by a brigade of the Indian 5th Division. The Bersaglieri fell back, but rallied in a wadi and then joined by German tanks they counter-charged. This time the Indians ran. Later the Bersaglieri were attacked by the British 22nd Armored Brigade, but they had hidden some 47mm anti-tank guns in sand depressions and behind sparse scrub brush, and they gave the British tanks a bloody nose. Following this, the tanks of the Ariete and 15th Panzer Divisions counter attacked and completely routed the British.

Nearby this day the 21st Panzer Division repelled the British 32nd Tank Brigade. The British were obviously in dire straits if they had to send the obsolete tanks of a 'tank' brigade against the panzers.

On Day Twelve the Ariete and 15th Panzer Divisions fought the Indian 5th Division for possession of Aslagh Ridge. It was a draw, as was the battle on the next day. Then, having suffered four thousand casualties, the Indians withdrew.

On Day Fourteen, angry at the failure at Bir Hakeim, Rommel now sent a sledgehammer to crush this French nut: attacking with the Trieste Motorized and 90th Light Divisions plus the panzergrenadiers of the Afrika Korps. They failed.

Rommel was really worried now, so he came to Bir Hakeim on Day Sixteen and personally directed these formations [equivalent to three divisions] against the French brigade. He failed. Shortly afterwards one hundred and ten Italian and German planes bombed the French.

That night Koenig asked for permission to withdraw and it was granted. In the darkness 45% of his troops managed to break out. The Bir Hakeim struggle was over.

Rommel agreed on a day of rest for his troops, while his reconnaissance units probed further eastwards.

On Day Eighteen (12 June) the next phase of the offensive began: the 90th Light Division drove to the coast then swung eastwards, while the Trieste, which was already further eastwards, advanced due north hoping to meet the 90th Light, and to their south the 15th Panzer Division maneuvered straight eastwards. Throughout the morning the Italian and German vehicles were sniped at by solitary British anti-tank guns and South African armored cars. Just before noon the 90th Light ran into the British 7th Armored Division and Indian 29th Brigade [of the Indian 5th Division]. But before long the Trieste came up and hit these Allies in the flank. The combat was deadly with no quarter.

On the afternoon of Day Nineteen the 90th Light and Trieste continued their advance, having destroyed one hundred and twenty British tanks.

Only now did the Allies on the Gazala Line begin to collapse. The Sabratha and Trento realized the South African 1st Division was running away, so they jumped up and chased after them. That night the Brescia and Pavia were taken by surprise when the British 50th Division in vehicles drove right through their lines. In the darkness the shooting was wild. The British kept on and eventually drove completely around the Italians to the south, thence east. It was obvious that the troops of the Pavia and Brescia were exhausted.

Indeed by Day Twenty all the Axis soldiers were in a state of stupor from mental and physical exhaustion. Many German and Italian officers suggested to Rommel that enough was enough. But Rommel knew the Allies had retreated towards Tobruk and he had no intention of advancing to that port only to repeat the previous year's siege.

On Day Twenty-One the Germans ran into a lone Indian infantry battalion of the Indian 20th Brigade [of the Indian 10th Division]. The sacrifice of these Indians held up Rommel for only two hours. Next day the 90th Light Division crushed another rearguard of two battalions, and 21st Panzer Division destroyed a solitary battalion.

On Day Twenty-three the Germans easily dispersed a British tank formation. On the morning of Day Twenty-five German reconnaissance troops lowered their goggles, wiped the gritty sand from their eyes and peered through binoculars at the defenses of Tobruk. That night Rommel prepared an assault plan. He had no reason to assume that Winston Churchill had changed his mind about holding Tobruk to the last man, but Rommel was in desperate need of this port. His nearest supply port was a hundred miles across the desert and his trucks were in full view of Allied pilots. He could not advance without taking Tobruk, nor could he afford to leave several divisions to besiege it. Furthermore, Tobruk had two airfields and he could certainly use them, not just to bring in supplies, but for Italian and German fighter planes, which only had a range of two hundred miles or so.

The Italians had another reason for taking the city, namely to eradicate the shame suffered here twice.

On the morning of Day Twenty-six the Sabratha arrived and began digging foxholes facing the western perimeter of Tobruk. The Trento arrived on their right. The Pavia joined them to face the southern perimeter. XXI Corps controlled these divisions. The XX Corps' Trieste and Ariete settled in to the right of the Pavia to face the southern perimeter, and the Germans dug in on their right facing the eastern perimeter. Rommel's excellent radio interception unit told him the city was defended by the fresh South African 2nd Division, the Indian 11th Brigade [of the Indian 4th Division], and the British 201st Guards Brigade with the famed Gurkha troops of the Indian Army. Tobruk's commander, newly promoted South African Major General Hendrik Klopper, held a reserve of the British 32nd Tank Brigade and some Czech infantry. The docks were ten miles from the Allied perimeter.

Rommel flabbergasted everyone by ordering a full-scale offensive this very afternoon. The troops were still digging holes. Some were still in the process of arriving. However, the Italian and German soldiers responded swiftly to his command, and within hours the Sabratha, Trento and Pavia Divisions began assaulting the South Africans, and the Trieste and Ariete charged the Indians. The Germans attacked the 201st Guards Brigade, but ran into a minefield, so they called for engineers. Italian and German engineers rushed into this sector and began clearing mines, tugging away barbed wire, filling in anti-tank ditches and disarming booby traps and all the while under direct enemy fire. They ignored their casualties and continued to work all night, and in some instances they had to fight off British infantry sallies.

By dawn the engineers had cleared a path wide enough for a few tanks, and the German panzers rushed forward, but instead of turning to hit the defenses in the rear they drove straight on for the docks. They ran right over British field guns in their path. Allied tank hunting teams were organized to hunt down these German metal monsters in the narrow alleys of the city.

Suddenly the news was radioed to all units. Klopper had surrendered! The order astonished everyone on both sides. Some Allied troops continued to resist until they received confirmation that it was not an Axis trick. A few Gurkhas ignored the order and fought on, preferring death to dishonor.

However, the Italians were leaping into the air with ecstasy. The more the news reached them the more they celebrated. They had erased the shame of Tobruk and had liberated the homes of Italian colonists. The revenge was even sweeter when they realized that among their prisoners was the South African 2nd Division, the same that had taken the surrender of the Savona Division five months earlier, and that another captured unit was the Indian 11th Brigade that had bested them at Sidi Barani, Keren and Sidi Rezegh.

The Italians had liberated the city of Tobruk, regained the precious docks, recaptured two airfields, and had taken a thousand armored fighting vehicles, four hundred artillery pieces, one thousand four hundred tons of fuel and five thousand tons of provisions, and had taken thirty-six thousand prisoners [two hundred Czechs, two thousand British colonial troops, two thousand five hundred Indians, one thousand seven hundred and sixty Black soldiers of the South African Army, nine thousand White soldiers of the South African Army, and twenty-one thousand six hundred Britons]. The door to Egypt was wide open.

As can be expected Fascist Italian and Nazi German propaganda gave the honors to their own troops: the Italians claiming that most of the attackers were Italian, and rightly so, and the Germans claiming that it had been their tanks that had broken through, equally correct. Truthfully the prize belonged to both. The conquest of Fortress Tobruk was an example of the kind of cooperation the Italians and Germans were capable of: both Italian and German infantry keeping the bulk of the defenders busy, while Italian and German engineers cleared the way for German tanks. Fortunately for the Allies this type of cooperation was rare, as the two Axis partners normally argued with each other and ruined any chances at fruitful teamwork. At Tobruk the Allies did not hold out long enough for the Axis partners to fall out of love.

Rommel was now full of praise for the Italians, making statements that he would have thought preposterous a year earlier. He claimed that their tank crews and artillerymen were brave and that the Bersaglieri were as good as any German infantry. He decorated several Italians.

The fall of Tobruk after a sixteen day battle in January 1941 did not mean its twenty-five thousand Italian defenders were cowards, any more than the fall of Tobruk after just twenty-four hours of fighting in June 1942 meant that the thirty-six thousand Allied defenders were cowards. Both incidents pointed to bad leadership.

Ritchie had already resorted to sacking key officers, such as Messervy, but now Auchinleck fired Ritchie and took over field command himself.

Rommel had already ordered his reconnaissance units forward and they found Auchinleck building a defense line at Mersah Matruh in Egypt. On 26 June the first German armored vehicles reached this area, but could do nothing as they were worn to a frazzle: the Afrika Korps was down to sixty tanks and one thousand five hundred panzergrenadiers. The Italians were in rough shape too and only reached the new battlefield late in the evening.

Reconnaissance units reported that the defense was built around a mine belt that stretched thirty miles inland from the coast and was covered by the British 50th Division. The Indian 10th Division defended the small port, while on the open desert flank the British 1st Armored, New Zealand 2nd and Indian 5th Divisions awaited

Rommel's customary flanking maneuver.

That evening the Italian XXI and XX Corps both searched for paths through the mine belt, and the Afrika Korps and 90th Light Division swung far wide in order to flank the mine belt. By 7pm the 90th Light had done so and had reached the coast behind the Allies.

Rommel was now reinforced by the Italian Littorio Armored Division, which contained an armored regiment of three battalions of M14s, an artillery regiment of four groups of towed artillery and sixteen Semoventi 75s, the 12th Bersaglieri Regiment of two battalions, engineers, support troops and reconnaissance forces - a battalion of L6s, a Bersaglieri battalion and two armored car sections. However, the division's personnel were already exhausted from many days of desert driving under continuous air attack. They were ordered to join Baldassare's XX Corps in finding a gap through the minefield and then to exploit it.

This evening the Afrika Korps overran the Indian 29th Brigade [of the Indian 5th Division].

Come dawn on 27 June the British 1st Armored Division counter attacked, but they were easily pushed aside by the Ariete, Trieste, Littorio, 15th Panzer, 21st Panzer and 90th Light Divisions. In reality neither side was at their optimum and the men were simply going through the motions like unthinking zombies. Allied aircraft were busy come sun up and they strafed the headquarters vehicles of XX Corps. To the shock of the entire corps the bullets killed Colonel Raffaelli and Major General Piacenza and mortally wounded Lieutenant General Baldassare. The latter, though knowing he was bleeding to death, continued to give orders, naming Major General de Stefanis as his successor.

That night in pitch darkness Freyberg's New Zealanders drove their vehicles right through the vehicle camp of the 21st Panzer. In some places they drove through tents mashing the occupants. The Germans ran around in the dark wildly shooting in all directions, but with only twenty-three tanks and a thousand panzergrenadiers they could not stop the trucks or the foot companies that ran through their camp. In the utter confusion the majority of the New Zealanders escaped into the darkness. Dawn saw the camp in turmoil with German privates and generals alike holding rifles and surveying the destruction of torn tents, broken down enemy trucks, abandoned equipment and the worst sight of all, a hospital tent in which the New Zealanders had run through bayoneting every wounded man and decapitating two of them. The word soon spread in Rommel's army. The New Zealanders already had a bad reputation from the Crete battle, where they had supposedly shot prisoners.

On the next night the entire Eighth Army drove and ran right through the camps of the 15th and 21st Panzer Division. The British knew this maneuver was risky, but they had gauged the exhaustion of the German troops accurately. By now the Germans were too fatigued to care.

Thus Mersah Matruh fell to the Axis in one of the most unusual battles ever fought. No one had performed well, with the exception of the 7th Bersaglieri Regiment.

On the 28th German reconnaissance units overwhelmed an Allied rearguard at Fuka.

On 30 June Lieutenant Umberto Musolini of the Carabinieri of the Littorio Armored Division, leading a few armored vehicles, ran up against a British tank force. He and his men defeated the British and liberated some Italian prisoners. Advancing, they soon encountered an Allied defense line consisting of a few holes in the sand that ran through a rail watering station called Alamein.

The Italians and Germans were well satisfied. Since 26 May they had suffered about eight thousand permanent casualties [killed, missing, severely wounded], but had inflicted fifty-eight thousand permanent casualties on the British Eighth Army, and had completely removed one division and six brigades from the Allied order of battle, and had advanced over four hundred miles. They now stood just sixty miles from the great British naval base at Alexandria, one hundred and thirty miles from Cairo and one hundred and ninety miles from the Suez Canal.

———————

Chapter Thirty-two
The Battle For Middle Earth

In December 1941 Mussolini was close to making real his boast of turning the Mediterranean [middle earth] into 'Our Sea', for the British Royal Navy was spread extremely thin. The Americans had been increasingly belligerent at sea, but as of 7 December 1941 they suddenly could no longer come to the aid of the Royal Navy, for they now had a total war against Japan on their hands. Indeed the Americans asked the British for help. The Royal Navy was also at war with Japan now and it was going badly for them. After just four days the Japanese had sunk their capital ships Prince of Wales and Repulse. In addition off the west coast of North Africa British warships were still engaging the French. Furthermore British merchant ships were in danger from German surface raiders as far away as the Pacific, were vulnerable to U-boats in the Atlantic, and were open to Luftwaffe air raids around the British Isles. Ships traveling through the English Channel even had to undergo German artillery fire.

December 1941 was a particularly deadly month in the Mediterranean: the Italian destroyer Alvise da Mosta (1,870 tons) was sunk while battling two cruisers and a destroyer; and the destroyer Alcione was torpedoed by the British submarine Truant, but miraculously this 640-ton warship survived by beaching. On the 12th the light cruisers Alberto di Giussano and Alberico da Barbiana sailed on a potentially suicidal mission, namely carrying thousands of full fuel cans to North Africa. They were intercepted by the Dutch light cruiser Isaac Sweers and British light cruisers Legion, Sikh and Maori. It took only a single torpedo burst into each Italian cruiser to ignite the fuel, and each blew up. A German e-boat (similar to an MAS boat) with them was also sunk. Over 900 lives were lost. The destroyer Cigno survived and was able to rescue five hundred sailors [where did she put them?]. This month the battleship Vittorio Veneto sortied, but was intercepted and torpedoed by the British submarine Urge: she limped back to port. The Italian freighter Sebastiano Venier was torpedoed by a British submarine while carrying two thousand prisoners of war: Britons, Australians, New Zealanders and South Africans. The explosion killed three hundred and nine prisoners and eleven Italians, but the captain beached the freighter and the rest of the passengers and crew survived. Elsewhere in the Mediterranean the German U-557 sank the British light cruiser Galatea. The forty-three man crew of the German submarine did not celebrate too long, for the very next day they collided with the Italian destroyer Orione and sank with all hands lost. The Italian submarine Caracciolo was crippled by the British destroyer Farndale and forced to scuttle. The British cruiser Neptune struck an Italian-laid mine and sank with seven hundred and sixty-five men. This minefield also claimed the destroyer Kandahar, and crippled the cruisers Penelope and Aurora. Days later an MAS boat found a life raft from the Neptune with one survivor and fifteen corpses aboard.

However, the most important incident this month was the most ambitious pig raid yet. On the night of 19 December the submarine Scire let loose three pigs ten miles from Alexandria. In the darkness these intrepid underwater warriors followed a British destroyer right into the heart of Alexandria harbor, and settled underneath the battleships Queen Elizabeth and Valiant and a tanker. This was a suicide mission in that the Italian pig riders had nowhere to go after this. British sentries saw their air bubbles and scanned the water with searchlights. Two of the pig riders were hauled out of the sea. They were taken aboard a battleship, where a British admiral demanded an explanation of what they had been doing. The two refused to talk, even after being incarcerated in the hold, where they knew they would be blown to bits in a matter of minutes. With seconds to spare the two were brought topside for another interrogation, when suddenly the pigs exploded. Both the tanker and the Queen Elizabeth exploded in flames, and the Valiant was badly crippled. As a bonus, the destroyer Jervis was damaged. Miraculously the two Italian prisoners survived.

Malta was the key to the Mediterranean, for this tiny island group sat halfway between Gibraltar and Alexandria in Egypt and provided British warships and submarines with a rest stop. And its airfields housed British planes. For a year and a half the Italians had been bombing the defenses, and the Italian fliers spoke with anger yet respect about the Allied fighter pilots and Maltese and British flak gunners based there. The British government was so impressed with the Maltese and so eager to boost their spirits that they awarded the George Cross (the highest valor medal for civilians) to the entire island nation.

1942 soon proved to be a continuance of the seesaw struggle for the Mediterranean. In January the Italian submarine Medusa was torpedoed and sunk by the British submarine Thorn. The submarine Saint Bon was sunk by the British submarine Upholder. The auxiliary cruiser Palermo with six hundred men was sunk by the British submarine Proteus.

In February the destroyer Carabinieri (1,620 tons) was badly damaged by a submarine torpedo. On 15 February the Italian destroyers Premuda and Polluce were unable to prevent the British submarine P-38 from sinking one of their charges, the Ariosta, which was carrying British prisoners of war: one hundred and thirty-eight prisoners drowned. On 27 February the Italian freighter Tembien was sunk by the British submarine Upholder, while carrying British prisoners of war. Three hundred and ninety of them drowned.

In the Indian Ocean the armed banana boat Ramb I was sunk by the New Zealand cruiser Leander. However in this same period in the Mediterranean Italian mines sank a British submarine, a U-boat sank a British destroyer, German planes sank a British destroyer, and the by now famous Italian destroyer Circe sank the British submarine P38. The Circe also captured the British submarine Tempest, but she sank under tow.

In March U-boats sank the British light cruiser Naiad and a destroyer, and German planes sank another destroyer, but the Italian submarine Guglielmo Motti was sunk by the British submarine Unbeaten, and the submarine Millo was sunk by the British submarine Ultimatum, plus the submarine Tricheco was sunk by the British submarine Upholder.

Despite the high losses suffered by the Royal Navy around the world, the British still considered the Mediterranean to be the toughest stretch of water. Several factors worried the British. The Regia Aeronautica had airfields in Sardinia, Sicily, Italy, Greece, and Libya, and several Luftwaffe squadrons had joined them. U-boats were operating here, having squeezed through the narrow Straits of Gibraltar. But the British were mostly apprehensive because of the presence of the Italian Navy with its war vessels ranging from battleships to two-man pigs. When convoy MW10 sailed from Gibraltar bound for Malta consisting of just four merchant ships, which in the Atlantic would warrant no more than two small escorts if that, the British provided an escort of three light cruisers, an anti-aircraft cruiser and eleven destroyers! Italian spies on the Spanish coast alerted Comando Supremo, and the main Italian battle fleet sailed on 21 March 1942, hoping to intercept the convoy. Admiral Iachino led personally sailing out of Taranto in the battleship Littorio accompanied by four destroyers. Vice Admiral Angelo Parona left Messina to join him with the cruiser Trento, light cruisers Gorizia and Giovanni delle Bande Nere and four destroyers.

Next morning an Italian reconnaissance plane sighted the convoy, and quickly Italian and German bombers struck. The flak was heavy especially from the anti-aircraft cruiser, and the maneuverability of the ships made accuracy a virtual impossibility for the pilots. At 2:27pm Parona's warships arrived and thirteen minutes later his cruisers opened fire at fifteen miles. For a quarter of an hour the Italian and British cruisers flung shells at each other, then the convoy turned and ran.

Parona did not follow, preferring to wait for Iachino. He was leery of being sucked into an ambush. It was a good decision, for the convoy soon met up with a British squadron of a light cruiser and seven destroyers. Shortly afterwards Iachino united with Parona, and now together they advanced on the convoy. The Italians with a battleship, a cruiser, two light cruisers and eight destroyers were going into battle against an AA cruiser, four light cruisers and eighteen destroyers. At 4:40pm the Littorio opened fire at very long range, and over the next two hours her superb gunnery struck the British light cruiser Penelope and three destroyers. As the two sides closed the range eventually all guns on all ships were able to open fire. The Giovanni delle Bande Nere was hit by shells, and at 6:35pm the Littorio took a torpedo launched from a destroyer. Iachino already knew that a gale was on its way, and now he ordered a return to port. The British AA cruiser Euryallus and light cruisers Cleopatra and Penelope had all been damaged, as had the destroyers Lively, Legion, Lance, Kingston and Havock. Indeed the latter was left dead in the water.

The gale was severe and caught many of the ships still at sea, sinking the destroyers Scirocco (1,417 tons) and Lanciere (1,620 tons) and causing much damage. The Second Battle of Sirte as it was known was a risk that Iachino felt he had to take despite the weather. In the action he had damaged an AA cruiser, two light cruisers and five destroyers, but his gamble had failed, for this profit was offset by the loss of two destroyers, the damaging of a light cruiser and the assignment of the Littorio to the repair dry-docks. Furthermore his target had been four merchant vessels, and they had escaped.

However, Iachino also knew that these merchant ships had yet to reach Malta, and he hoped that the following day with its clear skies would open them to air attack. He was not disappointed. The next day as the ships approached Malta, they were suddenly struck by German bombers peeling out of a clear blue sky. All four merchant ships were sunk. And a mine dropped by an Italian plane sank the British destroyer Southwold. Three days later Italian and German planes hammered Malta's harbors and sank the British light cruiser Legion and a submarine, and severely damaged the Penelope. Nearby an Italian mine sank a British submarine.

Elsewhere on 28 March the Italian ocean liner Galilea, which was being used to ferry members of the Julia Division, sailed as part of a convoy, but she was torpedoed by the British submarine Proteus. Almost a thousand Julia soldiers went down with her, as did some Greek prisoners of war and their Carabinieri guards.

In April 1942 the light cruiser Giovanni delle Bande Nere returned to sea only to be sunk by the British submarine Urge.

However, the Regia Aeronautica and Luftwaffe had not finished with Malta. Over the first eleven days in April they raided Malta again and again sinking the destroyers Kingston and Lance and a submarine and damaging two destroyers and the luckless Penelope once more. The British minesweeper Abingdon was wrecked beyond repair

At sea on 14 April the Italian destroyer Pegaso (840 tons) defended her convoy well by sinking the British submarine Upholder. Two weeks later she repeated the performance. Also in April the Italian submarine Aradam torpedoed the British destroyer Havock.

In May 1942 in the Mediterranean the British lost three destroyers to German planes and one to a mine. The only significant Italian loss this month was the destroyer Pessagno (1,870 tons), which was torpedoed by the submarine Turbulent. On 14 May the Italian submarine Amba launched three pigs off Alexandria, but the attempt failed.

In June in small actions in the Mediterranean the Italian submarine Veniero was sunk by a British Catalina flying boat, as was the submarine Zaffiro. The sloop Diana was sunk, and the destroyer Strale (1,205 tons) was crippled by air attack and forced to beach. However this same month in this sea U-boats sank the British light cruiser Hermione and a destroyer, the Grove; and a German e-boat sank a submarine. The crew of the submarine Alagi celebrated when they sank a destroyer, but later learned to their horror they had sunk their fellow Italians in the 1,870-ton destroyer Usodimare.

Aside from these small but deadly combats a greater battle was looming. On the evening of 9 June British planes raided Iachino's battle fleet at Taranto, but the Italians were not caught napping a second time. They were alert and had a good anti-aircraft defense. Two days later Italian spies reported an Allied convoy of six merchant vessels coming through the Straits of Gibraltar eastbound for Malta. Iachino realized now that the air raid on Taranto had been the opening round in this new convoy battle. Each time the British had attempted to send provisions to Malta they had been forced to pay a high price. Bound and determined to get some ships through, the British had denuded other areas of the world to provide an escort for these six vessels, and their escort was impressive: aircraft carriers Eagle and Argus, battleship Malaya, cruisers Kenya, Liverpool and Charybdis, a minelayer, two corvettes, ten minesweepers, twenty-seven destroyers and six motor gunboats.

Simultaneously other Italian spies reported that a convoy of eleven merchantmen was leaving Alexandria westbound for Malta and was accompanied by no fewer than thirty-three warships - minesweepers, cruisers, destroyers and corvettes - plus the battleship Centurion. To put things in perspective one must realize that the British had assigned more naval power to protect these seventeen cargo ships than the total Allied naval power currently protecting India, Burma, Ceylon, Australia, New Zealand, Alaska and western Canada from ongoing Japanese offensives! This month the US Navy went up against the main Japanese battle fleet with just three carriers. The American admirals would have given their eyeteeth to have the carriers Eagle and Argus with them.

This double convoy battle began on 14 June when Italian and German planes struck the eastbound convoy. Despite fighter cover from Fulmars and Hurricanes, and disregarding the wall of flak, the bombers crippled the Liverpool and sank a merchant ship. That night German U-boats attacked the eastbound convoy and German e-boats attacked the westbound. By midnight two merchant ships of the westbound convoy had been sunk and one was damaged.

Admiral Alberto da Zara left Palermo this night with the light cruisers Eugenio di Savoia and Raimondo Montecuccoli, five destroyers and fourteen submarines. Admiral Iachino sortied out from Taranto with the battleships Littorio and Vittorio Veneto, and cruisers Giuseppe Garibaldi, Duca D'Aosta, Gorizia and Trento.

By the early hours of the morning the eastbound convoy was sailing with a depleted escort of the anti-aircraft cruiser Cairo, nine destroyers and ten minesweepers, when da Zara's flotilla sighted them and opened fire at 5:39am. At once the British warships charged the Italians, but Italian gunfire disabled two destroyers. A shell destroyed the boiler room of the Italian destroyer Ugolino Vivaldi (1,870 tons). The convoy let off smoke and disappeared into it. The British warships then did the same.

This morning Iachino's fleet was assaulted from the air, and his flak gunners threw up a wall of flak, but it was not enough to put the Allied pilots off their aim, for the Trento was hit by a bomb that rendered her dead in the water, and the Littorio was struck by a bomb and an aerial torpedo. The Littorio limped home, but the Trento had to be towed at a painfully slow speed. Suddenly two geysers of water shot into the air as torpedoes rammed into the Trento: she had been caught by a British submarine. The surviving crew took to the boats and many jumped overboard, but the evacuation was only partly underway when she blew up. Italian warships picked up six hundred and two men: meaning that five hundred and forty-nine had gone down with her.

Incredibly the ordeal was not over, for now a wave of British four-engine Liberator bombers struck the battle fleet. A bomb savaged the Littorio.

This day Italian and German planes raided the westbound convoy and sank a destroyer and damaged two cruisers. Later an e-boat sank a destroyer. Having suffered crippling losses the westbound convoy returned to Alexandria. It had served its purpose anyway. It had been a decoy. In fact the Centurion was not a battleship, but had simply been disguised to look like one.

Italian and German planes were also attacking the eastbound convoy and they naturally informed da Zara where the ships were. Despite not having Iachino's flotilla, da Zara ordered his warships to forge ahead through the waves at high speed on an interception course. Gaining a visual sighting they opened fire and another surface engagement began. They sank three merchant ships, but the Savoia and Montecuccoli were damaged by shellfire. The Savoia damaged the destroyer Partridge and sank the destroyer Bedouin. [An SM79 also struck the Bedouin.]

Near dusk the two surviving merchant ships and their escort approached Valetta, Malta, but just as the people ashore began to cheer, explosions shattered their euphoria. Italian planes had dropped mines in the convoy's path: a Polish destroyer was sunk and a merchant ship and three minesweepers were crippled.

Da Zara was still at sea and his flotilla came upon two disabled enemy destroyers and they poured shells into them. MAS boats arrived to join the fight. One destroyer went down.

Late that night the westbound convoy was diverted to Port Said, Egypt, and just as the ships were about to berth, they were attacked by Italian and German planes. An Australian destroyer was sunk and the Centurion was damaged.

The idea of sending two convoys to Malta at once from opposite directions had been Churchill's, and like most of his interference in the running of the war it had been a total disaster. This was the greatest Axis naval victory since Crete, and both Germans and Italians were justly proud of their achievement. After all, with but a few shore-based planes, thirteen warships, some motor boats and a few submarines they had challenged the Royal Navy, which had shore-based planes, two carriers full of planes, several submarines and no less than eighty-one warships, and unknown to the Italians the British could read many of the Italian naval signals. The outcome, therefore, should have been a calamity for the Axis. Instead they were victorious. Italian casualties were one cruiser sunk, with damage inflicted on a battleship, a destroyer and two light cruisers, and some Italian and German planes were shot down, but they sank six merchant ships and six destroyers, and inflicted damage on the mock battleship Centurion, three cruisers, two destroyers, three minesweepers, and two merchant ships. Of greatest importance they only allowed one merchant vessel to reach Malta with a full cargo and they showed the Allies that this perhaps was 'Our Sea' after all.

Chapter Thirty-three
First Alamein

Naturally by June 1942 Mussolini was jubilant, for his air and sea forces had inflicted a naval defeat on the British, and his ground forces had liberated Tobruk and charged across Egypt. He had been planning an airborne invasion of Malta, but now he canceled it, as he truly believed the British were at the end of their tether. He decided to expand the Giovanni Fascisti Gruppo into an armored division, but not to fight, rather to march in a parade in Cairo. Pacing his palace in Rome he finally could take the suspense no longer and he flew to Libya to await the word that it was safe for him to enter Cairo.

But not even Rommel was in Cairo. He was still on the Alamein Line. Presently just a line in the sand, this could become a strong position, if he gave the British enough time to prepare it, because it lay between the Mediterranean and an area known as the Quattara Depression, a 'sea' of sand too soft for heavy vehicles. Thus his army only had a forty-mile wide doorway to Cairo. How quickly Auchinleck could slam that door remained to be seen.

Rommel was more realistic than Mussolini and he radioed that he needed fresh troops, and not for a parade either. He was expecting the unblooded German 164th Infantry Division any day, but this would not be enough. Therefore he asked for those units that had been earmarked for the aborted Malta invasion: namely the German Ramcke Parachute Brigade and the Italian Folgore Parachute Division. Mussolini complied, as he wanted to reach Cairo soon. Hitler agreed too, relieved that Ramcke would not have to drop on Malta and risk high casualties such as those received on Crete.

On 1 July 1942 Rommel sent his Afrika Korps against the Alamein line. The 15th and 21st Panzer Divisions, now down to fifty-five tanks, ran into the Indian 18th Brigade [of the Indian 8th Division], and they overcame these Indians and Brits, but lost eighteen valuable tanks and it took them all day. Simultaneously the 90th Light Division was repulsed by South African artillery. Rommel was perturbed. Every day he was held up gave Auchinleck another day to rest his armor and build up his defenses.

The next day the Germans went into the assault again, but bleary-eyed from lack of sleep they turned back at the first sight of British tanks.

On 3 July XX Corps joined the Afrika Korps, but these Italians were also exhausted. Ariete's towed artillery narrowly missed being captured by New Zealand infantry who attacked in trucks.

Meanwhile the Littorio Armored Division advanced, but was easily stopped. Lieutenant Musolini was captured this day, his tank having been knocked out. When Rommel saw for himself the depleted state of his troops he acknowledged the need for a halt to the fighting.

———————

For five days both sides slept, repaired, regrouped and replanned, while supplies and replacements arrived. Despite scattered air raids the Italians and Germans soon returned to a normal state, even laughing at their predicament.

The British received yet another American-built tank, the Sherman. It was heavier than a Grant or a Matilda, 30 tons, and thus was really too heavy for the desert, and at 9 feet high it stuck out above the horizon. However, it was armored up to 50mm and carried a good 75mm gun in a turret capable of firing armor piercing or high explosive rounds. All in all it was now the best tank in the British Eighth Army.

Rommel's armored units had been so ravaged that they were using many captured machines - Matildas, Valentines, Crusaders, Honeys, Grants. All received a new coat of paint and either the black cross of Germany or red square of Italy. Replacement vehicles also arrived. XX Corps received new M14s and Semoventi 75s from Italy, and the Afrika Korps received from Germany new Mark IIIs with a long-barreled 50mm gun and some Mark IVs with a medium-barreled 75mm gun.

Though members of the artillery, Semoventi commanders such as Major Pardi, who had been wounded at Halfaya Pass in 1941, had been retrained to use their vehicles as armor as well as artillery.

Rommel recognized that the Ruweisat Ridge, which lay at right angles to the Alamein line and divided it in two, was a key, because forward artillery observers here could see for miles. He chose to place his Italian infantry between the ridge and the sea, with on the coast the XXI Corps of the Trento Motorized and Sabratha Divisions. Between them and the ridge he put Lieutenant General Ferrari-Orsi's X Corps of the Brescia and Pavia Divisions. The Trento had been reinforced by the Giovanni Fascisti Gruppo [now consisting of three infantry battalions, 3/San Marco Marines, the Sardinian Grenadiers anti-tank battalion, some engineers and artillery]. The low Miteirya Ridge separated the two corps. Scouts concluded that they only faced one enemy division, the South African 1st, now commanded by Dan Pienaar. The British 1st Armored Division was in reserve at the eastern end of Ruweisat Ridge. Both divisions were controlled by Lieutenant General William Ramsden's XXX Corps.

South of Ruweisat Ridge Rommel placed XX Corps of Major General Adolfo Infante's Ariete Armored, Trieste Motorized and Littorio Armored Divisions facing the New Zealand 2nd Division. To hold the southern end of the line he chose the Afrika Korps [15th and 21st Panzer and 90th Light Divisions], which faced the Indian 5th Brigade [of the Indian 4th Division] and British 7th Armored

Division. Small German and Italian reconnaissance teams patrolled the Quattara Depression.

On 9 July Rommel launched his Cairo offensive with all of the above forces, but enemy resistance was tough. The Germans made no gains. The Italians gained some ground, but Italy lost one of her heroes this day. Major Pardi's Semoventi took a direct hit. Men ran to the burning wreckage to find three crewmen dead and Pardi badly hurt from multiple lacerations. He was placed in an ambulance, but the forty-mile ride over rocks to the rear finished him off.

Throughout the next day the Italians and Germans continued to try to break through, but made no further advances and that evening the Sabratha Division was counter attacked by Australians. British XXX Corps had just received Major General Leslie Morshead's fresh Australian 9th Division, and he had counter attacked at once. The Sabratha backed away, but several officers including Colonel Angelozzi, commanding the 84th Regiment, and even some sergeants begged, pleaded, ordered, threatened and cajoled and eventually convinced enough Italian soldiers to retrace their steps and hold the position. As they went forward, German infantry appeared out of nowhere and helped the Italians recapture their front line. The Italians of the Sabratha were most grateful for the timely appearance of these rescuers who were in fact members of the German 164th Division, who had been thrown into action the minute their trucks had hit their brakes. Though green troops these Germans were eager and were led by General Kurt von Liebenstein, who had fought in Russia.

However, Rommel was disappointed, and he called off his offensive following a consultation with his German and Italian staff officers. He ordered the Trieste to send some Bersaglieri to shore up the shaken Sabratha.

Following two days of repositioning his units, Rommel attacked again on 13 July. The 21st Panzer Division made an attempt to hit the Australians on their southern flank with the obvious intention of pinning them to the coast, but they ran into South African anti-tank guns and were stopped. The following day 21st Panzer tried again slightly further north, but were stopped by Australian anti-tank guns. That afternoon Colonel Angelozzi led the 1/85th Regiment of Sabratha into the assault. They were far more successful than the Germans, capturing several Australian positions.

However, Auchinleck had also recognized the value of Ruweisat Ridge, and he ordered Gott's XIII Corps to send Freyberg's New Zealand 2nd Division and the Indian 5th Brigade to crawl along the ridge to its western end. These Kiwis, Indians and Britons did as ordered, reaching the western end undetected just before dark. Then they poured down from the 35-foot high ridge to strike the Brescia Division in flank. For five hours these Italians stuck to their holes in the sand in the darkness fighting hand-to-hand, identifying the enemy by his shouts in a foreign language and by the sound of his weapons. Terrified, every Italian prayed that the body he had just sliced open with a bayonet or had put a bullet into was that of a foe and not a friend. Some New Zealanders ran down the ridge on the opposite side, and this caught many of the Pavia Division's soldiers unawares and there was some panic. Here some Italians hugged the ground and cried. Others ran, not knowing or caring in which direction. Some fired wildly. German troops also got caught up in the confusion. German tankers sat in their motionless vehicles with hatches shut. Blind at night they could not move for fear of running over a German or an Italian.

After what seemed the longest night of their lives, the dawn's light began creeping along the landscape, and the Italians and Germans saw that New Zealanders, Britons and Indians were all around them. The German tanks now awoke like vengeful dragons. Unlike infantrymen who crawled and could only see a few feet ahead, the tank crews could see for hundreds of yards and they recognized pockets of enemy soldiers. Spitting bullets and hurtling high explosive shells they made all the difference. Furthermore both sides began to throw undirected artillery shells onto the battlefield, killing men of both sides indiscriminately. Much of the ground here was too hard for holes so the shells impacted on the earth not in it, throwing their shrapnel sideways for many yards. The only way to survive was to lie between corpses. The tankers could sometimes see Italians crawling into harm's way but had no way of communicating with them to warn them. To add to the insanity the sun was soon glaring down with oppressive heat, burning the eyes of immobile wounded into blindness. Then the flies came, millions of them, to feed on the raw flesh of ripped open humanity. Such was the proximity of opposing troops that the sway of a hand to shoo away a fly drew a hail of bullets. The wounded and the overheated suffered greatly from thirst, but even if they had musty water in their canteen they could not reach for it for fear of attracting the enemy. Amid the blaring rattle of tank engines, explosions and gunfire were the screams of dying men. Some wished the wounded would go ahead and die, just so they would no longer have to listen to the blood-curdling screams.

Near dusk more German tanks and Italian infantry arrived and this broke the stalemate. Those New Zealanders who could, retreated, but nine hundred were taken prisoner.

The Brescia and Pavia Divisions had survived, but their officers had their hands full restoring morale. In the Sabratha morale had already been restored, it was believed, and the attack led by Colonel Angelozzi was evidence of this, but on the 16th the first line of the Sabratha was subjected to a heavy mortar barrage. Once it lifted the Sabratha troops could see a mass of Australian infantry charging them. Within minutes most of the Italians had cracked and run. A few stood their ground, feeling pity rather than anger for their comrades who were fleeing the battlefield. Fortunately there were some companies of Bersaglieri here from the Trieste and they fought well, as did a handful of German tanks. Rommel sent more reinforcements from Trieste and Trento and together they repelled the Australians. Even the Italian generals had to admit to Rommel that the Sabratha Division was no longer a fighting formation. However, it is noteworthy that Rommel still entrusted this sector to Italian officers. He knew they had some real warriors among them, such as Colonel Angelozzi of the Sabratha and Colonels Gherordo Vaiarini and Umberto Zanetti of the Trieste.

The Australians knew how close they had come to busting the Sabratha line, so they tried again the next day, but of course this time they ran into elements of the Trieste and Trento. However, these defenders were themselves at breaking point. The Trento's engineer battalion had suffered 80% casualties in six weeks and by now was down to one hundred and twenty men, yet they were thrown into this battle to fight as infantry. Here and there some Sabratha men were still resisting and others had regained their composure and had returned to the struggle. The Sabratha staff also sent many of their rear-echelon personnel into the fight.

Colonel Vaiarini led his unit of the Trieste into a savage counter attack and he fought until his last dying breath. For this he was posthumously awarded the Gold Medal, Italy's highest honor. Late in the day elements of the German 164th Division entered the fray. At last the Australians had had enough and they fell back. Trento's engineer battalion was now ordered to return to normal duty - all sixteen men!

On the night of the 20th British XIII Corps attempted to capture Ruweisat Ridge again, this time attacking at night with a fresh New Zealand Brigade and the fresh Indian 161st Brigade, but by coincidence German tanks were moving here at this very same moment. In the darkness the advancing infantry walked straight into the tanks, and the Germans made a banquet of this offering: for an entree the tanks slaughtered New Zealanders, then for the main course the tanks surrounded and annihilated an Indian battalion, and for dessert the tanks wiped out two battalions of Crusader tanks of the brand new British 23rd Armored Brigade.

On the morning of the 21st the Littorio Armored Division awoke under new command. Just one week earlier Major General Carlo Ceriana-Mayneri had been leading the Emanuele Filiberto Celere Division against Titoist partisans. He stared at his new battlefield and saw it was totally different than Yugoslavia: no houses, no civilians, no mountains, no snow, no fog, no trees and no roads.

Just after dawn this day the ad hoc formation on the coast consisting of men from Sabratha, Trento, Trieste and 164th were treated to the awe-inspiring sight of three battalions of bayonet-wielding Australians charging towards them. Within minutes they had the Aussies pinned down by machine gun fire and mortars. Soon British tanks arrived to support the Australians, and the first line of Italian defenders withdrew. However, this was part of their plan, for the second line was packed with 47mm anti-tank guns. The British tanks took the bait, believing that the 'Eye-ties' [as the Brits called all Italians] were on the run. The anti-tank gunners were as cool as cucumbers in the hot sun waiting until they could practically count the rivets and bolts on the tanks before they opened fire. It was a slaughter. They destroyed half the British tanks: the remainder fled.

The next day the Allies tried a similar attack in the same locality. The fighting was bloody and the Italians lost another fighting leader with the death of Colonel Zanetti of the Trieste.

On the night of the 26th Italian sentries in listening posts on Miteirya Ridge were silently stabbed to death by Australians, and by dawn the British 169th Brigade had infiltrated inside the Italian lines and had cleared a path through a minefield. Come sun up the Italians discovered the British in their midst and responded like a swarm of wasps, attacking the invaders with members of the Trento and Brescia plus German tanks and panzergrenadiers, until the British speedily retreated. But the Italians and Germans were in no mood for half measures, and they chased the British into an Australian formation and took many Australian as well as British prisoners.

Rommel finally accepted what his staff had been telling him for days, that the Italian infantry was in desperate need of rest, replacements and resupply. Rommel agreed to halt the fighting and he asked Comando Supremo to replace the worn out Italian divisions, whose men he had pushed to the edge of madness with his constant orders 'attack, attack, attack'. His medical officers informed him the Italians were suffering from battle fatigue, nervous exhaustion, desert loneliness, jaundice, diphtheria, sores, heat rashes, amoebic dysentery, wounds, injuries, paratyphus and malnutrition. They had lost all discipline and their trenches had become rat-infested sewage pits.

Rommel reported to Comando Supremo that since 26 May he had lost twenty-eight thousand five hundred men: specifically a thousand Italians and two thousand three hundred Germans dead; ten thousand Italians and seven thousand five hundred Germans wounded; and five thousand Italians and two thousand seven hundred Germans missing. The Afrika Korps, after replacement tanks and personnel had been absorbed, was still only at 22.7% of normal tank strength and 35% of normal panzergrenadier strength. The ratio of Italian dead to wounded seems odd for a 1942 battle. The German figures appear accurate. It is very feasible that some of the Italian missing were in fact dead, perhaps as many as two thousand. Identification was not always adequate in Mussolini's army. It is also quite possible Rommel's staff got the figures wrong, or even that they lied in order to inflate the German contribution and denigrate that of the Italians. After all, many of the Germans were Nazis.

But regardless, this was a great Italian-German victory. They had inflicted on the enemy a loss of eleven thousand killed and seriously wounded, and had taken sixty thousand prisoners, and had knocked out or captured two thousand armored fighting vehicles. In Alexandria the Royal Navy was making arrangements to move all ships further east, and orderlies were burning mountains of paperwork, lest the Axis capture it. In Cairo some staff officers were quietly packing their bags. Throughout Eighth Army there was an air of defeatism.

Chapter Thirty-four
Balkan Entanglement 1942

For two centuries Western European governments declared they
wanted no 'Balkan entanglements'. Politically the very word 'Balkan'
denoted intrigue, mistrust and defeat. Geographically the word meant
the area of Slovenia, Croatia, Bosnia-Herzegovina, Serbia, Kosovo,
Dalmatia, Montenegro, Macedonia, Bulgaria, Albania, Romania,
European Turkey and mainland Greece.

During World War I the British under pressure from Winston
Churchill and like-minded politicians had become involved here and,
as their political enemies had prophesied, the British had stumbled -
one army suffering an ignominious defeat at Gallipoli and another
becoming trapped on the beaches of Salonika for three years. Their
Bulgarian enemy described the precarious British beachhead as their
biggest prisoner of war camp.

A quarter century later Churchill, now prime minister, once again
ignored the 'curse of the Balkans' and sent sixty thousand troops to
Greece in 1941, only to see them scramble for their boats
ignominiously.

By early 1942 the Americans were warning Churchill that they
wanted nothing to do with 'Balkan entanglements'.

Italy and Germany had become entangled in the Balkans because
of Mussolini's greed for power and glory and Hitler's anger towards
the Serbs and his need to protect the Romanian oilfields. By 1941
both dictators had been seemingly victorious here, gaining Croatia,
Hungary, Romania and Bulgaria as active partners and occupying the
remainder of the Balkan states. The Croats sent Hitler a regiment and
a battalion to help invade the Soviet Union, but by 1942 they had
committed five army divisions and nineteen Ustaci battalions to battle
the Titoist partisans in their own country. The Bulgarians had to use
three and a half divisions to keep the Macedonians pacified. The
Hungarians had put two divisions into the campaign, but only to
reunite some small ethnic Hungarian lands with the mother country.

Hitler needed all the troops he could get to fight the Soviets, and
therefore he had not intended to leave any large formation of Germans
in the Balkans, hence his recognition of Croatia as an independent
nation, his creation of the Serb puppet state forces, his willingness to
let the Bulgarians have most of Macedonia, and his willingness to
allow the Italians to occupy the bulk of the territory. Yet, by April
1942 five German security divisions, two infantry divisions and an
infantry regiment had been drawn into anti-Titoist operations in
Serbia.

Since 1938 the Waffen SS, the military wing of the German SS,
had been a bona fide branch of the German armed forces, but the

German army, navy and air force had refused to allow the SS to conscript, hoping to keep it small. As a result the Waffen SS went abroad looking for cannon fodder. By 1940 the SS had induced thousands of naive young men to join up from Denmark, Norway, Netherlands, Belgium, France, Luxembourg, Sweden and Switzerland. With the invasion of the Soviet Union SS recruiters took in thousands of captured Red Army soldiers, who took the opportunity to fight the Communists. In Yugoslavia SS recruiters created the 7th SS Prinz Eugen Mountain Division using Volksdeutsch, i. e. Yugoslavs of German ethnicity.

The German police were also in need of people as most of their men had been conscripted into the German armed forces. Thus they came to Yugoslavia to recruit some field battalions of light infantry from the Volksdeutsch. They also recruited a large auxiliary police force of Croats. The German Nazi Party and its bullyboy organization the Sturm Abteilung (SA) organized a militia of Volksdeutsch in the Banat area of Serbia and a militia of Slovenes in German-occupied Slovenia.

The Italians had organized separate militias of Slovenes, Croats, Montenegrin Christians, Macedonians, Montenegrin Moslems and Kosovo Moslems in those regions they had occupied in April 1941. However, Slovenes and Croats from those lands occupied by the Italians since 1919 and the Dalmatians of Zara [a pre-war Italian enclave on the Yugoslavian coast] were already Italian citizens, so they were conscripted as if they had come from downtown Rome. Lastly ethnic Italians of Yugoslavia were encouraged to enlist in Mussolini's forces.

The Italian Second Army was still present in Slovenia and Dalmatia with the V and XI Corps, of four divisions each. The Ninth Army controlled the VI and XIV Corps, of four divisions each, serving in Montenegro, and the IV and XXV Corps, of two divisions each serving in Albania. The Eleventh Army occupied Greece with the III, VIII and XXVI Corps, with a total of eleven divisions.

The Albanian puppet-state had its own army, police, and Blackshirts. The Italians tried to cultivate a certain degree of nationalist feeling among all Albanians whether from Albania, Kosovo, Cham or Macedonia. It was perhaps somewhat akin to the Scottish-English situation. Scots are proud to be Scots and also British, but are ruled by the English. However, the English had been cultivating this situation for two and a half centuries by 1942. The Italians had only begun to cultivate the Albanians in 1939.

Mussolini dismissed the Albanian Prime Minister Shefket Verlaci in December 1941 and replaced him with Mustafa Merlika Kruja, who announced a policy of a fusion of the two nations. For the most part the Albanians were illiterate peasants who accepted any dictate dictated by any dictator. They are devoutly religious people, either

Orthodox Christians, Roman Catholics or Moslems, and therefore recruiters for the guerilla forces had little success preaching Communism or even Democracy. To these peasants the concepts of universal suffrage and Marxist Leninist Revisionism were as alien as Emersonian Existentialism would have been to an American hillbilly.

As a result the number one priority for the Albanian guerillas during the first two years of the Italian occupation was finding enough to eat in their mountain strongholds. However, their spirits were elevated when neighboring Montenegro erupted in revolt against the Italians in July 1941. This sparked an all-party congress of the Albanian guerilla factions, which was held in the town of Peza (illegally of course) with the intention of unifying into the National Liberation Movement. The general idea was to put political and religious differences aside until the last Italian swam back to Italy. However, the extreme right nationalists baulked when they suspected Communist machinations behind the scenes. Therefore, they established their own movement, the National Front with Midhat Frasheri as leader. Their avowed goals were to kick out the Italians, destroy the atheist Communists and unify all ethnic Albanians into a Greater Albania. The dedicated followers of Zog, the self-proclaimed 'king' of the Albanians, were in agreement with all this, but they insisted that the leader should be Zog and his 'Royal Family', so they set up their own movement, the Legality Movement, controlled by Abas Kopi.

Unfortunately these two anti-Communist movements were purely Moslem, and that left the Christians out in the cold, so they formed their own movements, the biggest being Jon Markagjon's Roman Catholic Movement, which conveniently ignored the Pope's love affair with Fascism. This left only the Communists and Socialists within the National Liberation Movement.

One wonders how these guerilla leaders were able to travel, meet and debate right under the noses of Italian military intelligence. The answer is that the Italians were perfectly aware of what was happening. They hoped that the meeting would not create unity amongst the guerillas, but would instead foment serious disunity. And that is exactly what happened. Full marks to the Italians! As soon as the guerillas returned to their separate mountain strongholds they began shooting at each other. The four Italian Army divisions in Albania were therefore not required to participate in the anti-guerilla war. They could be left alone to concentrate on the more important aspects of occupation duty: wine, women and song.

With the surrender of the Greeks in April 1941 Lieutenant General Carlo Geloso's Italian Eleventh Army took over occupation of all Greece, minus the small part given to Bulgaria. Crete was added in

June. Surprisingly there was no immediate guerilla activity to harm the occupation force, and their prime mission was to protect Greece from a potential British liberation attempt.

Mussolini chose no less a person than General Zolakoglou to head the Greek puppet government. This was the very man who had surrendered Greece to the Italians. Greek Fascists soon flocked to his banner.

Most Greeks were loath to accept such rule and guerilla bands popped up everywhere. For the first few weeks they jockeyed for position to gain acceptance among the people, and by autumn 1941 they had coalesced into a few major groups. The {EAM} National Liberation Front and its militant wing ELAS was a conglomeration of left-wing political parties including Communists and Socialists. The {EDES} National Democratic Greek League under the leadership of Napoleon Zervas set itself up in the Epirus Mountains and eagerly accepted everyone except Fascists and Communists. An ethnic Macedonian band remained in Greek Macedonia.

But this did not bother the Italians, for the Greek guerillas spent the first winter more or less building an infrastructure and if they made war it was against soft targets.

To defend the Bulgarian-occupied zone against guerillas the Bulgarians established a defensive militia among their ethnic brothers. For the same purpose the Italians sponsored an Arumanian (Vlach) defensive militia among that ethnic minority.

Come spring 1942 the Greek partisan rank and file were extremely disappointed, for the peasants were treating them like bandits. But this is understandable, because for the first year of Italian occupation these guerillas had spent their entire time arguing politics and strategy around the campfire. British and American agents had parachuted into the Greek guerilla strongholds with the goal of instructing the guerillas in weapons and tactics and also to coordinate the various bands, but they seem to have immediately fallen under the spell of whichever band leader they met. ELAS members convinced the Britons and Americans with them that the EDES were all Fascists. EDES leaders convinced the Britons and Americans with them that the ELAS were all Communists. Furthermore many band leaders denounced both EDES and ELAS, thus creating smaller splinter groups. It was these smaller bands that actually began the guerilla war in spring 1942.

The first to react to the guerilla raids were the Bulgarians, who brought in their II Corps to hunt guerillas in Thrace and Southeastern Macedonia. The Italians were slow to react, but in June an army truck convoy was ambushed on the Arta-Yannina road and all sixty soldiers were killed. That did it. Lieutenant General Geloso began to organize an anti-partisan campaign. He would start hunting down EDES guerillas in the Epirus Mountains with his XXVI Corps of the Casale

Division [with attached 23rd CCNN Legion] and Modena Mountain Division [with attached 36th CCNN Legion]. The III Corps with its Brennero Division [and attached 35th CCNN Legion], Forli Mountain Division and Pinerolo Division [and attached 136th CCNN Legion] of Major General Licurgo Zannini would begin hunting ELAS partisans and Macedonian rebels in the mountains of Roumelia and Greek Macedonia. In the Peloponnesus the VIII Corps with its Piemonte Division and Cagliari Mountain Division [with attached 29th CCNN Legion] would commence operations against several smaller bands and ELAS affiliated groups. The Siena Division [and attached 141st CCNN Legion] would wage a low key anti-guerilla campaign against several small bands. These were veteran units, except for the Casale. The Italian divisions stationed in the islands had little to do. Thus by the summer of 1942 fully half the Italian Army was tied down in occupation duty in the Balkans.

By June 1942 Tito had become tired of his pendulum campaign, swinging back and forth between Serbia and Montenegro, so he sent partisans into Bosnia-Herzegovina, while he ordered the Red partisans in Slovenia to launch a diversionary campaign.

In Slovenia the various armed factions had soon retreated to distinct regions. The Reds hid in the mountains. The Blues controlled the rural valleys. The Italians and their White allies owned the towns in the western, central and southern districts, and the Germans and their White allies governed the towns in the northern and eastern districts.

Mussolini ordered General Roatta's Second Army to counter this Titoist Slovenian offensive, so Roatta directed Lieutenant General Mario Robotti to assemble the V, XI and XXIII Corps with the following divisions: Cacciatore delle Alpi [with attached 105th CCNN Legion], Sassari [with 73rd CCNN Legion], Isonzo [with 98th CCNN Legion], Macerata, Sardinian Grenadiers, Re [with attached 75th CCNN Legion], Lombardia [with attached 137th CCNN Legion] and Emanuele Filiberto Celere [minus its 6th Bersaglieri Regiment]. Roatta reinforced these divisions with the Mountain Raggruppamento CCNN [of the 2nd CCNN Legion and 8th, 16th, 71st, 81st and 85th CCNN Battalions and the 3/311 of the army's Casale Division]. The Cacciatore had only just finished a campaign against the Titoists. The Macerata and Sardinian Grenadiers were new to combat. The troops took to the narrow roads and wound their way into the mountains of Slovenia with Whites protecting their flanks. Italian military intelligence had made a truce with the Blues for the duration of the campaign.

On successive days White scouts sighted Red guerilla bands, but usually by the time the slow lumbering Italian infantry arrived the quarry had skedaddled. There were a few engagements though, and the Sardinian Grenadiers, Cacciatore delle Alpi and Lombardia Divisions did inflict casualties on the Red partisans.

Meanwhile in Bosnia-Herzegovina the Axis partners launched a major response to Tito's invasion by counter attacking him with the German 714th Division and the Croat Army 1st Mountain Division. Two weeks of fighting saw the loss of 19 Germans and 200 Croats killed, 6 Germans and 169 Croats missing and 31 Germans and 250 Croats wounded. Yet the Germans and Croats had only been up against a portion of Tito's forces.

In late June Tito led four brigades into Bosnia-Herzegovina, but he ran into a line of Croatian Army and Ustaci units and some Germans and Cetniks. The Luftwaffe and Regia Aeronautica hounded the partisans continually.

By 6 July the Croats had identified Tito's headquarters by triangulation of radio signals. Field Marshal Kwaternik sent the Croat III Corps and several Ustaci battalions forty miles westwards from Sarajevo towards this location. Italian planes found Tito's main column in the Bugojno Valley and strafed it unmercifully. The partisans had few flak guns. Individual partisans who fled the column to hide from the planes ran the risk of being killed by roving bands of Bosnian Moslem militia and Cetniks.

Then Cetnik horse cavalry waving huge flags to identify them to the Italian pilots in the bright summer sun charged Tito's lines. The resulting battle was deadly.

Nearby some Titoists attacked Prozor, which was quickly abandoned by its Ustaci defenders. This gave Tito a loophole by which he could escape to the northwest. By climbing to 1,123meter Makljen Pass Tito's main column was able to reach the Vrbas River. Next day the partisans marched through Hurije, a Serb village. The villagers knew little of politics and took pity on Tito's column of men, women and children. The villagers gave what succor they could.

The Croats followed once Tito's rearguard pulled out and the next day the Ustaci Black Legion entered Hurije. The Ustaci judged these villagers guilty of the crime of helping Communists (and of the crime of professing the Orthodox Christian faith), and as punishment for both they massacred the entire village.

The Croat 1st Mountain Division attempted to block Tito on the slopes of the Kozara Mountains, but the Croats suffered badly fighting off waves of charging partisans, so they called for reinforcements. Kwaternik sent them his 3rd and 4th Mountain Brigades. A Cetnik unit rushed in and successfully defended Bugojno sixty miles northwest of Sarajevo, and the Croats advanced ten miles westwards of Bugojno, but by 31 July the Croats had fallen back from Zlosela. Next day aerial reconnaissance identified Tito's main force on Malovan Mountain, but the Croats were in no fit state to attack. Their 1st Mountain Division had suffered a thousand casualties and the remaining Croats had lost two thousand nine hundred.

All of these Axis formations plus the Cetniks had with them Italian liaison officers and forward air controllers and these Italians reported back to their generals not just the battle reports but also the atrocities they had witnessed. Tito's partisans were operating in such a way that they were covered by the Geneva Convention, which among other things meant that if captured they had to be looked after. However, the Croat and German authorities declared that all partisans were covered by the Hague Convention instead, which meant it was legal to execute them. Nonetheless most Croats and Germans were not mindless robots and they did take prisoners. As terrible as the massacres were, they were the exception not the rule even in this bitter struggle.

Chapter Thirty-five
Italian Victory in Russia

Those Italians under General Messe that had chased the Soviet Union's Red Army for five hundred miles in 1941 had remained at the front throughout the following terrible winter, eking out an existence in primitive challenging conditions. Messe had three divisions: the Amedeo Duca d'Aosta Celere of Major General Mario Marazzani, the Torino Motorized of Major General Roberto Lerici, and the Pasubio Motorized of Major Vittorio Giovannelli [with attached 1st CCNN Legion]. He also had the 63rd CCNN Battalion Gruppo. The Russians bragged that their best officer was 'General Winter', who had slaughtered the Swedes in the 18th century and the French in the 19th century and would now defeat the new invaders. Of all the Axis partners on the front line, only the Hungarians took the luxury of withdrawing their men for the winter. It was so cold that trucks could only be started by first building a wood fire under their engines. Yet there were still attacks and counter attacks. In one such on 12 December 1941 Brigadier General Ugo Carolis, commanding an infantry force from the Torino Division, was cut down by automatic fire. He was awarded the Gold Medal.

In February 1942 Messe's expeditionary corps was reinforced by Lieutenant General Enrico Francisci's '23 March CCNN Raggruppamento', which contained the Valle Scrivia CCNN Gruppo [previously 5th CCNN Legion] of three battalions, and the Leonessa CCNN Gruppo [previously 15th CCNN Legion] of three battalions. The latter had fought on the Greek front.

Mussolini reminded his people that Italy was engaged in a tremendous struggle and it was the Allies that were in the minority, not the Axis. By 1942 the Italians faced the Soviets, Americans and British (who of course had a great empire and were allied to the independent 'British' dominions of South Africa, Canada, Australia and New Zealand), but Italy's Axis partners were numerous: the French (and much of their empire), Finland, Albania, Hungary, Slovakia, Croatia, Romania, Bulgaria, Spain, Germany, Denmark, Japan, Thailand, Mongolia, Manchukutuo, the North China Republic and the Central China Republic. Moreover large numbers of volunteers served the Axis cause from about seventy-five other ethnic nations. A large portion of these were people who had been enslaved by the Communist Russians and were now aiding the Axis to kill the soldiers of the Red Army, an army that took orders from the anti-Christ himself: Stalin. Clergy from the Buddhist, Moslem and Christian religions supported this crusade against Communism, and (as Mussolini and his government contended) any Briton or American who continued to fight the Axis was aiding and abetting the expansion of Communism, and had become in effect the devil's disciples. With so much support for their endeavor it was difficult for any Italian to argue that they were fighting on the wrong side! Even the pope prayed for their victory and blessed Italian regimental flags.

At the Russian Front the 1942 campaigning season began in May following the melting of the snows, and it started with a massive Red Army pre-emptive strike. This backfired completely, and Stalin lost a quarter of a million men, and it did not alter Hitler's timetable to a noticeable degree.

Hitler planned to occupy the Caucasus oilfields and reach Asia this summer. However, his strategic eyes were bigger than his manpower stomach. Thousands of foreign volunteers were serving alongside his Germans: men from every country in Western Europe including a few Britons and Americans; and every German unit had recruited volunteers from among their Red Army prisoners and the Soviet citizenry. The latter were divided into actual combat troops [Osttruppen - Eastern Troops] and rear-echelon troops [Hiwis - Volunteer Helpers] and they included every ethnic group in the Soviet Union with the exception of Jews and Gypsies. By using these fellows the Germans had been able to offset their enormous casualties.

But for what Hitler wanted to do next, these were still not enough troops. Therefore he had to swallow his pride and ask his partners for additional assistance. The result was that while the Finns and Germans and their volunteers would hold the line in the north and center, a coalition of Axis partners would affect the main offensive itself in the south. On the northern flank of this southern offensive the German Fourth Panzer Army would aim for Voronezh. To their south the German Sixth Army would conquer Stalingrad. Far to their south German First Panzer Army would attempt to reach the Kalmyk lands and still further south German Seventeenth Army would invade the Caucasus. German Eleventh Army, which contained many Romanian units, would rid the Crimean Peninsula of the Red Army. This left a massive gap between Voronezh and Stalingrad, and to fill it Hitler inserted from north to south the Hungarian Second Army, the Italian expeditionary force and the Romanian Third Army. To link Stalingrad with the Kalmyk lands he inserted the Romanian Fourth Army. This still left a gap of two hundred miles between the German First Panzer Army and the German Seventeenth Army, and quite frankly Hitler did not have anyone left to cover it, so he ignored it. (Though German reconnaissance units and Kalmyk horse cavalry patrolled it).

At a meeting in Austria in April 1942 Hitler had requested that Mussolini reinforce Messe's expeditionary force. Il Duce was pleased that Hitler was asking him for help. Obviously the Italians had impressed the German generals. As a result Messe's expeditionary corps was retitled XXXV Corps and was reinforced by two battalions of Croats. Thousands of replacements were brought in to take the places of the dead, diseased, wounded and the frostbitten. The Amedeo Duca d'Aosta Celere Division was reinforced by the 6th Bersaglieri Regiment, veteran of many combats against Albanians, Yugoslav regulars and Titoists. Furthermore two more corps would be coming to fight alongside the XXXV Corps, namely the II Corps and the Alpini Corps. The II Corps consisted of the Sforzesca Mountain, Ravenna Mountain and Cosseria Divisions. The latter had fought in Ethiopia and briefly in France. The Sforzesca had fought in Greece. The Ravenna had fought French and Yugoslavs. The Alpini Corps was made up of Major General Umberto Ricagno's Julia Alpini Division, Major General Luigi Reverberi's Tridentina Alpini Division and Major General Emillio Batisti's Cuneense Alpini Division. The Julia was practically brand new, having suffered so many casualties in Greece and in a sinking at sea. The Tridentina had fought French and Greeks. The Cuneense had fought French, Greeks and Yugoslavs. Messe was ordered to transfer the 23 March CCNN Raggruppamento and the 63rd CCNN Battalion Gruppo to this corps. The latter would be renamed the Tagliamento Gruppo, and alongside the new Montebello CCNN Battalion Gruppo [30th CCNN Legion and 12th CCNN Battalion] would be assigned to the new 3 January CCNN Raggruppamento. The 30th had fought French and Greeks.

Messe was promoted and placed in command of these three corps. His new headquarters was designated Eighth Army, and the new Vicenza Division would protect his army's lines of communications from partisan raids. Messe did not want the job. Indeed he had argued against sending more Italians into the vastness of Russia.

The veterans of the first year of the conflict in Russia described their experiences in chilling detail to the newcomers: how barren the Russian Steppe was, how muddy the roads in October, how cold the winter, how inhuman the Red Army soldier.

There was a small Italian naval presence in the Black Sea and on one occasion an MAS boat captured a ship carrying a Soviet general. In another incident the midget submarine CB 5 was sunk by a Soviet torpedo boat. The MAS base at Yalta harbor was struck by low flying Soviet fighter-bombers, which inflicted serious damage on the facilities, sank two MAS boats and damaged three. The raid took place just one day after a German flak unit at the port had moved out. Obviously a Soviet spy had done his job well.

Hitler's great offensive officially began on 28 June 1942, but owing to the sheer size of the attacking force it was not until 11 July that the two hundred and twenty-seven thousand Italians were given the order to advance. They marched over hot dusty roads on a seemingly endless landscape of rolling steppe with the Don River on their left (northern) flank. Periodically they overcame enemy rearguards, which were not fierce, though fatal to some. Italian horse cavalry of the Amedeo Duca d'Aosta Celere Division performed well as scouts, and at Krasny Luch they dismounted and fought as infantry, wiping out a pocket of several hundred Soviets.

Some Red Army units retreated northwards until their backs were on the Don River, but rather than stop to destroy them, the Italians bypassed them and continued to advance eastwards, leaving these pockets for the Hungarians, who were following the Italians.

In August the Italians began reaching their assigned goals. Some Italian officers had thought it a mistake to leave pockets of Soviets behind them, perhaps not trusting the Hungarians, and on 21 August their fears were proven well founded. Red Army troops suddenly sprang out of one pocket near Yagodny and charged the Italians. The Italians poured artillery shells into them, but they did not desist, so the Italians fired mortars at them too, but they kept coming, and when they were within a few hundred yards of the Italian positions, the Italian infantry opened fire with rifles and machine guns, and they scythed down the charging Soviets like wheat. A few survivors fell back. Then Messe ordered the Amedeo Duca d'Aosta Celere Division to counter attack with L6 tanks and horse cavalry. At one point the Savoia Dragoons were maneuvering on horseback preparatory to dismounting to fight afoot when Colonel Bettoni saw a body of enemy infantry. With no time to lose he ordered his 2nd Squadron to charge at the gallop. When Captain de Leone received the order he did not ask for confirmation, for this was the dream of every cavalryman. While Italian artillery kept the enemy's heads down the horsemen moved out in ranks at a trot. Some men held their carbines ready to fire one-handed. Others strapped the carbines to their backs and drew sabers. A few crossed themselves in prayer. They were perhaps unaware that this would be the last great cavalry charge in Italian history. At a trot, then at a canter, then at the gallop they charged through tall grass under a blazing hot blue sky. The artillery barrage lifted and a few Soviets raised their heads to look around, and they yelled to their comrades as they saw the horsemen rushing upon them. As the grass was too tall to lie down and still be able to see, most of the Soviets fell to one knee and began firing their bolt-action rifles. De Leone went down, his horse riddled with bullets. The others charged on, many yelling words of encouragement. Soviet machine guns opened fire and more horses went down. But all too soon the Italian war horses were on top of the Soviet infantry, sabers glinting in the sunlight as they slashed the upturned faces of terrified Russians, and carbines fired pointblank into twisting bodies. The horses screamed as they slammed into the bodies of panicky soldiers, and the horsemen carried on clean through the enemy ranks into their rear. The surviving Soviets turned around and fell to one knee again in order to shoot into the backs of the cavalrymen, and therefore did not see a second wave of horsemen charging down upon them. This time the Soviets were taken even more by surprise as sabers and carbine muzzle flashes struck them in the back. Once this wave had passed through, the surviving Soviets tried to recover, but they now came under fire from yet another Italian cavalry squadron that had dismounted and was now shooting into the Soviet flank.

Suddenly the one thought among the Soviets was to flee the mad horsemen, and they took off like rabbits. When the forward artillery observers of the Amedeo Duca d'Aosta Celere Division saw the mob of Russians heading for the river, they called down artillery salvoes, which blasted huge gaps in the enemy ranks. After the last Soviets had fled the field, the horsemen counted one hundred and fifty Soviet corpses and six hundred prisoners most of them wounded, and they picked up over a thousand rifles, several machine guns and four artillery pieces. How many of those Soviets that escaped were wounded, was anyone's guess. The Savoia Dragoons had in fact devastated an entire regiment of three battalions at a cost to them of thirty-nine men killed and seventy-four wounded, and one hundred and seventy horses killed. This was a good culmination of the Italian victory in Russia, and Mussolini's propaganda machine made much of the affair.

Chapter Thirty-six
Italian Victory in the Mediterranean

While some Italians advanced ever deeper into the vastness of the Soviet Union and others prepared to assault Alamein once again, still others battled over and on and under the Mediterranean Sea. In one of the more ironic moments in the propaganda war the British press took time out from their 'all Italians are cowards' campaign to declare that the Italian pig riders were suicide warriors. They never said this about the Germans! In addition to pigs, one man boats and electric boats, the 10th MAS Flotilla had come up with Gamma swimmers. These fellows were definitely a suicide happy crowd. Unlike the pig riders these underwater swimmers had no machines of any kind. They simply swam towards their targets carrying limpet mines. After placing them, they swam away hoping to be out of range when the mines went off. Their first raid was 13 July 1942. Using a derelict ship on the Spanish coast as their base, with the tacit approval of the Spanish dictator Franco, they swam to the harbor at Gibraltar, where they placed mines. They swam back safely, and four merchant ships blew up.

The unit had another success on 29 August 1942. One man sailed his explosives laden motorboat into Alexandria harbor at night and crippled the British destroyer Eridge.

By 1942 Italian submarine crews had perhaps begun to think they too were on a suicide mission. In July the submarine Perla was damaged and captured by the British corvette Hyacinth, and the Ondina was scuttled after fighting a British Walrus seaplane and two South African warships. On 10 August the Scire attempted to launch pigs near Haifa, but was sunk by an anti-submarine trawler. The Pietro Calvi was sunk in the Atlantic by the British sloop Lulworth. The Italian submarine Morosini disappeared in the Atlantic. The Italian ship Nino Bixio was carrying two thousand British prisoners of war when she was torpedoed by the British submarine Turbulent. More than one hundred and fifty prisoners were killed and many were wounded, but the ship survived and was towed to safety by the destroyer Saetta.

Italian surface warships were suffering too. The destroyer Cantore (890 tons) hit a mine and blew up and the destroyer Strale was sunk for the second and last time. The light cruisers Bolzano and Muzio Attendolo were both torpedoed by the British submarine Unbroken, but they reached port.

The destroyer Pegaso had a good month. Though only 840 tons she sank her third British submarine.

These small actions counted, but they were not as newsworthy as a major event. That could only come in another convoy battle. In early

August Italian spies informed Comando Supremo that a British convoy of thirteen merchantmen and a tanker was due to stop at Gibraltar on its way to Malta. To escort this largest Malta convoy yet, the British pulled out all stops: battleships Nelson and Rodney, carriers Eagle, Indomitable and Victorious, cruisers Kenya, Nigeria and Manchester, anti-aircraft cruiser Cairo and fourteen destroyers. Ahead of the convoy British submarines were sweeping and British planes based at Gibraltar would fly overhead part way. Again the British were denuding the war against Japan in order to get one convoy past the Italians. Currently not one British carrier or battleship was engaged against the Japanese, whereas the US Navy admirals were battling for their lives against the Japanese at Guadalcanal and would have given their right arms for the three carriers and two battleships that the British assigned to this one convoy.

With so much power protecting these ships, the Italians knew they would have to hit hard and fast. As a result Comando Supremo chose to rely only on planes, submarines and small craft. In any case the main Italian battle fleet was low on fuel.

On 11 August the Axis submarines maneuvered into position and in doing so the Italian Dagabur was caught and rammed and sunk by the British destroyer Wolverine. In daylight a U-boat commander was offered a target too tempting to be worried about the risks of attacking through an escort in daylight, namely the aircraft carrier Eagle. He sent four torpedoes straight into her, and within seven minutes the mighty vessel sank beneath the waves. Just before dusk thirty-six German bombers flying from Sardinia struck the convoy. No hits were noticed owing to the resistance by heavy British flak and the British Fulmar and Martlet fighters flying overhead.

The next morning another twenty German planes attacked, but also without discernible effect. At 12:15pm seventy Italian and German planes from Sardinia assaulted the convoy. Despite fearsome opposition from flak, Fulmars and Martlets, the attackers sank a merchant ship. At 4pm the Italian submarine Cobalto surfaced in order to gain as much speed as a merchant ship, but was seen by the British destroyers Ithuriel and Pathfinder. She took too long to dive, and she was rammed, and started to sink. The crew evacuated before she went down, and two brave British sailors boarded her looking for documents and code machines. They went down with her. Nearby the submarine Emo tried her torpedo run submerged, but was driven off by barrages of depth charges.

At 6:40pm a hundred Italian and German aircraft arrived to do battle. One SM79 flew so low its crew could have qualified for sea duty pay and it placed a torpedo into a destroyer, the Foresight. A German Stuka dropped an egg squarely on the carrier Indomitable causing frightful damage. Two Stukas sent bombs into the Victorious, but they had released them too low for them to arm so the bombs did not explode.

Incredibly at this very moment most of the escort vessels abandoned their charges and returned to Gibraltar! The Italians were astonished. Surely the famed Royal Navy could not be so foolish?

As the sun began to set twenty German planes arrived from Sicily. Fewer flak guns and fewer fighters meant all the difference in the world, so these aircraft were highly successful. Italian reconnaissance planes followed them to study the scene - three merchant ships and the oil tanker were burning, the anti-aircraft cruiser Cairo was badly damaged and the cruiser Kenya appeared to be in rough shape.

The crew of the Italian submarine Axum did not care how many flak guns the Cairo carried, and they sent a pair of torpedoes straight into her. Within minutes the ship was a floating wreck that had to be abandoned and scuttled. Then the Italian submarine Alagi torpedoed the Kenya.

After midnight a flotilla of Italian MAS boats slipped inside the convoy area. The helmsmen of these boats aimed for the enemy ships as if to ram, while their machine gunners sprayed the decks of the ships. Of course the British flung everything but the kitchen sink at the tiny vessels, the shell explosions coming so near that they drenched the boats with water and shrapnel. Many an MAS crewman must have thought this was his last moment. Then after what seemed to be an agonizingly long time the two torpedo men saw the boat commander wave the signal, and they let loose the two torpedoes. Each boat's helmsman then spun the wheel in an effort to escape the danger zone. This night the MAS crews, whom the rest of the Italian Navy considered to be lunatics, did their country proud. They torpedoed seven vessels. Once back at their base on the island of Pantelleria these MAS crewmen would recount their deeds for days on end to anybody who would listen.

At dawn Italian reconnaissance planes peeked at the convoy: of the thirteen merchant ships only five were still afloat, and they were all badly damaged as was the tanker. The heavy cruiser Manchester was crippled by torpedo hits from two MAS boats. She was scuttled. There were a few destroyers left. Twelve German bombers from Sicily now struck these remnants. They hit the tanker again and blew apart a merchant ship. Later fifteen Italian planes arrived, striking the tanker yet again and sinking one merchantman and damaging another.

The Maltese at the dockside cheered as the oil tanker and three crippled merchant ships limped into harbor. After all only four merchant ships had reached the island nation in the past eight months!

Naturally the British politicians claimed a victory, but the British admirals knew that the Royal Navy could not afford many more such 'victories'. Mussolini also proclaimed a victory, with much greater justification. For the loss of two submarines and a few planes the Italians and Germans had sunk a carrier, two cruisers, a destroyer and ten merchant ships and had damaged two carriers, a cruiser, a destroyer, a tanker and three merchant ships.

The British still had an ace up their sleeve, namely their code breaking accomplishments. These enabled them in the last week of August 1942 to intercept and sink four Italian oil tankers that had sailed for Africa from four different ports filled to the brim with fuel for Rommel.

———————————

Chapter Thirty-seven
Alam al Halfa

Though Mussolini had long since returned to Rome, Rommel was still under orders to take Cairo. By late August 1942 Rommel knew he was as ready as he was going to be for his attempt to bust through the Alamein line. He had been desperate for reinforcements. What he wanted was several more armored divisions. What he received in July was one Italian armored division, the Littorio, and one German infantry division, the 164th. When he heard that the Malta air drop had been cancelled, he had even requested the paratroopers earmarked for Malta. He knew he was scraping the bottom of the barrel, because the German and Italian paratroopers, though courageous, were good for one thing only: a quick drop on the enemy's lines of communication. They were not equipped or trained to hold a front line and certainly not to attack one and moreover they were hopelessly outclassed against enemy armor. Yet, this is precisely what he now expected them to do.

By late August Rommel had raised his tank strength to two hundred and thirty-four Mark IIIs and IVs, one hundred and ten M13s and M14s, twelve M11s and a few L6s. Additionally he was unofficially using some captured tanks. Most importantly, he had received a major shipment of German anti-tank guns.

The forty-mile front line at Alamein was manned on the coast by von Liebenstein's German 164th Division (under a separate German corps command). Inland from there under Italian X Corps were the Trento Motorized Division, [German] Ramcke Parachute Brigade, Bologna Division and Brescia Division. In reserve Rommel kept the Afrika Korps [15th Panzer, 21st Panzer and Major General Ulrich Kleeman's 90th Light Divisions] and XX Corps [Ariete Armored, Littorio Armored and Francesco la Ferla's Trieste Motorized Divisions]. It is noticeable that Rommel allowed the German paratroopers to come under an Italian corps command, something he would never have done a year earlier.

Bastico, Rommel's boss, kept the XXI Corps of the Pavia, Pistoia and Folgore Divisions in his reserve, though he had permitted a few Folgore paratroopers to serve at the front. This gave Rommel a fighting strength of twenty-five thousand Germans and eighty-two thousand Italians with which to accomplish Mussolini's simple little order: destroy British Eighth Army, capture the great British naval base at Alexandria, take Cairo, cross the Suez Canal, capture the naval facilities there, conquer Palestine, cross Syria, cross Iraq and link up with the Germans on the Russian Front who would be coming down from the Caucasus!

Of course this was pie in the sky strategy and even Il Duce did not really expect to attain all of this. However, Rommel knew that the Suez Canal was within his grasp. Italian agents were trying to stir up anti-British revolts in Palestine and Egypt, but the Italian record of mistreatment of Africans did not endear them to the Egyptians. The Grand Mufti of Jerusalem was an avowed supporter of the Nazi/Fascist cause, but he had few supporters.

Rommel had been promised two thousand four hundred tons of fuel in August: he received a hundred tons. Obviously Rommel must have felt deserted. At least there was some good luck on his side: Auchinleck, the man who had turned Rommel's victory in November into an Allied victory, and who had fought like a cornered rat at Alamein, was inexplicably relieved by Churchill. This prime minister considered himself a strategist, but like Hitler his arrogance reached a higher level than his strategic knowledge could ever reach. Throwing out Auchinleck was one of his greatest mistakes. Churchill replaced him with General Harold Alexander, a competent infantry officer. Churchill was pure politician, and the fact that Alexander was an actual member of the British Army, whereas Auchinleck was Indian Army, may have had something to do with his decision.

However, Churchill had a good man in mind for command of the Eighth Army, Lieutenant General William Gott. But lady luck smiled on the Axis cause once more: Gott was killed in an air crash. Churchill knew he could not put Auchinleck under Alexander, as that would have shown political weakness, so he grabbed whoever was available, and that was General Bernard Law Montgomery, a British Army officer, who had recently been commanding troops in England. Both Montgomery and Alexander had fought in World War I, but the only combat in this war seen by either general was in retreat - both were at Dunkirk in 1940 and Alexander had retreated from the Japanese in spring 1942.

Quite frankly Montgomery arrived like a breath of fresh air or a thunderstorm depending on one's opinion, because he immediately replaced several senior commanders and promoted Major General Lumsden to lead X Corps. This pleased the Italians and Germans to no end, for now the Allies would be fighting under two new commanders who had no real experience of armored warfare with deputies whose only experience had been in defeat. The Italians already truly believed God was on their side. Had the pope not said so? As for the German soldiers - their army belt buckle was inscribed with "Gott Mit Uns" - God is with us. At last it appeared this was no hollow boast.

Nonetheless Rommel had been forced to put off the August 26 offensive, hoping for just one more supply ship, one more transport plane, to come from Italy. But by the 30th he felt he could stall Mussolini no longer.

He launched his attack on the 31st. At one signal the Italian and

German infantry went 'over the top', while their artillery blasted the Allied defenses and their planes bombed and strafed the Allied rear. Within minutes the Germans of the Ramcke Brigade and the 164th Division and the Italians of the Trento Division were running forward under fire, but soon the offensive was brought to a crawl along the hard sand under savage fire from the Australian 9th and South African 1st Divisions. The assault troops of the Bologna were stopped dead by the Indian 5th Division, and the Brescia was soon held up by the New Zealand 2nd Division.

Meanwhile the Afrika Korps and XX Corps were on the move on the southern flank skirting the edge of the Quattara Depression. They were under air attack from the onset. By now the Allied air forces in Egypt [RAF Desert Air Force] consisted of squadrons from the following air forces: British (RAF), Australian, South African, Polish, Greek and American. The latter were a group of B-25 Mitchell bombers under Brigadier General Edwin B. Lyon's US 9th Air Division. Besides Mitchells, the Allies flew Hurricanes, Spitfires, Blenheims, Fulmars, Swordfish, Barracudas, Wellingtons, Hampdens, Tomahawks, Marylands, Baltimores and Bostons.

Not until evening did Rommel's armor encounter Allied artillery fire, but unfortunately the German and Italian vehicles also drove into a newly laid minefield that they had not known about. No one was invulnerable to the deadly hidden devices: the commanding officers of the 21st Panzer Division and the Afrika Korps both became casualties; and the command vehicle of the Littorio Armored Division blew up, wounding two men, but Major General Ceriana-Mayneri escaped with minor abrasions and shock. Refusing to seek medical attention in the rear, he transferred to another vehicle. The Italian divisional staff was impressed with their new general. It seems they had a true warrior in command. Within hours though, Ceriana-Mayneri's new vehicle struck a mine. Not physically hurt, but obviously suffering from shock, the Italian general insisted on climbing into yet another vehicle and remaining in action. The Italian armored troops noted this with pride. He was their kind of general.

Yet courage alone was not enough, and by the third day the front line Italian and German infantry had still not been able to advance, and though the Afrika Korps and XX Corps had broken through the minefield, they had run up against Major General Horace Birks' British 10th Armored Division and were engaged in a ferocious battle. Rommel saw he would gain nothing but further losses, and like a professional gambler he knew when to quit. He ordered his infantry to hold what they had and he recalled his armor and placed the 90th Light and Trieste Motorized Divisions in a rearguard position. For another two days and nights these two divisions held off Montgomery's counter attack by Freyberg's New Zealand 2nd Division and British 23rd Armored Brigade. While this action was winding down some Folgore paratroopers in an 'on the job training exercise' captured the commander of a New Zealand brigade.

Though this was the second major struggle for the Alamein line, this affair is remembered as the battle of Alam al Halfa. The week long struggle was a serious defeat for Rommel's Armata Corazzini Africa. Reckless assaults on foot, vehicle charges across minefields and long distance truck supply journeys under air attack had cost his army one hundred and sixty-seven Italians and three hundred and sixty-nine Germans killed and nine hundred and eighty-seven Italians and one thousand and six hundred Germans wounded, plus the loss of fifty guns, fifty tanks and four hundred trucks. They had inflicted one thousand six hundred and forty casualties on Montgomery, but unlike Rommel he could afford this loss.

Montgomery had in fact used Auchinleck's plan to defeat Rommel, though he never acknowledged this. However, he was responsible for placing the new minefield, and most crucial of all he was exuberant in front of the men, wore several regimental badges on his beret to honor them, dressed like a combination of a civilian and an infantryman and gave inspiring pep talks. He came across to them as a soldier's general. No tank expert, fortunately he had excellent deputies. His XIII Corps was well handled by Lieutenant General Brian Horrocks in his first large battle command.

The Italians crawled back into their holes and silently dealt with their despair. They had lost friends and had nothing to show for it. One tragic loss was the Italian Sergio Bresciani. He had become a darling of the Fascist magazines, because he had required a special dispensation to fight in the ranks owing to his young age, and he had been decorated for bravery both by the Italians and the Germans and then decorated by both again for a later incident. At the time of his death he was sixteen years old.

The most depressing thought was that this battle would have to be fought all over again.

Bastico was informed by Italy's excellent spy network that the Allies were planning a major raid by special forces. If the report was to be believed the Allies were planning to hit every major Italian base in Libya. Bastico sat up and paid attention, because the Allies had some noteworthy special forces: the LRDG (Long Range Desert Group) of Britons, New Zealanders and White Rhodesians, who specialized in coming out of the desert in jeeps spraying machine gun bullets; the British Special Air Service, who parachuted behind enemy lines and performed sabotage; the British Special Boat Service, who raided ports in collapsible canoes; the Commandos (British, French and Palestinian (Arab and Jew), who specialized in attacking strongholds; the SIG (Special Interrogation Group) of European Jews, who could masquerade as Germans; and last but not least Popski's Private Army, a mixed-nationality force that did whatever the hell they wanted.

On the night of 13 September, having been warned to expect the unexpected, Italian sentries on the outskirts of Benghazi carefully studied a truck convoy coming towards them in the dark. The fact that the vehicles sounded like British and American trucks did not alert them, for both sides used them, but something was not quite right. So the sentries challenged the first vehicle, whereupon the convoy turned and drove into the desert. The sentries fired on them until they were out of sight.

This same night the Italian sentries at Barce airfield were also alert and when they tried to stop a convoy of jeeps that was approaching them in the dark the jeeps opened fire with machine guns. A fierce little battle developed as the jeeps drove across the airfield in the darkness firing machine guns, gunning down unarmed German and Italian ground crew, shooting at fuel dumps until they exploded, spraying the windows of buildings and riddling twenty-two aircraft with bullets When the jeeps fled into the desert and disappeared in the blackness, a group of brave Italians jumped into vehicles and followed them.

This same night Italian sentries at Tobruk recognized an approaching vehicle convoy as British and opened fire killing or capturing all the occupants - or so they thought: five men escaped. The prisoners were identified as members of the LRDG and SIG.

Simultaneously at Tobruk Italian coastal gunners, peering out to sea in the black night, sighted landing craft embarking from two ships. The Italian shore guns opened up at once. The British ships returned fire with 6inch shells, meaning they had to be light cruisers. (The Sikh and the Zulu). When the landing craft reached the shore British commandos leaped out, but Italians and Germans of all trades - Carabinieri, police, airmen, sailors, army clerks and mechanics, - grabbed rifles and began hunting down the British one by one in the dark night. Fortunately the 3rd Battalion of the San Marco Marines was here, and they quickly rushed into the fight.

Jalo Oasis, which was hundreds of miles from the coast had been captured by the Allies in 1941, but had then been abandoned. This night, as part of this multi-targeted raid, the Allies returned to Jalo with so much arrogance that they were sure the Italian garrison would simply surrender. They had even ordered a raiding party to stop here and rest on their way home!

As dawn began to shed light on this great series of events Italian planes found the LRDG column that had been driven off by the Benghazi defenses and they strafed the vehicles. Also this morning those Italians that had followed the LRDG from Barce airfield caught up with them. There was considerable shooting, but the LRDG vehicles scattered in different directions and the Italians gave up the chase. This same morning the Tobruk shore gunners received word from Italian reconnaissance planes that their shells had sunk the Sikh and had crippled the Zulu, which was limping back to Alexandria. The British anti-aircraft cruiser Coventry came to the Zulu's aid, but Italian and German aircraft sent the Coventry to the bottom of the peaceful looking blue Mediterranean.

The Italian garrison of Jalo did not capitulate, and they repelled attacks by British Sudanese troops for five days, until the British gave up and left.

By any calculation this series of raids was another great Axis victory. For the loss of a few men, some damage to minor facilities and the destruction or damaging of two squadrons of planes at the airfield, the Italians and Germans had inflicted major damage on the British, namely sinking two warships and crippling a third, and killing or capturing hundreds of Allied personnel, most of whom were highly trained specialists. Moreover, they had proven that their intelligence sources were impeccable. Indeed such had been the Italian response that never again would the Allies launch such an ambitious multi-targeted raid against the Italians.

––––––––––––

The Tobruk action was the only major destruction visited upon the Royal Navy in the Mediterranean in September 1942. Italian mines did sink a British submarine. The Italian submarine Alabastro was sunk by a Sunderland flying boat dropping depth charges, and Allied planes damaged the destroyers Castore and Lupo and sank the Polluce (640 tons).

On 12 September 1942 a German U-boat sent torpedoes into the British passenger ship Laconia. The Germans had thought she was carrying troops, and she was, some four hundred Polish and British soldiers, but also aboard were eighty British civilians and one thousand eight hundred Italian prisoners. The U-boat commander was horrified when he saw civilians and prisoners of war getting into life boats, so he sent a distress signal over open channels and over the next two days he was joined by another two U-boats and the Italian submarine Capellini, and they all began to tow the lifeboats to safety as the ship sank. The submarines were also packed with survivors, and their decks were full of them. However, an American warplane flew over and reported the scene, whereupon it was ordered to bomb the U-boats regardless of the effect upon the civilians and Allied soldiers. The bomber did as ordered. As a result the U-boats turned the lifeboats loose and submerged, the passengers on their decks having to swim for it. Admiral Karl Doenitz, commander of all U-boats, told his sailors from now on not to risk their lives by rescuing Allied personnel. Most of the survivors were eventually rescued.

The Italian submarine Archimede in the Atlantic torpedoed and damaged a Greek troopship, and later torpedoed and sank the British liner/troopship Oronsay.

On 19 October the Italian destroyer Verazzano (1,870 tons) was escorting a convoy from Naples to Tripoli, when she was struck by a torpedo. She went down quickly.

———————

PART THREE
The Long Road Home
Chapter Thirty-Eight
Second Alamein

Rommel had been ill during the Battle of Alam al Halfa, and following it he flew to Germany for treatment, part of the cure being an audience with Hitler and a promotion to field marshal. He had left General Georg von Stumme in command of Armata Corazzini Africa to preside over the resupply that would have to take place, if they were to halt the next enemy offensive. Rommel was sure the British would eventually attack.

The British Eighth Army, now firmly under Montgomery's grip, was building up at a rapid rate. Montgomery's armored divisions would soon have two hundred and fifty-two Shermans, one hundred and seventy Grants, seventy-six Crusaders and a few Honeys. The Sherman had proven itself to be a good tank, with one exception. When hit by a shell it had a tendency to explode. Montgomery's tank brigades [i.e. the units that were pledged to support the infantry] would soon have six hundred Valentines, Matildas and Honeys, and three experimental Churchills – the latter an 8 feet 2 inches high 39-ton tank armed with a 6pounder gun. The Eighth Army's artillery received some Priests, i.e. an American-made 105mm self-propelled gun, 9 feet 5 inches high and 22.7 tons.

The reliance on American-built armor is noticeable. The British armored brigades had the best tanks available to them, and almost 90% of these were American-built, though by now these armored brigades only used the Honey as a reconnaissance vehicle.

To counter this the Axis was also building up its forces on an impressive scale. Stumme would soon have two hundred and twenty M13s and M14s and sixty M11s in his Italian armored units, and eight Mark IVs with short 75mm guns, thirty Mark IVs with medium barrel 75mm guns, eighty Mark IIIs with medium barrel 50mm guns and eighty-six Mark IIIs with long barrel 50mm guns in his German panzer regiments. His German reconnaissance forces had Mark II tanks, Sd231 armored cars and the new 11.6-ton Puma armored car mounting a 50mm gun; and his Italian reconnaissance units used L6s, Autoblinda armored cars and some captured Matildas. Thus almost five hundred Axis tanks serving in panzer/armored regiments would face five hundred British tanks serving in armored brigades, an even match, but this did not count the six hundred British infantry support tanks in the tank brigades. Moreover the British had plenty of Bren gun carriers, a marvelous little lightly armored vehicle with an open top, good for rushing up provisions and personnel against machine gun bullets.

There was also a discrepancy in artillery. Counting self-propelled guns and towed guns Stumme raised his complement up to one thousand two hundred and nineteen guns (five hundred and seventy-five Italian and six hundred and forty-four German), but Montgomery had two thousand three hundred and eleven guns.

To support Stumme, the Luftwaffe and Regia Aeronautica provided two hundred Italian and one hundred and fifty German planes, including the superb German Bf109 fighter that had a top speed of 398 mph, the good Italian Mc202 fighter that had a top speed of 371 mph, the decent Italian Re2002 radial engine fighter that had a top speed of 333 mph, and the dependable Stuka dive-bomber used by both Italians and Germans. Sadly the remainder of the German and Italian planes in North Africa were obsolete.

Supporting Montgomery was Air Marshall Sir Arthur Tedder's Desert Air Force of five hundred and thirty Allied combat aircraft, including the Hurricane, Tomahawk and Spitfire fighters, which had a top speed of 340 mph, 360 mph, and 378 mph, respectively. In bombers he had the excellent Wellington, Mitchell and Boston. The remaining Allied planes in North Africa were obsolete. These were divided into ninety-seven squadrons [sixty-two British, thirteen American, eleven South African, five Australian, two Greek, two Yugoslavian, one Canadian and one French], though many of the flyers in the British squadrons were not from Britain - one whole squadron had White Rhodesian pilots.

In Libya and Egypt Bastico's manpower consisted of more than a quarter of a million men, but of these only ninety thousand Italians and seventy-one thousand Germans were serving under Stumme. The remainder consisted of twenty thousand Luftwaffe airmen and flak gunners, twenty thousand German Army support troops, and fifty-six thousand Italian airmen, sailors, flak gunners, Carabinieri, coastal gunners and army support troops.

The British Eighth Army and its support units contained troops from many nations - British, Australians, New Zealanders, Indians, White and Black South Africans, Greeks, French, Black African ascaris of the British Army (almost eighty thousand), Arabs and Jews from Palestine (four thousand five hundred, Cypriots (five thousand six hundred), and men from the Rodriguez, Mauritius and Seychelles Islands. There were also well over a thousand Italians in British uniform and some in French uniform.

By dawn on 23 October 1942 the Italians and Germans had done the best they could to prepare their defenses, but in such a barren landscape there was little they could do. Every scraggly bush, dip in the ground and sharp rock was being used as a natural defensive position. Man could add trenches, foxholes, barbed wire, minefields, camouflage nets and sandbags, but little else.

On both sides the main camps consisted of tent cities divided into platoon alleys, company streets and battalion avenues. Signs hung from tents to identify command posts to visitors, couriers and mail carriers. Letters from home arrived in batches, so each soldier organized them by postmark date and then read them in order. Then read them again, and again. At times Italian soldiers became angry that wives seemed more concerned about the color of new curtains or the price of table wine. In the hot Egyptian summer each soldier here would have given a day's pay for a drink of cold water, let alone a glass of wine, and in the winter he would have offered a week's pay for an extra blanket. Yet this mail was better than no mail.

On the coast this morning some Bersaglieri reported for sick call, only to be told by an obviously sick medic to wait for the doctor who was sick, who would tell them that everybody was sick, so what? Just inland perhaps some of the soldiers of the Trento Motorized Division were complaining about the food: 'tinned sausages again'? Just south of them were the Germans of von Liebenstein's 164th Division, the first ordinary 'Landser' to serve in the desert. Some troops watched as their divisional engineers prepared to place more mines. No one envied them this job. More than once an engineer had become disoriented and had trodden on one of his own mines. To the south of these Germans some Italians of the Bologna Division were straightening trenches. It was 'busy work' and they knew it. While working they most likely joked about their officers. To their south some fellow Italians of the Brescia Division were cleaning their weapons. They caressed the Breda light machine gun, but cursed the designers of their other hand-held weapons. The damned sand seemed to get inside the rifle barrels no matter how often they were cleaned. To their south some of the German paratroopers of the Luftwaffe's Ramcke Brigade underwent classroom type training from instructors with blackboards in the open air. Recent replacements were told how to tell the difference between the sound of a German Mauser rifle and a British Enfield at night, and how to charge with fire and movement tactics, and above all how to stay alive. To their south the paratroopers of the Folgore Division underwent similar instruction. They listened intently to every word, knowing that this information would save their lives. To their south many members of the Pavia Division cursed their officers, the Fascists, Mussolini, Hitler and Churchill. They talked about the strutting Blackshirts back home. In every company there were Socialists and Communists who tried to gain converts with their barracks rabble-rousing. Some vowed to defect the moment they got a chance. This day the Italian 31st Combat Engineers Battalion attended a ceremony held in their honor. Filled with pride, but tinged with sadness at the memory of lost compatriots, the entire battalion was awarded the Silver Medal for gallantry. This was practically unique in Italian history. Unlike the US Army the Italians did not have unit citations. Far to the rear the men of the 15th Panzer, 21st Panzer, 90th Light, Ariete Armored, Littorio Armored and Trieste Motorized Divisions attended to their vehicles and equipment: mechanics, tank crews, panzergrenadiers, Bersaglieri, armored car crews, self-propelled gun crews, fuel engineers, ammunition carriers, cooks, truck drivers and clerks working steadily; a sand-covered radiator could overheat at the crucial moment; a dirty ranging mechanism could cause inaccurate fire; a badly tuned radio could deprive the unit of artillery support; and so on. There were a hundred and one things to attend to. In this modern army the soldiers each had a specialty trade, and even in the lowly infantry, usually considered the 'dumbest' of the troops, each man had to be something of a mechanic, an athlete, a builder and a psychologist, for he had to second guess the enemy and be ready for him, whether the enemy attacked at noon or at night, with a bayonet or in a tank.

While flak gunners scanned the skies, the Italian and German generals planned; for it was not a question of 'if' the Allies would attack but 'when'.

In mid-afternoon the work details finished early. Food of sorts was dished out, to be washed down with musty water. Afterwards, the main form of entertainment consisted of complaining, storytelling, complaining, guessing, complaining, listening to rumors, complaining, joking and more complaining.

As the camps settled down for the night some Italians dreamed of climbing their beautiful Alpine mountains such as Monte Bondone, of spectacular views, of group singing in crisp mountain air. It was funny how the Alpine cold never bothered them, but in the desert the autumn nights were chilly. Others reminisced about the sidewalk cafes in Bologna and the sultry beauties who paraded along the thoroughfares in soft summer dresses in that fashion conscious city. They would have traded a year in the desert for one afternoon in Bologna. Others dreamed of meeting their girlfriends in the Brescia city center at the Piazza della Loggia in front of the large white building that was now the local Fascist Party headquarters. The more artistic-minded dreamed of exploring the historic structures in Italy, of viewing the magnificent art galleries and attending the opera. Romans in the desert boasted that their city put everyone else's to shame. No doubt some Sardinians and Sicilians wondered what they were doing here fighting an 'Italian' war.

As it drew towards a time to sleep and 'perchance to dream' the men of Armata Corazzini Africa sent their minds far from the desert, far from the war to the heart of Rome, of Berlin, of Munich, of Messina, of Milan, of Vienna, to the forests, the mountains, the beaches, to home. Little did they realize that in a few minutes a quarter of a million men from a score of nations would be trying to kill them.

At 9:40pm on the 23rd the sky over the Axis camps lit up like lightning as they were suddenly bombarded by the largest artillery concentration they had yet witnessed. Over two thousand three hundred guns were firing shell after shell at them, their gun crews quickly working up a sweat in the chilly night. The noise was deafening. Every few seconds the sky lit up as if it were daylight. Some Italians were blasted into fragments before they realized what was happening. Within one split second of time in Stumme's army there were no more Germans nor Italians, nor Fascists, nor Nazis, nor Communists, nor Socialists, nor Lutherans nor Catholics, not even any soldiers, just terrified men hugging the sand, trusting in their officers and begging for God to stop the noise, that oh so deadly noise.

After the longest twenty minutes in their lives the barrage lifted somewhat and became more selective. Those Italians stuck out alone in the desert in listening posts stared at the strangely attired men walking towards them in the dark lit by flashes of gunfire. The strangers were yelling at the top of their voices, but these Italians could not hear them above the din. Their ears were ringing from concussion. When the strangers motioned with their rifles for them to walk to the east, the Italians crawled out of their holes and obeyed. They were so dazed by the artillery barrage that they did not realize they had just been taken prisoner.

However, to the immediate rear of these posts Italian and German infantry who still had their wits about them were rushing to battle stations, experienced enough to know that such a barrage would assuredly be followed by an Allied infantry attack. They scanned the horizon, their night vision lost, hoping that gun flashes and flares would brighten the sky enough to see the enemy. Then they saw them, thousands of them, and they immediately opened fire with rifles, machine guns and mortars and called for artillery support. This was the largest offensive launched by a British-led army in the war to date: one hundred and four thousand front line defenders were under assault from one hundred and ninety-five thousand attackers.

The Bersaglieri along the coast began falling back in good order one meter at a time under pressure from the Australian 9th Division. To their south the Germans of the 164th Division were reeling back under a fierce bayonet charge by the famed 51st Highland Scots Division. The Scots were so confident they led with bagpipers. The Trento Motorized Division was under serious pressure from Pienaar's South African 1st and Freyberg's New Zealand 2nd Divisions. Still further south the men of the Bologna Division had forgotten all about their dreams as they battled for their very lives against the Indian 4th Division. Ramcke's paratroopers were under fanatic attack by men in British uniform, that later turned out to be Greeks. The Brescia

Division's soldiers fervently stood their ground against a full-scale charge by the British 50th Division. Still further south Major General Riccardo Bignami's Folgore Division paratroopers frantically defended their holes in the sand against an onslaught by the British 44th Division. On the southern flank of the line the Pavia Division fought against a French brigade.

Montgomery had divided his forces into three parts. Lieutenant General Oliver Leese commanded the northern part of the line, Lieutenant General Brian Horrocks controlled the southern stretch and Lieutenant General Lumsden kept the bulk of the armor in his X Corps in reserve.

The entire Axis line was fighting at bad odds: three Bersaglieri light infantry battalions on the coast against six Australian heavy infantry battalions; nine German heavy infantry battalions versus twelve similarly-armed British battalions; the Trento's six heavy infantry and three light infantry battalions facing fifteen New Zealand and South African heavy infantry battalions; six Bologna heavy infantry battalions against six Indian and three British of the same; Ramcke's three lightly-armed battalions against three Greek heavy infantry battalions; Brescia's six heavy infantry battalions fighting nine British of the same; and six lightly armed Folgore paratrooper battalions slugging it out with nine British heavy infantry battalions. Only the Pavia Division, which had some German reconnaissance troops attached, outnumbered its attackers.

By 1am all the defenders had fallen back somewhat, but then the Allies stopped to rest for thirty minutes. Then they resumed the onslaught.

Come dawn the Bersaglieri were still holding, firing at Aussies who ran towards them in short sprints. The German infantry reported they had the Scots pinned down in a minefield: the bagpipe music had stopped. The Trento was keeping the New Zealanders in a minefield and had also stopped the South Africans in the open desert. The Ramcke, Bologna, Brescia and Folgore were still withdrawing, but only one foxhole at a time and they made the attackers pay for everyone.

At 6:30am Trento's anti-tank gunners calmly waited while the vehicles of the British 10th Armored Division filled their sights. This was lovely, they thought, and when the tanks came so close that the Italians could read letters and numbers on them the anti-tank gunners opened fire, and continued to shoot for thirty minutes until the British withdrew. By now Italian and German planes were pummeling the attackers, and Allied planes were plastering the Italians and Germans. It was no picnic for either side.

By mid-afternoon the German infantry began falling back again. There was no panic, but they were in retreat nonetheless. In the past the Germans had had a habit of reinforcing Italian units with small detachments of Germans. They called it 'corseting' as it 'stiffened the backbone' of the Italians. This was extremely patronizing and often not necessary. Therefore, it was perhaps with some satisfaction that the Italian generals grabbed small detachments of Italians from several units and sent them to fill the gap vacated by the retreating Germans. Now who was it that needed corseting?

However, the Italians' feeling of regaining hurt pride soon turned to alarm as they found Scottish infantry, South African armored cars and the British 1st Armored Division pouring through the abandoned German line and penetrating fully six miles within an hour.

Lieutenant General Wilhelm von Thoma was worried about this situation. He had just been thrown in at the deep end: taking over command of the army when he heard that Stumme was dead. Von Thoma radioed Germany that he needed Rommel at once.

Fortunately for the Axis cause, the British did not exploit their breakthrough once they saw the Italian corseting force manning an emergency defensive position. In fact by the morning of 25 October, after thirty-two hours of battle, the situation had been stabilized. The Allies were still shooting, but not advancing. The German infantry had regrouped and was back in line again. The 15th Panzer Division now came up and attempted to regain the lost ground, but their effort failed.

Only the Folgore paratroopers were still under heavy pressure. By now casualties in this division were ridiculously high. Shrapnel and bullets were incoming so fast and furious that the wounded often had to be left unattended and were sometimes wounded again. The medics earned great praise from their fellow soldiers as they crawled from one wounded man to another. It was not just terrifying for the medics but heartbreaking, for they had to ignore those who were obviously not going to make it, even if it was a friend. The Folgore officers continuously yelled over the din into their field telephones and radios demanding reinforcements and artillery support and air support. They could not hold, they screamed. An Italian paratrooper does not run, but he does bleed.

At last von Thoma was able to send some aid to the Folgore: a few infantry companies and some artillery batteries from the Pavia, some artillery from the Trieste, and a handful of M13s and Mark IIIs. They were rushed straight into action. Later some artillery and anti-tank guns of the Giovanni Fascisti Gruppo arrived from strategic reserve.

On the 26th, the third full day of battle, the Bersaglieri and the 164th Division bore the brunt of an attack by the Australians, who were obviously trying to cut these defenders off with their backs to the sea. The 15th Panzer Division counter attacked again and failed again.

Finally Rommel returned and he identified Kidney Ridge as a strategic location, so he sent forces to hold it: some M14s and

Semoventi 75s from Littorio, panzergrenadiers from 90th Light, and the entire 15th Panzer Division. They got there just in time, for later that day the British 1st Armored and 51st Divisions attacked the ridge. The mixed Italian/German force was able to surprise the British completely. In fact they counter attacked and drove the British all the way back to their original front line.

By the fourth day of battle, the 27th, the shooting had not stopped, but Montgomery's plan had certainly been defeated. The Axis line had been restored, even if the Trento had begun pulling back somewhat. The Trento's 61st Regiment was particularly hard pressed, fighting at odds of two to one, but having fallen back a thousand meters they suddenly turned and counter attacked.

Montgomery realized the Folgore was near collapse and had been reinforced, so he reinforced the British 44th Division with a French brigade. The formations of young idealistic Italian paratroopers were being sliced up and cut to the bone, yet they stopped this new attack. By dawn on the 27th out of eighteen field grade officers in the Folgore, nine had been killed and four wounded.

Montgomery was stumped. The Italians and Germans were fighting magnificently. On the 27th the only good news for him was from Kidney Ridge where the 21st Panzer Division counter attacked the British 1st Armored Division and failed.

On the 28th Rommel ordered the 164th and Trento Motorized Divisions to counter attack. To reinforce the depleted infantry of the Trento, its divisional staff formed a provisional battalion of cooks, clerks, drivers and other rear echelon personnel and threw them into the slaughter. Within an hour the Trento and 164th had straightened out their line again. Meanwhile Rommel was sending the 90th Light Division to the coast.

On the 29th, the sixth full day of battle, the 90th Light tried to counter attack, but Allied aircraft had spotted their movement and was now giving them hell. Rommel studied the latest strength reports and was alarmed: the bulk of the Ariete was in reserve and still had one hundred and twenty-nine tanks, but the Littorio had sent packets to beef up the front and was now down to thirty-three tanks. The Trieste was down to thirty-four tanks, the 15th Panzer was down to twenty-one tanks and 21st Panzer was down to forty-five tanks.

On the evening of the 29th the 164th Division and the 90th Light Division were both struck by a major Australian assault. The Germans fought like wildcats for thirty-two hours solid, but on the morning of the 31st the commander of the 164th reported such terrible losses that Rommel asked his staff to plan for the retreat of the entire army, and he authorized the 164th to withdraw two thousand meters. As they did so, the Aussies attacked again and within an hour a large pocket of Germans was trapped, their backs to the sea.

On 1 November, the ninth day of battle, the 90th Light counter attacked and managed to rescue most of the trapped men. Obviously the 164th was no longer a viable formation. The Trento was also nearing its end, and by dawn of 2 November that division began to waver. By mid-morning many of its companies had been cut off. Lieutenant General Alessandro Gloria, commander of XXI Corps, organized a rescue attempt, but before he could implement it the trapped Italians were overrun by tanks of the British 9th and 23rd Armored Brigades.

The Trento Motorized Division, though cut in twain with a major enemy force between the two halves, nonetheless carried on the fight. Gloria now prepared a welcoming committee for the two British armored brigades, which would come on, he was sure. As the British tanks drove towards the tent city of the Trento Motorized Division camp, Gloria opened fire on them from both flanks with Italian and German anti-tank guns. The British tanks swerved towards their flanks to charge the gunners, but this was exactly what Gloria anticipated, for it opened their sides towards the tent city, and from this direction the Italians and Germans counter attacked with every tank that the Afrika Korps and the Littorio Armored Division could muster. The battle took place in a fog created by explosions, smoke from burning tanks and swirling sand churned up by maneuvering tank treads. In between the mechanical monsters ran Bersaglieri of the Trieste, who gymnastically dodged bullets and shrapnel and the heavy tank treads that could mash an arm or a leg into pulp without the driver even noticing it. Those Bersaglieri that survived this ballet of death joined with panzergrenadiers and charged the flanks of the New Zealand 2nd Division, which was currently busy facing the two halves of the Trento.

This was a mighty struggle. The Italian tank crews showed great bravery in mixing it with superior enemy tanks, because a solid shot could enter the M14 or M13, shower the crew with molten metal and spin around inside the tank, white hot, burning until the shell rammed into something more solid and stopped, and all within the time it took to blink one's eye! Most tanks simply stopped dead if hit, but some exploded, their turrets being tossed into the air like toys to land upside down by the hull. Crewmen often crawled out of these wrecks looking like blackened burned store dummies. Falling to the desert floor they were fair game for bullets or the treads of enemy tanks. The German tanks fared better than the Italians, for they traded one for one.

By nightfall the Italian and German tanks and anti-tank guns had destroyed two hundred out of the three hundred attacking British tanks, but the Littorio had lost all but a couple of its tanks and the entire Afrika Korps was down to thirty-five machines. The foot soldiers had suffered extraordinarily high losses.

This evening Rommel recognized the inevitable and ordered the Trento and Bologna to begin walking towards the rear. These men obeyed at once. They knew that if Rommel thought they were licked, then they really must be. Come dawn on 3 November, the eleventh day of battle, the survivors of these two divisions were strung out along tracks and the coast road, and as the sun rose the soldiers began to be subjected to bombing and strafing by Allied planes. This journey of fear was even more horrific than the front line fight. However, towards the end of the day the men were ordered to turn around and walk back towards the battlefield! Incredibly they obeyed, though it must have seemed to them that someone in the higher echelons was out to kill them off. That someone was in fact Adolf Hitler, who had personally countermanded Rommel's retreat order.

Surprisingly the Allies had not exploited the wide gap in the line created by the retreat of the Trento and Bologna! This was the first indication to the Italians and Germans that Montgomery did not understand a war of movement. He was an excellent planner, a terrific morale booster, and he was master of the set-piece battlefield, but a war of tank and truck was, quite frankly, beyond him.

Of course, lower ranking Allied officers had tried to push infantry through the gap, but Italian rearguards and forward artillery observers had stopped them. Indeed only after dark on the 3rd were the infantry of the Indian 4th and British 51st Divisions able to advance. Thus by the morning of 4 November the gap had been occupied by the British. This morning saw Rommel on the radio pleading for permission to retreat. By absolute coincidence one of Rommel's superiors, Field Marshal Albert Kesselring, was visiting his headquarters, and when he inquired of Rommel of the whereabouts of the army's reserves he was stunned to learn that the only force standing in the path of the British 1st, 7th and 10th Armored Divisions was the Italian Ariete Armored Division, which was already at low strength, because it had sent some battle groups elsewhere.

Ignoring Hitler's wishes, Kesselring and Rommel ordered the entire army to retreat, and Rommel asked the Ariete to sacrifice themselves to save his army, promising them reinforcements. A few Semoventi 75s and armored cars from the Littorio did reach the Ariete, but a column of German artillery ordered to the rescue arrived too late, and these gunners halted to stare in awe at hundreds of British tanks circling a large cloud of sand and smoke, while enemy planes flew overhead sending bombs into that cloud. The noise from the cloud was a deafening cacophony of explosions, tank engines and the rattle of treads. Inside the cloud was the proud Ariete Armored Division, and its men were being maimed, disfigured, burned, shot, sliced, blinded, peeled and mashed. Vehicles that were immobilized fought on like stationary bunkers. Dismounted crews searched for vehicles to clamber into. Bersaglieri fired rifles at oncoming tanks. It was a macabre scene as tragic as watching a city burn or a ship sink. It was the death of a division.

The last message Rommel received from Ariete was brief, stating simply that they were surrounded. The Italians, who are known for their bombastic flowery literary style even in official dispatches, must have decided that this event should take place in verbal silence. The simplicity of this last message was far more poignant than any poetry.

Rommel's army was on the run, Hitler or no Hitler. The weary remnants of the Trento and the Bologna arrived back at the front line just in time to be told to retreat again, but before many could do so they were assaulted by New Zealanders in trucks and South Africans in armored cars. Too tired to walk, let alone run, thousands of the Italians surrendered.

Elsewhere anybody who could climb aboard a vehicle did so and sped westwards away from the battlefield. Most of the Italians had to walk and they began their nightmare march under air attack, but some chose to die right here on this spot. Many surrendered.

Yet at midnight the overcautious Montgomery recalled his trucks and armored cars, fearing they would run into an ambush. Besides, his tanks were still busy massacring the Ariete. He then sat down to a late dinner with his guest von Thoma, who had been captured that day. It was not until dawn on 5 November that the last flickers of Ariete's resistance were extinguished.

The once mighty Armata Corazzini Africa was a battered bleeding remnant strung out along desert tracks for miles. It was impossible for units to regroup on the run and at one point Rommel personally directed traffic where two tracks intersected. The lines of vehicles were backed up twenty-five miles and all of it under air attack.

On the 6th Rommel chose the Folgore to man a rearguard to delay Montgomery. The surviving Folgore men knew this would be their last fight, for they were a division in name only. They opened fire at the approach of British tanks, but when part of their position was overrun the divisional staff officers debated their orders and they concluded it would be best to surrender. The British counted their prisoners: thirty-two officers and two hundred and seventy-two men, and were astonished to find that this was all that was left of the Folgore Division! [No fewer than thirteen officers and eight men of the Folgore were awarded the gold Medal]

This was the greatest land defeat suffered by the Axis in the war to date. As regards numbers of troops involved it was not a prominent affair - Mussolini had lost a far larger army in East Africa - but strategically speaking it was a defeat of tremendous magnitude. Mussolini's dreams of controlling the Suez Canal, of conquering the Iraqi oilfields and of safeguarding Mare Nostrum, had all been dashed. Hitler's dreams of conquering the Iranian oilfields and linking up with the Russian Front were also dashed. Few battles have had such repercussions.

In the thirteen day battle [known as Second Alamein] the attacking Allies had suffered thirteen thousand five hundred casualties. The British portion of this was 58%. Fully a fifth of the Allied casualties were incurred by the Australians.

Axis losses were devastating, over fifty-seven thousand: one thousand one hundred Germans and two thousand Italians killed; three thousand nine hundred Germans and one thousand six hundred Italians wounded; and seven thousand nine hundred Germans and twenty thousand Italians missing during the battle itself, plus five thousand Germans and fifteen thousand eight hundred Italians had been rounded up on the last day.

Partners always squabble in defeat and this calamity was no exception. The Germans began to blame the Italians for the outcome. Even Rommel, to his everlasting shame, joined the protest. German propaganda even denied the figure of two thousand Italian dead, claiming that Italian fatalities were more comparable with the German, say about one thousand two hundred. Despicably the Germans claimed that time and again they had been forced to take up the slack caused by Italian cowardice. They conveniently forgot to mention the Italian rescue of the German 164th Division or the sacrifice of the Ariete and Folgore that enabled the Germans to flee the battlefield. Likewise the Italian claim that all Germans were Nazis who deserted them when the going got tough was equally nonsense.

This author has accepted the Italian report of their casualties rather than the German report. Obviously the Italians knew more about their personnel strengths than the Germans did, and they could hardly have invented the names, serial numbers and addresses of an additional eight hundred dead, and to what end if they had? It must be remembered that the Germans were led by Nazis, who believed every non-German including the Italian was sub-human. A German move backwards was always described by the Nazis as a strategic withdrawal. The identical movement by Italians was described by the Nazis as a shameful retreat. In Africa the Germans, Rommel included, blamed all their woes on the Italians. In post-war books German historians invariably took the German point of view. This included German generals eager to whitewash their own mistakes.

It is unfortunate that this Nazi lie has been backed up by many British historians and even a few Americans, who began writing their books with a preconceived notion of Italian cowardice, and like all bigots they looked for evidence to confirm their opinions and discarded evidence that challenged them. Thus they quoted German sources avidly and ignored Italian sources. By lying about Italian deaths, the statistic gives the impression that for every 1 German killed or wounded another 1.6 Germans surrendered, whereas for every 1 Italian killed or wounded another 7.2 gave up. This suggests an Italian surrender rate of four and a half times that of the German. The inference is that the battle was lost owing to Italian cowardice and not because of a failure of German leadership.

However, if one takes the Italian statistics as reasonably accurate, then it appears that of all Italian casualties 8.5% were killed, and of all German casualties almost an identical percentage were killed. This seems more logical. On the last day of battle three factors caused a higher Italian loss in prisoners: first their lack of transportation meant that many Italian wounded had not been evacuated yet and thus were overrun, secondly it was harder for an Italian on foot to outrun an Allied armored car than it was for a German in a truck, and thirdly the Ariete was totally surrounded and all their wounded were captured. However, if the prisoner tally is looked at before the last day, then for every 1 German killed or wounded another 0.6 was captured, and for every 1 Italian killed or wounded another 1.2 was taken, thus the Italian rate of surrender is only twice that of the Germans. And as explained there were valid reasons for this.

The Germans had a far better medical evacuation system than did the Italians. On the battlefield itself the odds of a wounded German being rescued by an ambulance were greater than for an Italian. Some German wounded were even air lifted to hospital! Because of this the odds of Italian wounded being reached by an Allied medic first were greater than for German wounded. This battle was brutal but not cruel, and Allied medics treated German and Italian wounded, who of course were counted as prisoners of war. Knowing this, and assuming that the German and Allied counts of their own wounded are accurate, one would expect the ratio of Italian killed to wounded to be the same as for the Germans and the Allies, about 1 to 3.5. If Italian dead numbered two thousand, then by this assumption their wounded should have numbered seven thousand, and as the Italians retained one thousand six hundred of their wounded, then about five thousand four hundred of the Italian wounded must have been captured, which means the remainder of the Italian prisoners counted by the Allies were not wounded. [Though many could have been bedridden with sickness.] Looking at the Allied reports of prisoners one then sees that the number of Italian unwounded that surrendered was 7.3 times the number of Italian dead, and the number of German unwounded that surrendered was 7.2 times the number of German dead, almost exactly the same.

The infantry battalions suffered the highest casualty rate of course and in this battle there were twenty-six German infantry battalions (35% of the whole) and forty-nine Italian infantry battalions (65%), and these battalions were more or less similar in manpower strength. Therefore one would expect 35% of the total Axis casualties to be German and 65% to be Italian, and that is exactly what happened up to that last day, and it only changes to 31%/69% if the last day is taken into consideration.

Statistics can be misleading of course, but it does appear that the Italian performance at Second Alamein compared favorably with that of the Germans. To be sure the Allies did not notice any difference at the time! The Germans should be reminded that had it not been for the sacrifice of the Ariete and Folgore they would have all been lost.

The Italians suffered in the desert more than the Germans, in general because they had fewer motor vehicles, poorer equipment, fewer supplies, not as much ammunition and little fuel. It is a miracle they fought at all.

The truth is that neither cowardice nor bad generalship lost the battle. It was lost because an Austrian ex-corporal and an Italian ex-sergeant decided to send the young manhood of Germany-Austria and Italy into the desert in search of glory. They did not give their men the means with which to carry out their orders nor did they give them a sound enough spiritual ideal to fight for. This latter is truer of Fascism than it is of Nazism. If any Italian or German fought to the death, and countless did, it was for love of country and to save their comrades in arms. Few did so for love of Hitler or Mussolini.

———————

While the seeds of this international bickering were being sown, Rommel had other things on his mind. He had a hundred thousand men, but fewer than ten thousand were combat troops and the only fresh units on their way to help him were the Italian Centauro Armored Division and the Raggruppamento Sahariana. He believed he might have to parcel out his men in a series of rearguards to keep Montgomery at bay while he fell back on his supply dumps. After all, the further he traveled the shorter his logistics lines became and the more those of the Allies were stretched.

On 8 November Rommel was informed that American and British troops had landed in French-controlled Morocco and Algeria far to his rear [west]. The French there obeyed the government in France [unlike the French serving under Montgomery] and they were resisting the Allies, but if they collapsed and the Anglo-Americans were able to push eastwards into Libya, Rommel would be squashed between them and Montgomery. He asked Hitler if this would not be a good time to evacuate all forces from Africa.

———————

Chapter Thirty-nine
Italy's Home Front

Up until November 1942 the Italian people knew they were winning the war, though already things were not as they should be. Many goods were scarce. Prices were high. The black market flourished. Every day it seemed some woman in the market place was mourning a lost son or husband. Everywhere anti-Fascists were trying to galvanize the people with such pronouncements as: "Mussolini says we are advancing, but where to...a dry African desert.... a frozen Russian steppe.... a watery grave?'

On the night of 22 October 1942 the searchlights of the city of Genoa pointed their groping fingers into the black sky as sirens wailed. Soon flak gunners began punching holes in the night. Despite being offered a target of one hundred and twelve British four-engine Lancaster bombers they did not shoot down one aircraft. The bombs fell in a scattered pattern and several neighborhoods were devastated. The people hid in air raid shelters or in basements if they had them, except for the emergency personnel - flak gunners, searchlight operators, firemen, ambulance crews, civil defense volunteers and air raid wardens. The raid left fifty Genoans dead and two hundred hospitalized with injuries. The following morning the streets were filled with smoke and every survivor had a story to tell in their nervousness. That night the British returned to Genoa, this time with one hundred and twenty-two bombers. Turin and Savona were also bombed.

By the next day everyone in Northern Italy was agitated. Four major raids in two nights were unprecedented. Everywhere townsfolk began to wonder who was next. In Milan some speculated that the raids had something to do with the great desert battle going on at Alamein. After such a long break since the last raids, did this herald a new aerial offensive? While Milan housewives gossiped in the street and at the market, students at Milan's university engaged in the Fascist-democracy argument, and secretaries in the city's public buildings expressed concern for boyfriends at the front, and machinists at the Caproni factory mentioned the irony that British workers like them were making bombers too, workers killing workers. Many of the workers were Socialists and Communists who thought this not so much ironic as just plain despicable.

Suddenly the bombs tumbled out of the bomb bays in daylight onto an unaware Milan without warning. There had been no air raid sirens. The housewives in the open markets heard the planes, but as there was no sound from the air raid sirens they assumed they were Italian. Only when that terrifying screech of falling bombs reached their ears did they realize. Their first thoughts were: 'the children, the children!'

The secretaries were too busy talking and typing to hear the planes. The screech of falling bombs gave them just enough time to slide under their desks. At the Caproni factory the roar of machinery drowned out even the sound of falling bombs. The first they knew of the raid was when the windows blew in and the roof fell down upon them. For the next eighteen minutes eighty-eight Lancaster bombers leisurely dropped bombs.

As the last bomb fell, the air was filled with the sound of emergency vehicle bells: fire trucks turned their hoses on blazing buildings; ambulances swerved to miss rubble in the streets; civil defense workers dug with their bare hands through piles of rubble that had once been someone's home and hearth; police and Carabinieri rushed to stand guard on valuable items opened to looters by a shattered wall; flak gunners scanned the skies for a possible next wave, ashamed they had been caught napping and equally ashamed they had never actually hit anything yet; and surgery teams calmly and meticulously began to use tweezers to pick bits of clothing, wood and stone from the inside of desecrated bodies, while orderlies and nurses jammed more and more injured into hospital corridors. At the Caproni factory employees saw work stations they had known for twenty years become unrecognizable piles of scrap in one blinding flash. Men who were not crushed by bricks or sliced with shrapnel and broken glass were splashed with paints, acids, solvents and oils. Inside the city's public buildings the secretaries and their desks and filing cabinets were mashed into one. In the residential neighborhoods four hundred and forty-one homes had been obliterated. Over one hundred and seventy Milanese were killed, and more than a thousand were maimed.

That evening wives hugged husbands who returned from work alive, mothers hugged children whose school had not been hit, lovers reunited in silent bliss, and thousands made their way to the hospitals for word of loved ones. Civil defense teams continued to scratch through the rubble. Suddenly the air raid warning sirens wailed. The people cried in despair: 'No, not again. Please not again.' This time seventy-one bombers struck the city. Fortunately clouds hid part of the city and many bombs fell in fields.

On the night of 6 November seventy-two Lancasters hit Genoa. Fascist propaganda claimed the British were waging genocide against the Italian people. Looking around at shattered homes, at elderly residents sitting on the rubble in shock, at middle-aged women being carried away on stretchers, at the body of a lifeless child still clutching a toy, it was hard not to believe this.

The truth was that while British Royal Air Force policy was indeed to deliberately aim at civilians, which is the definition of genocide, this policy was only in effect for German civilians. British bombers over Italy aimed at factories, rail yards, docks and military installations. However, by 1942 high altitude bomb aiming was still very inaccurate in good daylight visibility, and in bad visibility or at night it was hopelessly inaccurate. For every bomb that hit the target many went astray.

On the evening of 7 November 1942 the industrial sector of Genoa was blasted by one hundred and seventy-five bombers, and six nights later it was struck again by seventy-six planes and two nights later by seventy-eight aircraft.

On the night of the 18th the Fiat vehicle factory at Turin was bombed by seventy-seven planes: most of the forty-two killed and seventy-seven wounded were members of the emergency services. Forty-eight hours later the factory was still burning, when a massive raid of two hundred and thirty-two bombers arrived to pour horrific death down upon twenty districts of this great city. Though the destruction was savage, casualties were relatively light: one hundred and seventeen killed and one hundred and twenty hospitalized. It took a week to get somewhat back to normality, but then the British slammed Turin again with two hundred and twenty-eight bombers. Another sixty-seven people were killed and eighty-three hospitalized. The following night thirty-six bombers hit the city, destroying commercial premises, hospitalizing fifteen and giving sixteen people eternal sleep.

The Neapolitans had at one time praised the Naples naval base as it meant jobs, but now they cursed it, for it attracted enemy air raids. Fortunately there had been little collateral damage in the city itself. However, nothing had prepared the people for the night of 4 December 1942. As the massive waves of bombers arrived the Blackshirt flak gunners and naval base gunners and warship gunners threw thousands of shells into the night sky that was now lit by pointing searchlights. Bombs rained down accurately on the light cruisers Eugenio di Savoia, Raimondo Montecuccoli and Muzio Attendolo, sinking the latter, but many bombs fell on the city inflicting hundreds of civilian casualties.

On the night of 8 December one hundred and thirty-three bombers struck Turin, starting over a hundred fires and killing two hundred and twelve and hospitalizing over a thousand. Twenty-four hours later civil defense crews were still digging people out of the rubble and firemen were still fighting fires, when two hundred and twenty-seven bombers returned to ravage the city once again, killing seventy-three and sending another hundred to hospital. More fires were started and others fanned. Forty-eight hours after this an extensive area was still in flames, when eighty-two bombers returned to blast away more parts of the city.

These British air armadas had taken off from airfields in Britain at sunset, had flown in the dark across the English Channel, had survived flak shells from German ships, had then flown over German-occupied France, dodging shells from countless German and French flak guns, and had then flown over Italian soil and more flak guns and then had entered the flak belt defenses of the target cities, and moreover they had done all this while under continuous attack from German and Italian night fighters, and following the bombing they then had to return along the same route to reach Britain before dawn. Yet out of one thousand eight hundred and nine sorties (sortie = one plane one mission) only thirty-seven planes failed to return, and some of those had probably suffered mechanical faults. Mussolini's victories overseas did not influence the Italian people half as much as his inability to protect them in their own homes.

————————

Chapter Forty
Russian Debacle

Naturally the Italians of Eighth Army on the Russian front were worried about their families back home under air attack, but they had their own problems. In stationary positions they had constructed a well-fortified line with thick minefields, and the mighty Don River lay between them and the bulk of the Red Army. The Italians had learned much since their first terrible winter in Russia, but only the Alpini corps was really equipped and trained to handle the severe conditions in Russia. They had skis, sleds, snowshoes, winter clothing and the know-how to survive freezing weather. The veterans taught the new recruits how to remove the oil from their weapons, lest they freeze up in cold weather, how to layer their clothing and that a coat used as a blanket was warmer than wearing it. They were taught to keep their heads, hands and feet warmer than their torsos. They were urged not to work up a sweat as the moisture would freeze and cause bad rashes. They were ordered to rub their hands and feet in snow periodically to prevent frostbite, and never to walk with wet socks. Sentries never stood still and were changed every few minutes, for otherwise a sentry could freeze to death, while the remainder of the troops huddled around pot-bellied stoves in crudely made huts. It was still autumn, but winter was on its way and the men were preparing for it.

By now the Axis advance had been stopped in Northwest Georgia, where the line was manned by the German Seventeenth Army, with the German First Panzer Army on their left [northeast] flank, but to their north in Kalmyk a stretch of two hundred miles was held by a single German motorized division supported by locally recruited Kalmyk horse cavalry.

If Hitler did not realize it, it was obvious to everyone else that the Germans alone did not have the manpower for this campaign. Some German armies had to be completed with Romanian divisions, and every German unit regardless of its mission had local 'Russian' volunteers in its ranks known as Hiwis [volunteer helpers]. In summer 1941 these helpers had been unarmed and had just worn civilian clothing and armbands and had been paid out of unit funds, but by 1942 they were semi-official, were armed, wore uniforms and had their own rank and awards structure. They primarily performed non-combat rear-echelon duties, but did pull sentry duty. By late 1942 there was approximately one Hiwi for every ten Germans.

In addition right from the start of the campaign the Germans had officially sanctioned combat units of Soviet citizens known as Ostruppen [Eastern Troops]. Invariably they were grouped by language for obvious reasons, such as the Kalmyks.

North of the Kalmyk lands was the Romanian Fourth Army facing east, and to their north was the city of Stalingrad in which the German Sixth Army was involved in a titanic struggle for every building, every cellar. Ten per cent of this army consisted of Hiwis. Stretching north from the city to where the Don River curves westwards and as far west as the Chir River was the Romanian Third Army. Their left [northwest] flank was manned by the Italian Eighth Army, covering the Don for fully two hundred miles. On the Italian left was the Hungarian Second Army also manning about two hundred miles of line, and their left was covered by the German Second Army.

The two most noticeable things about these dispositions were first that the Axis units were stretched so thin as to be practically transparent, and secondly that Hitler could never have come so far without the assistance of his partners, for on a front of one thousand four hundred miles fewer than half the troops were German.

In mid-November 1942 the Romanian Third Army launched a small offensive to clear some enemy pockets from the south bank of the Don, but suddenly on the morning of the 19th all hell broke loose in their sector. The Italians were informed by radio that the Soviets were counter-attacking the Romanians, and by midday it was understood that this was not a local counter attack but was in fact a major Red Army offensive. Within twenty-four hours the Romanian I Corps had been forced to sidestep into the protective arms of the Italians to avoid being overrun.

Now the Romanian Fourth Army south of Stalingrad was also struck by a major offensive. It was obvious that the Red Army was planning to crush the flanks of Stalingrad and then try to surround the German Sixth Army there. This same day the Soviets continued their advance on the north flank, chopping up the Romanian Third Army into pockets.

About twenty miles northwest of the Don-Chir confluence the Germans created a makeshift force of German armor and infantry and Luftwaffe ground crews, while they ordered the Italians to hold not only their own positions but those of the Romanian I Corps all the way up to the Chir.

Thanks to the bravery of Germans, Romanians and Osttruppen the Red Army north of Stalingrad was unable to break past the Italian right flank, but they were able to link up with the southern Soviet offensive, thereby surrounding Stalingrad.

German intelligence was permeated with Nazi ideology and this tainted their conclusions. They believed that the Soviets were deliberately challenging Germany's partners, whose soldiers in Nazi eyes were sub-human, weaker and less courageous than Germans. They were totally wrong. In fact after a year and a half of horrific warfare, the Soviet high command had concluded that Italians, Romanians and Hungarians were just as tough as Germans. However, the Red Army had no ambition to tackle tanks on the flat steppe, if they could avoid it, nor did they feel there would be much profit in pouring more troops into the Stalingrad mincing machine, so they attacked the infantry formations that flanked that city. In other words they attacked the Romanians [and eventually the Italians and Hungarians] not because of who they were but because of where they were!

Having said this, the Italian Eighth Army was in pitiful shape. Messe had been allowed to go home at last, and he was replaced by General Italo Gariboldi, veteran of Ethiopia and Libya. His two hundred and seventy thousand Italians were hopelessly overstretched with no more than about thirty infantrymen defending every hundred meters of front! Major General Ettore Blasio's Amedeo Duca d'Aosta Celere Division had fifty tanks, but they were useless L6s with 20mm guns. The Soviet T-34 tank had a 76.2mm gun and weighed 26 tons, and their KV-1 had a 76.2mm gun and weighed 47 tons, almost eight times as big as an L6. True the Italians had three hundred and eighty anti-tank guns, but these were useless because they were stretched out to an average of two per mile! In any case an Italian 47mm anti-tank gun could at best shoot through 50mm of armor plate at two hundred and fifty yards if it struck at the correct angle. The T-34 (at this stage of the war) had 45mm of frontal armor, thus the gunners would need luck on their side, but the KV-1 had 60mm of frontal armor. The Italian infantry was well able to repulse Soviet infantry, but the Soviets had learned their lessons and were no longer attacking with wave upon wave of infantry as if on parade. Morale was a serious problem among the Italians, as they wondered how they were expected to stop a Soviet armored offensive when the Romanians and Germans had been unable to.

The day everyone dreaded came on 11 December 1942. Following a short artillery bombardment, no fewer than three Red Army divisions attacked five battalions of Lieutenant General Filippo Diamanti's 3 January CCNN Raggruppamento. Facing odds of six to one against them, the Blackshirts fought like wildcats. Brigadier General Francesco Dupont's neighboring Ravenna Mountain Division answered their request for reinforcements, but soon they too came under attack. On the opposite flank the recently arrived German 298th Division, which had been loaned to the Italians, launched a counter assault, and their efforts together with artillery support provided by Lieutenant General Giovanni Zanghieri's Italian II Corps managed to repel the Soviets. A multitude of Italian guns were employed: 75mm, 105mm, 149mm and a few 210mm. The Italians sighed with relief. It had been a heart stopping moment.

In truth the Soviets had merely been testing the Italians. During this period Soviet engineers were laying bridges over the frozen Don and Chir Rivers so that tanks, artillery and trucks could join the infantry who had walked across the ice.

In the dark early hours of the 16th the Italian Eighth Army was struck with a terrific pounding of artillery shells, and the immediate front line was assaulted by Soviet tanks with infantry huddled behind them in deep snow. There was considerable power behind this assault: the First Guards and Third Guards Armies. Italian telephone lines were cut by shrapnel, and radios were jammed by the Soviets. Within minutes each Italian infantry company was fighting its own isolated battle. Cut off from all communications, the Italian infantry were convinced that only they had been attacked, and that if they just broke through to the rear they could rejoin the main defense line, but they did not realize that they were the main defense line! The Italian horse cavalry fighting on foot was annihilated when they challenged the Soviet tanks. In the sectors held by Carlo Pellegrini's Sforzesca Mountain Division, Francesco du Pont's Ravenna Mountain Division, Guido Boselli's Pasubio Division and Roberto Lerici's Torino Division the front line troops quickly disintegrated into mobs. However, Enrico Gazzale's Cosseria Division did retain cohesion. Lieutenant General Gabriele Nasci, and his chief of staff Major General Giulio Martinat, were sure that their Alpine Corps could survive, because their troops knew how to fight and maneuver in snow. They included three alpini divisions: Luigi Reverberi's Tridentina, Umberto Ricagno's Julia and Emilio Battisti's Cuneense.

The L6 crews abandoned their useless vehicles once they became stuck in snow or ran out of fuel. Even the self-propelled Semoventi 47mm assault guns were no longer of any use once they ran out of fuel. The Blackshirts of Filippo Diamante's 3 January CCNN Raggruppamento and Luigi Martinesi's 23 March CCNN Raggruppamento were on the run too. No one noticed what had become of the Croatian units attached to the army.

The worst nightmare of every Italian whether a lowly private or a general had come true: they were cut off from the Axis forces and surrounded by Communist armies. In bitterly cold weather, with numb hands and feet the soldiers stumbled along in deep snow, halting to jerkily catch their breath, merging into groups, then mobs, then masses of humanity. Spurred by the sound of gunfire these columns swerved away from it, first to the right, then to the left, often losing their bearings, but staying together in fear, believing there was safety in numbers, and in any case no one wanted to die alone. With rags wrapped around their feet and blankets over their shoulders, they were barely recognizable as humans let alone as soldiers. There were no proud crusaders here. The troop trains decorated with chalked Fascist slogans and the tossed flowers were just a cruel memory.

Every few hours the Soviets would appear, sometimes in tanks, often as foot infantry, and quite often on horseback, and like some gigantic green worm on a plain white flat landscape the column of

Italian soldiers would shift direction and slither to one side. Each man followed the one in front without the slightest care where he was heading. They hoped and prayed that someone at the head of the column knew where he was going. It was enough effort to just place one frozen foot in front of the other without worrying about navigation. Here and there an unfortunate fellow dropped by the wayside, too exhausted or wounded or sick to carry on. Priests attended them, giving last rites, as much to give comfort to themselves as to the dying man.

Reaching the town of Meshkov one retreating column found its way blocked by the Soviets, and the officers now appeared from among the mob, forgetting their own pains to gather together an actual fighting force. Enough of the 3rd Bersaglieri from the Amedeo Duca d'Aosta Celere Division were induced to attack. Charging as best they could in deep snow towards the buildings at the edge of town they were sliced down in swathes by machine gun fire, their scarlet blood polluting the pure white snow. Once the officers concluded that the path through Meshkov was well and truly blocked, they ordered the column to move off in another direction. Now and then an Italian straggler was picked off by a sniper or by Cossack horsemen who rode in wielding sabers.

On the fourth day of the retreat one column entered the Valley of Abrusovka, which was flanked by Soviet artillery. With the diabolical T-34s just a few hundred yards behind them, the survivors in the column had little choice but surrender or to try to run the gauntlet. They chose the gauntlet. Stumbling in the snow at walking speed they moved forward by the thousands, while enemy gunners on their flanks worked overtime pouring high explosive shells into them. Suddenly a few Germans appeared in trucks heading the same way and the Italians waved their arms hoping for a ride and some flung themselves in front of the vehicles to stop them. In blind panic the Germans shoved, kicked and shot the Italians off the sides of the trucks and ran over those in front. As the Italians stood and stared at the trucks as they drove away they were filled with disgust and hatred. Huge artillery explosions were blowing gaps in their ranks, filling the white landscape with bright red craters twenty feet across. Now the Soviet tanks caught up with the tail end of the column and began mashing the weaker men under their treads. Those who fled to the side were machine-gunned. Yet miraculously the majority of the mob escaped the valley of death, seemingly immune to the slaughter around them.

On the 23rd a rearguard tried to halt the chasing Soviets. Comprised of just the 63rd CCNN Battalion, a battalion of the 3rd Bersaglieri Regiment, some horse artillery and a few dismounted cavalrymen from the Savoia Dragoons, they knew they could accomplish little. Unbelievably they held for three days, and then when some Germans appeared and actually counterattacked the enemy, the 63rd CCNN

Battalion joined them and together they reached Voroshilov. After the action these Germans gave their Italian brothers an official salute to their bravery.

After sixteen days of retreat the Italian Eighth Army staff looked at the situation. Some Germans were still holding a major pocket to their east, and the Italians had more or less anchored their army on the Hungarians to their west, so that on the map it appeared that the retreating Italians were like a door that had remained hinged on the Hungarians, but had swung open to the south until the Eighth Army was at right angles to its original position. The collapse of the German, Romanian and Italian infantry was not the fault of the ordinary infantrymen. Indeed the fact that they were able to form rearguards shows great courage and fortitude.

By 11 January 1943 the front ran from a point twenty miles east of Rostov almost due north to the Donets River where it curves westwards, and was held by the German XLVIII Panzer Corps, Gruppe Hollidt [a provisional German-led formation of mostly Romanian divisions], and the German Fourth Panzer Army that also contained several Romanian divisions. From here westwards along the Donets to Voroshilovgrad the line was held by the German-led Gruppe Fretter-Pico, which had some Romanian units, and from there northwards to the Don the line was defended by the exhausted remnant of the Italian Eighth Army, which had finally outrun the Soviets. The Italians now relied greatly on their Alpini corps and on a provisional corps built around Major General Etelvoldo Pascolini's Vicenza Division that had been brought up from reserve. On the Italian left was the Hungarian Second Army, and beyond them the German Second Army, both of which had yet to be tested.

On 12 January the Soviets launched the next phase of their winter offensive, striking the Hungarians, and within twenty-four hours the Hungarian 7th Division had collapsed. The Soviets knew they were on a winner here, for their 'attack' had in fact been a reconnaissance in force. Their real offensive was not launched until the 14th using the Fortieth Army, Third Tank Army, XVIII Rifle Corps, VII Cavalry Corps and IV Tank Corps, plus smaller units including a brigade of ski troops. This Soviet juggernaut smashed into the German Second, Hungarian Second and Italian Eighth Armies at the same time. At once the Hungarian right flank broke apart, thus isolating the Italian left flank.

The remnants of the Italian Cosseria Division tried to stop a charge by twelve battalions of saber wielding horse cavalry, but the horsemen literally sliced and chopped their way through. Then the Soviet cavalrymen dismounted and faced back the way they had come and held a line in the snow with their carbines. This meant the Italians had to charge them and break through this line to reach safety. By dusk the Cosseria had lost a thousand men. The Italians were soon finding Soviet horse cavalry twelve miles behind Italian lines.

The Italians did not know if their minds could withstand another winter retreat. The more intellectual-minded remembered Napoleon's ill-fated retreat from Russia in 1812: three of his divisions had been Italian. At least the study gave them something to think about, because the constant never-ending trudging through white snow in a white blizzard under a white sky was mind numbing. The men became hypnotized, oblivious to the futility of the slaughter. It literally drove some men mad. Many woke up in prisoner of war compounds unable to remember how they had been captured. No one voluntarily became a prisoner of the Communists. Even the secret Communists within the Italian ranks did not want that.

At Nikolayevka an Italian column turned to fight. The chief of staff of the Alpini Corps, Major General Giulio Martinat, breathed his last here. The Germans were so impressed with his courage they awarded him the Knight's Cross posthumously.

The Soviet supply lines became stretched far too long and they eventually had to stop. The Italians outran their pursuers and managed once again to form a new defensive line.

The great Soviet offensive of November, December and January had cost the Hungarians thirty-five thousand killed, thirty-five thousand wounded and seventy-six thousand missing. The Hungarian Fascist dictator Miklos Horthy declared that henceforth his troops would no longer serve on the front line in Russia. The offensive had also crippled the Romanians, who suffered a permanent loss of one hundred and seventy-three thousand dead, missing or maimed. The German permanent loss was over four hundred thousand, including the entire Sixth Army inside Stalingrad, which surrendered in February. Additionally about thirty thousand Hiwis and Osttruppen were killed in their effort to protect their homes from Communism. Of the five thousand Croatians in the battle not enough survived to fill an infantry company.

Prior to the offensive since joining the crusade against Stalin the Italians had suffered nineteen thousand known dead and thirty thousand wounded, plus many thousands were being treated for lung ailments, frostbite, disease, malnutrition and complete and utter exhaustion.

As for the winter offensive the Alpini corps had fought superbly and as a result had not been overrun during the winter retreats, nor had its three divisions lost their cohesion, and of course its members knew how to survive in cold weather. Nonetheless their losses were atrocious - the Tridentina Alpini Division had come to Russia with sixteen thousand men and four thousand mules, but by February 1943 it was down to six thousand five hundred men and two hundred mules. The Julia Alpini Division, which had in effect already been wiped out once, had arrived in Russia with sixteen thousand men and four thousand mules and by February 1943 was down to three thousand two hundred men and forty mules, and its commander Umberto Ricagno was missing. It was now led by Brigadier Franco Testi. Of the Cuneense Alpini Division's fifteen thousand men only one thousand six hundred were now fit for duty, and its commander Emilio Battisti was missing. Brigadier General Carlo Fassi was now in command. The Amedeo Duca d'Aosta Celere Division and the infantry divisions suffered worse losses. The Vicenza Division had not taken part in the first retreat, only in the second, but by February of its eleven thousand men only one thousand three hundred had survived, and its commander Etelvoldo Pascolini was missing. In fact by February sixty-six thousand Italians were missing. As the Red Army bragged it had taken twenty-two thousand Italian prisoners, this meant that forty-four thousand of the missing Italians were lying dead under the snow. A rough estimate is that half of the Italians in Russia had become casualties during this winter campaign, and the actual combat formations had lost 90% of their manpower.

Many suspected that those twenty-two thousand Italians taken prisoner by the Soviets would not live long. They were right. At this stage of the war the Soviets treated their prisoners with the utmost brutality. The last of the prisoners died eating the feces of their guards to the latter's merriment in an effort to stave off death by starvation for just one more hour.

Mussolini did not want to appear weak like Horthy, so he declared that not only would Italians continue to serve on the Russian front, but those already there would remain in the line. The German generals, desperate as they were for manpower, could not in all humanity accept this and they sent the Italians home. In three months the Axis forces had lost eight hundred and fifty thousand men and had abandoned about three hundred and seventy-five thousand square miles of the Soviet Union, but throughout it all the soldiers of the various Axis armies, Italians included, had remained soldiers and they had fought tenaciously, inflicting upwards of seven hundred and fifty thousand casualties on the Red Army.

Chapter Forty-one
African Finale

Even Mussolini must have realized by late 1942 that his whole military system was rotten to the core. In October 1942 the British began a major aerial onslaught on his cities with impunity. In November his Armata Corazzini Africa began to retreat from Alamein. In December his Eighth Army in Russia suffered a defeat of catastrophic proportions. On 25 December French anti-Fascist troops under General Philippe LeClerc began pushing the Italians out of Southern Libya. In the last two months of 1942 his navy had lost three cruisers, two destroyers, six submarines and an MAS boat. Every convoy he had sent to Libya had been intercepted.

Yet because his greed was greater than his sense of proportion, Mussolini had in fact during this time gained new conquests and had launched a new ground campaign.

This had come about as a result of the schizophrenia in Washington. On the one hand the US was locked in a life or death struggle with the Japanese. The latter had already knocked out the US Pacific Fleet, conquered the Philippines, [which the Americans had been transforming from a colony into an ally], and had occupied Alaskan islands, preparatory some believed to an actual invasion of the USA and Canada. Already Japanese submarines were shelling Oregon and California, and balloon incendiary bombs were setting vast forests afire in the American Northwest. But then on the other hand, American warships had already been at war with the Germans for two years, and the American president Franklin D. Roosevelt was adamant that Britain be protected. He was not just an Anglophile, but was a distant cousin of Churchill, and he was adamant that Nazism/Fascism in Europe was the greater threat. He had his 'Germany-Italy First' supporters among his admirals and generals, but they were outnumbered by the 'Japan First' crowd. Certainly the vast majority of Americans were 'Japan First'. Millions of Americans were rushing to the colors to fight the Japanese, but few held a grudge against the Germans or Italians. Into this argument entered Churchill with his masterful oratory. The result was a compromise. The 'Japan First' crowd would be placated by being given the bulk of the US Navy and the entire Marine Corps, plus about a third of the US Army and a third of the US Army Air Force. The navy and marines each had their own air forces, too.

American propaganda now maintained that the attack on Pearl Harbor had been planned by Tojo [Japanese premier], Mussolini and Hitler. This was to convince the recruit that if he was sent to fight the Italians it would be the same war as if he had been sent to fight the Japanese.

The 'Germany-Italy First' gang would be given priority with the bulk of the ground and air forces. However, their main problem, and one which the 'Japan First' crowd was quick to point out, was that the Americans did not have the ability to reach the German Army nor the Italian Army for that matter. Rather than give up the troops that had been allotted to them, the 'Germany-Italy First' gang agreed to Churchill's proposal to use them to attack the French instead!

Churchill had been at war with the French for two and a half years, battling them at sea, in the air and on land in Gabon, Syria and Madagascar. He believed that French North Africa [Morocco, Algeria and Tunisia] would fall like a ripe apple. A landing here would place Allied forces on Libya's western border in Rommel's rear and put the Allies in control of ports just an overnight's sail from Malta. Once Rommel was destroyed, the Allies would be in a position to invade Italy itself.

Churchill described Europe as like a crocodile. The German Army in France was the croc's mouth ready to chew up a US invasion. The croc's tail was currently flaying about in Russia. But Italy was the croc's soft underbelly. The real reason Churchill wanted to draw the Americans into the Mediterranean was that his generals were terrified of having to fight in France again. Their experience there in World War One had put a bad taste in their mouths, having witnessed the slaughter of an entire generation of Britons, and this is why they had put up such a poor showing in spring 1940. However, they were willing to invade Italy, especially if it was as 'soft' as Churchill said it was. A second reason was that though British towns were still being bombed by the Luftwaffe [the Regia Aeronautica squadons that had been bombing England had gone home] and the sea lanes to and from Britain were infested by German U-boats, it was the Italians who were the greatest danger to the sea communications of the British Empire, because Mussolini still controlled the Mediterranean. Knocking Italy out of the war would free the empire's main sea route and would place American and British troops on mainland Europe, sort of like entering the theater's side door without having to buy an expensive ticket at the front box office.

The British had recruited a French general, Charles de Gaulle, to rally all anti-Fascist French, and these so-called 'Free French' had a small armed forces fighting alongside the British. The Italians had battled these French in Eritrea, Egypt and Libya. Churchill hoped that when a massive Anglo-American armada arrived off the coast of French North Africa the French troops there would lay down their arms and join de Gaulle. But they had to be convinced it was not really a British invasion, but rather some sort of American tourist visit. To this end he instructed British aircraft earmarked for the attack to be painted in US markings!

The Americans listened to Churchill and without committing

themselves to an attack on Italy they agreed to join the sightseeing trip to French North Africa. But the Americans loathed de Gaulle, because of a petty squabble between him and Roosevelt's cabinet ministers over two tiny French colonies off the coast of Canada. Therefore, the Americans secretly rescued a French general from German custody, Henri Giraud, intending to use him as a sort of Joan of Arc to rally the French soldiers in North Africa. The idea was absurd.

In late October 1942 Italian and German spies in the United States reported that major convoys of troopships were leaving the American Atlantic ports. American armor had been training in the deserts of California and was now boarding these ships, and as everyone knows there are no deserts in the Pacific or Northwest Europe. North Africa was obviously their destination. However, where in North Africa, the Italian and German intelligence community wondered? Did this point to an invasion of Spanish Morocco, French Morocco, Algeria or Tunisia, or to a reinforcement of Montgomery's forces in Egypt?

At dawn on 8 November the answer came. A huge armada of Americans invaded French Morocco at several locations under the command of Major General George S. Patton, with Major General Ernest Harmon's 2nd Armored Division, Major General Lucian Truscott's 3rd Infantry Division and Major General Manton Eddy's 9th Infantry Division. Simultaneously, Lieutenant General Lloyd Fredendall led Americans ashore at Oran in Algeria, with Major General Orlando Ward's 1st Armored Division and Major General Terry Allen's 1st Infantry Division. At that exact moment Major General Charles Ryder led his US 34th Infantry Division and a British brigade and some American rangers ashore at Algiers, the capital of Algeria. The French resisted on land, in the air and at sea, but before the first day was over many French officers began negotiating with the Americans. The fight was not easy. Two US warships were captured, and on land hundreds of Americans and Britons were taken prisoner.

The only good news, as far as Mussolini was concerned, was that the Allies had not invaded Tunisia, which lay between Algeria and Libya. The Americans had argued for a Tunisian landing, but the British admirals had refused to sail so close to Mussolini's fleet and airfields!

At once Hitler ordered German paratroopers to jump onto a Tunisian airfield and prepare it for transport aircraft. French troops at the airfield did not resist the Germans! Mussolini ordered General Bastico to send troops from western Libya into Tunisia immediately. Bastico chose the Giovanni Fascisti Armored Division, guessing that it would no longer be needed for the parade in Cairo. The French in

Tunisia did not resist the Italians.

Mussolini and Hitler agreed that German Lieutenant General Walter Nehring should command Axis forces in Tunisia. The French ground commander in Tunisia, General Louis Barre, was openly antagonistic towards the Axis, but the French naval commander, Admiral Esteva, was openly cooperative.

On 10 November all French forces in Morocco and Algeria ceased fire against the Allies. The invasion had cost the Anglo-Americans two thousand three hundred casualties. The French had suffered four hundred and ninety killed and nine hundred and sixty-nine wounded. However, all Frenchmen taken prisoner were released this day, in order to join the Allies under the guidance of Admiral Jean Darlan, a leading government figure who by coincidence had been visiting Algiers. After listening to such anti-Fascists as General Alphonse Juin the ground commander in North Africa, Darlan had negotiated the best deal possible with the Allied emissaries - French General Henri Giraud, American Lieutenant General Mark C. Clark and British General Kenneth Anderson.

By coincidence Mussolini, Hitler and Laval the French premier were in a meeting this very day. Hitler went into a tirade upon hearing the news. An entire French army of several divisions had gone over to the Allies. In anger he berated Laval and called off all deals and treaties with Laval's French government and he ordered German forces to occupy all unoccupied parts of France. The French Army did not resist the Germans. This bloodless conquest of France was Hitler's cheapest and swiftest campaign since his March 1939 invasion of Czechoslovakia.

Not surprisingly, Mussolini, who was as much of an opportunist as Hitler, also ordered his troops to rush in and pick up any scraps the Germans missed. Thus the Italian Fourth Army occupied southeastern France along the Riviera, in the process gobbling up the neutral nation of Monaco. This army controlled the I Corps [Pusteria Alpini, Rovigo and Mantova Divisions and 1st Raggruppamento Alpini Valle], XV Corps [Legnano, Piave and Lupi di Toscana Divisions] and XXII Corps [Centauro Armored, Taro and Piacenza Divisions and 164th CCNN Legion]. Most of these divisions were partially motorized. The new Parachute Battalion and assault troops of the San Marco Marines landed on the coast. In addition Lieutenant General Carboni's VII Corps of the Friuli Division [and attached 88th CCNN Legion] and Cremona Division [and attached 90th CCNN Legion] and the Bafile and Grado Battalions of the San Marco Marines sailed to the French island of Corsica. Mussolini's justification for this invasion was that the territory he was occupying had once belonged to Italians. There was no French resistance. However, the majority of Corsicans are fiercely independent. In the small villages they still spoke Corse, not French. After 174 years of French occupation they still had little loyalty to France, and they certainly saw no reason to accept Mussolini either. They began organizing guerilla bands in the mountains.

Meanwhile Italian and German air and sea forces tried to interfere with the Allied armada off North Africa. The Italian submarine Granito attacked the enemy ships, but was sunk by the British submarine Saracen, and the Italian submarine Emo was sunk by the warship Nuffield. However, Italian bombers sank the British minesweeper Cromer; and the Italian submarine Argo under the command of Lieutenant Pasquale Gigli sank a British troopship and the anti-aircraft ship Tynwald [already damaged by Italian aircraft]; and the submarine Ascianghi sank the British minesweeper Algerine. German U-boats sank two British destroyers, a Dutch destroyer and the British aircraft carrier Avenger. On 25 November the Italian destroyer Groppo sank the British submarine Utmost. On the 28th Italian and German planes raided the port of Bone, Algeria and wrecked the British destroyer Ithuriel. The British also sank one of their own submarines in error. The Italian submarine Dessie was sunk by a British Hudson bomber, and the famous Italian destroyer Circe was sunk following a collision. In her glorious career she had sunk four submarines and had damaged other vessels.

Elsewhere the Italian merchantman Scillin, carrying British prisoners of war, was sunk by the British submarine Sahib. Of the eight hundred and fifty on board only twenty-seven Britons and thirty-five Italians were rescued. The British government told the families of the dead that they had been murdered by the Italians in prison camps.

Days later the British ship Nova Scotia carrying eight hundred Italian prisoners was sunk by a U-boat. A quarter of the Italians drowned.

The submarine Antonio Sciesa was sunk during an American air raid on Tobruk.

Not only had the Allies landed four hundred miles from Tunisia, but the Americans and Britons were slow to advance along the coast road, despite no opposition except the odd Italian-German air raid. The Allies also created their own problems with their choice of commanders – Eisenhower, Anderson and Fredendall. British General Kenneth Anderson, a Dunkirk veteran, was aloof and would not cooperate with the Americans. American Lieutenant General Lloyd Fredendall, a blustery loud individual, had come close to panicking in his first combat at Oran and now he seemed eager to have his engineers build a bomb-proof concrete command center for himself in Algeria of such proportions as to rival the pyramids in case of an air raid on his person. Both should have had an Allied ground forces commander looking over their shoulder, but the overall invasion commander, American General Dwight D. Eisenhower, insisted on commanding the ground offensive himself. Completely out of his depth, he preferred to run the battle from his office in Algiers four hundred miles from the front using French road maps, while at the same time he attempted to control his air and naval commanders, and simultaneously he had many dealings with Allied diplomats and the volatile Darlan-de Gaulle-Giraud situation. This latter problem was not solved until Darlan was conveniently assassinated. Giraud wisely took a back seat to de Gaulle after this. This was all heady stuff for Eisenhower, a Kansas farm boy who had never commanded more than a battalion before and had never seen combat.

The Americans did have an armored warfare expert, a hero from World War I, Major General George S. Patton, but once he had captured Morocco, he was left to wither on the vine. As a result of all these Allied mistakes, the Italians and Germans were given eleven days to rush troops into Tunisia, at a rate of two thousand per day. Only then did a party of Britons and Americans reach the Tunisian-Algerian border. They found some Germans here and attacked them, but were repulsed quickly. The British troops here were as new to combat as the Americans were, and it showed. The Germans who had repulsed them belonged to a party of construction engineers.

The Americans did not know how they would do in battle against the Germans and Italians, but their swift victory over the French had given them far too much confidence in their abilities. They knew the Germans were tough from their World War I experience, but they could not understand how the British could have such a poor opinion of Italians as soldiers and yet have such a rough time fighting them. Something was wrong with this picture. By 1942 one American soldier in twelve was ethnically Italian. The luck of the draw meant that some platoons had none, while others were practically all Italian. Americans saw their own 'Italians' as brave to the point of rashness. The most decorated American enlisted man in the war to date was John Basilone, whose parents were Italian immigrants.

The French troops in Tunisia were mostly members of the Tunisian Division, which consisted of predominantly Tunisians with French officers and technicians, and they now joined the arriving Allies. Yet, the Germans with but a slight reinforcement were able to push all of these Tunisian troops out of Tunisia into Algeria.

Hard on the heels of the evacuating French an Italian unit occupied Sbeitla, but the next day these Italians were surprised by American troops and were forced to withdraw. Sbeitla had one significance. It marked the first time Italian and American ground units fought each other.

The Allied offensive into Tunisia had been ill prepared and badly coordinated, but the Americans, British and their new French/Tunisian allies soon got their act together and launched a real attack under Anderson's command using Major General Charles

Keightley's British 6th Armored Division, Major General Vyvyan Evelegh's British 78th Division and Major General Ryder's US 34th Division. This time it was the turn of the Germans to run. Nehring had decided to fall back onto a hastily dug defense line, and on 29 November the Allies reached it. Eisenhower, Anderson and Fredendall were all smug, for this line was just twelve miles from the Tunisian capital, the city of Tunis.

Meanwhile the Axis had continued their build up in Tunisia. Once the German force reached a strength of about 20,000, Hitler placed General Juergen von Arnim in control. This officer, a veteran of Poland, France and Russia, divided his men into a division of paratroopers, a grenadier regiment and a mortar regiment. Most impressive of all he was given three Tiger tanks hot off the assembly line and untried in combat. The Tiger was a grotesque monster of 55 tons and 9 feet 6 inches high, firing an 88mm gun. It could stay a half mile from enemy tanks and shoot through anything the Allies had. It could drive through a stone building like it was paper. Thus reinforced, von Arnim counter attacked the British, and perhaps to his surprise he won, inflicting two thousand casualties and knocking out 55 tanks.

Ward's US 1st Armored Division came to rescue the British, but one of his tank battalions ran into 88mm flak guns used in an anti-tank capacity, and was forced to pull back. A battalion of his infantry riding in half-tracks was strafed by German planes, whereupon they too turned back. On December 10 in the rain Ward's tanks held off an assault by German infantry, but they retreated when German tanks approached. Frankly the Germans were not impressed by the Americans.

The rain heralded the onset of the annual rainy season, turning Northern Tunisia's coastal belt into a lush verdant landscape, but it also turned the inland desert tracks into streams of mud. The Allies had lost the race for Tunis and more crucially they had lost the race for the weather.

On 22 December despite the rain Anderson agreed to an offensive and Major General Terry Allen's US 1st Division was brought up and ordered to jump off from Longstop Hill, currently in British hands, but when the soaking wet GIs clambered up the slope they found the Germans in possession. The spontaneous battle lasted three days and then the Allies withdrew. The British suffered two hundred and fifty casualties in the affair and blamed the 'Yanks' for everyone. The Americans had three hundred and fifty casualties and blamed the 'Limeys' for everyone.

To stop such bickering, Eisenhower decided to place his British, American and French troops into their own umbrella formations. Fredendall's US II Corps would control Ward's 1st Armored, Allen's 1st, Ryder's 34th and Major General Manton S. Eddy's 9th Divisions beefed up with rangers, four battalions of M10 tank destroyers and some Priest self-propelled guns. The M10 was in fact an 8 feet 5 inches tall 30-ton tank armed with a 3-inch gun. Its most notable feature was that the turret had no roof. Manned by artillerymen, they were not instructed in armored warfare and yet were expected to knock out enemy tanks. Fortunately for the Americans Eisenhower allotted them the southern sector, where no rain was falling.

French XIX Corps led by General Louis-Marie Koeltz had the Tunis Division [of Tunisians], Moroccan Division [of Moroccans], and the Algiers Division and Constantine Division [both of Algerians].

Anderson was given command of the British First Army, but he only had three divisions: 6th Armored, 46th and 78th and some smaller units.

Eisenhower commanded Fredendall, Koeltz and Anderson by retaining command of all ground forces for himself.

Meanwhile von Arnim received more reinforcements so he regrouped his command under the title German XXC Corps controlling a mortar regiment, Major General von Broich's Provisional Division of paratroopers and infantry, the 10th Panzer Division and two battalions of Tiger tanks. He also had operational control of Major General Vittorio Sogno's XXX Italian Corps of: Major General Dante Lorenzelli's Superga Mountain Division, Major General Sozzani's Giovanni Fascisti Armored Division and Brigadier General Giovanni Imperiali's 50th Special Brigade. The Giovanni Fascisti only contained three infantry battalions, the Sardinian Grenadiers anti-tank battalion, a unit of the Monferrato Mechanized Cavalry Regiment [of Autoblinda armored cars and L3 tankettes], some artillery and engineers. Mussolini had forgotten to send tanks to this 'armored' division. However, the division was soon reinforced by the new 8th Bersaglieri Regiment and the 10th CCNN Battalion Gruppo. As for Imperiali's 50th Special Brigade it possessed the 6th Infantry Regiment, engineers, artillery, a tank battalion and a unit of Semoventi 75 assault guns. The San Marco Marines were also represented here by the Bafile and Grado Battalions, and they performed well in raids and assaults. They included some Blackshirt members.

In December 1942 the savagery continued at sea. The Italian destroyer Folgore and four merchantmen were sunk in one convoy action. The destroyer Lupo (640 tons) was shelled into a wreck. The Italian submarine Porfido was sunk by the British submarine Tigris, and the submarine Uarsciek was sunk by the British destroyer Petard and Greek destroyer Queen Olga. The submarine Corallo was rammed and sunk by the British gunboat Enchantress. However,

Italian planes sank the British destroyer Quentin; Italian mines claimed two British submarines, P311 and Traveller; Italian SM79s torpedoed and sank the British corvette Marigold off Algiers; the Italian destroyer Fortunale sank the British submarine P222; the Italian destroyers Ardente (910 tons) and Ardito sank the British submarine P48 in the harbor of Bizerte; German aircraft sank a British submarine; and U-boats sank two Allied destroyers off Oran.

On the night of 12 December the Italian submarine Ambra let loose three pigs and ten Gamma swimmers in Algiers harbor. This was a suicide mission, in that the pig riders and swimmers knew they were not coming back. If lucky they could surrender to a sentry after swimming ashore. If their luck had run out the sentry would kill them. This raid was an outstanding success in that the sixteen Italians traded their freedom for the glory of crippling four merchant ships and a tanker. But this month three pigs failed to do damage at Gibraltar and only one rider returned to the Spanish coast and safety.

But small victories such as this were not compensation for the greater 'Big Picture'. This year alone Italy had lost one hundred and forty-eight merchant ships sunk or captured, for a total of four hundred lost since 10 June 1940. The Regia Marina had begun the war with one hundred and fifteen submarines and had launched another nineteen by the end of 1942, but had lost sixty.

During late November and early December of 1942 Rommel had been retreating across Libya hounded by the famed Desert Air Force, which had been reinforced by more US squadrons. Several German rearguards had prevented Montgomery's forces from catching up with the main body, and on 13 December 1942 it was the turn of the Italians to man the rearguard. They put together a battle group of Semoventi 75s, M14s, anti-tank guns and artillery manned by members of the Ariete and Littorio that had been on detached duty or recuperating in hospital on the day their divisions had been destroyed. The officers of this small force looked upon this mission as an honor, but most likely the rank and file probably thought Rommel was out to exterminate them. It certainly looked like it when the entire British Eighth Army finally arrived in front of them. First they were bombed and strafed by Allied aircraft. Then they were shelled by artillery, and then eighty British tanks charged them. For ten hours these Italians fought superbly, enabling the German 90th Light Division to escape. After knocking out twenty-two British tanks and two armored cars, the Italian rearguard delivered their surprise punch, a counter attack by the 31st Armored Regiment of the newly arrived Centauro Armored Division under the command of Major General Count Giorgio Calvi di Bergolo. These veterans of Greece sent the British reeling. Their job done, the rearguard then picked up, packed up and pulled out.

Sadly during the retreat Major General Alessandro Predieri was killed by a landmine.

Just before Christmas Rommel chose to make his first major rest stop at the hastily dug Beurat Line.

In Southern Libya the Italian garrison of Gatrun had surrendered to a Free French force coming out of Chad. Bastico now ordered the remaining garrisons in the southern desert to retreat and join Rommel.

In the northern mountains of Tunisia the rains were making it extremely difficult for both sides to resupply. The British here did not even think about attempting to advance against the Germans, especially when the Germans were reinforced by the Italian 50th Special Brigade.

In the dry southern mountains of Tunisia Lorenzelli's Superga Mountain Division and a few Germans cautiously watched the French XIX Corps and US II Corps. Quite frankly the Italians found the French here to be a tough opponent, but the Americans appeared timid and nervous. The American war correspondent Ernie Pyle learned of one reason the Italians might have believed this. An American observation post telephoned that two Italians were coming up the hill towards them. The response was a heavy barrage of American artillery fire. Naturally the two Italian scouts ran like jack rabbits. One can imagine the Italian surprise at the American reaction. However, it turned out that over the field telephone the recipient of the message misheard the words as 'two battalions' rather than 'two Italians'. Following this, the Americans began to use the British term 'Eye-ties' for Mussolini's troops to avoid such miscommunication in future.

January 1943 was not a good month for Italian destroyers at sea: the Aviere (1620 tons) was sunk in an air raid while loading at Palermo; the Bombardiere (1620 tons) was torpedoed by the submarine United and sunk; the Maestrale (1417 tons) struck a mine, though she survived to be towed to port; the destroyers Corsaro and Prestinari and corvette Procellaria sank when they struck mines; and the Ardente came to a sad end, sinking in a collision with the Grecale. Nor did the Italian submarine service do well: the Narvalo was scuttled after being crippled by aircraft. The Santorre Santarosa was blown up after running aground. The Tritone was sunk on her maiden voyage by the Canadian corvette Port Arthur. The cargo vessel Genoa carrying an Italian crew, two hundred Italian soldiers and one hundred and fifty-eight Greek prisoners of war was sunk by a British submarine. About half those on board survived. Of interesting significance was that the light cruiser Ulpio Traiani was sunk in Palermo harbor by British pigs! The Royal Navy was evidently not too old a sea dog to learn new tricks. On the plus side, the submarine Platino torpedoed the British corvette Samphire.

In North Africa the Allies confused the Axis partners with their lame strategy. Their failure to invade Tunisia from the sea was a colossal blunder. Their failure to swiftly seize the Tunisian coast with an advance by their armor coupled with an airborne drop by their paratroopers was yet another blunder. American General Eisenhower commanded the Tunisian campaign from the safety of his Algerian villa and seemed out of touch. The American Lieutenant General Fredendall was also in Algeria inside a bunker fit for a pharaoh. British General Anderson seemed to be in a quandary. French General Koeltz was adequate, but neither the British nor the Americans took him seriously because he was French. In Libya British General Montgomery seemed satisfied with following Rommel rather than chasing him. Montgomery was rather like the dog that barks at passing cars and then wags his tail because he truly believes he has chased them away. Montgomery truly believed he was pushing Rommel out of Libya.

In fact through British code breaking Montgomery knew that some defensive positions had been abandoned already, yet he insisted on full-scale assaults so that Rommel would not suspect anything.

The Allies in Tunisia had a decent air force consisting of British, American and French squadrons. The Italian Mc202 pilots had their work cut out for them when they encountered the American Lightning and Airacobra fighters and British Spitfires.

In January 1943 Hitler promoted von Arnim's forces in status, renaming them Fifth Panzer Army. By now the German components of this army were von Broich's division, which was now led by Major General Manteuffel, the 10th Panzer Division, the newly arrived Austrian-German 334th Division and the Hermann Goering Panzer Division. The Italian component was Lieutenant General Vittorio Sogno's Italian XXX Corps of the 50th Special Brigade, Superga Mountain Division and the Giovanni Fascisti Armored Division. On the southern open desert flank a German reconnaissance force and the Italian Raggruppamento Sahariana kept their eyes peeled. Also arriving here were the Italian 103rd Scouting Company and 10th Bersaglieri Regiment. Their war against American rangers and paratroopers would soon resemble a private feud.

Hermann Goering, commander of the German Luftwaffe, was in his element with this campaign, because many of the Germans in Tunisia were members of his Luftwaffe: the paratroopers who constituted the spearhead of the German invasion, the German air squadrons, the 20th Flak Division of anti-aircraft guns and the Hermann Goering Panzer Division.

———————

In Libya by 15 January Montgomery was finally satisfied enough with his dispositions to launch a major offensive against the Beurat Line, but his troops quickly reported they were opposed only by rearguards. Rommel's entire army had given 'Monty' the slip and was already driving westwards. Monty, of course, knew the state of the line through British code breaking, but he wanted Rommel to think he had been fooled.

To the south of Rommel the Italians had abandoned Murzuk Oasis as per Bastico's orders and were driving towards Tunisia.

On 19 January Marshal Ugo Cavallero the military head of Comando Supremo visited Rommel in the Libyan port of Tripoli to find out first hand just how far Rommel intended to retreat: he had already given up all that he had conquered since coming to Africa. Cavallero was alarmed by Rommel's reply. The German said he intended to evacuate all of Libya and link up with von Arnim in Tunisia until he could pursuade Mussolini and Hitler to abandon Africa altogether. His reasoning was obvious: while they talked an aide informed Rommel that fourteen fuel barges on their way to him had just been intercepted by the enemy and ten had been sunk, whereupon Rommel ordered his army to abandon Tripoli.

Next day the Italian garrison of Mizda Oasis in Libya capitulated to French troops, and on the 23rd Montgomery's armor entered Tripoli. Thousands of Libyans cheered. The minority Italian population of the city for the most part stayed indoors, fearful of Libyan mob rule.

It is unfortunate that Italian troops and others had to die in small rearguard actions across Libya - incidents that do not even have a name.

———————

Meanwhile in the rainy north of Tunisia the British finally launched further attacks. Imperiale's men and the Bafile and Grado Battalions of the San Marco Marines and the Germans on their flank stopped the British in their tracks. In central Tunisia the Superga Mountain Division gave up some ground to the French at Karachoum Gap. In the dry south four hundred Italians at Temout Mellor were attacked by French-led Moroccan camel troops. In a tough fight a quarter of the Italians were killed and wounded, and then they abandoned the place. Pursued by the Moroccans the Italians actually retreated into Libya!

On 12 January a unit of the Superga Mountain Division corseted by Germans was surrounded by a French thrust, and for two days they fought back until being forced to give up. Von Arnim replied to this in his customary manner, by attacking the flank of the victors: specifically hitting Britons and French-led Algerians on the 17th. The following day the Italian 50th Special Brigade launched an offensive. The French asked the Americans for help, and Fredendall responded on the 20th by sending CCB (a third of the 1st Armored Division) under Brigadier General Paul Robinett, but Fredendall's instructions were so vague, using terms like 'big boys' and 'elephants', that Robinett had to ask the French what they wanted. The following day Robinett refused to attack in the face of artillery fire and instead he withdrew to refuel. In disgust the French told Robinett to go home! By the 23rd the fighting had died down to a desultory artillery duel. Imperiale's men had suffered high losses and were praised by the Germans for their courage.

On the 28th more companies of the Superga Mountain Division were overrun by the Algerians, and once again von Arnim replied with a counter attack on the flanks against other French-led troops, forcing them out of the Robaa area.

On the last day of January German tanks easily pushed the French back from Faid Pass. This astonished the Allies, because the unit doing the pushing was the 21st Panzer Division of Rommel's army, which according to Montgomery was still three hundred miles away in Libya.

Marshal Cavallero returned to Rome and reported to Mussolini what Bastico and Rommel had said. In anger Mussolini dismissed both Bastico and Rommel, and for good measure he also dismissed Cavallero from his position as military head of Comando Supremo. Mussolini replaced him with 64-year-old General Vittorio Ambrosio, who was a combat veteran from the 1911 Turkish War, had served as a divisional staff officer in World War I, had led the Second Army in the Yugoslavian invasion, had fought Titoist partisans, and most recently had commanded the Italian Army. Mussolini gave command of the Italian Army to General Enzio Rossi. To the surprise of many, Admiral Ricciardi commander of the navy and General Fougier commander of the Regia Aeronautica kept their jobs.

Meanwhile Mussolini had asked the Germans for some equipment to rebuild his shattered forces. When his son-in-law and foreign minister, Count Galeazzo Ciano, reminded the Germans of this shopping list, which included such items as three hundred Mark III tanks, six hundred warplanes and one thousand two hundred flak guns, the embarrassed Germans had to hedge the issue. They simply did not have anything to spare.

Of course Mussolini already knew the state of the German war chest, and so did Ciano, and the latter was angry that his father-in-law had sent him on this fool's errand. He spoke with Il Duce in private and suggested that this German refusal could justify the Italians to seek terms from the Allies. It might be a chance to get out of this war.

Almost simultaneously Roosevelt and Churchill were meeting at the Casablanca conference and they came up with a new public announcement. They declared they would never discuss terms with any Axis partner. They demanded unconditional surrender or total destruction. It was an incredibly stupid strategy, because it was in effect a declaration of war against the people of the Axis nations, rather than against their governments. Suddenly the thought of Anglo-American generals sitting in Berlin and Rome disposing with the German and Italian people and lands at whim would now be enough of a spur to convince many an anti-Fascist Italian and anti-Nazi German to fight on against the Allies.

Having changed name tags in his military command structure, Mussolini now did the same with his political structure, announcing a new cabinet on 5 February. Many long-trusted Fascists were kicked out. Minister of the Interior Guido Buffarino-Guidi was replaced by Alberto Albini. Minister of Justice Dino Grandi was replaced by Alfredo di Marsico. Minister of Finance Thaon di Revel was replaced by Giacomo Acerbo. Minister of Education Giuseppe Bottai was replaced by Carlo Alberto Biggini. Other Fascist leaders who lost their jobs were Alessandro Pavolini, Renato Ricci, and most surprising of all Count Galeazzo Ciano. Mussolini declared he would handle foreign affairs himself from now on. Ciano, suspecting his father-in-law would exile him for having suggested they make peace, asked for the position of ambassador to the Vatican. Mussolini acquiesced. It was a shrewd move for the Vatican was sovereign territory and Mussolini could not touch him there, but it was also inside Rome, where Ciano could keep his finger on the pulse.

When Mussolini fired Rommel for abandoning Libya he also gave his Armata Corazzini Africa a new name: Italian First Army; and he sent General Giovanni Messe to command it. Messe loved this assignment. No more Russian winters for him, hopefully. However, Rommel remained at his headquarters. He was an officer whom the Italians and Germans would both follow. He had failed and taken the Italians on their longest retreat in history, yet his men still considered him far superior to other generals, most of whom were sycophants, 'yes men' for either Mussolini or Hitler.

Von Arnim, commanding German Fifth Panzer Army in Tunisia on the other hand was very much a Nazi political general, but he had done a fine job in Tunisia, considering he had a tenuous supply line, a provisional force and no time to plan. He and Rommel both proved that if properly led the Italians could be fine soldiers.

Now Field Marshal Kesselring stepped into the picture. A Luftwaffe general he was responsible for all German personnel in the

Mediterranean theater and that included von Arnim and Rommel. Kesselring was already toying with the idea of a counter offensive against the weakest link among the Allies in Africa, namely the Americans. Recently part of the US 1st Armored Division had tried another attack led by Brigadier General Raymond McQuillin, but the Americans had been slow, had been held up by air raids, including one by American planes, and had shown up too late to do any good. Clearly they were poorly led, badly deployed and their morale was low. Moreover the Americans were in southern Tunisia where the terrain was dry and fit for armor. Kesselring hoped that his counter offensive could put the Allies off their game for a while. Rommel loved the idea when he heard it and suggested doing far more. He wanted to advance a hundred miles into Algeria, swerve north to the sea and cut off all the Allies from their supply bases in Algeria. The other officers smirked. Here was the old Rommel and his flights of fantasy.

The final plan that they agreed upon put von Arnim in control in Northern and Central Tunisia, where he would hold the British and French and also lend support to the offensive. Messe would hold a defensive line on the Tunisian-Libyan border to keep Montgomery from interfering, though everyone agreed that the tortoise-like Montgomery posed no threat as yet. The actual offensive would be led by Rommel, who would have battle groups loaned to him by von Arnim and Messe amounting to forty-four Italian and two hundred and five German tanks and a thousand Italian and five thousand German infantry. Some of the German tanks were the new Panthers: a 44-ton tank armed with a long-barreled 75mm gun. To command such a small force was a terrible demotion for Rommel, but his alternative was to go back home in disgrace.

On 14 February under von Arnim's orders the German 10th and 21st Panzer Divisions slammed into the American mountaintop defenses through Faid Pass and Maknassy. The Germans even managed to summon up a sandstorm to hide their movements, and within hours they had surrounded two pockets of Americans - an infantry battalion of the 1st Armored Division and an infantry battalion of the 34th Division in one locale, and two infantry battalions of the 34th Division in another location.

Simultaneously Rommel struck in the Gafsa area with a battlegroup of the 15th Panzer Division and the Italian Centauro Armored Division, the latter commanded by General Calvi di Bergolo, son-in-law of the King of Italy. The Centauro had been whittled down by rearguard battles, air raids and rough desert terrain to the point that all that di Bergolo could spare for the attack were about two thousand personnel manning forty-four M14 tanks, some Semoventi 75s, a few batteries of towed artillery and the 5th Bersaglieri Regiment. Indeed just to make up these numbers some survivors of Ariete were brought in.

Following the sandstorm a heavy rain drenched the attackers, but the poor visibility did not prohibit Italian and German aircraft from devastating columns of American vehicles. Italian pilots were astonished to see that the bragging Americans were retreating and blowing up their massive supply dump at Gafsa. It was soon apparent that no American above the rank of brigadier had the will to fight!

Brigadier General McQuillin of the US 1st Armored Division did organize a counter attack with a battalion of tanks, a battalion of Priests and some infantry in half-tracks, but they came in line abreast like a horse cavalry charge. German anti-tank guns hiding behind 4 feet high bushes slaughtered them. The Germans destroyed twenty-six Priests, fifty-nine half-tracks, and forty-four of the fifty-one tanks.

The following day an element of the US 1st Armored Division commanded by Colonel Alexander Stark was ordered to counter attack, but Stark asked Colonel John Alger to lead the charge, as Stark had no tank experience! Alger attacked with fifty-eight Lee tanks, some infantry, a few 75mm guns on top of half-tracks (home-made self-propelled guns), some Priests and some M10 tank destroyers, but German aircraft dispersed them! Regaining their composure the Americans came on again and this time German artillery and anti-tank guns ambushed them. Only four American tanks escaped. Alger was captured. Upon hearing the news Eisenhower authorized a retreat of fifty miles!

By the evening of the 16th the Germans had reached Gafsa, and next day they captured Sbeitla. The 15th Panzer and the Centauro Armored Divisions cut off one American column and shot it up. Pilots reported several columns of vehicles fleeing to the west with American and French troops and Arab civilians intermixed, while on the American's northern flank the French had fallen back. An eighty-mile gap appeared in the Allied line. The Italians and Germans had achieved a remarkable victory. Suddenly Rommel's ambition of slicing through Algeria and cutting off the Allies did not seem so preposterous.

On 19 February the 10th and 21st Panzer Divisions attacked Sbiba, which was defended by remnants of US 1st Armored Division, part of the US 34th Division, a regiment of French and Algerians of Major General Welvert's Constantine Division and Brigadier Nicholson's British 1st Guards Brigade [of 6th Armored Division]. Anderson had hurriedly rushed in this latter brigade to help the Americans, and had also sent Brigadier Charles Dunphie's 26th Armored Brigade, which was still on the road. However, Nicholson refused to listen to no one but Anderson, whereas Welvert would only receive instructions from Koetltz, and the Americans looked to Orlando Ward for leadership. In truth no one was in charge of the whole scenario.

There was also bickering among commanders in the Axis camp,

prompting Kesselring to give overall command of the battle to Rommel. This afternoon Rommel personally led an assault by the 15th Panzer and the Centauro against Kasserine Pass, which he found to be defended by a regiment of the Constantine Division, remnants of US 1st Armored Division, a regiment of the US 1st Division and the US 19th Engineer Regiment, the latter fighting as infantry. Already the Americans were throwing rear-echelon personnel into the line without retraining them. Here too the defenders had a choice of commanders, Americans Robinett and Stark and British Brigadier McNabb.

Already Rommel was running low on tanks, mostly owing to bad terrain [throwing tracks on rocks, and sand blowing into radiators and thus overheating engines], and he demanded replacements. He suspected von Arnim was deliberately withholding help. Personal jealousies were still plaguing the Axis cause.

At dawn 20 February a battalion of German panzergrenadiers and the Italian 5th Bersaglieri Regiment attempted to infiltrate around the defenders at Kasserine Pass, but they ran into American engineers and other rear-echelon troops supported by French horse-drawn artillery. The combat was fierce and close, with the artillery firing over open sights. Some Italian tanks arrived to help the Bersaglieri launch several charges over sharp rocky slopes, during which the Italian regimental commander was killed.

The struggle continued into the next day, and at one point American tanks ambushed German tanks in a cactus patch. Outside Thala the Germans were stopped by British armor. At Bou Chebka hundreds of Bersaglieri lost their bearings in a heavy rain and walked right into a hastily prepared allied defense line. The shooting was quick and deadly.

On 22 February the 10th Panzer Division was met at Thala by ten British Crusader tanks supported by American artillery [9th Division]. The Germans destroyed seven tanks, but could not pass through the artillery fire. This day the various Axis units began receiving Rommel's order to withdraw. The nine day offensive had run its course. They had come within five miles of the Algerian border!

———————

Up north the Superga's troops had launched diversionary attacks, and at Siluno a thousand of them were cut to ribbons by British and Moroccans. Thereafter for five days around Pichon the Superga fought a steady withdrawal. Further north the 50th Special Brigade lost Cap Serrat to French-led Tunisians.

Rommel was not pleased with his offensive, known hereafter as the Battle of Kasserine Pass, for he had failed to achieve his personal goal. However, all the other Axis commanders were well satisfied. They had hurt the French and the British, inflicting about five hundred casualties on each, and they had devastated the Americans, who suffered a loss of three thousand four hundred wounded and five thousand five hundred dead or missing, and the destruction of three hundred and forty-five armored vehicles, two hundred guns and five hundred and thirty soft-skinned vehicles, and had abandoned several airfields and much needed supplies, and had been forced to retreat fifty miles. Most important of all the Italians and Germans had crippled American morale and caused considerable bitterness between the Americans and the British.

One reason for the bitter taste in the American mouth was that Montgomery told the press he was snapping at Rommel's heels as he chased him across Libya, but the British and Americans in Tunisia knew better. They had just fought Rommel and three of his divisions. This was the beginning of bad blood between Montgomery and the Americans.

Meanwhile General Messe could not believe his luck as he settled down to take command of Italian First Army. Montgomery seemed to have all the time in the world and as late as 26 February Messe had seen only one of Montgomery's divisions arrive anywhere near his defenses at Mareth in Tunisia. Rommel urged Messe to attack, but Messe was cautious especially as he had few tanks. Moreover his only real strength lay in the reinforcements he had been sent: Major General Giuseppe Falugi's Pistoia Division, Major General Gavino Pizzolato's La Spezia Division and Major General Nino Sozzani's Giovanni Fascisti Armored Division. The latter he placed in Lieutenant General Taddeo Orlando's XX Corps, which had remnants of the German 90th Light Division and Major General la Ferla's Trieste Motorized Division. Orlando had also been reinforced by the Italian 190th Reconnaissance Battalion, 5/7th Bersaglieri Regiment and 10th CCNN Battalion Gruppo.

Lieutenant General Paolo Berardi's XXI Corps took the Pistoia and La Spezia to add to his German 164th Division, 6th CCNN Battalion Gruppo, armored cars of the Aosta Cavalry Regiment and 3/San Marco Marines. South of Mareth in the open desert Messe placed elements of the Novara, Lodi, Nizza and Monferrato Mechanized Cavalry Regiments. The remainder of the Italian formations that had fought in Libya were currently regrouping behind the lines.

However, it was March before the units that Rommel had borrowed for his Kasserine Pass offensive were returned to Messe in any kind of shape to be useful.

By March Montgomery himself had arrived at Medennine in Tunisia and his forces had built a defensive position with his British 7th Armored and 51st Divisions and New Zealand 2nd Division. Several of his officers had wanted to chase Rommel across Libya, not just follow him, and thus prevent such things as Kasserine, but Montgomery continuously reined them in and he dismissed a few, including Generals Gatehouse and Lumsden.

Kasserine had been so much of a success that Hitler and Mussolini were willing to forget their squabble with Rommel, and he was appointed commander of all Axis forces in Africa, which included Messe and von Arnim, to the latter's indignation.

Thus Rommel's suggestion that Messe attack, now became an order, and Messe obeyed. On the morning of 6 March 1943 Messe's First Italian Army attacked Montgomery's defenses at Medennine, leading with one hundred and sixty German tanks [10th, 15th and 21st Panzer Divisions] and a few tanks from the Centauro, alongside the infantry of the Pistoia, La Spezia and Giovanni Fascisti Divisions. However, this was the sort of battle 'Monty' was good at, and he met the oncoming panzers with anti-tank guns backed up by field artillery, while his air support made merry over and behind Messe's lines. By day's end Messe had lost a quarter of his tanks and two hundred Italian and four hundred and thirty-five German casualties, and had failed to penetrate Montgomery's positions. Rommel agreed with Messe's request to call off the battle at once, and three days later he flew to Germany on sick leave.

If Messe learned that he could not break Montgomery at Medennine, he was equally convinced that Montgomery could not break him in his position at Mareth. Messe placed his twenty-five thousand Germans and fifty-five thousand Italians in such a manner as to stop the Allies, with XX and XXI Corps on the front line. Messe on the coastal plain faced southwards with his left flank (east) on the coast and right flank (west) in high inhospitable rocky mountains. To prevent Montgomery using mountain trails, Messe placed a trip wire unit in the mountains: Gruppo di Sahara under Brigadier General Alberto Mannerini. In reserve Messe had the Centauro Armored, 10th Panzer, 15th Panzer and 21st Panzer Divisions, all of them very weak, plus the Lodi Reconnaissance Battalion. Also in the rear was the tiny remnant of the 'old Alamein army'. Moreover he had good military intelligence, which informed him that Monty would hit him on the 22nd.

Actually Montgomery launched his offensive on the 20th with no fewer than one hundred and sixty thousand men. Near the coast the British 7th Armored and 51st Divisions assaulted the five thousand six hundred and fifty men of the Trieste Motorized Division, 190th Reconnaissance Battalion, 5/7th Bersaglieri Regiment and 10th CCNN Battalion, and the German 90th Light Division. The struggle was frantic from the outset. Inland the British 50th Division attacked the Giovanni Fascisti Division, which was already down to four thousand two hundred men. Further inland Major General Raymond Briggs' British 1st Armored Division charged the nine thousand men of the

La Spezia Division. On the flank Falugi's seven thousand four hundred and fifty troops of the Pistoia Division moved forward with their 47mm anti-tank guns to fend off a British tank assault from the open desert between them and the mountains. All day and into the next day the battle continued.

Messe was well pleased about one thing. Though the Allies controlled the sea in Tunisian waters they had not thought fit to use big gunned warships on the coast to shell Messe's troops out of their positions. Instead Montgomery was relying on field artillery followed by frontal assaults!

Late on the second day Mannerini's Gruppo di Sahara in the mountains radioed Messe that they were under assault by some infantry. This was a trip wire unit, consisting of four Italian and one Libyan battalions, some artillery, the Novara reconnaissance battalion, a machine gun battalion and some Frontier Guards. It was meant to alert Messe, not meant to hold ground, but throughout the night these poorly armed men fought frenziedly, constantly asking for reinforcements. Their pleas seemed so desperate that Messe sent them elements of the 21st Panzer and 164th Divisions. The Germans arrived at dawn on the 22nd, wondering what all the fuss was about, and why the Italians couldn't stop a handful of infantry, and only now did they learn that this small ad hoc force had been holding off an entire Allied corps commanded by Major General Freyberg - New Zealand 2nd Division, Greek 1st Brigade and the French Force L [a brigade-sized unit].

Messe continued to hold, even though Montgomery put in reinforcements including Major General John Hawkesworth's British 4th Division. Messe threw in his German and Italian armor. On the fourth day of battle Messe tossed in the last of his reserves, namely the bits and pieces of the 'old Alamein army', survivors of the Ariete, Brescia, Bologna, Folgore, Pavia, Littorio, Sabratha and Trento Divisions.

Next day von Arnim, who was in charge while Rommel was on sick leave, ordered Messe to retreat. Messe obeyed, but under protest, convinced he could hold. Even then Messe only withdrew his units piecemeal on his own timetable, while brave Italian and German rearguards kept Montgomery from interfering. The ground action finally ended on the 29th, the tenth day of battle. Messe's losses were a thousand Germans and five thousand Italians, many of which had been lost to air raids. Major General Pizzolato was killed in an airstrike. Arturo Scattini took over the La Spezia.

The Italian submarine FR 111 was sunk in an air raid. On March 14 the British troopship Empress of Canada carrying eight hundred and forty-six Polish and Greek refugees, some British civilians and military personnel and five hundred Italian prisoners was torpedoed in the Atlantic by the Italian submarine Leonardo da Vinci. As the large ship stopped all engines, the submarine crew hailed the ship and gave the passengers and crew thirty minutes to take to the lifeboats before they finished her off. This was about as much humanity as the submarine's captain could allow. However, the people in these open life boats had to undergo terrible privations of exposure before they were rescued. Some were eaten by sharks. Upon rescue it was found that forty-four of the crew, ninety civilians and two hundred and fifty-eight of the Italian prisoners had died. The extremely high loss among the Italian prisoners was the result of the actions of a British officer, who had refused to unlock the lower deck, thus ensuring that many Italian prisoners went down with the ship. In anger some of the rescued Italians threw him overboard in the path of sharks.

In the Mediterranean the Italian troopship Francesco Crispi was sunk by a British submarine with a loss of eight hundred soldiers.

––––––––––

Following the American debacle in Tunisia, Eisenhower sent Major General Ernest Harmon to advise Fredendall, but deep in his bunker Fredendall was in a state of panic and he effectively asked Harmon to take over! Eisenhower also sent Major General Omar N. Bradley to investigate the causes of the defeat. His and Harmon's reports convinced Eisenhower that Fredendall had to go. He sent him back to the USA, and sent several other officers too, including Stark and McQuillin. Eisenhower even fired himself, i. e. he brought in a ground forces commander, British General Sir Harold Alexander, who had worked well with Montgomery in Egypt and should do the same here once Montgomery blessed them all with his presence. Moreover, Eisenhower hoped Alexander would prod Anderson into action. There was considerable resentment among the Americans that Eisenhower put a Brit in charge of them. Patton said sarcastically that Eisenhower was "the best general the British have."

Patton now had a stake in this affair, because his son-in-law was among the missing, and because he was given Fredendall's job – command of II Corps. Patton was known for his bravery - he had beaten a Mexican officer to the draw in a wild west style shootout, and had led tanks in World War I. Famous also for his love of pomp and his obsession with spit and polish, he began his job at II Corps by firing people and by rewarding deserving heroes. Moreover, within days he went over to the offensive. However, this was no dashing charge, for II Corps was up against the Superga Mountain Division, which held the American advance to a snail's pace. Patton reported to his superiors that the Italians were fighting well.

Von Arnim was still convinced that the Americans were the weak link in the Allied chain, so he organized another offensive against them. His Germans had been reinforced by the 999th Light Division, a catch-all formation consisting of older troops including some criminal prisoners. To spearhead the offensive he chose the Centauro Armored Division and five battalions of all arms from the 10th Panzer Division. They struck at El Guettar, defended by Allen's US 1st Division [reinforced by a tank battalion and additional artillery]. Patton rushed to the battlefield to see it for himself and he forbade any thought of retreat. Here the Americans fought the Italians and Germans to a standstill. It was now clear to the Axis that the Americans had found a fighting general.

The news of Patton's victory made Montgomery anxious. Rumor had it that Patton had bested Rommel at El Guettar. Allied intelligence did not know Rommel was in Germany. Some troops under Montgomery's command had been fighting in the North African desert for almost three years and he wanted them to have the honor of administering the coup de grace to the Axis forces in Africa. He did not want Anderson's British newcomers to have the glory and most certainly did not want the Americans to have it, and definitely did not want the French to have that honor.

Alexander, now Allied ground forces commander in Africa, was trying his best to put an end to the 'Yank' vs. 'Brit' squabbling, but unfortunately he was the type of leader who never actually ordered anybody to do anything. He just made recommendations. As a result Montgomery did as he pleased, ignoring Alexander's latest 'advice', unless it suited him. Anderson understood these recommendations were in fact orders, and he obeyed them, albeit reluctantly. But often as not Koeltz and Patton ignored Alexander, because they did not understand his upper class British English speech and never knew they had been given an 'order'.

Messe was not aware of the problems of the Allied generals. He had his own problems, chief of which was that he was running out of room. His First Army had dug in at Wadi Akarit where impassable mountains came within four miles of the sea. Into this narrow front he crammed his entire army: infantry and assault engineers up front, anti-tank guns immediately behind them, armor right behind them and the artillery to the rear. To prevent the enemy from scrambling along the mountain slopes he put two battalions of infantry on mountain peaks. He prayed that Montgomery would still be arrogant enough not to ask the Royal Navy to bombard Messe's line.

On the night of 5 April 1943 Italian sentries of the 3/125th Regiment (La Spezia Division) and the 1/36th Regiment (Pistoia Division) peered into the darkness across the mountains from their cliff-top positions. Suddenly there was a silent black figure among them and then the glimmer of a blade. Gurkhas of the Indian Army armed with Kukri knives were literally cutting their way through the Italian mountain defenses.

This same night on the coastal plain British troops attacked head on against Messe's front line defended by XX Corps [Trieste Motorized Division, Giovanni Fascisti Armored Division, 190th Reconnaissance Battalion, 5/7th Bersaglieri Regiment and German 90th Light Division] plus the XXI Corps [Pistoia Division, La Spezia Division, 6th and 10th CCNN Battalion Gruppos, the Aosta Mechanized Cavalry Regiment, 3/San Marco Marines and the German 164th Division]. The line held. However, come morning Messe realized that General F. I. S. Tuker's Indian 4th Division spearheaded by the Gurkhas had turned his mountain flank. Messe had no choice but to order a retreat at once.

Once again Messe's skillful rearguards sacrificed themselves for the good of the army. The 3/San Marco Marines and some anti-tank guns drew the short straw. Messe assumed that Montgomery would have followed up his mountain advance by putting forward air controllers and forward artillery observers on the mountain peaks with adequate radios to bring down accurate fire on Messe's retreating forces. But unbelievably Montgomery had not done this. The Italians and Germans were left more or less in peace to evacuate the area, bar air strikes.

Meanwhile Anderson was under orders to break through General von Vaerst's Fifth Panzer Army, which besides German formations included the Italian XXX Corps [Superga Mountain Division, 50th Special Brigade, 5th CCNN Battalion, and Bafile and Grado Battalions of the San Marco Marines]. Anderson's plan was to crack open the Axis line at Fondouk with his British 1st Armored, 6th Armored, 46th, 56th and 78th Divisions, and Alexander made the suggestion that after this he should strike into Messe's rear. But the Italians and Germans defeated the attackers.

As a result by 11 April Messe's First Army was able to link up with the Fifth Panzer Army, and thus offer a solid front to the Allies. Because the front line was now shorter, Koeltz's French and Patton's Americans were pinched out, and suddenly unemployed, but not before French Major General Welvert was killed. However, Eisenhower demanded that the Americans be in on the kill for political reasons, so Major General Omar Bradley took US IInd Corps up north to attack along the coast.

Von Arnim was busy creating a continuous last-ditch defensive position named the Enfidaville Line, with the sea on both flanks, and to his back were the cities of Tunis and Bizerte and the sea.

The Italians and Germans knew that only a miracle could save them now, and Mussolini and Hitler appeared to have used up their genie wishes.

———————

As Messe watched his troops settle into this final position he saw that they were in tatters, and his units were mere shadows of their former selves. On the eastern coastal flank he placed Orlando's XX Corps, which had in line the German 90th Light Division (reinforced by a battalion from the Giovanni Fascisti). Slightly inland stood the remainder of the Giovanni Fascisti Division [reinforced by a regiment and a battalion of German panzergrenadiers]. On their right (west) lay the Trieste Motorized Division (five Italian infantry battalions and a provisional battalion of lightly armed Luftwaffe mechanics). Further west was Berardi's XXI Corps of the German 164th Division [three German and two Italian infantry battalions], the La Spezia Division [one German and five Italian infantry battalions], and the Pistoia Division [one infantry battalion and one battalion of the 5th Bersaglieri]. All of these divisions were sprinkled with a few survivors of Alamein.

On 19 April Montgomery's Eighth Army slammed into Messe's First Army. Monty's scouts had done their jobs well, identifying the two lone battalions in the Pistoia sector as a weak point, so Monty struck them with the British 1st and 7th Armored Divisions backed by the British 1st, 4th and 51st Divisions. Both Italian battalions would have simply disappeared had it not been for a timely counter attack by the rest of the 5th Bersaglieri and some German infantry. Meanwhile the New Zealand 2nd Division attacked the Trieste sector. All other defensive units were put under some kind of pressure. Incredibly the Italians and Germans held the line for five days, though the Trieste was completely destroyed. Indeed their resistance was so tough that Alexander decided that he would fare better if he assaulted the Fifth Panzer Army instead.

Alexander decided to strengthen his Anglo-American punch against Fifth Panzer Army along the western portion of the Enfidaville Line by borrowing two divisions from Montgomery. Monty sent him his best infantry: Freyberg's New Zealand 2nd and Tuker's Indian 4th Divisions, and they were given to Anderson to reinforce his 1st Armored, 6th Armored, 46th, 56th and 78th Divisions. To Anderson's north Bradley put his IInd Corps on the coast with Ward's 1st Armored, Allen's 1st, Truscott's 3rd, Eddy's 9th and Ryder's 34th Divisions. Alexander also found a slot for the French.

The defenders in Fifth Panzer Army consisted of Germans: the Manteuffel Division, Hermann Goering Panzer Division, 10th Panzer Division, 999th Division and 334th Division; and Italians: Superga Mountain Division, 50th Special Brigade, 5th CCNN Battalion, and Bafile and Grado Battalions of the San Marco Marines. In desperation von Arnim also threw in the Arab Legion, recruited from Arabs from North Africa and the Middle East, and a unit of Fascist French.

As soon as Alexander launched his offensive the combat was fierce, and by coincidence his French troops ran up against the Fascist French. No quarter was given. Only on 9 May 1943 after two weeks of vicious fighting did von Vaerst realize it was all over, and he surrendered his Fifth Panzer Army.

This same day Messe's Italians and Germans were still battling Montgomery. E. g. the British 167th Brigade suffered sixty-three killed and two hundred and twenty-one wounded and one hundred and four captured this day alone! But with the news of the German surrender, Messe learned that his right flank was wide open. He knew he had to retreat, but he had run out of dry land! He ordered his artillery to keep firing to hold the Allies at arm's length, while over the next four days his troops retreated until they literally had their feet in the surf. On this shore on 12 May von Arnim surrendered his personal headquarters and his last order to Messe was that he should give up too. Messe deliberated for another twenty-four hours, and then he commanded his survivors to lay down their arms.

In the last month of the Tunisian campaign including the last day the Allies captured a total of eighty-six thousand Italians and one hundred and sixty-four thousand Germans.

Chapter Forty-two
Africa in Perspective

When Mussolini became prime minister of Italy in 1922 he inherited an African empire consisting of the Libyan coast, Eritrea and most of Somalia. Over the next twenty years he expanded it to include all of Libya, Ethiopia, British Somaliland and parts of Kenya, Sudan and Egypt. Then he lost it all.

There is no doubt that one reason for his defeat was Mussolini's over reliance upon Africans. A few bande fought very well, but as a whole the bande program was disappointing. The uniformed ascari units did better, but this program too had mixed results. Having said this, in East Africa some of his ascari divisions won glory, such as the Eritrean 2nd Colonial Division at Keren in 1941, where the Eritrean/Ethiopian 4th Colonial Division also gained laurels. The Somali 101st and 102nd Colonial Divisions fared well on the Juba River in 1941, and the Somali 101st Colonial Division together with the Ethiopian 21st and 25th Colonial Divisions put up a magnificent fight at Soddu. The Ethiopian Harar Division fought nobly and bravely at Tug Argan Pass in 1940. But these were the exceptions. At best perhaps a quarter of the ascaris in the independent brigades and battalions were worthy of Italian trust. In North Africa the 1st and 2nd Libyan Divisions had been dangled like sacrificial goats and had been devoured by the British lion in one gulp. Even as late as 1943 the Italians were still using Libyan troops, but they did not rely on them. Some Libyans volunteered for the British Army in order to fight Fascism, but the British soon found they were capable of sentry duty at best.

The performance of the actual Italian soldier in Africa was very mixed indeed. In East Africa the Cacciatore d'Africa and Savoia Grenadiers Divisions both performed wonders fighting in detachments on various battlefields including Keren and Amba Alagi.

Alas in North Africa the 1st, 2nd and 4th Blackshirt Divisions made little impression on the Allies. The Cirene, Marmarica and Sirte Divisions recruited from Italian colonists in Libya fought courageously if poorly. The Catanzaro Division also fought badly, though some of its men showed spirit. The Sabratha began its war with a formidable resistance at Derna in January 1941 and then enhanced its reputation in 1942 at Second Gazala and First Alamein. The Bologna Division served commendably at the long siege of Tobruk, at First Alamein and Alam al Halfa. The Brescia became a fine formation in its long duty at Tobruk. The Brescia, Ariete, Trieste, Trento and Pavia fought in every one of Rommel's battles in Egypt and Libya at his request. The Littorio saw tough action at First Alamein, Alam al Halfa and Second Alamein. The Savona wrote a glorious page in history, that no one has bothered to read. The Folgore gained its page in history at Second Alamein.

But by December 1942 most of these divisions were at one-tenth strength or less and from now on would fight as emergency reserves only. The Centauro had gained a good reputation in Greece and fought with extreme gallantry in Libya in rearguard actions and in Tunisia at Kasserine Pass, Medennine, Mareth, El Guettar and Enfidaville. The troops of the Giovanni Fascisti fought well from November 1941 until May 1943, despite not being taken seriously by Mussolini. In Tunisia the Superga Mountain, Pistoia and La Spezia Divisions and the 50th Special Brigade earned admiration from both the Germans and the Allies.

The great tragedy of course is that these divisions did not go home with flags waving and crowds cheering. They were lost: dumped like so many discarded empty cans by Mussolini once he heard they had their backs to the sea. Of course the families of these men did not discard them.

The people of Ethiopia, Eritrea, Somalia and Libya hated Mussolini for the constant warfare and disruption of their lives and for the waste of their manhood, whether fighting for their own independence against the Italians or fighting for Mussolini's love of glory. But by 1943 they were all free of the Fascist yoke. It is no small wonder that these nations developed a seething mistrust of 'White' men.

The Italian colonists in Africa, many of whom had never seen Italy, were also free of the Fascist yoke now, and their hatred of Mussolini was just as fierce as that of the native Africans.

The people of Italy were not yet free from Fascism, but that possibility was becoming more and more probable with the Allied advance. Entire communities in Italy were devastated by the news of the surrender in Africa. What had become of their sons, brothers, boyfriends, fathers, uncles, cousins, neighbors, who had been whisked away to such an inhospitable land? Were they dead or lying crippled in a hospital or were they in a prisoner of war camp? And if the latter were they being fed, tortured, beaten? Their loved ones in Italy were plagued with a thousand nightmares.

The Germans blamed their predicament in Africa on the Italians, but is this fair? First of all the Italians had never asked them to get involved and secondly the Italians pulled the German chestnuts out of the fire as often as the Germans rescued the Italians. The Germans complained that the Italian supply line was ineffective and the supply personnel were timid in the face of Allied attack. Yet, if that was the case then why didn't the Germans rely exclusively on their own logistics? In fact the Allies were constantly astonished by the willingness of Italian sailors to run the gauntlet of firepower from Italy, past Malta to Africa. No less a person than Admiral Sir Andrew

Cunningham, Allied naval commander in the Mediterranean, praised Italian sailors: "It was always a surprise to me how the Italian seamen continued to operate their ships in the face of the dangers that beset them."

When one remembers the Allied advantage in code-breaking, the Italian feats in Africa are all the more startling. The British could read most of the Italian naval code, plus almost all of Comando Supremo's orders to its commanders, and they could also read some of the U-boat code and much of the Luftwaffe code, and last but not least they could read a high proportion of Hitler's directives!

Even Rommel, who was a hard taskmaster, found several of the Italian units to be laudable, and at no time did the Germans insist that Messe should be replaced by a German, or that Lieutenant Generals Orlando and Berardi should not command German divisions in their corps. Indeed it appears that Messe was more aggressive than von Arnim.

The war in Libya and Egypt had been a war of manoeuver, but not so in Tunisia, and the Italians were better equipped to fight a static battle. The German and Italian resistance in Tunisia is best summed up by pointing out one indisputable fact: it took the British, French and Americans almost six months to advance that last twelve miles to Tunis, and it cost them seventy-five thousand casualties!

The Allies suffered a major shakeup in their command structure owing to the Tunisian campaign. The number of officers that were dismissed would fill a book. The most noticeable US loss was Fredendall, sent back to the states ostensibly to train troops. After the campaign American General Ward was also 'kicked upstairs' and it was a year before he was rehabilitated. Also sent back were Stark and McQuillin.

One study, which has never really been made until now, is the hero's welcome provided by the British for their so-called war-winning generals from the campaigns in Africa. These battles should have been career stepping stones for the British generals, and if the Italians had put up as poor a show as British government propaganda wanted the British public to believe, then Africa would have been nothing but a string of laurels for British officers. The fact that some Axis generals in Africa were German is really irrelevant when it comes to soldiers' performance, because the only time that German troops outnumbered Italians was in Fifth Panzer Army in the last few months. Even a brilliant commander such as Rommel would have earned no spurs had his Italian troops not fought well. Yet a high proportion of British Army and Indian Army officers who served in Africa in combat units were treated shabbily - either demoted, shunted aside or kicked upstairs to rear echelon duties or backwaters. Why did this happen? By May 1943 the British suspected they would still have many more battles to fight and would need every battle-hardened victorious officer they could find. It is obvious that the major reason this happened was because Africa was not a string of victories, but rather a whole host of defeats within which were scattered a few victories, and many of the latter came about not because of Allied generalship or superior courage but because of consistently growing Allied materiel preponderance, especially that coming out of American factories. The numbers of British officers 'punished' in this way is alarming, and no doubt many did not deserve this fate. A cursory glance at generals treated in this manner identifies Cunningham, Wavell, Auchinleck, Anderson, Clutterbuck, Beresford-Pierce, Birks, Raymond Briggs, Chater, Creagh, Dunphie, Gatehouse, Godwin-Austen, Hughes, Lumsden, Norrie, Platt, Ramsden, Ritchie and Scobie.

It is also interesting that despite the so-called German lack of confidence in the Italian soldier, in spring 1942 Hitler asked the Italians to increase their presence in Russia. Surely if the German high command thought for a moment that the Italians would be a liability in Russia they would have sent the Italians home rather than ask for more of them? Had the Germans succeeded in Africa they would have had nothing but praise for their Italian brothers in arms. Victory has many fathers, but defeat is an orphan.

Chapter Forty-three
Bosnia

By November 1942 the British and Americans were taking a serious interest in the partisan war in Yugoslavia, where they hoped the Axis would be forced to reinforce their garrison. The Americans admitted they knew nothing of the true situation there, so they listened to the British, who told them they did. They didn't.

Tito's partisans were stronger than ever despite having fought off three offensives by Italians, Germans, Cetniks, Serbs and Croats. The realities of Fascist/Nazi rule such as draconian laws, arbitrary arrests, the shooting of hostages, execution of captured partisans, imprisonment of suspects on flimsy evidence, conscription of forced labor and the wholesale slaughter of villages because of their ethnicity or religion had all combined to drive many men and women into the ranks of Tito's partisans. Tito accepted anyone: Croats, Serbs, Slovenes, Macedonians, Kosovars, Montenegrins, Jews, Dalmatian Italians, Volksdeutsch, and his recruiters asked no questions, so he even took in deserters from the Fascist armies. Tito's Communism took a back seat. Priests, rabbis and Moslem clerics were even allowed to join his forces and perform their religious services. Women carried rifles just like the men.

By and large the Italians had not indulged in atrocities. Indeed they had rescued thousands of Jews and Moslems. However, as this guerilla war dragged on they became increasingly frustrated and prone to reactionary methods. Responding to messages from Mussolini to get tough, some officers complied, while others protested about the violence against the innocent and the helpless, but found themselves speaking out in vain. By late 1942 the shooting of Titoist prisoners by Italian firing squads was commonplace.

The Cetniks had also gained recruits, but Milhailovich never knew how many partisans he had because his band leaders only obeyed his orders when the mood took them. Probably he could rely on about thirty thousand, most of them infantry and horse cavalry. He had little artillery, no armor to speak of and almost no engineers.

He had hoped that by welcoming American and British advisers he would gain some new equipment, which could be parachuted to him the same way the advisers reached him, but he often had to apologize to these advisers, because his men appeared to spend more time fighting the Titoists than the Axis. However, the advisers indicated that this was all right, for the Allies would, they assured him, invade the country someday and then they would need the assistance of a strong Cetnik force. If his men were reduced to starving wretches on the run from Axis aircraft, they would be of no value at all to the Allied invaders: therefore, best he keep his men healthy. Besides,

Churchill liked the idea of killing Communists. Through Churchill's influence the Yugoslavian government-in-exile (with offices in Cairo) appointed Milhailovich to the position of Minister of War!

Also, Italian and German officers had been most appreciative whenever the Cetniks attacked the Titoists, and they had awarded medals to them for bravery and merit. Some Cetniks wore German medals and British medals for the same action!

In December 1942 Axis reconnaissance planes identified Tito's main force hiding in the Bihac region, one hundred and fifty miles northwest of Sarajevo. At once the generals gathered to coordinate a new offensive - Italians, Germans, Croats, Bulgarians and Serbs, with Cetnik liaison officers present.

Meanwhile the eight thousand Italian police and Carabinieri in Albania asked the Albanian Army, police and frontier guards [a total of another fourteen thousand Albanians] to join them in an anti-guerilla sweep. The object of the mission was not so much to destroy the Albanian partisans, but to drive them away from the main arteries and population centers.

The Italian Mountain Raggruppamento CCNN was renamed the '21 April'. By giving it this title [an important date in Fascist history] Mussolini thought it would steel the men's nerves for the coming struggle.

The fourth anti-Titoist offensive codenamed Operation White began to take form in January 1943. The action began with the Croat Army and Ustaci attacking into the Bihac region from the north. This included the Croat 369th Division, which had a German cadre. At the same time other forces advanced towards Bihac from the northeast - the German 717th Security Division and a regiment of the 187th Infantry Division plus the 7th SS Prinz Eugen Mountain Division, the latter consisting of Yugoslavian Volksdeutsch. Approaching Bihac from the west was General Robotti's Italian Second Army, specifically his V and VI Corps with the following divisions: Sardinian Grenadiers [and attached 55th CCNN Legion], Re [and attached 75th CCNN Legion], Lombardia [and attached 137th CCNN Legion], Emanuele Filiberto Celere, Messina [and attached 108th CCNN Legion], Marche [and attached 49th CCNN Legion], Emilia and Murge. The Emilia and Murge were new to combat. It was thus assumed Tito would have no choice but to retreat into the valley of the Neretva River where twelve thousand Cetniks were waiting to ambush him.

The main combat began on 16 January with full-scale Axis air onslaughts and artillery barrages on Tito's foggy mountain stronghold. As Tito had no fighter planes, the Axis air units could use any old obsolete aircraft here including captured machines. Within twenty-four hours Tito was on the move.

For three weeks the advancing Axis troops chased after Tito, and were dogged every step of the way by rearguards manned by wild looking fanatic partisans in long hair and full beards hidden in foggy and snowy mountain hideouts. Aircraft continued to harass the partisans, but in the higher altitudes of the mountains fog and snowstorms hid them from view. In addition to battle losses, the Italians, Croats and Germans were plagued by frostbite and respiratory ailments. Tito had twenty thousand partisans in his main column, but soon four thousand five hundred of them were wounded or sick and had to be carried on stretchers. The few horses he had were used to pull guns. The Axis artillery was also horse-drawn, and the Italians especially were faced with a daunting task, lowering guns down slopes on ropes, carrying them across stream beds, using men and horses to tow them through glutinous mud, heaving them over giant rocks, then hauling and pushing them up icy slopes. In some cases it took scores of men to manhandle one gun.

The Italian garrison of Prozor, one hundred and twenty-five miles south of Bihac, was informed that aerial reconnaissance had seen one Titoist column leaving the Bugojno Valley and moving through Makljen Pass towards them. This garrison of the 3/259th Regiment of the Murge Division knew they were the only troops that stood between this column and Jablanica on the Neretva, so they requested reinforcements. The Italian command assured them that Italian forces were rushing to their defense. However, what the Italian generals described as 'rushing' the Germans described as 'crawling'. The truth was that in their Fascist arrogance the Italian generals thought Prozor could hold on its own. On 16 February the Titoists attacked Prozor. These six hundred Italians had not been reinforced, but nonetheless they held their positions for twenty-four hours under fierce assault. Then the partisans brought up artillery. The garrison commander, perhaps believing his loyalty was to his men rather than to Mussolini's dreams of glory, opened negotiations for an honorable surrender. A few of his men did not trust the Titoists and they sneaked out that night. Next day the garrison marched out and formally capitulated. The partisans accepted the surrender, disarmed the Italians and then proceeded to massacre them.

The Italian generals apologized meekly to the Germans, and brought every available aircraft to bear on these partisans, who were now moving south from Prozor.

After a month of combat in appalling weather conditions and daunting terrain the Croats were worn out, having suffered a thousand killed and wounded and thousands laid low with sickness. German casualties were about four hundred. Apart from the loss of Prozor, Italian casualties were light. Between them the Axis troops had killed eight thousand five hundred partisans and captured two thousand. Actually, people lived in the middle of this battlefield and were killed by bombs, artillery and cross-fires, and the Axis troops counted every corpse as a partisan, whether it be that of a child or old woman. Furthermore many of the prisoners were not partisans, but helpless civilians caught in the wrong place at the wrong time. The few real partisans that were captured had fallen into Axis hands because they had become too weak to continue the march.

Beginning 19 February for three days the German 717th Security Division was held up by a rearguard, until Italian forces reached the Neretva River at Konjic. Whoever crossed the Neretva first would outflank the Titoist main column. It turned out to be the Germans, and once done the partisans fell back from their river defenses. The Italian soldiers in the snowy mountains wished that their generals in their warm coastal villas could be here to see the obstacles and conditions they had to endure. For example Prenj Mountain which dominates this area south of the river stands a thousand meters above the valley floor.

Yet again the Italian generals expected another one of their garrisons to stop the partisans, namely the few hundred Italians in Jablanica that were guarding a bridge. On the 22nd they were completely overrun by thousands of grubby bearded wild-eyed partisans. Then in an unbelievable order Tito directed that the bridge should be destroyed before his column crossed. He soon realized his error, but it was too late. His men were trapped on the wrong side of the river. It was his worst mistake of the war. Tito was no Robert E. Lee and he shamefully came up with feeble excuses to push the blame away from himself.

Robotti and his generals were overjoyed by the news. True, some partisans in this column had been able to climb over the broken bridge spans, but any who had heavy equipment to carry such as a laden stretcher or a machine gun had to double back several miles under Axis air attack to look for another bridge.

Beginning on 2 March for three days the German 717th Security Division and a band of Cetniks attempted to advance past Vilica Guvno, but were prevented by a rearguard. Only when joined by a brigade of Ustaci and the Croat 369th Division were the Germans and Cetniks able to bust through. On the 6th the last Titoists crossed the Neretva on a plank bridge.

The Titoists thought they were safe now, but the Axis generals had planned for just such an eventuality and had arranged for twelve thousand Cetniks to be waiting for them. With great courage but little tactical sense the Cetniks charged the Titoists. Thousands rode horses waving their gigantic flags and others ran behind. The Titoists had abandoned most of their artillery, but they still had plenty of automatic weapons and they mowed down great bunches of Cetniks. At day's end the Cetniks limped away, thoroughly defeated and demoralized.

There was only one possible direction for Tito to go and that was towards the Drina River to the east. Over the next week the Italian garrisons in the Foca-Brod district fought off these advancing partisans. The Cetniks recovered and harassed the Titoist flanks. When April arrived with a hint of spring the Italian command authorized the Italian garrisons here to evacuate and allow the partisans to enter Montenegro. But of course this placed the Italian XIV Corps of the Ninth Army in Montenegro in danger. The field divisions were alerted: the Ferrara [and attached 82nd CCNN Legion], Venezia [and attached 72nd CCNN Legion], Perugia [and attached 29th CCNN Legion], Taurinense Alpini and Alpi Graie Alpini. The Perugia was new to combat. The defenders of Podgoriza were overrun.

The Axis planners were angry at their failure and as is natural to humans, especially fervent nationalists, they blamed each other. The Germans and Croats said the Italians moved far too slowly, and their reliance on a few isolated garrisons to stop fanatic Titoists was stupid. The Italians, on the other hand, wanted to know why every lone partisan sniper could hold up the Germans and Croats for hours. The Croats declared that the Germans continuously pushed the Croats into action in front of them, hence their greater losses. It was noticeable to all that the young SS volunteers of the Prinz Eugen had performed no better than the 35- to 45-year old recalled German reservists of the 717th Division. Everyone praised Milhailovich and his Cetniks, but only to keep him on their side. He was in a deep depression, for casualties and desertion had chopped his forces down to nine thousand men. The Axis leaders consoled themselves with the knowledge that the Titoists had at least been driven away from the bauxite mines near Bihac. This material was a valuable commodity for war industries.

———————

Chapter Forty-four
Prelude to Disaster

In early 1943, having promoted General Ambrosio to the highest military command, Mussolini then gave him his mission: he was to keep the armies in Tunisia fighting as long as possible, for if Tunisia fell into Allied hands it would provide them with airfields which could support an amphibious invasion of Sicily, which would be a stepping stone to Italy. Mussolini was convinced that the only reason the Allies had not landed on the Tunisian coast was that their fighter planes could not reach that far, and the British admirals were not going to risk their aircraft carriers that far east, and they would not risk their troopships without air cover. He was correct in his assessment. Thus the Allies would have to possess Tunisia before they took Sicily and would have to own Sicily before they invaded Italy, and he was sure they would invade Italy, because that is where he lived and he was confident that the sole obsession of the Anglo-Americans was to get at him. Dictators always assume they are the enemy's number one target.

Just so Ambrosio would not get bored, he was given other missions too: destroy the partisans in Yugoslavia; convince the Germans to retain Italian units at the front in Russia; make it too costly for British bombers to continue raiding Italian cities, which meant retraining Italian night fighter pilots and flak gunners; create a safe corridor for Italian ships to sail the Mediterranean in peace; and build up the coastal units in case of Allied invasion. Ambrosio must have known that to accomplish any one of these missions completely would require a good deal of luck and to accomplish them all would require nothing short of divine intervention.

As if to emphasize the Allies' interest in Sicily, on 31 January 1943 the day Ambrosio was promoted, Allied long-range bombers tore up the airfields in southern Sicily, and three days later a British submarine sank an oil tanker off the Sicilian coast.

On the night of 4 February German radar and observation posts in France reported to the Italians that an Allied air armada was on its way flying from England across France towards Italy. CR-42 pilots of the night fighter squadrons scrambled all over Northern Italy, searchlight crews began scanning the night sky, flak gunners ran to their posts, air raid sirens sounded, civil defense workers and medical teams reported for duty, firemen were placed at the ready, and air raid wardens escorted civilians to shelters and scanned the streets for any lamps that had been left glowing, lights that could be seen by the planes. Just by appearing the bombers caused a tremendous amount of disruption. Everyone on the ground knew he was in danger regardless of his own personal feelings about Fascism.

Turin was the target and the city's flak guns opened up a heavy concentration of fire against the fleet of one hundred and eighty-eight heavy bombers. Despite the size of the raid and the terrible destruction unleashed on the city only twenty-nine people were killed and fifty-three were wounded.

La Spezia was also raided this evening.

This air armada was shot at by German fighters and German and French flak guns on its way to Italy, and on its return, and by Italian fighters and flak guns over Italy. This overwhelming military power managed to shoot down three planes!

On the night of 14 February a major Allied raid struck La Spezia, while another one hundred and forty-two bombers hit Milan. Hundreds of Milanese were killed and injured. The people were angry. Mussolini had sold them a phony idea, an idea of recreating the glory days of the Roman Empire. Instead, he could not protect his people in their own homes. They did not blame the Allies for the destruction, but laid the blame at Mussolini's door.

The Royal Navy was acting impudently again. On the evening of 8 February British carriers launched Swordfish, Fulmars and Skuas that darted over the coast and precisely laid their ordnance on target at La Spezia, Pisa and Livorno. Simultaneously the battleships Renown and Malaya stood out to sea in the darkness and shelled Genoa.

Also at sea in February Italian and German planes sank a Canadian destroyer. The Italian submarine Avorio was scuttled after being damaged by the Canadian corvette Regina. The submarine Asteria was scuttled after being damaged by the British destroyers Wheatland and Easton. The Italian submarine Malachite was sunk by the Dutch submarine Dolfijn. Italian submarine crews suffered from many shortages, but never a shortage of courage. The destroyers Saetta and Urgano sank when they struck mines. The submarine Accaio sank the British anti-submarine trawler Tervani.

Because Mussolini believed Sicily was the next Allied invasion target he took special interest in its defenses and he now placed General Mario Roatta in command of the island. Roatta had earned three gallantry medals in World War One, had risen to command Italian Military Intelligence, had led the first expeditionary force to Spain, had been wrongly blamed for others' mistakes, had succeeded in gaining forgiveness from Mussolini (no mean feat), had gone back to Spain to command a division, had led troops in the invasion of Greece and had finally become temporary commander of the Italian Army. He had then taken command of Second Army in its war against Tito. Now he was given Sicily. He was brave and highly intelligent.

When he attended Mussolini to receive his orders for Sicily, he was assured by Il Duce that the Sicilian defenses were strong - Sixth Army of two corps, each of four divisions and several armored formations; the local Blackshirt flak gun service; the local Blackshirt militia; several naval bases each with their own powerful shore defenses, marines and flak guns; a high number of active warplanes; and of course the Carabinieri and police.

However, upon reaching Sicily Roatta found that Fascist propaganda and Mussolini's wishes did not exactly match reality. First of all he looked at Sixth Army. Its XII Corps under Lieutenant General Mario Arisio and XVI Corps under Lieutenant General Carlo Rossi were responsible for defending the coast. Upon closer inspection he saw that to guard the coast of craggy cliffs and white beaches on this triangle-shaped island the 202nd Coastal Division had to protect no less than forty miles of coastline between Marsala and Castelvetrano on the western portion of the south shore [i.e. the base of the triangle]; eastwards from there to Licata the 207th Coastal Division of Major General Augusto de Laurentis was responsible for 120 miles of coves and inlets; while from there eastwards along the remainder of the base to Syracuse, a distance of 120 miles, the 18th Coastal Brigade and 206th Coastal Division stood watch; from Syracuse northwards to Messina the entire 80 mile shore was guarded by the 213th Coastal Division; and from Messina westwards to Marsala along the northwest coast, fully 320 miles, the only defenders were the 19th Coastal Brigade, 136th Coastal Regiment and 208th Coastal Division.

These frontages were ridiculous because they were so long. Most of the personnel in these coastal units were Sicilian Blackshirts, many from the 36 to 54 age-group. Those who had seen combat in World War I or other campaigns had no wish to push their luck. Most had wives and kids to be concerned about. As Sicilians it would be all too easy for them to desert in order to protect their families [a problem the Italians had seen in Africa amongst colonist soldiers]. Roatta noted that their officers were poor material and were often absent for extended periods. Training was either minimal or non-existent. Roatta organized an instruction program at once.

However, even excellent skills could not compensate for the scant and shoddy equipment. The coastal units had so few motor vehicles that they could not maneuver. Their flak defenses consisted mostly of 27mm and 37mm guns and a mere handful of larger guns, and what is more these were already in action almost daily and were suffering a high rate of casualty attrition.

Naturally the prime purpose of the shore batteries in these units was to sink Allied ships before they could disembark troops, but no one had seen fit to provide them with heavy anti-shipping guns. Instead they would have to make do with horse-drawn field guns! If an invasion took place, the Allies would use aerial bombing and would fire large caliber naval shells at them, but there were so few concrete bunkers that much of the coastal artillery would have to fire from open pits! Troops in defensive positions need to know what is happening on their flanks and they require constant reassurance they are part of an overall network of defenses and that there is a powerful army ready to come to their aid. This means radios and field telephones. Unfortunately the main form of communication for the coastal units in Sicily was the bicycle mounted messenger!

Roatta knew the Allies would bring tanks ashore at once, so he inquired about anti-tank weapons. The generals replied they had 47mm antitank guns. 'Excellent', he thought, until he learned there was but one for every five miles of coast! The Allies would naturally spearhead their invasion with infantry, who would try to break inland and then swerve to the flank and attack other coastal defenses from the rear. So the coastal units had to have an infantry component in order to counter attack. Someone had thought of this and they had been given thirty-six infantrymen for every half mile of front. Land mines were an important part of coastal defense in this war, but few had been laid. There was also a shortage of barbed wire.

Much reliance was placed on the naval base defenses: Palermo and Trapani on the north west coast, and Messina, Catania, Augusta and Syracuse on the east coast, but Roatta found that they only consisted of a few flak guns and about 700 riflemen for each base. Furthermore the admirals insisted that they retain control of their own defenses, and would not integrate them with the army and Blackshirts. One thing the island did not lack was administrative staff. Sixth Army headquarters was at Enna. Naval headquarters was at Messina. The Blackshirt militia, Blackshirt flak service, Carabinieri, police and emergency services were controlled from Palermo. The Regia Aeronautica staff was at Catania.

Roatta was glad that at least he had some mobile units and he placed them where he thought they could do the most good. On the southwest coast between Marsala and Syracuse he placed a battalion task gruppo. He sent Mobile Gruppo B to Marsala. Eastwards from there he put Mobile Gruppo C at Castelvetrano, a task gruppo at Sciacca and another at Licata, Mobile Gruppo E at Ponte Olivo, Mobile Gruppo G at Comiso, Mobile Gruppo H at Biscari, and a task gruppo and Mobile Gruppo F at Pachino. Behind the eastern shore stood a task gruppo and a small mobile gruppo. Behind the northwest coast lay Mobile Gruppo A near Trapani, and at Alcamo two task gruppos: the 1st Bersaglieri Anti-tank Battalion and the 10th Bersaglieri Regiment.

The term gruppo 'group' was a common Italian military term, but it was always decidedly vague and was used when no two such formations contained the same number of men or type of weaponry. The terms 'bunch', 'a few' 'some' could equally have been used. Primarily the gruppos were mixed bags of trucked infantry and armored cars and an assortment of tanks: L3s, L6s, M11s, M13s and R-35s. The latter was a French Renault 11 ton two-man tank with a

37mm gun. Against first-wave infantry these units might do well, but once the Allies brought ashore Sherman, Grant/Lee and Churchill tanks and Wolverine and Hellcat tank destroyers, they would not stand a chance.

Roatta reported to Rome what he had found and demanded reinforcements at once. He needed real motorized infantry and real armor and real authority. In response Mussolini asked Hitler for the aid he had been promised, and he did make it clear to everyone on the island that they had to obey Roatta.

Already Allied aircraft based in North Africa were bombing throughout Italy and Sicily. In February the Allies formed the North West African Allied Air Force. Its two combat arms were the Strategic Air Force [RAF Strategic Bomber Command and US Ninth Air Force] and the Tactical Air Force [RAF Desert Air Force and US Twelfth Air Force]. In this sense strategic meant heavy four engine bombers and tactical meant every other kind of bomber. Moreover, almost all these raids were in daylight. The first heavy bombers to raid Sicily were Halifaxes and Liberators in early 1943, flying from airfields in Eastern Libya and Algeria: and in March 1943 they were joined by medium bombers - Baltimores, Mitchells, Mosquitoes, Amiot 354s, Liore et Olivier 451s and Wellingtons flying from Algeria and Western Libya; and in the spring they were joined by short-range ground attack aircraft - Bostons [Havocs], Hurribombers, Bloch 174s and Marylands, flying from Tunisia.

Thus in Sicily and Southern Italy the flak gunners were kept busy: Blackshirts in the cities and along the coast, army gunners at military bases and airfields, and naval gunners at ports and aboard ship. On 1 March a massive air raid on Naples inflicted serious damage on the dockyards and sank the destroyer Monsono (910 tons). On 10 March Palermo suffered a particularly heavy raid, and this was repeated on the 22nd, when American heavy bombers devastated the port facilities and sank several merchant ships and the destroyer Geniere (1620 tons). On the 28th it was the turn of Livorno, where the destroyer Antares (640 tons) was sunk. On 4 April the Americans blasted Palermo, Syracuse and Naples, at the latter city killing two hundred and twenty-one civilians and wounding three hundred and forty-seven. Axis fighter planes - Italian CR42, Mc200 and Mc202 and German Bf109 - were hopelessly outnumbered by the bomber escort of Allied fighters - Spitfires, Tomahawks, Fulmars, Fireflies, Martlets, Hurricanes, Airacobras, Hawks, Dewoitine 520s and Lightnings. The pilots were Britons, Americans, French, Poles, Australians, New Zealanders, Canadians and South Africans.

American bombers struck the Italian naval base at La Maddalena and sank the cruiser Trieste.

In April Mussolini met with Hitler at Klessheim in Austria, where both tried to bolster each other. Mussolini was even more under the influence of Hitler now, and he also listened to Himmler. The German SS had originally been Hitler's personal bodyguard, but this organization under the direction of Heinrich Himmler had rocketed into a catch-all force that had its fingers in many pies. The SS absorbed the Concentration Camp Service, made money by running labor camps full of political prisoners, controlled the Gestapo (Secret State Police), provided German towns with security guards, and had recruited its own army primarily from foreigners. As if this was not enough, Himmler had also clawed his way to become chief of the German national police.

Seeing Mussolini's vulnerability to an Italian popular uprising, Himmler advised Il Duce that he should create the nucleus of a new SS-style army that would owe loyalty to him only. Mussolini liked the idea, especially if Himmler agreed to provide equipment for the unit. To man this new unit, which Mussolini modestly named the Mussolini Division, he brought in Blackshirts that had seen action against Titoists or in Russia, and he gave the top job to Consul Generale Losana. Its combat components were the 63rd Tagliamento and the Montebello Battalion Gruppos, each of two infantry battalions and a Semoventi 75 battalion, plus a Mark III tank company and a Mark IV tank company.

Himmler also expressed his concern for the lack of Fascist ardor shown by Carmine Senise, the head of the Italian National Police, who either could not or would not stop the current wave of industrial strikes in Italy. Mussolini took Himmler's advice and replaced Senise with a Blackshirt general, Renzo Chierici. He also fired Aldo Vidussoni the Secretary of the Fascist Party, and replaced him with Carlo Scorza.

─────────────

The war at sea continued to be ugly. Five British submarines were sunk: one to an Italian mine, one by an Italian convoy escort, one by the Italian corvette Cicogna, one by the German destroyer Hermes, and one by the Italian destroyer Climene (640 tons) and corvettes Gabbiano and Euterpe. German e-boats sank a British destroyer. Italian and German planes were still hitting Malta and on 28 March they sank a warship there.

The Italian submarine Delfino sank following a collision. The submarine Finzi was damaged by a mine in the Gironde River in France. The Italian destroyers Ascari (1620 tons) and Malocello (1870 tons) were crippled by mines, and the Ciclone (910 tons) was too small to survive her encounter with a mine. Air attacks seriously damaged the destroyer Pigafetta (1870 tons) and sank the destroyers Ulpino (1620 tons) and Tifone (910 tons).

The Italian destroyers Pancaldo II (1870 tons), Lampo (1220 tons) and the German Hermes were sent on a suicide run packed with ammunition for the troops in Tunisia. They were caught by Allied aircraft and all three were blown up and sunk.

On the night of 16 April the Italian destroyer Cassiopeia and minesweeper Cigno battled against the much bigger British destroyers Packenham and Paladin. They damaged the Packenham, but both Italian vessels were sunk. However, the following morning Axis planes caught the damaged Packenham and sank her.

The Italian destroyer Climene was sunk by a submarine and the destroyer Perseo (640 tons) was sunk by British warships.

Off Brazil the Italian submarine Archimede was sunk by an American Catalina flying boat.

In March labor strikes broke out in Italy, most notably in Milan and Turin. Ostensibly the workers were demanding better pay and conditions, but everyone knew the truth. They were demanding peace.

It was in this atmosphere that on 7 April Mussolini met Hitler again, this time at Salzburg, this Austrian town being chosen because it was equi-distant between Rome and Hitler's military headquarters at Rastenburg. Mussolini demanded a huge amount of German provisions and equipment in order to carry on the war, for the first time hinting that he might not be able to carry on if his demands were not met. Hitler had suffered disastrous losses on the Russian front, and he lowering his conscription age to seventeen in order to make good his manpower shortage, and he was conscripting more foreign labor and offering juicy inducements to foreign volunteer workers in order to relieve German workers for military service. As a result he could not fill Mussolini's shopping basket just yet. However, both men were verbally jousting. Mussolini urged Hitler to make peace with Stalin, so they could both turn against the Anglo-Americans. But this suggestion, that Italy's woes were more important than Hitler's conquests in the Soviet Union went against Hitler's political and military philosophy. Hitler, like many a German nationalist before him, had been preaching that Germany had a right to possess Ukrainia and Byelorussia, the two most western Soviet provinces. No one had ever preached that Germany had an obligation to defend Italy. The four-day conference ended with the usual smiling faces for the photographers.

On the night of 13 April no fewer than two hundred and eleven bombers struck La Spezia. Total Axis air defenses managed to knock down only four Allied planes. On the 16th American bombers tore huge chunks out of Palermo and Catania and sank the destroyer Medici (650 tons). Next day streams of American bombers hammered Palermo and Catania again and caused destruction in Syracuse.

The Italians assumed the Allies intended to invade Sicily then Italy, but this had not always been the Allied plan. In fact the only Mediterranean move the Americans had agreed to was the North African operation. They wanted to invade the French Atlantic coast in 1943, which they saw as the quickest route to Berlin. Furthermore the Americans felt the Italians would surrender once the Germans were knocked out of the war. But the Americans and British each saw potential battles in France in a different perspective based upon their own experiences in World War I. In that conflict the Americans had experienced nine months of sedentary trench warfare in France followed by three months of relatively mobile warfare, and the bulk of their divisions had seen just a few weeks of action. Their battle casualties had been high – two hundred and forty-six thousand killed and wounded, and they had been victorious in every fight. The British on the other hand had fought in France in that conflict for over four years, almost all of it stationary trench warfare, and had suffered many a defeat, and their victory had come at a price of over two million killed and wounded. As a percentage of their populations, British losses had been twenty times that of the Americans!

Then in 1940 the British had tried to stem the German tide in Belgium and then in France, and had suffered two terrible defeats, the worst humiliation of any army in British history. It is understandable that the British generals and politicians were not eager to return to France in 1943 or any other time. So they just firmly refused to invade France in 1943. "Fine", the Americans answered, for they believed they had enough troops to do it alone, but they needed British ports, British airfields and above all the Royal Navy, and without British approval they could have none of these. Thus the Americans had to agree to postpone the invasion for a year. Thereupon Churchill brought up the Sicily plan, a way of drawing the Germans into Italy, which would tie down several of Hitler's divisions uselessly, because the Allies had no intention of invading Italy. As the British were willing to put up half the troops and much of the air and sea forces too, the Americans agreed to the Sicily operation.

Now the FBI got into the act. This government crime busting body under the dictatorial rule of J. Edgar Hoover had been given a war-time role to seek out enemy spies. Hoover took on the job with relish and approached his contacts in 'This Thing of Ours' (La Cosa Nostra), a shadowy semi-secret criminal association of several gangs held together by a code of silence (Omerta) and regulated by its own rule book (Mafia). In the USA this body was often referred to as the 'Black Hand' or 'Murder Incorporated'. It was in effect the American branch of a Sicilian association. Mussolini had gained great public support in Sicily by crushing these thugs there, and naturally the gangsters of the American branch hated Mussolini. J. Edgar Hoover had protected them in the USA whenever possible! Perhaps this was because he knew they might blow the whistle on his sexual activity – considered a perversion in the 1940s. Or perhaps he actually thought he could control them. So, once Roosevelt had given Hoover the mission of stopping spies and saboteurs, Hoover approached Charles 'Lucky' Luciano for assistance. This man was the boss of bosses (Capo di Tutti Capo) of La Cosa Nostra. The fact that he was in prison had never prevented him from controlling this criminal empire. In return for favors Luciano agreed to help Hoover. From now on Fascist Italian spies and saboteurs in America were not just hunted by the FBI and other government agencies, but were hunted by La Cosa Nostra. Almost all were caught. The gangsters were especially successful in the ports and docks.

In early 1943 Hoover learned of the plans for the invasion of Sicily. He offered La Cosa Nostra a deal. If they contacted their relatives in Sicily to aid the invasion, then once US forces were in occupation of Sicily the gangsters of La Cosa Nostra would be allowed to take up their old habits again, free from Mussolini's police. The gangsters agreed. Their prime success was in approaching senior Sicilian army officers and government officials and inducing them to surrender to the Allies when the time came, using a sort of 'we know where your kids live' persuasive technique.

The Germans had a more global view. They knew the Allies were planning another amphibious landing in the Mediterranean, and they suspected it would be a stepping stone to an invasion of the European mainland. They considered such invasion routes as Sardinia-Corsica-France, Greece-Yugoslavia, or Yugoslavia directly. If the latter was the target the Cetniks would most assuredly join the Allies: the Germans were under no illusions about this. Therefore the Germans initiated Operation Black. Namely, two divisions of Germans and Croats moved against the Cetniks near the coast. They asked the Cetniks to willingly disarm, and naturally few complied. Many ran inland. Others fought back. The Italians had come to look upon the Cetniks as partners and they refused to be party to this treachery. Besides, their Second and Ninth Armies were too busy fighting Titoists in Bosnia and Montenegro, where they suffered a setback at Favorak. At Bioce their 3/83rd Regiment of the Venezia Division was under pressure from surrounding partisans.

In spring 1943 as part of their anti-Tito campaign the Italian XIV Corps of the Ninth Army joined Germans, Croats, Serbs and Bulgarians in launching a fifth offensive against Tito, whose main force was about thirty miles southeast of Sarajevo. This began 15

May with Axis troops attacking the Titoist main force from all sides: from the Sarajevo area the German 118th Jaeger and Brandenburg Divisions entered the fray, aiming southeastwards; on their left [east] flank were the Croat-German 369th Division and Bulgarian 61st Regiment attacking southwards into the Drina Valley; on their left [southeast] was the German 1st Mountain Division advancing southwestwards towards Kolos; to their left flank [south] the Italian Taurinense Alpini Division assaulted westwards towards Pljevlja on the Cehotina River; on their left flank [further south] was the German 7th SS Prinz Eugen Mountain Division attacking westwards; and from their southeast the Italian Venezia Division [with attached 72nd CCNN Legion] and Ferrara Division [with attached 82nd CCNN Legion] were push northwestwards into the Tara Valley. In reserve were the Bulgarian 62nd Regiment, German 104th Jaeger Division and an additional 11,000 Croats. In command of this offensive which covered 4,000 square miles was the German General Luetters.

Axis intelligence assured the troops that the partisans were on their last legs, but the Germans and Bulgarians were stopped at once by fanatic resistance. Aerial reconnaissance identified two Titoist columns, one heading for Sutjeska about fifty miles southeast of Sarajevo, and the other in the Zabljak district aiming for the Lim River another twenty miles southeast. Italian garrisons on the Tara River belonging to the Ferrara and Venezia Divisions blocked their path, and fought so courageously that Tito was forced to change course. By 5 June the Ferrara and Venezia Divisions were battling the Titoists as they approached the Sutjeska River. Tito was in a bind. At one stage in the battle he himself was isolated and wounded. Reaching a radio he ordered his followers throughout Yugoslavia to pull out all stops and attack everywhere. Unbelievably the Axis forces were fought to a standstill and Tito's main column escaped across the Zelengora River.

The Italians like the other Axis soldiers were extremely angry with their leaders. Some men of the Ferrara entered villages suspected of supporting the partisans and they ran amok arresting, burning, pillaging, raping and murdering. The Axis units claimed to have killed seven thousand five hundred partisans in this latest month-long offensive. Their own casualties totaled three thousand killed, wounded and missing.

On 9 May 1943 American bombers blanketed the island of Pantelleria sixty-five miles south of Sicily. The Italians had an MAS boat base on this thirty-two square mile island, and they were stuck out like a sore thumb, almost daring the Allies to attack. The island had a small indigenous population. The island's defenses were in the hands of Brigadier General Achille Maffei's Mixed Brigade of fifteen battalions of flak guns and coastal artillery. Most of the gunners were older men and some were locals. Counting these men, naval personnel, Carabinieri and police there were about eleven thousand uniformed men on the island. At the first bombing raid the civilians fled into the mountains. They were right to do so, for the Allied planes returned on an almost daily basis from now on.

On 8 May three pigs left Spanish soil for Gibraltar, sank three ships, and this time all six riders returned safely, swimming back to Spain. On 11 May heavy bombers plastered Catania in Sicily. By now it seemed that anything that moved in Sicily caught the attention of Allied fighter pilots. In some cases even donkey carts were strafed. On the 14th Mussolini went public, admitting to his people that now that Tunisia had been lost Sicily could expect to be invaded. It was a sobering admission. The people remembered Mussolini's speeches when he had declared war on Britain and later on the USA. He had said nothing then about being invaded.

At sea the Italian navy continued to do battle, but with no sign of their main battle fleet coming to help them. The submarine Leonardo da Vinci was lost, sunk by the British warships Active and Ness. She had been the most successful of Mussolini's submarines, accredited with sinking eighteen ships [120,243 tons]! The average for a submarine of any nationality was 9,000 tons. The second most successful Italian submarine, the Tazzoli, was credited with sinking eighteen ships [96,650 tons]. She disappeared in the Atlantic this month. She may have been depth charged by the USS Mackenzie. The destroyer Castore (640 tons) was sunk by surface ships. The submarine Gorgo was sunk by the US destroyer Nields. Of course these days Italian warships did not have to put to sea to fight the enemy. The destroyer Groppo (910 tons) was sunk in a heavy air raid on Messina, and the destroyer Bassini (650 tons) was sunk in an air attack on Livorno. During an air raid on Cagliari the submarine Mocenigo was sunk. In fact the only Italian naval bases not under air attack were at Trieste, Fiume and Pola.

On 30 May Naples suffered her sixtieth air raid of the war. But Pantelleria had been bombed twenty times in the past three weeks, and now the island was shelled by a cruiser. The coastal artillery retaliated as best they could.

In Sicily Roatta received welcome news: he was getting out of Sicily. Moreover he was promoted to replace Enzio Rossi as head of the army. This made six changes in the top army job in three years. In contrast George Marshall commanded the US Army throughout the war. Roatta's replacement, who inherited the Sicilian headache, was General Alfredo Guzzoni. A professional soldier who went by the rules, Guzzoni had conquered Albania in 1939 and had invaded

France in 1940 and had achieved the exalted rank of vice chief of the army and undersecretary of war before retiring in 1941. Now he found himself back in uniform and as soon as he arrived he was under incessant air attack.

Pantelleria, which came under Guzzoni's command, was bombarded by a warship on 1 June as well as being bombed from the air. Two days later the defenses were shelled by a cruiser and four destroyers and were bombed from the air, and were bombed again the next day. On the 5th the defenses suffered aerial bombing and shelling by a cruiser and two destroyers. Bombed again over the next two days, the island was shelled on the 8th by five cruisers, eight destroyers and three MTBs, and bombed. It is understandable that the dazed, shocked, exhausted and wounded defenders of the island must have thought the Allies had singled them out for special attention. They were right to think so. The Allied air commanders were conducting an experiment! They wanted to know if an island could be induced to surrender by air attack alone. In fact the naval shelling got in the way of the experiment. But the admirals were jealous of the 'fly-boys' and wanted to show it would take a naval bombardment as well as air raids to induce a surrender. This was not really part of the war between the USA and Italy, but rather part of the war between the US Army Air Force and the US Navy! On the 8th Eisenhower himself stood on a warship's bridge watching the bombardment.

By 11 June the defenses of Pantelleria had been ripped to shreds. In the previous ten days alone the Allies had dropped five thousand tons of bombs, equivalent to thirty-two 25 lb. bombs for every defender! In six days the Allies had flown three thousand seven hundred and twelve sorties against the island. One plane for every three defenders. This morning the defenders were bombarded by five cruisers and eight destroyers, and aircraft dropped leaflets demanding their surrender.

On Pantelleria Rear Admiral Gino Pavesi and Brigadier General Achille Maffei did not need to discuss the Allied request. Their coastal guns had been replying to the Allied ships, and their flak gunners had shot down forty-five Allied planes and damaged scores more, but they already knew their men had borne more than human beings are meant to withstand, and everyone's nerves were shattered. Besides, they were almost out of ammunition. As a result they agreed to the Allied demand. That afternoon Allied infantry came ashore. Only a few Fascist die-hards fired a potshot or two. The surrender of the island is often used as an example when pseudo historians speak of Italian cowardice. Yet when the Germans invaded the islands of Guernsey, Alderney and Jersey in 1940 the British did not fire one shot in their defense. In fact all such encounters between enemies should be looked at with more than just a cursory glance from the armchair.

Meanwhile Guzzoni had noticed that Roatta's training program was paying off, and fortunately for him reinforcements were arriving. Major General Erberto Papini's Assietta Mountain Division came to Sicily and was beefed up with two batteries of 20mm flak guns, the 126th Heavy Mortar Battalion and the 17th CCNN Legion. Also arriving was Major General Domenico Chirieleison's Livorno Mountain Division complimented by three batteries of 20mm flak guns, the 1st Medium Mortar Battalion, the 11th Commando Battalion, the 4th Anti-tank Battalion, and by enough trucks to make this one of the few truly motorized divisions in the Italian Army. Also coming to the island was Major General Giacomo Romano's Aosta Division, accompanied by two batteries of 20mm flak guns, the 28th Heavy Mortar Battalion and the 171st CCNN Legion. Another reinforcement was Major General Count Giulio Gotti-Porcinari's Napoli Division, aided by two batteries of flak guns and the 173rd CCNN Legion. Moreover half the artillery in the Aosta, Assietta and Napoli consisted of Semoventi 75s. There were also twenty-four of the new Semoventi 90mm! The Livorno had fought in France 1940, and the Assietta had fought in Ethiopia in 1936 and had invaded Yugoslavia. The others were green.

It appeared to Guzzoni that these were powerful divisions, but he did not realize that compared to the American infantry divisions they would be facing, they were no match. For example, though Allen's American 1st Division did not have any flak guns or any heavy mortars, or any self-propelled guns, it did have three times as much artillery as the Aosta. This American division, nicknamed the Big Red One, had nine infantry battalions versus the Aosta's eight, but the Aosta would soon lose its 171st CCNN Legion to another command. This would give the US 1st Division one hundred and sixty-two machine guns against the Aosta's seventy-two, and two hundred and forty-three sub-machine guns and automatic rifles for the Aosta's ninety-six, and eighteen anti-tank guns, fifty-four light mortars and two hundred and sixteen shoulder-fired rocket launchers, whereas the Aosta had few light mortars and no rocket launchers and no anti-tank guns. Additionally American infantrymen were liberally supplied with grenades, whereas the Italians had few, and those they did have were usually not fatal. Of course once the ground battle had begun, these figures would change, but they are a useful guide.

By June the Regia Aeronautica and Luftwaffe units in Sicily and southern Italy had been chopped down significantly, while the Allies were increasing their air strength daily.

The Italian submarine Barbarigo disappeared. In her career she had claimed to have sunk seven merchant ships and two battleships! Her captain, Enzo Grossi, was responsible for the claims and was highly decorated. However, only his merchant ship claims were valid. He had missed when firing on the battleships. He was not aboard when she went down. The submarine H8 was sunk in an Allied air raid on La Spezia.

To make up for a lack of artillery on invasion day the Allies would have scores of warships on call. Guzzoni could do nothing about this, except pray his gunners could cripple the warships. His only hope to destroy the first wave of incoming infantry was to counter attack at once with tanks, yet the only Italian armored fighting vehicle worth its salt was the Semoventi [either with 75mm or 90mm guns]. What Guzzoni needed was German tanks: big Panthers with long 75mm guns and even bigger Tigers with long barreled 88mm guns. He demanded that Roatta in his new position of army commander get him some German tanks. Roatta agreed and passed the request to Ambrosio, who tendered the request to Mussolini, who turned to Hitler. Il Duce begged the Fuehrer for six hundred and eighty tanks, nine hundred flak guns, eight hundred self-propelled guns and four hundred and thirty-two anti-tank guns. At current German production rates this was about six weeks output. Put another way, the German Army would have to go six weeks without a delivery of such weaponry if Mussolini got his wish.

Guzzoni studied the defense plans and tried to refine them. His coastal defenses were still intact because they were so thinly spread they could not be damaged by mass bombing by heavy bombers. However, many positions had been individually targeted by smaller planes, and his flak gunners had been in constant action for over five months by late June. Much of the civilian infrastructure had been damaged and many townsfolk had fled for the mountains. Not one airfield was in full operation. An inspection team arrived from Comando Supremo and in their report they predicted a disaster.

Comando Supremo expected the Allies to make two landings, one on the southeast to capture the bulk of the ports and airfields, the other in the northwest to seize Palermo, following which the two Allied armies would advance on Messina along the coast roads in a pincer movement. As time went on Guzzoni came to the conclusion that the Allies would only land in the southeast, because they had poor strategic ability. Furthermore, if the Italian intelligence reports were accurate then Montgomery would be commanding a significant portion of the invasion, and Alexander would be in overall control. That was good news for Guzzoni, because he had been informed that Montgomery was timid and Alexander incapable of controlling Monty.

However, German high command [OKW] believed the Allies would not invade at all! They favored Sardinia or Greece as a target. Hitler did not want to send troops to defend Italy and moreover Mussolini did not want German ground troops on his soil. He just wanted their equipment. Ambrosio mistrusted the Germans and therefore agreed with Mussolini. However, Roatta and Guzzoni were realists. Better the Germans in Sicily than the Allies, they argued. Field Marshal Kesselring, commander of all German forces in the Mediterranean, genuinely liked Italians and wanted to help them. He urged a German intervention and it was upon his recommendation that Hitler acquiesced in sending the new 15th Panzergrenadier Division to Sicily.

Guzzoni was elated. He said he wanted the division to reinforce the southeast. However, the Germans overruled him and ordered the panzergrenadiers to the northwest! Unknown to any of these parties Hitler had agreed to send troops to Italy not just to keep the Allies out, but also to disarm the Italians if they appeared to waver in their loyalty to the Axis cause.

On the night of 23 June fifty-two British bombers blew up the oil storage tanks at La Spezia. Having decoded Italian naval signals the British knew the Italian navy was short of fuel and that the main Italian battle fleet could not intervene in the invasion of Sicily if it had no fuel.

On 26 June Guzzoni received surprise visitors: Kesselring and Lieutenant General Fridolin von Senger und Etterlin. The latter was a devout Catholic German, a brilliant intellectual, fluent in English and Italian, Oxford educated, and a one-time Benedictine monk. With a warm smile Kesselring introduced him as his liaison officer with Guzzoni. Von Senger could clearly see the Allied, Italian and German points of view and he quickly sized up the true situation in Sicily. Moreover, having recently commanded the 17th Panzer Division in Russia he had no illusions. But Guzzoni was no fool and knew that von Senger was really a spy for Hitler and a potential German commander for Sicily. Nonetheless the gentlemen were all courteous to each other.

Guzzoni brought them up to date. The Allies were expending far too many bombs on Sicily for the island to be anything other than their real invasion goal. The Allies had taken the surrender of three small islands south of Sicily: Pantelleria, Lampedusa and Linosa, which would prove useful bases for an invasion of Sicily. Every North African port was filling with Allied troopships. Allied commandos had raided Sicily. He knew this because his alert Italian coastal troops had killed or captured them. Everything pointed to an invasion of Sicily.

Guzzoni also expressed gratitude for the 15th Panzergrenadier Division, though he wished he had more control over it, and Kesselring was able to confirm that the new Hermann Goering Panzer Division was also coming. It would be placed between Gela and Catania, right where Guzzoni wanted it.

The command structure was a problem, though. Italian sailors and marines took orders from Guzzoni and also from Regia Marina. Italian airmen took orders from Guzzoni and also from Regia

Aeronautica. The Carabinieri took orders from Guzzoni and also from Carabinieri headquarters in Rome. The police took orders from him and also from the National Police headquarters in Rome. The Blackshirts took orders from him and also from MSVN headquarters in Rome. The emergency services obeyed him and also obeyed the administrative headquarters in Palermo and also the Minister of the Interior in Rome. The 15th Panzergrenadier Division would report to him and also to Kesselring and also to OKW and also to Hitler. The Hermann Goering Panzer Division would report to him and to Kesselring and to OKW and to Hitler and to Hermann Goering. All Luftwaffe personnel on the island reported to Guzzoni and also to Goering. In other words there were too many chiefs. One of the many ways in which this command structure caused problems was in the case of the Tiger tank. Seventeen of these monsters were suddenly transferred from the 15th Panzergrenadier Division to the Hermann Goering Panzer Division, not by order of any of the various commands, but by personal order of Hitler himself. Evidently Goering had become jealous of the army's Tigers and he wanted some for his boys as well!

As each headquarters tugged at the fabric of the defenses it came apart in their hands, and by early July the 'wisdom' radiating from the various headquarters had managed to chop up the 15th Panzergrenadier Division into battle groups: its 115th Panzergrenadier Regiment was sent to Catania; its 129th Panzergrenadier Regiment minus a battalion was ordered to Enna; the single panzergrenadier battalion was trucked to Comiso; and the 104th Panzergrenadier Regiment stayed with the remainder of the division in the northwest. But then the 115th Panzergrenadier Regiment was ordered to report to Colonel Wilhelm Schmalz, whose battle group also included a panzergrenadier battalion and two artillery battalions from the Hermann Goering Panzer Division and three fortress battalions [German infantry aged 36 to 45].

The Italians were also affected by this conflict of command. The Assietta Division was ordered to hand over a CCNN battalion and a machine gun company to Task Gruppo Licata. The Aosta Division lost its 171st CCNN Legion to Task Gruppo Alcamo. The Napoli Division's 173rd CCNN Legion was divided amongst Task Gruppo Comiso-Ispica and Mobile Gruppo G.

Fortunately Guzzoni was informed that more Germans were on their way: two divisions and a corps headquarters, which would come as far as Calabria in mainland Italy and be on call if he needed them.

Guzzoni was grateful for the German reinforcements, but he wished they would keep them all in one place and not keep changing their structure. If he was right the Germans would be savaged by Allied fighter-bombers when they tried to concentrate on invasion day.

On the afternoon of 9 July 1943 Mussolini was inspecting troops at Lake Bracciano, when he was informed that the Allied armada had sailed.

———————

Chapter Forty-five
Invasion

At 4:30 pm on 9 July 1943 Guzzoni was informed that
reconnaissance planes had sighted five separate lines of ships south of
Malta all of them pointing towards Sicily. Each was estimated at one
hundred and fifty to one hundred and eighty vessels. Even allowing
for exaggeration Guzzoni knew that no previous convoys were ever
this large. There was no doubt this was the invasion, and he alerted
the defenses. The flak gunners and fighter pilots did not need an alert:
they were already in action at this very moment against four hundred
and eleven Allied bombers and seventy-eight fighters.

That night just after 10pm at Cape Passero gliders began silently
drifting to earth in the dark. The wooden craft landed by crunching
into jagged rocks and stonewalls. One after another they skimmed the
ground or bounced along the treetops. Troops of Major General
d'Havet's 206th Coastal Division were taken by surprise for a minute,
but then they realized these gliders contained Allied soldiers, so they
opened fire on the aircraft, hoping to inflict casualties before the
soldiers inside could shoot back. Flak gunners searched out to sea by
shooting star shells into the air and they identified more waves of
gliders and began firing on them. These gun flashes, searchlights and
flares destroyed the pilots' night vision, until they were flying blind
and then landing blind. At sea the approaching Allied ships thought
they were under air attack so their gunners began firing on the gliders
too!

Fifty-nine gliders landed between Syracuse and Cape Passero, a
distance of thirty miles. Such an aerial assault meant only one thing to
Guzzoni's staff: the purpose of the glider troops was to disrupt Axis
communications throughout a large sector. The attack also confirmed
that the southeast was one of the invasion targets. The Italians had no
way of knowing that the destination of the gliders was the Ponte
Grande near Syracuse, just one bridge! Strong winds had dispersed
the gliders and only twelve landed near the target. Sixty-nine had
crashed into the sea. Some had been released too soon by nervous and
inexperienced tow plane pilots. Some had deliberately come down,
because their blind pilots thought they were over land. Some had been
shot down by Allied naval gunners. Some had been blown off course
by the wind. The whole operation was a fiasco for Major General
Frederick Browning's British 1st Airborne Division. Not only did it
cause extraordinarily high casualties, but it told Guzzoni where the
invasion armada was heading.

Despite the size of the Allied fleet coming towards them, Italian
naval launches put to sea to rescue downed glider troops. This was a
very heroic and humane act.

Only a handful of British glider troops seized the Ponte Grande Bridge, and Lieutenant General Carlo Rossi at XVI Corps headquarters sent a message for the bridge to be retaken at once, but for some reason the message was never received - destroyed communications, human error, anti-Fascist sabotage?

Around Gela the defenders did not expect an airborne drop by gliders as the ground was too rough, nor did they expect a paratroop drop, because no paratroopers had ever launched a major drop at night or in winds stronger than fifteen mph. Tonight the wind blew at thirty-five mph. Thus they were taken totally by surprise when around midnight two hundred and fifty Allied planes approached them and amid flak bursts white shrouds appeared and began drifting to ground. At first the flak gunners thought these were air crewmen, baling out of crippled aircraft, but they quickly changed their minds when they saw so many of them. They were under attack by paratroopers of Major General Matthew Ridgway's US 82nd Airborne Division. The flak gunners only managed to shoot down eight aircraft.

Again the wide scattering of the paratroopers by the wind convinced the Italians that the Allied intention was to disrupt communications over a large expanse. Indeed, that was the end result. Paratroopers that realized they were miles from their targets resorted to 'Plan B' as it were, tearing down telephone lines and ambushing messengers and truck drivers. The infantry of the 18th Coastal Brigade and 206th Coastal Division began hunting the paratroopers in the dark and were joined by rear-echelon troops and Carabinieri. Sicilian civilians armed with shotguns and knives also attacked the paratroopers. Those paratroopers who had been wounded by flak or injured in the jump were easily rounded up, but the remainder offered sterling opposition. Paratroop generals are always in as much danger as their soldiers. Brigadier General Charles Keerans, deputy commander of the 82nd Airborne Division, was killed in action early on. Some captured paratroopers knew they had been blown off course and they asked their Italian captors if they were in Sicily! When taken prisoner the Americans gave name, rank and serial number, as they had been trained to do. But unknown to the Americans this could prove fatal, for in two incidents Fascist officers executed Americans with Italian surnames.

Guzzoni's headquarters was busy. Clerks were yelling at each other, running from room to room with reports, and officers were on telephones trying frantically to make sense of the news coming in: trucks had been ambushed, small outposts overrun, barracks sniped at, road junctions blockaded, and telephone lines were down everywhere. But most disturbing was that from some districts there was no word at all from the defenders. One thing was certain: Allied prisoners appeared ignorant of the fact that there were German units in Sicily.

Just before 3am on July 10 near Piano Lupo a road guard of forty

Italians and ten Germans was attacked by American paratroopers. Responding with a withering fire they quickly drove off the Americans.

Guzzoni told the navy that he had been outflanked by an airborne drop of an estimated twenty-four battalions, but that the amphibious invasion had yet to begin, so there was still time to intercept it. The navy replied they could not give battle. They had no fuel.

It was still dark when the flak gunners were offered a second helping of targets, but this time the one hundred and seven Allied planes dropped bombs on coastal artillery, barracks, airfields and the flak gunners themselves. Afterwards, Allied battleships, cruisers and destroyers began shelling the coastal defenses.

The 18th Coastal Brigade and 206th Coastal Division reported that they were under heavy naval gunfire, and with their searchlights they could see Allied landing craft approaching. Couriers had been sent on bicycles to order all guns to open fire.

The gunners at Cape Murro di Porco and Casibile were still awaiting orders when suddenly out of the dark night armed men burst into their open gun pits. Where was the infantry who were supposed to protect them, the gunners wondered, as they scattered from the bullets? The attackers yelled for the unarmed gunners to surrender, and some Italians yelled back defiantly and made threatening gestures, whereupon they were gunned down or grenades were tossed at them, wiping out whole groups. The surviving gunners threw up their hands in surrender. Their captors proved to be British SAS and commandos.

Meanwhile other Italian gunners began receiving orders to fire, and they set to work loading shell upon shell. Their forward observers sent messages back to correct the range as Allied landing craft came closer. But within minutes the gunners were themselves under fire from huge naval shells, which blew gun pits into the air, churning up both men, dirt and equipment. Some men were buried alive by falling earth; others fell to ground minus a limb. The survivors were deaf and dazed and shaking with shock, forgetting their duty, even their names for a while. In the Punta Castellazo sector British marine commandos easily rounded up scores of gunners in the dark whom they found in this state of shock.

Major General Antonio Calierno's 207th Coastal Division was firing upon ships and landing craft with twenty-two batteries of 75mm and 105mm guns and two batteries of 149mm, but the American landing craft kept coming. When Italian flak gunners saw the landing craft they opened fire on them with their 20mm and 37mm guns. Then as the Americans hit the beach the coastal infantry could see them in the dark night as black figures running across white sand, and they began shooting with rifles and machine guns. Suddenly, many of the coastal fortifications were assaulted by American infantry from the rear. These Americans had landed elsewhere along undefended stretches of coastline. The choice of the gunners was to live or die and they were not given but a second to dwell over this. Most chose to live and they surrendered. These Americans were members of Major General Lucian Truscott's 3rd Division. A die-hard cavalryman, he was an expert in mobility, and even retained a horse-mounted unit in his division.

A battery of Italian guns mounted on rail carriages was brought to the coast by a locomotive, and they soon began firing on the beachheads, where their shells slammed into American infantry, engineers, and medical teams and into Italian prisoners of war. Everyone hugged the sand. This ended when US Navy warships sent 6inch and 8inch shells right on top of the train.

By 4am Guzzoni was learning that there were solid lines of Americans on the beaches at three sectors. Truscott's US 3rd Division had landed on a front of seven miles centering on Licata. This was almost in the middle of the south coast. Twenty miles to the east General Terry Allen's US 1st Division had landed on a front of five miles stretching to the east of Gela. Ten miles further east General Troy Middleton's US 45th Division had landed on a front of five miles centering on Scoglitti. The 1st had seen much action in Tunisia, but the 3rd had only fought in the Moroccan landing. The 45th was green.

D'Havet's 206th Coastal Division reported a British landing of equal proportions beginning twenty-five miles east of the Americans. Major General G. G. Simonds' Canadian 1st Division landed between Pozallo and Cape Passero on the island's southeast corner, and encountered almost no opposition, fortunately for them as this was their first ground combat experience. On their right was Major General Douglas Wimberley's 51st Highland Division with two battalions of Royal Marines and the 231st Brigade at the cape itself, and to their north [on the east coast] at Avola was Major General Sidney Kirkman's 50th Division, and further north in the Syracuse was Major General Horatio Berney-Ficklin's 5th Division and commandos.

Both Canadians and British were under Montgomery's Eighth Army. The Americans were led by Patton's US Seventh Army. Both were controlled by Alexander's 15th Army Group.

This was the largest amphibious invasion in history to date, consisting of over two thousand five hundred ships and craft, protected by six battleships, fifteen cruisers and one hundred and twenty-eight destroyers. More than three thousand four hundred Allied planes flew over them. Total German and Italian air strength in this region was about one thousand seven hundred planes, but perhaps only half were currently airworthy.

Inland it seemed that every Italian and German was under attack by airborne troops at one time or another, and the naval shelling was devastating along the coast. There was complete confusion everywhere. To add to Guzzoni's problems many Italian-speaking Americans were telephoning Italian units and ordering them to surrender. The shore battery at Monte Desusino was obliterated by seven hundred and thirteen 6inch naval shells, before the gunners could even open fire. Guzzoni ordered Rossi at XVI Corps to send his mobile units to reinforce the Augusta-Syracuse sector.

At 4:30am two Italian fighter squadrons took off to attack the still dark waters off Scoglitti. The pilots must have felt like mosquitoes attacking crocodiles.

As the first rays of dawn could be discerned in the east an Italian artillery battery at Avola was straddled by 4inch shells from Dutch warships. Guns and equipment were destroyed and horses and men were sliced open. Near Torre di Gaffe several artillery batteries were giving the Americans hell, their gunners sweating to fire off their allotment of shells before American warships found their range. Then suddenly 4inch naval shells began to fall on them. Within minutes an entire battery was wiped out.

At 5:30am as dawn quickly approached, the small road guard near Piano Lupo was attacked by paratroopers again. This time the Americans had managed to find a couple of mortars and these pinned down the Italians and Germans, who hoped the Americans would run out of mortar shells before they ran out of blood. Suddenly the paratroopers were among them, shooting. The surviving members of the road guard gave up.

Guzzoni had been proven correct. The sole Allied invasion had come in the southeast. He was not fooled by a demonstration by British ships off the northwest coast. He gave out the following orders: all battle groups of the 15th Panzergrenadier Division to head southeastwards at once; all Italian mobile gruppos in the threatened sector to counter attack; the Napoli Division to prepare to counter attack; Gruppe Schmalz to prepare to receive an attack; and the Hermann Goering Panzer Division to assault Gela.

Offshore at Gela a lone Stuka bombed the destroyer USS Maddox. In just two minutes she went down with two hundred and ten men.

The Americans considered the Rangers to be their most elite troops, yet inside the town of Gela Italian coastal troops actually destroyed an entire ranger platoon. Inside Licata the 17th CCNN Legion and Task Gruppo Licata were holding off a ranger assault.

Near Monte Sole a battery was plunging shells into the Americans. In fact it became so dangerous that the beach masters ordered all landing craft to avoid this stretch of the shore. The Italian gunners were firing as fast as possible knowing the inevitable naval shells would soon start falling on them. Suddenly they fell - the 6inch naval shells annihilated the battery. The surviving batteries at Torre di Gaffe continued to fire until 7:15am, when they too tasted the hot slicing shrapnel of 6inch naval shells.

Rear Admiral Priamo Leonardi at Syracuse was under an air raid when he learned that the Ponte Grande Bridge was still in British hands, so just before 8am he organized a task force of San Marco marines and armored cars supported by armed sailors and sent them to recapture the bridge.

By the time bright July morning sunshine was glaring down on the battlefield of Gela, its two hundred defenders marched out with their hands on their heads. Yet at Avola a few survivors of the terrible bombardment managed to get some guns back into action, which they knew was a suicidal endeavor. Within minutes British naval shells wiped them off the face of the earth.

Guzzoni was informed that his armored counter attack was getting under way and there was further good news: no Allied tanks had yet been seen. Mobile Gruppo E had R35s, L6s and L3s, all tiny by Allied standards. Indeed L3s had proven worthless against Ethiopians armed with swords! Nonetheless Mobile Gruppo E's toy tanks rattled along the narrow roads towards Gela in two columns. The crews were tense. They reached a point ten miles inland from Gela and saw no sign of naval gunfire - eight miles from Gela and still no sign of shells falling - five miles from Gela and still no hint that the Americans were anywhere near. Only when they were within two miles of the town center did naval shells begin to fall on them - 6inch shells directed by spotter aircraft. The explosions were huge. A direct hit turned an L3 into a hole in the road with a black oily spot at the bottom. No fewer than two hundred and eight shells blasted the column into smithereens. Incredibly when the smoke cleared a few tanks had miraculously remained unscathed, and with a feeling of dread their drivers moved their vehicles forward again, so the spotter pilots called in another one hundred and eighty-four 4inch shells!

The second column was also targeted by the US Navy and a hundred 4inch shells struck these tanks. Astonishingly nine machines survived, but rather than turn back they continued on exhibiting incredible bravery. Within yards of the outskirts of the town they came under fire from American rangers armed with shoulder-fired bazooka rocket launchers. The first, second and third tanks were hit. The crews of the remaining six tanks finally came to their senses and withdrew.

The headquarters staff of Mobile Gruppo E wondered how things were going. They found out when heavy naval shells from a British battleship blasted them apart in their tents.

However, Guzzoni's counter thrust towards Gela was not over yet. The Hermann Goering Panzer Division's main battle group was approaching in several columns. One such, on the Biscari-Nisemi road was fired on by American paratroopers who had captured a

47mm anti-tank gun. The other columns were strafed by fighters. The bullets could not hurt the tanks, of course, but did chew up some trucks at the rear of the columns. Then the Germans, Herman Goering's pride and joy, retreated!

By late morning the defenders of Licata including the 17th CCNN Legion and Licata Task Gruppo had surrendered, and the batteries around Scoglitti were finally silenced by naval shells.

In the early afternoon Major General Chirieleison's Livorno Mountain Division assembled just outside Gela, its infantrymen psyching themselves up to do what Italian and German armor had failed to do, namely reach the beachhead. But, before they were fully prepared, Allied naval shells began falling among them slaughtering infantrymen and engineers in heaps.

By midafternoon a battery at Cadeini Point that was still in action was overrun by British glider troops attacking from the rear.

Inside the city of Syracuse the civilians were out in the streets by now. They smiled when they realized the authorities were not going to fight for the city – in other words the lives of the women and children would be spared - and they were especially happy that the first British infantry to arrive were behaving themselves. There were so many things to be thankful for: no more death and destruction at the hands of Allied bombers, no more of Mussolini's secret police or swaggering Blackshirts, no battle amid their homes, and possibly the end of the war. They laughed and sang, joyous just to be alive. They embraced the British soldiers. The Tommies thought it all a bit queer that Italian men had just been shooting at them and here Italian women were kissing them.

But at the Ponte Grande Bridge no one was kissing anybody. All day the marines and sailors battled elite British airborne troops and finally at 3:30pm they forced the British to surrender! The Italians checked their prisoners for hidden weapons, then began marching them towards Syracuse, when suddenly around the bend came, what appeared to be, the entire British Eighth Army. The Italians threw up their hands.

Throughout the day the battle was as confusing for the Allies as it was for the Germans and Italians. In some places Italians and Germans were resisting fanatically, yet a few yards away Italians and Germans were walking up to solitary Allied soldiers and asking to be taken prisoner. One US paratrooper accepted four prisoners and marched them towards an American unit, only to find when he arrived that twenty more had joined his little parade. Finding an officer he calmly asked: "Sir, what the hell do I do with these guys?"

The tiny garrison of Vittoria had been bombed, strafed and shelled this day, and now they were attacked by American paratroopers. Most of the garrison surrendered, but a handful of Fascists held out for another hour.

American paratroopers infiltrated into Avola, but the Italian garrison counter attacked them, only to be attacked themselves in the rear by British infantry. Caught between two fires the Italians gave up. At Santa Croce Camerina the five hundred Italian defenders were attacked from two sides at once. They capitulated. In both instances neither of the Allied units knew the other was present and had actually shot at each other.

By late afternoon thousands of Italian soldiers were milling around on the beach watching the Allies unload case upon case of food, clothing, ammunition etc., and drums of fuel. The wounded, both Allied and Italian, were being carried on stretchers aboard landing craft. Still in uniform, many wearing their boat shaped helmets the Italian coastal troops wandered around and stared sort of like tourists. No one seemed to notice them.

Near Priolo ten small Italian tanks burst into life and tried to make a run for the beach, but they ran into American paratroopers armed with bazookas. They halted. At 6:40pm these paratroopers were reinforced by American infantry.

As night approached the defenders of Ragusa withdrew and the airmen at Comiso airfield radioed headquarters that they were under ground attack. Admiral Leonardi knew the cities of Syracuse and Augusta had been lost, but he knew nothing of the situation at the two naval bases near those cities. He expected his sailors to fight to the death. As night fell in the Syracuse-Augusta area thousands of men in German uniform - flak gunners, sailors and rear-echelon troops - jumped into vehicles and began driving north helter skelter frantically trying to escape the Allies. The local Blackshirts were unnerved by the sight of panicky Germans, and the hysteria soon engulfed them too, so they commandeered vehicles and fled. Naturally the Italian sailors armed with rifles and a few bullets each felt pretty vulnerable by now, so they too fled in vehicles or on foot. Within minutes both naval bases had been abandoned.

Guzzoni was exhausted. It had been a long day. He knew the only chance of survival was a massive counter attack by German armor and a sortie by the Italian main battle fleet. Mussolini was demanding as much.

The Italian admirals had to put things into perspective. At Taranto they had the 29,000-ton battleships Andrea Doria and Caio Duilio, which were thirty-two years old and lightly armored, and therefore no match for a modern British fleet, although their 12.6inch guns could inflict heavy damage. At La Spezia lay the battleships Littorio, Vittorio Veneto and La Roma, each of 46,000 tons, excellent armor and nine 15inch guns. Alongside them was the Giulio Cesare {similar to the Caio Duilio}, plus five light cruisers and eight destroyers. This squadron would be able to counter attack the Allied armada, but it would require twenty-five hours sailing time. This would put them under the eyes of Allied aircraft. This of course was the problem. The battleship had had its day. The master of the sea no longer sailed in it, but flew over it. The smaller warships of the Italian navy had been culled extensively by the Allies and some of the remaining few were being used to carry cargo, because the Italian merchant fleet had been devastated with five hundred and fifty vessels sunk to date.

Given such difficulties Admiral Ricciardi's best suggestion was for ten Italian and six German submarines to sail south of Sicily, for German e-boats to sail to Messina in Sicily, for Italian MAS boats to patrol the Straits of Messina, for a few fast destroyers to patrol north of Sicily [but only at night], and for a couple of night sorties by the light cruisers. This was clearly an inadequate response.

Mussolini's Regia Aeronautica had once impressed the world with its size, innovation and daring, but in the last eight months he had lost two thousand one hundred and ninety aircraft. A high percentage of the surviving planes were grounded for lack of spare parts. Currently the flight schools were only graduating seventy-five pilots a month, because there was not enough fuel to train more.

Recently the primary mission for Mussolini's fighter planes had been to intercept Allied bombers. Over Sicily in the first nine days of July his Italian fighters flew six hundred and ninety sorties and Luftwaffe fighters flew five hundred. Together with flak guns they had accounted for three hundred and seventy-five Allied planes shot down. Yet by evening on 10 July not one Italian plane was able to take off from any Sicilian airfield and only ninety-four Italian fighters in mainland Italy were at airfields within range of Sicily. A few German machines were able to reach Sicily flying from Italy and Sardinia. However, this same day the Allies flew three thousand six hundred and eighty warplanes over Sicily, some of them making two missions. The sole damage inflicted on the Allied armada by Axis planes was the sinking of a minesweeper, a destroyer and a hospital ship.

The Allied ground troops that invaded Sicily were fresh, but the Italian coastal gunners were in their sixth month of air raids, and on invasion day they had been fiercely bombarded by Allied aircraft and warships. As most of these gunners were older men, they had come to like the taste of life. It should have been expected they would surrender when faced with certain death, especially as they had satisfied their honor by offering stout resistance during air raids and in the early hours of the invasion. And indeed by the end of the first day of the ground battle most had taken this chance for an honorable surrender. Yet by the morning of 11 July, over twenty-four hours into the invasion, several batteries were still flinging shells towards the Allies. For generations Italian artillerymen had consistently shown courage and the Sicily campaign would not prove to be an exception.

At 6:30am on the second morning of the invasion Italian aircraft challenged the mighty invasion armada, braving the largest concentration of flak guns in history. They succeeded only in damaging a transport.

Guzzoni's staff was already coordinating another ground counter-attack, despite knowing this one would be more foolhardy than that of the previous day, for the Allies now had artillery and tanks ashore, including Major General Hugh Gaffey's US 2nd Armored Division. Major General Conrath had been shamed by the feeble performance of his Hermann Goering Panzer Division the previous day, especially when compared to the Italian counter attacks, and he angrily dismissed two senior officers. Conrath, a policeman before the war and a Luftwaffe rear-echelon officer since 1939 he was in an enviable position as the only Luftwaffe officer currently commanding a panzer division. Goering had his eye on him. This was the second such division named after Goering himself. The other had been lost in Tunisia. For Conrath's young Luftwaffe Nazis to have retreated while Italians were fighting and dying was a disgrace that the German people would never have understood. Naturally, as Germany was a police state without freedom of the press, the German people were never told when their soldiers performed poorly. This morning Conrath was given a second chance when he was asked to provide a battle group to support the Livorno Division.

The Livorno had suffered badly the previous day from air raids and naval gunfire, and had yet to actually see an invader, bar a few paratroopers here and there. Major General Chirieleison put an infantry assault together of a battalion west of Gela, two battalions to the northwest of the town and one on the north. Each battalion would be accompanied by a few L6 tanks.

As his attack began this morning his infantry came under artillery fire at once, but this did not break them. Then they were strafed by low-flying American planes. Naturally this disorganized the assault troops, but they regrouped and leaped forward again. Suddenly huge 6inch naval shells exploded among them. The men threw themselves on the ground, as no fewer than eight hundred and sixty-seven shells annihilated them.

Elsewhere a thin line of Italian L6s, all that remained of Mobile Gruppo E, crept down a narrow road unseen by American spotter planes, but they ran into a team of rangers armed with bazookas. The fight was short and the rangers quickly pulled out. Thinking they had won, the tankers proceeded, but then realized the rangers had pulled out after having been warned that naval shells were on their way. Thirty-eight 6inch shells obliterated the tank column. The forward artillery observer who called in the shoot was none other than Patton himself.

Of today's counter attack plan only Conrath's forces remained, and his armored vehicles and panzergrenadiers were able to approach very close to the beach before encountering serious opposition. Once the startled Americans of the 1st Division realized what was happening they counterattacked with infantry, paratroopers, engineers, tanks and artillery. The German battle group broke apart and many men fled in panic.

This morning the headquarters of the 206th Coastal Division surrendered when Allied infantry overran them.

Mussolini was frantic. He demanded a major aerial onslaught to drive off the armada. The result was a massive raid (by Axis standards) of one hundred and ninety-eight Italian and two hundred and eighty-three German planes. By pure luck they found the fleet almost devoid of fighter protection, so all they had to worry about were the few thousand flak guns. They managed to damage a British destroyer and sink a US freighter.

Through faulty intelligence, or perhaps someone's wishful thinking, Guzzoni was informed the Americans were about to evacuate their beachheads. He knew this was surely nonsense, but would have been amiss if he had not tried to take advantage of the news lest it be true. So he ordered yet another suicidal counter attack on Gela.

The officers and sergeants of the Livorno Division harangued their surviving men with Fascist slogans and pleas to the baser instincts and managed to form another assault. They were supported by tanks and infantry from Mobile Gruppos G and H, 173rd CCNN Legion and the Comiso-Ispica Task Gruppo. At 5pm they ran into rangers armed with bazookas. This was bad enough, but what was worse was to see the Americans scamper out of the way. This meant only one thing - seconds later 6inch naval shells started falling. This time the Italians retreated.

Once the shelling was over the Livorno regrouped and unbelievably they began to advance again! This time they were met by ground fire from thousands of US soldiers of the US 1st Division. The Americans who shot them down in bunches would never forget the slaughter nor the courage of these Italians, and they marveled at the stupidity of such bull-headed tactics. Having lost two thirds of its infantry in two days the Livorno withdrew from the scene.

Guzzoni did not know if he had hurt the invaders. He did know that it had been a close run thing in some sectors, despite Allied claims to the world's press of speedy advances against 'slight resistance', The Americans were looking at almost four thousand casualties in the first seventy-two hours. 'So much for slight resistance', the GIs murmured.

Guzzoni studied his order of battle. The Livorno was crippled, the Hermann Goering was in a state of panic, Mobile Gruppo C had been shattered by air attack, Mobile Gruppos E, G and H had been devastated by air, naval and ground forces, and the 18th Coastal Brigade, 206th Coastal Division, 17th CCNN Legion and Task Gruppo Licata no longer existed. As yet none of the other Axis units had reached the battlefield, so he ordered Conrath to concentrate his division for another counter attack, this time against the British. Guzzoni was thankful to learn he was to be reinforced by a German parachute division.

During the night the Italian submarine Flutto battled British MTBs north of Sicily. She was sunk.

On the morning of the 12 July the survivors of the Livorno Division retreated, but even now they were unlucky, because spotter planes saw them and directed eight hundred and eight 6inch naval shells onto them. The survivors fell back to the airfields at Comiso, Ponte Olivo and Biscari just out of the range of naval gunfire. However, Middleton's US 45th Division was close on their heels, and by mid-morning the defenders of these airfields were under ground attack. They were manned by remnants of several units: the Livorno Division, Mobile Gruppos E, G and H, Task Gruppo Comiso-Ispica and the 173rd CCNN Legion; and the Regia Aeronautica ground crews also went into line armed with rifles. In mid-afternoon the defenders of Comiso and Ponte Olivo were ordered to pull out. The defenders of Biscari fought on and were joined by some panzergrenadiers.

This day the last of the coastal artillery that was still firing, a battery of 149mm guns at Monte San Nicola, was destroyed. Without doubt these men had earned their pay.

Guzzoni attempted to stop the Canadians and British near Pachino with his 542nd Bersaglieri Coastal Battalion, Mobile Gruppo F and Task Gruppo Pachino, but the Italians were overrun quite quickly.

The submarine Bronzo sneaked past or rather under the Allied fleet and entered Syracuse harbor, but as she surfaced she was fired upon by countless guns. The crew had not realized the port was in British hands. Nine men were killed before the crew surrendered.

Admiral Priam Leonardi personally surveyed his naval base defenses at Augusta. Everyone had long since fled, apart from one gun battery. When British troops approached he went out to meet them with a rifle in his hand.

North of Augusta Major Nino Bolla of the Napoli Division witnessed hundreds of soldiers, Blackshirts, airmen, sailors and police rushing past his positions in panic. He and his men grabbed as many as they could and formed provisional units, but as soon as his back was turned they fled. Everywhere officers were trying to stem the rout and in some cases they were shot by their own men. Bolla gave up in sheer frustration and ordered his men to prepare to meet the enemy. By nightfall he was battling for his life against the British spearhead.

Outside Gela a few of Hermann Goering's panzergrenadiers

wanted to regain their honor rather than obey the order to withdraw, so they attacked. It was a futile gesture.

By this third day of the Sicily land campaign Axis air activity was minimal. Allied ships were astonished to see one lone Italian fighter who weaved among them at wave-top height, his machine guns blazing. They were almost regretful when this heroic pilot's machine was sliced to ribbons by flak and he plunged into the sea.

At Kesselring's headquarters and at every German headquarters in Sicily the Nazis were all blaming the Italians, though even the most rabid of Hitler's followers had to admit that the Italian coastal gunners had fought bravely. But, being Nazis, they refused to admit that part of the fault lay with the Hermann Goering Panzer Division, which had performed abysmally, and that the 15th Panzergrenadier Division was too scattered to have done any good. Fanatics are never objective.

Off the coast Italian and German bombers attacked a British troopship, the Timothy Pickering. Of the one hundred and ninety-four still aboard, only twenty-eight survived the sinking. The Italian submarine Nereide was sunk by the British destroyers Echo and Ilex. The Italian submarine Accaio was sunk by the British submarine Unruly.

On 13 July the last remaining sailors at Augusta were overrun, and the sailors at Catania were evacuating. However, as the day's events were reported to him Guzzoni became quite pleased. The Napoli Division was still holding the British just north of Augusta, and this morning one of its battalions actually counter attacked and recaptured a seaplane base. The defenders of Biscari airfield were holding on by the skin of their teeth against American infantry and tanks of the US 45th and 1st Armored Divisions. Only the westward advance of the Americans seemed to be proceeding smoothly. Guzzoni could not know that Truscott's US 3rd Division was advancing westwards along the coast in violation of Alexander's orders. The day's most notable event was the dropping of the German 1st Parachute Division, which was accomplished without any major interference by the vast Allied air forces. It was a miracle. Furthermore, no sooner had the German paratroopers reinforced Gotti-Porcinari's Napoli Division north of Augusta than British commandos stormed ashore from the sea between Augusta and Catania, where the Primosole Bridge crosses the mouth of the Simeto River, which was close to the Malati Bridge over the Lintini River. Obviously the British were hoping to capture these two bridges in the rear of the Napoli Division. They would have succeeded too, had they landed a couple of hours earlier, but now they came up against the German paratroopers who immediately pinned the Britons down on the beach.

An incredible message reached Guzzoni. In a shrewd public relations move General Eisenhower ignored President Roosevelt's unconditional surrender policy and announced on public radio and by air-dropped leaflets that any Sicilian in uniform who surrendered would be allowed to return home as soon as his village was in Allied hands. Those from Gela, Augusta and Syracuse could go home at once. It was a brilliant move and within hours tens of thousands of Sicilians began walking towards the invaders looking for someone to accept their 'parole'.

Just after midnight, now the 14th of July, Italian flak gunners near the Primosole Bridge were offered a splendid target - a steady stream of transport planes full of British paratroopers towing gliders. As the chutes began to pop open hundreds of guns were trained on them. Trigger-happy Allied ground and naval flak gunners joined in the shooting. The mission drop zone for these British paratroopers and glider troops was the Primosole Bridge, but only 15% landed on target. Still this was enough, and by 3am they had defeated the German paratroopers and had linked up with the British commandos on the beach. Within minutes they moved on to capture the Malati Bridge. Gotti-Porcinari's Napoli Division and Gruppe Schmalz and the mixed defenders of Biscari were still fighting, but they were now trapped.

At dawn German paratroopers counter attacked the two bridges. And now these paratroopers, who were just as lightly armed as their British counterparts, gained a lovely reinforcement, a small battle group of Tiger tanks. With these monsters they were able to push the British off Malati Bridge and recapture Primosole Bridge.

Unfortunately later in the day the Napoli's line collapsed, and by dusk the Italians had lost the seaplane base, and then they and Gruppe Schmalz retreated to a point six miles south of the Primosole Bridge. They anchored with the Italian garrison of Lentini together with elements of the 115th Panzergrenadier Regiment and were constantly shelled by accurate artillery fire. British observers were directing the fire from a nearby mountain. Twenty miles to the southwest at Vizzini the Hermann Goering was under attack by the Canadian 1st Division.

At Biscari most of the defenders fell back, but only because they had run out of ammunition. Several were cut off and taken prisoner. The Americans of the 45th Division were extremely angry at having lost friends in this their first battle. In two incidents American soldiers used this as an excuse to show how 'manly' they were. Sergeant Horace West lined up prisoners and began shooting. He killed thirty-four Italians and two Germans. Captain John Compton shot dead forty Italian prisoners. There were in fact several shootings of Italian and German prisoners by the Americans, including a mass execution of upwards of two hundred Germans at Comiso. These were all cold blooded murders and had not taken place in the heat of battle. At Canicatti an American officer fired his pistol into a crowd of looters, killing eight, including an eleven-year old girl, who was looking for food. [The US Army went through the motions of justice. Despite plenty of witnesses to these atrocities only Compton and West were court martialed, and only West was convicted, being sentenced to life imprisonment. After serving barely a year he was quietly released.]

General Vittorio Ambrosio, military head of Comando Supremo, finally worked up enough nerve to ask Mussolini to stop the war. His pleas fell on deaf ears. Ambrosio then reminded Mussolini that his new bodyguard, the Mussolini Armored Division with its excellent German equipment, might be able to help the boys in Sicily. Il Duce refused to commit it. However, he did make one concession. He placed the division under army command.

By morning of 15 July the Napoli Division and Gruppe Schmalz had retreated across the Simeto River and had saved themselves for the time being. The Hermann Goering troops were still holding Vizzini under Canadian pressure.

Guzzoni was much more worried about Western Sicily, for he had only one major mobile defense unit there to challenge the American advance. The Americans were advancing westwards along the south coast rolling up the positions of the 207th Coastal Division one by one from the rear. Von Senger, Guzzoni's German 'observer', thought the drive was the beginning of an American attempt to take Palermo from which they would swing eastwards and head for Messina. Therefore, he took it upon himself to order all Germans to concentrate on defending the northwest of the island, in direct contradiction to Guzzoni's orders.

The Italian Navy was conspicuous by its absence. This day the submarine Remo was sunk by the British submarine United. British warships shelled Empedocle and Agrigento at leisure.

16 July marked the end of a full week of non-stop combat in Sicily, and Guzzoni allowed this to be an unofficial rest day. However, Truscott's Americans did not rest and continued to advance westwards in trucks, jeeps and on horseback, taking rear-echelon personnel and artillery gunners by surprise. This day alone they seized six thousand prisoners.

Guzzoni was informed that still more reinforcements were on their way: the brand new German 29th Panzergrenadier Division; and with it would come Lieutenant General Hube and his XIV Panzer Corps headquarters. Hube, a veteran of the 1940 French campaign, had brought his XIV Corps direct from the Russian Front with orders from Hitler to hold the line northwest of Catania. This placed von Senger and Guzzoni in an awkward position, as Hube was to take command of all Germans in Sicily and would report directly to Kesselring. Guzzoni recognized this for what it was. The Germans would fight their own battle in Sicily from now on. The Nazis justified their actions by a whole sling of racist insults, such as 'the Italian coastal infantry had folded up', 'the Napoli and Livorno had run away', 'Italian tanks were useless', 'Guzzoni was incompetent for he had yet to commit his Aosta and Assietta Mountain Divisions', and 'the Italian admirals refused to sail'. In Nazi eyes the Italians no longer wanted to fight and so the Germans had a right to take over.

The Italians saw things differently, claiming that the only worthwhile German ground reinforcements they had received were the lightly armed paratroopers, and that the Allies had only been able to advance forty miles in seven days owing to tough Italian opposition. While there was some truth in all these accusations, they were systematic of an alliance of two partners that were ultra nationalist beyond all reason.

At sea the submarine Dandolo was not afraid to fight. She torpedoed a British destroyer. The light cruiser Scipio Africano fought off British MTBs, sinking one. At Trapani a coastal battery fought a duel with British warships for several hours. On the 18th and 19th nine coastal batteries of the 213th Coastal Division near Catania were bombarded by British and Dutch warships.

————————

Chapter Forty-six
Balkan Battles

Greek partisan activity did not become serious until spring 1942. And it was spring 1943 before it required major Axis attention. Near Domenico the partisan ambush of an Italian truck convoy killing eighty Italians including a general woke up the complacent Axis authorities.

The XXVI Corps was tied down occupying the Epirus Mountains one hundred and fifty miles west of Athens, the stronghold of the EDES partisans. Troops of the Casale Division [with attached 23rd CCNN Legion] and Modena Division [with attached 36th CCNN Legion] patrolled the roads. The III Corps began hunting ELAS partisans and Macedonian rebels in the mountains of Roumelia and Greek Macedonia two hundred and seventy miles north of Athens. with its Brennero Division [and attached 35th CCNN Legion], Forli Mountain Division, Pinerolo Division [and attached 136th CCNN Legion], 2nd Bersaglieri Regiment and Aosta (horse) Cavalry Regiment In the Peloponnesus the VIII Corps with its Piemonte Division and Cagliari Mountain Division [with attached 29th CCNN Legion] continued operations against several small independent bands and ELAS-affiliated groups. The Germans also responded to the increase in partisan activity in May 1943 by bringing in their 1st Mountain Division from Yugoslavia. The Greek partisans had an excellent intelligence network and they learned of this reinforcement, so several bands from different political persuasions joined together to stop the division at Leskovik just inside Albania before it reached the Greek border. However, these Germans were veterans of the war against Tito, and they discovered the ambush and attacked the partisans in flank. Seriously defeated, the partisans scattered. Behind these Germans more were coming: the 117th Security Division, 1st Panzer Division and the headquarters of LXVII Corps.

In order to keep the Greek partisans at bay without soaking up any more German units, the Axis partners authorized the current Greek Prime Minister, Joannes Rallis, to establish the Security Battalion of a thousand Greek Fascist volunteers.

In June 1943 this Security Battalion joined German LXVII Corps in attacking the partisans in the mountains of Roumelia. As part of the Italian contribution to this offensive III Corps sent Major General Adolfo Infante's Pinerolo Division, 2nd Bersaglieri Regiment and Aosta Cavalry Regiment into the mountains. Within hours the Italians were pinned down by ELAS rearguards. After another three days of fighting Infante withdrew his men. He had suffered five hundred casualties and had gained nothing.

The Germans were impressed by the enthusiasm of the Greek

Fascists and they asked Rallis to raise another fourteen thousand of them!

Inside the Kournoso rail tunnel an Italian military train was blown up by saboteurs, killing or wounding over five hundred soldiers. In retaliation the Italian garrison at Larissa one hundred and sixty miles northwest of Athens emptied their jail of one hundred and eighteen Greeks, currently being held as suspected partisans, and executed them. In response the ELAS announced that henceforth they would take no prisoners.

This summer at Bougazi an Italian battalion was ambushed and forced to retreat. At Rovilista another battalion was repulsed, losing one hundred and twenty casualties. At Monotiano the garrison of eighty-five Italians was overrun.

The Italian defenders of Almyros one hundred and twenty miles northwest of Athens drove off their attackers. These Italians were convinced that local men had aided the partisans, so they picked out thirty-eight of them at random and murdered them.

A Bulgarian column was all but wiped out in an ambush.

———————

Meanwhile in Albania by December 1942 General Pirzio-Birolli and the staff of Italian Ninth Army had come to the conclusion that the Albanian police and army, despite having been reinforced by a considerable Italian police presence, could no longer control the partisan situation in Albania. Italian intelligence estimated there were about twenty thousand Albanian partisans, half of them Communists. As a result the Ninth Army joined this war and advanced into the freezing mountains with its IV and XXV Corps: the former consisting of the Puglie Division (with attached 115th CCNN Legion) and Firenze Division (with attached 92nd CCNN Legion); and the latter consisting of the Parma Division (with attached 109th CCNN Legion), Arezzo Division (with attached 80th CCNN Legion) and Raggruppamento Monferrato.

On 2 January 1943 two battalions of Italian infantry were ambushed at Gjormi. No doubt these Italians had become a little soft after a year and a half of endless boring occupation duty, and they retreated quickly. Later an Italian company was wiped out at Voskopoja.

Comando Supremo decided that the Albanian problem needed a firmer hand, so they sent General Alberto Pariani to seize the initiative. He paid his respects to Viceroy Francesco Jacomoni and Prime Minister Kruja and then set to work. One of his first recommendations following a study of the situation was that Kruja had to go. Mussolini agreed, and on 19 February he replaced this Albanian puppet with Ekrem Libohova. However, this new marionette found it impossible to rule, and he resigned after just twenty-eight days. His successor was Maliq Bushati. He found the same problems, and declared that he could not rule, so Mussolini asked Libohova to try again. He agreed, but on the condition that Albania be given greater autonomy. Mussolini acquiesced, even removing Comando Supremo's control of the Albanian Army.

This game of musical chairs did not impress the partisans. In a major confrontation at Permet the Communist partisans inflicted over five hundred casualties on Albanian and Italian troops. In July there were large-scale battles at Mallakastra and Tepelene, both of which the Italians won, but their losses were high.

———————

In Yugoslavia once Tito's main column had survived the fifth offensive against him, the big war in that nation came to an intermission. However, the Italian soldiers did not cease fighting the small war, i. e. the war of arrests, sniping, road ambushes, assassination, major thefts, anti-black market operations and executions.

———————

Chapter Forty-seven
Dethronement

On 19 July 1943 a very important meeting took place in Rome among several leading Fascists. Dino Grandi demanded that the Fascist Grand Council meet in emergency session. This leading body of the Fascist Party had not met since 1939, many of its twenty-nine members being too lazy to meet. Mussolini had bribed them all with money, land, titles, jobs, mistresses and business contacts. At least some of them had served in uniform in Ethiopia, Greece and elsewhere, unlike Hitler's cronies who never even visited the front.

The 47-year old Grandi was a member by virtue of his long service to the party. A hero in World War I he had fought as a Fascist in the street war, that period before Mussolini gained control of Italy. He had served as an Alpini officer in Greece 1940-41 and had at various times been Minister of Justice, Foreign Minister and Ambassador to Britain. Grandi's purpose in calling the council together was to ask Mussolini to give up control of the war and place it in more capable hands. This would still leave Mussolini with the office of Prime Minister.

It was perhaps symbolic that the two submarines Remo and Romolo, named after the two founders of Rome, had been sunk in the last few days, the former by a submarine, the latter by aircraft, but Mussolini needed no omen to inform him how bad things were. He too was in a meeting this day at the Villa Gaggia in northern Italy. His guest was Adolf Hitler, and Mussolini sat patiently listening to one of the Fuehrer's monologues. This very day the German armies had begun to retreat in Central Russia. Yet as always Hitler was optimistic with his talk of Nazi/Fascist will triumphing over the unholy alliance of Russian Communism, Jewry, British Imperialism and American Democracy. The Italian officers with Mussolini, including Ambrosio, listened in disgusted silence, ashamed that Mussolini did not challenge such blatant nonsense.

Even Hitler eventually ran out of words and when he did the discussion became heated. While the German and Italian generals argued with each other, American mechanized forces were charging westwards from Agrigento, Sicily. The German generals demanded they be given command of all Italian forces! At this very moment Task Gruppo Sciacca in Sicily was under attack from the rear by American infantry. As Mussolini stood up to plead for more German aid, American bombers were on their way to Rome. As the Italian generals reacted angrily to the German demands, Italian truck drivers were being ambushed by partisans in Greece. While the German generals calmed down and rephrased their demands, the Blackshirt flak gunners of Rome were astonished to see American Flying

Fortress and Liberator bombers overhead. Hitherto the Allies had promised not to bomb Rome because the pope's Vatican Palace was inside the city limits. As Mussolini and Hitler tried to work out a compromise, Italian sentries in Albania were stabbed. While Hitler ranted about his generosity to Italy, German and Italian troops retreating just south of Mount Etna in Sicily were attacked by Allied fighter-bombers. While Mussolini pleaded, an Italian patrol in Yugoslavia was ambushed by Titoists. While Mussolini was interrupted by an aide informing him of the raid on Rome, a second wave of Mitchells, Marauders and Lightnings was on its way to Rome. While Mussolini pleaded, Hitler demanded, and while the conference became an all-out shouting match, back in Rome Grandi plotted.

That afternoon King Vittorio Emmanuele pondered the situation. He had been king for longer than most of his soldiers had been alive. But as the head of a constitutional monarchy he had been a powerless king, as he reigned, but did not rule. When he heard the bombs fall in Rome he was visibly shaken and he rushed to the bombed-out neighborhoods of Tiburtino, San Lorenzo, Ciampino and Littorio, where one thousand five hundred civilians had been killed or wounded, and where he intended to give solace to his subjects. However, the surviving residents that had just faced five hundred and twenty bombers, only two of which were shot down, jeered and booed their king. What good was this short, frail, impotent old man! By contrast the pope also visited the wreckage [in his capacity as Bishop of Rome] and he was met with deep reverence. The king was stunned by his reception. Naturally he blamed Mussolini. He felt even worse when informed that one of the dead amid the ruins was a friend, General Azolino Hazon the commander of the Carabinieri. This day was the one thousand eight hundred and seventy-ninth anniversary of the burning of Rome, and like Nero the king had fiddled while his capital was in flames. He was determined not to suffer the fate of Nero.

The following day General Ambrosio handed his resignation to Mussolini. He was at the end of his tether and Mussolini had failed to support him at the meeting with Hitler. Il Duce refused the resignation. Heartbroken, Ambrosio returned to his office and confided in his aide, Brigadier General Giuseppe Castellano. Of Sicilian parentage Castellano was one of the youngest generals in the army. He was also a friend of Ciano, Mussolini's son in law. Ambrosio queried him about the possibility of asking the king to dismiss Mussolini. Thus within twenty-four hours three plots had been hatched, by Grandi, by the king and by Ambrosio, although these plots had been incubating for some time.

Before the day was out Castellano met with representatives of the king, so that they could inform his majesty of Ambrosio's wishes.

They came to a decision to arrest Mussolini in six days' time. It would take that long because the arrangements would have to be made under the eyes of the OVRA secret police.

Meantime over the next few hours these plotters maneuvered Mussolini into appointing General Angelo Cerica, a known anti-Fascist, to replace Hazon as head of the Carabinieri. They also met with Carmine Senise, who had recently been dismissed from his job as head of the National Police. Senise agreed to resume his position once Mussolini was removed.

The plotters also met with Lieutenant General Giacomo Carboni. This officer was brilliant and loyal, though to many Italians he was not a 'real' Italian. He was half Sardinian and half American. His position as head of Military Intelligence in 1939 had exposed him to some stark truths about Nazism and he had worked against the alliance with Germany ever since. Mussolini had dismissed him because of this and had placed him in command of the officer's academy. In 1942 he was given the Friuli Division and later he led VII Corps in the bloodless invasion of Corsica. On 14 July 1943 he was relieved of his Corsica command by General Giovanni Magli, so that he could come to Rome to command a motorized corps, where he would report to General Alberto Barbieri. The plotters visited him this day and asked him if he would order his troops to arrest all Blackshirts in Rome on their signal. He agreed.

The plotters also spoke with Major General Giunio Ruggiero, commander of the Sardinian Grenadiers Division based just outside Rome. Castellano wanted Ruggiero to act at once to occupy Rome, even before the coup. Ruggiero stated that to do so would arouse suspicion, but he did agree to send two battalions to Rome on 'exercises'.

The most important personage approached by the plotters this day was Marshall Pietro Badoglio. His first reply was that at seventy-two years of age he was beyond such escapades, but was then informed that eighty-three year old ex-prime minister Vittorio Orlando, his mentor, was also in on the plot. Ambrosio wanted Badoglio to become interim prime minister once Mussolini was ousted. Some plotters preferred asking ex-prime minister Ivanoe Bonomi to take over, especially when they found out he had already hatched his own plot. Still others preferred asking eighty-one year old Marshal Enrico Caviglia to take the reins. An outspoken anti-Fascist, only Caviglia's military reputation had prevented the OVRA from arresting him, but they had arrested three of his nephews to force him to keep his mouth shut. However, the king refused to consider Caviglia because he was a freemason! The king knew he would need the support of the pope, and the pope hated freemasons. But the pope smiled upon Badoglio.

———————

Meanwhile this day Mussolini had returned to Rome and he studied the reports coming to his desk. The OVRA informed him there were several plots afoot, but this was nothing new. He had survived plots and assassination attempts before. Grandi's move to call a meeting of the Fascist Grand Council was not considered a plot, for he had been quite open about it, even placing his purpose on the agenda. The OVRA suspected that Grandi might gain five or six supporters on the council at most. Worst case scenario was that the entire council would vote against Mussolini. So what, thought Mussolini? This would only be a vote of no confidence. The council had no power and the seven hundred thousand card carrying Fascists in the country would still support him, he was sure. In fact he was convinced that the twenty million anti-Fascists in the country would also support him.

His cabinet, some members of whom also sat on the council, did have the power to vote him out of his position of Minister of War, but he would still be prime minister. As for the plot by the generals - he did not worry about it. He, who had never risen above the rank of sergeant, had little regard for generals. Each one owed his current position to him, and if they did revolt the Blackshirts would defend him.

Only the king had the right to dismiss him as prime minister, but this weak unintelligent old man had been useful at times and he liked the trappings of power without the effort to earn them. He had not refused when Mussolini made him Emperor of East Africa, nor had he baulked when Mussolini made him King of Albania.

As for the Roman Catholic Church? The priests would not be a problem. Two popes had done his bidding like lackeys, blessing Italian soldiers on their way to kill the enemy, whether Christian Ethiopians, Communist Spaniards and Russians, imperialist Britons or capitalist Americans. The Church owed the very existence of the Vatican State to him, and there was no guarantee a succeeding Italian government would continue the arrangement. In fact a succeeding government might be Communist-controlled, which would outlaw the Church completely. When Mussolini had imposed anti-Jewish legislation at the behest of Hitler, the pope had feebly requested that racial Jews who were Roman Catholics should be exempted from the new laws. Il Duce had willingly acquiesced. It meant nothing to him, for he did not dislike Jews, and it put the pope deeper in his debt.

Mussolini in fact had far greater worries. He would be 60 years old in a few days and he was not as active as he wanted to be. His nerves and stomach cramps had become so painful at times that he collapsed on the floor writhing in pain. Like Hitler, who also suffered from serious health problems, he felt himself destined to lead his people through this hour of turmoil and therefore had to fight his own ailing body to see the nation through the trial.

Hitler? Ah, yes, he was a problem. In the last few weeks nine German divisions had entered Italy: currently four were in Sicily, one was in Sardinia and four were on the mainland. The German ambassador Hans Georg von Mackensen was as ever quite polite, but he was only window dressing. The real German power in Rome was SS Standartenfuehrer Eugen Dollman, the head of the embassy's security section. He was also the darling of the Rome social scene. His deputy, SS Obersturmbannfuehrer Herbert Kappler, chief of the Gestapo section, was a much more studious individual, who shunned cocktail parties, but he had made some friends, especially in the Vatican. Mussolini knew Hitler was one step away from seizing power in Italy. The question was would there be a role for Mussolini in the new state? He thought there would, honestly believing that Hitler's friendship was more than mere rhetoric.

As a result of collecting his thoughts over this eventful week he was confident. However, his Blackshirt and police bodyguards were not nearly so sanguine and they expressed concern for his safety, so he compromised with them. For the council meeting the police would sit in a nearby room and the Blackshirts would stand guard outside.

––––––––––––

On the afternoon of the 24th Il Duce's ever-loyal wife Donna Rachele suddenly begged him not to attend the meeting, suggesting he should have the entire council arrested or at the least he should imprison Grandi. Il Duce smiled and reassured her. He probably did not realize that one thousand nine hundred and eighty-seven years earlier another wife in Rome begged her husband not to attend a meeting: the wife of Julius Caesar.

At 5pm on 24 July 1943 the Fascist Grand Council assembled at the Palazzo Venezia in Rome. As each member entered the conference room Mussolini stared at him, sizing him up. He believed he could bully some of them: Carlo Pareschi, his Minister of Agriculture, Luciano Gottardi, Frattari, Rossoni. Others were fence sitters who would join the majority: Annio Bignardi, Luigi Federzoni, Tullio Cianetti his Minister of Corporations, Giuseppe Bottai the law professor and Alpini officer, who was an ex-minister of education, and Giovanni Ballela the President of the Confederation of Industry. He was certain of the loyalty of some: Blackshirt General Roberto Farinacci one-time Fascist Party Secretary, General Enzo Galbiati the commander of the Blackshirts, Gaetano Polvarelli the Minister of Popular Culture, Carlo Scorza the Fascist Party Secretary, Count Giacomo Suardo the President of the Senate, Carlo Alberto Biggini the Minister of Education, Antonio Tringali-Casanova Chief of the Special Tribunals, Umberto Albini the Minister of the Interior, Baron Giacomo Acerbo the Minister of Finance and a Blackshirt officer, Alfredo di Marsico the Minister of Justice, Giuseppe Bastianinni the

Deputy Foreign Secretary, Guido Buffarino-Guidi ex-minister of the interior, Alberto de Stefani ex-minister of finance, and his own son-in-law Count Galeazzo Ciano, currently Ambassador to the Vatican. Indeed his only real concerns were Giovanni Marinelli, Dino Alfieri the Ambassador to Germany, Blackshirt General Count Cesare Maria de Vecchi an enemy of Mussolini for twenty-one years, Blackshirt Marshal Emilio de Bono a long-time enemy of Mussolini, and of course Dino Grandi himself.

Mussolini was unconcerned as the introductory pleasantries gave way to serious discussion. They began taking turns to speak their mind, but often they were interrupted by someone. Everyone offered compromises. Everyone demanded. Everyone gave way. Everyone refused to budge and the argument continued, an example of Machiavellian intrigue at its best. Only Mussolini was off form, at a loss as to what to say. He had mentally dismissed the Fascist leadership too often to take them seriously now and he had prepared nothing in his defense. When he did speak it was haltingly about trivialities. He was also ill and tired, and several times he broke up the meeting for short breaks. However, he wanted a vote quickly so he would not have to listen to insults any further. At one point an aide brought a message - Bologna was under a heavy air raid. He had expected to bully the entire council within an hour. Instead the insults and jibes went on interminably. Finally after nine and a half hours he demanded a vote. He had let them all have their lira's worth and now it was time to put up or shut up. Grandi was tense, knowing the police were just outside the door. He silently fingered the pistol in his pocket. The result of the vote was: Suardo abstained, eight voted against Grandi's motion to remove Mussolini from control of the war, but the remaining two thirds including Ciano voted to strip Mussolini of his war making power.

Il Duce did not at first understand what had happened. It took a moment to sink in. The members rose and left the room. He had been outvoted, but what did it mean? Most of the members went home and packed a small suitcase lest they had to go on the run.

The following morning was a Sunday, and despite having had only a few hours of fitful sleep Mussolini arose just before 9am as usual and went to work. He read the dispatches from the front lying on his desk. In Albania guerillas were stepping up their attacks. In Greece the vying partisan bands had seemingly put their differences aside and were uniting to attack Italian truck convoys. In Yugoslavia hundreds of thousands of Italian troops were kept busy hunting Titoists. In Corsica guerillas were testing the Italian garrison. In the previous twenty-four hours Livorno and Bologna had been bombed with forty-seven civilians killed in Bologna.

The news from Sicily was catastrophic. Mobile Gruppo B had counter attacked the advancing Allies, and had been totally vanquished, and the seven hundred and fifty survivors of the unit had surrendered. Mobile Gruppos A and C had collapsed under American pressure. Trapani naval base, Corleone, Castelvetrano and Marsala had fallen to Americans attacking from the rear. At Trapani members of the 3/San Marco Marines [who had been rescued from Tunisia in the nick of time] were now taken by the Allies from the rear. Task Gruppo Alcamo and the 171st CCNN Legion had collapsed. The mayor of Palermo had surrendered his city of four hundred thousand civilians and all his police, flak guns and coastal guns. What little was left of the 10th Bersaglieri Regiment, Mussolini's old regiment, was backing away from the Americans. Brigadier General Giuseppe Molinaro had surrendered his command in a pompous official ceremony! Telephone calls from Fascists in Palermo said the people were behaving as if they were being liberated not conquered. Guzzoni, who had removed his headquarters to Messina, reported that forty-four thousand of his uniformed personnel were missing in action, and that the Napoli Division's headquarters had been overrun and so he had withdrawn the division and was attempting to rebuild it. He said the Germans were no longer obeying his orders. In fact the Germans were holding the line Catania-Adrano-Nicosia-San Stefano, a very mountainous line crossed by just one inland road in addition to the coastal road. At the north end of this line the Italians were trying to hold back the Americans with the Livorno and Aosta Divisions and remnants of many smaller units, including the 177th Bersaglieri Regiment, 1st Anti-tank Bersaglieri Battalion and 51st and 58th Bersaglieri Battalions. However, Guzzoni had ordered the Aosta Division to fall back from Nicosia owing to desertions in its ranks. Of all the Italian ground forces only the Assietta Mountain Division had not yet been committed. The Germans were under a British assault, and their troops within ten miles of the coast were being shelled by British and Polish warships. The submarine Ascianghi tried to sink the British heavy cruiser Newfoundland, but was shelled and sunk by British destroyers Laforey and Eclipse.

Also on the desk was a letter from Cianetti. He had changed his mind and was now voting against Grandi. Moreover Cianetti resigned his government post and asked to be sent to a front line military unit. Mussolini recognized this shameful letter for what it was: a typically Fascist method of crawling to save one's neck.

———————

Meanwhile the king was panicking. He had planned his coup for Monday, when Mussolini was scheduled to deliver his daily report to him, but here it was Sunday and Mussolini was asking for an audience immediately. The king was aware of the vote by the Fascist Grand Council, but he still had to reckon with Mussolini's bodyguards and the police. The chief of police in Rome, Renzo Chierici, was a staunch supporter of Mussolini. There were also the Rome Blackshirt legions to be considered and the Blackshirt flak gunners. Just thirty miles north of Rome was the all-Blackshirt Mussolini Armored Division equipped with German tanks and Semoventis. There were also German forces just outside the city. The king's dismissal of Il Duce might well create civil war. However, gaining confidence from his advisers, the king finally gave approval for Castellano to arrest Mussolini. Castellano, not wishing to be the actual arresting officer, ordered General Cerica the commander of the Carabinieri to arrest Il Duce. Cerica, not wishing to be personally involved, passed the order to Lieutenant Colonel Giovanni Frignani, who was to call up fifty Carabinieri reservists to ostensibly search for enemy paratroopers. Frignani was also nervous, so he ordered Captain Paolo Vigneri to take command of the detachment.

At 4pm General Ambrosio on his own authority ordered Chierici to return to duty with the army and hand over the Rome police to Carmine Senise. Chierici did not argue. He was glad to be getting out of this nest of backstabbing traitors.

At 5pm Mussolini arrived at the palace in civilian clothes and was quickly ushered in to see the king. He went to great lengths to explain to the king that the vote of the council was a mere formality. Nonetheless the king summoned up enough courage to interrupt the fiery orator and tell him he was fired. At first Mussolini did not understand. When it was plain the audience was over, the stupefied Il Duce wandered out of the palace, where he was met by Captain Paolo Vigneri and his 'paratroop hunting' detachment of Carabinieri. They politely but firmly pushed him into an ambulance and drove off.

Evidently Mussolini thought he was being whisked away to safety owing to some assassination attempt, and it was only at journey's end when he was marched into a prison cell that the truth dawn on him. No one informed him of what was happening.

What was happening was a coup d'état. Army troops surrounded government buildings and Blackshirt barracks in every town in Italy as per Ambrosio's orders. Ruggiero rushed the remainder of his Sardinian Grenadiers Division to Rome. The Carabinieri began arresting known supporters of Mussolini. The rank and file did this in ignorance of the reason.

On the evening radio news everyone learned the reason, that Mussolini had 'resigned' and the king had named Marshal Badoglio as the new prime minister. The king assured the people and the armed forces and of course the Germans that the war against the Allies would continue. The Italian people flooded the streets at once, then linked arms and marched down the avenues of their hometowns singing and laughing and cheering, and jeering at the Fascists. They did not know if Il Duce had really resigned or had been arrested, but he was gone and that is what mattered. When they encountered hometown Fascist bigwigs and Blackshirts they responded with insults, spat upon them, jostled and beat them to the ground. In several instances Blackshirts fired on the crowds from windows. Some Fascists shot themselves.

One of Badoglio's first orders was that all Blackshirts and their units would henceforth be inducted into the army. The legions serving with the army's infantry divisions would become regiments numbered in the 300 series. The Mussolini Armored Division was renamed Centauro II and Major General Calvi di Bergolo the king's son in law was ordered to command it.

General Enrico Galbiati, commander of the Blackshirts, ordered his men to fire upon the army's troops outside his Rome headquarters, but he was soon talked into surrendering.

Come dawn the streets were still filled with forty-three million joyous people. No one had slept. They sang songs long forbidden by the Fascists and tore down emblems of Fascist power, ripping down banners and posters, daubing friezes with paint and toppling giant statues of Mussolini. They smashed, scarred, disfigured, wrecked, cut, sliced, marred, pounded and pulverized until they were exhausted. Political prisoners were liberated from the jails.

Naturally Badoglio had to restore discipline and order at once, and at first his methods appeared acceptable. After all the workers had to go back to their factories, and instead of attacking the Blackshirt flak gunners the people should have allowed them to continue to peer at the skies. There was a war to be fought. Most important of all Badoglio had to reassure the Germans that they still had a partner. There was obviously a lot of tension among the Blackshirts. How should they react to Mussolini's arrest/resignation? Ironically the Fascist propaganda that had claimed that Mussolini, the Fascist Party and the Blackshirts were all one and the same had convinced most people that this was the truth. Many army officers expected Blackshirts to come out shooting at any moment. But the truth was that the higher one's rank in the Blackshirts the less one trusted the Fascist Party or Mussolini. Most Blackshirt generals were glad to see the back of him. As for the rank and file Fascist Party members, the fact that the Fascist Grand Council had fired Mussolini the day before his arrest suggested to many that the Fascist leadership was involved in his removal. [They were not.] To be true Mussolini had his supporters, but few of these Mussolini-ists had any power or prestige.

So the police and Carabinieri went into the streets and good naturedly asked the revelers to disperse. So far so good.

Chapter Forty-eight
Seeking an Exit

Upon hearing of Mussolini's overthrow General Eisenhower the commander of Allied forces in the Western Mediterranean called off all air raids on mainland Italy for one day as a message to the new Italian government. Badoglio took this as a sign that the Allies might negotiate rather than continue their demand for unconditional surrender. Eisenhower was going out on a limb here, as he had done when allowing Sicilian POWs to go home, and now he formally asked his superiors if he could offer the Italians a compromise peace. Anthony Eden, Britain's foreign secretary, and a rabid anti-Italian, convinced Churchill and Roosevelt to stay firm and offer nothing.

Badoglio did not know this. But he had more immediate worries. Now that Mussolini was imprisoned and his Fascists knocked off balance, the long-dormant Communists, Socialists and Christian Democrats began pestering Badoglio to make a decision about Italy's future. Those who knew him well knew exactly where he stood politically: he was a Badoglio-ist. His choice of cabinet astounded everyone. Not one member was an anti-Fascist or even anti-Mussolini. In fact many had been members of Mussolini's cabinet including Domenico Romano, Leopoldo Piccardi, General Carlo Favagrossa a veteran of Spain, and Brigadier General Antonio Sorice. The latter had been undersecretary of War and would now become the new Minister of War. Others were high profile Fascists such as Gaetano Azzariti, the chief of the anti-Jewish trials who would now be Minister of Justice; and Guido Rocco, Director of the Fascist Press, who would now be Minister of Popular Culture; and Giovanni Acanfora, the Director of the Bank of Italy, who would be Minister of Exchange and Currency. Rear Admiral Raffaele de Courten was promoted to Minister of the Navy, and Major General Renato Sandalli, who had become a hero after bombing helpless Ethiopian tribesmen, was named Minister of Air.

The public could not understand that Badoglio was performing a dangerous high-wire act. He needed the Fascists, because they were the only ones with experience over the last twenty-one years in controlling the civil service, finances, media, education and courts. In any case his cabinet was window dressing. He had no intention of consulting them on major issues. Furthermore, he placed trusted supporters in positions that held the real power: the national police, the various city police forces, the Carabinieri and units of the armed forces. To keep the OVRA secret police happy and busy he gave them new tasks.

He also needed to keep the Germans off balance. Hitler, he knew, was eager to take over the country. To counter the German reinforcements coming into Italy, Badoglio ordered General Vercellino of the Fourth Army in France to send him two divisions at once.

All was quiet on the streets. A dusk to dawn curfew was in force, and every community was patrolled by police, Carabinieri and soldiers with orders to prevent gatherings and arrest anyone caught without identity papers. All meetings were banned. All front doors were to remain unlocked. All private cars were immobilized. Freedom of speech was outlawed and any violators were to be tried by military courts martial. Anyone resisting arrest could be shot dead on the spot.

The great irony was that at no time had Mussolini ever introduced such draconian laws. In other words the Italian people had leapt gleefully out of the frying pan into the fire.

In Turin workers gathered to voice their complaints. General Enrico Adami-Rossi ordered his troops to fire on them. They did, and the result was a mass scampering of hundreds of workers, but they left behind eight of their comrades lying still on the ground and scores writhing in the agony of their wounds. In Reggio Emilia soldiers killed nine demonstrators and wounded others. In Bari Blackshirts killed twenty-three demonstrators and wounded sixty. In Florence eleven demonstrators were shot. In La Spezia two were killed and eleven wounded. Some suspected Italy was drifting towards civil war.

However, there were far more demonstrations than these and in most cases the local authorities refused to open fire. Badoglio dismissed Major General Salvi because he dispersed a mob in Savona by talking rather than shooting.

Mussolini knew none of this. On the 28th he was secretly taken to the island of Ponza and placed under house arrest, oddly enough in the same building that Mussolini had once used to hold an Ethiopian general under house arrest.

Those members of the grand council that had voted against Mussolini were in fear of their lives. In the first few days of Badoglio's tyrannical rule his police arrested eight hundred and fifty Fascists, but these were all small fry. Most of the important Fascists were still in power especially in the provinces. The pope was pleading that Badoglio not harm them. Of course the pope did not plead for the lives of demonstrating workers.

In any case Badoglio knew there was more than one way to skin a Fascist. All Italian males had a military obligation up to the age of 54. Most older men held essential jobs or had health problems and therefore had not been called up. There was never enough equipment for those who were called in any case. Badoglio took advantage of this and began to send conscription orders to many leading Fascists sending them off to war.

But Badoglio considered the Germans to be the greatest threat. On the day after Mussolini's fall some Germans in Yugoslavia disarmed neighboring Italians. It was obvious that Hitler had issued orders to prepare to disarm the Italians and these particular Germans had jumped the gun. On 30 July the German 44th Jaeger Division and 163rd Mountain Brigade entered Italy through the Brenner Pass and the 76th and 305th Divisions entered from France all without permission from Badoglio. These were all new formations and well equipped. Reports reached Badoglio that many Germans were behaving like conquerors: e. g. insisting that Italian retailers accept German money. Ambrosio, still military chief of Comando Supremo, formally complained to Kesselring.

Lieutenant General Alessandro Gloria commander of XXXV Corps in the South Tyrol (Alto Adige) reported that the local people, most of whom were ethnic Austrians, cheered the arriving Germans.

The war was still on, of course, and in Sicily Germans and Italians were fighting as one, or at least that was the propaganda message. In fact by late July they were each fighting their own war. At the front two thirds of the Aosta Division were in reserve at Troina, and on the north coast a mixed force of Livorno and Aosta troops held the front line. Elsewhere the front was held exclusively by Germans.

To placate Hitler Ambrosio had agreed that all Italian forces in Sicily should now come under German command. This decision stuck in his throat, because he was angry at German claims of Italian cowardice and German courage. Like all bigotry these claims were nonsense. On 31 July the fresh German 923rd Battalion entered the line, only to run away a few hours later! At sea Italian sailors continued to exhibit great bravery. The submarine Micca was sunk by the British submarine Trooper.

On 1 August at Troina in Sicily the Germans beat back three US battalions. During the fight the Aosta troops in reserve came under artillery fire. Patton's Americans were now pressing the Italians and Germans from the west with Gaffey's 2nd Armored, Allen's 1st, Truscott's 3rd, Eddy's 9th, Ryder's 34th and Middleton's 45th Divisions. Montgomery's Eighth Army was pressing the Germans from the south with Major General Evered Poole's new South African 6th Armored Division, Simmonds' Canadian 1st Division, and the following British divisions: Evelegh's 6th Armored, Berney-Ficklin's 5th, Kirkman's 50th, Wimberley's 51st and the fresh 78th. Poole had fought in North Africa for two years. Perhaps the South African Major General Dan Pienaar would have taken this new division, but he was killed in a plane crash.

On 1 August the German 1st SS Panzer, 24th Panzer and 65th Divisions entered Italy through the Brenner Pass, again without permission. This evening coastal settlements in the toe of Italy were bombarded by five Allied cruisers and ten destroyers.

On 2 August at Troina the Germans stopped Patton, who had attacked with one Moroccan and six American battalions. Following this the Germans and the Aosta troops in their immediate rear were blasted by one hundred and sixty-five Allied field guns.

On the 3rd Patton threw one Moroccan and twelve American battalions against Troina. Guzzoni knew the Germans would crack open soon, so he ordered Rear Admiral Pietro Barone to begin preparations for an evacuation of all Italian uniformed personnel from Sicily to mainland Italy. Within hours the Germans also began evacuating non-essential personnel.

On 4 August the Germans fell back from Catania, and typically they did not bother to inform neighboring Italian units. Suddenly an Italian ad hoc force, coddled together by Major Bolla of the Napoli Division, found itself under assault. He told his men to make their own way to the rear and to ignore the Allied artillery, naval bombardments and air raids, an order easier given than obeyed.

On the morning of the 5th the German defenders of Troina pulled out. This day a heavy Allied air raid struck Naples, crippling the destroyer Pallade. This evening the light cruisers Raimondo Montecuccoli and Eugenio di Savoia sailed to raid the Allies, but they were sighted, and rather than risk ambush they entered port at La Maddalena Island off Sardinia.

On 6 August representatives of OKW (German High Command) met with Comando Supremo at Tarvisio. Both Italian and German generals made plans to defend Italy. Both declared an intention to fight together to the bitter end. Both were lying through their teeth and both knew it.

Even street peddlers in Italy knew that the most northern landing site for an Allied invasion of mainland Italy had to be the Gulf of Salerno, owing to the short range of Allied fighters now based in Sicily. The Allied admirals would not sail beyond fighter cover. But Badoglio reinforced Gloria's corps on the Austrian border! Soon eight Italian divisions would be north of - and three northwest of - the Po River, and one was at Florence just south of the Po, and three were around Rome. Yet where the Italians expected the Allies to land Badoglio had only placed two divisions to reinforce the local coastal units. It was obvious Badoglio had a secret agenda.

The Germans claimed to be rushing southwards to meet the Allies, but were moving so leisurely they were in fact strung out along the length of the Italian boot. The Italian people did not have any illusions. The Italian dispositions suggested Badoglio expected to be attacked from Austria not from the sea. The German dispositions suggested they intended to fight the Italians not the Anglo-Americans.

Rear Admiral Franco Maugeri, the Chief of Naval Intelligence, personally took Mussolini to La Maddalena Island and imprisoned him there.

On 7 August the light cruisers Giuseppe Garibaldi and Duca d'Aosta attempted to attack the Allies, but retired when they ran into a fog bank. Without radar they could not see into it, whereas Allied warships had radar. This night Allied bombers hit Genoa, Milan and Turin causing widespread destruction. The next day they bombed Genoa again, sinking the destroyer Freccia. On 9 August off La Spezia the destroyer Gioberti (1600 tons) was sunk by a submarine.

On the 9th General Roatta, still commander of the Italian Army, ordered all Italian personnel in Sicily to embark on ships at Messina and sail across the narrow strait to Italy. Already ships had embarked the wounded and sick and seven thousand rear-echelon troops. Rear Admiral Pietro Barone and Brigadier General Ettore Monacci, who were given responsibility for the evacuation, did not relish the task. Their problems seemed insurmountable. Though the strait was so narrow – three miles - that individual buildings could be discerned on the far shore, it would still require ships. Barone began to confiscate anything that floated: boats, coasters, trawlers, tugs, transports, lighters, ferries and barges. In such confined waters they would be fish in a barrel to Allied pilots. Furthermore the Allied fleet could sail up the straits and sink anything they wanted to. This could become the greatest slaughter in Italian history. Furthermore, the Sicilian port of Messina was a mess as months of bombing had rendered it useless, and eleven partially sunk ships blocked the harbor entrance.

On the bright side for Barone, there were plenty of German and Italian flak gunners on both sides of the straits and there were some Italian shore batteries: specifically several batteries of light 3inch and medium 4inch, plus two batteries of heavy 152mm (6inch), four batteries of very heavy 170mm, and four batteries of massive 280mm (11.2inch).

On 9 and 10 August the Germans sent across the straits four thousand four hundred and eighty-nine of their sick and wounded, and eight thousand six hundred and fifteen other troops, three thousand one hundred and sixty-two vehicles, four hundred and forty-six metric tons of ammunition, five hundred and twenty-seven metric tons of fuel and five thousand one hundred and fifty-five metric tons of equipment and provisions. The Italian records were later lost, but it can be reasonably assumed that the Italian figures were similar to the German. This is startling when one considers that during these two days the Straits of Messina were under air attack from one thousand two hundred and eighty-seven Allied warplanes!

On 12 August Castellano approached Ambrosio with the idea that he be allowed to bear an olive branch to the Allies. Ambrosio knew that Badoglio had already sent emissaries to the Allies, but he wondered if the Allies believed them. Castellano assured Ambrosio that he could dodge German spies, reach the Allies and convince them of Badoglio's sincerity. Ambrosio dismissed the thought that

Castellano might be just another boastful Sicilian, and he agreed to let him go, but he sent Franco Montanari with him, who was not only Badoglio's nephew, but also half-American and a Harvard man.

That night five hundred and four bombers attacked Milan, smashing the Alfa-Romeo plant and flattening La Scala Opera House. More than a thousand Milanese were killed or wounded. This night one hundred and fifty bombers smote Turin.

The following day Rome's air raid sirens blared, her flak guns opened fire and bombs fell. The next night one hundred and forty bombers returned to Milan. A futile victory occurred off Corsica when the corvette Minerva sank a British submarine.

Castellano and Montanari had intended to travel by train from Italy into France then to Spain and Portugal, but owing to a train re-routing they ended up in Madrid the Spanish capital, so they used their initiative and visited the British ambassador to Spain Sir Samuel Hoare. Officially neutral, Spain was a de facto Axis nation. Italian underwater swimmers were using Spanish soil as a base from which they swam to Gibraltar with small mines and to date they had sunk eleven ships there. Spanish troops were fighting on the Russian front. If the Spaniards realized what Castellano and Montanari were up to, they would arrest them and hand them over to the Germans.

On 15 August in Bologna near some bomb ruins General Roatta, his deputy Lieutenant General Francesco Rossi and his aide General Giacomo Zanussi, met with General Alfred Jodl, Chief of OKW Operations, and Field Marshal Erwin Rommel, who had just been appointed commander of all German forces in Northern Italy. Roatta pleaded for German reinforcements to come to Italy to fight the Allies. This took the Germans aback, for up to now the Italians had been complaining every time another German soldier entered Italy. Roatta was sincere in his plea, which was supported by Badoglio, and did not realize he had been duped by Badoglio. Badoglio's request for reinforcements was just a ruse to gain more time. Moreover, Badoglio had a new idea. He did not want to surrender to the Allies, but he did want to fight the Germans by seizing control of the Brenner Pass and then disarming the Germans in Italy!

Despite his surprise, Jodl was fooled by this request, and he agreed at once to send more Germans and even gave his approval for the Italian Fourth Army in France to transfer three more divisions to Italy.

That night two hundred bombers pummeled Milan.

Meanwhile the naval evacuation of Sicily had been completed. Between the morning of the 11th and the 17th of August 1943 the Germans embarked another forty-one thousand six hundred and nineteen troops, six thousand six hundred and twenty-seven vehicles, forty-eight tanks, one hundred and sixty-three guns and twelve thousand five hundred and thirty-seven metric tons of equipment, fuel, supplies and ammunition. During this same period without any coordination with the Germans, the Italians evacuated sixty-two thousand personnel, two hundred and twenty-seven vehicles, forty-one guns and several thousand tons of supplies. They would have brought more vehicles, but the Germans had stolen them at gunpoint!

In spite of having fallen out of love, both Axis partners had performed wonders. It is true that sixteen German and Italian vessels were sunk, but not one Italian soldier was lost while afloat. Barone and Monacci and their staffs could only surmise that the largest concentration of flak guns ever seen in the Mediterranean was enough to keep Allied planes from taking careful aim, for in two weeks the gunners had only shot down thirty-one planes.

Allied warships had decided not to risk facing the array of Italian shore guns in the straits, and only on the night of the 15th did they come close enough to shell Messina. At dawn on the 17th Monacci and a small party of Italian engineers were the last Axis troops to leave Sicily. Allied infantry were nowhere to be seen, though their artillery was already shelling mainland Italy.

The evacuation itself was a victory. It was Italy's 'Dunkirk'. And much was owed to the Italian shore gunners and flak gunners, fighter pilots and sailors and planning staff. The Germans told the world they had evacuated Sicily because the Italians had fled the island. Actually the Italians were the last to leave. True to form the British believed the Nazis and disbelieved the Italians, because it fit their perceptions of the Italians. Furthermore had it not been for the Italian coastal gunners and flak gunners remaining at their posts, none of the Germans would have got out. Moreover, most of these Italian gunners were Blackshirts.

But there was no disguising the fact that the Sicily land campaign was a massive defeat for Italy. Not only was Sicily with its valuable agriculture and ports and naval bases and airfields and people lost, but the Allies gained them to use as a stepping stone to mainland Italy. The Italian military losses were horrendous: over two hundred and twenty-six thousand uniformed personnel were missing. As the Allies claimed to have captured one hundred and thirty-seven thousand, it must be assumed that about eighty-six thousand must have doffed their uniforms and melted into the civilian population, and perhaps as many as three thousand had been killed. Of those registered by the Allies as prisoners of war, thirty-four thousand were Sicilians and were soon paroled to go home. Eisenhower was a man of his word.

On August 16 the US freighter Benjamin Contee, transporting Italian prisoners, was torpedoed by a U-boat. She did not sink, but the explosion killed two hundred and sixty-four Italians and wounded one hundred and forty-two.

Chapter Forty-nine
Countdown

As the last troops left Sicily Badoglio ordered Dino Grandi to go to Spain in secret to contact the Allies. Grandi felt honored, yet could not help but be suspicious. He was right to be. Badoglio was in fact using him as a decoy, hoping the Spanish police would recognize him and arrest him.

All Italians would have been quite hurt in the pride department had they known that the Allies had no intention of actually invading Italy. Only some of the British were eager, especially Churchill, because the narrow Italian boot would allow only a few divisions to participate, and Churchill did not want to put too many of his divisions in harms way, hoping to hold down casualties. He preferred to wage war on the cheap, the way the British had done during the Napoleonic conflicts and the Crimean War, and he went one bit further, namely preferring to use non-British infantry if possible, and even sending in Black Africans and Indians before risking actual Brits. The British people like other white imperialist nations of the day did not really even count the deaths of 'foreigners' in their service, let alone care about them. Between June 1940 and late 1941 not one infantry division raised in Britain had gone into action. Ostensibly Churchill wanted to keep actual British troops home in case of a German invasion, and while that excuse may have held water in summer 1940, it certainly had no substance once Hitler invaded Russia in June 1941. And when the Japanese attacked the British and Americans in December 1941 Churchill only sent one actual British infantry division to help the Americans battle the Japanese Empire.

A much better reason for Churchill's strategy was that within the vast British Empire and the British Commonwealth, only the residents of Britain and Northern Ireland could vote in a British election! The others could not vote, so their attitude towards casualties was irrelevant.

By August 1943 the Americans had only been in the war twenty months, whereas the British had been at war for four years. During this time seventeen divisions raised in Britain had seen combat. But seventeen US divisions had seen action in the previous twelve months! In fact eight divisions recruited in Britain had already been disbanded! Another two had surrendered. In spring 1940 the British had twenty-two divisions recruited in Britain and ready for action against the Germans. Over the next eighteen months they gained more enemies: Italy, France and Japan. Yet by August 1943 after an extra three years of recruiting from the 18-45 age group they had only twenty-one divisions. In other words in net divisional terms their army had shrunk. Only an increasing reliance on independent brigades rather than divisions gave the British a ground combat manpower capability similar to that of early 1940. By contrast almost ninety divisions raised in Italy had seen action in the last three years.

It is true that in the early part of the war British troops made up a third or more of the Indian Army divisions, but as the Indian Army recruited to meet the Japanese threat fewer Britons were assigned to their divisions. The British found that after providing their war factories, air force, navy, home guard and merchant fleet with sufficient manpower there was not enough left to make a major contribution on the ground. Frankly one cannot help suspect that the British allocation of manpower was badly managed. Even Churchill complained when the coal mines confiscated two hundred thousand recently conscripted soldiers! Furthermore throughout the war many thousands of British troops were stationed in backwaters. Even in Britain they were often given 'busy work', such as hanging paintings in museums. And this while units at the front were desperate for replacements. When the Home Guard was formed in Britain of teenage boys and men over 45 it required a cadre of regulars to whip them into shape, and after two years they were pretty efficient, yet most of the cadre was never sent back to the regulars.

One of the reasons for a shortage of British warm bodies at the front was the health classification system introduced by their army in 1939. 'A' meant one could be sent anywhere to do anything, but 'B' meant one could not be sent into combat, and 'C' meant one could not be sent outside of Britain. Theoretically this should have meant that men normally unfit for military service could be put into uniform to 'do their bit'. But it did not work that way. Serving soldiers healthy enough to fight Arabs in Palestine in 1939 were sent home because they were not healthy enough to fight Germans in France. Hitler also badly managed his manpower, initially limiting his infantry to men under age thirty-six, but military necessity brought an end to that idea. Roosevelt also handled his recruitment badly. Despite Pearl Harbor so few Americans aged eighteen to twenty volunteered that he had to resort to conscripting them, but the recruitment doctors rejected a high percentage of recruits on laughably flimsy grounds. Mussolini was even more guilty of maladministration, drafting some men as old as fifty-three, while twenty-five year-olds were sitting at home without a job!

As a result of the manpower crunch Churchill was convinced that the British Army would be hard put to wage open warfare in France. The adventurous side of him was as willing as the Americans to fight there, but his practical side knew better. Churchill had actually fought in the French trenches in World War I. He knew what a mincing machine it could become.

The Americans could of course afford to wage war in Italy, for most of their divisions had yet to see action. Manpower was not a problem. But they did not believe the gain would be worth the fight! They were fixated on invading France. They didn't give a damn about liberating the French, it was just that it was on the road to Berlin, they said. There were no Alps between France and Germany. There were Alps between Italy and Germany. Therefore, the preparation they seemed to be making to invade Italy was a bluff.

———————

As part of the bluff Allied bombers hit Turin again, damaging the Fiat works. This attack brought about an anti-war strike by the workers, who this time did not disguise their motives. Badoglio's troops soon arrived and dispersed them with gunfire.

Interestingly enough the ordinary German soldiers coming to Italy sincerely thought they were here to help the Italians and they began setting up coastal defenses. On August 18 they created the Gulf of Salerno Defensive Zone, which would be guarded by the new Tenth Army of Colonel General Heinrich von Viettinghoff. He was a veteran panzer commander with experience in Poland, France and Russia. His combat units were those Germans that had recently evacuated from Sicily.

Meanwhile Badoglio began shifting his balance. He gave Carboni his old job back at military intelligence. This was a strong indication that Badoglio was making an overture to the Allies – the half-American Carboni was known to be anti-Nazi.

———————

After meeting with Hoare in Madrid, Castellano and Montanari moved on to Lisbon, dodging German agents. There they met British Brigadier Kenneth Strong and American Major General Walter Bedell-Smith, Eisenhower's intelligence chief and chief of staff, respectively. The four were in civilian clothes, not wishing to alert the Portuguese police.

It was soon obvious to Castellano that the Allies thought Italy was about to surrender, but what Castellano was authorized to offer was not a capitulation, but an alliance, so that together they could destroy the Germans in Italy. Both Allied emissaries were surprised, and they concluded this would have to be dealt with at a much higher level.

On 20 August on Badoglio's orders the Carabinieri arrested General Soddu, but the king thought this an unwise move, and feeling his oats now he ordered Soddu's release. This angered Badoglio, who ordered Soddu's re-arrest. The Carabinieri could be forgiven for thinking the power struggle in Rome was not yet over.

Badoglio ordered General Giacomo Zanussi to join Castellano in his talks, and as a sign of good faith he was to take an Allied prisoner of war with him, British Lieutenant General Sir Adrian Carton de Wiart, who had been captured by the Italians.

On 21 August the Carabinieri arrested Ettore Muti, a leading Fascist. Not willing to risk the king's interference again, Badoglio had Muti murdered in a poorly played out 'ambush by unknown assailants'. This was a sad end for Muti. Whether one agreed with his politics or not, he had been a gallant warrior, who had earned fifteen medals for bravery. The Carabinieri and police now began stepping up their arrests of leading Fascists, taking into custody Achille Starace, Giuseppe Bottai, Antonio Tringali-Casanova, Blackshirt General Attilio Teruzzi, Blackshirt General Enrico Galbiati and others. They even arrested Clara Petacci, Mussolini's current mistress, but not his wife Donna Rachele.

Ciano was in a bind. He had voted against Mussolini in the council meeting, so he could expect no support from those loyal to Il Duce, but he was still the dictator's son-in-law, so he could expect no support from Badoglio, and as he was still a leading Fascist he could expect no support from the anti-Fascists. So he asked the Germans to help him escape to Spain. He evidently did not realize the Germans had been trying to get rid of him for years. Promising to fly him and his family to Spain, the Germans redirected the aircraft in mid-flight to land in Germany, where he was arrested by the Gestapo.

On 28 August while the 640ton destroyer Lince was sinking from a British submarine's torpedo, General Zanussi was being taken to Algiers by the Allies, supposedly to meet Eisenhower. But once there he was ignored. The Americans had no intention of fighting in Italy with or without the Italians at their side.

Moreover, the Italian offer to hand over several German divisions to the Allies on a silver platter seemed too good to be true. Long used to Fascist lies, many of the Allied leaders could not believe this was a genuine offer. They sensed a gigantic trap. The Americans did not trust the Italians, believing they were all Fascists. The British did not trust the Italians, because they were Italians. However, a few American and British officers and diplomats were willing to take a chance the offer was in good faith, and they urged Eisenhower to meet Castellano in Sicily.

On 29 August Standartenfuehrer Otto Skorzeny and his team of SS commandos raided La Maddalena to rescue Mussolini. They found the house empty. Hitler demanded they continue to search for Il Duce.

Meanwhile with the use of secret coded telegrams Badoglio learned that Castellano might pull off the deal after all. Badoglio surmised that Hitler's other partners wanted out of the war too, and Italy's defection from the Axis might bring about an end to the war completely. After all, the previous day the Danish government had tried to get out of the war, and combat was now taking place between Danish and German forces! An invasion of Italy by, say, fifteen Allied divisions while at the same moment the Italians turned against the Germans should bring about a swift collapse of German forces in

Italy. The Allies had invaded Sicily with fifteen divisions, so surely this was not beyond their capability?

On the 31st Castellano, Montanari and Zanussi were finally united and they met Allied representatives in Sicily, and here they became ecstatic to hear that the Allies had suddenly stopped playing hard to get and would accept their proposal. The Allies agreed to invade Italy with fifteen divisions and give Badoglio dates and times and locations of the assaults.

Unknown to these three Italians, the Allies did not have fifteen infantry divisions to spare. Two British and two US divisions were already preparing to leave the Mediterranean for Britain. This left the Allies with twenty infantry divisions in the entire Mediterranean, but that was for all eventualities, and obviously some had to be left in reserve. Furthermore the Allies did not possess sufficient shipping to land that many. Many of the ships and landing craft used in the Sicily invasion were already on their way to Britain. Nonetheless the Allies were willing to lie to the Italians. Indeed if it meant turning the Italians against the Germans, the Allies would have promised the second coming of the Messiah.

Informed of the Allied acceptance, Badoglio now laid other conditions on the conference table through his secret telegrams. E.g. he wanted guarantees of Italy's sovereignty after the war. General Alexander became tired of this horse-trading and he informed the three emissaries that if they did not sign the existing agreement now he would order his air forces to destroy Rome. The three called Alexander's bluff, saying they had to confer with Badoglio first. They knew they were taking a chance. Just a few weeks earlier the British Royal Air Force had destroyed the German city of Hamburg, burning alive fifty thousand civilians!

At dawn on 3 September 1943 the largest British artillery barrage of the war to date blasted holes in the toe of Italy, firing from Sicily. The British 5th Division then crossed the narrow straits. As the Brits set foot on mainland Europe, thousands of Italian soldiers and civilians charged towards them - to join them!

The Regia Aeronautica was still full of fight, however, and Italian planes bombed the invaders. Italian airmen shot down four Spitfires, but three Italian bombers were shot down, one of them piloted by Major Giuseppe Cenni. He had earned fame flying in the Spanish Civil War, and was regarded as a great test pilot, and had been the man responsible for convincing Mussolini to buy Stukas from Germany. He was just twenty-eight years old at the time of his death.

The British invasion of the toe of Italy was a feint designed to draw German forces away from the Gulf of Salerno, but the Germans did not take the bait.

Almost within earshot of the bombardment Castellano in Sicily received a telegram from Badoglio agreeing to the Allied terms.

Therefore, he signed for Italy. Bedell-Smith signed for the Allies. Unknown to Castellano, Eisenhower was supposed to have signed, but this amiable shy American had morals and he always kept his word, and knowing that the Allied promises were just so much hot air he refused to be party to such a despicable trick. He knew the Allies had no intention of abiding by the details, the letter or even the spirit of their agreement. Castellano asked if the Allies would invade at Salerno. No answer. "On the 18th", he asked? He received silent cold stares from everyone.

The Germans saw evidence of Badoglio's betrayal - Badoglio and his senior officers began sending their relatives to neutral Switzerland; not one Italian unit was moving towards the British invasion beachhead in the toe of Italy; known Fascist officers were being reassigned or arrested. On the other hand the Italian air and naval forces were still fighting the Allies. On 5 September Admiral de Courten sent twenty-two submarines to the north of Sicily to seek the impending invasion fleet. Surely, the Germans thought, the Italians would not make a deal with the Allies and then endanger it by sinking an Allied troopship?

But Castellano had informed Badoglio that the invasion was set for 18 at the earliest, so Badoglio could afford to keep his submarines at sea for several more days without risking an encounter.

On 6 September the Allies warned Badoglio to be ready to receive an important message after 9am the next day and also told him that the BBC World Service radio would broadcast in an agreed code when the invasion was imminent. The secret Italian alliance had removed all American obstacles to their participation in the invasion of Italy. It would be a cake walk, the British claimed.

Badoglio told Carboni to have his radio listening teams monitor the BBC constantly. Carboni told him he suspected the Allies would come earlier than the 18th. He also told Badoglio that some Italian troops might not fight the Germans. He was especially concerned about the Blackshirts. The new Centauro II and Littorio II Armored Divisions were manned by Blackshirts. Additionally some known Fascists were still in positions of power. The new commander of the Sardinian Grenadiers Division, Major General Gioacchino Solinas, was a fervent Fascist.

There was also a good possibility that those Italians who resisted the Germans might be defeated. General Ugo Tabellini of the Piave Division complained of a lack of equipment and spare parts, as did Major General Raffaele Cadorna, commander of the new Ariete II Armored Division. The Ariete's reconnaissance battalion [Montebello Lancers] was issued with Lancia 269 armored cars armed with a 47mm gun. The division's 135th Armored Regiment had some

Semoventi 75s and a few of the new 45P, a good tank armed with a 75mm gun, but most of the division's tanks were obsolete M13s and M14s. The divisional artillery was not yet fully formed and still had light 75mm field guns, and had yet to receive its full complement of 105mm guns.

Carboni also reminded Badoglio that the region's flak gunners were Blackshirts. He was obviously worried about a civil war breaking out and he was getting cold feet. Badoglio's next order did not make him feel any better. He ordered Carboni to welcome an American agent and help him organize an airborne drop on Rome.

On 7 September Carboni went to see Ambrosio, but learned the general was out of town on 'personal business'. He informed Ambrosio's deputy, General Francesco Rossi, that he could not possibly receive an American parachute drop yet.

On the afternoon of 7 September the Allied invasion fleet was sighted. Obviously Anglo-American forces would be landing in a few days. The Germans instituted defensive plans at once. The new 16th Panzer Division moved to the coast at Salerno to reinforce the Italian 222nd Coastal Division. The Italian soldiers were glad to see the Germans come up right behind them. Badoglio wondered if this armada was a feint, for he was still waiting for that secret message he was promised, and the BBC had not broadcast the code words yet.

This evening Rear Admiral Franco Maugeri took the corvette Ibis to a rendezvous at sea, where he met a British MTB. There he exchanged ten Italian hostages for two Americans, Brigadier General Maxwell Taylor and Colonel William T. Gardner. Once docked, the two uniformed Americans were driven to Rome. This night Naples was under a terrific pounding by bombers. Obviously the Allies wanted to remind Badoglio who the senior partner was in this new alliance.

This evening the submarine Valella was sunk by the British submarine Shakespeare.

At Comando Supremo headquarters the Italian staff was embarrassed by the appearance of the two Americans. Carboni began to vent his fears in front of them – he had no fuel, no ammunition, no spare parts, not enough good tanks, too many Fascists, too many Germans etc. What shocked the Americans was not what he said, but how he said it. They certainly recognized the fear in the man. He was half-American, so there was no mistranslation of his words. Then it was the turn of the Americans to shock Carboni. They told him the airborne drop was scheduled for the very next day!

Carboni rushed to see Badoglio, taking Taylor with him. The Prime Minister was incensed that he had not been alerted about the invasion. Where was the secret message he had been promised?

Where was the BBC code? He sent off a telegram insisting the Allies put off the attack for several days.

The Italian people knew nothing of the great crossroads that their fortunes had reached. On the morning of 8 September Italian warplanes were still taking off to attack the invaders in the toe of Italy. Flak gunners in the cities scanned the skies for Allied bombers. Italian sentries in Yugoslavia, Albania, Greece and Corsica were alert in case of guerilla attack. The navy was no longer safe in its own harbors, and shipboard flak gunners had to be ever wary even when in port. The coastal defenses were in a quandary. On the one hand they had no ambition to risk their lives for the new Prime Minister Badoglio, any more than they had been willing to do so for Mussolini, nor did they appreciate having to join with the hated 'Tedeschi' - Germans. Many of the older troops had fought the Germans in World War I. Yet the people looked to them to keep out the invaders. The soldiers of the 222nd Coastal Division at Salerno were glad to have the 16th Panzer Division at their backs, but they also had the odd feeling that the German guns were aimed at them. The aristocratic commander of the 222nd, Major General Don Ferrante Gonzaga del Vodice, was uneasy having to work with the Germans. Not only was he not a friend of the Nazis, but he was racially Jewish.

To the south of Salerno the Italian Sixth Army that had evacuated from Sicily was retreating northwards from the toe. Its main units were the Aosta, Assietta, Livorno and Napoli Divisions. The few Germans on the road with them were sullen and uncommunicative. Their coastal flanks were secure as they were protected by the Italian Seventh Army, now commanded by Lieutenant General Mario Arisio, with its 24th, 210th, 212th and 227th Coastal Divisions and the 31st Coastal Brigade, and they would soon reach a defense line manned by the Piceno, Mantova and Legnano Divisions. Of these three only the Legnano had fought in battle [Greece] and was now commanded by Major General Vincenzo Dapino, who was known to be anti-Fascist. These divisions did not have Blackshirt elements.

Between Salerno and Rome and ready to defend Rome were ten divisions: the Centauro II Armored, Ariete II Armored, Littorio II Armored, Piave, Piacenza, Pasubio, Sassari, Re and Sardinian Grenadiers. The three armored divisions had many Blackshirts and the latter four divisions had Blackshirt elements. Of these ten divisions only the Sassari, Re, Sardinian Grenadiers and Pasubio had seen action [in Yugoslavia and the Pasubio in Russia too], but the Pasubio was still rebuilding from its Russian adventure and was full of new recruits.

North of Rome there were sixteen coastal divisions. In addition General Mario Caracciola di Feroleto's Fifth Army was in command in Northern and Central Italy with several divisions, including the Torino, Amedeo Duca d'Aosta Celere, Sforzesca Mountain, Tridentina Alpini, Julia Alpini, Ravenna Mountain, Cuneense Alpini, Vicenza and Cosseria which were all still rebuilding following their experience in Russia. He also had the new Novara, Ciclone [Cyclone] Parachute and Veneto Divisions. And he controlled the veteran Eugenio di Savoia Celere that had fought the Yugoslavs and Titoists, and the Pusteria Alpini, that had fought Ethiopians, French, Greeks and Titoists.

In Northwestern Italy and France was General Vercellino's depleted Fourth Army of four divisions: Emanuele Filiberto Celere that had fought Albanians, Yugoslavians and Titoists, Lupi di Toscana that had battled French and Greeks, Taro that had faced Greeks and Titoists, and the unblooded Rovigo Division. Also under Vercellino's orders was Lieutenant General Magli's VII Corps on Corsica with the Friuli and Cremona Divisions, that had both invaded France in 1940. The Friuli had also fought the Yugoslavs. The shore defenses of that island were in the hands of the 225th Coastal and 226th Coastal Divisions. Sardinia was defended by Lieutenant General Antonio Basso's XIII Corps, consisting of the Bari, Calabria, Nembo Parachute, Sabauda, 204th Coastal and 205th Coastal Divisions, and the 4th and 25th Coastal Brigades, plus a mobile gruppo and an armored gruppo. The Sabauda, named after the royal family, had last seen action in Ethiopia 1935-36. The Bari had invaded Greece. The Nembo and Calabria were unblooded. Both Corsica and Sardinia also had flak units and Carabinieri.

In Yugoslavia the Second Army of General Mario Robotti and the Ninth Army of General Lorenzo Dalmazzo controlled fifteen divisions between them and were currently in battle against the Titoists. These divisions were the Emilia, Alpi Graie Alpini, Taurinense Alpini, Perugia, Venezia, Ferrara, Messina, Marche, Murge, Bergamo, Zara, Isonzo, Macerata, Cacciatore delle Alpi and Lombardia. There were four divisions on anti-partisan duty in Albania – Puglie, Firenze, Parma and Arezzo. General Vecchiarelli's Eleventh Army had eleven divisions facing Greek partisans – Acqui Mountain, Siena, Cuneo, Regina, Brennero, Forli Mountain, Pinerolo, Piemonte, Cagliari Mountain, Casale and Modena Mountain.

By 8 September German intelligence saw conflicting evidence of Italian loyalty to the Axis cause. The Allies had bombed Naples during the night and this afternoon a massive Allied air raid struck the little inoffensive town of Frascati, population eleven thousand. Initial civil defense reports suggested that half the townsfolk had been killed or wounded. Would the Allies inflict such punishment on the Italian people if the Italians had already secretly surrendered, the Germans wondered?

This afternoon Roatta was in conference with Kesselring, the latter asking permission for the 3rd Panzergrenadier Division to drive through the streets of Rome on its way south. Roatta responded by saying he would pass on the request.

At 3pm Badoglio received a secret message from the Allies. The airborne drop had been cancelled, no doubt owing to Taylor's findings. That was the good news. The bad news was that the amphibious invasion had not been called off and would begin the following morning. Moreover the news of Badoglio's alliance with the Allies would be made public in three and a half hours' time!

Badoglio went white with shock. Already the Allies had betrayed him by not sending the required coded messages as promised. And two hundred and ten minutes was not enough time to ensure that every member of the Italian armed forces received the order to resist the Germans, without alerting the Germans. First off, he had to convince the soldiery that the Allies were coming as friends not as enemies, a reversal of three years of propaganda. Then he knew everyone would want confirmation of the orders, suspecting initially that it might be an Allied ruse. And of course it would only take one Fascist in the armed forces to warn the Germans. Only an open broadcast by Badoglio would circumvent this, but that would cause instant combat between the Italians and Germans. He set the works in motion immediately. But he knew his efforts would be futile.

In any case, the Allies were not finished betraying him, for just sixty minutes later Allied entertainment radio stations began interrupting their normal broadcasts to announce that Italy had surrendered! The cat was out of the bag now!

———————

PART FOUR
CIVIL WAR
Chapter Fifty
The Blackest Twenty-four Hours in Italian History

When German radio interception units informed Hitler of the surrender news, he did not panic. He had expected betrayal any day and was well prepared. He knew that once Mussolini was knocked out of the driver's seat, Italy would career towards the Allied side of the road. Therefore he had given to every one of his German units secret plans to disarm the nearest Italian military formation, and he informed them that they should open these sealed orders upon receipt of the single word 'Axis' and that confirmation was not necessary. Now Hitler issued the word.

Within minutes throughout the Mediterranean and Balkans German troops started up their vehicles, slammed magazines into their rifles, broke open ammunition belts for their machine guns and called for air and artillery support should it be needed.

As it was against the law for Italians to listen to Allied broadcasts, few knew of the announcement. Those who had heard it were assured by their officers it was an Allied trick. General Caracciola di Feroleto, commander of the Fifth Army, telephoned Roatta's headquarters for orders. He received none. Lieutenant General Basso in Sardinia informed his men it was a hoax: he had received no orders to the contrary. Major General Carlo Biglino commanding the Pasubio Division on the coast west of Rome equally assured his men that he had received no indication of surrender. General Lorenzo Dalmazzo commander of the Ninth Army, who had fought against the British in Egypt and lately against Titoists, telephoned Comando Supremo and was told nothing untoward was happening. Regia Aeronautica General Renato Sandalli was ordered to attend a meeting at the Royal Palace in Rome. He was in a quandary. His pilots were asking him should they take off. And if so, whom should they bomb? Sandalli was one of the few who knew the truth already, but if he alerted General Eraldo Ilari the commander of the Rome airfields, would Ilari's Blackshirt flak gunners calmly watch while the planes took off, or would they begin shooting at the planes they had once sworn to protect?

Already, smiling Germans were walking up to Italian sentries at barracks gates as if to ask directions, and then pointing their weapons at them they disarmed them. They then drove straight to the arms rooms, confiscated the weapons, and then informed the unarmed Italian soldiers in the barracks that they were now prisoners. Everywhere along the coast Germans began approaching Italian artillery gunners from their unprotected rear and arresting them. The coastal guns were dug in and could not be turned around. By ruses and tricks Italians were being arrested by the thousands.

However, the Germans were also in the process of dividing the wheat from the chaff. In Greece the Germans surrounded a unit of four thousand Italian truck drivers and asked who would join them. Three quarters agreed to serve under German orders. A quarter refused and was taken prisoner. At Ostia Colonel d'Auria and Lieutenant Colonel Bianchedi voluntarily handed their commands over to the Germans.

At 6:30pm Eisenhower went on the air to formally announce the surrender. Moreover, the wording Eisenhower used was in complete contradiction to the signed agreement. Eisenhower told the world that Italy had surrendered unconditionally. This was a bald faced lie. It was pretty obvious to Badoglio that he had been screwed. The Allies had no intention of honoring their treaty. They wanted to own Italy!

In Rome the king met with Badoglio, Admiral de Courten, Generals Sandalli, Carboni, Ambrosio and Sorice, the king's aide General Puntoni and Foreign Minister Raffaele Guariglia. Accepting the fait accomplit they decided that Badoglio should make his own broadcast. As a result at 7:45pm he announced to the Italian people that Italy was no longer at war with the Allies.

The reaction was mixed. Certainly most Italians ran into the streets to publicly celebrate. However, the Fascists took this as an unbelievable betrayal and they approached the Germans with apologies. Many offered their services. Ironically some German soldiers thought the news meant that the war was over for them too and they joined in the celebrations.

Only now did Comando Supremo issue effective orders to units, namely to refrain from attacking the Germans but to resist all attempts by the Germans to disarm them. It was still daylight as Italian troops throughout the Mediterranean began to take up defensive positions. In every town in Italy soldiers, city police, national police, Carabinieri and Blackshirts began to occupy government buildings, bridges, major road intersections, rail stations and airfields. The Sassari Division took over key installations in Rome.

The Piacenza Division asked for orders from XVII Corps, but Lieutenant General Zanghieri could not or would not offer any. At 8pm smiling members of Major General Kurt Student's German 2nd Parachute Division walked up to members of the Piacenza in the villages of Lanuvio and Albano just south of Rome and suddenly swung their Schmeisser machine pistols in the faces of the Italians before they realized what was happening. Hundreds of Italians were quickly surprised and taken captive. However, at the nearby villages of Risaro and Ardea members of the Piacenza were more alert. They opened fire on the approaching smiling Germans, who turned and fled.

Major General Edouardo Minaja, commanding the 221st Coastal Division, finally received orders from Zanghieri to resist the Germans, whereupon he sent couriers to his gun positions, but unknown to him his men were already being rounded up by the Germans. With their big guns pointing out to sea and few of them carrying personal arms the Italians were sitting ducks for panzergrenadiers.

At 9pm just north of Rome Major General Cadorna of the Ariete II Armored Division was asked by the commander of the 3rd Panzergrenadier Division if he would allow his Germans to pass through. Cadorna replied: "Negative."

At 9:45pm elements of the Sardinian Grenadiers Division in the village of Cecchignola were approached by German paratroopers. They shot back.

By this time many units of the Fifth Army were in a shooting battle with German forces, but the army commander General Caracciola di Feroleto still refused to believe it.

At 10pm with dusk falling fast the 1st Regiment of Sardinian Grenadiers at La Magliana was approached by Germans asking to be let through to Rome six miles away. The Sardinians refused. Minutes later the Germans returned and, when the Sardinians stood up to converse once more, hidden German machine gunners suddenly sprayed them with bullets. All the Sardinians opened fire and quickly drove off the Germans, but the firefight had cost the lives of thirty Sardinians.

Elsewhere near Rome other Germans tried the same trick with a Carabinieri patrol of thirty men. When the Carabinieri agreed to talk, the Germans suddenly opened fire, killing thirteen, and wounding the rest and taking them prisoner.

Germans approached the town of Marargone cautiously: Piacenza troops opened fire on them. In the short battle the Germans were ultimately successful.

At Gaeta the Hermann Goering Panzer Division asked permission to enter an Italian naval base. The sailors refused, though they knew their resistance with rifles against tanks would be suicide.

At Sassuolo Major General Ugo Ferrero ordered his troops to resist the Germans. For two hours they fought back, but when Ferrero realized he would not be rescued, and the Germans promised humane treatment for his men, the general surrendered.

In Albania General Ezio Rosi, commander of all Italian troops in the Balkans, was still trying to get clarification of orders when he was arrested by a group of visiting Germans.

The 222nd Coastal Division was bombed by Luftwaffe planes, and the dust from bomb explosions had barely cleared when panzergrenadiers overran the gun pits. They surrounded del Vodice's headquarters and demanded immediate surrender or else. The Italian general chose the 'or else', and a short fierce fight ensued. The general was soon gunned down. He had known that as a racial Jew he probably would not have lasted long in Nazi hands.

In like manner the 220th Coastal Division was overrun.

At Ciampino aircraft mechanics grabbed rifles and ferociously defended their airfield against a German attack. Their flak gunners also resisted. Some Italian fliers were Fascists, of course, and a few attacked the Allied invasion armada: four were shot down. Still other Fascist pilots attacked Italian formations. Other Italians rose into the air to bomb German formations. The flak gunners shot at everything.

By now Major General Biglino was on the telephone frantically trying to get some direction, because his Pasubio Division was under attack by the 15th Panzergrenadier Division.

Just after midnight the Sardinians in La Magliana were assaulted again, and again they drove off Hitler's elite paratroopers.

Roatta at last issued sensible orders - the Ariete II Armored Division leading with its Montebello Lancers was to advance into Rome.

No orders were coming from Badoglio. The 'hero' had run away.

At sea Italian admirals seized the moment. De Courten's orders were for all ships currently at Taranto to sail for Malta, and for all ships on the west coast to head for Bone in North Africa, and for all other ships to make it to the closest Allied port. Admiral Luigi Sansonetti, Deputy Naval Chief of Staff, ordered the cruiser Scipione and corvettes Scimitarra and Baionetta to make for the port of Pescara to pick up waiting dignitaries.

Rear Admiral Nomiss Pollone in the Corsican port of Bastia needed more provisions for his flotilla of four corvettes, twelve destroyers and small craft, but German shore batteries looked down on him. Slowly his ships got underway and sailed completely out of danger before the Germans realized what he had done. However, running away was anathema to this fighting admiral, so he ordered his ships to turn around and he blasted the German shore guns to pieces. Shortly after this Lieutenant General Magli ordered Generals Clemente Primieri and Ugo de Lorenzis to capture the port of Bastia using their Cremona and Friuli Divisions and 43rd and 60th CCNN Battalions. They moved out and before dawn they took the city from its German garrison, and now Pollone's flotilla could sail back into the harbor and resume loading provisions. However, about two hundred Blackshirts fled into the hills where they defected to the Germans and formed the '9 September Battalion'.

In the early hours of the morning of 9 September the Allied invasion began as troops of General Mark C. Clark's US Fifth Army began climbing into landing craft off Salerno. The Americans had in fact provided just two infantry divisions for the invasion – Major General Fred Walker's 36th and Major General Troy Middleton's

45th, plus rangers and a few smaller units, all packaged into Lieutenant General John Lucas' VI Corps. Clark's other corps was British – Lieutenant General Richard McCreery's X Corps of Major General John Hawkesworth's 46th Division and Major General Gerald Templer's 56th Division, plus some British, Polish and Belgian commandos. So much for the fifteen divisions promised by the Allies. Middleton, Lucas and Hawkesworth had already commanded in battle in Sicily, but Clark, Templer, McCreery and Walker were new at this!

While aboard ship the troops had heard of the surrender and most of them expected a tourist excursion. Only when coastal guns opened up on them at 1:30 am, did they realize they were in for a fight. Germans of the 16th Panzer Division were manning these shore batteries. British warships returned fire, but US warships refrained from doing so for hours, owing to very stupid orders. The invasion had started badly and it would get worse.

By dawn on the 9th it was apparent to all Italians that Badoglio had traded one war for three. The world war with some Italians fighting the Allies was still on, plus many Italians were now fighting the Germans in a new war, and most terrifying of all Italians were fighting Italians in a civil war.

Some Italians had been fighting the Fascists for years. They had fought openly with their fists, clubs, pistols and rifles in the Street War 1919-1922 when the Fascists were just one of many political camps bidding for power. Since 1922 anti-Fascists had fought in a more clandestine manner offering passive resistance. Some had joined the Republican Army in Spain in 1936 to fight Franco's Fascists. On occasion they faced Mussolini's troops on a Spanish battlefield. In 1939 some had joined the French Foreign Legion and others the British armed forces to fight Hitler's Fascists. Some had fled to the United States, and come the entrance of the USA into the war they had eagerly joined the American armed forces. By June 1943 thirteen thousand of the Italians that had been captured by the British had volunteered to leave the safety of their prison camps and serve as British Army pioneers or as Royal Navy artisans to fight Mussolini's Fascists. Of those captured by the British in Sicily three thousand had volunteered to serve the British and had been inducted.

Nonetheless all of this anti-Fascist activity prior to 8 September 1943 was not true civil war. That monstrous beast did not raise its ugly head until now, when every scenic village and populous city in Italy was suddenly turned into a battleground with brother versus brother, father against son.

Already by dawn on 9 September tens of thousands of Italian soldiers were prisoners of the Germans. Totally bewildered, they were almost suicidal. However, their depression turned to anger when they saw a few among them volunteering to work for the Germans. In everyone's eyes everyone else was a traitor. Those who turned against the Germans, their partners in this great Fascist cause, were traitors. Those who refused to obey Badoglio's orders were traitors. Those who refused to join either side and simply ran off were traitors. Others had more noble reasons to desert: namely to protect their families from arrogant roaming Germans.

However, the greatest number of Italians in uniform were still in fighting trim, and despite having no direction from above they were ready to tackle the Germans and they were also on the lookout for Fascist tricks. Fascists were now aiding the Germans by giving misinformation on the telephone, by radio, at traffic intersections and so on.

At 5:15am as the sun was rising over Rome, General Roatta ordered the entire Rome garrison to move twenty miles to Tivoli. Only the police and Carabinieri would remain to keep order. This was a sensible directive for it would take the battle away from the populated areas and relieve him of the headache of feeding the Romans, and in any case Rome had no strategic significance. He himself then left the city.

Obeying this order, Carboni put on civilian clothes and drove towards Tivoli. On the road he ran into the Centauro II Armored Division commanded by Major General Count Carlo Calvi di Bergolo son-in-law of the king. The two generals conferred. Bergolo assured Carboni that the Centauro, despite being a 'Blackshirt' division, would hold its ground.

Come dawn the Sardinian Grenadiers were still holding back the German 2nd Parachute Division at La Magliana and Cecchignola. In the latter town about one hundred and eighty officers and sergeants were besieged at a supply depot, having refused a request to surrender. They offered such tough opposition that the Germans brought up an 88mm gun to shell them point blank.

The Piacenza Division was holding back German paratroopers at Risaro and Ardea, and here the frustrated Germans brought up powerful Marder 75mm self-propelled guns.

In the Monterosi area thirty miles north of Rome Major General Cadorna of the Ariete II was again asked by the 3rd Panzergrenadier Division if they could pass through. Again he refused. This time the Germans advanced anyway. In their path was a bridge that Lieutenant Ettore Rosso and his team of the 134th Engineers was ordered to destroy. They worked feverishly, but had not completed their task when German tanks arrived. Most of the engineers scampered quickly, leaving Rosso and some others to finish. Seeing the Germans, Rosso knew that if he ran off the bridge it would give the lead German vehicle time to cross too and perhaps sabotage his fuses.

Therefore as the first vehicle reached the bridge he blew up the bridge and himself.

Halted by this literally suicidal resistance the Germans opened fire from their side of the river: the Ariete replied. The two divisions now battled each other. When Cadorna received Roatta's order to withdraw to Tivoli, he refused to move until someone could get the Germans off his back.

Along the Austrian border XXXV Corps was under attack. Alessandro Gloria the commander, who had fought under Rommel in North Africa, was now under siege in Bolzano by the German 44th Division, which was taking orders from Rommel. In Milan General Vittorio Ruggiero was also under siege by Rommel's troops. The 3rd Bersaglieri Regiment was here in the process of rebuilding with twenty year old conscripts, and most of the unit sided with the Germans. At Verona the Bersaglieri was training twenty year old conscripts for the new 120th Provisional Regiment. Most of them joined the Germans.

General Caracciola di Feroleto in his headquarters in the town of Orte forty miles north of Rome, finally woke up to reality, accepting that his Fifth Army was under attack from the Germans. He ignored Roatta's order and commanded his units to move towards Rome. Almost at once his own headquarters building was attacked by elements of the 3rd Panzergrenadier Division.

In mid-morning the headquarters of the Piacenza Division was overrun by German paratroopers riding on tanks and self-propelled guns.

Seventh Army headquarters at Potenza was speedily overrun by the Germans. Ashamed, one staff officer shot himself.

Lieutenant General Pentimalli ordered his XIX Corps to leave Naples and head for Rome, in disobedience to Roatta's order. But when his men encountered Germans on the road, Pentimalli issued orders that scuppered any chance of resistance.

When the base commander of Foggia airfield, General Giovanni Caperdoni, realized his staff officers were welcoming the Germans, he shot himself, but the bullet only blinded him.

In Fiume General Gastone Gambara, that well-known Fascist veteran of Spain and Greece, and who had fought under Rommel in Libya, was currently commanding XI Corps in combat against Slovenian Titoists. He now made arrangements to hand over his entire command to Rommel, including the Isonzo, Cacciatore delle Alpi and Lombardia Divisions. There was already shooting outside his window.

General Enea Navarini, who had served under Rommel in the desert, offered his services to the Germans.

In mid-morning Caracciola di Feroleto was informed by his divisional commanders that they could not continue to move towards

Rome, because they were under German air and ground attack.

By now major battles were underway at Futa Pass, Pisa, Livorno [where a mob of the Anarchist political party stormed the naval academy], Ascoli Piceno, Chiusi, Orvietro, Viterbo and Tarquinia. In the Fourth Army sector major confrontations were taking place at Turin, Tortona, Cuneo, Bergamo, Savona, Genoa, Parma and Pavia. In the northeast serious combats were ongoing at Trieste, Fiume, Treviso and Trento. In the Seventh Army sector there was heavy fighting at Naples and Aversa.

In some places generals were fighting with rifles in their hands. Barracks exploded in violence as roommates now shot each other. Civilians showed up at defensive positions asking to be armed against the Germans. In many battles civilian men and women dragged wounded out of harm's way, carried ammunition and grabbed rifles from the fallen. On the island of Sardinia the Nembo Parachute Division split apart into violent civil war.

In Genoa the Fascists seized the naval base. In Turin General Adami-Rossi joined the Germans. At Novara General Cosentino helped the Germans arrest his own men.

In keeping with de Courten's orders Vice Admiral Carlo Bergamini in the new battleship La Roma left La Spezia harbor at 2:30 am in company with the battleships Vittorio Veneto and Littorio (recently renamed the Italia), light cruisers Attilio Regolo, Raimondo Montecuccoli and Eugenio di Savoia and eight destroyers. La Roma, at 46,500 tons, with nine 15inch guns, had in fact been launched in 1938, but poor quality administration and a lack of funds had held up construction. Though she had not been in action at sea she had been bombed in port on 5 June 1943. As she slipped out of the harbor her crew could hear the sound of gunfire between the port defenses and attacking Germans.

By 6:30am Bergamini's battle fleet was off Corsica under a blue sky and he linked up with the light cruisers Giuseppe Garibaldi, Duca d'Aosta and Duca degli Abruzzi, two destroyers and small craft that had sailed from Genoa. They all made for La Maddalena off Sardinia.

However, at 1:00pm Bergamini was alerted that a German force had taken La Maddalena and had sunk two destroyers there, so he ordered all his ships to head straight for Malta. At 3pm aircraft buzzed the fleet. They were large four engine planes and the flak gunners assumed they were Allied Liberators and did not open fire. Only when it was too late did someone recognize them as German Dornier 217s. Immediately the ships' gunners opened up with 20mm, 37mm and 3.9inch. The bombs fell and thankfully the swerving ships managed to dodge them all. At 3:52pm a wave of twin-engine bombers arrived and all guns began firing at once. Then suddenly two radar-guided 'smart bombs' dove straight for La Roma. In a blinding flash the superstructure crumpled like paper and her guts were wrenched apart. Then a magazine blew up, snapping the great ship in two. Hundreds of sailors, many of them on fire, jumped into the sea. As the two shattered halves began to sink, destroyers sped to the scene to pick up survivors. Of the battleship's one thousand nine hundred and thirty crew, only five hundred and sixty-five were rescued. Bergamini was not among them.

Several other ships were damaged including the Italia before the planes flew off.

––––––––––––

The generals and staff officers of Comando Supremo who had plotted Italy's global strategy with colored pins on wall maps in the cozy safety of their Monterotondo headquarters twenty miles from Rome now saw the ugly side of war at first hand, for at 9am this morning a battalion of the German 1st Parachute Division parachuted on top of them. Well, that was their intention, but the flak gunners surrounding the headquarters put up such a tremendous volley of fire that the paratroopers had to drop anywhere from one to four kilometers away.

The paratroopers quickly regrouped and launched a ground attack on the complex, and at once the Carabinieri sentries opened fire and were quickly joined by others that grabbed rifles and pistols from privates to generals. Everyone participated in defending the nerve center of an army that had not yet lost its nerve. Civilian employees aided the defenders.

Unfortunately the Germans knew all the complex's weak points thanks to Fascists who had joined them. Nonetheless the resistance was so ferocious that after two hours Hitler's elite paratroopers resorted to pushing Italian women and children in front of them as human shields. The defenders did not slacken their fire one iota, and the surviving women and children and paratroopers scattered amid a hail of bullets. Inside the rooms filled with shattered glass and splintered wood the casualties were mounting as radio operators begged for rescue. Nearby at Ponte del Grillo and Mentana other Italian rear-echelon soldiers were attacked by elements of the 1st Parachute Division, and they too put up a fanatical fight. Major General Tabellini of the Piave Division heard their pleas by radio and he sent two battalions to rescue them: all he could spare. Close to noon these infantry counter attacked the German paratroopers. In early afternoon two battalions of the Re Division joined the battle. By day's end the Germans in the region were in a bad way, having suffered six hundred casualties.

––––––––––––

Major Giovanni Licari seemed to be a man others would follow and armed with his personal charisma he gathered together a provisional force made up of troops from the Sardinian Grenadiers Division, including infantrymen, engineers, artillerymen, clerks, cooks, drivers etc., and together with cadets from the Carabinieri school and a host of civilian men and women he created a blocking position in the southern outskirts of Rome. When German paratroopers approached, Licari's people opened fire. The Battle of Rome had begun. The defenders were hard pressed by the Germans. But just in time the cavalry came to the rescue - the Montebello Lancers, that is, in their Lancia armored cars armed with 47mm guns, and this unit of the Ariete II Division drove back the Germans, following which Licari ordered a counter attack. The Germans were thrown totally off balance and retreated a mile. Later a Major d'Ambrosio organized a more thoughtful counter attack with infantry and armored cars and he recovered even more territory.

Brigadier General Dardano Fenulli, deputy commander of the Ariete II, led a battle group towards the Ciampino district.

––––––––––

Meanwhile German paratroopers had talked their way into La Magliana, swearing to the Sardinian Grenadiers that they just wanted to pass through. However, when they sighted a group of Italian officers they gunned them down. Angered by this perfidy the Sardinian defenders fought back with a vengeance. Soon these Germans reached a bridge and they forced one of their captives Lieutenant Colonel Giuseppe Ammassani in front of them. With a pistol in his back he was ordered to command his men to surrender, otherwise he would be shot. Instead, though knowing this was suicide, he shouted to his men to fight on. Both sides opened fire. Amazingly the bullets missed Ammassani and he survived.

By noon Cadorna was reporting that his Ariete had defeated the Germans everywhere, and his Montebello Lancers were already in Rome, and now that the Re Division was arriving to take over his position, he could comply with Roatta's orders. Within an hour his armored division was on the road and that afternoon they reached Rome. They were met by tens of thousands of cheering and celebrating civilians, and they heard the gunfire to the south, where the Montebello Lancers were still in action. But they were under orders to turn eastwards towards Tivoli.

Once he arrived at Tivoli, Cadorna conferred with Carboni. He had to report that unfortunately some of his men had deserted en route.

Carboni had little data. Reports from the country at large were sketchy. The Germans had captured Orvietro, Chiusi, Viterbo and Tarquinia. The Re Division having taken over from the Ariete was already under attack, but was holding. Every Italian unit was receiving contradictory orders either caused by confusion or by Fascists. Di Bergolo was even approached by some of his own

Blackshirt officers suggesting he hand over the Centauro to the Germans! The Sardinian Grenadiers were ordered to abandon their defenses in Rome, but no one knew who gave the order. Carboni ordered them to stand fast and obey no one else but him. Those Sardinians led by Licari and d'Ambrosio in south Rome actually counter attacked again, but they lost heavily this time.

General Italo Gariboldi, who had worked so well with Rommel, was arrested by German troops and sentenced to death. Fortunately this sentence was never carried out.

The Scipione, Scimitarra and Baionetta sailed into Pescara harbor, but their captains were told that the dignitaries were now waiting at Ortona instead. So the three warships turned around and sailed there. They met the dignitaries at that port: they turned out to be Badoglio, the Royal Family and several generals. Badoglio ordered the warships to take them to Bari further south along the coast. That port was in Italian hands and still in good order because General Nicola Bellomo had gathered an ad hoc force of customs police, Blackshirts, sailors and troops and had attacked a German engineer unit, hoping to prevent the Germans from sabotaging the port. Bellomo succeeded, but was wounded in the encounter.

By dawn on 9 September the Allies were ashore in mainland Italy at three locations: Montgomery was still at the toe; a few British troops sailed into Taranto like tourists; and Clark's US Fifth Army was ashore at Salerno. Only Clark met opposition. Unbelievably one lone German division, 16th Panzer, was holding up Clark's entire Anglo-American invasion force! Even taking into consideration that half of the invaders at Salerno were green troops, their lack of progress was disappointing, especially as they could call upon warships galore and a plethora of warplanes for support. Indeed it was only the naval gunfire and air strikes that prevented the Germans from shoveling the whole horde back into the sea. This was Clark's first battle as a senior commander and it showed.

The Italians could not help but notice they were on their own. They were not even getting Allied air support, though they were radioing the Allies and asking for it. They had been hung out to dry. The Italians wondered if the Allies secretly wanted them to be annihilated!

In every Italian unit there had been betrayals and gunplay, but as a whole the armed forces were intact. When the battleship Giulio Cesare received orders from Admiral da Zara to sail to Malta, the Fascists aboard wanted to disobey and join the Germans. Fistfights among the one thousand two hundred and thirty-six crewmen settled the issue. The ship sailed for Malta.

The Italian naval drama was also unfolding in the western Pacific and tributary seas. The warships Lepanto and Carlotto were scuttled by their anti-Fascist crews before the Japanese could confiscate them. The gunboat Eritrea arrived at Ceylon to join the British, and the submarine Cagni surfaced off Durban South Africa to do the same. However the submarines Capellini, Giuliani and Torelli joined the Japanese. The Japanese did not know what to do with these Italians so they imprisoned them. Eventually they were allowed to sail their submarines into action with mixed German-Italian crews.

There were five Italian midget submarines in Romanian ports. The fifteen crewmen were arrested and the vessels were confiscated.

———————

Chapter Fifty-one
Civil War

By dawn 10 September 1943 Hitler was very angry indeed. Not only did he have a war to fight, but now he had a new war on his hands, namely the campaign to neutralize the Italians. Ten months earlier he had conquered the larger part of France in one day. Two weeks earlier he had crushed the Danes in a couple of days. Why could his armed forces not crush the Italians, he wished to know? He knew the Hungarians were already making peace overtures and he was afraid the entire Axis might collapse, leaving Germany alone in Europe. Whenever he was in a tough position he always resorted to outrageous lies. This time he ordered Radio Berlin to broadcast that the entire Italian armed forces had been peacefully disarmed.

Those Germans currently in combat against the Italians could not believe their ears. Not only were they under fire from some Italians in uniform, while others asked to fight at their side, but in Italy the civilian population was decidedly anti-German. Women in clinging summer dresses armed with rifles had become femme fatale in the truest sense.

However, there were some British leaders including Anthony Eden, the British Foreign Secretary, who were so blindly prejudiced against Italians that they actually believed Hitler's broadcast! To accept Hitler's word, because it fits into one's bias is a sign of insanity. They now tried to justify their cowardly refusal to help the Italians by repeating Hitler's lie, that there were no Italian soldiers left to help. Incredibly the vast majority of British, American and German so-called 'historians' repeated this lie for the next fifty years. They believed that the Italian Army in Italy could be disarmed in the twinkling of an eye by eighteen German divisions, because 'all Italians are cowards, right'? Yet they come up with outlandish excuses why Clark at Salerno could not defeat one lone German division and why Montgomery with his quarter of a million troops in the toe of Italy could not defeat a few companies of German engineers! Most British and American 'histories' of the Italian campaign do not even mention the Italians, which is sort of like writing about the colonization of America without mentioning the Indians! As such the whole library full of 'histories' that claim to be about the Italian campaign are of passing interest at best, and are worthless as so-called comprehensive histories.

At 3:30am 10 September Carboni, believing himself to be the highest ranking officer still fighting the Germans, offered to surrender to the Germans if they agreed to certain conditions. He was undoubtedly extremely bitter that the Americans, whom he knew so well as he was half-American, had let down the Italian Army. Where were those fifteen divisions they had promised? The Germans listened to his offer. They were desperate and would have agreed to anything, but OKW did not believe Carboni had the authority to make the deal. His conditions were quite agreeable: retention of all Italian police and Carabinieri; retention of the Piave Division as Rome's garrison; and Rome to be declared off limits to all German soldiers. General Siegfried Westphal, Kesselring's chief of staff, ignored OKW and agreed to confer by radio with Carboni, but he refused even these paltry conditions and demanded Carboni's unconditional surrender, threatening to command the Luftwaffe to demolish Rome if Carboni refused.

Carboni was a wily negotiator, so he ordered the Piave Division to move into Rome, and for the Ariete to reinforce the Sardinian Grenadiers in the southern suburbs of the city. Such political confusion destroyed many a man this day. Colonel Rabbi of the Ariete shot himself.

The Sardinian Grenadiers and the Montebello Lancers had counter attacked again and had recovered yet more ground, whereupon the Germans asked for a truce to recover their wounded and dead. The Italians honorably agreed, but within minutes they realized the Germans were using the truce to bring up artillery. Therefore they opened fire and the battle was renewed. Under a heavy pounding by the German artillery the Italian armored cars withdrew and the mob of foot soldiers and accompanying civilians had to follow suit. So far, the Sardinians had registered over a hundred dead and several hundred wounded.

About five hundred Sardinians set up a rearguard in the suburb of La Montagnola, but by 8am artillery salvoes made this position untenable. Therefore they retreated and placed a small rearguard inside Fort Ostiense. Within thirty minutes the fort was under assault by automatic weapons and artillery firing point blank. This resulted in a slaughter in which fifty-four defenders were killed and scores were wounded.

At least this gave the bulk of the defenders of Rome a chance to regroup. The Sardinian troops, armed civilians, Carabinieri cadets and Montebello Lancers fell back to the Garbatella district and they were now joined by police and Carabinieri, and in the Tormoranci sector Sardinian infantry were joined by two batteries of artillery from their division. Among the civilians was a sixteen year hunchbacked boy, Giuseppe Albano. He refused to let his handicap stand in his way.

In mid-morning they were all assaulted by the Germans, and they fired back from windows and street barricades made from vehicles and furniture. The defenders began to give way, but then rallied, counter attacked and regained their barricades. However, once the line was stabilized, their leaders ordered them to make an organized withdrawal.

On the Via Ostiense Captain Romolo Fugazza of the Montebello Lancers impressed his men with his bravery. Wounded, he refused evacuation. But a shell struck his Lancia and he was wounded again. Still refusing evacuation he drove the wreck to an advantageous point, where he could continue the fight. Suddenly the car took a direct hit and blew up.

The defenders withdrew through the Porto San Paolo, a gate in the city's medieval wall, and here Captain Count Sigismondo Fago Golfarelli rallied one hundred and thirty-six Sardinians. When the Germans arrived Golfarelli's men charged them, six of his men falling quickly, and then the Germans counter charged and Golfarelli ordered his men to fall back.

On the Via Ostiense and Via San Saba reinforcements arrived as Lieutenant Colonel Enrico Nisco brought up his armored cars of the Genoa Mechanized Cavalry. On his flanks came Sardinian infantry under Captain Giulio Gasparri and more Lancias of the Montebello Lancers under Captain Camillo Sabatini. Among them were factory workers, housewives, police, Carabinieri, veterans of World War I, Spain and Ethiopia, and veterans of the current war who had been invalided home with wounds or sickness or were on leave. They stood up under artillery fire and infantry assault, risking their lives for their country. If this was the saddest time for Italy it was also one of her proudest moments.

Suddenly German tanks approached. The defenders realized this was the end for them. But again, just in the nick of time more reinforcements arrived: Bersaglieri of the Ariete II Armored Division and infantry of the Sassari Division. The German paratroopers and tanks retreated. Every Italian here cheered, but it was too late for the gallant Captain Sabatini.

Noticing that a pocket of Germans had been cut off, Lieutenant Guido Cordano led a charge against them, but almost at once he was cut down. But he then raised himself up on one arm and waved his men on. They continued and drove back the Germans.

The hot afternoon sun was blazing down now on the city of smoke, flames, sweat, blood, pain and confusion, while in the center of the city a new drama was unfolding. Carboni had returned to his headquarters, and from there he was negotiating with the Germans. Listening to advice from several sources, he made his decision. He ordered the Rome garrison to capitulate.

The news was received in the streets with varying degrees of shame. The Montebello Lancers had lost half their officers and many men, and in the Laterano district some of them refused to give up. Only when divisional staff officers arrived to convince them they should obey to prevent retributions by the Germans, did they cease-fire. Those members of the Sassari Division who had fought here were thoroughly disillusioned, but those who had been ordered to remain in barracks and had not fired a shot felt even worse. They were all ashamed. The defenders of a palace in Viminale flatfooted refused to surrender and fought on. Along the Via Appia soldiers of the Ariete II Armored and Piave Divisions accepted the order reluctantly, though here too some fought on. Brigadier General Fenulli refused to surrender and he hid. The Piave men were surprised to learn they would become the new garrison of Rome. Along the Via Cavour armed civilians continued to fight: military orders meant nothing to them. On the Via Gioberti army engineers and rear-echelon troops were still shooting Germans. In the Piazza dei Cinquecento an ad hoc formation of soldiers from several units fought on. Major Carlo Benedetti's armored train in the rail station fired on the Germans whenever they came near. Throughout the night the battle continued. Major General Solinas joined the Germans, explaining that his Sardinian Grenadiers had fought them without his approval.

Cleverly Carboni had only surrendered the Rome-Tivoli defenses, and elsewhere the Italian armed forces continued to resist. Although this day the garrisons of Livorno and Florence surrendered.

————————

Forgotten by the Italian people were two tiny garrisons in Japanese-occupied China to protect trading missions. At Peking and Tientsin they resisted the attacking Japanese for about twenty-four hours.

————————

Only the British had been happy with the results of the Badoglio treaty so far. Their prime purpose in all of this had been to settle the question once and for all, was the Mediterranean 'Mare Nostrum' as Mussolini claimed, or was it 'Mare Britannia'. With the surrender of the Italian fleet and the Regia Aeronautica, the matter was indeed settled. The sea was now firmly in British hands. That was the meat and potatoes for the British. And if the landing at Salerno had forced the Americans to grab a tiger by the tail, where they could not evacuate, but nor could they advance, and were forced to ask for American reinforcements, which might delay the Allied invasion of France another year: well so much the better; this was the gravy on the British meat and potatoes.

The treaty had certainly not pleased the Americans. They had invaded at Salerno merely to accept the surrender of the Italians and enable them to turn on the Germans. This is why they had not preceded their landing with the customary naval bombardment, and why they had provided only two divisions, one of them green. Their discovery here of a German panzer division, whose members had taken over Italian shore batteries, came as a rude shock.

Certainly the ordinary anti-Fascist Italians in the street were displeased by the deal. They had not known how many divisions the Allies had promised, but they did know that the Allies had plenty of troops, planes and ships, which at the moment were oh so conspicuous by their absence.

The German soldiers were angry, because they had honestly come to help defend the Italians, and now the Italians had turned on them: biting the hand that fed them, so to speak.

The Italian Fascists were outraged, for they were suddenly persona non grata in their own country, and they were embarrassed to tell the Germans that they needed protection from their own people. Unfortunately the anger of the Fascists and Germans towards their Italian enemies spilled over into atrocities.

The Carabinieri at Aversa were forced to give up when they ran out of ammunition. Marching out with their hands up they were then forced to dig their own graves by Germans and Fascists, and then they were all shot.

The Taro Division surrendered after a fight, and the Germans executed its artillery commander in front of his men, because they had resisted.

The sailors and marines at Gaeta naval base held out for forty-eight hours, and then only surrendered when the Germans advanced with women and children in front of them as human shields.

At La Spezia the crews of the cruiser Taranto, MAS boats and merchant ships had scuttled their vessels rather than let the Germans take them. In retaliation the Germans executed the captains of these vessels. By nightfall members of the naval garrison and troops of the army's XVI Corps were still holding out in the port. Everywhere surrendering Italians were disgusted to see Fascists aiding the Germans.

After protracted talks General Ruggiero surrendered Milan. At Verona elements of the Pasubio Division, including many veterans of the Russian front, under the leadership of Major General Orengo continued to fight against the 15th Panzergrenadier Division.

In Sardinia Italian troops outnumbered the Germans considerably: Lieutenant General Basso's XIII Corps, consisting of the Bari, Calabria, Nembo Parachute, Sabauda, 204th Coastal and 205th Coastal Divisions, and the 4th and 25th Coastal Brigades, plus a mobile gruppo and an armored gruppo faced the German 90th Panzergrenadier Division, but nonetheless Basso was under orders not to take offensive action against the Germans, so he agreed not to fire on them if they left the island. He had fought alongside the Germans in Africa and perhaps he did not want to see war between Italy and Germany. In any case the shooting had already begun, because the Nembo Division was having its own mini civil war, Fascists fighting anti-Fascists. Colonel Alberto Bechi Luserna tried to convince the Fascists in his unit to remain and welcome the Allies. They shot him.

Eventually Basso agreed that any Fascists that wanted to leave with the Germans could do so.

At the naval port of La Maddalena Island the Blackshirt coastal gunners and Major Mario Rizzati's battalion of the Nembo had gone over to the Germans.

At Monterotondo the defenders of Comando Supremo finally gave up. They had suffered one hundred and twenty-three military and thirty-three civilian deaths and hundreds of wounded during their resistance. They had inflicted twenty per cent casualties on the attacking German battalion.

Meanwhile Mussolini knew very little of what was happening. He was suffering the worst punishment a megalomaniac can suffer: he was being ignored. Having reached the depths of total despair Benito Mussolini the fighter, the bully boy, the warrior, the rabble rouser, the man who wanted to make the world tremble, slit his wrists in a suicide attempt. An alert Carabinieri guard saved his life.

At sea this morning of 10 September Admiral Romeo Oliva led the Italian battle fleet into harbor at Malta. The Maltese lined the shore to stare at the battleships Vittorio Veneto and Italia, light cruisers Attilio Regolo, Raimondo Montecuccoli, Eugenio di Savoia, Giuseppe Garibaldi, Duca d'Aosta and Duca degli Abruzzi, and ten destroyers. Launches were soon taking Italian wounded to hospital. The British declared that these crews were now prisoners of war. However, in a very odd move the British told the crews to remain aboard for the time being, and their vessels would remain armed! Admiral da Zara's flotilla soon arrived, including the battleships Caio Duilio and Andrea Doria and light cruisers Cadorna, Scipione and Pompeo Magna. This day Admiral Pollone's flotilla left Bastia for Malta.

So far two hundred and three Italian aircraft had landed at Allied airfields.

In mainland Italy the supply lines of the anti-Fascist Italians were in tatters and most of these troops were surrounded in pockets. Some men deserted as soon as possible, and some surrendered, while others fired a few shots to satisfy honor and then surrendered. Here and there a few resisted until they had run out of ammunition. A few fought to the death. Some went into the mountains determined to carry on as guerillas. However, the largest portion obeyed orders whatever those orders might be.

On the morning of 11 September General Mario Vercellino, commander of the Fourth Army, ordered his engineers to blow up the

Monte Cenis tunnel, and he told Major General Giuseppe Andreoli of the Emanuele Filiberto Celere Division to hold the Alpine passes against the Germans. But Andreoli replied he had no such division - it had disintegrated. Throughout the day further bad news filtered through to Vercellino. That evening he ordered the remaining soldiers of Fourth Army to go home.

This day the last defenders in La Spezia surrendered, but the Germans were still being resisted in the cities of Piombino [an Anarchist stronghold], Teramo, Orbetello, Udine, Reggio Emilia, Piacenza, Cremona, Mantova, Bologna and Modena.

In Naples Lieutenant General del Tetto had withdrawn his garrison from the city, but the ordinary people were still attacking Germans whenever they saw them. Just east of Naples at Nola the Germans took the surrender of forty-eight soldiers that had been fighting them, and they murdered them all. Villagers who saw this were so outraged they attacked the Germans.

South of Naples most of the Italian Army formations had retained integrity and were awaiting Montgomery's advance from Taranto and the toe of Italy. However, Montgomery was as usual advancing at the speed of a tortoise - an aged arthritic lame tortoise. However, his British soldiers were becoming frustrated, knowing that Britons and Americans were dying at Salerno, while they sat around sun bathing and waiting for orders. Montgomery was like a child who wants all his toy soldiers lined up before he begins to play. Some of Montgomery's men finally reached breaking point and advanced without orders, claiming there were no Germans in front of them. Montgomery actually recalled them! The Italians awaiting Montgomery were equally angered, for every day he delayed meant another day they would spend under German air and ground attack. The problem with Monty was that he was a 'World War I' general in a 'World War II war'.

By the end of 11 September most of the Italian Navy was safe in Allied harbors. But some warships were still in danger, and their captains felt they could not escape the German net as it grew tighter, so they scuttled their vessels, including the battleship Conte di Cavour and the destroyers Zeno, La Masa, Ghibli, Maestrale, Corazziere, Dezza and Pegaso. The Germans captured few warships.

On their way to an Allied port the two 1870-ton destroyers Antonio da Noli and Ugolino Vivaldi ran into a small German convoy in the Strait of Bonifacio. Despite being within range of German shore guns the two Italian ships attacked. Both were quickly damaged by the shore guns, but nonetheless they destroyed several German vessels, before resuming their journey. Unfortunately the Antonio da Noli struck a mine and was wrecked. The survivors were taken aboard the Ugolino Vivaldi, and then the Antonio da Noli was scuttled. But survival was against the odds, and German bombers caught the Ugolino Vivaldi and sank her.

This day the 970-ton destroyer Quintina Sella was trapped by German e-boats, and she was sunk in a ferocious little action.

On 12 September the submarine Topazio was unable to answer a signal from a British bomber, so the aircraft dropped depth charges, which blew the sub apart. This was an example of the kind of confusion that permeated the Allied ranks as well as the Italian. As late as 13 September Allied air and naval commanders were asking their superiors how to treat the Italians. Were they prisoners or allies? For example, thirty-five Italian planes had landed on Allied airfields in Sicily, and their pilots were demanding fuel and bombs in order to fight the Germans. Already thirty-nine Italian aircraft based in Sardinia were flying bombing missions against the Germans.

The Italian sailors in Allied ports handed over their own Fascist prisoners and then asked for fuel and orders. They offered the use of a powerful fleet if the Allies were willing to use it: five battleships, nine light cruisers, thirty-five destroyers, nineteen corvettes, thirty-five submarines, scores of small craft and a large merchant fleet.

In Corsica Lieutenant General Magli controlled the 225th and 226th Coastal Divisions and the Cremona and Friuli Infantry Divisions. On the evening of 8 September his infantry had captured Bastia from German coastal gunners and rear-echelon troops, and since then his forces had been battling the SS Reichsfuehrer Brigade. Meanwhile General von Senger und Etterlin, the German commander on the island, met Magli for several discussions. While they sipped wine like gentlemen in a mountain villa and discussed a possible solution to their problem, outside the walls their soldiers were locked in bitter combat with each other. It was as if they were playing human chess.

The fledgling Corsican guerilla movement made a truce with Magli, and soon the guerillas were fighting alongside the Italians, and they both radioed the Allies for help. But the German garrison was being reinforced by those Axis troops that were evacuating Sardinia, namely the German 90th Panzergrenadier Division and a host of Fascist Italians, many from the Nembo Parachute Division.

In the Balkans [Albania, Slovenia, Croatia, Serbia, Bosnia, Kosovo, Macedonia, Montenegro and Greece] there were initially few ground clashes between the Italians and the Germans, because many miles separated the garrisons of these Axis partners. And where they were in close proximity the Germans were usually outnumbered.

However, since the evening of 8 September the Luftwaffe had been raiding Italian bases, and the Regia Aeronautica had been bombing German bases. Not until 11 September were the Germans ready to launch ground assaults on the Italians, having asked the Bulgarians to protect their base in Serbia. To disarm twenty-eight Italian divisions and those indigenous units raised by the Italians the Germans had at their disposal eleven divisions - 1st Mountain, 100th Jaeger, 104th Jaeger, 114th Jaeger, 118th Jaeger, 7th SS Mountain Prinz Eugen, 173rd, 181st, 187th, 297th and 373rd.

Major General Francesco Giangreco's Zara Division was in an unusual position. Recruited in Zara, an Italian enclave on the Dalmatian coast of Yugoslavia, this division had taken part in the invasion of Yugoslavia and had then withdrawn to safeguard the city and its home base. Many of these Italians were thus defending their own homes. When the Germans drove up, the Italians opened fire.

At Spoleto (Split) Major General Alfonso Cigala-Fulgosi made a truce with the local Titoists, and his Bergamo Division provided these guerillas with arms and ammunition. When the German 7th SS Mountain Prinz Eugen Division arrived, the Bergamo and the local Titoists gave them a good thrashing.

Throughout Bosnia outposts of Lorenzo Vivalda's Taurinense Alpini Division were under assault by Germans. They were used to fighting off Titoist partisans, but unlike the Titoists the Germans had air support and artillery.

In the mountains of Slovenia outposts of Guido Cerruti's Isonzo Division, Luigi Maggiore-Perni's Cacciatore delle Alpi Division and the Lombardia Division were surrounded and under attack.

At the ancient city of Dubrovnik on the Dalmatian coast German troops took Major General Giuseppe Amico prisoner and at gunpoint put him on a balcony in front of a large gathering of his Marche Division to order them to surrender. The Marche had invaded Yugoslavia in 1941 and had battled Titoists on and off since then. Amico, a veteran of Spain, who had led the Catanzaro Division against the British in North Africa, astonished the Germans by shouting orders to his men to fight the Germans. Immediately a hellacious battle developed. Unbelievably Amico survived and was liberated by his men.

With the normal military chain of command ruptured in all Italian units, new leaders arose among the anti-Fascists. One body of anti-Fascists from the Emilia Division chose to fight their way to the coast, hoping to find a ship.

When the German XXI Mountain Corps of the 100th Jaeger and 297th Divisions entered Albania, the Italian formations in that nation collapsed because Fascists had sabotaged all efforts at resistance. The Albanian government that had so recently danced to Mussolini's tune and then to Badoglio's music now got in step with Hitler's marching band. In return Hitler allowed these politicians to keep their armed forces.

Throughout Albania Italian barracks rabble-rousers convinced many of their fellow soldiers to march into the mountains to join the Albanian partisans. Many did so, and the Communist Albanian partisans accepted soldiers from all Italian units plus Carabinieri and Italian civilian workers, including men from Luigi Clerico's Puglie, Enrico Lugli's Parma and Arturo Torriano's Arezzo Divisions. The largest such band came from Gino Piccini's Firenze Division. However, Lugli, Clerico and Torriano were captured by the Germans.

General Carlo Vecchiarelli, a Fascist sycophant who had commanded a corps in the 1940 invasion of France, and who now was responsible for the safety of the whole Eleventh Army in Greece, ordered his men to hand over their weapons to the Germans! But while the Brennero, Forli Mountain, Cagliari Mountain, Casale and Modena Mountain Divisions obeyed his orders, the Acqui Mountain, Siena, Cuneo, Regina and Pinerolo Divisions did not. In fact the Pinerolo Division of Major General Adoles Infante was currently in combat with the Greek ELAS partisans, but notwithstanding this. Infante and the commander of the Aosta Cavalry Regiment approach ELAS with an idea for a truce. The ELAS commander General Stefanos Serafis was totally unscrupulous, but highly intelligent. He agreed to a pact.

On the island of Rhodes Admiral Campione did not have to obey Vecchiarelli's orders, as he was a naval officer, but he was also a Fascist. When German planes raided one of his bases, he ordered a total capitulation, but not all of his men were so willing to walk into captivity or side with the Germans, and gun play broke out between Fascists and anti-Fascists. The Fascists won and arrested most of the anti-Fascists, but a few of the latter found boats and sailed to neutral Turkey.

On Crete members of Major General Angelo Carta's Siena Division tried to make contact with the Cretan partisans, but the latter refused a truce. The Siena had performed with mixed results in the invasion of Greece, and since then they had been softened by two years of easy occupation duty, bar the odd air raid and a few sabotage incidents by partisans. But on 9 September British agents appeared, hoping to help coordinate opposition to a German invasion of the island. While the Siena troops conferred they came under serious German air attack.

On 12 September in the Balkans the garrisons of Rabac and Cattaro came under heavy German ground assault.

———————

On 13 September Skorzeny and twenty-seven of his SS commandos accompanied by a prisoner, Major General Franco Soleti, landed in gliders on top of Gran Sasso Mountain in Italy. Spies had located Mussolini here at the luxury Hotel Alberto Rifugio. As the gliders landed, Inspector Giuseppe Gueli ordered his Carabinieri sentries not to resist. This was not his decision. He was in fact obeying the orders of police commander Carmine Senise. The bewildered Mussolini was led into the open air in front of a newsreel camera and then shoved aboard a single-engine Fieseler Storch aircraft next to the pilot and the tall Skorzeny. After a hair-raising take-off the Storch flew to a nearby airfield. Transferred to a slightly roomier He-111 Il Duce was flown to Vienna, and from there he was flown to Hitler's headquarters at Rastenburg in eastern Germany for a tearful reunion.

At the same moment that Hitler was liberating one Italian, he was enslaving millions of others. He told his generals to ignore Carboni's terms of the Rome armistice and to march into the city.

The Germans approached Marshal Cavallero at Frascati and asked if he would openly declare for the Fascist cause and establish a new Italian Army. He refused, unwilling to become a German puppet. He was fearful, though, that the Germans would use his name even if he refused. Caught in this dilemma he sought an honorable way out. A few hours later he was dead: an apparent suicide.

The Germans also asked Major General Count Calvi di Bergolo, the king's son-in-law, to join them. He too refused, and in violation of both Carboni's terms and the Geneva Convention he was denied prisoner of war status, was arrested by the Gestapo and hauled off to a concentration camp.

In the Balkans the Germans overran Major General Guglielmo Spicacci's Messina Division, but not without a fight. Because he had resisted them the Germans denied Spicacci prisoner of war status and sent him to a concentration camp. It was the last ride he ever took.

Major General Ernesto Chiminello announced that his Perugia Division would resist the Germans.

At Priboj Colonel Graziani and his eight hundred men were under attack by Cetniks for twenty-four hours until he realized he would receive no support. Therefore he negotiated with the leader of these Cetniks. The Cetniks replied that they really just wanted his weapons and provisions, and he and his men could leave. So they struck a bargain. However, once the Cetniks disarmed the Italians, they handed them over to the Germans.

In many localities small groups of Italians were approaching Cetnik strongholds asking to join them if together they could fight the Germans. The Cetniks accepted them, but then disarmed the Italians often by a trick, and then handed them over to the Germans. British and American liaison officers serving with the Cetniks were disgusted by this treachery. However, when Brigadier General Carlo Isasca led a significant number of his soldiers of the Venezia Division to join the Cetniks, they were accepted if they agreed to fight against the Titoists rather than the Germans. Isasca agreed.

Tito was far more pragmatic and he looked upon the anti-Fascist Italians as valuable manpower. He knew they were good fighters, for he had been battling them for two years, and he already had Dalmatian Italians within his ranks. He put out the order that all Italians were to be accepted as partners. His partisans were especially happy at this decision when they saw that the Italian defectors brought their equipment with them including flak guns, artillery and armored vehicles, and they also freed eighteen thousand Titoist prisoners they had been holding.

Eventually the Titoists accepted thirty thousand Italians, including the majority of Lorenzo Vivalda's Taurinense Alpini Division, Major General Giovanni Batista Oxilia's Venezia Division, the Aosta Artillery Gruppo of Colonel Carlo Ravnich and some members of the Emilia Division. The combat troops were reorganized as the Titoist Garibaldi Division commanded by Oxilia with Vivalda as his deputy, while the engineers and support troops began forming a real regular military infrastructure, something that Tito had so far lacked. At Kolasin Carlo Isasca's Italians and some Cetniks attacked Oxilia's Italians and some Titoists. Oxilia won.

If the situation was traumatic for the Italians in the Balkans it was doubly so for the Italian-sponsored formations. The Slovenian Legion of Death was locked in mortal combat with a Titoist force. To rescue them, the Slovenian Anti-Communist Volunteer Militia began to assemble at Turjuk, where they had a vague idea of declaring Slovenian neutrality, now that their Italian overlords had disappeared. However, only one thousand six hundred troops had reached the town, when they were attacked by Titoists, the latter assisted by some of their new Italian partners. As a result of this incident, the Anti-Communist Volunteer Militia sought to join the Germans. In the city of Ljubljana the Germans accepted these Slovenians and assigned them to a force of Slovenian 'Blues', henceforth to be known as the Domobranci under the leadership of Leon Ruprik and Franc Krenner.

Meantime the Germans were taking over Trieste and Western Slovenia, and they organized one thousand five hundred Slovenes into the Littoral National Guard. The port of Trieste was extremely valuable and to add to its flak defenses the Germans used two new Italian anti-aircraft cruisers, the Etna and the Vesuvio, which they had captured.

The Italian-sponsored militias in Montenegro and Bosnia also asked to join the Germans and were accepted at once.

On the night of 13 September the first real Allied aid reached Italian anti-Fascist troops, and ironically it did not come from the British or Americans. The French navy arrived in Corsica with French and Moroccan regulars of the 4th Moroccan Division in response to the call for help by the Corsican guerillas and the Italians. Lieutenant General Giovanni Magli welcomed them. Von Senger ordered an immediate evacuation of all German forces from the island.

On the Italian mainland at Piombino the 215th Coastal Division was still in its gun positions, perhaps owing to the fact that its commander Major General Count de Vecchi was a staunch Fascist, though an enemy of Mussolini. However, when the first German evacuation convoy arrived from Corsica some of the division's shore batteries opened fire. The anti-Fascists in the division aided by sailors and civilians were not about to let the Germans ashore. Naturally Fascist officers ran to the gun pits to call a cease-fire, but not all were obeyed. The guns sank two German corvettes and several small craft and damaged a destroyer, killing eight hundred Germans. Over the next day the anti-Fascist gunners were disarmed by German infantry.

By the morning of 14 September the only full-scale battles between Fascists and anti-Fascists still raging in mainland Italy were at Naples, Fiume and in small mountain outposts. Colonel Duca surrendered the Military Academy at Modena to the Germans.

In the Balkans the major centers of Italian resistance to the Axis forces were at Spoleto, Dubrovnik, Rabac, Cattaro and Zara.

After forty-eight hours of battle in Dubrovnik the Marche Division collapsed. The Germans recaptured Major General Amico and this time they shot him.

On the evening of 13 September the Germans landed on the Greek island of Kephalonia, defended by elements of Major General Antonio Gandin's Acqui Mountain Division, the 19th CCNN Battalion and 27th CCNN Legion and some customs police and navy shore guns. Gandin had been decorated for bravery in Russia by the Germans. His deputy was Brigadier Luigi Gherzi. About two thousand German infantry with self-propelled guns and tanks under Colonel Hans Barge were already on Kephalonia. The Italians opened fire on these German reinforcements [elements of the 1st Mountain and 104th Jaeger Divisions]. Ever since their bloody battles in the invasion of Greece, the men of the Acqui had been on peaceful occupation duty. They may have become flabby, but they still had honor and the Germans found few Fascists among them. The Italian flak defenses were good and they shot down several German planes. The 670-ton destroyers Stocco and Sirtori also fought back, but were wrecked by German dive-bombers.

On 15 September on Corsica Lieutenant General Magli coordinated his resistance to the Germans with the commander of the newly landed French forces, Brigadier General Henri Martin. Italian and French planes supported their efforts. The French were bringing in troops as fast as their limited sea power would allow. They had received almost no assistance from the British and Americans. Having said that, the French troopships were escorted by a powerful French Navy escort of one cruiser, three light cruisers, four destroyers and three submarines.

Magli's Italians had lost Bastia to the Germans, but were now advancing again towards that port. The Corsican resistance, declaring loyalty to France, asked Martin to provide them with weapons and ammunition. Martin had none to spare, but he agreed to ask the Italians for them, as he was under orders to remove the Italians from the scene as quickly as possible. This was after all French territory.

On 16 September Benito Mussolini made an announcement on Radio Vienna, which could be heard in parts of Italy. He was back in business.

On 17 September the last Germans and Fascists to leave Sardinia reached Bastia in Corsica to reinforce von Senger. The latter, feeling stronger now, ordered a counter attack against the Cremona and Friuli Divisions. Meanwhile the French captured the Corsican city of Ajaccio.

On 20 September the Slovenes at Turjuk capitulated after a week of battle. Their Titoist captors shot all of the officers and brutally imprisoned the other ranks.

By now on Corsica the Italians, Corsicans, Moroccans and French had pushed the Germans back to St. Florient. Martin assumed his position was now stable, so he started withdrawing the Italian units from his order of battle: the length of the front line was shrinking in any case, and naturally Martin wanted his own troops to be in on the kill. The Italians agreed. However, Martin asked that Magli's artillery remain in the line as they were doing good service. The partners repelled another German assault and then Martin advanced.

On 22 September Cattaro fell to Germans and Fascists, but Rabac still held out.

On Kephalonia the Acqui Mountain Division continued to offer fierce opposition. Gunner Corporal Benedetto Maffeis died earning the Gold Medal. Alfredo Sandulli, a Carabinieri lieutenant on Kephalonia was executed by the Germans for having resisted them. He too was awarded the Gold Medal.

But on 22 September Major General Gandin surrendered Kephalonia, because his troops had run out of ammunition. So far, one thousand six hundred and forty-six Italians had been killed or wounded resisting the Germans.

In mainland Italy the citizens of Naples and Fiume were still resisting the Germans. At Teramo a Carabinieri unit finally surrendered.

On 23 September Magli's and Martin's formations captured Bonifacio and Porto Vecchio on Corsica.

On 24 September German troops landed on Korfu, where they were opposed by members of the Acqui and Brennero Divisions. For two days the battle raged. Finally, the Italians agreed to surrender if they could be repatriated home. Of course the Germans agreed, and the guns went silent. Once they had disarmed the Italians the Germans shot two hundred and four officers.

After more than two weeks of dithering and countless messages from London, British Admiral Cunningham the Allied Naval Commander Mediterranean decided to allow Italian warships to take part in the war. Even then the British government refused to allow him to release the battleships. The first mission he gave to the Italians was to take supplies to the beleaguered Italian garrisons on the Balkan coast and on the Greek islands.

On Kephalonia the Germans had begun to massacre their Italian prisoners as per Hitler's direct order. Just before he was shot, Major General Gandin threw his iron cross in the dirt. His deputy Brigadier General Luigi Gherzi was also shot. Twenty Italian sailors were also executed. In fact the Germans and the Fascist Italians executed five thousand Italians. However, the remaining Italians were saved by the lack of discipline among the Germans, for despite the order coming from the Fuehrer himself many of the Germans refused to obey it. Actually most of the troops of the 1st Mountain Division were Austrians, and it seems that in this case there was an argument between the Austrians and the 'real Germans'. The bodies of the dead were burned in gigantic funeral pyres. The Greek islanders claimed they could smell the burning flesh for years afterwards.

On 27 September the Bergamo Division capitulated at Spoleto, having suffered heavy losses. Their conquerors, the 7th SS Mountain Prinz Eugen Division of Yugoslavian Volksdeutsch had fought with an intact supply line, air support, without desertions and with Fascists on their side who gave valuable military intelligence, but it had still taken them two weeks and serious losses to force this capitulation. In grief because of their own casualties, they executed all captured Italian officers including Major General Cigala-Fulgosi.

On Korfu, Major Luigi Ottino refused to surrender and he and his twenty-two men escaped on a ship and they took their four hundred and thirty-three German prisoners with them.

Throughout the war zone Fascists and Nazis were embittered by the Italian resistance and they often reacted violently on the helpless.

The German ship Donizetti sailed with one thousand five hundred and seventy-six Italian prisoners aboard. They never reached port. British destroyers sank the ship with all aboard lost.

On Crete a minority of the Italians joined the local Greek resistance, calling themselves the Italian Volunteer Legion of Crete. But most Italians obeyed orders from their Fascist commanders and surrendered to the Germans.

When the Zara Division finally surrendered, the Germans refused to give Major General Francesco Giangreco and Major General Paolo Grimaldi prisoner of war status and sent them to a concentration camp.

By 3 October the Perugia Division's outposts in Albania and Kosovo had been overrun by the German 1st Mountain Division. As per orders the Germans executed Major General Ernesto Chiminello and fifty-eight other officers.

On 3 October the French, Corsicans and anti-Fascist Italians drove the last Germans and Fascists from Corsica. The anti-Fascist Italians here had suffered about three thousand casualties in the twenty-six day campaign.

Chapter Fifty-two
Fatal Errors

By October 1943 the most confusing series of battles in Italian history had finally dissipated into a sensible front line. The anti-Fascist Italians still held Sardinia and the southern third of mainland Italy, and with French help they had kicked the Fascist Italians and Germans out of Corsica. Some of Badoglio's forces were clinging to the smaller islands of the Aegean.

However, the vast majority of the northern two thirds of Italy, plus that part of the French Riviera that Mussolini had seized the previous year, plus Crete, Rhodes, and all of the Balkans including mainland Greece were all now in German hands.

It is noticeable that the Corsican affair was settled by the intervention of troops, aircraft and ships under French command. The British and Americans had been invited to the Corsican party, but had better things to do, evidently. However, launching a serious attempt to destroy the German forces in Italy was not one of them.

One wonders how the battle for Rome might have gone had the US 82nd Airborne Division dropped on the city, supported by Allied warplanes. The Italians kept wondering: where was this mighty Anglo-American sword that had supposedly brought them to their knees?

What had actually happened was a total military and diplomatic failure on the part of the Anglo-American war leaders. With hindsight it is obvious that many Allied officers, especially British officers, did not believe that most Italians would resist the Germans and that those few who would resist were not worth helping at the cost of Allied blood. Not only was this a bigoted attitude, but like all bigoted attitudes it was stupid. The Allies would pay for this racist attitude in Allied lives: thousands of them.

Montgomery's 'invasion' did not meet any ground opposition for an entire week after landing, and that was only at Brindisi where the British 1st Airborne Division overcame a small rearguard. In his first two weeks in Italy his mighty Eighth Army of a quarter of a million men suffered only 700 hospitalized cases, and moreover this was from all causes: air raids, sniping, mines, accident and sickness. The only obstacle to his advance was road demolitions by German engineers. Montgomery's people did not encounter serious resistance from German troops until day sixteen, and on that day three battalions of the Canadian 1st Division were repulsed at Potenza.

Ever overly cautious, Monty withdrew the Canadians and pelted the enemy position with a massive artillery barrage, destroying the entire town and killing two thousand civilians into the bargain. The Germans, who had numbered fewer than a hundred, had already pulled out!

These Canadians were veterans of Sicily, and for two thousand five hundred of them to have been repulsed by a few score Germans was a national disgrace, and one can only assume they were reined in from above by high ranking British officers, because Canadians are not cowards.

All this time Clark's US Fifth Army was locked in major battle at Salerno. His Anglo-American army was supposed to aid Montgomery by attacking hundreds of miles into the enemy rear. [Salerno was one hundred and fifty miles from Taranto] Montgomery was not supposed to rescue Clark. And he certainly saw no reason to alter his orders. Of course his boss General Alexander commanding 15th Army Group could have given him a direct order to rush forward, and General Alan Brooke, Chief of the Imperial General Staff in London, could have ordered Alexander to do this, and Churchill most definitely had the power to order this. Monty was not solely to blame for this lack of moral courage and common sense. He had plenty of company.

Yet for three days the solitary German 16th Panzer Division held up Clark's army. On 12 September, after the fall of Rome to the Germans, the Hermann Goering Panzer Division and 29th Panzergrenadier Division rushed down to Salerno to join the defenders. The Germans counter attacked and came within 800 yards of the beach before naval gunfire stopped them!

Clark demanded reinforcements and received the US 82nd Airborne Division and British 7th Armored Division. Clark was still not satisfied, and he convinced the British to send him one thousand five hundred replacements, but when they arrived they mutinied! This debacle of morale did not end until three men were sentenced to death. [Not carried out]

A reinforcement of anti-aircraft guns at Salerno helped shipboard gunners and Allied fighter pilots destroy the Luftwaffe in the beachhead area, and German air raids lessened until on 18 September only one German plane attacked.

This day the Germans concluded they could not hold Salerno. But their fighting withdrawal kept Clark to a crawl.

On 27 September Eighth Army troops reached Foggia Air Base and found it abandoned by the Germans. So far they had advanced at the rate of three miles a day, which would have been adequate had they faced daily ground opposition, but they did not. Indeed some of the terrain they covered was already in anti-Fascist Italian hands, namely that terrain occupied by the Piceno, Mantova, Aosta, Assietta, Napoli, Livorno and Legnano Divisions! Fascist members of these units, such as Major General Chirieleison, had already fled with the Germans. At times British and American war correspondents attached to Eighth Army got so frustrated waiting for Monty to order an advance that they drove ahead on their own to prove there was no enemy in front of him! There is something wrong with a general if his soldiers can't advance with tanks, but four journalists in a jeep armed with typewriters can advance. The Americans were so exasperated by the British by this date, that Eisenhower had a tough time keeping the Anglo-American alliance together.

The Canadian 1st Division had an unusual situation in that they ran across some Italian paratroopers of the new Folgore Parachute Division that asked permission to tag along with the Canadians to kill Fascists and Germans. Yet near Cittanova they ran into a hundred Fascist members of the Nembo Parachute Division, who resisted them spiritedly.

Only on 2 October did Monty's famous Eighth Army reach a German defense line, on the Biferno River.

The British people had no right to attempt to shame all Italians with the stain of cowardice, when in September 1943 Italian men and women and even children were battling German troops with their bare hands, while Monty's British combat troops sunbathed and got drunk on stolen vino! At Naples Italian boys as young as ten armed with rifles were in street battles with German troops! Moreover Britons and Americans were dying at Salerno at the hands of Germans whose backs were turned to Montgomery. As the GIs and Tommies died, they asked: 'Where's Montgomery?'

If the British contribution to the Italian campaign to date was a joke, then the American contribution had proven to be a farce. Major General Taylor had been right to call off the airborne drop, considering the information available to him. But what a pity he never interviewed the warriors of the Sardinian Grenadiers or of the Montebello Lancers.

But the real American farce was Salerno. Because of bad American leadership, both in General Clark and in one of his corps commanders Lieutenant General Lucas, British and American troops were dying in this three-week battle, though for the first four days they outnumbered the enemy four to one: four reinforced divisions, with an impressive supply system, naval gun support and massive aerial superiority against one German panzer division manning some Italian shore guns. Soon Clark had one armored and five infantry divisions facing three badly depleted German armored divisions. Only on 23 September did Clark's Fifth Army begin to move out of the beachhead, and even then his advance was held down to a snail's pace for four days by just two thousand Germans. When Clark's men finally entered Naples they found that the Germans had been unable to completely destroy the great docks because of an uprising by armed civilians including children. At least five hundred and sixty Italians had been killed in the struggle. But instead of acknowledging these heroes, the Americans looked upon Italian men as worthless cowards and Italian women as fair game for sexual activity. Only those

Americans of Italian ethnicity had a different opinion, and they were embarrassed by their comrades.

———————

Hitler's initial plan had been to disarm as many Italians as possible so that he could withdraw his forces in safety from all of Italy south of the Po River. He knew that the Allies could land troops on either coast and outflank his men, so holding the boot of Italy was impossible. But he wanted northern Italy because that is where the industrial sites lay. Then he was approached by Kesselring. That German had been watching the Anglo-American way of war for two years and he convinced Hitler that they were timid and if given an army he could keep the Allies south of the Po River for an entire year. As evidence, he pointed to Montgomery's lethargy and Clark's inability to walk off a beach. Of course there was some personal boast involved. Kesselring had always wanted to command an army in battle and had left the German Army in a huff after realizing it would never happen. He had then offered his services to Hermann Goering, who made him a senior Luftwaffe commander. Kesselring had sent waves of bombers over Britain in 1940, but since then had been more or less just a glorified administrative clerk. Nonetheless Hitler took him at his word and gave him control of all German troops in Italy.

For two years the Nazis had blamed their defeats on their partners, usually the Italians. Now the Allies were blaming the Italians for their own failures.

———————

Winston Churchill was somewhat different from the run of the mill British leader. A fantastic orator and a brilliant political strategist, he was however completely out of his depth in military/naval affairs, though as a soldier/war correspondent he had seen combat in India 1897, the Sudan 1898, the Boer War 1899-1902 and World War I. Like any good tactician he was always looking for the enemy's weak spot, but like the bad tactician that he was he always found it in the wrong place.

His influence had sent British forces into two campaigns in the Aegean in 1915, both of which proved to be disasters to a varying degree [Galipoli and Salonika]. He had then sent British forces right back there in March 1941 only to see them humiliatingly evacuate twice [from the Greek mainland and from Crete].

Having learned nothing from these four episodes, he decided to go there again. However, this time his generals and admirals argued so vehemently against it and were avidly supported by the Americans, who wanted no Balkan entanglements, that he was left without the necessary troops to implement his plan. But they did not reckon on his obduracy, and he chose to attack in the Aegean regardless, by stealing a few units when his generals weren't looking.

In any case most of the Aegean islands were still held by anti-Fascist Italians. Lesbos was garrisoned by part of Major General Giacomo Scaroina's unblooded Regina Division, and it had a small naval base that harbored the destroyer Euro (1070 tons), sloop Ago, minelayer Legnano, and the 3rd MAS and 39th Minesweeper Flotillas. Air support was provided by the 147th Seaplane Reconnaissance Squadron. The Italian commander of these islands was Admiral Luigi Mascherpa.

Samos was garrisoned by elements of the Cuneo Division [with attached 24th CCNN Legion] commanded by Major General Mario Soldarelli. The Cuneo had fought in the invasion of Greece. Soldarelli had led the Sabratha Division in Libya. Several smaller islands were defended by a few platoons: Kithnos, Khalki, Simi, Stampalia, Patmos, Lipsoi, Nikario and Kos. The war had seemingly passed these men by over the last two years.

Since 8 September the Germans had shown interest in these islands, the evidence of this being their constant air raids on the garrisons, each time followed by a surrender demand. Each of these garrisons had refused Eleventh Army orders to capitulate and they refused the German demands too. They resisted as best they could with a few flak guns and infantry machine guns. Churchill saw these men as the nucleus of his Aegean force and he began to reinforce them with about four thousand personnel that he had managed to scrape up, all that he was able to sneak past the scrutiny of the Americans.

Furthermore British planes flew over the islands in daylight to challenge the Luftwaffe, and every night British ships darted in to patrol for a few hours. In late September Italian warships were released from British ports to run supplies to these islands at night.

However, German planes were still very active here and they sank the British destroyer Intrepid and several Italian MAS boats, and they crippled the Euro.

By October the Germans had begun to formally organize those Italian Fascists who had joined them, and they chose a tried and true method learned in Russia. They came up with two names for their Italian volunteers. The rear-echelon Fascist troops, such as truck drivers, mechanics, supply clerks, maintenance troops etc., were assigned positions in the German rear as Hilfeswillige (Volunteer Help). Hiwis for short. This term was in use in Russia, as was the term 'Osttruppen' (Eastern Troops) meaning foreign volunteers from the east that served in combat units. However, the Germans chose the name 'Kampfwillige' (Battle Volunteers) - Kawis for short - to describe Italian volunteers in combat units.

In addition to the Italian kawis and hiwis, many Italians volunteered to join the new armed forces that Mussolini was putting together. In Greece enough of the Piemonte's gunners volunteered to form an artillery battalion. Other members of this division formed an infantry battalion and a machine gun battalion. The 24th CCNN Legion was reformed in the Aegean Islands. In Yugoslavia the 49th, 72nd and 86th CCNN Legions and the 33rd, 40th, 49th, 81st, 82nd, 111th and 114th independent Blackshirt Battalions were reformed.

On 3 October Germans and Italian kawis invaded Kos. By now this small sunny island was defended by some Italians of the Regina Division under Colonel Felice Leggio, plus Britons and Indians. British officers were in overall command. After a twenty-four hour fight the British commander surrendered the island. The Germans and kawis took all the Britons and Indians prisoner, as they did the Italian enlisted men, but they shot one hundred and two Italian officers including Colonel Leggio.

On 5 October German bombs rained down on Leros once more, sinking a minesweeper and the Legnano and damaging three merchant ships.

The Germans and their kawi helpers followed the Kos operation with the invasion of Simi, which was only defended by one hundred and fifty Italian sailors under Lieutenant Andrea Occhipinti, who had recently been reinforced by thirty Britons of the Special Boat Service (saboteurs) and forty Royal Air Force mechanics. Thus the garrison was poorly armed and untrained in infantry combat. Nonetheless the garrison fought back viciously and was joined by local Greek civilians armed with knives and shotguns. The Germans and kawis had not expected such a response and they withdrew to their boats leaving behind sixteen dead and thirty prisoners. Allied casualties were one dead and three wounded Britons and ten wounded Italians. Next day German Stukas plastered Simi Island killing three Britons and twenty civilians. On the 12th the garrison evacuated, leaving the islanders to their fate.

On 20 October the ship Sinfra left Crete with two hundred and four Germans and two thousand four hundred and sixty Italian prisoners aboard, mostly from the Siena Division, when she was caught by American Mitchells and British Beaufighters. Their bombs sank her with the loss of two thousand and ninety-eight Italians.

———————

The British and Americans had still not formally accepted the Italians as Allies. Their politicians wanted to play out the niceties of diplomatic arrangements even if it damaged their war effort. Yet the French on Corsica had already accepted the Italians as allies. Admiral Cunningham had already released Italian ships to help him fight the naval war. And surprisingly Montgomery had treated with a modicum of respect those Italian units that he encountered in Southern Italy. On 3 October Eisenhower's operations staff recommended to him that he make the use of Italian forces 'official'. He agreed, but his political bosses insisted that the Italians were not to be recognized as members of the Allies. Instead those who served Badoglio and King Vittorio Emanuele would henceforth be known as Co-Belligerents. Furthermore, those Italians who prior to 8 September had enlisted out of the prisoner of war camps into the British armed forces would be recognized as 'Co-Belligerents temporarily assigned to the British', which finally clarified their status, but those Italians who had been civilian resident aliens in Britain, France and the USA and who had enlisted in either of those armed forces would retain their status as 'Britons', 'French' and 'Americans'.

As Badoglio's armed forces had been in combat with the Germans since 8 September someone in his office thought it might be a good idea to recognize this, so on 13 October 1943 Badoglio's government declared war on Germany. By now Badoglio's forces, henceforth known as Co-Belligerents, consisted of a much reduced armed forces in the air, at sea and on land.

In the air the ragged remnants of the Regia Aeronautica [now known as Co-Belligerent Air Force] were scattered throughout Sardinia, Corsica, Sicily, Southern Italy, Malta and the Aegean islands. Of all the fighter pilot aces only Teresio Martinoli had remained with Badoglio's air force. He was a magnificent pilot with twenty-one confirmed kills.

On the ground the Co-Belligerent Army had troops in Corsica, Sardinia, Southern Italy and the Aegean islands. The Co-Belligerents had a powerful navy and a large merchant fleet. These merchant ships were exceedingly valuable and were put to work sailing the world's oceans in the Allied cause. Italian warships (but not the battleships) were given a second combat mission. In addition to running supplies to the hold-outs in the Aegean, they were now to protect Allied convoys all over the world from raids by German aircraft, surface craft and U-boats.

It was decided that Italian submarine crews needed more training and they sailed off to the Caribbean to get this. However, some were kept back to run spies, saboteurs and equipment to the partisans. The MAS boats were soon in action again, but the still untrusting British placed a British officer in command of each one. The British had already begun picking the brains of the Italian Navy's Decima MAS including the pig riders and Gamma swimmers.

Allied officers toured the Italian formations in Corsica, Sardinia and Southern Italy and declared them battle ready. This included the Nembo, though it only stood at two-thirds strength owing to Fascist defections. Throughout this 'liberated area' Italian flak gunners of the coastal units, naval bases and cities had been in constant combat against German air raids since 8 September.

————————

Mussolini's war against the French, British, Greeks, Yugoslavs, Russians and Americans from 10 June 1940 to 8 September 1943 had cost Italy one million two hundred thousand casualties, of which one hundred and sixty-three thousand had died in uniform or on merchant ships, and about three hundred thousand had been wounded. Approximately five hundred and fifteen thousand Italians and two hundred and thirty thousand ascaris and bande were missing. Many of the missing native troops had deserted. About one hundred thousand Italians had also deserted, most of these being the Sicilians who took advantage of Eisenhower's pardon and simply went home. About four hundred thousand of the missing Italians had been captured and were in prison camps, and sixteen thousand Italians taken prisoner by the British had volunteered to serve the British.

Civilian casualties from bombing and battles in built up areas had reached several thousand by 8 September 1943, and of course the population of Sicily and the colonial Italian populations of Libya, Eritrea, Somalia and Ethiopia had been placed under Allied occupation. Despite such losses, on the morning of 8 September 1943 Badoglio had still controlled an armed forces of one million and ninety thousand.

However, over the next thirty-six days from 8 September when the Allies acknowledged on public radio that the Italians had surrendered until Badoglio's declaration of war on Germany 13 October about five hundred and twenty-two thousand Italian servicemen had been seized by the Germans by one method or another. Of these at least eight thousand were seriously wounded. About sixty thousand Italians had managed to join the partisans in Albania, Yugoslavia and Greece. About thirty-five thousand anti-Fascist Italians had been killed in combat against the Germans and Fascist Italians or had been executed by them for resisting, or had been drowned when their ship was sunk by Allied forces. Thus by October 13 about four hundred thousand soldiers, sailors and airmen remained under Badoglio's control. Interestingly enough many were Blackshirts. This leaves a large discrepancy of seventy-five thousand men, but this can be accounted for by adding up those who had simply gone home, those who were organizing guerilla units in the mountains of Italy, and of course those who were serving the Germans as kawis and hiwis.

None of the above numbers reflect the involvement of Italian civilians during this 36 day period. Civilian casualties during this period are unknown.

On Corsica Badoglio had control of Lieutenant General Magli's VII Corps of the Cremona, Friuli, 225th Coastal and 226th Coastal Divisions, plus airmen, sailors and Carabinieri. On Sardinia he had Lieutenant General Basso's XIII Corps of a mobile gruppo, an armored gruppo, 4th and 25th Coastal Brigades, and the following divisions: Nembo Parachute, Bari, Calabria, Sabauda, 204th Coastal and 205th Coastal; and there were also city flak troops, police and Carabinieri, as well as sailors and airmen, for a total of about 188,000 men in uniform. Despite having driven the Germans from the island, Sardinia was not as peaceful now as one might imagine, for German air raids plagued the defenders, as did large robberies by gangsters and small-scale sabotage by Fascist guerillas.

In Southern Italy Badoglio had his city and national police, the Carabinieri, sailors, airmen, a host of army rear-echelon troops, the 31st Coastal Brigade and the following divisions: 24th Coastal, 210th Coastal, 212th Coastal, 227th Coastal, Piceno, Mantova, Legnano, Assietta Mountain, Aosta, Napoli and Livorno Mountain.

In the Aegean twenty-five thousand Italians were still holding on, including the Cuneo and Regina Divisions and sailors and airmen.

Even before the Allied decision to formally accept anti-Fascist Italians, they had in fact begun doing so at small unit level in southern Italy. The British under Monty immediately began using them as drivers, clerks, dock workers, painters, mechanics, technicians, radio operators, ammunition specialists, fuel engineers, construction engineers, administrators, medical staff, cooks and general manual laborers, and even as teamsters, muleteers, farriers and veterinarians for Italian horse-drawn wagon and mule convoys. The duties of such soldiers were inglorious, but they were of the utmost importance if the Allies were to retain a ground presence in Italy and keep their planes flying and their ships sailing and their supplies moving.

By 13 October south of the main front line in Italy Badoglio had just over ten thousand police and they continued their duty, just as before, as did the eighteen thousand seven hundred Carabinieri in this region, and these two formations were a god send to the Allies, because it relived them of the necessity of bringing in tens of thousands of their own military police. Furthermore some Fascists in the south had formed guerilla bands and were periodically sniping at the Allies and sabotaging equipment. Badoglio's police and Carabinieri began hunting them.

Every Allied supply dump, tent, truck and rail car had to be guarded from Fascist guerillas and saboteurs [and from good old-fashioned gangsters]. Some localities were so dangerous that Allied truck drivers were warned to stay out. The Allies asked Badoglio for help, and he responded by assigning ten thousand five hundred of his soldiers as permanent sentries.

Italian gunners who manned shore batteries now peered out to sea on the lookout for German raiding parties, e-boats, destroyers and surfaced submarines. Many an Allied ship convoy was grateful once they came within the range of these shore guns that had so recently been aimed at them.

Italian flak gunners who retained allegiance to Badoglio's

government, whether they wore Blackshirt, army, Regia Aeronautica or Regia Marina uniform, continued to shoot at German and Fascist Italian aircraft flying over Corsica, Sardinia and Southern Italy. However, as both Fascists and anti-Fascists used the same markings on their aircraft it was confusing. On 16 October the gunners were informed that Co-Belligerent aircraft would drop the old national emblem and would henceforth carry the emblem of the Italian flag. The Co-Belligerent Air Force was slowly undergoing retraining to fly British-built and American-built machines, and currently consisted of five hundred and fifty-seven flight crewmen and fourteen thousand four hundred and twenty-three ground crewmen. Additionally Badoglio loaned another seven thousand seven hundred ground crewmen to British and American squadrons.

Between 8 September and 13 October forty-eight thousand Italians that had been captured by the Allies prior to 8 September opted to join Badoglio's anti-German forces, but the Allies refused to hand them over to Badoglio! Instead they preferred to use them to their own advantage: those in British hands were sent to the British Army Pioneer Corps or Royal Navy Artisan Corps; those in French custody were sent to French Army labor battalions; and those in American camps were sent to US Army labor battalions. Within the United States, Canada, in Britain and throughout Africa these fellows could be seen working for the war effort. Their duties were as varied as helping with the harvest, unloading trucks, digging ditches, fighting fires caused by accident or sabotage, sentry duty and manning flak guns. The Allies refused to give these men Co-Belligerent status, which would have put them under Badoglio's orders. They came up with a name for them: Cooperators.

At the end of October the French took responsibility for the defense of Corsica, freeing Italian VII Corps. Magli's Italians were now shipped to Southern Italy and Sardinia in troopships escorted by Co-Belligerent warships.

Badoglio was a military man and he knew that the duties being performed by his personnel were of extreme value, but he was also keenly aware that after the war their record would count for naught. Only the record of infantry formations on the front line would gain any recognition at the peace conference table, and currently none of his infantry formations were in action in Italy. What he needed was a ground formation winning battles and gaining headlines.

The greatest hindrance to this dream was not a shortage of troops, nor a shortage of battlefields, but rather the shortsightedness of British politicians and generals. The British were faced with a serious credibility gap that threatened to become a public relations disaster. Since 1917 the British press, all too often imitated by the man in the street and by the radio comic and the film actor, had decried the Italians as poor soldier material, sometimes even blatantly calling all

Italians 'cowards'. Anti-Italian jokes in this vein were popular. Even British motion pictures sprinkled their scripts with such clap-trap, such as: "You can tell those planes bombing us are German, for 'Eye-ties' don't have the stomach for battle". Those who knew better cringed when they heard such blatantly idiotic racist statements. But now in autumn 1943 if the British government suddenly announced that they were entrusting part of the front to Italian soldiers, then this would point to one of two conclusions: either the war was going so badly that they had to resort to putting Italian cowards into the line, or this business about Italian cowardice had all been a complete and utter myth right from the start perpetuated by politicians for their own ends [and by generals to cover up the fact that they could read many of the Italian coded signals]. It was easier to explain an Italian defeat by using words like 'feint-hearted Italians' than it was to tell the public and hence the enemy that the British knew all of the Italian battle plans having read their signals! Obviously the latter conclusion was the truth, but the British dare not let the Germans know about their expertise in reading coded signals. Certainly it would prove politically embarrassing for politicians to admit they had been lying about Italians for twenty-six years. Nor did the newspaper and newsreel editors look forward to admitting their complicity in the great deception.

The Americans on the other hand were not embarrassed by this dilemma, because they had never accepted the lie about Italian cowardice. [Their racial prejudice was aimed at others.] Indeed the Americans enjoyed seeing the British generals squirm with this dilemma. One American soldier in twelve was of Italian ethnicity and there had never been any indication that they were poor military material. The Garibaldi Battalion had earned distinction in the American Civil War. In World War I Italian-Americans and Italian immigrants had fought with tremendous courage. They were doing so in the current conflict. However, the Americans needed the British, and therefore they agreed to protect their 'sensitivities'.

Nor were the French bothered by this dilemma. They too had never accepted the cowardice myth. In fact their Foreign Legion, which contained Germans, Italians, Britons and Americans and others, consistently considered Italian members as second only to German members in bravery and efficiency - rating Americans and Britons much lower!

Yet the British generals had to admit they needed Italian troops at the front. The Americans had quickly come to the conclusion that Germany would only be defeated by an invasion of France, but the British were loath to return there, hence their involvement in Italy and Greece. However, as the Americans owned the bat and the ball the British were forced to let the Americans choose the ballpark. Italy could not be abandoned to the Germans: honor demanded the Allies remain, but there were not enough first-class British and American troops to fight here and in France and against the Japanese all at the same time. The USA was a populous nation of one hundred and forty million, but was stretched thin: the American ground force facing the Japanese was larger than the entire British Army. As a result the Allies compromised, deciding to assign a few first-class combat troops to Italy and if the campaign continued they would reinforce them with second-class troops. In the mindset of the US Army the term 'second-class' meant American Negro troops. Most of the white American generals and politicians were so racist that they assumed all Negroes were cowards. They also had a unit of Americans that were racially Japanese. Obviously, they did not consider these Nisei to be cowards, but the American politicians and generals did distrust these soldiers, and they had imprisoned thousands of Nisei women and children. In the mindset of the British Army the term 'second-class' meant anybody who was not British. The thinking of the Brits and Yanks was that if the war was to be won in France they had to have troops there they could trust.

As a result of this 'second class' decision the British and Americans agreed to use Italian infantry, though the Italians would have to concede many of the accepted rights allotted to other Allied partners: namely they would only serve under US command, neither Italian nor British, and their units would have titles assigned by the British. The purpose of the latter was in case the press reported the activities of these Italian units. The British generals did not want their own press mentioning Italian 'divisions' and 'brigades', because the British public were used to such terms by now and knew how many troops were involved. A brigade was about three thousand men. A division was about ten thousand or more. The British hit upon the idea of using the name 'gruppo'. It was a common enough Italian term, but even in the Italian mind it did not identify the numbers of men involved. While the British term 'group' was a fixed term in the RAF, it was never used by the British Army except in conjunction with another term, such as 'brigade group' [a reinforced brigade] and 'army group' [two or more armies]. However, the Americans did use the term 'group' to mean two battalions.

In fact the British politicians and generals were hoping the Italians would receive no publicity at all, so that they would never have to explain the use of Italians to the British people. Allied ground forces in Italy were controlled by Alexander's 15th Army Group, and Alexander had already given his British press officers secret strict priorities: to whit, British troops were to get the lion's share of publicity, with the Americans coming in a poor second. Other Allies such as the Canadians and Poles would receive some press mentions on occasion, and the Italians would have little if any at all. Moreover, victories by troops that were not British would sometimes be described as 'British victories': literally stealing someone else's glory. Naturally this caused bad faith and poor morale among non-British troops. It especially hurt the Americans to read in a newspaper that a hill that they spilled blood to capture was a 'British victory'.

The basic truth is that the Allies were caught completely unprepared by the Italian surrender, which is a shocking indictment of Allied military and political planners. In September while the Italians carried the ball the Allies fumbled. This condemned the British and Americans to suffer twelve thousand casualties just to crawl off the beach at Salerno, while Montgomery's forces might just as well have remained on the playing fields of Eton for all the good they accomplished. Additionally, Churchill's 'invasion' of the Aegean would have been comical, had it not been for the human loss.

Following their military errors the Allies compounded them with political mistakes. The Badoglio regime was anathema to most Italians. No one had elected him and he did not have a political party power base. The Ethiopians, who were bona fide members of the Allies, had actually indicted him as a war criminal. He was probably the worst possible choice to lead a shattered and fragmented Italy. At least the king was useful as a symbol of continuity. The Allied leaders knew Badoglio was hopeless, and some had toyed with the idea of producing an Italian 'De Gaulle', a champion of anti-Fascism, and they had negotiated with Lieutenant General Bergonzolli [old electric whiskers] to this end. Nothing ever came of it, though.

Perhaps it was human nature that the British who had struggled for three years against the Italians could not now embrace them as friends. Even some Americans felt like that. However, for the good of their war effort they should have made the overtures. After all they were currently treating the Soviets like friends though they despised them intensely.

The Americans had the muscle to curtail all of this nonsense, but they did not have the moral courage. Quite frankly the American generals were overawed by their British counterparts. The USA was still a young country. Veterans of the Wild West Indian Wars were still alive. Parts of the USA had yet to be explored by white men. In 1939 Eisenhower had been a mere lieutenant colonel. Some of the National Guard generals were more politician than soldier. The Americans saw the British with their history of castles and knights and kings and parliament and literacy and arts as the finest example of politician or general or admiral the world could produce. Practicality said that the British must know something or they would not have conquered the largest empire the world had ever seen. Yet at the same time the Americans looked down despairingly at the French who could claim a similar lineage and history and empire. It is obvious therefore that Anglo-Saxon racism was at the heart of the Anglo-American alliance. America's soldiers might be ethnic 'Germans',

'Poles', 'Italians', 'Irish', 'Swedes', 'African Negroes' and so on, but her generals were 90% Protestant Anglo-Saxon. The British lapped this up of course and often offered 'advice' to the Americans on how to fight a war. As a result the British were far more influential than their numbers would suggest. The breadth of their influence can be judged when it is remembered that the Americans had never wanted to go to Morocco, Algeria, Tunisia, Sicily nor Italy, but had been enticed, lured, cajoled, conned and pressured into these countries by the British.

British rear-echelon soldiers echoed their generals' prejudice against Italians, a case of the blindly ignorant leading the blindly ignorant, but those Tommies who had actually fought them had a different opinion. Veterans of Keren, Sidi Rezegh, Alamein, Kasserine and Enfidaville knew better. But of course generals never ask corporals for their thoughts.

Needless to say this attitude frustrated the Co-Belligerents. Their army of twenty-three divisions was ready to liberate their country. As most of them came from Italy north of the front line, they worried constantly about their families under German occupation. Would the Fascists imprison their families as relatives of a 'traitor'? Once the Co-Belligerents saw the Allies try to reach Rome with just four divisions they realized how desperate the Allies were for trained manpower. With everyone else in the Co-Belligerent forces doing the job he was trained to do, such as medical orderly, radio operator, driver and mechanic, why was the infantry stuck in barracks awaiting orders?

Marshal Giovanni Messe had been a prisoner of war since his surrender in Tunisia. But come 8 September he sided with Badoglio and at the latter's request he was released from a British prisoner of war camp with the status of cooperator. Badoglio requested the British send him home to become commander of the Co-Belligerent Army. The Allies had known him as an intelligent and resourceful foe in Tunisia. They trusted he would exhibit those same qualities on their side now. Therefore they agreed to his promotion.

Messe immediately urged the Allies to use his infantry at the front. Only with blood, he believed, could Italy buy a seat at the post-war peace conference table. These were not his standards, but those of the world. No one goes to a military parade to see marching clerks carrying laptop computers led by a color guard in greasy mechanics' overalls. They go to see men carrying guns. In the mind of the public only combat soldiers are real soldiers.

Once Messe agreed to Allied restrictions he began to put together a division to serve under Clark's Fifth Army. Clark, who had never seen Italians in action, had an open mind. The British insisted that the unit be given an ambiguous title: 1st Motorized Group, which in British terminology could mean fifty men or a thousand. To the

Americans it sounded like two battalions. To Italians it roughly suggested about two thousand men. However, 15th Army Group also referred to this unit on occasion as the 1st Motorized Brigade, which to the Italians meant four battalions, and to the British meant three battalions and to the Americans four or six battalions. At times the British also called it the 1st Motorized Brigade Group, a name that to British ears meant a brigade with added engineers and artillery, but which was confusing to the Italians and Americans. Additionally the unit was also named the Dapino Brigade after its commander Major General Dapino, who had recently commanded the Legnano Division. Furthermore it was also called the Dapino Brigade Group. And some Italians referred to it officially as the 1st Raggruppamento, a vague term. All these titles were used in official dispatches at random. The purpose behind this absurdity was to keep the press guessing as to the correct size, and thus belittle the Italian contribution. It was not a division, the British insisted. However, the plan backfired with ludicrous results, because the hard pressed ordinary GIs of Fifth Army expressed euphoria, believing they were soon to be reinforced by a whole Italian corps containing the Dapino Brigade, 1st Motorized Group and 1st Motorized Brigade!

Moreover the British did not want to use an existing Co-Belligerent unit in its entirety, such as the Legnano Division. Therefore Dapping's formation was a composite force consisting of the independent 4th Bersaglieri Regiment of two battalions [some members were from 11th Bersaglieri Regiment], plus the 11th Artillery Regiment from the Mantova Division, and the 68th Infantry Regiment [three battalions] from the Legnano Division, with support troops from both divisions. The 4th Bersaglieri had fought in the French Alps in 1940 and in the Greek campaign. The Legnano had seen combat during the Greek campaign. By Anglo-American standards it was small for a division, but it was a division nonetheless. But to call it a division would have placed it in the public eye more than the terms 'group' or 'brigade' would have. It currently numbered eight thousand five hundred personnel. The US 82nd and 101st Airborne Divisions each had a normal complement of eight thousand five hundred and five personnel and no one has ever suggested they did not have the right to call themselves 'divisions'.

Chapter Fifty-three
Mussolini the New Lazarus

There was another reaction to the Badoglio surrender, that of the Germans and Fascists. They were taken completely by surprise by the Allied radio broadcasts, but the Germans had been preparing for such an eventuality and their precision in implementing Operation Axis was impressive indeed. However, it is to their everlasting shame that some German soldiers resorted to cowardly tactics like hiding behind women and children. This is evidence that they were extremely scared: understandable as they were surrounded by Italians, not knowing who their enemy was and in expectation of Allied paratroopers dropping on them any moment. The one ace up their sleeve was the number of Fascists willing to sell out their countrymen. At this stage of the war there were no Germans willing to sell out theirs.

The vast majority of Germans had not witnessed Italian battlefield courage and was therefore gullible victims of their own government propaganda, which was racist to the extreme. In the mind of the German soldiers they had come to Italy to defend a partner and that partner had stabbed them in the back. Some of the incidents where Germans massacred Italians were the result of sheer blind fury at the loss of a comrade. It is bad enough to lose a friend to the enemy, but when one loses a friend to a so-called partner it creates a violent reaction.

The Fascists were plainly embarrassed. Their own Grand Council had voted against Mussolini. Their king had fired him. Their people had celebrated in the streets by attacking Fascists, and now had come the great betrayal following which ordinary Italian civilians began hunting Fascists down like dogs. Even most of the Blackshirts had turned against the Fascists.

The only escape route for the Fascists led straight into the arms of the Germans, and once within the relative safety of German firepower they began to take revenge. This did not mean the Fascists trusted the Germans. On the contrary, the nature of their political ideology meant they did not trust foreigners, but the choice was simple: hang out with Hitler or be hanged alone.

The German goal was not just to disarm the Italians in their midst, but to gain control of northern Italy, because that was the region where most Italian industry lay. Furthermore they needed to deny northern Italian airfields to the Allies. Additionally Hitler had another need: to convince his other partners they could not slip out the back door when the going got tough. The French in North Africa had done so the previous November. The Danes had tried to do it in August 1943, and now the Italians had tried. The inference was clear: remain

Hitler's partner or be crushed by Hitler. Furthermore he had one eye on the German people. The German public believed they were in the right in the current conflict, and one indication of that righteousness was the number of partners they had. Hitler set about creating the illusion that Italy had not changed sides at all, but was still a staunch member of the Axis. These are some of the reasons why Hitler jumped at Kesselring's offer to hold northern Italy for a year.

The search for and rescue of Mussolini was also part of this plan. The resurrection of Il Duce was paramount in Hitler's efforts to convince the German people 'you can't keep a good man down'. Hitler was under constant danger of assassination by his own people and he wanted to show them that it was all but impossible to overthrow a Fascist dictator. Naturally Mussolini would be forever grateful to Hitler and would dance to any tune he whistled from now on. When Mussolini was rescued it is noticeable that Hitler ordered that he be brought to him. No more would Hitler journey to meet the Italian dictator half way. The welcome was genuine enough, but Mussolini was still made to feel like a beggar, which of course he had become.

Only now did the Italian dictator learn what had become of his followers. Many had been arrested by Badoglio's police before 8 September, and some had been captured by anti-Fascists after 8 September. A few were trapped in Allied territory and were in hiding or trying to form guerilla bands. Most had sided with the Germans and were aiding them either in a civilian capacity or as soldiers.

By 18 September when Mussolini made his radio broadcast the Germans had already begun to bring order out of chaos. Thousands of Fascists were helping the Germans: kawis were fighting as infantry, artillerymen and combat engineers; and hiwis were instructing Germans how to use captured Italian equipment and were working as interpreters, guides, radio operators, mechanics and technicians. The German navy, army, air force and SS all began using Italians. Soon a platoon of forty kawi infantry would be assigned to every German infantry battalion. Kawis and hiwis had their own rank and uniform structure. On Rhodes alone four thousand Italians became kawis and hiwis. Civilians were aiding the Germans as informers, spies and workers.

This was not good enough for Mussolini. He immediately established a new government and armed forces and a new political party: the Fascist Republican Party. The word 'Republican' was added to reflect the fact that they owed allegiance to Mussolini and not to a king. He named Alessandro Pavolini as Secretary of the Party, and he urged all Fascists to acknowledge this new party and go back to their original jobs if possible. Il Duce also made the MSVN [Blackshirts] independent again and indeed gave them more freedom than ever. He named Lieutenant General Renato Ricci as their commander. Ricci was a staunch Fascist: Bersaglieri in World War I, with D'Annunzio in the Fiume Revolt, had seized Zara for Fascism, had fought in Greece, had once commanded the Blackshirts, had been undersecretary of the Fascist Party and a cabinet minister. Mussolini hoped Ricci would put some backbone into the force.

As his Minister of Interior Mussolini picked Guido Buffarino-Guidi. He had been arrested by Badoglio, but liberated by the Germans.

Temporarily Mussolini was living in the Villa Feltrinelli in Gargagno in northern Italy. Hitler had not allowed him to return to Rome. The new government was spread all over the Gargagno district. As all propaganda edicts were issued from the village of Salo the public began to refer to Mussolini's authority as the Salo government. Its official title was the Italian Social Republic.

Badoglio dismissed Mussolini's rival government as powerless, but in truth it was strong and growing stronger every day. Covered by German guns Mussolini's orders reached 80% of the Italian population and three quarters of Italy's landmass. To enforce his orders he had the National Police, which he soon weeded of anti-Fascists. To cement their loyalty he demanded an oath from each man. This gave police chief Tamburini a force of twenty thousand. General Riccardo Maraffa also had two thousand men left over from the now defunct colonial police. Mussolini gave them security jobs. However, Maraffa was not amenable towards the Germans, so the Gestapo arrested him and sent him to Dachau concentration camp where he died. Wisely Mussolini ignored his fate. No fewer than eighty thousand Carabinieri had remained loyal to Mussolini and he immediately set them to work in the rural districts.

With internal security taken care of for the immediate moment Il Duce could concentrate on creating a new armed forces. To command it as Minister of War he needed someone who was wily, experienced in counter-insurgency operations, a front line leader, a recognized figure, without a hint of Badoglio-ism, and who wanted the job. There was only one man who fit this bill: Marshal Rodolfo Graziani, the butcher of Libya and Ethiopia. To head the army Mussolini chose Lieutenant General Gambara, who had recently shown good Fascist judgment by handing his entire corps to the Germans. The most loyal of Mussolini's sailors was Prince Junio Valerio Borghese, who had helped the Germans seize La Spezia naval base. Graziani authorized him to recreate the navy.

Hitler had already set up a controlling body for Italy: Reichsminister Albert Speer was in charge of all war industries, SS Gruppenfuehrer Karl Wolf was in command of internal security, and Field Marshal Kesselring was in charge of the front line, military lines of communication and all air, land and sea bases. The German Reichsarbeitsdienst arrived with its teenage workers to perform light construction and take on Italians as workers and sentries. Organisation Todt arrived to perform military construction using German and foreign volunteer workers, and it recruited Italians as employees and sentries. Its sentries not only protected construction sites from saboteurs and thieves, but also guarded slave workers, some of whom were Italian. The NSKK also arrived to provide drivers, traffic directors and mechanics for armed forces and government departments. They too hired Italians. By October the SS alone was using ten thousand hiwis and kawis, either in their front line units (Waffen SS), or as sentries for SS regional and local headquarters, or as guards at labor camps and concentration camps. The '9 September Battalion' of Blackshirts was still serving the Germans and was now on security duty just behind the front line.

To man Mussolini's new armed forces Graziani called upon all soldiers, sailors and airmen to report to the nearest police station for orders. This included those serving as hiwis and kawis, and naturally this immediately placed him in confrontation with the Germans. But they needn't have worried, because German pay for volunteers was good and conditions were excellent, and as a result few Italians were willing to leave to serve in one of Mussolini's organizations.

Perhaps knowing that few would leave his service, Hitler readily agreed to Graziani's call to arms. However, he refused to meet Graziani's next demand, to release those prisoners of war held by the Germans that now agreed to serve Mussolini. The Germans were treating their Italian prisoners despicably. They had murdered some of them. Given the restrictions of war-time the Germans treated their British and American prisoners relatively well, especially early in the war, but the Germans did not look upon these Italians as honorable soldiers fighting for their country, but as traitors. These prisoners only had one chance of escape from this hell - volunteer for German service. Therefore many had done so. Hitler trusted these men, but he did not trust those who refused to serve Hitler but were willing to serve Mussolini. Hitler's advisers assured him that once freed they would desert.

It was becoming apparent to many that though Mussolini might call himself head of state, it was Hitler who really called the shots. There was no better example of this than the fate of the South Tyrol. This terrain, known to the Italians as Alto Adige, had been sliced away by the Italians from a defeated Austria in 1919 along with its Austrian population. Now in September 1943 Hitler was demanding the region should be returned to Austria, which really meant to him, as he had controlled Austria for the past five years. Only Hitler's special relationship with Mussolini had prevented him from pressing the argument before. However, Mussolini had agreed back in 1939 that citizens of the region could serve in the German forces rather than the Italian. Many had chosen to do so. However, in September

1943 Hitler tired of this charade and organized a border commission to judge the situation. Its two most influential members were Friedrich Rainer a Nazi Party official and Odilo Globocnik an SS Obergruppenfuehrer in the Concentration Camp Service. Objectivity was never one of Hitler's strongpoints and he chose these men well. Neither was German. Both had grown up in the Austrian city of Trieste while it was part of Austria and had seen their home town handed over to the Italians in 1919. In fact Globocnik was not even racially Austrian, but was half-Slovene and half-Hungarian. One did not have to be psychic to guess how the border commission would vote. On 19 September they declared that all the territory grabbed by Italy from Austria in 1919 should be returned. And this was done. The South Tyrol districts of Bolzano and Belluno would henceforth be administered as the Alpenvorland Gau by Friedrich Hofer the leading Nazi in South Tyrol, and the Italian districts of Udine, Gorizia, Trieste and Pola would be governed as the Kuestenland Gau by Friedrich Rainer. Globocnik would be head of security in both gaus. The Italian-speaking district of Trento, once ruled by Austria, was also taken from Italy, but it was declared to be an autonomous state, perhaps as a sop to Mussolini who had once lived there.

However, Hitler agreed that any citizen of the two gaus or the Trento state could volunteer for Mussolini's new armed forces rather than serve the Germans. In Alpenvorland lived one hundred and fifty thousand Austrians, fourteen thousand Friuli-Ladins and a few thousand Italians. The former chose to serve Hitler, and the latter two were divided in their loyalty between Hitler and Mussolini - surely a choice of the lesser of two evils. The population of Kuestenland was a mixture of Italians, Austrians, Croats, Slovenes and Friuli-Ladins, and only the Austrians overwhelmingly chose to serve Hitler.

Once the hand over celebrations had ceased, the Austrians of these districts began to learn the truth about Nazism. They were given third class citizenship, rather than first class like a German. The Alpenvorland police force was designated Ordnungsdienst (Order Service) rather than Ordnungspolizei (Order Police) as a deliberate insult and was assigned German overseers. The Kuestenland police force was named the Civic Guard and consisted mostly of Fascist Italians, many of them ex-cops. The Trento police force was named the Trient Security Corps and was almost exclusively Italian. However, Heinrich Himmler did comb his SS for people who had grown up in these areas and who by definition had been Italian citizens until 19 September 1943 and he placed them into the new Bozen [Bolzano] Police Regiment. The regiment also took in new recruits.

By now Italian manhood, whether military or civilian was divided into the following: those serving the Germans; those serving Mussolini; those serving Badoglio; those in hiding in the mountains;

and those languishing in somebody's prisoner of war camp.

Mussolini was desperate for manpower. His recruiters visited the Piave Division, which was the garrison of Rome. But when few of its members stepped forward to join him, the Germans realized this was a potential enemy in their midst, so in violation of the Armistice at Rome they surrounded the city and disarmed the Piave Division and marched its personnel off to a prison camp.

As a result Mussolini told Gambara to concentrate on building a small army initially. He also turned to other cronies to help him form an 'army'. Ricci controlled four hundred and eighty-seven thousand Blackshirts, but this figure was misleading as it included women, and macho Fascists did not want to give rifles to women. As the Blackshirt retirement age was sixty many were in their fifties and in poor physical condition. Furthermore, as most were reservists they held essential civilian jobs. The full-time Blackshirts were already serving in such units as the Forestry Militia, the Port Militia, the Post and Telegraph Militia, the Anti-Aircraft Militia, the Frontier Militia and the Highway Militia. These had continued to perform their duties, under Mussolini, then under Badoglio and then under the Germans. Most now agreed to serve Mussolini again. Though the Germans had already recruited many of the flak gunners to serve in Luftwaffe anti-aircraft artillery units.

Within a week of being asked to recruit a new navy Borghese had collected no fewer than twelve thousand marines and thirteen thousand sailors. No mean feat. Many of these fellows had been serving the Germans as kawis and hiwis and others had simply gone home to await events. He formed the marines into the San Marco Division and put some of the sailors into the following: MAS boats, a midget submarine flotilla, a sub-chaser flotilla, a minesweeper flotilla, a pig unit and a gamma unit. But this still left most of his sailors unemployed, so he formed them into an infantry division under the name Decima MAS. The name bore no relation to their duties, but was the name of the most famous of the sea going units once commanded by Borghese. In normal parlance this naval infantry formation would be known as the Condottieri Division [after 16th century Italian mercenaries]. It would contain thirteen infantry battalions, three artillery battalions, an engineer battalion and a reconnaissance unit.

For this incredible effort Mussolini promoted Borghese to Undersecretary of the Navy. However, the Germans did not like the idea and demanded Mussolini cancel the promotion. He did. Seeing Mussolini weaken, Ricci had his Blackshirts arrest Borghese, a potential political rival. Mussolini ordered him released. Borghese still felt vulnerable, so he bought protection from Gambara. The price was the San Marco Division, which Borghese signed over to Gambara's control.

Gambara needed the marines, because by the end of September only sixteen thousand five hundred men had stepped forward to join his army. There appeared to be no other way to gain recruits except to conscript them. Mussolini had never conscripted all his available manpower because he never had enough equipment for them. E. g. in terms of a percentage of their population the Americans had conscripted twice as many men as had Mussolini. In fact Il Duce had not yet called up the classes of 1921-24 [i.e. men born in those years], though some had volunteered. Graziani suggested calling these classes now. Ricci was against it, citing with some sense that if they had not already volunteered their heart was obviously not in it and they would be useless to the cause. Mussolini ignored Ricci, because he knew Ricci was jealous of Graziani and Gambara. Mussolini declared that only with new armed forces could he regain the independence he had sold to Hitler. Like all his decisions it had a political motive.

Everything in Mussolini's new armed forces was haphazard and make-do. The uniforms were a good example. The hated puttees were thrown away and enough regulations of the old royal army were discarded to allow each soldier to make a fashion statement. In Italy even warriors were fashion-conscious. Borghese's beached sailors of the Condottieri Division and Major General Amilcare Farina's marines chose army-style tunics but without collars or lapels, and forage caps. Gray roll neck sweaters were for winter wear. The troops of the Nembo Parachute Division that had sided with the Germans wore camouflage smocks and German paratrooper helmets, being almost indistinguishable from Germans [a few chose Italian infantry helmets]. Members of Gambara's army could wear collared or collarless tunics, and they had a new badge, the 'Gladius' (emblem of a Roman Empire short sword) in place of the royal crown. The Alpini in the army retained their distinctive feathered hats, and the Bersaglieri retained their black cock feathers in their helmets. Officers tried at first to remain standard in their mouse gray collared tunic, flat cap and cavalry pants, but as time went on they wore what they could get. Many a soldier adopted German clothing.

By mid-October Gambara could inform Mussolini he had fifty coastal artillery batteries [manned by Blackshirts], ten mobile gruppos of artillery, and three divisions - Italia Bersaglieri, Monterosa Alpini and Littorio Grenadiers [the latter was half alpini]. To man this army he currently had sixteen thousand five hundred volunteers, but conscription was bringing in more. The nucleus of the Italia Bersaglieri Division was a body of veterans from the 3rd and 8th Bersaglieri Regiments, [the latter had been the 120th Provisional Regiment], and the new recruits were put into the 1st and 2nd Bersaglieri Regiments and into a battalion of combat engineers and an artillery gruppo.

Finally, Mussolini convinced Hitler to allow the Italians living in Hitler's filthy prison camps to volunteer for the new army. The fuehrer put a limit of thirteen thousand on this.

Mussolini also clawed back some airplanes confiscated by the Germans and asked Lieutenant Colonel Botte to form a new air force. He even managed to gain the new 385 mph Fiat G55 inline engine fighter aircraft that was just coming off the assembly lines. He was fortunate that most of the fighter pilot aces of the Regia Aeronautica now volunteered to serve him, including Luigi Gorrini who had fifteen aerial victories, Carlo Magnaghi, Mario Veronesi and Ennio Tarantola each the victor in nine fatal encounters, Amedeo Benati, Giulio Torrese and Natalino Stabile who each had eight kills, Giovanni Bonet, Giuseppe Robetto and Antonio Camaioni each credited with seven shot down, Ugo Drago, Adriano Visconti and Fausto Fornaci each with six confirmed enemy knocked down, and Guido Fibbia, Antonio Longhini and Dino Forlani with five victories each.

———————

Chapter Fifty-four
The Partisans

Surprisingly those members of the Pinerolo Division and Aosta Cavalry Regiment that had joined the Greek ELAS would soon suffer a worse indignity than those in German prison camps. The Yugoslavian and Albanian Communist leaders, Tito and Enver Hoxha, had agreed to use Italian defectors, and they kept their word. But the ELAS leader Stefanos Serafis was a fanatic Communist and a Greek racist and unwilling to compromise. One of the British agents working with ELAS was Anthony Quayle.[The movie star] He had no love for the Italian turncoats any more than did Serafis, but he was humane and he advised ELAS to give the Italians a chance. After all the ELAS had found the Italian to be a formidable foe in battle. Reluctantly the ELAS band leaders assigned missions to the Italians, but they either chose extremely difficult ones or hindered the Italians at every turn. Following these defeats, they convinced themselves the Italians were useless and they began to separate the Italians into small manageable groups, and then by trickery they disarmed them. Then they stole their equipment. Later they ordered them to perform manual labor. Within weeks they were treating them like slaves. During the Italian occupation of Greece the Italians had murdered about nine thousand civilians, and the Greek Communist partisans could not forgive this, and they went out of their way to be brutal. When the first cold temperatures arrived the partisans began to steal the clothes of their Italian slaves. By late October the literally naked and starving Italians began to die. At the risk of his life Quayle extracted Major General Infante and took him to southern Italy.

———————————

Throughout Italy north of the front line [i.e. Mussolini's Italy] the ordinary people went back to their humdrum lives after the heady days of September, and now survival was a full-time job, first of all because the British and Americans were continuing their air raids; secondly because the Germans had declared martial law and their patrols were everywhere; and thirdly because the Italian OVRA was back in business advised by the Gestapo and they sought out anyone who spoke against Fascism or Mussolini, and they would arrest and torture them on the merest suspicion. Rationing was worse than ever and black market prices were extortionate. Finding food for the children was a major undertaking. Only the Fascists lived the good life.

Not unnaturally many Italians wanted to fight back against the Fascists, but only the soldiers who had fled into the mountains had the weapons, ammunition and training to become guerillas [i.e. partisans].

One such was the Julia veteran Germano Baron. Another was the sailor Augusto Bazzino. But how could an ordinary civilian simply walk into the mountains and become a partisan? It took more than courage. It took food, knowledge, weapons, ammunition and equipment.

Yet some civilians had done this. Many were military veterans, like Franco Anselmi, who had fought for Mussolini in Ethiopia and Spain. Many were political rabble-rousers. Gian Luigi Banfi was a famous architect. Anyone was welcome to join a partisan band if he or she brought his or her own food, weapons and ammunition. For pure convenience individual guerillas accepted the political ideology of their band leader. It would have been a miracle if by coincidence all the Communists lived in one valley and all the Christian Democrats in another. The Communists were more successful in establishing bands, because they had been running clandestine passive resistance to the Fascists for twenty-one years. They had the infrastructure.

In the three regions annexed by Hitler many of the partisans were Slovenes, Croats and Friuli-Ladins and there were even some Austrians among them.

As early as 9 September the leaders of political parties long dormant under Mussolini had met to organize resistance to the Germans and Fascists. The main parties represented were the Communists, Socialists, Conservatives, Christian Democrats and Liberals. They formed the Committee of National Liberation of Northern Italy (CLNAI). There were also several smaller parties including Catholics, Anarchists and Democrats.

On 20 September northern representatives of the CLNAI met in secret to form an umbrella organization that would attempt to control the partisan bands springing up in the mountains. Designated the CLN – National Corps of Liberation, it would provide liaison between the partisans and Allied headquarters.

Of Italy's population of forty-five million [1940 statistic], approximately ten million were men between the ages of eighteen and fifty, of which by October 1943 about one million eight hundred thousand had been killed in the war or had been imprisoned or were serving Badoglio. Of the remainder one million seven hundred thousand were living in Badoglio's Italy, and six million five hundred thousand were living in Mussolini's Italy.

Excluding Fascists, therefore, within Mussolini's Italy there were roughly five million eight hundred thousand Italian men that could have joined the partisans. But most were family men and had the responsibility of protecting their loved ones. Furthermore a family man who leaves home for the mountains is noticed by his absence and in retaliation the Fascists might arrest the family he left behind. Moreover, guerilla warfare is a young man's game, and the older men might have figured they would be a liability to a partisan band. In addition it takes extreme courage to climb into the mountains at night without a destination, with little food, without weapons and ammunition, without medicines, stumbling around and hoping to run into partisans before encountering a German or Fascist patrol. In any case the vast majority who did find partisans were told to go home and await the call to rise up.

There will never be an accurate count of anti-Fascist partisans. The hundreds of thousand s that resisted the Germans in the heady days following 8 September eventually returned home to live as 'model citizens' either in Badoglio's or Mussolini's Italy. They never bothered registering their name, and with whom would they register it? Does one include them? An untold number that did not formally join a partisan band for whatever reason nonetheless performed valuable service behind enemy lines: cutting a telephone line, slitting a tire on an army truck, pouring dirt into an army fuel tank, creating false alarms, giving misinformation to the authorities, misdirecting a German troop convoy, and so on. Does one include them? How about those who aided the partisans with food or a safe house for a night. Does one include them? The Fascists certainly called them all partisans and if caught they could be sent to a labor camp or a concentration camp, and some were shot. The members of the Squadre Azzione Patriotico [GAP or SAP] were a branch of the partisans: i.e. law-abiding citizens by day, saboteurs by night.

Italian men of the mid-twentieth century were sexist, and because of this the partisans refused to acknowledge the women among them as bona fide partisans, referring to them as 'staffete' rather than 'partigiani', though in truth there was little difference. Staffete risked their lives just as much as partigiani, and many fought with rifles in their hands.

In October the Socialists reported they had about five hundred partisans in their Matteoti Brigade, and the Christian Democrats and Liberals acknowledged they had about one thousand five hundred partisans in their three 'Justice and Liberty' brigades. The Conservatives reported they had one thousand five hundred men in their People's brigades. There were also some small Anarchist units and Catholic formations. The Communists, who were more experienced at this sort of thing, declared they had twelve thousand partisans in their Garibaldi brigades. They took the name of Giuseppe Garibaldi the great Italian nationalist hero to convince naive recruits they were true Italians and not lackeys of Moscow.

About eight thousand soldiers of the Fourth Army had gone into the mountains of Piemont to continue the fight and they had no specific political loyalty. Whole platoons had kept their cohesion, many of them Alpini who were trained to fight like this in winter and summer.

The term brigade was consistently used by partisans. There were two reasons: the leaders assumed they would eventually expand their band to true brigade size, and secondly it made them seem larger to potential recruits. Guerilla fighting is a lonely business and the larger the band the more safe recruits would feel. Though in truth it should have been the opposite. Perhaps there was a third reason: vanity. A commander of a 'brigade' had more prestige than the commander of a 'battalion'. And soon there developed a fourth reason: once the Allies agreed to the CLN suggestion that they parachute supplies and agents to the partisans, the term brigade came in handy, for the Allies dropped enough for a real brigade, that is for three thousand men not five hundred.

By now the main partisan strongholds were in Piemont, where the remnant of the Fourth Army held out, in Carnia-Friuli where the Garibaldi brigades dominated, the Northern Apennines which hid Garibaldi brigades and 'Justice and Liberty' brigades, and the shores of Lake Maggiore dominated by Garibaldi brigades.

Mario Ricci, an anti-Fascist who had fought against Mussolini in Spain, joined with Osvaldo Poppi to set up a Garibaldi brigade near Sassuolo southwest of Modena. Mario Lizzero, whom Badoglio had freed from prison, organized a Garibaldi brigade in Friuli, choosing Lino Zocchi as his military commander. Candido Grassi organized People's brigades in the Osoppo area, where there were also Catholic and Conservative units. Grassi was as much afraid of Communists as he was of Fascists, and there were some skirmishes between the Communists and other partisans.

In early November several Garibaldi brigades gathered in the Val d'Ossola northwest of Lake Maggiore and they attacked into the next valley. This went against the first rule of guerilla warfare, attacking a large formation with a large formation. For three days they battled with the Germans, following which about five hundred surviving partisans dragged their wounded bodies back into the mountains under the first snowfall.

Despite this defeat and nothing to show for their efforts anywhere, the partisans were causing the Axis major concern. No military or police vehicle could be parked without a sentry. Vehicles could not travel through mountains without a truckload of troops as escort. Telephone and telegraph lines were always down and the repair parties had to be escorted by armed men. All information coming from civilian sources had to be thoroughly confirmed. Troops were often thrown onto the alert at night, causing sleep deprivation. Every sentry was terrified of having his throat slit. High profile Fascists had to have bodyguards. In November alone twenty-eight Fascist officials were assassinated.

In the last week of November strikes broke out in Turin and soon spread to Milan and other industrial centers. Buffarino-Guidi described the situation to Mussolini as chaos – e. g. in Milan there were only nine hundred policemen and not all were armed. As a result the police had to ask Blackshirts for help, but some of them were as young as fifteen and untrained.

The situation became so bad that the Germans decided to bring in their own anti-partisan troops, and the varied ethnic composition of these reinforcements was evidence to the Italians that Hitler was running short of manpower: the Security Corps of Belorussians, the Savage Division of Tatars and Caucasians, several squadrons of Kalmyk horse cavalry, a battalion of Lithuanian auxiliary police, three French NSKK companies, five regiments of Cossacks. These men did not understand the Italian language and barely spoke any German. The Germans, knowing these reinforcements were devoutly religious and therefore hated Communists with a passion, convinced them that all Italian partisans were atheistic Communists.

Mussolini's personnel were also drawn into the anti-partisan conflict early on whenever they came under attack, and naturally the police and Carabinieri immediately set off in pursuit of the 'bandits'. The police would rarely ask the Carabinieri for aid and vice versa owing to political jealousies.

Soon even the Germans were asking Mussolini for help! Borghese's Condottieri Division of ten thousand naval infantry seemed to be unemployed, so Mussolini ordered them into the anti-partisan conflict. They fought primarily in small groups in the mountains of Piemont, Lombardy and Gorizia in a series of winter sweeps to flush out partisans. On the rare occasions that they sighted partisan bands they tried to hold them in place until artillery or air support could be brought into play, but the partisans usually managed to scatter. Often the Condottieri had to retreat when partisans doubled back around them and attacked their supply lines.

As Minister of the Interior the partisan problem really fell at the feet of Buffarino-Guidi. He created a new anti-partisan force from select policemen and new recruits called the Auxiliary Police, who were expected to stay on the trail of partisans for days on end. Eventually they formed nine battalions.

Motivated as much by envy of Borghese and Buffarino-Guidi as by a desire to help in the cause, Ricci organized anti-partisan formations among his Blackshirts. Each formation took a different name. The largest was the four thousand strong Ettore Muti Legion, named after the Fascist martyr murdered by Badoglio.

The Germans wanted Gambara's army to join in the partisan conflict too, but Graziani was insistent they should be trained for front line combat against the Allies, and what's more he asked for German help in training his divisions. The Germans agreed if the training was done in Germany. This was acceptable. As a result the three army and one marine divisions were entrained for Germany.

This still left Gambara with some smaller units in Italy. Most were for coastal protection: one mountain infantry battalion, eight battalions and twenty independent companies of infantry, four Bersaglieri battalions, ten coastal artillery gruppos [some had three battalions, some four], and fifty independent coastal artillery batteries. Many of these troops were Blackshirts. There were also twenty-seven engineer battalions. Behind the coastal fortifications by November he had two armored gruppos: the Leoncello [part of the old Centauro II Armored Division], and the new San Giusto. They used any armored vehicle they could find from Semoventis and M14s to the old L3s. There was also the 63rd Blackshirt Tagliamento Battalion Gruppo [of the Mussolini Division], now redesignated as a regiment of four battalions. With the Allies in control of the seas the importance of coastal defenses could not be overemphasized. Furthermore the flak sections of these units were in action constantly, because Allied aircraft would fly over the sea northwards before turning inland to strike their targets. The coastal flak belt of German and Italian guns was always a gauntlet the Allied aircraft had to run, twice.

In the Alpenvorland the Ordnungsdienst could not manage anti-partisan operations and normal police work too, so Himmler authorized members of the Bozen Police Regiment in the gau to fight off partisan raids. A militia, the Landschutz, was also created: each member spent a few hours per week guarding an installation.

In Kuestenland the Slovene Littoral National Guard was created to hunt partisans, while the Civic Guard remained on normal police duties. Its commander Cesare Pagnini proved adept at negotiating with the SS, the German Army, Fascist Italians, Italian partisans, Slovene nationalists and Titoists. Obviously he intended to survive the current situation.

In Trento the Trient Security Corps was only involved in partisan problems when they were attacked.

The partisans were poorly coordinated, many of their band leaders only paying lip service to a political party or to the CLN, but they were far more coordinated than the Axis forces they were up against - German Army soldiers, SS troops, Italian police of some kind, Italian anti-partisan formations owing allegiance to Ricci or Buffarino-Guidi or Gambara or Borghese, and the foreigners brought in by the Germans. There was no anti-partisan headquarters in Italy and each local German and Italian boss behaved like an independent warlord.

In November Gambara's coastal units came under attack by partisans and no one seemed able or willing to help him, so he created from his small army several anti-partisan formations of his own: the Reparti Autonomi Bersaglieri [two regiments strong]; Reparti Anti-Partigiani Gruppo [five battalions]; and the Cacciatore degli Appenini Gruppo [nine Alpini battalions]. Almost at once one of the Bersaglieri battalions was hot on the heels of a partisan band in the upper Isonzo

Valley.

Conscription had caused arguments among the Fascist leaders. Ricci was convinced they would all run away. In order to placate Ricci Mussolini gave him more power. He made him head of the new Guardia Nazionale Repubblicana (GNR) a body that would hunt partisans and defend the national soil. The nucleus of this GNR would be the entire eighty thousand man Carabinieri and the two thousand-strong Colonial Police, and new guard formations would be established using twenty-five thousand fresh conscripts. Ricci took the bait, just as Mussolini thought he would, and of course by using conscripts himself Ricci could hardly continue to argue against their use by others.

These twenty-five thousand conscripts were to come out of the pool of the 1921-24 classes, a total of one hundred and eighty thousand names, which would still leave plenty for Gambara's army, but there were two flies in this ointment: first, Hitler demanded forty-four thousand of the conscripts to serve as workers in Fritz Sauckel's labor organization in Germany and in Albert Speer's Organisation Todt all over Europe. As conscripts they came under the description of forced labor and would not receive the same pay and conditions as volunteers, but they would be paid and have time off. The second fly in the ointment was that ninety-three thousand of the 1921-24 classes refused to report for duty and went into hiding. Gambara ended up gaining only eighteen thousand conscripts for his new army.

Still Ricci was not bothered. His warning about mass desertion had been somewhat proven correct and at the same time he had increased his personal power. Gaining the Carabinieri was quite a coup, for this paramilitary police force contained several sections: mail investigation, mountain warfare, seaport defense, forestry patrol, rail security, frontier guards, the highway patrol and nine legions of light infantry, including some paratroopers. Though primarily regulated to rural districts and to serious crime activity such as gang busting and partisan hunting, the Carabinieri did have jurisdiction throughout the nation and did not answer to the police. Their myriad of uniforms reflected their duties. In cities they patrolled in a uniform first seen in the early 1800s.

Ricci went further in his power struggle by ordering every Blackshirt man that was not already doing a legitimate war job to 'volunteer' for the GNR. Thus, with his conscripts and these new 'volunteers' and with the Blackshirt security formations he had already formed, he managed to establish, in addition to the Carabinieri, a force of four regiments [Isonzo, Istria, D'Annunzio and Tagliamento], sixteen independent infantry battalions, the Tagliamento Legion of four battalions, the Leonessa Tank Battalion, a parachute battalion, two anti-tank battalions and the Vesubio Anti-Paratrooper Battalion. He also convinced several thousand Blackshirt flak gunners to leave the Germans and serve him, and he placed them in the new Etna Flak Division.

To placate Buffarino-Guidi Mussolini gave him nominal authority over the GNR.

Thus over a period of two months Mussolini had put together a significant armed body of men with allegiance to him: three thousand sea-going sailors, ten thousand Condottieri, twelve thousand marines, forty-seven thousand five hundred army volunteers and conscripts, eighty thousand GNR-Carabinieri, two thousand GNR-Colonial police, twenty-five thousand GNR conscripts, forty-three thousand Blackshirt GNR 'volunteers', twenty thousand National Police, about five thousand airmen and ten thousands Etna flak gunners: a total of over a quarter of a million men.

The number of Italians serving in German formations as members, hiwis or kawis was at least one hundred thousand and growing. For some Italian teenagers a German uniform was more prestigious than an Italian one. Hitler had told his recruiters not to take any more Italians out of his prison camps for obviously any who volunteered now did so only to escape their brutal treatment. The recruiters ignored him and continued to accept volunteers. E.g. at Debica in Poland the German Waffen SS had gathered about six hundred volunteers mostly from the Julia Alpini and Lombardia Divisions and had placed them into SS Battalion Debica under the command of Major Guido Fortunato. In addition to armed men, millions of Italian workers in Axis Italy were aiding the Axis cause, but only God knows how many did so willingly.

––––––––––

Chapter Fifty-five
Allied Italy

Churchill still refused to hand over the Italian cooperators to Badoglio, making feeble excuses such as a lack of shipping. In Britain many of them worked in road gangs or on farms. With a paycheck for the first time in years, freedom and the close proximity of British girls the Italians were happy enough, but they had volunteered to fight like Italian soldiers not to live like English civilians. Churchill had already forced millions of British women to work in war industries and on farms, because he needed to release British men for military service. For every Italian he put to work another British male worker could be inducted into uniform.

Oddly enough much of the British public could not understand what was going on. Frankly, they just couldn't 'get it'. They did not see the Italian Recalcitrants, i.e. those Italian prisoners that refused to serve Badoglio, because they were still behind barbed wire. The public only saw the Cooperators. The British people came to the lunatic conclusion that if a German surrendered he was sent to a prison, but if an Italian surrendered he was given a bicycle and a ticket to the cinema! In a society where information was strictly censured the rumor-mongers and story tellers were in their element. Housewives in food queues and workers in lunch canteens would believe just about any farcical tale that came their way.

When Montgomery's Eighth Army had finally come across a German defensive position at the Biferno River, he had quickly outflanked it by a seaborne landing, but had then been held on the Trigno River until 3 November. After another short advance Montgomery was stopped again on the Sangro River. Clark's US Fifth Army since its terrible time at Salerno had waged bloody battles on the Volturno and Garigliano Rivers and had been fought to a standstill by November 15. It appeared that having reached Italy the Allies had no other plans but to butt their heads against the German wall.

Whereas the Germans had performed magnificently, especially considering the few units they had available. Against Montgomery's quarter of a million men they had only committed the 1st Parachute Division, a battle group of the 26th Panzer Division and the 65th Infantry Division, the latter consisting of Polish conscripts. Any kawis who showed up at the front line to help the Germans were very welcome.

In the Aegean the Germans also relied on Italian kawis and hiwis. By November the Germans and kawis had overrun the islands of

Simi, Kos and Stampalia and had bombed to destruction two Italian, one Greek and five British warships. German air raids had worn the Regina Division on Leros to a frazzle. The island's seaplanes were all shot up and the artillery positions were demolished. On 12 November Germans and kawis invaded Leros. Their landing barges met heavy opposition from the Regina's artillery. Even German air strikes could not prevent the Italian gunners from fighting back. In fact the Germans aborted their invasion in this sector. Elsewhere on the island the invaders fought their way ashore versus British resistance, and some German paratroopers dropped to capture key installations. For five days British, New Zealand and Italian defenders fought vigorously, but they were hopelessly outgunned owing to German air supremacy. However, the majority of the infantrymen of the Regina refused to leave their barracks and would not fight the invading Fascists! Finally the British commander of the island surrendered. A few managed to escape in small boats. Needless to say most of the Regina's infantry now joined the kawis, but those Italians that had resisted were taken prisoner, and over the next few days the kawis and Germans executed the officers including two admirals.

By the end of November all the Aegean islands had been conquered by the Germans and kawis, except Samos. Here the British and the Italian Cuneo Division held out under air attack until the last minute, and then the British evacuated by sea. The British claimed not to have sufficient shipping to evacuate the Italians on the island, and thus abandoned these men to the Fascists. Though they did evacuate Major General Soldarelli.

Churchill's venture into the Aegean had been a detour, and it had cost five thousand Allied casualties and twenty-five thousand Co-Belligerent casualties.

***

In late November 1943 General Harold Alexander overruled the fears of many of his subordinates and gave approval for Messe to place his first new combat formation into the front line. As commander of Allied ground forces in the Mediterranean Alexander was already in charge of troops from a score of nations and he had experience commanding 'yesterday's enemy' - he had once commanded German troops in battle. Messe gave the necessary orders to Dapino's 1st Motorized Gruppo (or whatever it was called on a given day) to move up to the front. Just about every British officer in the loop had misgivings.

The first members of Dapino's unit to see action were the gunners of the 11th Artillery Regiment. It was cold on the last night of November 1943, but they worked up a sweat manhandling their 105mm, 100mm and 75mm pieces into position under orders from US Fifth Army. Though few of the gunners spoke English there seemed to be no shortage of Americans who spoke Italian and the guns were soon coordinated into the Allied firing plan. They were excited, for this would be the first time Co-Belligerent forces took offensive action against the Germans. They knew what was at stake. If the Allies lost the war the British would hide behind their navy in the English Channel, and the Americans would be safe across the Atlantic, but where would the Co-Belligerents go? And the possibility of the Allies losing was very real indeed. To suggest these Italians had deliberately joined the Allies only because they were winning is utter nonsense. In the war against Japan the Americans had yet to conquer any Pacific island of major importance, and the British were still on the defensive on the India-Burma border. On the Russian front the Red Army had put the Germans on the defensive, it was true, but they had a long road ahead of them. At sea Allied propaganda could not hide the fact that the German U-boats could still go where they wished. In Italy the Anglo-American generals had shown extreme caution.

On the chilly damp morning of 1 December 1943 when Dapino's artillerymen opened fire on the Germans along the Garigliano River front in Southern Italy, alongside French, American and British gunners, they did so with a mixed feeling of apprehension and vengeance. For two days their shells churned up the muddy positions of Germans and kawis [and of course they suffered from counter battery fire], after which French, British and American infantry advanced. The Italian gunners continued to give fire support for five days, but did not have to move their guns because the Allied infantry only managed to advance a few hundred yards.

On 8 December the remainder of Dapino's unit entered the line and was given the mission of occupying the Mignano Gap, which US Army intelligence assured them was practically undefended. They were correct, and the Italian infantry gained an easy little victory here. However, the Germans quickly realized their mistake, and the following day they counter attacked with a battle group from the Hermann Goering Panzer Division and the 15th Panzergrenadier Regiment. The Italian infantry was hopelessly outclassed against tanks, self-propelled guns and panzergrenadiers armed with a plethora of automatic weapons, but they stubbornly fought back nonetheless. They wondered why the Americans had failed to warn them about the sleeping giant at the north end of the Mignano Gap. Cursing the fool Americans and the Germans with the same breath the Italians clung to their rock positions, foxholes and ditches. Officers ran to their men encouraging them with such exhortations as 'you are not fighting for a sand dune in Libya or a frozen steppe in Russia, but for your homeland and more importantly for Italian national honor' These men felt that every Allied general had his eye on them. At the end of the day it was the Germans who withdrew.

The next morning the Germans came on again and now the Italians began an authorized fighting withdrawal, halting at their original jump-off line.

Looking at this incident objectively the Italians did as well as any light infantry would have done under similar circumstances, but many a bigoted Briton took the opportunity to blame the Italians with an 'I told you so'. Some Britons even wanted to remove the Italians and use them only as rear-echelon. Fortunately in US Fifth Army Mark Clark was calling the shots, not the Brits, and he praised the courage of these Italians and allowed the unit to remain in line.

Clark had already become impressed by the bravery of Italian muleteers. The Americans had come to the conclusion that mules were a necessary form of transportation in the mountains of Sicily and Italy and had sent out a call to bring over American mules by the thousand. Many an American farm boy had handled a mule, but they were not able to lead mules in military convoys on steep mountain slopes with a sheer drop on one side in the rain across patches of ice at night without lights while under artillery fire, but that is exactly what was required. Obviously this activity called for a different type of muleteer indeed. The Italians had such mule units and Clark began to use them. He also asked them to train his Americans to do this job. Though in theory a part of the rear-echelon these mule units suffered high losses to artillery, mines and accidents.

On 15 December Dapino's men rewarded Clark's trust in them by raiding the Germans. Reinforced by the 51st Bersaglieri Battalion they first gave the hated 'Tedeschi' a forty-five minute artillery barrage, and then they assaulted, capturing fifty Germans and two 88mm flak guns. The German prisoners were astonished to find their captors were Italian. Next day the 4th Bersaglieri Regiment captured a hill at the end of the Liri Valley. With these two minor 'victories' under their belt the Italians now agreed to be withdrawn. Clark withdrew them, but not because he was dissatisfied. On the contrary, he had arranged for them to be given British uniforms and equipment.

On the night of 21 December eighty Polish commandos held off an attack by two hundred German mountain troops, having been alerted by Italian civilians that had risked their lives to infiltrate through the front line to warn them. In little incidents like this, in the courage of Italian muleteers, in the ferocity of Dapino's unit at the front, the Italians were proving themselves to the skeptical Allies.

More and more the Allies came to the conclusion that they needed the Co-Belligerents. Eight German-Austrian divisions, some Polish conscripts and the kawis were holding back fifteen Allied divisions [five American, four and two-thirds British, one French, one New Zealander, one Canadian, one Indian and one Moroccan, plus Dapino's unit and several smaller combat formations of Poles, Belgians, Newfoundlanders and others]. In reserve Alexander kept six divisions [one British, one Indian, one Algerian-Tunisian, one

Moroccan, one Canadian and one Polish], but he concluded that the Italian campaign would soon soak them up too.

Because of this Alexander approved an amphibious flanking maneuver near Rome to lever the Germans out of their defenses. The result was a landing at Anzio-Nettuno on 22 January 1944 on a stretch of undefended beach.

Mussolini was shaken by the news. Suddenly Allied tanks were just thirty miles from Rome and there was nothing to stop them. German planes counter attacked and were bewildered by their choice of targets. Mussolini warned the Fascists in Rome to be ready to evacuate. Fortunately the authorities there had recently caught the leading partisan in the city, Colonel Giuseppe di Montezemolo. So far, torture had not made him talk. They had also caught General Vito Artale, who had been fighting the Fascists since the Battle for Rome in September.

If Kesselring was worried, he did not show it, and he still put his faith in the timidity of the British and Americans. Having landed, the invaders under the American Lieutenant General John Lucas did not go anywhere, and this gave Kesselring two full days in which to rush long-range artillery to Anzio and then another six days to bring up infantry. Lucas had been cautioned by Clark not to do anything rash, and he interpreted this as an order not to do anything at all. A frustrated Churchill described him as a 'stranded whale'. However, Lucas reported to Clark, who in turn reported to Alexander, and these two must also bear much responsibility for the Anzio fiasco. Clark even visited Lucas' command post, and still did not press him. Only on the ninth day did Lucas order an advance, and then it was into the waiting arms of a German ambush prepared by von Senger und Etterlin. The Allies were slaughtered. Of one thousand one hundred rangers in the assault, the best troops in the US Army, only two hundred survived.

In fact the fiasco was a double blow, because Alexander had also ordered Clark to simultaneously attack the main front line along the Garigliano-Rapido River. On the banks of the Rapido the US 36th Division was massacred.

In February 1944 Harold MacMillan, British political representative in the Mediterranean, was asked to report to parliament on the state of the Co-Belligerent forces. He replied they were doing 'good work'.

For example, of Badoglio's seventy-five thousand man navy: his submarines were now hunting U-boats in the Atlantic, sneaking spies and saboteurs ashore on enemy coasts and escorting vessels; his surface warships were protecting Allied convoys in the Atlantic and Mediterranean; his MAS boats were raiding German coastal traffic.

Unfortunately in the Atlantic these Italian submarines had to be wary of both sides in the conflict. The submarine Settembrini was rammed by the USS Frament, having mistaken her for a U-boat. Only fourteen of the fifty-six man crew survived.

Furthermore, tens of thousands of Italian merchant seamen were risking their lives to help keep the Allies supplied.

Badoglio's air force of twenty-eight thousand fliers and ground crew were performing a variety of missions: Re 2001, Re 2002, Mc202 and Mc205 fighters were intercepting German reconnaissance planes and bombers, and they were escorting Allied bombers. Transport planes of several makes were entering enemy air space to parachute supplies to Greek, Albanian and Titoist partisans. Small aircraft were landing behind enemy lines to pick up agents. Float planes were rescuing downed fliers at sea. SM79, SM82 and Z-1007 bombers were patrolling the seas for signs of enemy ships and u-boats, and between 9 September 1943 and 29 February 1944 they had sunk or damaged eighteen Axis vessels. Also many Allied squadrons were using Italian ground crews.

As for Badoglio's army, by now the Allies trusted the Co-Belligerents enough to give them the job of protecting Sicily as well as Sardinia and Southern Italy. Sardinia was defended by the Italian VII Corps of the 4th Coastal Brigade and the following divisions: Calabria, Friuli, Cremona, 204th Coastal and 226th Coastal, and also by the XIII Corps of the 25th Coastal Brigade and the following divisions: Bari, Nembo Parachute, 203rd Coastal, 205th Coastal and 225th Coastal; plus some mobile units. There were also forty-two thousand Italian rear-echelon personnel on the island, thousands of Carabinieri and ten thousand eight hundred flak gunners. These troops were not redundant. This was not 'busy work'. The Allies did not have superfluous soldiers. No one got a free ride. Everyone had a valuable job to do. And the Allies certainly did not look upon Sardinia as a backwater. German nightly air raids were continuing and Fascist guerillas were still performing sabotage. In fact the Americans reinforced the island with their own 44th Anti-Aircraft Brigade.

Though the French had reclaimed Corsica, relieving the Italians there, they had retained five thousand nine hundred Italians as necessary personnel.

For propaganda purposes the British and Americans did not publicize the fact that six months after having conquered Sicily from the Italians, they had in effect given the island back! The garrison now consisted of the Sabauda Division, ten thousand Carabinieri and several thousand Italian rear-echelon soldiers and flak gunners. The latter were necessary, because the Germans were still bombing the island. For this reason the Americans retained their 34th Anti-Aircraft Brigade here.

Behind the scenes the Sicilian Major General Castellano was

negotiating again, this time with the mafia. He needed their help to prevent Sicilian nationalists from seceding from Italy!

The Allies on mainland Italy faced north against the Germans and kawis, but this left their rear very vulnerable, especially as they had their backs to the sea on three sides. This coast was now guarded by Italian troops of the 24th, 210th, 212th and 227th Coastal Divisions and the 31st Coastal Brigade. Elements of the Mantova and Legnano Divisions were fighting as part of Dapino's unit, and the remaining soldiers of these divisions were serving as sentries, as were the men of the Piceno, Assietta Mountain, Livorno Mountain, Napoli and Aosta Divisions. There was also the separate ten thousand five hundred man Sentry Force.

Throughout southern Italy eighteen thousand seven hundred Carabinieri and twenty thousand police waged their own 'war' against gangsters, black market operators and Fascist partisans. And ten thousand Italian firemen were now under military orders fighting fires caused by accidents, air raids and sabotage.

The Luftwaffe was still active - flying no fewer than two thousand five hundred sorties on Anzio alone - hence the need for Allied flak gunners in Sicily, Sardinia and southern Italy. The six thousand one hundred Italian flak gunners in southern Italy were kept busy. The Italian coastal divisions also had flak gunners. The Americans recognized the seriousness of the situation and had brought to southern Italy their 35th and 45th Coastal/Anti-Aircraft Brigades. In addition the British had plenty of flak guns in the rear. The front line units had their own flak defenses.

As if to emphasize the importance of flak gunners, on the evening of 2 December 1943 the Luftwaffe dealt the Allies a major blow. Recently the port of Bari had only been visited by German reconnaissance planes, and the town's Italian flak gunners and the port's British flak gunners had ceased to 'waste' ammunition on these solitary targets. Indeed to keep accidents to a minimum and facilitate round the clock dock operations the British no longer enforced the blackout here. On this evening the town was well lit. The crews of the one hundred and five German JU88s could not believe the scene below them. They could see everything, and the flak defenses were uncoordinated, with some gunners delaying their fire until the bombs were falling. As a result German aerial casualties were low. But down below was a veritable hell's inferno. Because many of the ships were unloading fuel and ammunition when they were hit by the bombs, the resulting explosions were horrendous, and the fires that broke out aboard ship and in warehouses continued to cause more explosions throughout the night. No fewer than twenty-seven Allied merchant vessels were sunk or destroyed [eleven of them Italian] and thirteen were damaged [one Italian]. Casualties were horrific on the ships and ashore. The old medieval part of the city was destroyed and the docks were wrecked. The sea was layered thick with oil, which soon caught fire, and sailors were flung by explosions into the burning ocean. But even those who managed to stay out of the sea of flames were overcome by toxic fumes from blazing oil and shattered chemical containers and a substance that almost no one in Bari knew was even there – mustard gas carried in the hold of one of the destroyed American ships. It took almost twenty-four hours before Italian and British doctors were able to identify that six hundred and twenty-eight of their two thousand wounded patients were suffering from exposure to mustard gas, by which time several were already dead. About ten per cent of these 'gas wounded' died within two weeks. Over two hundred Americans died, mostly merchant seamen and navy sailors, and a thousand Italians died - seamen, flak gunners, civilian dockworkers and townsfolk. Statistics are in fact vague, because wartime governments are notoriously reticent about admitting losses, and when the Allies learned that mustard gas had been carried in one of their ships they put the security lid on the whole affair. The USA had broken international law by shipping this lethal substance, and it would have been a propaganda coup for Mussolini and Hitler if they found out.

By November 1943 the British Eighth Army, now under General Oliver Leese, was using seven thousand three hundred and twenty Italian rear-echelon troops and US Fifth Army was using four thousand Italian rear-echelon troops. The term rear-echelon did not necessarily mean non-combatant, for many of these men were serving at the front as muleteers, stretcher-bearers, medics, engineers, linesmen and radio operators. Impressed by the Italians, Clark was asking for more such troops. He also asked for an Italian mountain division. Furthermore, he was using a special commando section of one hundred and fifty Italian paratroopers called 'F-Force' – the F stood for Folgore. Some of these Italian paratroopers had been tagging along with the Canadian 1st Division since September.

On 8 February 1944 Clark put Dapino's unit back into action, and he brought up the Legnano's 67th Infantry Regiment in reserve.

Alexander's 15th Army Group, in addition to controlling Fifth and Eighth Armies, had its own rear-echelon troops and thirty-two thousand of these were Italian. Badoglio too had his own rear-echelon including four thousand four hundred and seventy personnel at his headquarters.

By February 1944 one hundred and ten thousand Italian Cooperators were serving the Allies throughout the world. In total over six hundred thousand Italians were serving the Allied cause in a 'military' capacity. Of course without the millions of Italian civilian workers the rail lines and ports would have ceased to function.

———————

Despite the massive industrial wealth of the Allied nations it was 'the poor bloody infantry' who would win or lose this war. At Anzio, on the Garigliano and Rapido and at Cassino these fellows were fighting and dying in a bloodbath reminiscent of World War I. Von Senger had halted Lucas' half-hearted advance out of the Anzio beachhead, and now Major General von Mackensen organized a German counter attack at Anzio on 17 February to drive the Allies into the sea. For two weeks his troops gallantly sacrificed themselves in front of the Allied guns. By 4 March he had to call a halt, the slaughter was so sickening.

Kesselring was so desperate for manpower that he asked for anti-partisan units to be used at the front. One such unit thrown into the horrendous struggle at Anzio was the Barbarigo Battalion of the Condottieri Division. Also arriving were two thousand Nembo paratroopers. Some of these had fought their fellow barracks mates in Sardinia and had evacuated with the Germans. Others belonged to Major Mario Rizzati's battalion that had gone over to the Germans at La Maddalena. Heinrich Himmler, who was ever on the lookout to expand his personal army, the Waffen SS, thought so highly of the Fascist spirit of these paratroopers that he honored the unit with SS status. The Germans thus referred to the Nembo as SS Sturmbrigade 'Italien'. Its members called themselves the Vendetta Legion. To complicate matters, according to Mussolini they were members of his air force!

Von Mackensen launched a renewed effort to destroy the Anzio beachhead on 17 March. The Vendetta Battalion of SS Sturmbrigade 'Italien' under the command of SS Obersturmbannfuehrer Frederico degli Oddi, took part in this attack and over the next eight days these six hundred and fifty men suffered an incredible three hundred and forty killed and most of the others wounded. Then the remainder of the brigade was brought up to hold a static line. The Germans praised their bravery.

On the main front the US 36th Division was withdrawn in February having been reduced to a skeleton. Clark's army had suffered so much that Alexander transferred to him Tuker's Indian 4th and Freyberg's New Zealand 2nd Divisions of the Eighth Army. These divisions were legendary by now because of their experience, quality and battle honors. For the Indians: Nibeiwa-Tumar, Agordat, Keren, Massawa, Halfaya Pass, Crusader, First Gazala, Second Tobruk, First Alamein, Second Alamein, Mareth, Wadi Akarit and Enfidaville. For the New Zealanders: Greece, Crete, Crusader, First Gazala, Mersah Matruh, First Alamein, Alam al Halfa, Second Alamein, Medennine, Mareth, Wadi Akarit, Enfidaville, the Sangro and Orsogna.

The new mission for these two fine formations was to capture the town of Cassino, but of course by now there was no town, only rubble. For miles on either side of the line Italian civilians huddled in caves, churches, tents and isolated farmhouses living off the kindness of the Allies and Co-Belligerents [south of the line] or of the Germans and Fascists [north of the line]. They could not go home while the armies fought over their olive groves and village streets and fields, over and over and over again. On 15 February the New Zealanders and Indians attacked Cassino. These two legendary divisions gave up the attempt after one night.

Major General Dapino was ordered to hand over his formation to Major General Umberto Utili, who had been Messe's chief of staff in Russia in 1941, and later chief of operations at Comando Supremo. Dapino described the situation of the Cassino line to Utili. His Italian soldiers were holding on by gripping their rifles in the snow and mud. The freezing nights were filled with tension as both sides sent patrols to kidnap prisoners. At dawn the Germans always said 'Guten Morgen' with an artillery salvo. During the day every moving figure caught the attention of a sniper's bullet.

The formation Dapino handed over was growing in size. Though still plagued by its asinine British nomenclature, it now consisted of the 51st Bersaglieri Battalion, 1st Battalion/185th Parachute Infantry Regiment [Nembo], 4th Bersaglieri Regiment, 68th Infantry Regiment [Legnano], 11th Artillery Regiment [Mantova], and the 51st Combat Engineer Battalion.

From now on the Italians would unofficially refer to the formation as the 'Utili Division'. The unit still only fielded seven assault battalions, but then again so did many an Allied division in this war. The US Army currently had fourteen armored divisions each fielding only six assault battalions. Yet the Allies continued to refuse this unit the honor of the title 'division'. This prejudice was petty and childish.

In March Clark brought forward one thousand three hundred men of the Legnano's 67th Infantry Regiment, but the men were told to lay down their rifles and carry stretchers instead. Naturally they were disgusted, and they felt the Americans had insulted them. Or at least they thought that until they reached the front and saw what the conditions were like. In places it was taking four stretcher-bearers fully eight hours to carry one wounded man down from the mountains to a waiting ambulance. Artillery shells, aerial bombs and long-range machine gun fire do not recognize a medical armband and so the job required courage as well as stamina. Many an Allied soldier owed his life to these brave fellows.

The use of this Italian regiment in such a manner was not a reflection of American disdain for Italians. On the contrary, the Americans were entrusting their own wounded to the care of these Italians. The Indian 11th Infantry Brigade, one of the finest in the Allied arsenal, was also given a non-infantry mission. They were ordered to serve as porters to carry water, ammunition, food, medical supplies and stretchers.

On 15 March the Allies [Indians, New Zealanders and British] began an eight-day struggle for Cassino. They gained nothing and it cost them two thousand one hundred killed and wounded and hundreds felled by sickness. The Italian stretcher bearers were kept busy.

Of course the partisans behind Axis lines did not see this futile bloodletting. All they saw was the war map: it never changed. Their hopes of being liberated by the Allies grew dimmer each day.

Between Lake Maggiore and the Swiss border in freezing snow-covered mountains several hundred of them huddled together for warmth, attempting to remain invisible to enemy aircraft and ski patrols. Filippo Beltrami had created one band by gathering men together mostly from Milan, and he had recently been joined by young men escaping Mussolini's conscription. In February the CLN urged partisans to make major attacks. So, despite their pitiable condition Beltrami felt his band was strong enough for a raid. On the 13th they struck Megolo. It was a terrible misjudgment, for the Germans responded fiercely with troops of all types. Beltrami and most of his men were massacred.

Nonetheless by March the surviving partisans in the Lake Maggiore region had managed to assemble three bands: Bruno Rutto and his two hundred guerillas; Alfredo di Dio, who commanded three hundred and seventy irregulars; and Dionigi Superti, whose brigade numbered five hundred partisans. They too took the war to the enemy, but this time with carefully planned small-scale raids. It was this type of guerilla warfare that did the most harm to the Axis.

The Germans responded by reinforcing the region. One new arrival near Turin was the Italian SS Battalion Debica.

The month of March 1944 saw terrible battles at Cassino and Anzio, and none of the Allies achieved anything, none that is except for the Utili Division. This formation had been expanded yet again with a company of Alpini and a battery of 20mm flak guns. On 31 March the division launched an offensive against Monte Marrone 5,300 feet up in the snowy Apennines. They made a considerable impression on the Germans, forcing them off the summit. Next day they attacked again, shoving the Germans off a spur, and by the third day they had conquered Monte Castelnuovo and Point 1344. However, this placed the Italians in a salient surrounded by the enemy on three sides. On 3 April the Germans counter attacked with three battalions and tried to cut off the most forward troops, but the entire Utili Division fought back ceaselessly. As these Italians were wearing

British uniforms it was only now that the Germans realized they were up against Italians. They splattered leaflets all over the area each asking the Italians to save their lives by surrendering to their Fascist brothers. The Italians allowed the insulting leaflets to flutter in the breeze. That afternoon the Germans attacked again, and again the Italians met them with artillery, machine guns, rifles and bayonets. When the Italians launched a counter thrust, the Germans withdrew.

Since ensconcing himself in the town of Brindisi King Vittorio Emanuele had reigned over a fantasy world. Convinced he had saved Italy he could not understand those politicians who kept asking him to abdicate. He was tainted, they said, because he had tolerated Mussolini for twenty-one years. Prime Minister Badoglio ruled Sardinia, Sicily and the south Italy provinces of Bari, Lecce, Taranto and Brindisi with an iron hand, which is exactly what the Allies wanted. In fact just in case he relaxed his grip an Allied Military Control Commission peeked over his shoulder now and then. The Allies themselves ruled the terrain between the front line and these provinces with a military government. They claimed they would release more territory to Badoglio as the front was pushed northwards, but would hold onto Naples, as it was vital to their war effort. Naturally Badoglio was angry. The only reason the Allies had Naples was because its people had risen in revolt against the Nazis and Fascists. The only reason the port was vital was because of the tens of thousands of Italians who worked there for the Allies. To suggest that a handful of American cowboys and British aristocrats could rule this great city better than the Italians who had ruled it for over two millennia was a tremendous insult.

Suddenly on 17 April 1944 the king made the announcement that everyone was awaiting. He stated that on the day Rome was liberated he would abdicate not just for himself, but also for his House, though he would designate his son Crown Prince Umberto as Lieutenant General of the Realm. Throughout Italy on both sides of the front line the public reacted joyously for two reasons. It would mean the end of the king and the end of Badoglio.

Despite the Utili Division having proven itself there were still stubborn bigots at Allied headquarters and within the British government who wanted to belittle the Italians. On 3 April in answer to a British questionnaire about his usage of Italians Clark replied that he was currently using seventeen thousand four hundred and fifty Italians in the front line - circa nine thousand in the 'Dapino Brigade', plus one thousand eight hundred and fifty combat engineers, five hundred radio operators and telephone linesmen, one hundred and fifty gunners manning an independent artillery battery, one thousand seven hundred medics, surgeons and ambulance crewmen, one thousand three hundred stretcher bearers, one hundred and fifty paratroopers of F-Force and two thousand eight hundred muleteers. He considered all of the above to be combat echelon. It is noteworthy that the mule convoys were suffering a higher percentage of casualties than the infantry! As for rear echelon troops, he was using one thousand two hundred Italians as sentries, nine thousand one hundred as manual laborers and twelve thousand seven hundred in technical positions. Thus US Fifth Army contained more than forty thousand Italians.

By now the British Eighth Army together with units directly under the command of 15th Army Group were using eight hundred Italians as sentries, one thousand five hundred as drivers and mechanics and twenty-seven thousand six hundred as rear-echelon technicians and manual laborers. Many of the Italian laborers served in companies of the British Pioneer Corps, which by 1944 was a catch-all branch that could mean practically anything. Italian pioneers dug trenches and foxholes, filled sand bags, strung barbed wire, lifted and planted landmines, poured concrete for bunkers and air raid shelters, refurbished roads, strengthened culverts to bear tanks, built bridges, drove and maintained vehicles, pulled sentry duty, fought fires and even manned flak guns. By March 1944 more than half of all British-controlled pioneers in Italy were in fact Italians, either Co-Belligerents or Cooperators, manning one hundred and ninety-five companies. Furthermore much of these duties were performed under air raids and long-range artillery fire. In recognition of the pioneers' courage under fire and their dogged determination the British officially renamed the road running up to Cassino "Pioneer Way". This public honoring of Italian and other pioneers was evidence that the British had certainly softened in their attitude towards the Italians. Despite their initial reluctance to use Italians in battle, by April 1944 the British Eighth Army was using four thousand Italians at the front, to whit a reconnaissance company of one hundred and fifty commandos, three artillery batteries (four hundred and fifty gunners), two thousand four hundred combat engineers, five hundred and fifty radio operators and telephone linesmen and four hundred surgeons, medics, stretcher bearers and ambulance drivers.

Badoglio was expanding his armed forces by taking in young volunteers: e.g. three thousand additional airmen. In April alone Co-Belligerent warplanes sank or damaged a hundred Axis vessels.

The Allies thought so much of the Carabinieri, that they asked for more of them. Badoglio recruited another eighteen thousand. The new men came from new volunteers and by transfers from the army.

Most encouraging of all the Dapino Brigade/Utili Division was finally recognized by the Allies as a 'division'. Unofficially the Allies had already begun to recognize it as such. Even in official documents Allied commanders had slipped up now and then. They began their messages by addressing the unit as a 'brigade' or 'group', as per instructions, but further down the page they mentioned the unit's 'divisional' supply line!

As Utili had done such a fine job Messe agreed the division should bear his name. Thus it became official – the Utili Division. Its new composition, effective 17 April was as follows: 51st Combat Engineer Battalion; the divisional support troops [Mantova]; the 11th Artillery Regiment [Mantova], which now contained four batteries of 75mm howitzers, two batteries of 100mm, two of 105mm and two of 149mm. It also had two batteries of 57mm anti-tank guns. The divisional infantry was divided into two brigades: the 1st that contained the 4th Bersaglieri Regiment, 1st Battalion/185th Parachute Infantry Regiment [Nembo], 4th Alpini Regiment [ex-Taurinense Division], and two batteries of mountain 75mm howitzers; and the 2nd Brigade that consisted of the 68th Regiment [Legnano], IX Assault Unit [one battalion], and the Bafile Battalion of the San Marco Marines. This gave the Utili Division a total of twelve thousand five hundred personnel.

The Nembo Parachute Division was also brought up to the front in reserve. It contained the 183rd and 184th Parachute Infantry Regiments [each of two battalions], the 184th Combat Engineer Battalion, and the 184th Artillery Regiment, which had seven batteries: two of 75mm howitzers, two of 75mm guns, two of 100mm guns and one of 20mm flak guns. With support troops the division controlled seven thousand one hundred and thirty-two personnel.

To control both divisions Utili was promoted to corps command and his new headquarters was named the Corps of Liberation. The British, despite their earlier reluctance to recognize the Dapino Brigade as a division, now regularly called the corps by its real name. However, their bigotry was still present. Though calling Utili a corps commander, they refused to treat him as such and ordered Clark to place him under the thumb of an American corps commander.

In February the Allies had asked the CLN to order major partisan attacks to coordinate with the next Allied offensive. Many partisans had obeyed, often of necessity revealing their intelligence sources and hidden weapons caches. Unfortunately the planned Allied offensive fizzled out. Many a partisan died in this premature onslaught.

In March the Allies launched another offensive and again asked the CLN to order a full-scale assault. The Allies gained no ground and the partisans were once again left out on a limb with no sign of liberation. The survivors scurried back to their mountain hideouts.

Now here it was May and the Allies were planning yet another attempt to break the Anzio and Cassino lines. As the British considered Utili's corps to be a 'second-class' formation it could not be given the honor of making a major offensive, so the corps was transferred to the eastern side of the Apennines. Once again Utili was insulted by being told to take orders from an Allied corps commander, in this case British V Corps. This corps reported to British Eighth Army. By now Utili had twenty-two thousand soldiers in his corps. He put both the Utili and Nembo Divisions into the front line.

Once more the CLN ordered an all-out attack to support the Allies. This time many partisan brigade commanders chose to wait to see if the Allies actually broke out of their self-made trap before they risked the lives of their men.

————————

Inside Axis Italy a very confusing and deadly situation had developed. Fascists in the cities felt themselves besieged by the partisans in the countryside. Anti-Fascists in the cities did not consider the partisans to be the enemy, but they and the Fascists were equally besieged by Allied air forces.

It is true that Italian civilians were not the targets of the bombs, but their close proximity to the targets meant they died anyway, whether they were a rabid Fascist or a secret agent for the partisans. They died because they lived near rail lines or bridges, or because they worked at factories, rail yards, docks or on construction sites. Their defenses against air raids consisted of the Luftwaffe fighter force, Mussolini's small fighter force, German flak gunners including their Italian hiwis, and Italian flak gunners of the coastal units and the Etna Flak Division.

Popular magazines praised the heroes of the air, who defended the people. E.g. Adriano Visconti had added another nine kills to his record since September 1943. In January 1944 his squadron handed in their obsolete Mc200 and Mc202 fighters for the better Mc205.

In one dogfight a squadron of Mc205s challenged a squadron of American Thunderbolts, both sides losing two planes. One of the Italian victors in this incident was Sergeant Major Luigi Gorrini. This was his fourth victory since September 1943. Prior to that he had shot down fifteen Allied planes. A few days later he was seriously wounded and forced to quit flying.

However, everyone knew these defenses were insufficient. Between 8 September 1943 and 1 April 1944 more than ten thousand Italian civilians were killed and as many again wounded by Allied bombs.

The whole situation was backwards. Most city folk were vehemently anti-Fascist, whereas many country folk were Fascist, yet the Fascists felt safer in the cities, and the partisans felt safer in the mountains. Furthermore, the percentage of Fascists among the population of Sardinia, Sicily and southern Italy was far higher than in northern Italy, yet the Fascists now ruled in the north – the Allies and Badoglio ruled the other regions.

It was noticeable to the Italians that the Allies did not bomb near great architectural treasures or museums. It was obvious to them that the Anglo-Americans cared more for Italian art than they did for Italian children. In this manner the air raids altered the politics of many. Seeing is believing, and seeing the death and destruction caused by Allied planes swayed many a person towards the Fascist cause. Others blamed the Fascists and Germans for the air raids, especially as the local swaggering Fascists become more insufferable than ever. Witnessing a screaming woman being dragged out of her house by policemen in front of her crying children and trucked off to an unknown destination was enough to unnerve anyone. Usually the neighbors never learned why the person in question had been arrested or what became of her.

To add to the soul-searching and the terror of living in a police state and the fear of air raids was also the knowledge that Mussolini's Italy had become a vassal state of Germany. In Italian eyes there was little difference between Germans and Austrians, the latter being the traditional enemy of centuries. Often in normal conversation the words 'German' and 'Austrian' were used interchangeably. Austria was under Germany's thumb these days, but the Italians were aware that many of the leading Nazis were Austrians, including Hitler himself. Austria's population was about ten per cent of the Third Reich, but Austrians accounted for far higher than ten per cent of the Nazis.

Many Italians deliberately damaged the Axis cause by passive resistance. The most damaging was the industrial strike. Strikers were always careful to choose a non-political reason for their actions. Finally Hitler tired of Mussolini's refusal to crack down on strikers, and on 6 March 1944 he interfered, ordering Gruppenfuehrer Karl Wolf to punish all strikers in the following manner: the rabble-rousers would be sent to a concentration camp, and twenty per cent of the strikers would be arrested and sentenced to slave labor, and any striker known to be a Communist would be executed. As soon as the rules were published the strikers went back to work.

Naturally the Fascists saw things differently. To them a victory for the Allies would be a victory for the Soviet Union and by inference for atheistic Communism. The pope and his church were still very supportive of Fascism. Some Roman Catholic priests and nuns had already been murdered by Communist partisans, and what made things worse was that outlaw bands were roaming the countryside raping, stealing and murdering under the guise of calling themselves 'partisans'. Mussolini was a tough dictator, but he had never massacred workers in the streets like the Allied puppet Badoglio had done. As for the Germans, to be fair they were well mannered most of the time and always paid their way.

Many a Fascist did not want to live and let live, but insisted on knowing whom his friends and enemies were. Such a man was Mario Carita of Florence. To him and his two hundred Blackshirt Squadristi anyone who was not for Mussolini was an enemy. He arrested suspects on flimsy evidence. If lucky the poor victim was just given a beating and an overdose of castor oil, a favorite Fascist treatment. If not so lucky the victim was imprisoned and tortured. On occasion Carita executed some. Eventually the commander of the local German garrison could stand it no longer and he made a formal protestation to Mussolini's government about Carita's brutality. To the relief of the Florentines Mussolini moved Carita to Padua, where he was allowed to continue his insanity there.

In Milan Francesco Colombo behaved in a similar manner. Backed up by the GNR Muti Legion and other Fascists he and his men were able to push their way through the main thoroughfares as much as they wished. They dare not leave the city, though, unless escorted by a powerful armed force: partisans liked nothing better than to capture a Blackshirt and have fun with him for a few hours before killing him.

In Rome the Blackshirt leader was Pietro Koch, who because he was half German could command respect from the Germans. Lieutenant General Mischi, commander of the Rome Carabinieri, tried to curry favor with Koch, because he did not trust his own men, suspecting some of them were partisan spies.

Every few days it was announced that some anti-Fascists had been executed by the Fascists. Only the high profile ones were named. Admiral Inigo Campione and Admiral Luigi Mascherpa, who had surrendered to the Germans after offering serious resistance, were both executed by Blackshirts for not surrendering sooner.

Then again it was hard to trust anyone in Axis Italy, especially when Mussolini proved he did not trust his own leading Fascists. It was announced that his forces and the Germans had arrested Luciano Gottardi, Emilio de Bono, Carlo Pareschi, Giovanni Marinelli, Tullio Cianetti and Count Galeazzo Ciano and had imprisoned them in Verona and that they would be tried for the crime of voting against Mussolini at the last session of the Fascist Grand Council. Everyone assumed they would receive light prison sentences and that perhaps Ciano, who was after all the father of Mussolini's grandchildren, would not even receive that. For three days the accused listened to testimony against them and then they were found guilty. As Cianetti had retracted his vote within hours he was sentenced to just thirty years! The others were given the death penalty. Less than twenty-four hours later a squad of GNR Blackshirts drove the bewildered prisoners to Forte San Procolo, and then sat them down reversed on hardback chairs, and then riddled them with bullets from behind.

One wonders what words of consolation Mussolini had for his grandchildren.

The partisans had not ventured into the major cities, apart from spying and some light sabotage. Yet it was always their intention to deny the Fascists any sanctuary, and when a group of SAP in Rome came up with a plan, the Rome partisan movement accepted it. Himmler had sent elements of the Bozen Police Regiment to Bologna, Florence, Perugia and Rome, and every day a company of them marched through Rome along the same route, in flagrant disregard of Carboni's truce with the Germans made the previous September. It was Himmler's way of reminding the Italians that the Germans were in charge. But as these men were recruited from ethnic Austrians from northeast Italy, and had until recently been Italian citizens, it was as if the old Austrian Empire had been resurrected and the partisans saw them as a symbol of ancient oppression.

On the morning of 25 March 1944, chosen because it was the twenty-fifth anniversary of the founding of the Fascist Party, a team of men and women of the SAP set off a bomb near the Spanish Steps as the unit paraded past. The resulting slaughter was horrific: thirty-two killed and one hundred and two severely maimed.

The Rome police and Blackshirts demanded action at once. Himmler took the attack personally and ordered retaliation. The Nazis in South Tyrol demanded a response. Under such pressure Hitler ordered Herbert Kappler head of the Gestapo in Rome to execute ten of his prisoners for every 'German' killed.

Kappler was no Nazi robot. After arriving in Rome he had taken pains to warn the Jewish population of what lay in store for them. He was even party to an attempt to buy the Jews from his SS superiors, and he and his immediate supervisors warned the Pope and asked him to intervene to save the Jews. Meantime German diplomats in Rome urged the Jews to go into hiding. The Jews were as naïve here as in Germany and they refused to believe the horror stories. In any case Mussolini would protect them, they believed. After all many of the Jews were Fascists! But the SS leadership refused to sell 'their' Jews, Mussolini did nothing, the pope remained silent and the Jews did not heed the warnings. Then one day the order arrived, and at once the Gestapo and SD began mass arrests of Jews. Only now did some Jews go into hiding. So the Gestapo employed Jews to help find these hold outs. One of the more successful Jew catchers was Celeste di Porto, an eighteen year old Jewess! She did it for money, and spent the money on the latest fashions.

And now because of the Spanish Steps incident Kappler had been given another distasteful order personally by Himmler, namely to execute three hundred and thirty prisoners. Quite shaken by the order Kappler found that he only had two hundred and eighty prisoners in his jail. So he asked Pietro Caruso, the Rome police chief, to let him have enough Socialists, Communists, trade unionists and anti-Fascist rabble-rousers to make up the difference. Caruso complied, throwing in a few extra for good measure.

The Gestapo and SD, commanded by Kappler and his deputy Erich Priebke, drove three hundred and thirty-five prisoners in trucks to the Ardeatine Caves. There they shot them in the back of the neck. One of the victims was Colonel Giuseppe di Montezemolo, the partisan leader. Another was Lieutenant General Vito Artale, an artillery officer that had joined the partisans, but had been captured in December. Yet another was Brigadier General Dardano Fenulli, who had organized partisans, but had been caught in January. The executioners were highly nervous and sick at the stomach and as a result they aimed badly, wounding more than they killed. They ended up climbing over mounds of corpses to finish off the wounded.

On 22 April 1944 Mussolini met Hitler at Klessheim in Germany. The topic for discussion was Italy's role in the Axis. Il Duce was beaming, happy to report the high degree of Fascist ardor among his people. He had recreated an air force, which was bombing the Allies as well as defending the homeland, and he was preparing a squadron for the Russian front. Also defending the homeland were ten thousand gunners of the Etna Flak Division. He had recreated the navy, albeit only manning MAS boats and small craft at the moment, but the navy's Condottieri Division was fighting partisans and one of its battalions was at the front. SS Sturmbrigade 'Italien' was also at the front. One marine and three army divisions were training in Germany. The GNR now numbered one hundred and fifty thousand personnel and was hunting partisans, as were twenty-five thousand policemen. Thus about two hundred and seventy thousand Fascists were serving in Italian uniform.

Part of the talks centered on the number of Italians in German uniform. The German Army now admitted to having over one hundred thousand Italian hiwis and kawis serving against partisans in Italy, Greece, Albania and Yugoslavia, and some were on the Italian front line. The Luftwaffe was using fifty-one thousand hiwis, mostly as flak gunners, some of whom were defending German cities. The German Navy had a few thousand Italian hiwis serving aboard German warships. The SS admitted to possessing twenty thousand hiwis and kawis, but did not clarify if this included SS Battalion Debica and SS Sturmbrigade 'Italien'. The Civic Guard and Trient Security Corps together accounted for three thousand policemen. The Gestapo and SD would not disclose how many Italians were on their payroll, but it certainly numbered in the thousands. In addition Italians served in the NSKK, RAD and Organisation Todt as sentries and members. Thus a minimum of one hundred and ninety thousand Italians were wearing German uniform. Thus either serving Hitler or Mussolini, there were four hundred and fifty thousand Italians 'fighting' on the Axis side.

In March 1944 the submarine Bagnolini was sunk by Allied planes. She had a mixed Italian and German crew. Under German orders she was referred to as UIT-22.

Hitler was also concerned about the number of Italian workers making materials for his war machine. Mussolini promised to conscript more workers.

The day following the meeting Mussolini visited the San Marco Division at its German training camp. Farina and his marines told him they were anxious to return to Italy to defend their homes.

The CLN was consistently at loggerheads with Allied headquarters. It must be understood that regular officers have always mistrusted irregular units. American generals disliked their rangers immensely as they did their 1st Special Service Brigade, and in fact they were calling for the disbandment of such units. Churchill had formed the LRDG, SIG, SAS, SBS and commandos only over the protests of British generals. If regular officers would not tolerate irregulars who were of the same nationality, who owed allegiance to the same government and who had often entered the military in the same fashion as the regulars, it is evident that they would certainly not trust foreign partisans, whose allegiance and motives were unknown and whose training was minimal at best.

In the case of some British officers their anti-irregular attitude was exacerbated by their prejudice against all Italians. If, as they believed, Italians made cowardly soldiers, then surely sending supplies to a partisan, who had the ability to desert and go home at any time, would be a poor investment indeed. Bigots are never influenced by reality, for they are too arrogant to recognize it. Britons who had escaped from German prison camps in Italy commented on how they had been aided by brave and resourceful Italian partisans, but many senior British officers called these men 'liars', because it did not fit their racist fanaticism. British agents had parachuted behind the lines to inspect Italian partisans and they brought back mixed results. The British senior officers did not believe those agents that reported the partisans were a viable force. In fact they suspected these agents of being gullible or worse - of having a personal agenda such as Communist sympathies. However, those agents who brought back stories of Italian incompetence, panic and indecision were praised for their honest and insightful reports!

Thank goodness there were some wiser officers in British Intelligence, and they believed all the reports, for they reflected the reality of guerillas. [Similar reports came in about French, Greek and Yugoslav partisans]. Not all partisans were well led or nobly motivated. In addition to this tainted view of Italian partisans was the political situation. No one knew just how many of the partisans were really Communists. Unlike the Americans, Churchill had never been fooled by the Communists, and he had no intention of liberating Italy from Fascism only to see it fall to Communism.

Given the realpolitik and the bias of many Britons and the uneasiness of most regulars when dealing with irregulars, it is amazing that the Allies aided the partisans at all, but they did. Allied and Co-Belligerent planes flew behind enemy lines to drop parachuted supplies. Allied and Co-Belligerent submarines and small craft sailed inshore at night to unload supplies. Badoglio's MAS boats had been given British commanders, and whether involved in these resupply missions or in attacks against German shipping, the British boat commanders consistently lauded the bravery and efficiency of their Italian crews.

It would have opened the eyes of the Allies considerably had they been able to listen in on Axis headquarters conferences about the partisans. In frustration the Axis security forces became ever more brutal. When the Fascist authorities discovered that their Major General Filippo Caruso of the Carabinieri was in fact a major partisan leader, he was tortured to make him talk. He died without giving anything to his tormentors. Every day scores of people were arrested and some were executed. Every day local Fascist dignitaries were assassinated, telephone lines were cut, trucks blown up, tires slashed and sentries stabbed or strangled.

In May 1944 sixteen thousand Axis troops of several anti-partisan formations swept the mountains northwest of Lake Maggiore, surrounding Dionigi Superti's partisan brigade. He ordered his men to scatter into tiny parties and try to infiltrate through the Axis units. Most survived and later reunited elsewhere, but skirmishes continued for several weeks.

Also in May between La Spezia, Modena and Montefiorino the Ricci-Poppi brigade attacked the German garrison of Carradolo and destroyed it. Then they captured Fanano. With these successes under their belt they easily attracted other partisan bands and together they laid siege to Montefiorino, which was defended by Germans and GNR.

Meanwhile northwest of La Spezia near Bonassola GNR units and Germans surrounded and destroyed a partisan band.

Simultaneously Major Enrico Martini-Mauri led four thousand veterans of Fourth Army down out of the Ligurian Mountains between Turin and the sea to attack the rear of German and Fascist coastal units. This impressive partisan force was quickly joined by Giovanni Latilla commanding the 16th, 18th and 48th Garibaldi Brigades, totaling another two thousand men. Some of these partisans were Provencal-speaking Italians and French-speaking Italians, and a few were Italian-speaking Frenchmen, a reflection of the badly drawn border. On 21 May partisans attacked the Carabinieri headquarters in Vicenza. In the month of May the security forces registered no fewer than two thousand separate partisan incidents ranging from vehicle sabotage to all-out frontal assaults.

Chapter Fifty-seven
Roman Spring

On the evening of 11 May, 1944 Allied artillery opened a massive
barrage on the Cassino position. The Germans and the Italian hiwis
and kawis with them hugged the ground praying for an end to the
horrific pounding. Already Allied infantry were walking forward. The
courage of Polish troops in Allied uniform was awe-inspiring in this
offensive, and this enabled the Canadian 5th Armored Division to
break through into the Liri Valley with Britons and Indians on their
flanks. In the mountains Americans, French, Moroccans, Algerians
and Tunisians pushed ahead very fast. In fact Moroccan mountain
infantry moved faster in the mountains than did tanks on the roads!

By the 17th German paratroopers were showing suicidal resistance
on Montecassino, and only at the last minute did they withdraw to
another defense line just two miles to the rear.

Kesselring was worried, and when the Allies attacked out of Anzio
on 23 May and the Canadians crossed the Melfa River next day he
knew his entire army group had to retreat northwards. At 7:30am on
the 25th the Anzio Allies linked up with the Cassino Allies. Suddenly
the word 'Rome' was on every Allied soldier's lips.

This day Utili's Corps of Liberation also began advancing.
Spearheaded by Alpini the Italians moved quickly, but what looked
like one mile on the map proved to be five miles on the ground owing
to the steep slopes and winding mountain trails. The 4th Bersaglieri
Regiment, 1st Battalion/185th Parachute Infantry Regiment, 4th Alpini
Regiment and IX Assault Unit had a tough struggle capturing
Picnisico 7,000 feet up, but they did it. Further combats took place
that enabled the Italians to enter the Fondillo valley.

Kesselring declared Rome an 'Open City', i. e. he would not fight
for it. At once German and Fascist orderlies began burning paperwork
they could not remove, and thousands of sped northwards in countless
vehicles. Roberto Rosselini the filmmaker and his assistant Federico
Fellini could not believe their eyes. Filthy black smoke belched forth
from the chimneys of every Fascist office. These two and some
friends had already risked their lives filming Blackshirts arresting
suspects and now they took their camera into the streets again,
believing that one day every decent Italian would want to see the
actual footage of the Fascists running for their lives. They smiled to
see the city's Auxiliary Police Battalion flee in panic. Pietro Koch
jumped into a car and did not halt until he reached Milan.

Just north of Rome the partisans were in clover. Any casualties
they suffered now would not be in vain. There would be no more
shameful scampering back into the hills. They intercepted every
fleeing Axis vehicle convoy in some manner: ambush, sniping,

misdirection, felling trees across roads etc. At Teramo partisans prevented German engineers from blowing bridges. At Subiaco partisans inflicted heavy losses on one column. To add to the discomfort of the fleeing Germans and Fascists, Allied and Co-Belligerent planes strafed them.

General von Mackensen was afraid his German combat soldiers would run away, so he put straggler-catching roadblocks of military police just south of Rome. After five months stuck in one place this advance must have seemed like a cavalry charge to the Allies. In fact it took them two weeks to cover the thirty miles to Rome.

In Rome on 3 June a Fascist firing squad shot Major General Pietro Dodi. This partisan leader had been captured in March.

Just after 6am on 4 June 1944 jeeploads of Americans and Canadians of the 1st Special Service Brigade cautiously drove through an archway on the Via Tuscolona. Seconds later German bullets streamed toward the jeeps, and the Allied infantry flung themselves into the roadside ditches. The second battle for Rome had begun.

This fight was almost as confusing as the last battle. Fascists frantically struggled to free themselves from mobs of angry civilians. Policemen turned their pistols on one another, one of them suddenly becoming 'anti-Fascist'. The Rome partisans and SAP came out into the open, jumping on cars and trucks with crude slogans chalked on them. Rural partisans rushed into the city. In one street Carabinieri gave fleeing German trucks accurate directions. In another street the Carabinieri opened fire on the Germans. Elsewhere Carabinieri fought among themselves.

Individual Americans squeezed through densely packed crowds of civilians who were laughing, crying, singing, cheering and kissing, until the crack of a rifle bullet sent everyone diving onto the road surface. Miniature battles were fought all over the city as Fascists and Germans tried to flee. When cornered the Germans usually surrendered, but the Fascists fought like trapped rats, only surrendering to the Americans when they were assured they would not be handed over to the partisans. The partisans hunted down every last individual Fascist. There were shooting incidents in parks, offices, apartments and courtyards, at power stations, on trains, even in churches. At one point an American unit had a nice little skirmish with another American unit.

Throughout the day and all night the gunfire continued. There is no way to ascertain how many casualties were produced by this battle. Thousands of Germans and Fascists were captured by the Allies and partisans, of which eight thousand were in need of medical attention. By dawn on 5 June Rome was free.

In part the Romans secured their own freedom, and the partisans must get much of the credit too, but the lion's share of the praise without doubt goes to the gallant Allied soldiers of a score of nations (including Italians) who fought their way up the Italian boot. Since landing in Italy on 3 September the Allies had suffered one hundred and twenty-five thousand casualties.

To date Co-Belligerent forces had suffered a thousand casualties while serving under British and American command in Italy.

King Vittorio Emmanuele kept his word and stepped down from the throne. Badoglio, knowing he had no support from the people, resigned. An old favorite of the people now stepped into the driving seat, Ivanoe Bonomi. He had never supported Mussolini. At once he called an assembly of the leading political parties to meet in Rome. The Allies asked him to bring an extra thirty thousand Carabinieri to Rome to keep order in the liberated city. Their prime duty was to disarm the SAP and partisans.

Inside the assembly building Bonomi and the politicians began an ancient argument...who shall rule Rome? An argument that had plagued many an Italian before them, such as Caesar, Caligula, Nero, Constantine and Matteoti. Count Sforza arrived with a flourish and a bag full of Allied credentials. Bonomi fobbed him off with a minor cabinet role. Bonomi had been prime minister once before over twenty years earlier and he had some experience with jobseekers. He chose a liberal, Marchese Alessandro Casati, as Minister of War. Casati had a son serving with Utili.

One of the highlights was when the pope appeared in public and blessed the Allied soldiers who had liberated Rome and who were on their way north to kill Fascists. Most Italians saw the hypocrisy in this, for the pope had often blessed Fascists on their way to kill Allied soldiers. There was one complaint from the Vatican. Clark had assigned American soldiers to guard the perimeter of the Vatican in case Communist partisans tried to attack 'His Holy Father'. The Vatican asked Clark to remove these soldiers as they were Negroes. An incensed Clark replaced them with white Americans.

Bonomi repeated Badoglio's demand that Roosevelt and Churchill release the Cooperators, so they could be placed in Co-Belligerent units. But unlike Badoglio he also wanted the Recalcitrants released, i.e. those prisoners of war who had refused to join the Allies or Badoglio. There were currently twenty thousand Recalcitrants in American prison camps in Italy, sixteen thousand in Australia, fifty-three thousand in Allied camps in North Africa, thirty-six thousand in East Africa, sixty-six thousand in the Middle East, thirty-nine thousand in South Africa, thirty-three thousand in India, forty-seven thousand in the USA, one hundred and fifty-four thousand in Britain and about three thousand scattered elsewhere. The best response Bonomi got was from Roosevelt who agreed to ask the Recalcitrants in his care if they wished to join the Americans, but any who did so would not be allowed to serve in Italy lest they desert.

———————

There were two reasons why Alexander was not as happy as he should have been. A day after Rome was taken the Anglo-Americans invaded France, and every newspaper editor in the English-speaking world suddenly had a bigger and better story to tell. The news of the liberation of Rome was quickly shunted to the back pages. The second reason was that the Allied governments confirmed their previous contingency plans to transfer the bulk of their first-rate troops from Italy to France and leave Alexander with just second-rate troops corseted by a handful of first-rate men. Specifically, of the twelve US and twelve British divisions that had fought in Sicily and Italy four American and four British had already been withdrawn, and now he would lose another three American divisions. Furthermore he would lose his four divisions of French, Moroccans, Algerians and Tunisians. In compensation for the loss of these fifteen divisions he would receive three divisions - an untried Brazilian division, a recently formed American mountain division and a new division of American Negroes. Furthermore he was to lose seventy per cent of his air power. And most important of all he was to lose his naval ability to launch a flanking amphibious invasion.

Therefore it is understandable why he lent a favorable ear to Messe's plea that more Italian divisions should be sent to the front. Messe had reorganized his ground forces, disbanding the Aosta, Assietta Mountain, Livorno Mountain and Napoli Divisions and reassigning their personnel. The new Prime Minister, Bonomi, was informed by reliable sources that his Co-Belligerent Air Force was certainly respected by their Allied counterparts, and the Co-Belligerent Navy was doing sterling service. E.g. in June the Royal Navy entrusted the Italian pig program with an important mission: the 1,417-ton Italian destroyer Grecale sailed as close as she dared to the Axis coast in the dark and let loose a pig. The pig silently slid inside and under La Spezia naval base, settling below the light cruiser Bolzano, which now had a mixed German/Italian crew. The operation went like clockwork and the explosion sank the Bolzano.

British reports of the Utili and Nembo Divisions were also highly favorable. Utili gained the Grado Battalion of the San Marco Marines, which he placed into the 2nd Brigade of the Utili Division. Advancing northwards as the Corps of Liberation under the control of British V Corps, Utili's Italians captured Sulmona on 11 June and reached Popoli. From here one prong struck out for the coast hoping to take Chieti and Pescara, while another prong continued northwards towards L'Aquila and it captured that town on the 13th. The northbound column then crossed the Tordino River near Teramo on the 15th thanks to partisan control of this region.

On this day British V Corps pulled out, but the British were still not willing to leave Utili unsupervised, for propaganda reasons, so they placed his corps under the command of Lieutenant General Anders' Polish II Corps. Anders and his staff were almost apologetic to Utili when informed of this arrangement. As the Poles did not have any anti-Italian feelings they treated Utili and his men as equals, and quickly a very fine relationship developed between them.

Anders wanted to concentrate on Pescara, especially when on 18 June the Italians gained control of Ascoli Piceno forty miles north of Pescara and were already attacking Macerata. Three days later having covered thirty miles of steep foothills the Alpini of Utili's corps crushed a German rearguard at Fermo. Only on 25 June did the Italians halt, when they reached a major defensive position held by the German LI Mountain Corps on the Chienti River. To their west the Germans had already stopped the Allies: east of Lake Trasimene the German LXXVI Panzer Corps held back the British X and XIII Corps; westwards from the lake to Siena the German I Parachute Corps including the Italian SS Battalion Debica and SS Sturmbrigade 'Italien' had brought the French to a halt, though it cost the life of Major Rizzati; and from there to the west coast the German XIV Panzer Corps had slammed the door on the US II Corps.

As eager as Alexander was to salvage his shrinking army group, he did not want to use partisan bands in his front line. The current rules were that once partisans were liberated they were to be disarmed and sent home. Moreover, the Co-Belligerent forces refused to accept them as volunteers. The reason for this had been Badoglio's unwillingness to have Communists in his army. In practice, however, the rules were being bent: some partisans did join the Co-Belligerent air force, navy and army, and others remained with their liberators to work as guides, scouts and interpreters. Some were even allowed to infiltrate back behind enemy lines. In June Eighth Army encountered the Maiella Brigade raised by Ettore Troilo, which had been battling the Germans and Fascists for eight months. This was not a mob of half-starved wretches, but a well-disciplined force that was willing to take orders, and General Leese, having become convinced of Italian prowess and courage, flagrantly broke the rules by accepting the entire brigade as a reconnaissance force.

In the midst of this carnage the partisan leaders set up a new chain of command. The CLNAI would continue to make political decisions, but all military orders would now issue from the CLN commanded by a professional soldier General Raffaele Cadorna, who had led the Ariete in battle against the Germans. He was the son of a World War I hero. His deputies would be Luigi Longo, a Communist veteran of the Garibaldi Brigade in the Spanish Civil War, and Ferruccio Parri a politician. Cadorna could have remained safe in his office in Allied Italy, but he decided to earn the respect of the partisans by parachuting behind enemy lines and operating from a hideout. However, the Allies refused to recognize Cadorna's authority!

Chapter Fifty-eight
Summer of Blood

The partisan situation was becoming so serious that Mussolini concluded he needed yet another anti-partisan force. Ricci had definite ideas how to stamp out guerilla activity and he urged Mussolini to increase the size of his GNR, but instead Il Duce turned to Alessandro Pavolini and asked him to form an 'army' out of the Fascist Republican Party rank and file membership. This was obviously a slap in Ricci's face. Mussolini also asked Graziani to coordinate all anti-partisan operations by Italians and to coordinate them with Gruppenfuehrer Wolf.

Like all of Mussolini's sycophants Pavolini accepted the new mission without any idea how he was to accomplish it. When a man signs on as a member of a political party he might reasonably expect to have to pay annual dues and even attend a meeting once in a while, but he does not expect to be handed a rifle and sent into the mountains to hunt down guerillas. But that is exactly what Mussolini wanted the members of his Fascist Republican Party to do.

Graziani set about his new mission with a vengeance. He made it known that if a partisan act took place in a village or city neighborhood then the entire village or neighborhood would be burned to the ground and all of its inhabitants would be sent to a concentration camp, unless they could prove their loyalty. If the community was actually proven to have assisted the partisans then every male aged eighteen and over would be executed instead of being sent to a camp. Of course this law was as stupid as it was brutal.

The partisans just north of the Chienti River were very active because the Allies were near. In fact the partisans could hear the artillery fire from the front line, but when the Allies suddenly halted on that river line the partisans became quite exposed. Anti-partisan units rushed in and surrounded Major Filipponi and his band and killed or captured all of them. Following a fruitless interrogation the prisoners were hanged.

At Sasetta a sizeable German rearguard opened fire on the advancing Americans, but almost at once they were attacked in the rear by partisans. The Germans quickly surrendered. On 22 June at Lucca a Fascist Carabinieri unit mutinied and freed several political prisoners and together they headed for the hills.

In Parma partisans destroyed thirty German vehicles. Near Milan partisans destroyed the Greco rail tunnel. Near Turin partisans smashed the hydroelectric power station. Partisans ruined another three power stations along the Genoa-Turin rail line.

The citizens of Siena were deliriously happy to see Allied troops arrive: French-led Africans. The French were relieved to find partisans already in possession of key buildings.

By late June the partisans were becoming very bold indeed and in effect ruled large sections of mountainous terrain in Piemont, eastern Friuli, Liguria, Sondrio, the Milan countryside, Bobbio, the shores of Lake Como and Lake Maggiore, Gorizia, Carnia, Treviso, Asiago, Vicenza, along a line Grosseto-Siena-Florence, several Alpine passes and the following valleys: Ceno, Enza, Parma, Maira, Varaita, Taro, Lanzo and Sesia.

Tens of thousands of Fascists had fled Rome and Central Italy ahead of the Allies and now that they had no jobs Mussolini ordered them to organize anti-partisan formations or join existing units. Lieutenant General Mischi had fled Rome bringing only a handful of his Carabinieri with him and he received orders from Mussolini to go to Parma and organize an anti-partisan unit. He was an experienced partisan hunter, having served in Yugoslavia. Mussolini also assigned three thousand five hundred of these fleeing Fascists to Major General Montagna in order to pacify Piemont. At least two thousand Fascists had not fled fast enough and had been caught by partisans and killed in the three weeks following the fall of Rome.

Mussolini wrote to Hitler again, demanding that he release more of those soldiers in his prison camps that had expressed an interest in serving Mussolini but not Hitler. So far only thirteen thousand had been released. In defiance of Hitler's orders the German prison camp authorities were still recruiting Italians, but for German units not for Mussolini. Thus, by late June 1944 the Luftwaffe admitted to having eighty thousand Italian flak gunners, most of them serving in Germany. So, Hitler compromised with Il Duce, agreeing that any prisoners who wished could leave their camp and work in Germany as volunteer industrial or agricultural laborers.

Just as Mussolini started to calm down, Field Marshal Wilhelm Keitel caused another row. This arrogant Prussian proposed that the four Italian divisions currently training in Germany should be disbanded and the personnel transferred to the Luftwaffe as flak gunners. Actually this reflected Germany's manpower shortage and her crucial need for greater anti-aircraft protection more than it did Keitel's insensitivity towards Italian pride. However, the damage was done and Graziani hit the roof and threatened to resign if Mussolini allowed this. Hitler, knowing that Graziani was one of the few Italian generals who commanded respect among Italian soldiery, ordered Keitel to retract his suggestion. Mussolini felt quite smug about this, because he knew that Keitel would not urinate without a written directive from Hitler. The suggestion had most likely been Hitler's all along.

Naturally Graziani was suddenly Mussolini's golden boy, causing Ricci, Buffarino-Guidi and Pavolini to feel snubbed. Graziani seized the opportunity to ask Il Duce for control of the GNR.

Of course the public in Mussolini's Italy could not be made aware of the incident. For their 'education' the Fascist press reported nothing but a warm loving feeling between the two Axis partners. As part of this propaganda campaign Mussolini used publicity stunts that gave his people some pride. One such stunt was an air raid by his bombers on Gibraltar, which had begun to think of itself as a backwater. To be fair, the raid was impressive, but it was small consolation for the loss of Rome.

On 8 July Utili's corps spearheaded by the Nembo Parachute Division crossed the Musone River under fire and reached Fillotrano, which was in partisan hands. The meeting was joyous, but within hours the Co-Belligerent troops moved out on their way to the Esino Valley, hoping to outflank Ancona. The partisans petitioned the Nembo officers for provisions so that they could join them. The Nembo troops were glad of the help, as they had suffered upwards of three hundred casualties in the last few days. Anders' and Utili's troops received formal praise from British Eighth Army for their audacity. The Maiella Brigade was still performing very nicely in this region as a reconnaissance unit for the Poles.

Hundreds of miles to the north there was no succor for the partisans. At the beginning of July anti-partisan forces made another sweep northwest of Lake Maggiore and within days had killed over two hundred partisans and captured forty-three, most of them wounded. The Fascists tortured each one to death for information, but learned nothing.

At Montefiorino the partisan's political commissars declared their zone of fire to be an autonomous republic. Paying lip service to Bonomi's government they asked through their Allied radio operators for Cadorna to assist them with provisions and troops. Cadorna agreed and eventually gained Messe's permission for the Nembo Parachute Division to parachute onto Montefiorino. It would take the Nembo about three weeks to pull out of the line and prepare for the jump.

Down below in the valleys and in the major cities the Fascists still ruled and were still a major threat to the very existence of the partisans. Mussolini asked Pavolini how his new anti-partisan formation was coming. Omitting those party members who were already serving in a uniformed capacity the party had four hundred and eighty-seven thousand men and women on the books. However, Pavolini chose not to arm the women, and he placed an age limit of sixty upon the men. This reduced his available manpower even more, but some of the men were too infirm for military duty, and most of them held valuable jobs in war-related industries or were necessary to local government. This left one hundred thousand men available for his new 'army. Most were those that had fled their homes ahead of the advancing Allies. Pavolini decided to use these men by superimposing a military structure on top of the administrative structure of the party. A good decision. Therefore, while retaining the title of Party Secretary he also now took the title of Lieutenant General of the Armed Party Militia. His forty-six regional deputies would each wear a second hat as a brigade commander. As black was the official Fascist color these regional brigades were known as Black Brigades, each taking the name of a Fascist martyr. These brigades would fight in the immediate vicinity of their region. In addition Pavolini formed seven mobile brigades for duty nationwide, a few independent companies and an operations 'arditi' brigade to perform commando-style missions. He provided the units with an official code about equipment and uniforms and age, but it was ignored almost at once. Boys as young as fifteen and men in their seventies were recruited to fill the ranks. Eventually an all-female brigade was established in Trieste, the Norma Cossetto.

Mussolini was pleased when Pavolini reported that he now had one hundred thousand troops. Hitler was pleased too, but for a different reason. Italian commercial enterprises were contracted to the war effort and their millions of workers were doing good service, and tens of thousands of Italians were working in Italy for German companies. In terms of war production Hitler could not afford to lose northern Italy's industrial basin.

Furthermore, by July 1944 three hundred and sixty thousand Italians had volunteered to work in Germany, and thousands more worked for the Germans in other countries. As volunteers they were paid well and had time off. Whenever the Germans saw an Italian chatting up a pretty German girl in a park they were reminded that Germany still had partners.

In fact by this date the number of foreign workers in Germany was phenomenal, up to half the work force in some towns. This included volunteers, forced workers and slaves. The volunteers were treated as well as Germans. The forced workers were treated almost as well, if they were of the right racial grouping, such as Dutch, Norwegians and Volksdeutsch. However, Russians, Ukrainians, Poles and other Slavs were treated poorly, though they were still paid, allowed time off, a week's vacation per year and emergency leave. Many a Ukrainian girl worked as a maid for Nazi party members. The slaves were exactly what the name suggests. Supposedly they had committed a crime to have warranted their arrest and they were treated like inhuman chattel and confined to camps. Many a German slave was guarded by an Italian sentry!

Of course in Axis Italy most Italians worked for the war effort under protest, knowing it could mean death if they refused and possibly the arrest of their family. Nonetheless whenever possible many sabotaged the production facilities.

In mid-July a band of partisans was surrounded near Arezzo, and forty-eight including their leader Eugenio Calo were captured. For two days the Fascists tortured them, but gained no information. Finally in desperation the Fascists buried Calo up to his neck and placed a lit stick of dynamite next to his head with a long fuse. The countdown to the end of Calo's life burned away. A split second before the explosion he was probably thinking of his wife and four children. He did not know they were already dead: arrested by the Gestapo, entrained for Poland, and murdered in an extermination camp. The Gestapo had not known of their relationship to a partisan. They had been arrested because they were Jews.

After the IX Assault Unit captured Cingoli, the Maiella Brigade reconnoitered the Esino Valley, following which Utili's Corps of Liberation captured Jesi and struck out for the Misa River. Seizing Ostra and Villa Spada from German rearguards they then rested. Meanwhile, the Maiella Brigade scouted the Ceseno River.

Polish II Corps praised the Italians for this action. In fact the Poles asked for more Italians, so Eighth Army sent them an eight hundred man battalion of infantry. Because of the continuing absurd British attempt to hide the truth about the use of Italians, this battalion was given the unusual name of 111th Bridge Watching Company. The Poles used them at once to help capture Monte Freddo. By 29 July Anders' Poles and Utili's Italians were poised to take the Metauro River on the run and charge towards Pesaro.

Alexander wanted to cross the Arno at Florence and anchor his flanks at Pisa and Ravenna before Kesselring discovered how much Alexander's forces had shrunken. Just south of Florence SS Sturmbrigade 'Italien' and German paratroopers held up the New Zealand 2nd Division for three days until the night of 28 July. In a humanitarian gesture Kesselring declared Florence an Open City to spare its great treasures, but oddly enough this caused the Allies as many problems as it solved for they soon had a salient with enemy on both flanks and the Arno in front of them. Inside Florence, as the Germans withdrew, the local Fascists began setting up defensive positions in violation of Kesselring's order.

In the last two days of July Utili's Corps of Liberation fought off fierce German counterattacks. During this same period SS Sturmbrigade 'Italien' counterattacked the New Zealanders. By 4 August a team of partisans had bravely crossed the Arno at night under fire to string a telephone line from Allied headquarters to partisan headquarters inside the city. In the Florence suburb south of the river the partisans hunted down Fascist suicide snipers, the latter being members of the GNR and the local black brigade. Men who knew each other, had perhaps been friends or were related now fought to the death in a deadly game of cat and mouse. When possible the Allies and Germans stayed out of this 'Florentine Civil War'.

On 12 August near Florence a unit of the SS Reichsfuehrer Division took fire from partisans. The men of this German unit were full of hatred. Raised as a bodyguard for Heinrich Himmler, they had never expected to be asked to fight, and they had been humiliated by their defeat on Corsica at the hands of the Italians. And now with this latest incident they lost their composure. They picked a village, probably at random, Sant' Anna di Stazzema. Despite the long name, the community only had a small population. The SS troops butchered every man, woman and child they could find at short notice, about five hundred and sixty.

Between 16 and 18 July in Germany Mussolini visited the Monte Rosa Alpini Division at Muenzingen, the Italia Bersaglieri Division at Paderborn, the San Marco Marines at Grafenvoehr and the Littorio Grenadier Division at Sennelager. Major General Tito Agosti boasted his Littorio was ready and should return to Italy at once. Agosti had been seriously wounded in East Africa and captured by the British, but owing to his injuries they had repatriated him. The other three divisional commanders begged the same. Their German instructors complained the troops needed more training. Mussolini wondered if these German pronouncements were based on sound military sense or on Hitler's orders. He planned to bring this to Hitler's attention when they met again 20 July 1944.

On that day when the train pulled into Rastenburg Mussolini alighted to find Hitler waiting for him on the platform, but this was a shaken, wounded and highly-strung Hitler. Just hours earlier, Mussolini learned, a time bomb had exploded in Hitler's war room during a major conference, inflicting heavy casualties. Despite being wounded and in shock, the Fuehrer insisted on personally receiving Il Duce, the only friend he had left, he might have thought. German Army garrisons had mutinied and though the day was not yet over it appeared that the Nazis had retained control.

Mussolini expressed genuine relief that Hitler had survived. He knew that if the Fuehrer went down the drain, he would spiral down alongside him. However, surely there must have been a sense of satisfaction in Mussolini's mind. Ever since his rescue by Hitler he had been forced to eat umble pie. But now no German would be able to mention the shame of the 25 July 1943 overthrow of Mussolini or the 8 September 1943 turnabout by Badoglio without an Italian reminding him of the 20 July 1944 army mutiny against Hitler.

Eventually the meeting got down to brass tacks: Mussolini promised the new black brigades would make a difference in the partisan war; Hitler promised to graduate the San Marco Marine Division early and send it home. Furthermore the Hermann Goering Panzer Division was taken out of the front line to beef up the anti-partisan forces.

———————

On 29 July the Hermann Goering troops began advancing through the Secchia Valley towards Carpinelli. Allied radio operators at Montefiorino just ten miles away notified Cadorna, who called off the jump by the Nembo in the nick of time. The paratroopers would not have been able to fight a panzer division any better than the partisans could. On the 30th a large formation of GNR and Condottieri advanced towards Montefiorino. The partisans resisted, but they were surrounded.

In early August Mischi's new anti-partisan formation went into action against partisans in Piemont. Simultaneously the partisans northwest of Lake Maggiore were attacked yet again by Germans, but this time they evaded the enemy and slipped into the Cannobio Valley. Once there Armando Calzavar and Filippo Frassati gathered all the partisans in the valley to form the Piave Partisan Division.

In the Sesia Valley Vincenzo Moscatelli unified two fragmented bands of Communists into a solid force.

Meanwhile the Montefiorino Republic was dying. Two brothers, Gino and Guglielmo Cacchioli, both Christian Democrats, gathered stragglers together and formed the Beretta Brigade. They hoped to hold out until relieved by the Allies.

However, the Allies were still stuck at Florence. There on 11 August the last Germans pulled out of the city, abandoning the Fascists that were still holding out. It took another seven days of fighting before the partisans declared the southern suburb free from Fascism. Yet the shooting continued in the rest of the city north of the river. On the 21st a German long-range artillery salvo obliterated a civilian church congregation. In fact not until September were the last Fascist gunmen in Florence run to ground and killed. A figure of five hundred Italians killed on both sides in the month long 'Florentine Civil War' is as accurate as any.

Mussolini was getting angry again. His anti-partisan offensives had not crushed the partisans, but had merely pushed them from one location to another like a spoon through soup. He was also angry that he now only controlled half of Italy. He was also angry that ten per cent of the San Marco Marine Division had deserted the moment they arrived back in Italy. The other three divisions returning from

Germany also suffered desertions. One small group from the Montrerosa led by Lieutenant Omero Ciai joined a Garibaldi partisan brigade in the Val d'Aosta.

This put Mussolini in the mood to set his house in order. He had had enough of Ricci, so he gave the GNR to Graziani. The Carabinieri had been autonomous within the GNR, but Graziani immediately gave this paramilitary police force its independence again. However, because there had been desertions and mutinies by Carabinieri, Graziani insisted on a new oath of loyalty and a review of individual track records. As a result seven thousand six hundred Carabinieri failed to pass muster, so they were sent to Germany to perform sentry duty or serve as flak gunners. Surrounded by ninety million Germans it would be hard for them to desert.

––––––––––––

By 14 August Anders decided reluctantly that Utili's Corps of Liberation needed a rest, and it was agreed the Italians would be withdrawn from combat at month's end. This would mark seven months of continuous action for some members. On the 19th the corps captured Pergola on the upper Ceseno River, and next day took Santa Maria Carpinata. Fighting their way forward up and down mountains at the rate of two miles a day they reached the Metauro and Burano Rivers on the 22nd. A day later they charged forward four miles to conquer Cagli, and the following day captured Acqualagna. Now the corps could be withdrawn.

The 111th Bridge Watching Company and the Maiella Brigade were not under Utili's command, so they remained to fight under Anders' orders. Despite casualties, the Maiella had expanded to about one thousand five hundred men by recruiting partisans from other bands as they were liberated.

At the central part of the front line a Co-Belligerent reconnaissance unit had been assigned to a Sikh battalion of the Indian Army. In one location an Italian officer telephoned the next village to ask if the Germans had left yet. Assured they had, he led his troops cautiously forward and scanned the village with binoculars. Seeing no signs of enemy he informed the Sikhs. A full Sikh company now marched up the road as the Italians watched. Just short of the first building a withering fire from several machine guns mowed down the Sikhs. The Italians gave covering fire. A second Sikh company charged forward to help, but ran into the bullets of the Italians. The village was eventually cleared, and no Germans or Fascists were found. The enemy had in fact been firing from the heights above the village on the far side. The Sikhs suffered sixty-nine casualties. Really this action was no one's fault, but it did nothing to enhance Indian trust of Italians. These Indians and their British officers belonged to the Indian 4th Division, which had fought the Italians at Keren, Alamein and Enfidaville. It is understandable that passions ran high.

———————

In the same manner that Hitler looked fondly upon Nuremberg, the heart of Nazism, so Mussolini looked proudly upon Milan, the heart of Fascism. Yet the city was also an industrial center and as such the majority of its inhabitants were Communists or Socialists. The casualty telegrams received by mothers and wives over the last twenty-two years and the bombing of the city over the last four years had spread the gap between the Fascists and non-Fascists ever wider. The Fascists and Germans had won the Battle of Milan in September 1943, but its ferocity showed just how strong anti-Fascist feelings ran.

Lieutenant General Diamanti, a Blackshirt veteran of Ethiopia, Yugoslavia and Russia, was responsible for security here, but to pacify this great metropolis he had but a few hundred policemen, plus the Caruso Police Legion, five hundred Blackshirts of the GNR Muti Legion and six hundred members of the city's new Resega Black Brigade. Germans in the area were not his to call upon. Yet he could not curtail the activities of SAP saboteurs. The result was a buildup of frustration among the authorities. On 8 August 1944 someone blew up a truck, a common enough incident in the city. However, the Muti Legion had become tired of these actions and was angry at the wall of silence erected by the public. No one saw anything, as usual. Four days later in sheer bitter frustration Muti members grabbed fifteen innocent people at random, put them against a wall in the busy Piazza Loreto and publicly shot them. The partisans just outside the city reacted by executing forty-five Fascists they had recently kidnapped.

———————

Mussolini and Graziani were too busy to worry about tit for tat killings in Milan, because German intelligence alerted them that another Allied armada was assembling at ports in Corsica, Sardinia, southern Italy, Sicily and North Africa. German reconnaissance planes could not get close because of Allied and Co-Belligerent flak batteries and fighter planes. Fascist spies could not learn the destination of the armada owing to vigilant security by Allied and Co-Belligerent sentries. But one thing was certain. It heralded an invasion bigger than that of Salerno or Anzio. German forces were alerted as far apart as Greece, Yugoslavia, Italy and France. Graziani put the Army of Liguria on alert. He had only just formed this army and had given its command to General Gambara with the mission of protecting Genoa and Italy's northwest shore, and it consisted of coastal batteries, the San Marco Marine Division and some German formations.

The Allied armada set sail and on the 14th Gambara's heart almost stopped when he was told the ships were pointing straight towards him. Mussolini's navy had been given little opportunity to show its mettle, but this threat could not go unchallenged. The Fascist MAS boats slid out of their harbors and charged into the mass of ships. It was a suicide run, every crewman knew, and their effort made little impact on the Allies. In fact the fleet was so large that most Allied sailors did not know they had been under attack!

During the night Gambara began to breathe easier as he was informed the armada had changed course towards the south coast of France, and in the early hours of the 15th it disgorged the US Seventh and French First Armies on the French shore.

Gambara, Graziani and Mussolini knew they had only been given a temporary reprieve, because with the Americans already streaming across Northern France and with Paris in revolt, this invasion would be the coup de grace for the German forces in France. Graziani instructed Gambara to take up defensive positions along the Franco-Italian border. Graziani hoped the terrain of high alpine passes and mountains would be a sufficient stumbling block for the Allies. He remembered how difficult it was for the Italians to attack here in 1940.

The Allies advanced quickly in Southern France, as the Germans were on the run, and within days American and French troops arrived on the Italian border. But here they stopped. From now on Gambara's Army of Liguria would pepper the Allies with artillery fire and prick them with raids and nightly patrols. His army was reinforced and divided into two corps: the Italian Lombardia Corps of the San Marco Marine Division and a German battlegroup, and the German LXXV Corps of the German 5th Mountain Division and 34th Division and the Italian Monterosa Alpini Division.

On 23 August the partisans northwest of Lake Maggiore burst forth from the Antigorio Valley to attack the GNR strongpoint of Baveno and after three days of bloody struggle they captured it. They then went on to take Varzo, Crevola, Ossola and Iselle and block the road coming out of the Simplon Pass from Switzerland.

In early September the Piave Partisan Division, now numbering about three thousand guerillas, captured Cannobio on Lake Maggiore, and then attacked the three hundred strong black brigade garrison of Domodossola. The garrison called a truce and asked to be allowed to leave, whereupon the partisans agreed, and then in jubilation they declared the autonomous Republic of Domodossola.

Mussolini was furious. Despite sweeps by German police and soldiers and Italian police, Carabinieri, GNR, army, black brigades and Condottieri the partisans seemingly did as they wished, blowing up bridges, derailing trains, destroying factories, burning down warehouses, smashing power stations and making travel all but impossible. In addition in June, July and August of 1944 the partisans had inflicted twelve thousand casualties on the Axis!

In September the Italians of SS Battalion Debica, following successful anti-partisan sweeps in the Chisone and Susa valleys, joined their compatriots in SS Sturmbrigade 'Italien'.

Graziani launched another anti-partisan offensive. This one had the goal of eliminating the so-called Republic of Carnia, a partisan stronghold along both sides of the border of Italy and Kuestenland. Coordinating the attack with Gruppenfuehrer Karl Wolf, who put twenty thousand Cossacks into the field, Graziani sent twelve thousand members of the black brigades and several thousand Condottieri, and together they advanced through the Cadore district and the Cellina Valley. Suspecting all villages of helping the partisans they razed most of them to the ground.

The Fascists proved just as ruthless as the Cossacks. Indeed the Fascist fanaticism of the black brigades had attracted the attention of Himmler, and he honored the 1st and 82nd Black Brigades with the titles 1st and 2nd SS Mountain Regiments (Italien) and he honored a black brigade artillery formation with the title 29th SS Mountain Artillery Regiment (Italien). These Italians were entitled to wear SS insignia and would have the same rights as German SS. They accepted the dubious honor with grace. Once they had swept through Carnia, they did an about face and repeated the sweep.

When the US Fifth and British Eighth Armies approached the line Pesaro-Pistoia they realized they had at last reached Hitler's main defensive position in Italy. The army of retreating Germans and Italian hiwis and kawis had long suspected that this line was a myth created by the propagandists, but now they found it was very real. The Gothic line had been built by the German Organisation Todt using German and Italian and foreign volunteer labor, and plenty of slaves, many of them Italians. They had cut grass, plucked bushes, dug trenches, placed sandbags, strung barbed wire, laid mines and poured concrete.

On 30 August Allied artillery [including Italian gunners] opened a massive barrage on the eastern half of the line. The shells fell on top of German troops, Polish conscripts and Italian hiwis and kawis, and those Todt members who were putting finishing touches to the line, and everyone dove for cover. After just one hour of shelling the Allies attacked with Poles, Britons, Canadians and Indians. Also making the assault were Italian infantry of the 111th Bridge Watching Company, while members of the Maiella Brigade sought for routes through the defenses, and other Italians followed closely behind: stretcher bearers, combat engineers, medics, radio operators and telephone linesmen. After three days of battle Kesselring ordered a retreat along the eastern half of the line! Next day the Poles took Pesaro.

However, there was method in Kesselring's seemingly mad decision. His forces withdrew to the Conca River and then turned to offer fanatic resistance yet again. By the eleventh day of the offensive the Allied advance had been slowed to a crawl, almost to a stop. Kesselring had succeeded, but the eleven-day struggle had cost him eight thousand killed and wounded and three thousand seven hundred missing.

The US Fifth Army had been conspicuous in this battle by its absence. Indeed Clark was only ready to attack his half of the line on 10 September. His reconnaissance units, including the Co-Belligerent F-Force, had been given plenty of time to learn they were up against the German 4th Parachute Division and 334th Division, plus the SS Battalion Debica and SS Sturmbrigade 'Italien'. Clark's American and British forces launched their offensive, ably assisted by thousands of Co-Belligerent troops – combat engineers, radio operators, telephone linesmen, artillery gunners, medics, stretcher bearers, ambulance crewmen, and muleteers. Fifth Army broke through the Gothic Line, but it took six days of bloody battle.

Meanwhile an unusual situation had arisen in Eighth Army sector. San Marino is surrounded by Italian territory, but it is an independent country. Mussolini had 'protected' the state, though the San Marinese had never asked for his protection, but in September 1943 the state had reaffirmed its independence and Hitler had respected that. Over the next year the nation became home to thousands of refugees fleeing the bombing and fleeing the Fascists. Now the Germans requested permission to place artillery observers inside the country. The plucky little government refused and mobilized its three hundred man army! The Germans invaded and swept them aside. A week later British and Indian troops invaded and chased the Germans out. The German occupation of San Marino was the shortest occupation of a country in the war.

West of the Apennines Fifth Army was now advancing, but finding it tough going. The 36th Garibaldi Partisan Brigade noticed that the strategic importance of Monte Battaglia had not yet been recognized by the Germans, so this formation of grubby, exhausted, hungry wild-looking guerillas climbed the mountain and radioed the Americans.

Initially US Intelligence was skeptical, but the 88th Division staff agreed to take the Italians at their word and ordered their 305th Regiment to join them, which gave its 1st Battalion orders to advance, which told C Company to investigate, which picked out a platoon to infiltrate through German lines and climb the mountain to see if these Italians were truthful or just 'full of it'. Partisan guides led the handful of Americans up a winding trail in the dark with a sheer drop on one side. Once at the summit the Americans radioed C Company that the partisans had spoken the truth. Thereupon the remainder of C Company also climbed to the summit. They were barely in place by dawn, when the mountain was suddenly shelled by German artillery. When the shelling stopped and the sun burned off the morning fog the partisans and Americans saw hundreds of German infantry climbing uphill towards them. The battle was on. The Germans were easily repulsed. The partisans suspected the Germans had not expected to encounter an American infantry company with its mortars, bazookas and tripod machine guns. Throughout the morning the partisans and Americans fought off German infiltrators. That afternoon the Germans attacked with four battalions leading with flamethrowers. This seemed to work at first, for the partisans and Americans had to abandon their positions or fry, but soon realizing they had nowhere to retreat to, the defenders turned and charged the Germans, sending them streaming down the mountainside. That night another American company reinforced them and brought much needed supplies on mules. During the next two days the partisans and Americans flung back several attacks, hugged the ground during artillery salvoes and shot down night infiltrators. On the night of the 30th they were reinforced by another two US companies, and on 1 October they repelled a major German onslaught. Shortly after this the defenders were all relieved by an entire British brigade.

As early as 1 September partisans had begun nightly infiltration into the great city of Bologna in the belief that liberation was just days away. GNR Blackshirts and the Facchini Black Brigade were ordered to hunt down these partisans and the city took on a surrealistic appearance. During daylight the city was at peace. Come sunset the shooting began again! By October it was apparent the city was not going to be liberated after all, for Kesselring had a new ally: the autumn rains. Mountain dirt roads were turned into rivers of mud, and the Allied armies, which relied heavily on motorized traffic, became stuck, literally.

On the 19th there was slight movement: Cesena was seized when partisans hit the Germans in rear while the British attacked in front. Otherwise the line was immobile.

By September 1944 the Allies had advanced up the Italian boot for an entire bloody year, but unknown to them they had only arrived at a line where Hitler had intended to retreat to the previous year. Kesselring had kept his promise to Hitler. He had held the Allies south of this line for an entire year! This advance, as spectacular as it was, was a gory affair and it drained the Allied armies. Manpower shortages were growing daily. The Americans had a massive armed forces of thirteen million men, which on the face of it sounds tremendous, but they were spread all over the globe. In fact by September 1944 they had no more divisions left. All were either in battle or in transit to battle.

So far Clark had only received three divisions as reinforcements: the first-rate US 10th Mountain and the second-rate US 92nd and Brazilian. Much was expected of the American mountaineers, but once in Italy it was realized they needed further training in the peculiarities of the Apennines, before they could enter combat. The Americans had trained them as best they could, but now they had to turn to the real mountain experts - the Italians. Fortunately there were plenty of Co-Belligerent Alpini who could provide that training, and Clark made the necessary arrangements.

The 92nd Division was ready for combat according to some and would never be ready according to others. The difference in opinions was a result of the fact that the division was all Negro, except for some white officers. The vast majority of white Americans in 1944 were bigots, and most wanted nothing to do with the formation. Objective white Americans believed the Negroes would make good soldiers - they had in all American wars to date - but even these liberal whites wondered if the Negroes would fight for a society that spit upon them.

As for the Brazilians, they were truly of unknown quality. They might as well have come from the moon. One thing was noticeable to the USA Americans. Negroes served in Brazilian units with equal treatment.

In any case these three divisions were not enough, because by now two thirds of Clark's units had been siphoned off to the French campaign (the Western Front). He was so desperate he was forced to turn an entire US anti-aircraft brigade into an infantry unit. Moreover, he was not getting sufficient replacements to compensate for his casualties, so he had to comb his rear-echelon units for infantry replacements, leaving some units dangerously short. He begged for thousands of trained infantrymen to be sent to him from France. The best response he got was three thousand rear-echelon personnel, and a few air force mechanics. He threw them into the line as infantry replacements without retraining them. In truth the Americans were short of personnel in France, and had only been able to let Clark have these few thousand, because thirty thousand Italian cooperators had arrived in France to help fight the Germans.

Unbelievably some British staff officers at 15th Army Group were still so anti-Italian that they suggested Clark pull all of his Italians out of the firing line. Clark could have replied with a simple 'No thank you', but this suggestion incensed him so much that he replied in stark blunt terms, the meaning of which comes through even though his words were hedged in military jargon and with an effort to be 'polite' to the British: "Imperative no reduction in number of Italian troops allotted Fifth Army...Italian troops assigned now fully employed essential service operations." With words like 'imperative' and 'essential' this answer shows how much Clark appreciated his

Italians.

British Eighth Army was also in serious straits, yet its commander Lieutenant General Oliver Leese was ordered to release a British division and his Greek 1st Brigade for the upcoming invasion of Greece, and he was told to disband his British 1st Armored Division, and to prepare to lose his Canadian corps, which was needed on the Western Front. Already short of British replacements, he had been forced to reduce most of his British infantry battalions from four companies to three. He still had the excellent New Zealand 2nd Division, but the only way the government of New Zealand could keep this unit at full strength was by disbanding their 3rd Division currently fighting the Japanese.

Anders' Polish Corps was so desperate for manpower that he asked the Allies to release Poles whom they had captured in Italy and France wearing German uniform! This was agreed and thousands of Poles were soon on their way to Anders. Naturally the Italians were outraged. The Allies could not see fit to release Italians from Cooperator status, let alone Recalcitrant status, but they could release Poles of dubious political loyalties! The Italians had thought they had proven themselves. Actually, they had done as far as British combat officers were concerned. But British staff officers and politicians were still bitterly biased.

The only new unit that Eighth Army received reflected the Allied attitude of sending second class troops to Italy. It was one of Churchill's pet projects, an all-Jewish brigade. Most British Army officers were raised in the staunch Anglican Church of England or the Presbyterian Church of Scotland, and anti-Semitism was rife. The generals accepted the brigade most reluctantly indeed. However, the regimental officers in the British Army had been supportive of creating the unit, for it gave them the chance to kick Jews out of their own regiments, sending them to the Jewish Brigade with a sort of 'you'll be happier there' attitude.

Thus not only were the Allied forces in Italy being short changed in the number of combat formations, but they were being fobbed off with second-rate infantry [or at least what was considered to be second-rate]: namely Jews, Negroes, Brazilians, anti-aircraft gunners, rear echelon soldiers and air force mechanics.

Alexander was still in charge of this mess, robbing Peter to pay Paul, as it were, and he knew he just absolutely had to overcome the objections of his British staff officers and ask Messe to provide more Italian infantry units. It was a simple matter of arithmetic. Of the forty divisions sent to the Italian campaign he would soon have only eighteen left. If the Allies were to hold in Italy let alone advance they needed more warm bodies. Therefore, Alexander accepted Messe's offer of four divisions: Friuli, Cremona, Legnano and Folgore.

The men of the Friuli had fought the French briefly, the

Yugoslavian Army briefly, Corsican guerillas for a few months, and on Corsica they had fought the Germans. The division consisted of the 87th and 88th Infantry Regiments under Colonels Carignani and Ciancabilla, the 35th Artillery Regiment of Colonel de Biase, a battalion of combat engineers, and support troops. Its commander was Major General Arturo Scattini, who had been the deputy commander of the La Spezia Division in Tunisia and had spent several months in an Allied prisoner of war camp. He was informed that his ten thousand seven hundred and thirty men would be issued British uniforms and equipment, some US equipment and no fewer than one thousand three hundred and sixty-three vehicles. The latter figure astonished him. Only a few of his men knew how to drive, and driving lessons would thus extend the division's training schedule. Most of the weaponry would remain Italian, giving him a firepower strength of seven thousand nine hundred and sixty-seven rifles and carbines, four hundred and forty-five, five hundred machine guns, one hundred and forty 2inch mortars, forty 3inch mortars, one hundred and seventy-eight anti-tank guns and sixty-four field guns.

Major General Clemente Primieri's Cremona Division had fought the French briefly, Corsican guerillas for a few months, and against the Germans on Corsica. It consisted of the 21st and 22nd Infantry and 7th Artillery Regiments, a battalion of combat engineers, and support troops. The Cremona would be refitted like the Friuli.

The Legnano Division would soon be commanded by Major General Utili. This division had fought the Greeks. Its 67th Infantry Regiment was already serving admirably at the front as stretcher-bearers, and its 68th Infantry Regiment had only recently been pulled out of the line, having been part of the Dapino Brigade/Utili Division. The Legnano also contained the 58th Artillery Regiment, a combat engineer battalion, and support troops. Clark did not want to lose his veteran stretcher-bearers of the 67th, because they were performing sterling service, so it was decided to assign the new 69th Infantry Regiment in place of the 67th. The original 69th had been destroyed in Libya in 1941. This newly designated 69th was created by renaming the 4th Alpini Regiment, and adding to it a battalion of the 4th Bersaglieri Regiment. The 4th Alpini had fought the French and the Titoists, and for several months had fought the Germans as part of the Utili Division. The 4th Bersaglieri had fought the French and the Greeks, and for the last few months had been fighting the Germans as a part of the Dapino Brigade/Utili Division.

It is surprising that Messe gave Major General Morigi's new formation the name Folgore, to honor the division that had been annihilated at Alamein. Incredibly a few members of the original division had survived, like Ugo Siva. After the death of the original division, those members that had been detached or recovering from wounds or sickness were formed into a battle group that was destroyed in Tunisia, but Siva had been transferred out in the nick of time. Siva then served with the Nembo and fought in the mini-civil war in that division on Sardinia. Following this as a lieutenant colonel and an instructor he helped prepare the Co-Belligerent Nembo for combat on the Italian front. This new Folgore Division would consist of the 185th Parachute Infantry Regiment, a battalion of which had fought as part of the Dapino Brigade/Utili Division. The other infantry regiment of the new division was made up of marines, including the Bafile and Grado Battalions that had fought as part of the Utili Division. The divisional artillery was named the 155th Artillery Regiment honoring the Emilia Division that had disappeared into a German prisoner of war camp. A battalion of combat engineers and support personnel made up the remainder of the Folgore.

Alexander believed that once they were reequipped and retrained the Cremona, Folgore, Friuli and Legnano Divisions would be a valuable and welcome addition to the Allies. Unfortunately he still had to deal with politicos at home and on his own staff (British officers could and often did serve as members of parliament, too). Many had the attitude that the 'Eye-ties' had switched sides once and therefore might do it again. In a continuation of their childish behavior they told Alexander he could use the divisions, but could not inform the press they were real divisions. Instead they would be referred to as 'combat groups': in Italian 'gruppo di combattimente'. The silliness of this can be seen in official dispatches that described an Italian combat group and then mentioned its 'divisional' lines of supply.' Bonomi's government went along with this charade, but Messe absolutely refused and always called them 'divisions'. After all the British had never described Italian formations of this size as 'combat groups' when they were fighting against them. They had always used the term 'division'.

There was another source of manpower and that was the partisans, but here Alexander was up against the prejudice of Italian politicians as well as British. The partisans were useful as long as they were Mussolini's headache. Once they became Bonomi's headache he wanted rid of them. He had made one concession: he would allow ex-partisans to join the Co-Belligerent forces, but each had to undergo political screening. He wanted no Communists preaching in the barracks. However, in flagrant violation of the rules most Allied units used partisans as guides, scouts and interpreters, and the Maiella Brigade was still fighting alongside the British as a regular unit.

Chapter Fifty-nine
Death in the Balkans

There were other land campaigns that involved a considerable
number of Italians after September 1943, and they were fought in the
Balkans. Here Italians fought on both sides, just as the people of the
Balkans did. Here the war was truly a European Civil War.

Of all the Italians that had joined the partisans in the Balkans in
September 1943 the largest number and the best treated were those
that had been accepted by the Titoists. In addition to combat troops,
many were rear-echelon. Of course, surrounded by Axis forces these
'rear' troops were often in as much danger as the 'front' troops. The
largest Italian unit serving under Tito was the Garibaldi Division, now
commanded by Major General Vivaldi. Those serving with the
Albanian partisans, including Enver Hoxha's Communists, were
treated well enough, but were usually trusted only in rear-echelon
duties - i. e. if a partisan army can have a 'rear'. Those Italians that
had joined non-Communist Greek guerilla bands were now fighting
alongside the Greeks as equals. Most of the partisan leaders were
intelligent, though often brutal, such as Tito and Hoxha, but Stefanos
Serafis was brutal and stupid, and most of those Italians that had
joined his Greek Communist ELAS were dead by spring 1944,
murdered by ill treatment and neglect. The survivors were a pitiable
bunch.

In April 1944 the Germans decided to clear guerillas out of the
Helicon district in Greece, and they chose to do it by an amphibious
invasion. The attacking troops consisted of Germans, Fascist Italian
kawis, Fascist Greeks and Arabs. The sweep they made through the
region would leave a lasting impression on the villagers. These
peasants witnessed that the Germans obeyed orders to the letter, no
matter how ruthless, and were disciplined and behaved well if left to
their own devices. The Italian kawis were obnoxious, looting and
raping every female in sight. The Arabs behaved quite abominably,
even worse than the kawis. However, the worst were the Greeks of
the security battalions, who pillaged, beat, raped, tortured and
murdered their own countrymen. However, these invaders were soon
counter attacked by a significant partisan force, and after losing two
hundred and fifty casualties they evacuated the area in ignominy.

There is no accurate count of the number of Italians serving in
Greece on either side in 1944, but there are some indications. E. g. in
the Pindus Mountains Greek EDES partisans were attacked by two
Axis divisions, one of Germans and one of Russians. The partisans
had to flee and abandon their bedridden wounded and sick...of which
nine hundred and seventy-two were Greek, three hundred and forty-
one were Italian and seven were British. In July ELAS raided the

German naval base at Stylida and found a significant number of the defenders were Italian hiwis of the German navy. In August Greek partisans wrecked a military train and captured thirty-seven injured guards, of which twenty-five were Fascist Greeks, ten were Italian hiwis and two were German.

———————

In October 1944 the Titoists became extremely bold because of the arrival of the liberating Soviet Red Army. By now Tito's main force had evolved into a regular army. He even had airfields and squadrons of bombers. Titoists attacked the Italian city of Zara on the Yugoslavian coast, which was defended by Germans and Italian kawis and hiwis. Many of these Italians were citizens of the city. The battle lasted for three savage days and no quarter was given, especially when Italian partisan encountered Italian Fascist. The Germans then surrendered.

The approach of the Soviets marked the beginning of the end for the Germans in Yugoslavia, Albania and Greece, and as they retreated northwards they and their many supporters including Italian hiwis and kawis had to battle their way through bands of guerillas along winding mountain roads. At the same time on the eastern border of Yugoslavia the main German combat forces were trying to fend off a full-scale offensive by the Soviets. Romania and Bulgaria ditched Hitler and joined Stalin.

On 19 October the Germans surrendered Belgrade the Yugoslavian capital. Most of the Serb troops and police had already fled.

On 30 October Enver Hoxha's Communist Albanian partisans, accompanied by his Italians, launched a major assault on the Albanian capital Tirana and in a two-week battle they killed most of the Albanian Fascists, many Italian Fascists, and a few Germans. The nation was now liberated from Fascism and enslaved in Communism in one fell swoop.

As the political complexion of the Balkans was changing, Allied agents serving with the various partisan bands began to ask their superiors at Allied headquarters if the anti-Fascist Italians here could not be taken to Italy, as they were in dire straits indeed. They could be classified into three groups. The healthiest were those Italians who had married Greek girls during their tour of duty and who in September 1943 had doffed their uniforms and become 'Greeks'. They wanted to come home, but they also wanted to bring their wives and kids with them. The second group of Italians was the partisans, who suffered from wounds, sickness and injuries, all exacerbated by a poor diet and a lack of the most rudimentary medical attention. However, it was the third group that required urgent relief, namely the slaves of the ELAS. More than half had died, leaving only seven thousand five hundred, many of whom did not even have underwear let alone clothes and a second cold winter was fast approaching. Without making any political decisions the Allies agreed that Allied and Co-Belligerent planes could drop supplies to them.

In October the Garibaldi Partisan Division made a formal request to be repatriated home. This caused another problem for Bonomi, because he knew that the leadership of the division was politically, if not entirely 'red', certainly 'dark pink'. Though he suspected few of the rank and file were Communist. But Bonomi still had a rule that all partisans had to be politically screened. The Garibaldi had performed wonders under Tito's command, but their travails had been difficult indeed. Of the eighteen thousand who joined in September 1943 only five thousand were still alive. Tito praised them and wanted to keep them, so the divisional leadership eventually agreed to remain if they could be supplied by the Allies.

The Operations Branch of Allied Forces Headquarters Mediterranean gave its opinion that the partisans in the Balkans should be repatriated and placed into Co-Belligerent units. Tito agreed, but only if Bonomi formally requested it. Suddenly Bonomi saw a snake in the grass. No one, not even the Soviets, had formally recognized Tito as head of the Yugoslavian government, and a formal request from Bonomi could be construed as doing exactly that. There was already a Yugoslavian government as far as the Allies were concerned: a group of politicians living in Egypt. Moreover, prior to the war Italy had ruled portions of Slovenia, Croatia, Istria and Dalmatia. Bonomi had no indication from Tito that he would agree to those pre-war boundaries. The fate of five thousand courageous men who just wanted to fight Fascism would have to remain in doubt for the time being.

On 12 October Marshal Messe expressed his indignation that the Allies had not yet rescued the Italian slaves of ELAS. Evidently the parachute supply drops had not taken place, owing to flimsy excuses. Only at the end of the month did Bonomi and the Allies agree: the slaves would be repatriated as soon as Allied regular troops reached ELAS. Meantime supplies would be dropped.

This conclusion sounded good at the conference table, because the British had already landed in Greece. The Germans and Fascist Greeks were evacuating their troops from mainland Greece, but owing to British control of the air and sea they had been forced to abandon their island garrisons manned by fifteen thousand Germans and five thousand Fascist Italians.

However, ELAS had made a deal with the Germans. In return for German deliveries of small arms and ammunition, the ELAS partisans would not harass retreating German convoys. It was obvious to the British that ELAS was going to try to seize control of Greece. Furthermore, British agents reported that the parachuted supplies meant for the slaves had been stolen by ELAS guerillas. Indeed these

British agents had no influence on the guerillas anymore and were in fear of their lives.

It was mid-November before British regulars reached the slaves in northern Greece. At last they could be clothed, fed, repatriated to Italy and sent to hospital.

The Allies were also contacted by the fifteen thousand Italian partisans in Albania. They too wanted to come home.

In addition a thousand Italians that had been captured by the Bulgarians during the last year were released, now that Bulgaria had switched sides. They also wanted transportation home.

At this stage in history all non-Communists believed that all Communists were alike, and that they were lackeys of Stalin. In truth Tito had nothing to do with Hoxha and neither had anything to do with Serafis, and none took orders from Stalin anymore. But Bonomi and the Allies were convinced that Hoxha and Tito and Serafis and even the Communist partisans in Italy would attack the Allies as soon as Stalin gave the order.

Yet Bonomi was under considerable pressure from many quarters to recognize Tito and get those 'boys' of the Garibaldi division home. In desperation on 28 November he resigned. This ploy had been done before in Italian history and it worked again. His opponents backed down and asked him to reconsider. He did, and allowed them a few minor cabinet changes to save face. One change was that Count Sforza became Foreign Minister.

To prove Bonomi right, in early December Serafis began a war against the British and any Greeks that opposed him. On 6 December the Allied agents with Tito asked Bonomi once again what was going to happen to the Italians in Tito's forces. Bonomi fobbed them off. The Allies, he replied, were preparing to ship them from Dubrovnik to Taranto where a convalescent camp had been set up for Italians coming from the Balkans. Italians were already arriving from Bulgaria, Albania and Greece.

Finally on 23 December Bonomi caved in and asked Tito to release all his Italians, including any Fascist prisoners he had. Tito refused! It was going to be a long cold winter for Colonel Carlo Ravnich and his Garibaldi Division.

Chapter Sixty
Fratricidal Autumn

Mussolini continually tried to woo the Italian kawis and hiwis away from the Germans, and he repeatedly asked the Germans to release them. Instead the Germans recruited more. Indeed in October 1944 Hitler pressured Mussolini into sending another 8,000 Italian conscripts to Germany to man flak guns. Allied air power was obliterating Germany's cities and Hitler was desperate for anything to alleviate the destruction and suffering of his people. The scale of this air to ground conflict can be understood when one looks at the flak defenses of the Leune oil refinery in Germany. Manning the guns were 28,000 members of the German Luftwaffe Flak Service, and they were assisted by 6,000 German boys as young as twelve, 3,050 German girls as young as fifteen, several hundred Italians, a few hundred Hungarians and 3,000 'Ost hiwis' [Russians, Latvians, Lithuanians and Ukrainians]; plus another 3,000 military and paramilitary Germans were serving as aircraft observers, rescue workers, air raid wardens, emergency repairmen, drivers, mechanics and gun emplacement maintenance personnel; plus hundreds of German firemen and medical staff were fully employed; and 18,000 German seventeen-year old boys stood by to repair bomb damage. In other words a total of 62,000 people were defending one installation! And this does not count nearby Luftwaffe fighter pilots and their ground crews.

Himmler united the three black brigades he had honored with SS status and now he called them the 24th SS Karstjaeger Mountain Division (Italien). They were assigned an Austrian SS battalion as an anchor. He also began to issue them orders. With SS pay and equipment the men continued to fight partisans in Italy, but from now on reported to Obergruppenfuehrer Karl Wolf not to Pavolini.

In October the Littorio Grenadier Division returned from Germany, but as the front lines in central Italy and along the French border were stable Graziani put them on anti-partisan duty.

On 9 October a large formation of GNR accompanied by some German battalions invaded the so-called Republic of Domodossola. On Day One they captured Cannobio, then advanced towards Domodossola, covering the twenty-five miles of alpine foothills in six days of combat. After taking Domodossola they still had another nine days of combat before the partisans scattered into tiny groups.

Meanwhile another operation was under way in Friuli by 2,000 GNR and 1,500 Germans against the west bank of the Tagliamento River. Soon another body of 2,000 GNR and 4,000 Germans advanced through the heart of Friuli and attacked along the Tagliamento in the Carnia and Tolmezzo Districts. On the 12th

Germans and Cossacks attacked through the Piave Valley and seized San Stefano. These three offensives squeezed the partisans into the Ampezzo area, where they were forced to melt into the mountains in small groups.

The type of combat in these operations can be understood better by looking at the casualty statistics kept by meticulous German Intelligence officers. In one operation imaginatively named Large-Scale Mussolini's casualties consisted of 33 Fascist Italians killed, 183 wounded and 28 missing (either dead, captured or deserted), and among Hitler's forces, which included Italian kawis and hiwis, there were another 50 killed, 183 wounded and 4 missing, but they succeeded in liberating 161 Germans and 125 Italians that had been captured by the partisans in earlier actions, and they killed 1,539 partisans and captured 1,248, plus they arrested 1,973 peasants suspected of aiding the partisans. In another operation named with equal imagination Small-Scale Mussolini's casualties were 53 Fascist Italians killed, 155 wounded and 7 missing, and Hitler's forces, including Italian hiwis and kawis, lost 53 killed, 116 wounded and 4 missing. They killed 532 partisans and captured 868, caught 13 deserters, rounded up 1,097 men of military age who would be sent to forced labor or inducted into Mussolini's armed forces, and arrested 1,101 peasants suspected of helping partisans.

The deserters would have been shot. Most of the captured partisans would eventually be executed or sent to a concentration camp. The suspects would be sent to slave labor. In the above two operations in terms of live humans the partisans lost 8,371 and the Axis gained 511. Such major actions were fatal to the partisan struggle.

In August through to October elements of the SS Reichsfuehrer Division massacred about two thousand civilians at Bardine San Terenzo, Monzuno, Grizzana Morandi and Marzabotto, including forty-five babies. Most of these massacres were committed by the divisional reconnaissance battalion commanded by an Austrian, Sturmbannfuehrer Walter Reder.

Near Lucca SS personnel discovered sixty Jews hiding in the Farneta monastery. They killed them all and also executed the priests and monks who had hid them.

By contrast behind Allied lines in southern Italy between 8 September 1943 and 31 October 1944 the Allied and Co-Belligerent forces only caught 223 Fascist partisans, spies and saboteurs. They executed a few. However, anti-Fascist partisans usually cleaned house themselves, and never bothered to inform the Allies how many Fascist partisans they had killed. E.g. the above figures do not include the casualties of the 'Florentine Civil War'.

The anti-Fascist partisans were frustrated by the Allies. Why had the Allies stopped at the Franco-Italian border? The only major fight on the Franco-Italian border was in October when French troops captured Monton and Sospel on the coast. The partisans were unaware that the Americans did not trust their French allies, suspecting they intended to annex a good deal of Italy. In fact the US government ordered US 6th Army Group to provide the French Alpine Command with just enough materiel to enable them to fight off an Axis counter-attack. Indeed when Italian partisans infiltrated through the snow-covered mountainous front line and asked the French to enter Italy and bring mule supply trains with them, the Americans refused to authorize it. However, the Americans did set up rest centers on the French Riviera for any partisans who managed to reach Allied lines.

However, Alexander's 15th Army Group and his British superiors, not knowing of this American mistrust of the French, asked US 6th Army Group to aid the partisans. Therefore, 6th Army Group rescinded their ban and allowed Italian partisan mule convoys to come into their lines and resupply. Some French and American mule convoys also took supplies to the partisans. The Axis did not have enough troops to man a contiguous front line here.

By November 1944 Alexander was faced with a terrible decision. Since May he had inflicted on the Germans losses of 90,000 killed or missing and 104,000 wounded, yet they were still strong and were preventing him from advancing. His forces had been just outside Bologna for three months. In November the Polish Corps, including the Italians of the 111th Bridge Watching Company and the Maiella Brigade, was given a one-day objective. They succeeded, but it took eight days of bloody struggle. To lever the Germans out of Modigliana took several days of attacks by British and Indians. And now bad weather was shutting everyone down. Alexander realized he was not going to accomplish anything until spring, therefore he made his painful decision: he ordered the partisans to "prepare and wait until the moment comes for the next blow", and everyone knew that would not be for at least six months!

This was heartbreaking news for the partisans, especially those within an arm's length of liberation. The 28th Garibaldi Brigade outside Ravenna was lucky. Immediately after they attacked that city the Allies arrived. But those who died around Montefiorino did so within earshot of Allied artillery. Partisans had invaded Bologna on 1 September, expecting a swift liberation. It had not come. The nightly combat inside Bologna was so nerve-wracking for the Facchini Black Brigade and the Bologna GNR Battalion that the latter asked to be sent to the front instead! The Germans agreed and placed the unit in the line. They reported these Italians were soon fighting bravely.

A band of partisans fled Carnia heading for Titoist territory. In order to prevent this union several Condottieri battalions chased them into Kuestenland. Gauleiter Rainer in charge here complained of the Condottieri's 'invasion' of German soil.

By November two of the largest anti-partisan formations in Italy were the 24th SS Karstjaeger Mountain Division (Italien) and the 1st SS Cossack Division. Hitler gave the Cossacks an incentive. If they cleared Tolmezzo District of partisans he would give it to them as a national homeland. This was welcome news for the Cossacks, because they had their families with them.

Mussolini offered an amnesty: up to 10 November any deserter from the partisans would be accepted into his armed forces with 'no questions asked'. His prime purpose was to attract those partisan formations that had once been Fourth Army regular units. However, he got few takers. Having failed with the carrot he now tried the stick. On 15 November he launched a major offensive in northwest Italy using the 24th SS Karstjaeger Mountain Division (Italien), the Littorio Grenadier Division, several battalions of GNR, some black brigades and some German troops.

––––––––––

Alexander was now promoted to command the Mediterranean Theater, and his successor to head 15th Army Group was none other than Mark Clark. Alexander was no doubt glad to be rid of Italy. In December British troops, Canadians, and the Poles and their Italians launched an offensive and the sum total of their gains was the town of Faenza. The Brazilians attacked Monte Castello and received a bloody nose. A planned Fifth Army offensive was called off and Clark ordered everyone to shut down for the winter.

15th Army Group lost the two Canadian divisions at year's end, who went to the Western Front, but gained Major general Guido Bologna's Italian Mantova Division [as the Mantova Combat Group]. This division's infantry consisted of the 113th and 114th Regiments, but rather than retain its own 11th Artillery Regiment, which had seen considerable action with the Dapino Brigade/Utili Division, Messe gave it the 184th Artillery Regiment of the Nembo Parachute Division. These gunners had fought in the 'Nembo Civil War' and had then spent three months in the line under Utili's corps.

This now gave Clark a Co-Belligerent reserve of five divisions – Cremona, Friuli, Legnano, Folgore and Mantova - totaling 55,537 personnel [with an extra 4,062 men in a replacement pool].

In addition to these five divisions the 9 December 1944 strength returns showed that 56,518 Italians were serving the Allies in Italy either reporting to Eighth Army or directly to 15th Army Group, and another 70, 801 reported to Fifth Army, while 5,549 were undergoing training by the Allies.

In addition on this date Bonomi directly controlled the Bari, Sabauda, Piceno, Nembo Parachute and Calabria Infantry Divisions and the following coastal divisions: 204th, 226th, 203rd, 205th, 24th, 210th, 212th, 227th and 225th. He had another 120,000 personnel serving in smaller army units. And he had circa 20,000 flak gunners.

For internal security he had access to 40,000 police, 70,000 Carabinieri and 10,000 firemen under military orders. His Co-Belligerent Air Force had 31,000 airmen, and had been issued American Baltimore bombers and Airacobra fighters and British Spitfire fighters. His navy possessed 75,000 sailors, plus his merchant seamen served all over the world. Outside of Italy the Allies were using 140,000 cooperators.

Thus the Italians with over 900,000 uniformed personnel [not counting partisans] were now one of the largest national contributors to the Allied cause. But this was not enough. The Allies wanted more, so Bonomi now agreed that any liberated partisan could join the Co-Belligerent forces, and the Allies asked Bonomi to begin conscription to expand his army!

———————

Chapter Sixty-one
The Last Winter

In December 1944 the Allies ceased their major offensives throughout Europe, primarily owing to the weather, a shortage of fuel and long supply lines. Stalin did not care about individual soldiers, but he did want to retain his army and had no intention of sacrificing his men in frontal assaults while the Anglo-Americans shut down for the winter. In any case his generals had been begging him to halt in order to resupply. In 1944 his army had performed wonders, throwing the Germans out of the Soviet Union, conquering Poland and forcing Romania, Slovakia, Finland and Bulgaria into changing sides.

The Anglo-Americans had also won magnificent victories. To date in this war they had knocked the Fascist French out of the equation, gained most of those French as Allies, emasculated Mussolini's Italy and gained most of the Italian armed forces for themselves, conquered Madagascar, Gabon, Somalia, Ethiopia, Eritrea, Libya, Tunisia, Morocco, Algeria, Sicily, Corsica, southern and central Italy, France, Belgium and part of the Netherlands. This was all the more impressive when it is remembered that a third of the American forces were hotly engaged against the Japanese on the other side of the globe.

This war had cost much in manpower, and the British had suffered more casualties in the last half of 1944 than in the previous five years. They had been forced to disband one of their divisions on the Western Front to provide replacements for the others. They also had to withdraw a British corps from the Canadian First Army on the Western Front, hence the transfer of the Canadians from Italy. In December the British on the Western Front were forced to shut down by a shortage of manpower as much as by the weather. On the Western Front the Allies had eight armies: British Second, Canadian First, French First, US First, US Third, US Seventh, US Ninth and US Fifteenth, plus the French/US Atlantic Command and French/US Alpine Command, the latter on the French/Italian border. Obviously the Americans dominated the Western Front.

Hitler, ever the opportunist, decided to take advantage of the cessation of Allied movement in December by launching his own offensive. Overcoming all his generals' objections Hitler not only produced a pretty good plan but produced the manpower to make it work, by expanding his conscription age to include all men aged fifteen to sixty. He planned a triple maneuver. In the Colmar Pocket of France he would assault a French and a Moroccan divisions with an Austrian mountain division and a German panzer regiment. In Lorraine France he would strike a line of depleted troops of an American and an Algerian-Tunisian Division with no fewer than eleven divisions. His major effort would come in the Ardennes, a thick forest on the Belgian-Luxemburg border, where twenty-one German divisions would smash into four US divisions, one of which was new and another sadly depleted.

Mussolini was not privy to Hitler's plans, but he knew something serious was about to happen. Not to be outdone, he wanted to launch his own winter offensive. After all, apart from the Hungarians and Croatians who were fighting fanatically on home ground, Mussolini's Italy was Hitler's last remaining Axis partner in Europe, and he wanted to remind the world of this.

Hitler's offensives had sound military judgment behind them, even if they were over ambitious, but Mussolini's offensive had no basis in strategy and his troops would be attacking for one purpose only, to inflate his own ego.

On 16 December Hitler launched his Ardennes offensive. Within days he had destroyed one US division and trapped two others. In mileage terms his forces were gaining little, but the shock of the impact was felt all the way to Washington DC. The Americans were already short of manpower and now they became desperate. They assigned tens of thousands of rear-echelon soldiers and air force ground crew to infantry regiments as replacements with no more instruction than a pep talk. The British were forced out of their winter slumber to put divisions on the American flank.

Mussolini, Graziani and their staff approached the Germans with their plan. They would attack with Major General Guido Manardi's Italia Bersaglieri Division that had just returned from Germany and with Major General Mario Carloni's Monterosa Alpini Division, which had done a three month stint on the French-Italian border and had just been relieved by the Littorio Grenadier Division. GNR and black brigades would beef up both the Italia and the Monterosa. Some of the black brigade troops were only fifteen years old, their brains full of Fascist spirit and little else. The offensive would target an American Negro division and an independent Negro regiment. The Italians knew the American generals did not trust these Negroes, and Graziani's staff assumed they would probably fold up quickly. They were aware of American racism, and that the Negroes knew that the white men in the US Army thought the Negroes were good enough to die for the USA, but were not good enough to eat in the same mess hall as white men. The Germans liked the plan. The Nazis thought the Negroes would collapse because they considered them to be racially inferior. However, the Germans insisted that their 148th Division spearhead the offensive. Mussolini agreed.

On 16 December Mussolini spoke in public at a carefully staged rally in Milan. He praised the efforts of the Germans in defending Italy, but reminded his audience that there were now 786,000 Italians serving the Axis cause. He arrived at this figure by counting those in

Italian and German uniform and volunteers serving in Germany. He did not tell his audience that 30,000 of his men were writing 'last letters', hearing mass, checking their weapons for the umpteenth time, going over assault plans, and most difficult of all, waiting for the order to attack.

In the early morning hours of Christmas Day Mussolini launched his offensive. The assault troops were divided into three battlegroups. One contained an infantry company of the Italia Bersaglieri Division and an Alpini infantry battalion and a reconnaissance unit of the Monterosa Division: the second had an Alpini infantry battalion of the Monterosa and a German battalion of the German 148th Division; and the third was a portion of the German 148th. They struck the sleeping Negro Americans of the 1st Battalion of the 370th Infantry Regiment of the 92nd Division, and the divisional reconnaissance platoon, and the 2nd Battalion of the independent 366th Infantry Regiment. Caught completely by surprise there was considerable confusion. Two of the eight Negro infantry companies panicked and ran, but the other six fought a disciplined withdrawal. In the afternoon the remainder of the German 148th and Italia Bersaglieri Divisions entered the fray, joined by another Alpini infantry battalion plus engineers and artillery of the Monterosa. By late afternoon they had struck other units of the Negro division. And by dark the Germans and Italians had captured Gallicano, Bargo and Sommacolonia in the Serchio Valley.

US Intelligence had learned of a possible offensive, and prior to 16 December they would probably have ignored the warning signs, but since Hitler's offensive in the Ardennes they had done a complete somersault and were now apt to believe anything. As a result the Americans were expecting Mussolini's attack. However, they had not alerted the poor fellows who would bear the brunt of the assault! Their reasoning was that they did not want the enemy to gain a prisoner who blabbed 'we're expecting you'. The fact that it was Negro soldiers who were hung out to dry is probably coincidence. There were plenty of examples of US Intelligence doing this to white GIs. However, they had brought reserves closer and had coordinated an artillery firing plan from several divisions.

On Day Two of the battle the Allies counter attacked with several battalions of white Americans, plus British, Indians, and the American Negroes of the 2nd Battalion, 370th Infantry Regiment of the 92nd Division. The Italia Bersaglieri Division, part of the Monterosa Alpini Division, some GNR and black brigades and the German 148th Division held their ground.

However, on the third day of battle the Italians and Germans began falling back slowly, and on the fourth day they withdrew past their original jump-off line. The Allies were content to stop now.

Of course the Germans blamed the failure on the Italians. But it is noticeable that they now pulled out and left the front line between the

Serchio Valley and the west coast in the hands of the two Italian divisions.

———————

On 27 December thirty-four members of the elite British SAS-Special Air Service parachuted north of the Serchio Valley with the ambitious mission of convincing the Germans that a major airborne drop had taken place. The mission was created by a moron and planned by simpletons. The British had not even bothered to notify the local partisans. By chance near Borgeto they ran into a Justice and Liberty Brigade and asked the Italians to join them. Naturally the partisans were apprehensive. Alexander had told them to lie low. Now here were British soldiers asking them to attack. Furthermore by the 29th it was obvious the Allies had ceased to advance following Mussolini's little riposte. Not surprisingly only fourteen partisans chose to join the British.

On New Year's Day 1945 these SAS and their fourteen helpers raided Borgeto, garrisoned by Germans and GNR. A few days later in Montebello five SAS men and their partisan guide were captured by soldiers of a black brigade. The Fascists treated the Britons as prisoners of war, but they tortured the partisan guide into a wreck and then shot him. This brought it home to the British SAS that the partisans were at greater risk than they. On the 11 January the SAS raided Borgeto again. In retaliation a black brigade drove to nearby Brugnato, arrested the whole population as hostages and set the entire village alight. The partisans and SAS saw the smoke, ran to the area and managed to catch the Fascist vehicle convoy as it was leaving. The fight was short and bitter, and most of the Fascists escaped. Moreover few hostages were freed. By coincidence the truck column was then strafed by four US fighters.

The SAS now openly complained that the partisans were ineffective, but their insulting remarks were made in arrogance and bigotry. The families of these SAS men were safe back in Britain. The families of partisans were in constant terror of being arrested. The SAS men had spent months in healthy barracks, eating regularly with periodic leisure time. The partisans had been on the run for fifteen months often going days without food. Furthermore the partisans explained that they had been ordered to lie low by someone with far more insight than these lowly SAS adventurers.

Nonetheless twenty partisans joined the SAS for their next venture, an ambush on a truck column near Aulla. After the fight the twenty partisans moved off and spent the night in Cedolo. They awoke to find themselves surrounded by Germans, who had been tipped off by a local Fascist sympathizer. The partisans knew they were dead men, but if they fought back surely the Germans would destroy the village in anger. To spare the village they surrendered. This put the Germans in a good mood, so they only executed six of their captives.

So far the SAS mission had caused the deaths of few enemy, but had also caused the deaths of seven partisans, the imprisonment in a concentration camp of fourteen others, the destruction of a peaceful village and the imprisonment into slave labor of scores of innocent villagers. Moreover the activity of these Britons attracted more Fascists to the area, and days later a black brigade discovered a large partisan band and attacked it. The partisans scattered into the high snow-covered forests.

The SAS then moved off to the front line and infiltrated through it to Allied lines, where they reported their valiant escapades and great victory.

––––––––––––

At Cima Valsolda a partisan band was surrounded and only gave up when they ran out of ammunition. One of the staffete, Livia Bianchi, was given a chance of survival as she was a woman. She refused. She and the others were put up against a wall and shot. She was honored with the Gold Medal. On 22 January some partisans were trapped in Boschetto and overrun by a German battalion. On the 25th a partisan band was destroyed in Buzzo by 400 Mongolians in German uniform. The worst partisan loss this month was the capture of Ferruccio Parri, deputy commander of the partisan movement.

On 28 January on a frozen road in Poland starving Italian prisoners of war were marching westwards under German guard. Fifty-two year old Major General Ugo Ferrero finally reached the end of his strength and layed down in the snow to die.

In February Daniele Bucchione led his Justice and Liberty Brigade on a raid into La Spezia naval base.

The partisans in Carnia had also been having a rough time as Germans, Condottieri, black brigades, Cossacks, and Italian SS sought them out and never let up. On 3 January a black brigade chased the partisans out of Gova into the alpine foothills. Elsewhere for several days a Justice and Liberty brigade and three Communist brigades were trapped on a snowy mountainside, before they could scatter into small teams. The Condottieri were in action so much in Kuestenland that Gauleiter Rainer ordered them to leave, hoping the partisans would then follow! Of course the Condottieri ignored him.

West of Lake Como the partisans tried to obey Alexander's order to lie low, but in January they were attacked by Germans, black brigades and a Milice formation of French Fascists.

In February the Piero Balbo partisan brigade was in action at Valdivilla. Piero's father Giovanni Balbo was killed. [Giovanni was later awarded the Gold Medal.]

This hive of activity had come about because Graziani and Wolf were in fact making a conscientious effort to destroy the partisans before the expected Allied offensive in the spring. Secretly they both knew the war was lost and had no ambition to be captured by partisans. They hoped to negotiate a surrender to regular Allied forces. Even high profile Fascists had suffered terrifying treatment in the hands of anti-Fascist Italians. For example, Pietro Caruso, the ex-chief of Rome police had been captured and put on trial in Rome for his part in the Ardeatine Caves massacre. During the trial a Fascist prison warden, Donato Carretta, was brought in as a witness. Recognizing him, the crowd seized him away from his Carabinieri guards, manhandled him out of the courtroom and threw him into the river and made sure he never came up for air. Caruso was found guilty on the second day of his trial and within hours he was executed with a shot to the head. Most Romans complained that the proceedings had taken far too long.

General Ettore del Totto and General Riccardo Pentimalli had both opposed the Germans in September 1943, but the Bonomi government still sentenced them to twenty years imprisonment, because their actions had been lukewarm. Obviously Bonomi intended to use as much force as necessary to separate himself from his enemies, no matter how moderate. A well-known member of the SAP, Giuseppe Albano, was killed in Rome in a shootout with Carabinieri. Bonomi felt he had to bring these ex-partisans to heel if Italy was to see real peace in the post-war world.

Though Hitler's three-pronged winter offensive had failed, it had cost the Americans over one hundred thousand men. There was now no chance of any US reinforcements coming to Italy, and Clark had to make do with what he had. Therefore, he began to commit his Italian divisions. The presence of these Italians plus the many thousands of others serving the Allied cause was of absolute paramount importance. The Allies had kept an average of about one hundred and seventy infantry battalions in the line in Italy, but for their spring offensive they would be down to just over one hundred and twenty, that is without the Co-Belligerent divisions, and just over one hundred and fifty with them. Obviously without these Italians there could be no spring offensive, and even with them it would be a tough proposition.

In early January 1945 in British Eighth Army sector the Folgore Division of Major General Morigi entered the line southeast of Bologna under British VIII Corps, while Major General Primieri's Cremona Division and Major General Bartolomeo Pedrotti's Friuli Division settled in at the front between Faenza and the east coast under the command of British V Corps.

According to the press the front was quiet. The Italians found that this was true, that is if one did not count sniping, daily artillery salvoes, nightly infiltrators, nightly patrols into enemy territory, platoon-sized raids and periodic company-sized attacks to 'adjust' the line.

On the Axis side of the line on the west coast the Italia Bersaglieri Division continued to hold, flanked by Colonel Giorgio Milazzo's task force from the Monterosa Alpini Division [an infantry battalion plus engineers and artillery]. The Germans noted that the desertion rate of these Italian divisions was higher than the German rate, but did not think it was serious enough to withdraw them.

On 4 February the Italia was assaulted in the Serchio Valley by Negro troops of the US 365th Infantry Regiment of the 92nd Division, and initially some Italians fought poorly and many surrendered. However, the majority held steadfast and prevented the Americans from breaking though. They held off another attack on the next day. On the third day they stopped an assault by most of the 92nd Division and the independent 366th Infantry Regiment [also Negro], and they held again on the fourth day, and that night having received some German reinforcements the Italians counter attacked and hurt the Americans. They repeated this counter attack the following night. There was less chance of Allied aircraft intervening if the Italians attacked at night. Both sides rested somewhat on the next day, but the day after that the Italia was struck by five Negro battalions and was forced to withdraw. Yet that night the Italia counter attacked again and each night for four more nights. Then both sides lay exhausted. The Italia had inflicted one thousand one hundred and thirty-one casualties on the Americans in the eleven-day battle.

On 18 February the US 10th Mountain Division justified its training by capturing Monte Mancinella, and three days later together with Brazilians they captured Monte Castello. The American mountaineers had relied on Italian partisan guides and had been aided by an Italian mule unit.

Also in February, while the Friuli Division guarded his flank, Major General Primieri attacked with his Cremona Division and captured Tre de Primaro, taking two hundred German prisoners.

At the beginning of March the Friuli Division was switched to British X Corps high in the Apennines, and Utili's Legnano Division went to the US Fifth Army sector southwest of Bologna, settling in between the US 91st and Indian 10th Divisions. The Mantova Division remained in immediate reserve.

On 3 March the US 10th Mountain Division and the Brazilians attacked German outposts on precariously high mountain peaks. The combination of the Brazilians charging in the valleys and the Americans climbing cliffs and ridges was a workable system. In five days they took one thousand two hundred German prisoners. Again Italian partisans and muleteers had aided the Americans.

This month the Germans pulled the Monterosa Alpini Division out of the line for a rest to salvage its flagging morale.

————————

Chapter Sixty-two
Spring Offensive

By March 1945 Mussolini's Italy was the only effective partner Hitler had left. Finland, Romania and Bulgaria had switched sides. Estonia, Latvia, Lithuania, Byelorussia and Ukrainia had been overrun. The Fascists of France, Greece, Serbia and Albania had fled their homelands for Germany or were in hiding. The Slovakians and Croats were collapsing fast. Spain had suddenly decided to be neutral again, and the Hungarians had been decimated and driven from their homeland. Japan still held out, but was in no position to help Hitler.

Though Mussolini had lost two thirds of his country he was still powerful. Of his army divisions the Monterosa Alpini was resting after six months in the line, though it still had a battlegroup on the Franco-Italian border, the Italia Bersaglieri was still in line west of the Serchio Valley after three months and two major battles, and the Littorio Grenadiers were in their fourth month of front line duty along the Franco-Italian border. On his coasts Mussolini had eight artillery gruppos (of three or four battalions each], eight infantry battalions, twenty independent infantry companies and fifty independent artillery batteries. Inland to protect the coastal fortifications from attack by partisans he had the Cacciatore degli Appenini (effectively a division), the Reparti Autonomi Bersaglieri (of two regiments), the Reparti Anti-Partigiani [five battalions], the Tagliamento Regiment and the Leoncello and San Giusto Armored Gruppos. In total his army had seventy thousand personnel.

As for his navy, the twelve thousand man San Marco Marine Division was currently in its seventh month in line on the Franco-Italian border [some of its personnel had periodically been withdrawn to fight partisans], and the ten thousand man Condottieri Division had battalions everywhere hunting partisans, and one battalion, Barbarigo, was at the front. None of these units were actually under navy orders. About ten thousand sailors manned MAS boats and maintained naval bases. Allied bombing raids on Pola had sunk the few midget submarines Mussolini had.

Mussolini's police had their hands full trying to prevent armed robberies, for not only were partisans stealing money for their 'cause', but ordinary thieves were masquerading as partisans. The Police Auxiliary was always hard on the heels of partisan bands. Currently twenty-five thousand men wore Mussolini's police uniform. His Carabinieri still had seventy thousand men and did a very good job simply by their high-profile presence and their vigilance.

The GNR-National Republican Guard now had sixty thousand troops divided into seventy battalions, and they were constantly hunting partisans.

The black brigades had become a serious anti-partisan force, but had been reduced to sixty-five thousand personnel owing to casualties and owing to Himmler who had commandeered thousands of them to man two SS divisions.

There were still about ten thousand troops serving in semi-private armies that did as they pleased, such as Mischi's CARS and the Muti Legion.

Mussolini's air force was continuously low on fuel and short of spare parts, but its ground crews were dedicated to their work despite constant air attacks on them, and their flyers showed extreme courage in fighting at such tough odds. Major Adriano Visconti, a fighter pilot, eventually had twenty-six kills to his credit, and yet only in January 1945 had he acquired a really decent plane, a German Bf109. And every day the ten thousand gunners of the Etna Flak Division were in action.

Thus around three hundred and fifty thousand men were serving in Mussolini's uniforms.

Then there were those Italians in German uniform. The Trient Security Corps and Civic Guard together contained about three thousand cops. The 1st SS Sturmbrigade (Italien) was still at the front, alongside SS Battalion Debica. Himmler's 24th SS Karstjaeger Mountain Division [Italien] and his new 29th SS Infantry Division [2nd Italien] were fighting partisans. In addition to these combat troops the SS had another eighty thousand Italians serving as members, hiwis or kawis in such sections as: Algemeine for administration, supply and sentry duty; SD for counter-espionage; Gestapo for investigation of political crimes; Kripo to hunt black marketers; Border Police to guard the Swiss border; Economics Department to guard installations and slave labor; and the Concentration Camp Service to guard the pitiful wretches that had been sentenced to a life of horror.

Other Italians were taken on as uniformed members of German paramilitary units including: OT-Organisation Todt to build military fortifications and guard slave workers; NSKK to provide drivers and mechanics to whoever needed them on a temporary basis; and the Werkschutz to guard German-run factories and slave labor. In addition to its uniformed Italian members the OT also employed Italian civilians.

In Italy and northern Yugoslavia the German Army was using one hundred thousand Italian hiwis and kawis. Sailing the coasts of these territories were ten thousand Italian hiwis of the German Navy. The German Luftwaffe had eighty thousand Italians: some were sentries and ground crewmen, but most served as flak gunners, many of them in Germany. Thus well over three hundred thousand Italians served in German uniform. In total, therefore, more than six hundred and fifty thousand Italians were 'soldiering' for the Axis cause.

Hitler was worried about the situation in Italy, fearful Mussolini's people would make a separate peace with the Allies, and he was equally afraid that the Germany Army in Italy would collapse, especially as this army relied heavily on Polish conscripts and Italian, Russian and Turcoman volunteers. He placed his faith in Obergruppenfuehrer Wolf and the supposedly racially superior SS. However, the joke was on Hitler, for of the one hundred and sixty-two thousand SS men under Wolf's command in Italy no fewer than one hundred thousand were Italians, and of the remainder there were ten thousand Slovenes, ten thousand Croats, five thousand Slovaks, two thousand Indian Moslems and twenty thousand Cossacks, Mongols, Byelorussians, Russians and Caucasians. This left only fifteen thousand 'Germans' and many of them were in fact Austrians, South Tyrolers and Volksdeutsch from Eastern European countries. And as for Wolf himself: he had his own agenda.

Thus inside Axis Italy by March 1945 about 75% of the defenders were Italian and fewer than 20% were German.

While Mussolini's followers prepared for the great struggle ahead, he played politics. He dismissed several cabinet members and replaced his Minister of the Interior, Buffarino-Guidi, with Paolo Zerbino.

In preparation for their spring offensive the Allies gathered their forces. On the Franco-Italian border they planned to attack with French Alpine Command consisting of the French 1st and 27th Divisions and two regiments of African ascaris from French colonies. Furthermore, of the thirty thousand Italian cooperators assisting the Allies on the Western Front, many would be assigned to French Alpine Command for the coming battle.

Outside of Italy and France another one hundred and ten thousand Italian cooperators were supporting the Allied cause.

Inside Allied Italy Italian soldiers, police, sailors, airmen and partisans were poised to assist the Allies in any way possible to complete the liberation of their country. By March 1945 the Co-Belligerent Air Force was manned by thirty-one thousand personnel, one third of who served in British and American squadrons, and two thirds of whom served in Italian squadrons. The latter were equipped with one hundred and seventy-eight SM79s and other Italian made bombers, forty-five American-built Baltimores, one hundred American-built Airacobras, ninety-seven Italian-made Mc202s and Mc205s, and thirteen British-constructed Spitfires.

The seventy-five thousand sailors of the Co-Belligerent Navy hunted German u-boats in the Atlantic and Mediterranean, raided the coast of Axis Italy, carried supplies and agents to partisans, and defended convoys from German submarine, surface and air attack. Bonomi also planned to send Italian warships to aid the Americans in their war against the Japanese.

Italian merchant seamen sailed all the seas of the world, a most dangerous occupation indeed in these war years.

Bonomi had already called back to duty all Italians who had been serving in the Royal Army up to September 1943, including those Sicilians that had been sent home by the Allies. Few able-bodied young men were now left in the villages and towns, and under Allied pressure Bonomi had begun conscription in January 1945, calling up all able-bodied Italian men aged 21 to 31 that were not involved in essential war work. This law brought in another thirteen thousand conscripts from Sicily, fourteen thousand from Sardinia and thirty-one thousand four hundred from mainland Italy. Furthermore, thirty-five thousand ex-partisans and ex-prisoners of war had been repatriated from Yugoslavia, Bulgaria, Albania and Greece, and the doctors had decided that ten thousand six hundred and ten were fit enough for continued military service after a short recuperation.

However, it was March 1945 before Bonomi and Tito worked out a deal that brought the Garibaldi Division home, and by now only three thousand members were still alive. Of these, two thousand six hundred were deemed to be fit enough for further military service after recuperation.

By the end of March 1945 thousands of partisans in Italy that had been liberated by the Allies had been allowed to join the Co-Belligerent forces, eleven thousand and nineteen since 1 January. Italian partisans had proven to be very effective as reconnaissance forces for the various Allied divisions in Italy, therefore Alexander, as head of Allied Forces Mediterranean, ordered the creation of five new reconnaissance battalions of five hundred partisans each, with one battalion to be assigned to each of the Cremona, Friuli, Folgore, Mantova and Legnano Divisions.

By now in addition to the Co-Belligerent troops serving in Fifth and Eighth Armies and 15th Army Group, Messe personally controlled an army of about three hundred and fifty thousand. On Sardinia were VII Corps, consisting of the Calabria Division, 204th Coastal and 226th Coastal Divisions and 4th Coastal Brigade, and XIII Corps, which controlled the Bari Division and 203rd, 205th and 225th Coastal Divisions and the 25th Coastal Brigade, plus some mobile units. There were also forty-two thousand rear-echelon personnel and ten thousand eight hundred flak gunners on that island.

In Sicily were the Sabauda Division, flak gunners and several thousand Italian rear-echelon soldiers.

In mainland Italy south of the front line Bonomi controlled the 24th, 210th, 212th and 227th Coastal Divisions and the 31st Coastal Brigade, a ten thousand five hundred strong sentry force, six thousand one hundred flak gunners, eighty thousand recruits in training and about twenty thousand men in convalescence, plus thousands of rear-echelon troops. He also had those parts of the Nembo and Mantova Divisions that were not currently being used at the front.

In addition to the army about twenty thousand Carabinieri and twenty thousand police were keeping order on Sardinia and Sicily, and fifty-five thousand Carabinieri, forty thousand police and ten thousand firemen were assisting the Allies in mainland Italy.

The Allies received great assistance from these Italians, and it was of comfort to the Allied generals that someone was protecting their rear. Security was necessary because Fascist saboteurs and spies and good old fashioned gangsters were still active. In fact the Carabinieri was doing such a sterling job the Allies asked Bonomi to recruit another ten thousand of them. The presence of Italian coastal troops was quite valuable. It is true that the prospect of a major German amphibious invasion of Sardinia, Sicily or Southern Italy was mere fantasy by March 1945. But then again just four months earlier the idea that Hitler would suddenly produce an extra half million troops and launch them in a counter-offensive on the Western Front was also considered pure fantasy, and yet Hitler had pulled it off. The Allies would really have been caught with their pants down had they omitted to defend the shores of Southern Italy, Sicily and Sardinia. Moreover, the flak batteries of the coastal units were still in action. The Luftwaffe was by no means dead. Furthermore, Spain was a problem. Though diplomatically neutral, Spain was a de facto Axis partner and Spanish troops were still fighting alongside the Germans. Franco owed Mussolini and Hitler his very existence. And he certainly suspected the Allies would turn on him as soon as they had disposed of the other two. Likewise, the Allies could not be sure he would not launch an attack against them at the last minute.

Clark's 15th Army Group [of Fifth and Eighth Armies] was now six hundred thousand strong, of which fully a third was Italian, namely one hundred and thirty-five thousand eight hundred rear-echelon personnel and seventy-four thousand seven hundred combat troops. The number of Italians serving under Clark was greater than the number of either Americans or British, thus Italy was the largest contributor of manpower to the Allied presence in Italy. They included Brigadier General Enrico Mattioli's Piceno Division, which Clark had just accepted from Messe. Its ten thousand seven hundred and thirty members were divided into the 235th Infantry Regiment commanded by Colonel Ferdinando Borello, a veteran of the Sicily campaign, the 236th Infantry Regiment and the 152nd Artillery Regiment, combat engineers and support troops. While under Clark's orders this division would be known as the Piceno Combat Group, and the 235th would be called the 1st Regiment, the 236th would be named the 2nd, and the 152nd would be referred to as the 3rd and the engineer battalion and support units as the 4th Regiment. Neither Mattioli nor his staff, including Lieutenant Colonel Ugo Siva the chief training officer, liked this idea, but they paid lip service to this ridiculous Allied request.

Clark planned to make his spring offensive with Lieutenant General Sir Richard McCreery's British Eighth Army in the eastern sector and Lieutenant General Lucian Truscott's US Fifth Army in the western sector. For this operation he provided McCreery with two divisions and seven brigades of Britons, two divisions of the Indian Army, two divisions and a brigade of Poles, a New Zealand Division, an all-Jewish brigade, and three Italian divisions. Truscott would have a Brazilian division, a South African division, an Italian division and six divisions and two regiments of Yanks. Clark would hold in reserve two divisions and two brigades of Britons, a US division and two Italian divisions. In the assault Clark would have fifty-five American infantry battalions, thirty British, twenty-nine Italian, nineteen Polish, twelve Indian, nine Brazilian, six New Zealand, six South African and three Jewish. In other words the Italian percentage of Allied assault troops would be 17%.

Clark outnumbered the enemy front line 2:1 in infantry, 2:1 in artillery and 3:1 in armor, and he had enough ammunition for one month of liberal use and sufficient fuel to drive to Austria. The Axis forces on the other hand were so low in ammunition their field guns were limited to twelve shells per day per gun, and they did not have enough fuel for even routine trips.

Clark also had air supremacy and control of the sea: e. g. Allied aircraft destroyed the battleship Conte di Cavour once more: the Germans had been trying to refit it.

Most important of all, though, were the partisans. The coordination of their activities by General Raffaele Cadorna head of the Volunteer Corps of Liberation was smoother than a year ago. However, as victory seemed close at hand the political commissars within the guerilla bands began to make waves. Even Cadorna's deputies were becoming more pronounced: Luigi Longo representing the Communists and their three hundred and fifty-seven Garibaldi Brigades; Enrico Mattei speaking for the Christian Democrats, who together with the Liberals controlled one hundred and ninety-one Justice and Liberty Brigades; and Giovanni Battista Stucchi spokesperson for the Socialists and their fifty Matteoti brigades. Ferruccio Parri, representative of the Action Party was still in a Fascist prison. Other partisans were manning the People's Brigades, and there were no fewer than eighty-seven brigades that claimed no particular political loyalty, many of them formed by veteran soldiers.

The Communists claimed they represented the bulk of the partisans, but this was blatantly untrue, and even within the Garibaldi Brigades few guerillas were died in the wool Communists. Indeed there was a considerable number of Anarchists within the Garibaldi ranks. Perhaps a third of the partisans were Communists, and about a quarter of the Italian people could have been considered Communist [going by post-war voting patterns].

Nonetheless Churchill's British government lived under the assumption that all partisans were Communists and he planned to disarm them as soon as possible. With British soldiers not yet cold in their graves, killed at the hands of Greek ELAS Communist partisans, it is understandable that the British did not want to trade one war in Italy for another.

Cadorna was good at his job, but even he did not know how many partisans he controlled. In August 1944 he and Allied intelligence had come up with a working figure of eighty thousand, but they admitted this did not count females, known officially as Staffete, nor did it count the SAP in the cities. Certainly if these people were included a figure of well over one hundred thousand would be more truthful. Furthermore the partisans had told many would-be recruits to go home and wait. If this were to be the final offensive of the Italian campaign then every would-be partisan would now come out into the open. Additionally many who had never tried to join the partisans, perhaps owing to family commitments, might do so as their town was being liberated. Postwar these fellows, called Johnny-come-lately, would be branded as cowards, but this is uncalled for. Cowards do not join armies in the midst of battle even on the last day, for a coward knows that the last bullet fired in a war is just as deadly as the first. Besides what guarantee was there that this would be the last day? Partisans entering Bologna on 1 September had thought this, but here it was seven months later and the Battle of Bologna was still in progress.

By March 1945 almost half of all partisans were in the mountains of Piemont, and about 10% were in Liguria, 10% in Emilia, 20% in Lombardy and 20% in Veneto-Carnia. Bonomi informed them that upon liberation they could either retain unit integrity by following Allied orders or they could join the Co-Belligerent forces as individuals, but under no circumstances could they remain an independent armed band. Ostensibly this was to rein in those bandits masquerading as partisans, but it was also to destroy the armed might of the Communist Party.

Thus by March 1945 there were around nine hundred and seventy thousand Italians serving the Allies in a uniformed capacity, not counting those partisans still behind Axis lines. Italians comprised three-quarters of the Axis forces in Italy, and Italians comprised two-thirds of the Allied forces in Italy. Far more Italians were under arms now than on 8 September 1943, the day that, according to both German and Allied propaganda, the Italians quit the war! For so-called historians to ignore a million Allied troops and six hundred and fifty thousand Axis troops simply because they were Italian is a sad reflection of the victory of racist bigotry over truth.

Morale among Italians serving the Allied cause was extremely high, because they sensed this next offensive would liberate the remainder of their homeland and erase the Fascist scourge from Italy once and for all. Ironically morale among the other Allied troops was low. The Poles in Italy were still fighting bravely to liberate their homeland too, but unfortunately of the two armies that had crushed their native land in 1939, Hitler's Wehrmacht and Stalin's Red Army, one of those armies, namely Stalin's, was back in control in Poland and was there with British and American blessing! The Poles would fight in this up and coming battle, but many were thinking that they had already lost the war.

In the case of the Britons and Americans, they had always been confident of victory. There is something in the English spirit that cannot contemplate defeat. There is an old saying: "the English only win one battle per war, the last battle". The Americans were also highly confident of victory in Europe, perhaps because they had not lost any territory here and they saw every battlefield accomplishment as a plus, no matter how futile. So there was no air of defeatism among the British and Americans in Italy. However, the poor morale was caused by a sinking feeling that they might be killed in a mere sideshow, an event staged to please an audience of generals who did not have enough medals. Already wives and parents had been writing to these gallant soldiers asking why were they wasting their time in Italy when the 'real European war' was on the western front. Such letters were devastating to morale.

As early as September 1944 Allied troops had reached Germany on her western border. By January 1945 the Soviets were but fifty miles from Berlin. In March the Americans and British conquered the Rhineland and crossed the Rhine. Over a third of Germany was already in Allied hands by late March. Why therefore was a battle in Italy so necessary? Surely without the Germans the Italian Fascists would fold up? By March 1945 the Americans still had seven divisions of their dwindling manpower pool in Italy, but they had forty-eight divisions on the Western Front and twenty-five divisions facing the Japanese, plus they employed in those theaters many smaller formations that added up to an equivalent of several more divisions. In Italy the British had four divisions and nine brigades, but on the western front they had twelve divisions and several brigades. The assignment of a US Negro division to Italy was proof to many a white GI that the American government considered Italy a side show and that the Americans stationed there were second-class.

The Battle of Salerno had been the only glory the Anglo-Americans gained in Italy, for several reasons. It came at the time of the Italian 'surrender' and in civilian minds the invasion had caused the 'surrender', whereas in truth the surrender had caused the invasion. Also it had been the first return of the British to mainland Europe in two years, and of course it took the war to an Axis homeland. However, after Salerno all battles fought in Italy were devoid of glory. Even the glory of conquering Rome was stolen by the D-Day invasion of Normandy a day later. Normandy pushed Rome off the headlines. With typical American humor the GIs in Italy began calling themselves the D-Day Dodgers, a play on the name of a popular baseball team the Brooklyn Dodgers. The joke was that they had escaped [dodged] the danger of fighting on D-Day by hiding in the middle of an Italian battlefield. At home in the USA and Britain names like St. Lo, Paris, Aachen, Arnhem, Bastogne and the Rhine had become household terms. No one spoke of Garigliano, Liri, Cesena, the Gothic Line or Pesaro. Of what could the Allies truly boast: Anzio? That was a sick joke. Cassino? There it had taken them six months to conquer one mountain. By March 1945 the Allies in Italy had been holding the same line for six months. It was clear to the lowliest army private that an attack in Italy was redundant. No one seriously thought Mussolini's Fascists would fight on without German support.

And yet there was a very sound reason for launching another offensive in Italy, but Allied Intelligence could not blab the truth. In this war scores of nations had been overrun, only to see their armed forces rise from the ashes in another land. For example, Poland had been conquered in 1939, yet now in March 1945 Polish troops were currently fighting in Italy, on the Western Front and the Eastern Front. Would the same thing happen to Hitler's German troops? There was no guarantee that all German troops would ceasefire if Germany was overrun. They might retreat to Northern Italy to carry on the fight. Even if the Germans in Germany surrendered, the Germans and Fascists in Northern Italy might carry on the war. After all they had nothing to lose. The British and Americans could not afford to keep troops in Italy much longer. There were two reasons for this. One was that their populations wanted their boys to come home, and as both the British and American governments were democracies, which relied on votes to retain power, they had to listen to their people eventually. Furthermore, Japan had not yet been invaded and that nation currently had twenty million armed troops and militia awaiting the Allies! The British had earmarked one lone division for the invasion of Japan, so it would obviously be an American show. Therefore the Americans needed to pull their men out of Italy as soon as possible and send them to the Pacific.

Initially the idea that the Axis forces in Northern Italy might fight on to the death was only supposition. But then Allied Intelligence learned startling news: Hitler was planning to fight on in the half-moon shaped region of the German Alps, Austrian Alps and Italian

Alps. He was already stockpiling supplies there to wage a defensive war in this 'Alpine Redoubt' for years if necessary. The fortifications were already being constructed deep inside mountains. The crawl up the Italian Apennines had been a nightmare for the Allies, but compared to the Alps the Apennines is merely a row of pimples. The Americans and British had but one mountain warfare division between them. Neither Roosevelt nor Churchill could afford to commit to an attack on well-entrenched and well-supplied forces in the Alps, nor could they stand idly by while the Axis waged a protracted guerilla war from their mountain stronghold. A few generals thought Hitler's talk was all hot air, but Intelligence officers reminded them of how the Allies had ignored the signs of Hitler's Ardennes offensive in December 1944 to their everlasting regret. As recent as early March 1945 Hitler was still launching major offensives [currently in Hungary]. The Allied generals simply had to assume Hitler was telling the truth and they had to conquer the Italian, Austrian and German Alps before the Germans could finish stockpiling supplies there. Likewise they could not let Hitler know they knew of the Alpine Redoubt. Therefore, the attacking Allied soldiers would have to be kept in the dark.

———————

The Allied spring offensive would come in five stages, which can be labeled Silent, Alarm, Diversionary, Positioning and Full-Scale.

The Silent Stage consisted of spying, disinformation and diplomacy. Spying was done by Allied agents, including Co-Belligerents, who parachuted into northern Italy to learn details of a particular installation. Partisans were asked to do likewise. In addition reconnaissance flights photographed routes of advance and enemy positions.

Disinformation consisted of lies and false evidence deliberately planted so that the Axis would be misled.

Diplomacy primarily involved talking to neutral states that conversed with Mussolini's people, hoping to gain an insight into what they might do in case of a German collapse. Mussolini had already opened a channel of communication with the Allies. All he demanded was life and freedom for himself. He cared not a damn for the Fascists who were about to lay down their lives for him. Unknown to him the Allies had also received a communication from Karl Wolf. This SS general met American agents in Switzerland and to show his good faith he brought with him his most illustrious prisoner, Ferruccio Parri. The Allies were also conversing with Axis diplomats and business leaders.

Diplomacy also involved negotiating a deal with the Swiss. The Swiss guarded their neutrality with a powerful army. Sometimes their flak gunners and fighters shot down Allied aircraft that strayed over their air space. The Swiss now agreed that they would turn away every Axis soldier or politician who tried to seek sanctuary in Switzerland. No Axis unit would be admitted, not even disarmed ones, lest they suddenly escape back into Italy to restart the war with hidden weapons. The Swiss border would be a veritable wall, through which no one could pass. By denying an escape route to the Axis forces the Swiss became a de facto member of the Allies.

The second stage was the Alarm Stage and this began in the last week of March when the partisans and SAP began making life for the Axis troops a sheer misery by the use of sabotage, ambushes, sniping, assassination and raids. Of course this caused a swift response by the Germans and Fascists. In defense of Monte San Giulia the partisan Mario Allegretti was killed in action. This twenty-five year old would be awarded the Gold Medal.

Allied special forces joined in this stage too. For example, the Co-Belligerent submarine Grecale sailed close into Genoa harbor at night and let loose a pig team. The pigs silently slid into the naval base and sank the aircraft carrier Aquila.

Elsewhere, several raiding teams infiltrated behind Axis lines by parachute and by boat. The British SAS were prominent in these operations and they accepted two Italian formations to help them, F-Force and a company from the Nembo Parachute Division. Furthermore Co-Belligerent Italians were actually assigned to the SAS. In one operation fifty SAS men [Britons and Italians] parachuted to join a hundred members of a Justice and Liberty brigade. This brigade had also recruited seventy Russians that had escaped from German prison camps. The combined force then attacked the German administrative center at Albinea, killing thirty Germans and driving off the others, and then burning the buildings and destroying thousands of valuable documents. In the melee a few partisans and three SAS members were killed. One of the SAS dead was Italian.

Just west of Modena the Axis retaliated against partisans in the Secchia Valley. By their very presence these partisans tied down thousands of Axis troops.

The partisan campaign was no longer one of spectacular stunts, but of solitary acts of brutality on both sides. E.g. near Udine partisans captured twelve Carabinieri in their sleep. After torturing them, they beat them to death.

The Diversionary Stage began on 30 March. French troops on the Franco-Italian border launched a major attack through the snowy St Bernard Pass 6,564 feet up in the Alps. The Americans did not like the idea of unleashing the French to invade Italy, but in their eagerness to swiftly occupy the Italian Alps they had to take a gamble.

Clark now reviewed his order of battle: on the east coast was the

British 2nd Commando Brigade, British 24th Guards Brigade and Italian 28th Garibaldi Brigade; west of the Comacchio Lagoon was the British 56th Division, then further west the Italian Cremona Division now led by Major General Giacomo Zanussi, Indian 8th Division, British 78th Division and New Zealand 2nd Division. All of these forces came under the powerful British V Corps, which had three British brigades in reserve.

On the left [west] of V Corps was the Polish Corps, containing the Polish Carpathian and Kresowa Divisions and 2nd Armored Brigade plus the Italian Maiella Brigade. In corps reserve were the British 7th Armored and 43rd Infantry Brigades.

To the left of the Poles was British X Corps, which only controlled the Friuli Division and the Jewish Brigade. This was further evidence of British politics. Never had they created a corps headquarters without at least one division subordinate to it. Nor had they now. They may call the Friuli a 'combat group', but they were treating it as a division. On their left high in the Apennines was British XIII Corps containing the Folgore and Indian 10th Divisions. All of the above corps came within British Eighth Army.

To the left of Eighth Army was US Fifth Army with on its right the Legnano Division due south of Bologna, then to its left the US 91st, 34th and 88th Divisions and the South African 6th Armored Division. These forces came directly under US II Corps. Further westwards were the US 1st Armored and 10th Mountain Divisions and the Brazilian Division. US IV Corps controlled these. From here to the west coast lay the 92nd [Negro] Division and two regiments, which reported directly to Truscott at Fifth Army headquarters.

In his personal reserve Clark had one US and two British divisions and the Italian Mantova and Piceno Divisions.

In the beginning of April came the Positioning Stage. All along the front in north central Italy Allied units began sending out extra patrols to capture prisoners and gain information. The Axis responded in kind. Also some small-scale attacks were launched to gain better jump-off positions. The reconnaissance battalions of the Cremona, Folgore, Friuli and Legnano Divisions performed well in this, as did the Maiella Brigade, but it was heartbreaking to see a comrade killed in this pre-battle stage.

On 2 April on the east coast the British 24th Guards Brigade (three battalions) [of the 56th Division] and the battalion-sized 28th Garibaldi [Partisan] Brigade attacked the German defenses along the Reno River. There was little resistance and during the day no fewer than six hundred and fifty Turcoman soldiers in German uniform surrendered. Simultaneously the British 2nd Commando Brigade launched an amphibious invasion a few miles to the north of the

Comacchio Spit. This spit was nine miles long and varied in width from two miles to just a few hundred yards. It separated the Adriatic Sea from the Comacchio Lagoon. The British and the partisans continued to attack, soon entering the southern entrance to the spit, hoping to reach the commandos. British warships protected the eastern flank with naval gunfire, but the lagoon side was dominated by the Germans who had placed troops on the tiny islets of the lagoon. On the second day the Turcomans began to fight better and their German cadre resisted fanatically. This resistance stiffened over the next two days, so that after four days of combat the British and partisans had yet to advance far enough along the spit to reach the commandos. The British reported that the Garibaldi partisans fought very well.

———————

On 3 April on the Franco-Italian border the French launched major attacks hoping to pin down the Axis forces here. Soon all the Axis units were under pressure: the Italian Lombardia Corps of the German Battlegroup Meinhold and Italian San Marco Marine Division, and the German LXXV Corps of the German 5th Mountain and 34th Divisions and the Italian Monterosa Alpini and Littorio Grenadier Divisions.

———————

On the night of 5 April the British SBS-Special Boat Service and members of the 28th Garibaldi Brigade sailed into the Comacchio Lagoon in small boats and began conquering the defended islets one by one. Some islets were no more than ten yards across, containing a machine gun team. The advance was a whole series of miniature amphibious invasions, often by just five or six men in a boat. In one incident an SBS team was pinned down, but was rescued by partisans. It took another three days and four nights for the SBS and partisans to clear the lagoon. Meanwhile the British on the spit finally reached the commandos. All in all it had been a tough week long fight.

———————

On 5 April on the west coast the Italia Bersaglieri Division and a battlegroup of the Monterosa Alpini Division together with some German units and their Italian kawis and hiwis came under attack from the Americans: 92nd [Negro] Division, 679th [Negro] Anti-Tank Battalion, 758th [Negro] Anti-Tank Battalion, 473rd Regimental Combat Team, 442nd [Nisei] Regimental Combat Team and 100th [Nisei] Separate Infantry Battalion. In the first twenty-four hours of combat these defenders inflicted one hundred and forty-three casualties on one US battalion and one hundred and forty-two casualties on two others and lesser losses on the remaining

Americans. The combat proved deadly on the second day too, and the third, with the Italians and Germans inflicting seventy-three casualties on one American battalion and further casualties on the others. The Axis did not know if this was part of the final stage of the offensive or not. For many a soldier on both sides it was final.

The Full-Scale Stage of the Spring Offensive finally began at dusk on 9 April when the British, Italian and Polish artillery of the V and Polish Corps opened a continuous fire on the German 26th Panzer, 42nd, 98th, 278th, 305th, 1st Parachute, 4th Parachute, 362nd and 162nd Divisions. Southwest of the Comacchio Lagoon, just to the right of the main Ferrara road, the British 56th Division charged forward, meeting fierce opposition from the Germans and their Italian kawis and hiwis. On the road itself the Cremona Division calmly advanced to find the first village crawling with Germans: immediately the fight was on. West of the Cremona around Lugo on lower ground the British 78th, Indian 8th and New Zealand 2nd Divisions attacked. The fighting was terrible, and many an Allied soldier thought that this offensive, like so many others in Italy, was going to fail. To the west of V Corps lay the Bologna road along which the Poles advanced. All along this front Co-Belligerent Italian troops worked under fire as engineers, artillerymen, telephone linesmen, medics, stretcher bearers, surgical teams, ammunition resupply teams and such.

By dawn on 10 April the Cremona's infantry and combat engineers were battling for every house in Alfonsine, an affair that took all day. The divisional gunners continued firing.

On this day the Legnano Division began preliminary assaults along another road leading to Bologna. They found German opposition to be fierce.

On 11 April the men of the Cremona crawled and ran at a crouch under heavy artillery fire for three miles towards the Senio River. The divisional gunners gave counter battery fire as best they could. Once the reconnaissance battalion had scouted the river, the divisional combat engineers moved up and built a bridge, seemingly oblivious to German shelling and automatic weapons fire.

During the night the infantry of the Cremona crossed the river, and by the morning of 12 April the reconnaissance battalion of the Cremona Division was studying the enemy defenses along the Santerno River.

This day to the west the remainder of Eighth Army now joined in the offensive. The Folgore and Friuli Divisions found the Senio and Santerno Rivers to be just narrow mountain streams on their frontage, that they could jump across or wade through, but the Germans defended them heroically all the same. Members of the Folgore quickly found themselves locked in hand to hand combat.

It was 13 April before the Italians, British and Poles could cross the Santerno River. In five days of heavy action they had advanced only twelve miles.

On the 14th those units of the US Fifth Army not already locked in mortal combat now launched their offensive. At once that army's Italian engineers, stretcher-bearers, medics, telephone linesmen, muleteers and others began supporting the assault, ignoring enemy artillery fire. Opposing them were the German 188th Mountain, 237th, 155th, 29th Panzergrenadier, 8th Mountain, 65th, 94th, 114th, 334th, 232nd and 148th Divisions, each with their Italian kawis and hiwis. In fact the Germans fought back so ferociously that none of Fifth Army's attacking divisions made any gains this day.

And on the coast the Italia Bersaglieri Division and a battle group of the Monterosa were still involved in major action after ten days, offering such stout resistance that the Americans had to be reinforced by their 365th Regiment [Negro].

The Legnano troops in their fifth day of battle were at least happy that there were no rivers between them and Bologna.

This day the New Zealanders broke through and crossed the Sillaro River, but on the Bologna road fanatic German paratroopers stopped the Poles at Imola. The Poles asked for help and at once the Friuli Division made a right turn and came down from the mountains, following the Santerno River into Imola. Meanwhile the Folgore continued on course, crossing the upper Sillaro. That division now had a clear run into Bologna.

By late on 15 April Fifth Army had made some slight movement. This day the Friuli together with the Poles conquered Imola, and the Folgore's 185th Parachute Infantry Regiment took Tossignano just twelve miles from Bologna.

However, as the Friuli got back on track for Bologna, the Folgore was ordered to shift to the left. This order angered many of its soldiers, for the repositioning placed three rivers and the Gaiana Canal between them and Bologna. By now everyone wanted to be first into Bologna. It was a goal: something to aim at; something to brag about later. The capture of a famous city always has and always will be a major morale booster for soldiers. Bologna was also a major road network and its capture was strategically essential.

Already the Indian 10th Division had fought its way across the Gaiana Canal, and during the night the US 10th Mountain Division had overcome opposition and by dawn was advancing swiftly, but the Legnano was still stopped by tough resistance.

On 18 April Clark gave the go-ahead for an all-out partisan uprising. Now at last the partisans, staffete and SAP could come out into the open, some in makeshift black uniforms and others with armbands. They had to win now. It was do, or die. Their goal was not to destroy facilities but to occupy them. They had come to stay.

On the 19th the Friuli was stopped along the Quaderna River by German teenage paratroopers who had chosen to die for Hitler. Far to the east the partisans of the 28th Garibaldi Brigade took off on their own, wading through flooded fields towards the Po River.

On 20 April one hundred and twenty-five members of the Italian F-Force and one hundred and eleven paratroopers from the Nembo Parachute Division parachuted behind Axis lines. Their mission was simple: raise as much hell as possible.

This day the Friuli ran into more desperate German paratroopers. However, the Folgore began to advance quicker and the enemy opposition became lighter, but these Italians could not understand how they could still be so far from Bologna. The Cremona did not have Bologna in their sights, but in any case they had their hands full trying to overcome the German defenses of the Idice River. This day British troops captured Argenta on the Ferrara road, thus outflanking the Idice.

The German ground commander General von Viettinghoff studied his Intelligence reports, noting that Argenta was just twenty-five miles from the Po River, the last great water barrier in Northern Italy. If the Allies crossed the Po, all would be lost. He had his orders from Hitler, to die rather than retreat, but he ignored them. He ordered all units to cross to the north bank of the Po at once before they were cut off.

Inside Bologna the garrison panicked when they received the order. Within minutes no vehicle was secure as the fleeing Germans and Fascists stole them to get away: German soldiers, SS, Luftwaffe and paramilitary personnel, and Italian police, Carabinieri, Blackshirts, soldiers, flak gunners, GNR, Black Brigaders and their families all tried to run way. However, on almost every street they ran into partisans. Sniping and ambushes caused huge traffic jams. Any fleeing vehicles that cleared the city had to run the gauntlet of Allied fighters.

On 21 April the US 34th and 91st Divisions, the Poles, the Maiella Brigade and the Legnano Division all converged on the great city of Bologna along different roads. There were plenty of Fascists still loose, but the partisans were taking care of them. Incredibly the partisans and Fascists had been shooting it out in this city for seven months and three weeks. This was a proud moment for Major General Utili. This man had performed wonders leading the Dapino Brigade/Utili Division, Corps of Liberation and now the Legnano Division. Along with Allied generals he was invited to the city's public buildings to be feted by the crowds. A little embarrassed, he was eager to get back to his duties, but nonetheless he must surely have gushed with pride in his troops.

In fact some members of his Legnano were already skirting the city and by doing so they caught many Germans who had been held up by partisans. The Germans usually threw up their hands when they realized the Legnano troops were regulars and would accept their surrender on honorable terms.

Of course Bologna had become a bottleneck, so the front units were now reorganized. The Friuli and Folgore were placed in reserve. These two divisions had performed exceedingly well in their three and a half months in the line and during their ten day offensive.

Meanwhile the Cremona was crushing the German opposition that had been holding up their drive to the Po, and by 23 April they had killed scores, captured two hundred and fifty and forced thousands to run. Major General Primieri was justly proud of his men.

Behind the advancing Allies some Fascists went into hiding. Those partisans who had been liberated were best equipped to deal with these die-hards, and they spent the next few days hunting them down. Almost all the partisans that had been liberated willingly placed themselves under Allied orders.

The staff of the US 92nd [Negro] Division was worried about Carrara, because the village looked down a thousand feet upon the coast road, and the entrance to the village was by two circuitous mountain roads open to observation all the way. It would be a tough nut to crack and many an 'American boy' would die taking it. However, just before their attack began they were informed that local partisans had seized the village from its garrison!

On 23 April partisans poured into Genoa, joined up with the local SAP and began a full-scale rebellion against the six thousand man Fascist/German garrison.

On 24 April the city of Cuneo rose in revolt to the astonishment of the Lidonnici Black Brigade. This day the Americans entered Modena to find partisans already roaming the streets and hunting down members of the Pistoni Black Brigade. It took another twenty-four hours to kill off the fanatics, bringing the city's Fascist death toll to one thousand four hundred. At Tirano near the Swiss border a large partisan force attacked five hundred French Milice under the French Fascist Joseph Darnand. The struggle was ferocious and only after losing twenty-five killed and sixty-five wounded did Darnand choose to talk his way out. He asked for permission to make it to Switzerland and surrender to the Swiss. The partisans agreed and escorted the Frenchmen to the border.

Mussolini moved to Milan. There he received countless visitors, most of them urging him to make some kind of deal with the Allies. The Fascists were terrified of the partisans and as a result Il Duce put out the word that he wanted to meet representatives of the CLNAI. On 21 April 1945 when the full knowledge of von Viettinghoff's retreat order reached Mussolini he knew the chances of a compromise peace were gone. There would be no rescue from Hitler this time. The Nazi dictator was himself trapped inside Berlin surrounded by the Red

Army.

On the morning of the 25th Graziani received the overnight reports. On the west coast the Americans had captured the naval base at La Spezia. In the northeast the Titoists had invaded the Istrian Peninsula of Italy by land and sea. Near the east coast the Allies had reached the great Po River. The 28th Garibaldi Brigade had finished their wading and had liberated several hamlets and had also reached the great river. The Cremona Division's combat engineers had brought up boats and were ferrying their infantry across the Po. The Legnano Division was rapidly pushing up to the Po.

The worst news for Graziani was that full-scale rebellion had broken out in Milan, Como, Turin, Parma, Pavia, Trento, Brescia, Ferrara, Legnano and many smaller towns. Everyone was besieged: police, Carabinieri, flak gunners, GNR, black brigades. The streets were full of veteran partisans including female Staffete and SAP, who were joined by new volunteers and they were attacking everyone and everything Fascist and German. In Turin the Auxiliary Police 2nd Mobile Assault Unit was trying to use its vehicles to get out of town, while the Cappelli and Ponzecchi Black Brigades remained to fight to the death. In Ferrara the Ghisellini Black Brigade and a local GNR Battalion were holding out, but suffering very high casualties. In Brescia the Tognu and Meattini Black Brigades were under heavy attack and suffering badly. In Parma the Gavazzoli Black Brigade was under assault and franticly looking for a way out - there was none. In Pavia the local Auxiliary Police Battalion and the Alfieri Black Brigade were surrounded and taking heavy fire. In Milan partisans were hunting down every member of the Auxiliary Police Caruso Legion, 2nd Arditi Black Brigade, Resega Black Brigade and the Muti Legion. It did no good for these Fascists to doff their uniforms and go into hiding, for the neighbors knew every member by sight. In Trento the policemen of the Trient Security Corps were abandoned by the Germans.

Female Fascists were sometimes killed, but more often than not they were arrested, publicly humiliated and their heads were shaved. Girlfriends of Germans suffered a similar fate.

This day 25 April the four most powerful men in Fascist Italy began seeking surrender terms, each in his own way: Mussolini, von Viettinghoff, Graziani and Wolf. This afternoon at the Milan Prefectura Mussolini received Cardinal Schuster the Roman Catholic Archbishop of Milan who was accompanied under a flag of truce by representatives of the CLNAI. They informed him that Wolf's proposals had offered the best solution to the Allies so they had already made an agreement with him. Mussolini was not part of the equation.

Following the meeting Il Duce studied his three options: be believed he could flee to Switzerland. He did not know that the Swiss were refusing to take refugees. This day they had turned back the French Milice, who had been forced to surrender to the partisans, though their leader Darnand had gone into hiding. Secondly, Mussolini could surrender, but to whom? The partisans would butcher him on sight, surely. Thirdly he could fight on, but not inside Milan. Already he could hear shooting as building after building was falling to the partisans. He decided to fight, and for this last glorious stand he would join Alessandro Pavolini, who had three thousand members of his black brigades in the Valtellene District.

A little before 5pm he was informed that a violent mob of civilians was gathering outside, trying to work up enough nerve to attack. It was time to go, he concluded. Mussolini ordered GNR Blackshirts to sweep the mob aside and this they managed to do without gunfire. Then he strutted out of the building dressed in a Blackshirt uniform with a sub machine gun hanging around his neck. He paraded in front of the mob, as defiant as ever, and climbed into an open-top Alfa Romeo. In another car was his mistress Clara Petacci accompanied by her brother Marcello and his wife and children. Mussolini's son Vittorio followed in a third car. Mussolini had ordered the Blackshirts to escort the little convoy, but a junior SS officer Fritz Birzer, who had two truckloads of SS flak gunners, insisted on escorting the cars. There were awkward glances between the Fascists and Germans, but Mussolini agreed to Birzer's demand, though surely he must have wondered if he was being escorted or arrested? The convoy drove off, leaving the mob behind and left the city without incident and reached Como at 9pm. Here Mussolini insisted on spending the night at the local prefectura. His sleep was no doubt interrupted by the sound of the battle in the streets as Blackshirts fought partisans in the small town.

The Allied advance was unstoppable now. In twenty-five days they had taken forty thousand German prisoners [including kawis and hiwis].

At 4:30am Mussolini arose and tried to take his SS escort by surprise and leave early, but the sentries outside his door actually grabbed him and held him until Birzer was ready. Mussolini was now more suspicious than ever. After driving alongside Lake Como for an hour Mussolini called another halt at Menaggio. He wanted to see Emilio Castelli, a local Fascist. Once the amenities were over, the dictator and Clara spent three hours alone in a room in Castelli's house.

About 8:30am the convoy moved off again, but after just three miles Mussolini called another stop, and went into the Miravalle Hotel in Grandola. Here he learned that the Swiss were refusing to accept Fascist refugees. They had even turned away Mussolini's wife Donna Rachele.

Quickly Mussolini and Clara made a break for it, but the SS guards ran after them and this time stopped the pair at gunpoint. Not knowing their hidden agenda he did not call their bluff. The two returned indignantly to the hotel where Mussolini insisted on waiting for Pavolini and his men, so that he could dismiss his SS escort.

During this day open revolt broke out in Padua as partisans rushed in from the countryside to battle the local auxiliary police battalion and the Begon Black Brigade. At Verona the Rizzardi Black Brigade was besieged by partisans that seemed to be everywhere. The Gramsci Garibaldi Partisan Division assaulted Casteggio. One of its more colorful officers, Franco Anselmi was killed this day. The partisans were in no mood to take prisoners. In Bergamo the Cortesi Black Brigade was also trapped. In Genoa after a four day battle the Germans surrendered to the partisans. However, the Fascists dare not surrender. The men of the Parodi Black Brigade, auxiliary police and the sailors at the naval base vowed to fight on. However, the partisans maintained that they would accept all Fascists as bona fide prisoners of war. As a result most of the Fascists gave up. The partisans massacred them.

The Cremona Division was now advancing swiftly. Usually a few shots were sufficient to induce an enemy rearguard to surrender. The men of this division also liberated hundreds of partisans, who willingly accepted orders and joined the advance. One of them, twenty-year old Cristoforo Bendazzi, was killed earning the silver medal.

Just before dawn on 27 April Pavolini arrived at the Miravalle Hotel, but he reported to Mussolini that most of his three thousand men had already surrendered or had fled southwards hoping to be captured by Allied regulars, and the remainder, the Rodini Black Brigade, was still fighting in Como. Pavolini had only brought twelve men and an armored car.

At 6:30am the convoy prepared to leave. They had also been joined by a few local Fascists and thirty-five trucks carrying a Luftwaffe signals unit. Pavolini warned Mussolini to ride in the armored car in case of a partisan ambush. He agreed, and this proved to be sound advice for just six miles down the road the column was ambushed. The armored car's machine gun sprayed the undergrowth and a partisan tumbled dead into the road. The firing died down and the partisans called out that they were willing to negotiate. Captain Davide Barbieri of the 52nd Garibaldi Brigade agreed to negotiate with the Germans and Italians in a nearby house. Mussolini remained in the armored car. At 2pm Barbieri agreed that the Germans could move on, but not the Italians. Furthermore, the German vehicles would be searched at Dongo a little bit further along the road. Barbieri had already been informed by spies that Mussolini was in the column, but he did not let on that he knew. The SS guards put a Luftwaffe coat and helmet on Mussolini and shoved him into the back of a truck along with other Germans. As the truck drove off Clara Petacci, who of course had to stay, had to be prized away from the truck's tailgate, tears in her eyes.

At 3:15pm in Dongo on Lake Como the partisans searched the vehicles. Giuseppe Negri recognized Il Duce at once and brought Political Commissar Urbano Lazzaro to the truck. They dragged Il Duce from the vehicle and marched him to the prefectura. The Germans stared at the armed partisans and did nothing to protect Mussolini. The villagers cheered when they saw what was happening. A partisan officer Count Pierluigi Bellini delle Stelle interrogated Mussolini until 7pm.

Mussolini, that most belligerent of dictators was captured like a green recruit. This most nationalist of Italians was found hiding in a foreign uniform. This dictator who had his own bodyguard and a Hitler-sent bodyguard was captured by partisans while his bodyguards idly stood by.

During this eventful day the French broke through on the Franco-Italian border and captured Ventimiglia. After twenty-nine days of battle the Littorio, San Marco and Monterosa Divisions were in full and speedy retreat.

South of Vicenza the US 88th Division ran into serious opposition from what the Americans described as 'elite infantry'. It was a battalion of the Condottieri Division.

This day partisans liberated Aosta, having overcome the Picot Black Brigade. In Milan Fascists fought like trapped rats, their days, their hours numbered. Fascist French journalists in the Milan area claimed that ten thousand Fascists were killed in that city in the last days. If this figure is true it includes those killed in battle as well as those executed.

Partisans surrounded Gallarate Airfield, where Major Adriano Visconti the well-known fighter ace agreed to surrender his men if they were treated as bona fide prisoners of war. The partisans acquiesced and kept their word, but on the march one partisan let his anger get the better of him and shot Visconti in the back.

When Fascist Customs Police recognized Buffarino-Guidi trying to escape to Switzerland they arrested him, hoping to use him as a bargaining chip with the partisans. They were successful. In return for their freedom they handed him over and he was quickly executed. The partisans also arrested many foreign Fascists, including the American Ezra Pound.

This day was not easy for Italy. Fascists betrayed each other in a desperate effort to survive. Innocent people were 'turned in' to the partisans by neighbors who had a grudge against them – perhaps a long standing debt or a rival in love. The partisans were ready to believe the charge of 'Fascist informer' as quickly as medieval peasants believed the charge of 'witch'. Some with evil in their heart committed murder, claiming their victims were secret Fascists. Thugs robbed and killed in the name of 'liberation'.

In Milan the CLNAI leadership met and concluded that Mussolini should be handed over to the Americans, who were but thirty-five miles to the south and closing. They ordered Colonel Valerio to get Mussolini and bring him to them. Valerio, whose real name was Walter Audisio, was not happy about this and he spoke with his Communist colleagues before leaving. He had been killing Fascists since 1936 in Spain and now he was supposed to bring in Mussolini alive.

At 11:30pm Mussolini was put into a car. Count delle Stelle agreed they could stop and pick up Clara. When they did so, she was adoring of Mussolini as usual, though she must have known her fate if she stayed with her lover. Approaching Moltrasio they heard firing from the direction of Como. Not wishing to lose his prisoner to a Fascist rescue attempt, the count ordered the driver to turn back. Retracing their journey through the rainy night they halted at Mezzegra at the farm of Giacomo de Maria. The lady of the house kicked her two sons out of bed and offered it to Mussolini and Clara. Outside the door two partisans stood guard: Guglielmo Cantoni and Giuseppe Frangi.

On the morning of 28 April, as Colonel Valerio drove towards Dongo, all over northern Italy towns and villages were being liberated by partisans or Allies. In some communities the Allies arrived to find all enemy presence eradicated. Generally speaking by now the Germans were giving up like lambs to the advancing Allies and even to the partisans. The Fascists were also surrendering to the Allies by the thousand, but when faced with the choice of surrendering to partisans or fighting to the death, they usually chose the latter course.

Venice witnessed the German retreat. Fascists fled with the Germans hoping to make it to Switzerland before the Cremona Division arrived.

In Trieste the partisans realized they had bitten off more than they could chew as the Germans and Fascists vowed to fight on. These included the Cividino and Cossetto Black Brigades, the latter all-female. In the city's prison Fascists were still executing captured partisans.

At 2:10pm Valerio arrived in Dongo, to be met with a fusillade of shots until he was identified. The partisans here were few in number and jittery owing to the number of high-ranking Fascists they had captured. Valerio was surprised to learn he had driven right past Mussolini in Mezzegra. He was also informed that these partisans were holding senior Fascists prisoner. Valerio agreed that the fifteen most prominent should be executed. Yet, he ordered these few partisans to stay the execution until he took care of Mussolini. As the area was crawling with Germans and Fascists this seemed to some like an unwise move. The fifteen might be rescued before he returned.

However, he knew that the Communists had already informed the Americans of Mussolini's execution!

Along the Ligurian coast this day the French were advancing rapidly and handing leaflets to the villagers they encountered. The leaflets asked the people to vote to become French citizens! The Americans had been right to be concerned about French ambitions. [The French did indeed move the border in their favor.]

In the last three days the Allies had captured eighty thousand Germans and Fascists, and this did not count those in partisan hands. On the 28th advancing Allied troops reached those one hundred and twenty-five paratroopers of F-Force and one hundred and eleven paratroopers of the Nembo that had been fighting behind enemy lines for a week. These courageous few had inflicted a thousand casualties on the Germans and Fascists.

In Padua the German garrison surrendered to the partisans after four days of bitter fighting in which they had suffered roughly five hundred killed and a thousand wounded. Partisan losses here were two hundred and twenty-four killed and several hundred wounded.

There was heavy fighting in Savona, as the men of the Briatore Black Brigade fought for their lives against partisans A leading partisan, Augusto Bazzino, was killed here. He would be awarded the Gold Medal.

Valerio arrived in Mezzegra bringing with him Guido Conti the vice commandant general of the Garibaldi brigades, [real name: Aldo Lampredi], and Pietro Gatti the vice commander of the 52nd Garibaldi Brigade, [real name: Michele Moretti]. He had also brought a staffete with him, a blonde. They took Mussolini and his mistress from the farmhouse and loaded them into the small car, and with the two partisan guards Cantoni and Frangi riding on the running boards they drove up the hill. But they halted just three hundred yards up the hill at the gates to Villa Belmonte. There Valerio stood Il Duce and his mistress up against a wall. Clara realized what was happening and screamed for mercy, not for herself but for her dear Benito. Mussolini stubbornly looked Valerio in the face and demanded to be shot in the chest. Without fuss Valerio pulled the trigger on his sub machine gun. The weapon did not fire. He dropped it and used his pistol. It too misfired. He then borrowed a French-made sub machine gun and pointed it at Clara. A stream of bullets flung her against the wall and she fell like a rag doll. Then he emptied the weapon into Mussolini. He crumpled like an empty sack. Then Valerio fired his pistol into the dictator's corpse. It worked this time.

The above is the accepted story of the demise of the great dictator. Yet the story is, frankly, quite preposterous. This author believes this pathetic cover story was made up to suit a bad situation. Why did Valerio abandon his high-profile prisoners in Dongo, thus risking their rescue? As long as the partisans in Dongo had valuable prisoners they were in danger of Fascist attack. Why therefore did Valerio risk their lives? Why did he not order the executions to take place as soon as he arrived? Why bother to drive Mussolini and Clara away from the farmhouse instead of shooting them there? Why put them in a car to go just 300 yards? Why stop at a highly visible spot in the road? Indeed why kill Clara at all? Why did two weapons belonging to Valerio, a veteran guerilla fighter, misfire? Why did he honor Mussolini by shooting him in the chest rather than in the back, the traditional end for Italian traitors, or even hang him like a common criminal? Valerio had hated Mussolini for a decade, yet he now showed him respect? Why were there no bullet holes in the wall after the shooting? Was Valerio that good of a shot, and with a borrowed foreign weapon? Lastly why did he not photograph his crowning glory? He knew a photographer was available.

There is no doubt that Valerio was ambitious, and no doubt he had been given secret orders by the Communist leadership to execute Mussolini. Certainly all anti-Fascists wanted Il Duce dead. It is possible that when Valerio arrived at Dongo he learned to his dismay from Conti and Gatti that Mussolini and Clara were already dead, that they had attempted to escape and had been shot by their two guards? This would have nipped in the bud any chance of glory for Valerio. After all why wouldn't Mussolini try to escape when he had just two sleepy men guarding him? He had tried to escape from his SS escort twice. Then again a fleeing victim is usually shot in the back not in the chest. What if Valerio learned that Mussolini had grabbed a gun and turned it on himself as an act of suicide? Or had Mussolini tried to grab the weapon and was shot in the struggle? Mussolini had tried to commit suicide during his 1943 incarceration. Surely he was depressed enough to try it again now? Cantoni or Frangi might then have shot Clara to keep her from telling the truth. Valerio may have been informed that only he, Conti, Gatti, Cantoni and Frangi knew the truth. If so, this explains why he put the prisoners at Dongo on hold, knowing time was of the essence and why he grabbed a blonde staffete to go with him to Mezzegra. Inside the farmhouse they could have dressed Conti or Gatti and the staffete as Mussolini and Clara, then driven them covered in the car under the gaze of the prying eyes of villagers to a spot where everyone could see, but far enough away that faces could not be recognized. Perhaps he ordered the staffete to scream to ensure every villager looked up. The story about the misfires was possibly concocted to explain why Mussolini and Clara were not killed by bullets from Valerio's own weapons, but from a French made weapon. Most likely there were no bullet holes in the wall because Valerio fired the French made weapon into the air. Valerio had not brought a photographer with him for obvious reasons.

Of course this author's theory is pure conjecture, but surely it fits the known facts more easily than does Valerio's fantasy?

Communists were just as fanatical as Fascists, and all fanatics are unscrupulous and murderous. A few days after the 'execution' at Mezzegra a staffete was found drowned in the nearby lake. Cantoni was shot dead, supposedly accidentally while cleaning his weapon. If they had started to talk then perhaps they had to be silenced?

The anti-Fascists wanted Mussolini executed. They wanted revenge and Valerio gave it to them. For the Communists it was the end of a battle going back thirty years, and they boasted for the next half-century how they shot him. If the Italian people had learned Mussolini had taken his own life they would have felt cheated. Worse, the surviving Fascists would have felt pride if Mussolini had gone down fighting. [After all, when the Allies learned Hitler had committed suicide they felt cheated.]

At 4:12pm Valerio left the two corpses under guard and returned to Dongo. There he learned that Alessandro Pavolini and Marcello Petacci had tried to escape and had been shot, though Pavolini survived his wound. Valerio ordered the prisoners to be lined up against a railing facing the lake. He did not permit them the honor of facing their executioners, which he had supposedly given Mussolini. Each of the fifteen stood with a partisan behind him. They were Pavolini the commander of the Black Brigades, Idreno Utimperghe a Black Brigade officer, and members of Mussolini's government: Fernando Mezzasomma, Ruggero Romano, Paolo Zerbino and Augusto Liverani; plus leading Fascists Paolo Porta, Francesco Barracu [who had won the Gold Medal in Ethiopia], Mario Nudi and Alfredo Coppola; and to make up the numbers Vito Casalinuovo Mussolini's adjutant, Nicola Bombacci an old friend of Mussolini, Luigi Gatti Mussolini's private secretary, Ernesto Daquanno a journalist and Pietro Calisti an air force pilot.

Valerio made sure a photographer was on hand to record the execution for posterity and then he gave the order. As each partisan fired into the man in front of him not everyone fell at once: some clung to the railing. The guns fired again. The bodies writhed on the ground. The guns fired again. It was a messy affair. Valerio ordered the bodies thrown into a furniture van. On their way to Milan they would pick up Mussolini's corpse.

At dawn on 29 April passers-by in the Piazza Loreto in Milan noticed a group of partisans staring at twenty corpses. Added to Valerio's victims were the bodies of Roberto Farinaci, Carlo Scorza and Achille Terazzi, executed hours earlier by Milan partisans. When the gathering crowd recognized Mussolini they vented their fury on his lifeless hulk. They kicked his corpse in revenge, yelling and screaming. They kicked him for all the victims of Fascism who could not be here. They kicked him for Giacomo Matteoti, murdered because he dared suggest the Fascists had rigged an election. They kicked him for Giovanni Palatucci a police officer who refused to arrest Jews and who therefore was sentenced to die in Dachau concentration camp. They kicked him for Gian Luigi Banfi, architect turned partisan, who died at Mauthausen concentration camp. They kicked him for young Rita Rosani, an SAP member who was arrested, tortured and shot. They kicked him because five hundred and sixty-three Milan citizens had been executed simply for being Jewish. They kicked him for the thousands killed in Allied bombing raids, the result of his declaration of war on Britain and America. They kicked him for their young men who had died of thirst in the Libyan Desert, who had died in the mud of a Spanish trench, who had frozen on the Russian steppe, who had died of fever in Ethiopia, who had burned to death when their plane fell in flames, who had drowned in submarines that were not seaworthy. They kicked him for those countless soldiers who in September 1943 were enslaved by their own commanders.

Eventually they strung the bodies upside down from the edge of a garage roof. Then a loud cheer was heard as a live Achille Starace was marched into the square. He was turned to face away from his executioner, and a newsreel camera caught the whole proceedings as he was shot.

Several other Fascists were shot in Milan this day, including Carlo Borsani, who had been wounded and crippled in the Greek campaign, and Father Tullio Calcagno, a priest who had defied the pope and had run a Fascist publication.

———————

On 29 April after six days of bitter no quarter killing the partisans captured Cuneo. At Vicenza the Faggion Black Brigade and elements of the Condottieri Division surrendered to the US 88th Division. This day the Italia Bersaglieri Division and a battlegroup of the Monterosa formally capitulated to the Brazilians.

Graziani now radioed the Allies, agreeing to surrender the armed forces of the Social Republic. Near Cernobbio he was met by two officers, one American and one Co-Belligerent, and they took him in a car to the signing location. On route the car struck a mine (or was hit by a grenade). The Co-Belligerent officer was killed and the American and the driver were wounded. Graziani, the great survivor, lived to sign the capitulation.

On 30 April partisans took the surrender of the Axis garrison in Turin, after having killed two thousand Fascists. The US 92nd Division [Negro] arrived hours later.

Meanwhile New Zealand troops reached the Piave River at Santa Dona, and American forces crossed the Po near Mantova. Inside Mantova the Turchetti Black Brigade was already in its death throes at the hands of hundreds of partisans. Just north of the mighty Po the US 10th Mountain Division was struck by a counter attack by the fanatic German 1st Parachute Division. The German 148th Division was trapped south of the river and surrendered to the Brazilians.

At Trieste, where the partisans were clinging to their few gains, the Titoists arrived, now uniformed and equipped as a regular army. These Yugoslavian partisans joined with the Italians to continue their attack. The battle was ferocious.

This day Wolf and von Viettinghoff conversed and decided it was all over. They issued orders to their joint forces to ceasefire at once and surrender at 6:30pm on 2 May. Naturally Berlin picked up this signal and countermanded the order and furthermore informed von Viettinghoff that he was to be relieved of command by General Schultz.

By the morning of 1 May most of Italy was in Allied hands. Only Trieste and the Alps were still nominally under Axis control. In Trieste the garrison fought like wild animals for none of them wished to be taken alive by the Italian partisans or the Titoists.

The Maiella Brigade joined with the Seven Communities Partisan Brigade to attack the Fascist garrison at Asiago.

This morning General Schultz arrived at von Viettinghoff's headquarters and was immediately arrested by SS guards under Wolf's orders. Wolf and von Viettinghoff then explained the true situation. While talking they heard on the radio that Hitler had been killed in action fighting in Berlin. [Even in death Hitler could not resist a lie. He had in fact committed suicide.] Finally at 10pm Schultz agreed to confirm von Viettinghoff's call to surrender.

The following morning as New Zealand forces reached Trieste, the Axis garrison of ten thousand agreed to surrender to the New Zealanders. Following a symbolic 'attack' by Titoists, the garrison gave up and received the New Zealanders' protection. About four thousand Fascists and several hundred Germans had been killed here.

At 2pm this day Schultz broadcast the order for all German-controlled forces in Italy to surrender. This was all well and good for those who could find an Allied regular to surrender to, but those surrounded by partisans were not so eager to capitulate. A bus belonging to the pope's armistice commission was ambushed by partisans and its sixty passengers were murdered. The partisans were not about to let the Fascists off lightly. Around Lake Como they killed a thousand. Another three hundred Fascists were killed at Varese, and one thousand seven hundred at Brescia, and one thousand five hundred at Mantova, and four thousand at Bergamo. The Allies found many fresh mass graves of Fascists. At Codenigo three men claimed to be the only survivors of a two hundred man GNR unit. Of Mussolini's entire navy including the Condottieri Division only two thousand two hundred were handed alive to the Allies. How many Fascists hid and survived will never be known, but the bloodletting went on for days after the official surrender.

Partisan losses were high too, of course. In Gorizia District on 21

April alone one hundred and seventy of them were killed. Fascists had been executing captured partisans just hours before they threw in the towel. Passions ran high.

Owing to their location by 2 May French Alpine Command and US Fifth Army had nowhere to go, having reached the Swiss border, but British Eighth Army, including its tens of thousands of Italians, headed straight into Austria, where the Germans were still fighting. However, Eighth Army was told to keep its Cremona, Folgore and Friuli Divisions in Italy for political reasons. On 7 May the new German chancellor Admiral Doenitz arranged a complete capitulation. The war was over in Europe.

This day an entire artillery battalion of the Monterosa Division came out of the mountains to surrender, the last cohesive unit of Mussolini's republican armed forces.

———————

It turned out that the Alpine Redoubt had existed only in Hitler's mind. This does not mean the Italian spring offensive was redundant. German and Italian guerillas could have led the Anglo-Americans a merry chase for years had they chosen to.

The Italian people had never considered the spring offensive redundant. It freed them from a hateful tyranny that was growing more insane each day. It gave them an opportunity to regain their self-respect. It gave them the chance to emerge from the war victorious. Following this, they could get back to doing what they do best: living. A whole new cultural renaissance lay ahead of them.

———————

There was a footnote to this two sided coin known as World War Two. One side was ended, the war against Nazism and Fascism. But the flip side of the coin, the war against the Japanese was still on. With the destruction of the Fascist and German armed forces, Bonomi sent Co-Belligerent warships to the Pacific to challenge the Japanese. There Italian Fascist submarines and warships were still fighting alongside the Japanese. The submarine Torelli with a mixed Italian-German crew sailing under Japanese orders actually shot down an American bomber in August. The Japanese agreed to surrender on 15 August 1945.

———————

Chapter Sixty-three
Conclusions

When Mussolini was appointed prime minister by the king in 1922 he inherited two conflicts: one military, the other political. Both consisted of killing, imprisonment and exile. The military affair was in the far off deserts of Libya. The British and French had grown fat waging this type of war, as a cat grows fat killing mice. Mussolini saw no reason why his regime could not grow fat killing tribal 'savages'. However, it was the political struggle that worried Mussolini, because his Fascist Party never attracted more than four per cent of the populace, and the Blackshirts, his own paramilitary force, despised him. The Blackshirt generals were jealous of him. Nonetheless, he used them in a shaky precarious alliance, and he never crushed them, as Hitler crushed his SA stormtroopers when they were no longer useful, but neither did Mussolini allow the Blackshirts to have the status and wealth that Hitler allowed his SS.

As time went on Mussolini became one of the most popular leaders in Italian history. At first the peasants did not like him, but he convinced them he was one of them and he gave migrant workers, farm workers and tenant farmers a structured wage and labor system, which coupled with government investment and major projects like the draining of marshes gave Italy a streamlined and profitable agricultural industry for the first time in history. Prior to Mussolini the only hope for a poor farm worker was to emigrate.

At first industrial workers did not like him, but he convinced them he was one of them, and he led many a campaign for shorter hours, longer contracts and better pay, and his government's investment in new equipment and training and his long term plan of military expenditure gave Italy a boom economy that helped her sail through the Great Depression practically unharmed.

At first the moneyed classes did not like him, but his removal of the need for strikes, his emasculation of the Communists and Socialists and his opening of new investment opportunities soon brought them around to his way of thinking.

At first the nobility did not like him. The nobility's power had been removed by previous governments, but they still retained privileges. However, once they realized that Mussolini was willing to use their system, by ennobling some of his own cronies, they soon concluded that noblemen in other lands might sleep with a pistol under their pillow, but in Italy they slept like babes with the assurance that their privileges would still be there in the morning.

At first the priests did not like him. But he bought off the Roman Catholic Church with the greatest gift of all: he gave the church its own country, the Vatican. No matter it comprised only a few buildings and a courtyard: it was a sovereign state. Mussolini turned the pope into a president and his bishops into diplomats, and gave the church the right to place an embassy in every capital in the world. In return the Church turned a blind eye to his excesses.

At first the moralists did not like him, but he brought an end to the street battles of political violence, and he whittled down the nation's major criminal families, including the 'Mafia' in Sicily.

At first the nationalists did not like him, but within a few short years he gave all Italians something to be proud of, with victory in Libya, a major warship and commercial ship building program, and an air force that was the envy of the world, with Italian pilots as popular in the public imagination as race car drivers.

Therefore in Mussolini's Italy of the first two decades it was quite common for an Italian to support Mussolini and yet remain a Socialist, a Communist or a devout Catholic. People that would cross the street rather than walk next to a Blackshirt and that silently insulted all Fascists under their breath would still praise Mussolini in the privacy of their dinner table.

The Italian people were therefore guilty of the sin of omission. They omitted to see what went on in the streets after midnight...the beatings, the arrests, the castor oil tortures and the disappearances. This omission led the fanatic Blackshirts and Fascist police to believe their acts were condoned by the silent majority. Most nations have experienced this at one time or another, such as the British police in their attitude to Irish rebels in the latter third of the twentieth century, or the American police during the Nixon years, and more recently during the presidency of George W. Bush. And of course racists the world over survive because of the omission of others.

As a result of this conviction the Fascists became ever more brutal in their war against the Libyan Senussi, turning a sniping affair into a war of genocidal proportions. Much of Moslem Libya's attitude to the world can be attributed to their treatment at the hands of the Christian Italians. This horror existed because the Italian people omitted to see it. This blinkered view, which they shared with many other 'white' nations of the time, resulted in their 1935 invasion of Ethiopia. This war was described by jingoists with flowery oration and rich vocabularies of romantic poetry naming high moral arguments similar to those that had spurred on medieval crusaders. Even such anti-Fascists as Cardinal Schuster praised the war. In truth the war was a cruel exercise in bullying. Mussolini, the onetime schoolyard bully, had found a bigger schoolyard. As far as Mussolini was concerned Ethiopia had owed Italy a rematch since the Italian defeat there in 1896. At first he tried to seduce Ethiopia. When that did not work he resorted to rape. It was fully two years after the invasion before anyone remembered the supposed reason for the war, namely to bring civilization to a backward land.

This complacent attitude of the Italian people transmuted into verbal approval when the Spanish Civil War broke out. Originally Italian involvement was a token show of strength to affirm solidarity with their Christian brothers in Spain, but it degenerated into a bigger and better schoolyard for Mussolini to show off his war toys. Did the civilians of Barcelona really die because their love of their Catalonian homeland threatened Italy, or because Mussolini wanted to impress the world with his new airplanes?

This complacency: this silent approval; this refusal to shout 'enough'; led to the invasion of Albania in which a Christian people taught a predominantly Moslem people the meaning of Christianity by invading and conquering them on Easter weekend!

In 1939 Mussolini kept Italy out of the Polish-German War, which the British insisted on calling the Second World War. In Italy many wanted their country to do exactly what she had done in World War One, namely join the British to fight the Germans. Il Duce prevaricated making a decision, and then suddenly entered the fray in the most shameful manner possible, after France was half overrun and after the British Army of a half million had been thrown into the sea. Moreover his purpose was immoral: war for profit. The Germans publicly welcomed the Italians, but in private they too thought Mussolini's timing was despicable.

To say Mussolini's greedy eyes were too big for his military stomach is a major understatement. Within hours of his declaration of war on Britain, a supposedly defeated enemy, his people were subjected to death and destruction in the form of British air raids and naval bombardments. So far the Italian people had seen only what Mussolini's strictly controlled cinema newsreels, radio broadcasts and newspaper articles wanted them to see. British air raids had a reality about them that Mussolini's propaganda machine could not stifle. The death of one old woman in a city by a British bomb was more shocking than the deaths of a hundred soldiers in a far off desert.

Mussolini's invasion of Greece began to remind villagers of World War One, because of its stream of casualty notices. In the first four months in Greece Italy lost more sons than she had in Libya, Ethiopia, Spain and Albania put together.

Of course it was far too late for the Italians. Shocked out of their complacency they could now only hold on for dear life like the passengers of a drunken bus driver. There was never a popular uprising against Mussolini. It was the king's move in July 1943 that gave them license to show how they really felt about this war. Mussolini while imprisoned never saw the all-night parades of massed citizens cheering his removal. He did not see the images of his face being smashed and disfigured throughout Italy. When he tried to commit suicide was it shame at having been duped by the king, or was it a spoiled child's attempt to gain attention?

Once rescued, he created a new Fascist Italy without a hint of suspicion that the people no longer wanted him. He refused to believe that the Italian people had seized control of the war, and that he was their enemy. Hitler refused Mussolini's request to release the captured Italian soldiers, knowing the majority would not fight for Mussolini. It is obvious that Hitler had a much more accurate grasp of reality than did Mussolini.

Among the political fanatics of the mid-twentieth century the Fascists and Communists were the most feared. No single man could ever personify Communism, though Lenin, Stalin and Mao Zhe-Dung tried to. However, Mussolini was Fascism. Without Mussolini the history of Fascism in Italy would have been a mere footnote. Without Mussolini there would have been no Hitler, Franco, Salazar, Peron, Saddam Hussein or Noriega, at least not in the way the world knew them. Therefore the argument that ninety-eight per cent of the Italians were innocent of the horrors of warfare does not hold water. The truth is the Italian people allowed Mussolini to get on with the job while they busied themselves with more private pursuits. This is perhaps only human nature. Even in democratic nations few involve themselves in politics, many do not vote, and in colleges poetry has always attracted more students than political science. The only Italians who can truly be called innocent are those who had no ability to speak out, such as the children, the very aged and the handicapped.

Having established the guilt of the people it is then necessary to categorize a degree of guilt. E.g. who was more guilty? Sergio Bresciani, a teenager who died trying to kill Englishmen, and who had not known a split-second of life without Fascist propaganda, or the educated English newspaper editors of the 1930's who used their freedom of speech to praise Mussolini?

It is much easier to judge a criminal after the crime has been committed than before. In 1922 no one, not even rabid anti-Fascists, could have foreseen where Mussolini was going to take Italy. Count Galeazzo Ciano was Italy embodied. Italy personified. He became a follower of Mussolini, then a friend, married his daughter Edda, became his puppet, his soldier, his confidant and last of all, his victim. The millions of Cianos who followed Mussolini were equally betrayed by him. Ironically the young Mussolini was also betrayed by the elder Mussolini. Mussolini the warrior, who charged out of the trenches in 1916 against Austrian-German machine guns, was not the same Mussolini who silently surrendered in 1945 while hiding in a German uniform.

The same had happened to Mussolini's spirit as had happened to the spirit of the Italian armed forces. In World War I the Italian soldier fought in miserable conditions, suffering unbelievably high casualties, recovered from a defeat that would have destroyed most armies, and won a brilliant victory. However, in World War Two the performance of Italian men at arms was quite varied. The image of the Italian fighting man was battered and bruised by British propaganda during World War I, and come World War II this image was dragged through the dirt. Furthermore after 1945 this image was murdered and buried by American, British and German historians, each with their own agenda. Even Allied veterans who published their memoirs, and who should have known better, fell into the same trap of blatant anti-Italian racial prejudice, with such comments as 'the Italian warships advanced reluctantly'. How on earth can a ship move reluctantly? It either moves forward or backwards. Others maintain that Italian dive-bombers were not as aggressive as German dive-bombers, but did they know that some of those German-made Stukas were flown by Regia Aeronautica pilots? Or were they so foolhardy as to stick their head up during an air raid to identify aircraft insignia? Whenever a multitude of writers spin the same web it is worth delving deeper to see if this is a result of truth or of bias. The truth is that the Italian forces of the twentieth century were efficient, generally speaking. Without efficiency there would have been no Vittorio Veneto, no Teruel, no destruction of British armor in the desert, no charge across Russia, and no impressive last stands at Keren, Amba Alagi, Alamein or Enfidaville. There would certainly have been no partisan uprising, no heroic police work against the 'Mafia' and other criminal organizations, no war on terrorists and no splendid aerial performance in the 1991 Gulf War.

In 1917 during World War I the British were on their last legs. Their Serbian ally had been overrun. Their Russian ally had collapsed. Their French ally was suffering huge mutinies. Their American ally was hopelessly unprepared to help. Only their Italian ally was holding fast. Britain's own Irish subjects had rebelled. The British people were questioning the morality of the war. Poor showings at Gallipoli, the Somme and Ypres had increased the casualty lists for no noticeable gain. Then in October 1917 came the Italian defeat at Caporetto. It looked like Britain would be left to battle on alone. The British government grabbed at straws and tried to shame their soldiers into fighting on with such slogans as 'our boys can take it', implying that though the Russians might surrender, the French refuse to advance, the Americans dawdle and the Italians run away, the British Tommy could stand and take it on the chin. This British belief that Russian military prowess had died in 1917 was prevalent even after the war when the British fought the Red Army during the Russian Civil War. The British belief in French cowardice was part of their reason to refuse to stand beside the French in 1940. British anti-Italian prejudice might have faded away, but it received a shot in the arm periodically to keep it alive: e. g. the slowness of Italians to defeat Ethiopians armed with swords and spears, and the lies and distortions of the Spanish Republican press regarding the

Battle of Guadalajara. In 1940 as the British began to decode Italian secret messages it was imperative that no one find out, so the old myth of Italian cowardice was dusted off and once again put to work. It became a convenient answer when the press asked why British forces were so victorious against Italians but not against Germans. British infantry recruits were so imbued with this bias that when they came up against Italian infantry they commented it was just their luck to be thrown against the only Italians who had backbones.

The Italian surrender in 1943 only made things worse. The Italians expected to be welcomed by the British as a priest welcomes sinners who have finally seen the light. Instead the British scorned them for betraying a friend - even if that friend was the devil.

It was this betrayal that caused the rift between Germans and Italians. Austrians and Italians have fought each other for centuries, but Germans have nothing to do with Austrians, bar a common language. However, in World War I Germany and Austria were partners, and by World War II the two nations had become one. Therefore Austrian prejudice towards Italians became a factor in Germany's dealings with their new Axis partner, especially as a high proportion of the German Nazis including Hitler were in fact Austrians not Germans. In 1940 just as the Italians would have been happier fighting alongside the British against the Germans, so the Germans would have been happier fighting alongside the British against the Italians. The German position in September 1943 was very much like Britain's position in 1917, therefore when the Italians joined the Allies the Germans began to blame all their woes on the Italians. The Italian fighting man became a very convenient scapegoat. Post-war German historians added to this myth and German generals in their memoirs willingly took the opportunity to blame their defeats on someone else.

Actually not one German defeat can be laid at the door of their Italian partners! The Germans in Stalingrad were doomed to failure by Hitler's poor strategy, not by the collapse of the Italian Eighth Army. Rommel was defeated in Africa, but he would have been beaten much quicker had it not been for outstanding performances by some Italian units such as the Savona and Ariete. In Tunisia the Germans surrendered before the Italians did. Sicily was not so much lost by the Germans as abandoned. They had no need of Sicily. The Germans surrendered in Italy in 1945 because they were 'bludgeoned to death' by Allied military force. [As John Ellis put it.] They did not fall because of Italian perfidy. In fact the Germans were in the minority in the last campaign, outnumbered three to one by Fascist Italians.

The truth is that Italy was not the first nor last to desert the Axis cause. The French armed forces in North Africa defected to the Allies in November 1942. The Danish government deserted Hitler in August

1943. Badoglio's move in September 1943 was only in keeping with the trend. The Hungarians would have defected in March 1944, but a German invasion put a stop to that. The Romanians, Bulgars and Finns turned on the Germans in summer 1944. The Slovaks then rebelled, and Franco's Spaniards began skipping out the back door when they saw the Allied 'cops' approaching the front door. It is odd, therefore, that of all these defections only the Italian one still rankles in Germany. Few Germans know that in summer of 1943 Hitler was in secret negotiation with Stalin regarding a truce. If Hitler had had his way he would have abandoned his Axis partners including Italy to the Communist wolf.

None of the lost Axis partners ever rose again to fight alongside Hitler, bar a few small units, except Mussolini's Italy, which rose out of the ashes and rebuilt a viable partnership. Mussolini died only hours before Hitler and on that day Mussolini controlled more acreage in Italy than Hitler did in Germany.

Surprisingly after 1945 most Italians actually joined their own hecklers. The basic reason for this was social survival. All Axis partners were forced to pay some sort of compensation to the Allies after the war. Italy lost her African Empire, the Dodecanese Islands, Dalmatia and Istria. However, compared to Germany the Italians got off practically Scott-free, because the German people were branded with a collective guilt, the most damning ever stamped on a nation by the world community. For two generations after the war the world feared every German as a Hitler-in-waiting. However, the suggestion that the Italians, that fun loving, artistic, musical, comic people could be guilty of mass murder or warmongering brings a smile to the lips of Britons and Americans alike.

In their campaign to convince the British and Americans that they were innocent the Italians have been one hundred per cent successful. In agreeing with their detractors that all Italians are cowards they have managed to deny their military conquests and thus the guilt associated with them. Rather like a member of a gang of robbers who when arrested pleads mental incompetence. As a result Italy has never paid serious compensation to the Soviet Union, France, Ethiopia, Libya, Albania, Greece or Yugoslavia. Brigadier General Carlo Isasca fell into Yugoslav hands at the end of the war and was executed. But not one Italian of high military or civilian rank was ever handed to these nations by the British or Americans to answer charges of war crimes, though there were hundreds of names on the extradition requests. After the war the British only executed one Italian, General Nicola Bellomo, for the killing of a British prisoner. This was a gesture. The Americans did not punish any Italian severely. Genuine war criminals such as Graziani, Badoglio, Ambrosio and Roatta were protected by the Allies.

Only when it comes to the partisans, that is the Italians who fought to liberate rather than to enslave, are the children of Italy allowed to be openly proud. They can call them heroes without contradiction, even in the company of foreigners. But anyone who praises the bravery of the Julia Division in Greece, the Trieste Division in North Africa, the Savoia Grenadiers in East Africa or the sailors at the Battle of Cape Matapan is labeled a neo-Fascist. In order to maintain this attitude the enemy of the partisans as depicted in novels, television and movies is almost exclusively shown as German. Heroic good Italian partisans versus heroic evil Germans. There is an almost mathematical equation to this: a partisan cannot be considered to have been heroic unless his opponent was heroic, and if his opponent is depicted as being Fascist Italian, then either the heroism of the partisan must be denied or the heroism of the Fascist must be acknowledged. And as the latter cannot be admitted for political and social reasons, the Fascist Italian is suddenly transformed into a German in the book, film or TV show, even when they are about known historic incidents where the protagonists were Fascist Italians.

Oddly enough the British fall into this same trap. They awarded many bravery medals including Victoria Crosses for actions against Italians, yet then turn around and say without a blush that the Italians always ran away! Racist bigotry only sounds logical to another racist bigot.

The stories of Italian partisan heroism were often promulgated by the Italian Communist Party. They put forward the lie that the only heroic partisans were the Communists, and that only they were responsible for Italy's liberation. In other words an Italian is a coward until he becomes a Communist. This lie was responsible for the good showing of the Communists in the elections of the immediate postwar period. Not only did Communists vote for them, but many a moron voted for them too.

In this post-war climate it has been difficult for Italy's armed forces to maintain morale. Full praise must be given to those Carabinieri, police and servicemen that risked their lives in conflict with terrorists, gangsters and in foreign adventures such as peacekeeping operations.

It is interesting to note that few Americans have become involved in this myth of Italian cowardice. Though one American general was fired for telling an 'Italian cowardice' joke to journalists - and rightly so. On the contrary, most Americans look upon Italians as brave to the point of being reckless. There are distinctive reasons for this. The American experience of fighting against Italians was gained in Tunisia, Sicily and Italy, where they encountered courageous opposition. In the USA ethnic Italian gangsters and policemen are both looked upon as courageous by the American public. It is not an easy choice to challenge the 'Mafia'. The American experience of fighting alongside Italians at Cassino and in the 1945 spring offensive was a positive one. Furthermore, by the time of World War II one GI in twelve was ethnically Italian. The lists of American heroes in the American Civil War, World War I, World War II, Korea, Vietnam, Iraq and Afghanistan contain many Italian names.

This narrative has attempted in a small way to bring justice to Italian arms. In the 1920s and 1930s Italian aviation led the world. But the Regia Aeronautica was not seriously challenged until 1940, by which time their planes had become obsolete. The 399 mph Mc205 was excellent, but the phrase 'too few, too late' fits this aircraft exactly. The tallies of Italian fighter aces are therefore all the more impressive...Adriano Visconti with 26 kills, Leonardi Ferrulli with 21, Teresio Martinoli with 22, Franco Bardoni-Bisleri with 19, Luigi Corrini with 19, and so on.

At sea even the most biased anti-Italians had to admit their fear of the pigs. And look at the size of British escorts in the Mediterranean. The Royal Navy had a healthy respect for the Italian Navy.

As early as 1941 the Regia Marina knew their submarines lacked quality. They compared them to the German U-boats and found they had a somewhat lower surface speed and a much lower speed in adverse weather conditions. Engine performance was poor. In some cases the submarines couldn't even catch a fully laden merchant ship. Many of the submarines had a high conning tower, and some had a longer one as well, which gave them better visibility than the German boats, but this also gave them a higher profile. No wonder so many were sunk by British submarines. Italian subs were noisier than German ones, making it easier for Allied sonar systems and hydrophones to hear them. Poor training, a lack of experience and bad design meant it took much longer for an Italian submarine to dive than a German or Allied boat. In general, Italian subs were not as maneuverable as German ones. Italian submarines were easier to spot than German ones because firing a torpedo left an air bubble that rose to the surface and their torpedoes left a longer trail. Italian torpedo warheads were not as powerful as they should have been. Italian boats had few torpedoes, therefore they usually only fired one at a target, then waited to see the result. German and Allied boats usually fired two, and some American boats fired four. Newer vessels built in late 1941 and later did remedy some of these problems, but it was too late to have an effect.

On land the Italian war machine was more unreliable. The Blackshirts never came up to anyone's expectations and definitely not up to their boasts. In Ethiopia and Spain some Blackshirts volunteered for the excellent pay check and fought in such a way that they would live to spend it. The Blackshirts fought better once under army control from 1940 onwards, especially in East Africa.

Mussolini's reliance on Ethiopian and Libyan troops was ill advised. The Italians were no more racist than the British at this date, and their treatment of Eritrean ascaris was good and in return they got a very fine soldier. But how could they seriously expect Ethiopians and Libyans to fight for Mussolini? The British tried Libyan volunteers, and soon relegated them to sentry duty. They did not even attempt to use Ethiopian troops outside of that country.

To judge the Italian Army one must look at the different branches. In general the infantry performed well. Sometimes they panicked, but at other times their bravery was outstanding...Franco-Italian Border 1940, Greece, Egypt/Libya, Eritrea/Ethiopia, Tunisia, the first few days of the Sicily campaign, Cassino, the crawl up the Italian boot, the battles of 1945 on both sides of the line. The Bersaglieri soldiers were elite and consistently good, showing great audacity. At Sidi Rezegh they reassured a nervous Rommel. At Kasserine Pass they worried the Americans. On the Russian front they sliced their way through Russian hordes. The Alpini were also impressive, but often were given too much to do. The horse cavalry had their moments, but they had not been a war winner for over a century. Italian armor possessed courage and that was about all. Their equipment was laughable. The combat engineers of the Italian Army are without doubt the unsung heroes. Their actions were consistently dependable, whether at Tobruk in 1942 or just north of Rome in 1943.

The most praised branch was the artillery, whether facing a German amphibious invasion on Leros or grappling hand-to-hand with British infantry in 1940. Even Nazis in Sicily praised Italian artillery. In Tunisia in 1943 companies of Semoventi self-propelled guns acted as armored assault units. When the French took over the battle for Corsica they insisted on keeping the Italian artillery in action.

However, the operations of Mussolini's army were hampered by bad leadership and shoddy equipment. Decent leadership, such as provided by the Duke D'Aosta, Lorenzini, Nasi, Utili, Bergonzolli and Messe, was all too rare.

After 8 September 1943 Italian gallantry was the norm not the exception. Whether looking at partisans, the Condottieri Division, the SS Sturmbrigade 'Italien', the Italia Bersaglieri Division, the Utili Division or the 'combat groups' of the 1945 spring offensive, the word courage keeps coming to mind. The US 88th Division had fought Germans for a year, but when they ran up against the Italians of the Condottieri they described them as 'elite'.

As the British Eighth Army began to see more and more the performance of their own Italian troops and as the war neared its end and some of the censorship restrictions were lifted, the British senior officers began to openly praise their Italian troops. British officers are the masters of understatement. A defective idea would be described by them as 'could do with improvement', whereas the plain-speaking Americans would call it 'crap' and the excitable Italians would name it 'impossible'. When one of these British officers described a victory as 'It was a good show', the Americans would describe it as 'It was great' and the Italians as 'It was fantastic'. Moreover, regardless of their national characteristics all military officers have a habit of being reticent. Therefore it must be realized that when a British senior officer praised an Italian he really meant it and one should perceive a stronger emotion that the words alone suggest. The British officially reported the quality of the Co-Belligerent Friuli and Folgore Divisions as 'invaluable'. They made such statements as 'the Italian combat groups have exceeded expectations'... 'the bravery of the Italian troops in action is beyond question'…'they are paying a very worthwhile dividend'...and 'morale in these groups is very high'. The highest praise came from the Americans, who reported the Italian performance as 'valuable, without which [Fifth Army] could not have operated'.

It was the general belief in Fascist Italy that war was not a woman's affair, though Mussolini allowed his daughter Edda to serve as a nurse on a hospital ship. However, the war was forced upon women through air raids, the black market and the battles fought in their streets. Rape by invaders and liberators alike was a serious problem. Rape was not considered a war crime in this war, and most men looked upon rape as a lack of salesmanship rather than as an assault. Poverty forced many a woman into prostitution in order to feed her children. On 8 September 1943 women ran into the streets to fight German soldiers and eventually the staffete became a well-respected branch of the partisan movement. The CLNAI registered thirty-five thousand women as staffete, of which six hundred and twenty-three were killed in combat and four thousand six hundred and fifty-three were tortured to death or died in concentration camps. Another two thousand seven hundred and fifty were wounded in battle or maimed by torture. Fifteen received the Gold Medal, Italy's highest military honor. One such was Ines Bedeschi, who never talked despite being tortured and put in front of a firing squad.

The British and Americans tend to look at the European conflict between 1939 and 1945 as one war, but the Italians lived this period under the impression it was a series of wars. Only for the long time active anti-Fascists was it one war, and their conflict had not begun in 1939 but twenty years earlier. Certainly those Italians that actively fought Fascism from the moment they were able should be lauded by the rest of the world. In the first twenty years of Mussolini's rule the active anti-Fascists numbered fewer than one Italian in a thousand. Some of these men had fought in Spain against Fascism, at times opposing Mussolini's soldiers, and when that war ended in March 1939 they had fled to France, where they joined the French armed forces just six months later to fight Hitler's Fascists. When France collapsed some escaped to join the British forces, but others joined the French underground until September 1943 when they returned to Italy to fight as partisans until May 1945. As far as these men were concerned it was not a matter of they joining the Italian popular revolt against Hitler and Mussolini in September 1943, but rather a matter of the Italian people joining them in the war that they had been waging since 1919. It is their war that the Italian people won in May 1945! Not Mussolini's war that he launched in June 1940!

The Italian people did not consider their conflict against the Soviet Union as having any link to their war against the British. They looked upon their conquests of Greece and Yugoslavia as separate again. The civil war that began on 8 September 1943 was altogether another war, and as the bulk of the Italian people supported the Co-Belligerents and partisans, then it truly can be seen that the Italians emerged victorious.

Between 10 June 1940 and 8 September 1943 one hundred and sixty-three thousand Italian servicemen died serving Mussolini, and from then until May 1945 another twenty thousand Italians died in battle serving Mussolini. [Post-war Fascists claim forty thousand] Plus about seven thousand Italians died in German uniform. Additionally between 1940 and 1945 sixty-four thousand Italian civilians died in bombing raids, by far the majority at the hands of the Allies. The number of Dalmatian and Istrian Italians that were murdered by the Titoists will never be known. Therefore the number of Italians who died at the hands of Mussolini's enemies will never be known for sure. Should one include the prisoners of the ELAS, for example? The figure of just over a quarter of a million dead at the hands of the Allies and anti-Fascists is about as accurate as one can get.

Then there were those Italians who fought against Mussolini. They served in the Garibaldi Brigade in Spain and from 1939 onwards in the French or British forces. For example, no one expected the Italian immigrant Fortunato Picchi to give up his cushy job at the London Savoy at the age of forty-two to become a British paratrooper. But he did, and he died in a Fascist prison under torture refusing to give information that would endanger his fellow British paratroopers. Enzo Sereni, an Italian Jew, safely emigrated to British Palestine, but then joined the British Army and parachuted into Fascist Italy to aid partisans. He died in Dachau concentration camp.

Furthermore the US Army recruited so many Italian immigrants that they toyed with setting up all-Italian battalions.

In September, October and November 1943 fully thirty-five thousand Italian regular soldiers, airmen and sailors died at the hands of the Nazis/Fascists either in battle or executed or died of maltreatment. The casualties of Co-Belligerent personnel December 1943 to war's end numbered four thousand seven hundred and twenty-nine killed and wounded. Those who were taken to a German prisoner of war camp were soon offered a chance to serve Hitler in some fashion or other. Those who refused knew they were opting for pain and misery, for their treatment was horrendous and became worse in summer 1944 when the SS took over administration of their camps. The courage of these men who lived in horror daily rather than sign on the dotted line is highly commendable. By the war's end thirty thousand of them had died from the brutality.

Of the anti-Fascist partisans forty-five thousand, including staffete and SAP, died in Italy and twenty thousand Italian partisans died in Greece, Albania and Yugoslavia. The famed Maiella Brigade suffered fifty-five killed and one hundred and fifty-one wounded. The Allies eventually recognized two hundred and fifty thousand men and women as having served as 'partisans' and granted each of them or a surviving relative a Certificate of Commendation.

A complete count of civilians killed in the midst of battle or murdered by the Nazis/Fascists is impossible to achieve. The figure of eighty thousand seems to be as accurate as anyone will arrive at. It is known that four thousand five hundred Italians were murdered by the Nazis simply because they had more than two Jewish grandparents. Some of these Jews were Catholics and some were Fascists.

The Italian people believe that they have a right to be numbered among the Allied nations of the war in 1945, and that this right was purchased with the blood of two hundred and sixteen thousand Italians killed by the Nazis/Fascists.

Thus, total Italian deaths in World War II were probably just under a half million. For comparison as a percentage of population this was one and a half times the British loss and four times the American loss.

At war's end Italy was a shambles: bridges were destroyed and replaced by temporary military structures; tens of thousands of buildings were demolished; five million people were homeless; the black market still had a strangle hold on the economy; crime was rampant; millions suffered from malnutrition; major epidemics had broken out of septic skin sores, malaria, enteric fever, diphtheria and typhoid. Infant mortality was thirty per cent. Each day Allied and Co-Belligerent medical personnel threw up their hands in despair as more and more refugees arrived from the mountains suffering from a host of ailments including untreated wounds. The dying continued long after the official end of the war.

The problems facing Bonomi were nightmarish and the possibility of a Communist uprising was very real. The Allies soon agreed that Dalmatia and Istria were to be handed over to the Titoists. But at least they stood their ground in Trieste. That city remained Italian. Tito's refusal to allow Soviet troops to remain in Yugoslavia, coupled with the Allied stand in Trieste, Austria and Germany meant that the Red Army advanced no further. Stalin was in fact pleasantly surprised the Allies were letting him keep as much as they did. This sounded the death knell of any hopes of rebellion in the minds of Italian Communists. They might rant and rave and act ugly now and then, but they would confine their political efforts to the ballot box.

Within a couple of years the tourists began to come to Italy again. They came to see the ancient buildings of Rome, the classic architecture of Florence and Venice, the ski slopes of the Alps and the beautiful beaches. They did not come to see Monte Cassino, Anzio, the ruins of the Gothic Line or the Ardeatine Caves. The Italians liked it that way. Unlike Mussolini they had never wanted to make the world tremble with the sound of marching boots.

THE END

SOURCES

A work of this magnitude draws upon many sources, not the least of which is my own forty odd years of study of the subject matter. Therefore I only list below those sources that had the greatest bearing on this work.

First of all: telegrams, letters, memos and orders etc. as stored in the British War Office and Foreign Office sections of the Public Records Office at Kew, United Kingdom. This is an invaluable source for material on the activities of British, American, Italian, Polish and other armed forces during World War Two. Some of this material is available for perusal, but not direct quotation, and some is semi-secret and must be used with discretion, all owing to the peculiarities of the British Official Secrets Act.

Secondly: documents prepared by US Military Intelligence and authored by captured German prisoners of war in 1945 and 1946:
von Bosse, Colonel Alexander: The Cossack Corps, MS P-064, USAREUR
Gaisser, Police Colonel Karl & Lieutenant General Hubert Lanz: German Anti-Guerilla Operations in the Balkans,   MS DA-20-243, Dept. of the Army
von Geitner, Major General Curt: German Military Government in the Balkans, MS P-033, Dept. of the Army
Kesselring, Field Marshal Albert: Guerilla Warfare in Italy, MS C-032, Dept. of the Army
 Reinhardt, General Hellmuth: Voluntary Service in the German Army, MS 23A6, USAREUR
Thirdly: edited works:
Colonialism in Africa, L. H. Gann & Peter Duignan, Cambridge,
Dictionary of Modern Italian History, Frank J. Coppa, Greenwood Press,
European Fascism, S. J. Woolf, Random House,
Finito: Po Valley Campaign, 15th Allied Army Group Military History Section,
History of the Second World War, UK Military Series, HMSO
Hitler's War Directives, H, R. Trevor-Roper, Pan Books
L'Italia e la Seconda Guerra Mondiale, E. Faldella, Capelli
L'Italia Nell' Europa Danubiana durante la Seconda Guerra Mondiale, Istituto Nazionale per la Storia del Movimento di Liberazione
The Official History of the Indian Armed Forces in the Second World War, Bisheshwar Prasad, Combined Interservices Historical Section of India and Pakistan, Orient Longman's
The Rommel Papers, Basil H. Liddell-Hart, Collins
2194 Days of War, Cesare Salmaggi & Alfredo Pallavisini, Mondadori
War in the Aegean, Smith and Walker, William Kimber

Who Were the Fascists? Oslo Universitets Forlaget
Fourthly: authored books:
Abbott, Peter & Nigel Thomas: Partisan Warfare 1941-45; Osprey
Absolon, Rudolf: Die Wehrmacht im Dritten Reich; Schriften des Bundesarchivs, Harald Boldt Verlag
Adams, Henry: Italy at War; Time-Life Books
Alexander, Bill: British Volunteers for Liberty; Lawrence & Wishart
Archer, Jules: Twentieth Century Caesar; Bailey Bros. & Swinfen
Ash, William: Pickaxe and Rifle: the Story of the Albanian People; Howard Baker
Auty, Phyllis: Tito; Ballantine
Badoglio, Marshal Pietro: L'Italia nella Seconda Guerra Mondiale; Mondadori
Barclay, Glen: The Rise and Fall of the New Roman Empire; Sidgwick & Jackson
Barker, A. J.: Eritrea; Faber & Faber
Barker, Elisabeth: British Policy in South East Europe in the Second World War; MacMillan
Beevor, Antony: The Spanish Civil War; Orbis
Behrendt, Hans Otto: Rommel's Intelligence in the Desert Campaign; William Kimber
Bennett, Geoffrey: Naval Battles of World War II; B. T. Batsford
Bennett, Ralph: Ultra and Mediterranean Strategy; Hamish Hamilton
Breyer, Siegfried: Battleships and Battlecruisers; MacDonald
Caccia-Dominioni, Paolo: Alamein: An Italian Story; Allen & Unwin
Cannistraro, Philip V.: Historical Dictionary of Fascist Italy; Greenwood
Cervi, Mario: The Hollow Legions: Mussolini's Blunder in Greece; Chatto & Windus
Coverdale, John F.: Italian Intervention in the Spanish Civil War; Princeton
Cox, Geoffrey: The Race for Trieste; William Kimber
Davis, Melton S.: Who Defends Rome? Allen & Unwin
Dawidowicz, Lucy S.: The War Against the Jews; Holt, Rinehart & Winston
Deakin, F. W.: The Brutal Friendship; Weidenfeld & Nicolson
Djilas, Milovan: Wartime; Harcourt, Brace, Jovanovitch
Ellis, Chris: Tanks of World War 2; Octopus Books
Ellis, John: Brute Force; Viking
D'Este, Carlo: Bitter Victory; Collins
Fricke, Gert: Kroatien 1941-44; Verlag Rombach
Fuller, Major General J. F. C.: Military History of the Western World;
Gallo, Max: Mussolini's Italy; Abelard Schuman
George, Margaret: The Warped Vision: British Foreign Policy 1933-39, Univ. of Pittsburgh

Gigli, G.: La Seconda Guerra Italiana; Laterza

Gilbert, Martin: Final Journey: The Fate of the Jews in Nazi Europe; Allen & Unwin

Gilbert, Martin: Second World War; Weidenfeld & Nicolson

Goldschmitt, Arthur Jr.: A Concise History of the Middle East; Westview

Gorla, G.: L'Italia nella Seconda Guerra Mondiale; Baldini e Castoldi

Hammond, Nicholas: Venture into Greece; William Kimber

Hargrove, Hondon: Buffalo Soldiers in Italy; McFarland

Hawes, Stephen & Ralph White: Resistance in Europe 1939-45; Allen Lane

Heckmann, Wolf: Rommel's War in Africa; Granada

Hehn, Paul N.: The German Struggle Against Yugoslavian Guerillas in World War Two; Columbia University

Hoptner, J. B.: Yugoslavia in Crisis 1934-41; Columbia University

Hoxha, Enver: History of the Party of Labour in Albania; Naim Frasheri

Jurado, Carlos Caballero: Resistance Warfare; Osprey

Kedward, H. R.: Fascism in Western Europe 1900-45; Blackie

Kirkpatrick, Sir Ivone: Mussolini: Study of a Demagogue; Oldham

Klein, Harry: Springboks in Armour; South African National War Museum

Krejci, Jaroslav & Viteslav Velimsky: Ethnic and Political Nations in Europe; Croom Helm

Lazzaro, Ricciotti: Le SS Italiane; Rizzoli

Lenzi, Loris: Dal Dnieper al Don: La 63a Legione CCNN Tagliamento Nella Campagna di Russia; Volpe

Littlejohn, David: The Patriotic Traitors: A History of Collaborationism in German-occupied Europe 1940-45; William Heinemann

Lucas Phillips, C. E.: Alamein; William Heinemann

MacGregor-Hastie, Roy: The Day of the Lion; MacDonald

MacIntyre, Donald: The Battle for the Mediterranean; B. T. Batsford

Macksay, Kenneth: Crucible of Power: The Fight for Tunisia; Hutchinson

MacMillan, Harold: War Diaries; MacMillan

Martin, David: Patriot or Traitor? The Case of General Milhailovich; Hoover Institution Press

von Mellenthin, Major General F.: German Generals of World War Two; Univ. of Oklahoma

von Mellenthin, Major General F.: Panzer Battles; Univ. of Oklahoma

Messe, Marshall Giovanni: Come Fini la Guerra in Africa; Rizzoli

Messe, Marshall Giovanni: La Guerra al Fronte Russo; Rizzoli

Messe, Marshall Giovanni: La Guerra in Africa; Rizzoli

Milazzo, Matteo J.: The Cetnik Movement and the Yugoslavian Resistance; Johns Hopkins University

Mitchell, David: The Spanish Civil War; Granada

Mockler, Anthony: Haile Selassie's War; Oxford University

Mollo, Andrew: The Armed Forces of World War Two; Orbis

Mollo, Andrew & Malcolm McGregor: Army Uniforms of World War II; Blandford

Moorehead, Alan: An African Trilogy; Hamish Hamilton

Mussolini, Rachele: The Real Mussolini; Saxon House

Novak, Bogdan C.: Trieste 1941-54; Univ. of Chicago

O'Neill, Richard: Suicide Squads; Salamander

Pack, S. W. C.: Night Action off Cape Matapan; Ian Allen

Pack, S. W. C.: Operation Husky: The Allied Invasion of Sicily; David & Charles,

Pallotta, Pietro: Revista Militare, Anno XI-3

Pollo, Stefanaq & Arlsen Puto: The History of Albania; Routledge & Kegan Paul

Preston, Paul: The Spanish Civil War; Weidenfeld & Nicholson

Ramsey, Winston G.: After the Battle, Number 7

Ready, J. Lee: Forgotten Allies: The Military Contribution of the Colonies, Exiled Governments and Lesser Powers to the Allied Victory in World War II, Vol. 1; McFarland

Ready, J. Lee: Forgotten Axis: Germany's Partners and Foreign Volunteers in World War II; McFarland

Ready, J. Lee: World War Two: Nation By Nation; Arms & Armour

Ready, J. Lee: Arrogance on the Battlefield, Arms & Armour

Ready, J. Lee: SS und Polizei: Myths and Lies of Hitler's SS and Police; Monticello

Roberts, Walter R.: Tito, Milhailovich and the Allies; Rutgers

Rosignoli, Guido: The Allied Forces in Italy; David & Charles

Rusinow, Dennison: Italy's Austrian Heritage; Clarendon Press

Segre, Claudio G.: Italo Balbo; UCLA

von Senger und Etterlin, General Fridolin: Neither Fear, Nor Hope; MacDonald

Serafis, Major General Stefanos: ELAS: Greek Partisan Army; Merlin

Shores, Christopher F. & Brian Cull & Nicola Malizia: Malta, the Hurricane Years; Grub Street

Shores, Christopher F.: Mediterranean Air War; Ian Allen

Smiley, David: Albanian Assignment; Chatto & Windus

Smith, Denis Mack: Mussolini; Weidenfeld & Nicolson

Strawson, John: El Alamein, Desert Victory: J. M. Dent & Sons

Sugar, Peter F.: Native Fascism in the Successor States; ABC-CLIO

Tillman, Heinz: Deutschlands Araberpolitik im Zweiten Weltkrieg; Veb Deutscher Verlag der Wissenschaften

Thomas, Hugh: The Spanish Civil War; Eyre & Spottiswoode

Tomasevich, Jozo: War and Revolution in Yugoslavia: the Cetniks; Stanford

Toscano, Mario: Alto Adige-South Tyrol; Weidenfeld & Nicolson

Villari, Luigi: The Liberation of Italy; C. C. Nelson

Whiting, Charles: Skorzeny; Ballantine

Whitley, E. M. J.: Destroyers of World War II; Arms & Armour

Whittle, Peter: One Afternoon at Mezzegra; W. H. Allen

Willmott, H. P. : The Great Crusade; Michael Joseph

Windrow, Michael: Waffen SS (Revised Version); Orbis

Wistricht, Robert: Who's Who in Nazi Germany; Weidenfeld & Nicolson

Woodhouse, C. M.: The Struggle for Greece 1941-49; Hart-Davis McGibbon

Zuccotti, Susan: The Italians and the Holocaust; Peter Halban

Printed in Poland
by Amazon Fulfillment
Poland Sp. z o.o., Wrocław